Economic Issues and Policy

Economic Issues and Policy

Sixth Edition

Jacqueline Murray Brux

Emeritus Professor of Economics

University of Wisconsin-River Falls

CENGAGE
Learning®

Australia • Brazil • Mexico • Singapore • United Kingdom • United States

CENGAGE
Learning®

**Economic Issues and Policy,
Sixth Edition**
Jacqueline Murray Brux

Vice President, General Manager:
Erin Joyner

Product Director: Michael Worls

Senior Product Manager: Steven Scoble

Content Developer: Ted Knight

Product Assistant: Mary Umbarger

Marketing Manager: Katie Jergens

Marketing Coordinator: Chris Walz

Manufacturing Planner: Kevin Kluck

Art and Cover Direction, Production
Management, and Composition:
Lumina Datamatics, Inc.

Cover Images: © iStockphoto.com/bjdlzx,
© iStockphoto.com/ssuaphoto,
© iStockphoto.com/ macky_ch,
© Konstantin L/Shutterstock.com,
© AshDesign/Shutterstock.com, © Joe
Gough/Shutterstock.com, © iStockphoto/
Thinkstock, © Ingram Publishing/
Thinkstock, © DigitalVision/Thinkstock,
Ryan McVay/Digital Vision/Thinkstock

Intellectual Property
    Analyst: Jennifer Nonenmacher
    Project Manager: Betsy Hathaway

For product information and technology assistance, contact us at
Cengage Learning Customer & Sales Support, 1-800-354-9706
For permission to use material from this text or product, submit all
requests online at **www.cengage.com/permissions**
Further permissions questions can be e-mailed to
permissionrequest@cengage.com

Library of Congress Control Number: 2015932320

ISBN: 978-1-285-44877-0

Cengage Learning
20 Channel Center Street
Boston, MA 02210
USA

Cengage Learning is a leading provider of customized learning
solutions with employees residing in nearly 40 different countries and
sales in more than 125 countries around the world. Find your local
representative at **www.cengage.com**.

Cengage Learning products are represented in Canada by
Nelson Education, Ltd.

To learn more about Cengage Learning Solutions, visit **www.cengage.com**

Purchase any of our products at your local college store or at our
preferred online store **www.cengagebrain.com**

Printed in the United States of America
Print Number: 02   Print Year: 2016

Brief Contents

Contents

Economic Issues and Policy

Sixth Edition

Jacqueline Murray Brux
Emeritus Professor of Economics
University of Wisconsin-River Falls

CENGAGE
Learning·

Australia · Brazil · Mexico · Singapore · United Kingdom · United States

Economic Issues and Policy, Sixth Edition
Jacqueline Murray Brux

Vice President, General Manager:
Erin Joyner

Product Director: Michael Worls

Senior Product Manager: Steven Scoble

Content Developer: Ted Knight

Product Assistant: Mary Umbarger

Marketing Manager: Katie Jergens

Marketing Coordinator: Chris Walz

Manufacturing Planner: Kevin Kluck

Art and Cover Direction, Production Management, and Composition:
Lumina Datamatics, Inc.

Cover Images: © iStockphoto.com/bjdlzx, © iStockphoto.com/ssuaphoto, © iStockphoto.com/ macky_ch, © Konstantin L/Shutterstock.com, © AshDesign/Shutterstock.com, © Joe Gough/Shutterstock.com, © iStockphoto/ Thinkstock, © Ingram Publishing/ Thinkstock, © DigitalVision/Thinkstock, Ryan McVay/Digital Vision/Thinkstock

Intellectual Property
  Analyst: Jennifer Nonenmacher
  Project Manager: Betsy Hathaway

For product information and technology assistance, contact us at
Cengage Learning Customer & Sales Support, 1-800-354-9706
For permission to use material from this text or product, submit all requests online at **www.cengage.com/permissions**
Further permissions questions can be e-mailed to
permissionrequest@cengage.com

Library of Congress Control Number: 2015932320

ISBN: 978-1-285-44877-0

Cengage Learning
20 Channel Center Street
Boston, MA 02210
USA

Cengage Learning is a leading provider of customized learning solutions with employees residing in nearly 40 different countries and sales in more than 125 countries around the world. Find your local representative at **www.cengage.com**.

Cengage Learning products are represented in Canada by Nelson Education, Ltd.

To learn more about Cengage Learning Solutions, visit **www.cengage.com**

Purchase any of our products at your local college store or at our preferred online store **www.cengagebrain.com**

Printed in the United States of America
Print Number: 02   Print Year: 2016

Brief Contents

© iStockphoto.com/bjdlzx

© iStockphoto.com/bjdlzx

Contents

Economic Issues and Policy

PART III

Global Poverty, Agriculture, and Trade   235

CHAPTER 10 World Poverty   237

CHAPTER 11 Global Agriculture   261

PART IV

Efficiency and Stability Issues   313

PART V

You and the World Around You   425

Preface to the Instructor

T hank you for examining and/or choosing this new edition of my textbook. In each successive edition, aside from updating, I've tried to make the book superior to the previous edition. I've listened to students, instructors, and my own intuition. I hope you will be pleased with the textbook and the changes, and I also have some requests to make of you. But first let me tell you about the book.

About the Book

This text is intended for a nontechnical, issues-oriented economics course, usually a 100-level course at four-year universities. It is often a general education course. The book is also appropriate for two-year colleges and other institutions, as well as economic education programs for elementary and secondary teachers. Chapters are designed so that they can be taught in any order after Chapter 1. Each chapter includes references to other chapters that mention similar topics. Some of these references are provided in the "Roadmap" that begins each chapter.

I have over 25 years of experience teaching issues-oriented economics. Usually, my students have not been economics majors, although many have decided to major or minor in economics after taking this course. My goals in writing this book have always been to make students aware of social issues in the world around them and to facilitate their understanding of these issues and related policy options from an economic perspective. I have also always hoped that it would inspire students to become involved with the issues in order to make this a better world. Students are often unaware that the important issues of our day, even ones that directly affect them—the environment, our health care systems, our educational system, crime and drugs, and matters as weighty as war and peace—are rooted in economics. Furthermore, students often set aside as too complex the issues that *are* recognized as economic, such as unemployment and inflation or trade and budget deficits. They believe that these issues are better left for the experts. Students need to know that all of these issues are indeed relevant and within their ability to understand. They need to comprehend these issues to make sound choices and form intelligent opinions. Of course, before students are willing to commit themselves to the lifelong learning of economics, they first need to be convinced that it *is* relevant to their lives and that it *is* interesting!

The discussion of issues in this book is lively, relevant, and current. I have deliberately included and highlighted issues of gender, race, and ethnicity throughout the text, as well as issues that are international in scope. (Diversity issues are highlighted with a "Diversity" icon and are carefully discussed in Chapter 3, and international topics are highlighted with an "International" icon and are carefully discussed in the four international chapters.) Students are invited to broaden their sensitivity to global and multicultural issues through topics such as migrant farm workers, Colombian coca growers, immigrants to the United States, court rulings on affirmative action, the incidence of hate crimes, and others. Further, they are offered an understanding of the incredible poverty found in Africa, Asia, and Latin America, not to mention the poverty that takes place in the United States.

Economic theory is used to analyze social and economic issues and the implications of potential policies. The level of technicality is deliberately appropriate for an economic issues course with no prerequisites, unlike other issues texts that attempt to incorporate all relevant principles and theory into pages better focused on the issues themselves. The text is written in a clear and student-friendly manner. Graphs are straightforward and normally illustrate only one concept per graph. Except for the appendices, only two basic types of graphs are used in the text: production possibilities and demand and supply (and aggregate demand and supply). More technical material and additional examples are frequently placed in appendices.

This text generally presents economic theory in a straightforward, market-oriented framework, but the policy discussion is not limited to such a narrow context. Instead, diverse policy perspectives are offered. As a result, the book contains a more liberal orientation than one that would rely on market analysis only. *Indeed, the careful presentation of both economic conservative and liberal viewpoints is one of the unique characteristics of this book.* Students generally have opinions, and they often consider themselves to be either conservative or liberal, but they rarely have the sophistication to understand the economic meaning of these terms and how their viewpoints tie into one or the other general philosophy. The ViewPoint section at the end of each chapter clarifies these notions, giving students a framework within which to understand their own economic philosophies. *Please point out to your students the importance of reading the ViewPoint sections, which clarify the economic conservative and liberal views on the topics of the chapter.* Otherwise, as you know, students are inclined to skip the "boxes." The ViewPoint section of Chapter 1 is especially important, insofar as it introduces students to what it means to be an economic conservative or an economic liberal. It sets the stage for further discussion of this topic in relation to the issues in chapters to come.

The Economic Toolbox at the beginning of each chapter lists the key economic concepts addressed in that chapter, providing instructors with a helpful course-planning tool and students with a proven effective pre-reading strategy. Additional Internet exercises are included in the "Discussion and Action Questions" at the end of each chapter to help students learn to use the Internet for data collection and research. The summaries at the end of each chapter, and the glossary and index at the end of the text will also be helpful to students.

The order of chapters has remained the same as the previous edition (though some sections have been added, deleted, or certainly updated). In Part I, Chapter 1 has always presented the introductory concepts of scarcity, production possibilities, and demand and supply. Also, one of the important features of this text—the economic conservative versus economic liberal viewpoint—is explained and emphasized, along with a basic explanation of the capitalist versus socialist economic model. Also, in Part I, Chapters 2 through 4 were chosen both for their interest to students and their order of presentation of economic concepts. Chapter 2 on crime and drugs presents an example of public good, that of crime prevention. Cost-benefit analysis is utilized, and elasticity is introduced. Pollution as a negative externality and education as a positive one are introduced in Chapters 3 and 4, respectively, and cost-benefit analysis is utilized once again.

Part II is entitled *The Economics of Social Issues*, contains Chapters 5 through 9, and covers the topics, in order, of discrimination, U.S. poverty, housing, health care, and social security.

Part III focuses on global topics, including Chapter 10 (World Poverty), Chapter 11 (Global Agriculture), and Chapter 12 (International Trade). While international content permeates through all of the chapters, these three chapters are interconnected in such a way that makes the new ordering more appropriate. Chapter 17 focuses on the three separate regions of the world: the Western industrialized world, the Eastern industrialized world, and the developing world.

Part IV addresses efficiency and stability issues, with Chapter 13 covering market power, 14 addressing unemployment and inflation, 15 considering government macroeconomic policy, and 16 addressing taxes, borrowing, and the national debt. And finally, Part V (*You and the World Around You*) contains the final international chapter just mentioned, Chapter 17 (Globally Free Markets for the Twenty-First Century?), and the Epilogue.

Once our students begin to understand the economic issues around them, the text has the final explicit objective of *involving* our students in the issues and *challenging* them to have an impact on our world. This is evidenced throughout the text and especially in the sections, "You, the Student," and the "Discussion and Action Questions" at the end of each chapter, as well as in the Epilogue entitled "You and the World Around You." The Epilogue is personalized to the students, and clearly challenges them to make a difference in the world.

Changes in the Sixth Edition

First, the world has changed enormously in the few years since the fifth edition. As I write this, we have our first African-American president. Our economy is recovering from the Great Recession. The stock market crashed and rebounded. Unemployment spiked, but is recovering. Budget deficits hit record levels, but have since fallen. But, of course, you know all this, and textbook authors had to make mad dashes to update suddenly obsolete books. Naturally, data, policies, and topics have been updated.

Aside from updating the data as much as possible at the time this was written, some general changes include the following. A section entitled, "You, the Student" has been added at the end of each chapter. This section invites students to take a specific action on a topic related to the issues in the chapter. It is meant to encourage students to make a difference in their world. (As mentioned, the Epilogue and the "Discussion and Action Questions" do the same.) I've improved the structure of many chapters by revising headings and the order of material in order to streamline and clarify. I've also moved material to the appendices in an effort to reduce the length of chapters and give instructors greater option over coverage. Many graphs have been revised to provide more realistic numbers and examples. Some specific examples of changes include the following.

In Parts I and II (introduction and social Issues), Chapter 2 includes more discussion of hate crimes and other diversity issues. Two sets of material in Chapter 3 have been moved to appendices, including the "Effects of an Externality on Society in the Case of a Single Industry" and the "History of Federal Efforts to Limit U.S. Pollution." The former was done in order to streamline and clarify, and the latter leaves only more recent policy on the environment within the text. There is also new discussion of the Keystone Pipeline. In Chapter 4, there is updated information focused on jobs and studies for the future intended to help students planning their academic and work careers, as well as added discussion of the Common core curriculum. Some material has also been moved to appendices, including the figure on the cost-benefit analysis of a college education (though the topic is still discussed within the text) and the material on differential tuition. Chapter 5 utilizes an improved example in the figure on occupational crowding. In Chapter 6, portions that may have been confusing have been eliminated, the appendix on the Lorenz curve has been improved, and the material on measurement problems with the poverty line has been moved to an appendix in order to shorten the chapter and provide instructors with an option on including this. In Chapter 7, the housing market has been updated to show changes since the housing crisis, and the consumer specifics of traditional mortgage lending have been moved to the appendix. Chapter 8 has an improved structure pertaining to factors that cause a rise in health care costs, and the consumer specifics of private insurance (premiums, deductibles, coinsurance, and so on) have been moved to an appendix. And, of course, there is quite a bit of expanded information on the Affordable Care Act.

Part III on global topics includes an expansion in Chapter 10 to include a recent report on success toward meeting the Millennium Development Goals and a recent U.S. Agency for International Development report on the effectiveness of U.S. aid. It also includes a new section on micro-enterprise credit for poor women entrepreneurs, relying on recent on-site research by the author. Chapter 11 includes a new introduction on Farm Aid concerts and musicians and an update on recent farm bills. Chapter 12 includes a link between the recent U.S. recession and crisis in financial markets to global conditions, including trade; an expansion of G-8 and G-20; and an updated "Politics and Trade" section to include the new Cuban policy declaration by President Obama and the new sanctions on Russia. It also includes expanded discussion of poor global work conditions and fair trade issues.

Part IV on efficiency and stability issues includes updated examples of monopoly and the effects of market power in Chapter 13. Chapter 14 naturally includes updates on the economy, and again, includes updated information on jobs and study areas for the future. It updates the discussion of immigration to include the new Obama policy, and it adds global unemployment and inflation rates from selected countries around the world. Chapter 15 logically includes updated fiscal and monetary policy, as well as a new section on the post-Great Recession economy, and shifts most of the discussion of supply side policy to the appendix (though this topic is still discussed briefly in the text). In Chapter 16, the effect of government borrowing on interest rates, including the graph and the concept of crowding out, is moved to an appendix. There are better hypothetical examples of the effects of government sales and social security taxes on income distribution, and the effects of taxes on the macroeconomy. Federal income tax rates and brackets are updated, and a global comparison of tax revenue as a share of GDP in the Western industrialized world is added. Some discussion of the sequester is added as well.

Finally, in Part V on "You and the World Around You," Chapter 17 adds data on tax rates as a share of profits and an ease of doing business index (that focuses on regulatory behavior) in the Western industrialized world. And lastly, the Epilogue has become quite a bit more personalized about myself, in the hope that students can relate to me not just as an author, but a person, and by doing so, can gain greater insight into what other people do and into the world around them.

My Request to You

First, instructors and reviewers tell me that they *like* the global content as it weaves throughout the textbook and as it takes particular focus in Chapter 10 on world poverty, Chapter 11 on global agriculture, Chapter 12 on international trade, and Chapter 17 on global markets; yet they often complain that they don't have time to include these chapters. *Please do make a point of utilizing these chapters, or at least some of them!* The developing world of Africa, Asia, and Latin America will soon include close to four-fifths of the world's population, and our students need far more education about these parts of the world than they typically receive. Please at least review these chapters before making a decision on whether to include them on your syllabus. I hope that you will like them too!

Second, some studies suggest that today's youth are disinterested in the world around them. I don't believe this is true. In the post 9/11 era, students are indeed looking at the world around them, struggling to understand the relevance of global and socioeconomic issues to their own lives, and trying to discern the role they themselves will play in our complex and interdependent world. We can help them. The sections "You, the Student" and the "Discussion and Action Questions" at the end of each chapter are designed to make students think about what they can do, and the Epilogue encourages them to take action. *Please ask your students to read this material, and let's challenge them to make a difference*, whether it is fighting for fair trade coffee on campus, seeking an end to cocoa slavery in West Africa, boycotting big-box stores with poor labor practices, or conserving and protecting our global environment. *Thank you for your impact on your students, and through them, your contributions to our world!*

Preface to the Student: *Please Read This!*

The world has changed before your very eyes! Within the last few years, we've elected the first African-American president. Our nation tumbled into severe recession and then rose to a remarkable recovery. We endured a housing crisis and a financial crisis. The stock market crashed and rebounded. The budget deficit soared and then fell. You probably know people who went bankrupt, lost their homes, or became unemployed; but many of those people have now found jobs, albeit many of those are part time and low wage-paying.

This book will help you understand many of these topics. It focuses on the economics of social issues. It includes those issues that you would normally consider to be economic by nature, like those mentioned earlier. But it also includes a variety of other social issues that you might not ordinarily think of as economic ones: illegal drug use, the plight of our nation's homeless, the degradation of our environment, the problems in financing your higher education, and the issue of affirmative action. These and many other issues are addressed in this book.

The basic economic tools in the text can be used as a framework for understanding the various social issues and policies in the world around us. They can help us comprehend events in other countries, including those countries making a transition from socialism to capitalism in Eastern Europe and those countries struggling with poverty in the developing world. In short, these tools can be used again and again to examine problems and issues present in our world today.

The book is intended to be student friendly. The graphs are straightforward and clear, and boil down to just two basic types: production possibilities and demand and supply. The definitions of economic vocabulary in the margins of each chapter help you cut through any economic jargon. The "Roadmap" (which points you forward and backward to related topics in other chapters) and "The Economic Toolbox" at the beginning of each chapter, as well as the glossary and index at the end of the text, will also assist you. The issues in the text are current. The writing is clear, lively, and to the point, with a minimum of technicality.

The book is intended to get you to think. As you acquire a basic understanding of economics, you also acquire a framework within which to form and justify your personal opinions about economic issues. Are you a conservative or a liberal? Do you even know what these terms mean in the context of economics? Briefly, an economic conservative has the view that *less* government involvement in the economy is best. An economic liberal believes that *more* government involvement is best. Both of these are further explained in the ViewPoint section of Chapter 1, and the ViewPoint sections in subsequent chapters focus on specific issues and policies from both an economic liberal and economic conservative perspective. You will do yourself a great service by carefully reading the ViewPoint section in each chapter.

Finding solutions to economic problems is not easy. People of different philosophies can hold very different viewpoints, despite a common understanding of economic concepts. Here is where you, the student, come in. This book will provide a basic economic framework for discussing social issues and problems, but *you* must determine your own viewpoint on these issues and problems.

The material is presented in a way that you should find relevant to your personal life. It includes issues of gender, race, and ethnicity throughout, often highlighted with a "diversity icon." And, because the world is so rapidly becoming interdependent, there is plenty of discussion of international topics throughout the text. This discussion is generally highlighted with a "global icon." If your teacher does not assign at least one or two of the international chapters (Chapters 10, 11, 12, and 17), ask him or her to include them on the syllabus. Finally, the book challenges you to use your knowledge to make a difference in the world. Otherwise, to what benefit is your new knowledge? You are challenged in the sections, "You, the Student" and "Discussion and Action Questions" that end each chapter; and in the Epilogue at the end of the book. *Since I've addressed this Epilogue personally to you, please read this whether it is assigned or not.*

Now, enjoy your discovery of the world of economic issues!

Acknowledgments

I appreciate the help provided by some wonderful student assistants in prior editions, especially Anna Andahazy and Christina Brux Mburu. They have now gone onto providing wonderful global and community service. I am also grateful for the love and support of family and friends, including Clementine, Wesley, Adrian, Maliyah, and Nathaniel, who keep me going. I appreciate Pat, Corey, and Eric for their loving parenting. I am grateful to Keith, who continually teaches me what love is. I also thank Steve, Ted, and Joseph for all of their hard work, patience, and support.

Jacqueline Murray Brux

About the Author

Jacqueline Murray Brux received her Ph.D. in economics in 1983 from the University of Michigan in Ann Arbor and is an emeritus professor of economics at the University of Wisconsin-River Falls. Her area of expertise is the economic development of developing countries. Her research encompasses the area of economic development, with special focus on women in development, the effects of structural reforms, and credit for poor women's entrepreneurial activities. Dr. Brux's international experiences include work and research in the countries of Burkina Faso and Ghana in West Africa; Kenya and Uganda in East Africa; Mexico, Chile, and Cuba in Latin America; Russia; and Vietnam. She regularly travels to Norway to visit her daughter, son-in-law, and grandchildren.

Part I

Introduction to Economics, Scarcity, Public Goods, and Spillovers

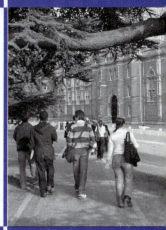

© Joe Gough/Shutterstock.com

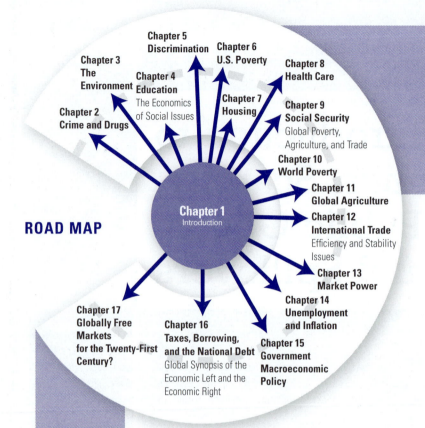

Chapter 1

ROAD MAP

Chapter 1
Introduction

Chapter 2
Crime and Drugs

Chapter 3
The Environment

Chapter 4
Education
The Economics
of Social Issues

Chapter 5
Discrimination

Chapter 6
U.S. Poverty

Chapter 7
Housing

Chapter 8
Health Care

Chapter 9
Social Security
Global Poverty,
Agriculture, and Trade

Chapter 10
World Poverty

Chapter 11
Global Agriculture

Chapter 12
International Trade
Efficiency and Stability
Issues

Chapter 13
Market Power

Chapter 14
Unemployment
and Inflation

Chapter 15
Government
Macroeconomic
Policy

Chapter 16
Taxes, Borrowing,
and the National Debt
Global Synopsis of the
Economic Left and the
Economic Right

Chapter 17
Globally Free
Markets
for the Twenty-First
Century?

The Economic Toolbox

The Economic Toolbox is a feature of each chapter. It points out specific economic topics that will be covered, alerting you to watch for these concepts in the chapter.

- Scarcity
- Resources
- Production possibilities
- Opportunity costs
- Unemployment
- Economic growth

- Demand and supply
- Equilibrium
- Microeconomics
- Macroeconomics
- Economic conservative
- Economic liberal

Introduction

Welcome to economics! Welcome? To the dismal science? To the colorless pages of *The Wall Street Journal*? To the realm of boring statistics, intimidating jargon, complex graphs, and middle-aged men and women in three-piece business suits carrying leather briefcases?

Welcome? To terms such as *budget deficit*, *balance of trade*, *national debt*, *money supply*, *exchange rates*, and even newer terms such as the *fiscal cliff*, *Obamacare*, *le budget dangereux*, *WikiLeaks*, *Abenomics*, and other phrases that are not even found in my computer dictionary?

Do we really want to know what these phrases mean? Do we really want to look at the graphs, charts, numbers, and newsprint? Can these possibly have meaning for our lives? Can they possibly be understood by average citizens such as you right here in this classroom?

Perhaps surprisingly, the answer to all of the preceding questions is a resounding yes … not because we enjoy jargon and numbers, but rather because we want answers to important questions. Will I be able to get a job when I graduate? Why does a marketing professor make more than an English professor? Will I be helped or hurt by a raise in the minimum wage? Why are college costs so high? Should students receive greater financial aid? Why do female workers earn only 81 percent as much as male workers? Why do we go to war? Why does hunger persist in a world of plenty? Why does poverty exist in the midst of affluence? Who will eat, and who will not? Who will find jobs, and who will not? Whose children will have quality education and health care, and whose children will not?

If you've ever wondered about these questions or questions like them, then you are interested in economics. This is because **economics deals primarily with scarcity: how should we allocate our limited resources to satisfy seemingly unlimited human wants and needs?** Once you understand a little economic reasoning, you will be able to answer the world's (and your) pressing questions better than most of the politicians, newscasters, and opinionated people who persistently tell you what to believe. Survival in the face of scarcity is what economics is all about. Understanding a few economic concepts allows you to analyze these issues yourself and come up with your own answers to these questions. So, let's get started.

In economics, hope and faith coexist with great scientific pretension and also a deep desire for respectability.

—*JOHN KENNETH GALBRAITH, U.S. ECONOMIST*, THE NEW YORK TIMES MAGAZINE,/CL: STYLE> JUNE 7, 1970

Scarcity
Limited resources relative to wants and needs.

Economics and Scarcity

Resources

Land, labor, machinery, and other inputs used to produce goods and services.

Production possibilities

An economic concept explaining scarcity and the need for choices; alternate combinations of the maximum amounts of two different goods that can be produced during a particular time period if the economy's resources are efficiently and fully employed.

Let's begin by discussing scarcity. **Resources** (land, labor, factory buildings, timber, minerals, machinery, and the like) are the basis for producing the food, shelter, medical care, and luxury goods that we want. Some of these are natural resources (land and timber), some are capital goods resources (factories and machinery) and some are human resources (labor). These resources are scarce in the sense that there are not enough of them to produce everything we need and desire. Even when using all resources as efficiently and completely as possible, and using all modern technology to its fullest extent, there is some limit to the amount we can currently produce. Scarcity forces us to choose among competing uses for society's resources. What to produce and how to distribute this output to society's citizens are the most basic economic choices to be made.

The easiest way to think about the problem of societal choice is by looking at a basic economic concept and graph called production possibilities. (I promise that only two basic graphs will be used to analyze almost all of the issues in this book.) **Production possibilities shows the maximum amounts of two different goods that can possibly be produced during any particular time period using society's scarce resources.** Because reality is complex, economists try to simplify it by making assumptions about the basic elements involved in analyzing an issue. In examining production possibilities, we must make these simplifying assumptions about our economy:

1. All available resources are used fully.
2. All available resources are used efficiently.
3. The quantity and quality of available resources are not changing during our period of analysis.
4. Technology is not changing during our period of analysis.
5. We can produce only two goods with our available resources and technology.

Let's consider the implications of these simplifying assumptions. First, all available resources are used fully, so that no workers are unemployed, no factory buildings sit idle, and so forth. (This does not mean that we fail to conserve some of our resources for the future. If we think that the habitat of the snowy owl is important ecologically, we simply do not make that part of the available resources.) Second, *efficiency* means that we use our knowledge and technology to produce the maximum amount of output with these resources. These first two assumptions mean that our economy is doing the best that it can; it is operating fully and efficiently. Third, the quantity and quality of our resources are not changing. This means that over the current time period, workers do not begin new training programs to make them more productive, new natural resources are not discovered, and so on. The next assumption is similar. Technological change—which might give us a better means of producing more goods with the same resources—is not occurring. We make these last two assumptions to deal with the world as it is right now, and not how it might become in the future. And finally, to simplify our analysis (and because here we graph in only two dimensions), we assume that we can produce only two goods with our resources. Let's pick bread and roses as the goods.

One of our choices is to put all of our resources and technology into the production of bread. This choice might give us 150 units of bread. Whether these bread units are loaves, cases, truckloads, or tons is irrelevant here. Let's suppose they are tons.

Two old adages suggest that man (and woman) cannot live by bread alone and that life is richer if we stop and smell the roses. So, let's allow another choice and take some resources and some technology out of bread production and use them to produce roses. Now, we might end up with 20 units of roses and only 120 tons of bread. Again, the nature of the units is irrelevant; our rose units might be bouquets, boxes, truckloads, or tons. Let's suppose they are tons. (Note, however, that we had to give up 30 tons of bread production to produce the 20 tons of roses.)

Another alternative might be to give up even more bread, leaving us with bread production of only 90 tons, to produce 40 tons of roses. (Note that, once again, we had to give up 30 tons of bread production to get the additional 20 tons of roses.) The alternatives could go on and on and might be summarized in a production possibilities table such as Table 1-1. Note that each alternative A through F represents one possible combination of bread and roses that we could produce.

The information in Table 1-1 can be easily displayed in a production possibilities curve, or graph. Don't let graphs intimidate you. They can be very useful. Every graph has just two axes, and each axis shows the amounts of one variable. As you move along the axes away from the origin, the amounts of the variables increase. In Figure 1-1, the horizontal axis represents tons of roses, and the vertical axis represents tons of bread. Each point in the graph represents a row in the table, and the labeling of the points corresponds to the alternatives in the table. Connecting all points gives us a production possibilities curve, which shows the alternative combinations of maximum quantities of bread and roses that our country is capable of producing. (Even though we end up with a straight line, we still call it a production possibilities *curve*. The appendix to this

TABLE 1-1 • Production Possibilities Table

Alternative	Bread (tons)	Roses (tons)
A	150	0
B	120	20
C	90	40
D	60	60
E	30	80
F	0	100

© Cengage Learning

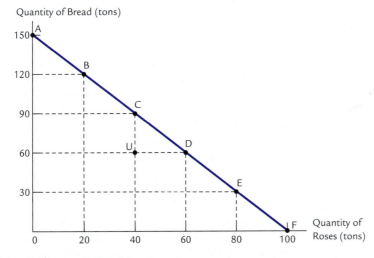

Quantity of Bread (tons)

Figure 1-1 • Production Possibilities Curve
Points A through F show alternative combinations of bread and roses that the economy can produce, whereas point U represents unemployed (or inefficiently used) resources.

© Cengage Learning

Opportunity cost

The best alternative forgone to produce or consume something else; what you give up to get something else.

Unemployment

A situation in which resources are not fully used in production.

Economic growth

A sustained increase in production, represented by an outward shift of the production possibilities curve.

Services

Activities such as haircuts, health care, and education that are consumed (used) by consumers.

Consumer goods

Goods that are consumed (used) by consumers.

Capital goods

Goods such as machinery and factories that are used to produce other goods.

Private goods

Goods produced or purchased by business firms and individuals.

Public goods

Goods produced or purchased by government.

chapter considers the more realistic production possibilities curve that is actually bowed outward.)

A number of important concepts are illustrated by the production possibilities curve. The most basic concept is that there is some limit to what we can produce. Thus, to produce more of one good, we must give up production of something else. This reality is what economists refer to as opportunity cost. **Opportunity cost** is the best alternative that is forgone to produce or consume something else. The opportunity cost of producing roses is not measured in dollars but in the bread that we give up when we produce these roses. And the opportunity cost of producing bread is the roses we give up when we produce this bread. As economists are fond of saying, there is no free lunch! There is an opportunity cost to everything.

The second economic concept that is illustrated by production possibilities is that of **unemployment**. Realize that our alternative combinations of the two products represent *possible* quantities. We have explicitly assumed the full use of our resources, knowledge, and technology; hence, the phrase production *possibilities*. In actuality, we rarely if ever produce to our full potential. In reality, some resources may go unused: factories are idle and workers are laid off. Nor do we always use resources in the most efficient manner. In these cases, we will not be on the production possibilities curve, but at some point below it, such as U (representing unemployment) in Figure 1-1 on page 5. At point U, we are producing only 40 tons of roses and 60 tons of bread, though we could produce more of both if we had full employment. Clearly, we could do much better by putting idle resources to work and moving our way back out to the production possibilities curve.

Finally, it is evident that our country need not be restricted to a single production possibilities curve forever. Economies may grow, and the variables that we assumed are unchanging (resources and technology) certainly *do* change over time. **Economic growth** may occur if the quality or quantity of society's resources increases, or if new technologies are developed so that we can produce more output with our available resources. Such growth would be reflected in an outward shift of the entire production possibilities curve, as illustrated in Figure 1-2. Such a shift would enable us to move to a point such as point G (representing growth) on the new production possibilities curve. Clearly, point G (with 80 tons of roses and 90 tons of bread) is superior to a point such as D (with 60 tons of roses and only 60 tons of bread) on the original curve. Such growth is possible only over time, and not in the current time period illustrated by the first production possibilities curve.

Of course, our country and world are capable of producing more than just two goods. We produce trucks, spaghetti, gasoline, smart phones, swimming suits, and a bewildering array of merchandise that fills our shopping centers. We also produce **services** such as health care, education, road repair, and cellular phone service. We can easily imagine infinite combinations of all the goods and services that an economy can potentially produce. We cannot graph these infinite combinations, however, because our graphs have only two axes. So, bread and roses simply represent one of an infinite set of choices. We can make our graph a bit more realistic by redefining the axes. We might redefine the horizontal axis as staple goods and the vertical axis as luxury goods. Or we could divide our economy's output into agricultural goods and manufactured goods, or **consumer goods** (goods that are purchased by consumers) and **capital goods** (goods such as factory buildings and machinery that are used to produce other goods). We may examine the choice between military goods and civilian goods. Or we may look at the production possibilities for **private goods** (such as cell phones and hamburgers, which are provided by businesses) and **public goods** (such as police and fire protection, which are provided by government). Thus, we can realistically consider many choices involved in the production of various types of output.

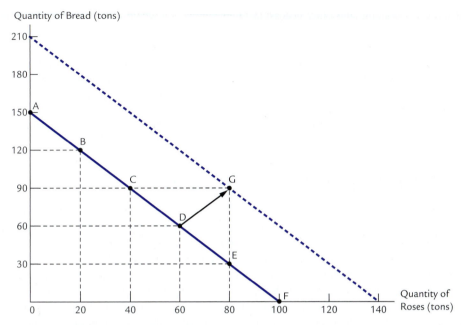

Figure 1-2 • Production Possibilities Curve With Economic Growth
Note that more of both bread and roses can be produced when the production possibilities curve shifts outward as a result of economic growth.

© Cengage Learning

I hope you don't suspect that the purpose of the production possibilities exercise was merely to illustrate some economic concepts and drawings. It wasn't. It has very important real-world relevance. It suggests to us first of all that we can never be absolutists when it comes to our nation's spending priorities. If we wish to devote more of the country's current resources to environmental protection, for example, we may have to give up part of our space program. If we wish to expand public education, we may have to give up some of our national defense. Or if we wish to have more government goods and services overall, we must give up some private goods. We can't have more of everything. We can't insist on any spending priority without limit, because there are always opportunity costs to consider.

The production possibilities curve also helps us realize that the costs of unemployment are not limited to personal hardships experienced by the unemployed person and his or her family, although these personal costs may be severe. Costs are also borne by our nation and our world as a whole in the form of reduced production. If we waste our resources through inefficient production techniques, output is similarly reduced. In a world of scarcity, we must see to it that our resources are fully and efficiently employed in the present, and we can then seek to expand our productive potential in the future.

And the problem of scarcity is real. Worldwide, more than 22,000 children die every day from poverty-related causes. Many of the world's citizens lack basic nutrition, health care, education, shelter, clothing, clean water, and hygiene. Many of the world's nations lack basic infrastructure in the form of communications, transportation, sanitation, and electricity. Any time a poor country makes a decision to improve transportation, for example, as an investment in the future, many of its citizens may die of hunger in the present. Even in a prosperous country such as ours, some 15 percent of the population is poor. As we shall see in Chapter 6 on U.S. poverty, these people do not receive adequate food, shelter, health care, clothing, and other necessities. Our nation as a whole lacks sufficient environmental protection, first-rate educational opportunities, and quality health care for all.

The issue of opportunity costs was widely discussed in the context of the war in Iraq. Beginning with the U.S. invasion in 2003, some economists estimated that the full cost of the war would ultimately be between $1 trillion and $2 trillion. Imagine the education, health care, and other important services that could have been provided to U.S. citizens, as well as poor citizens abroad, with the same amount of resources. Choices as to what we produce and how much we produce are clearly important to our citizens and the citizens of the world.

Economics and Distribution

Although production choices are important, they really tell us only half of the story. At least as important are choices relating to the distribution of goods and services. *The reason there is hunger in a world of plenty is not a problem of production but of distribution. Poor people and poor governments lack the income to purchase the food that is produced.* In terms of our current example, who should receive the bread and roses after they are produced? Should the decision be based on equality so that everyone receives the same amount of every good that everyone else does? Should people receive a share of the goods and services that is proportional to their contribution to producing those goods and services? Should the government make the distribution decisions, perhaps giving higher rations to those most "deserving" (however that might be determined)? Should the government ensure that all residents receive adequate housing, health care, nutrition, and education, with less-vital goods distributed on the basis of people's incomes and desires? Should all goods and services be distributed on the basis of people's incomes? On what basis should distribution choices be made?

As we will see, in a market-based economy such as ours, the choices of distribution as well as production are based primarily on prices. And prices are determined by demand and supply.

Demand and Supply
Demand

Have you ever had to hire a tutor to help with your coursework? (I hope you haven't had to in economics, at least not yet!) What are some of the factors that would determine the number of tutoring hours you would wish to purchase? Probably the degree of difficulty of the coursework is important, and so is your income, which will determine how much tutoring you can afford. Most likely, the price of tutoring services is important to you as well. All other things being equal, you would probably be inclined to purchase more tutoring service hours at $1 per hour than at $5 per hour. Most of us tend to behave in the same way. At very high prices, we would tend to be frugal in our use of tutoring services. We would ask more questions in class, study with a friend, or visit the teacher during office hours (maybe bringing along an apple or two). We would perhaps study harder (or take the consequences) rather than pay the fee for many hours of tutoring services if the price is high. At lower prices, we would be willing and able to purchase more hours of tutoring. Let's focus on the price variable for a moment.

Let's assume that you attend a large university where there are many students who want tutors as well as many students willing and able to tutor. Suppose we consider all your school's students and their desire to purchase tutoring services. Let's assume that the time period is one week and that all factors other than price (such as course difficulty and student income) are held constant. (Economists usually say "all other things equal" to specify that all other factors that might influence the quantity demanded are unchanging.)

To illustrate this example further, let's put this information into a tabular format. Let's consider people's willingness to buy tutoring services, where P stands for alternative possible prices of tutoring services and Q^D (quantity demanded) stands for the amounts of tutoring that students are willing and able to purchase at these various prices. This is reflected in Table 1-2, which shows alternative prices and the quantities that people are willing and able to purchase at these prices. This is called a **demand schedule**. It is clear that if tutoring prices are low (say, $2 per hour), the quantity demanded will be high (80 hours). If tutoring prices are higher ($4 per hour), the quantity demanded will be lower (40 hours). **This simple commonsense idea that people will be willing and able to buy more of a good or service at low prices than at high prices is a fundamental economic principle, the law of demand, which is usually stated as follows:** *price and quantity demanded are negatively related, all other things equal.* This means that when price goes up, quantity demanded goes down, and vice versa.

We can place the information from Table 1-2 into a graph of demand, illustrated in Figure 1-3. A graph of demand is referred to as a demand curve (even though demand curves are often drawn as straight lines). The price of tutoring services (P) is on the vertical axis, and the quantity of services demanded (number of hours) is on the horizontal axis, which is labeled Q for quantity. Plotting the information in each of the rows a

Demand schedule
A table showing the quantities that consumers are willing to buy at alternative prices during a specified time period.

TABLE 1-2 • Demand Schedule for Tutoring Services, One Week

Alternative	P ($ per hour)	Q^D (hours)
a	$1	100
h	2	80
c	3	60
d	4	40
e	5	20

© Cengage Learning

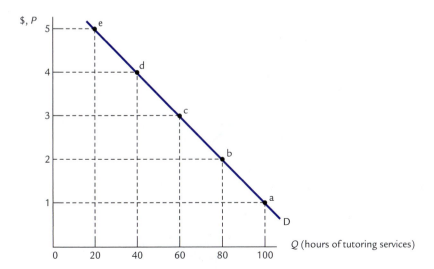

Figure 1-3 • Demand for Tutoring Services, One Week

© Cengage Learning

Demand curve

A graph showing the quantities that consumers are willing to buy at alternative prices during a specified time period.

Law of demand

There is a negative relationship between price and quantity demanded, all other things equal.

through e in the table gives us points a through e in the graph. Connecting these points gives us the demand curve in Figure 1-3. The **demand curve** (labeled D for demand) indicates all possible combinations of alternative prices and quantity demanded, assuming that all factors except price that could affect quantity demanded are held constant.

Note that the demand curve is downward sloping, reflecting the **law of demand**. A higher price is associated with a lower quantity demanded (40 hours at $4 per hour), whereas a lower price is associated with a larger quantity demanded (80 hours at $2 per hour).

What if one of the other factors affecting demand was to change? Course difficulty might increase, for example. Or student incomes might increase, making students better able to afford tutoring. Each of these examples would increase the demand for tutoring services. You probably can add to the list of things that would increase the demand for tutoring.

An increase in the demand for tutoring services will result in an entirely new demand schedule, such as the one in Table 1-3. We can plot this new information in the same graph as before, and we end up with an entirely new demand curve, D′. (See Figure 1-4.) Demand has increased so the demand curve has shifted forward, or to the right. Note that for every price that existed before, a higher quantity demanded now exists.

If an event causing a decrease in demand were to occur (say, a decrease in student incomes), the demand curve would shift backward, or to the left. For every price on the new demand curve, a smaller quantity would exist.

TABLE 1-3 • Increased Demand Schedule for Tutoring Services, One Week

Alternative	P ($ per hour)	Q^D (hours)
a′	$1	140
b′	2	120
c′	3	100
d′	4	80
e′	5	60

© Cengage Learning

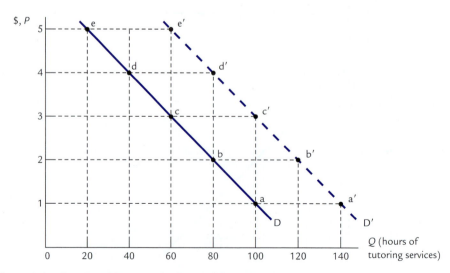

Figure 1-4 • Increased Demand for Tutoring Services, One Week
Demand curve D′ represents larger quantities demanded at each price than does demand curve D.

© Cengage Learning

Supply

Now let's consider the other side of the market for tutoring services, the supply side. Imagine the students at your school who not only don't need tutoring but who are actually able to tutor. This is the group of students who might supply tutoring services for a fee. What are the factors that influence these students' willingness to offer their tutoring services for sale? Probably the costs associated with providing the service are important. The most obvious cost is the value of the tutor's time. Remember that opportunity costs are always important. The opportunity costs of a tutor's time may be quantified easily if an adult tutor hires a babysitter while he or she tutors or if the tutor forgoes income from alternative employment. Some costs that are less easy to quantify are just as real. The tutor might be giving up precious study time, quality time with friends and family, or simply valued leisure time. Although it's hard to attach a dollar value to these costs, they remain important. Remember that there is no free lunch; *every choice has an opportunity cost; every activity chosen entails another activity given up.*

Another factor affecting the total quantity of tutoring services supplied will be the number of tutors available. If we experience an increase in enrollment of top-notch students who are dying to become tutors, we can expect more tutoring services suddenly to be supplied.

The price that tutors can receive for their services will also be an important determinant of their willingness to supply these services. Let's focus our attention on this price variable for a moment. Let's look at the supply of tutoring services in a one-week time period, when all the factors except price that might affect the number of tutoring hours supplied are held constant. It is realistic to assume that individual tutors will be more willing to provide tutoring services at a high price than at a low price. The higher price will allow them to cover their babysitting expenses more easily or will serve as a stronger inducement to give up leisure or time with friends and family. It will compensate them better for other job prospects they don't pursue because they are tutoring. In simple terms, the higher the price, the greater the incentive to provide tutoring services. Tutors (and business firms) will offer for sale a larger amount of the good or service at higher prices rather than at lower prices. **This is known as the law of supply, which is usually stated as follows: price and quantity supplied are positively related, all other things equal.** This simply means that price and quantity supplied (the amount offered for sale) change in the same direction. If price goes up, so does quantity supplied; if price goes down, so does quantity supplied.

The behavior of all tutors as a group might be summarized in Table 1-4, which is a **supply schedule** showing different quantities of tutoring hours supplied (Q^S) at the alternative prices (P) that the tutors might receive. The quantities represent the total number of hours supplied by the group as a whole at each alternative price over the specified one-week time period. All the factors other than price that might affect the tutors' willingness to tutor do not change. Thus, the only thing changing is the price determinant.

We can place the information from the supply schedule in Table 1-4 into a graph of supply, or a **supply curve** in Figure 1-5 on page 12. The axes are identical to those in the

Supply schedule
A table showing the quantities that suppliers are willing to sell at alternative prices during a specified time period.

Supply curve
A graph showing the quantities that suppliers are willing to sell at alternative prices during a specified time period.

TABLE 1-4 • Supply Schedule for Tutoring Services, One Week

Alternative	P ($ per hour)	Q^S (hours)
v	$1	20
w	2	40
x	3	60
y	4	80
z	5	100

© Cengage Learning

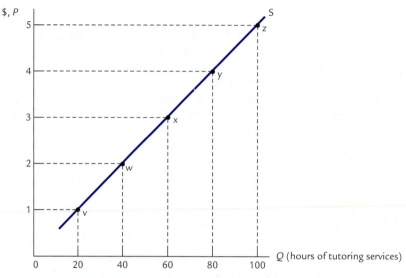

Figure 1-5 • Supply Curve for Tutoring Services, One Week
The graph shows amounts of tutoring supplied at various prices.

© Cengage Learning

Law of supply

There is a positive relationship between price and quantity supplied, all other things equal.

demand graphs, with price on the vertical axis and quantity on the horizontal axis. Plotting the information in each of the rows v through z gives us points v through z on the graph. Connecting these points gives us the supply curve S in Figure 1-5. The supply curve indicates all possible combinations of quantity supplied and alternative prices with the assumption that all other factors affecting supply are held constant. Note that the supply curve is upward sloping, reflecting the **law of supply**: price and quantity supplied increase together.

What if one of the other factors affecting supply was to change? Babysitting costs might decrease so that some tutors would be more willing to provide tutoring services, for example. This would increase the supply of tutoring services. You can probably list other factors that would increase the supply of tutoring. Changes in the costs of producing or supplying a product are among the most important factors causing a shift in the supply curve.

An increase in the supply of tutoring services as a result of lower babysitting costs will result in an entirely new supply schedule, such as the one shown in Table 1-5. Note that for each price, a larger quantity supplied now exists.

If we plot this new information on the same graph as the original supply curve, we have an entirely new supply curve S′, as indicated in Figure 1-6. Supply has increased, and the supply curve has shifted forward, or to the right, showing increased quantities supplied at each of the given prices. Lower costs always cause a forward shift in the curve, whereas higher costs always cause a backward shift in the curve.

TABLE 1-5 • Increased Supply Schedule for Tutoring Services, One Week

Alternative	P ($ per hour)	Q^S (hours)
v′	$1	60
w′	2	80
x′	3	100
y′	4	120
z′	5	140

© Cengage Learning

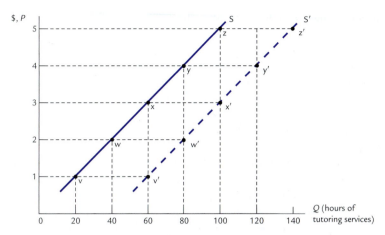

Figure 1-6 • Increased Supply of Tutoring Services, One Week
Supply curve S′ represents larger quantities of tutoring supplied at each price than does supply curve S.

If an event (such as an increase in babysitting costs) causing a decrease in the supply of tutoring were to occur, the supply curve would shift backward, or to the left. There would be a smaller quantity supplied at every price on the new supply curve.

Putting Demand and Supply Together

We can now consider the entire market for tutoring services at your school for the time period of one week. We have a demand schedule (or curve) that reflects the buyers' (students') attitudes toward purchasing tutoring services. And we have a supply schedule (or curve) that reflects the sellers' (tutors') attitudes toward supplying tutoring services. We simply have to put demand and supply together. Let's put them together graphically first. We will consider the original demand curve D and the original supply curve S, which are shown together in Figure 1-7.

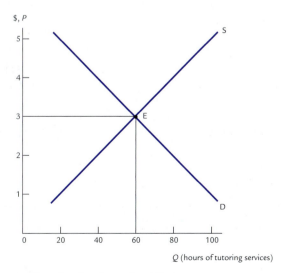

Figure 1-7 • Market for Tutoring Services, One Week
The market will clear at point E. At $3, quantity demanded equals quantity supplied.

As you can see, there is only one point in the graph (point E) where quantity demanded (which we read off the demand curve D) is equal to quantity supplied (which we read off the supply curve S). This point occurs at the intersection of demand and supply and corresponds to a price of $3 and quantities demanded and supplied of 60 hours a week. **At point E, the market for tutoring services is in equilibrium, or a state of balance, because the amount of tutoring services that students are willing and able to purchase is identical to the amount that tutors are willing to provide.** This equilibrium can also be seen in Table 1-6, which shows the original supply and demand schedules and (in bold) the equilibrium price and quantity.

Equilibrium
A state of balance; a point at which quantity demanded equals quantity supplied.

The market for tutoring services naturally tends to move toward the equilibrium point. To illustrate this tendency, consider what would happen if tutors were charging less than the equilibrium price of $3 an hour. Suppose that the tutors were charging only $1 an hour. At $1, the quantity demanded (100) exceeds the quantity supplied (20) by 80 hours. There would be a **shortage** of tutoring services of 80 hours, because at $1, buyers regard tutoring as a bargain, whereas sellers have little incentive to provide tutoring. (Note that in a technical sense, shortages *only* occur when market prices are below the equilibrium price.) Students will bid for the tutoring services that are available, and in the process the price will be bid up. Put yourself in the position of a student who needs tutoring. You would quite likely offer slightly more than $1 to a tutor so that you would receive the tutoring instead of your friend. Your (former) friend would probably be trying to do the same. In this process, the average price of tutoring would be pushed up. The bidding up of the price will continue only as long as the shortage exists, and as the price rises, the shortage will disappear. Two things happen as price increases: (1) buyers decrease the quantity they demand, and (2) sellers increase the quantity they offer for sale. This process of rising price, decreasing quantity demanded, and increasing quantity supplied is shown in Figure 1-8. The process will come to a screeching halt when equilibrium is reached at point E. Because the shortage no longer exists, the price will rise no higher. Economists usually refer to this phenomenon as the rationing function of price. This means that the movement of the price has ultimately rationed away the shortage. Without the ability of prices to adjust by moving upward, the shortage would have persisted indefinitely. Socialist countries have often done just that—they have prohibited prices from adjusting upward. As a result, shortages have been commonplace.

Shortage
A situation in which quantity demanded is greater than quantity supplied. This occurs only when the price is lower than the market level.

Surplus
A situation in which quantity supplied is greater than quantity demanded. This occurs only when the price is higher than the market level.

Now consider the opposite possibility. Tutors might be charging a price—say, $5— that is above the equilibrium price. Perhaps they feel that they can make a lot of income at this high price. There is, however, a problem in the market at this price. At $5 an hour, the quantity (20 hours per week) of tutoring services demanded will be very small. But tutors will be willing to supply a large quantity (100 hours per week) because they have so much incentive. The difference between the quantity that tutors supply and the amount that students actually buy (quantity demanded) is a **surplus** of unsold services in the market. (Note again that in a technical sense, surpluses *only* occur when market prices

TABLE 1-6 • Supply and Demand for Tutoring Services, One Week

P ($ per hour)	Q^S (hours)	Q^D (hours)
$1	20	100
2	40	80
3	60	60
4	80	40
5	100	20

© Cengage Learning

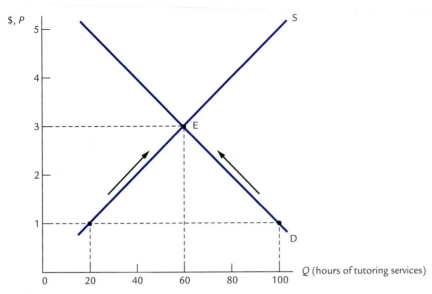

Figure 1-8 • Response to a Shortage of Tutoring Services
At a price of $1, quantity demanded exceeds quantity supplied by 80 hours. The 80-hour shortage will cause price to rise to the equilibrium price of $3.

are above the equilibrium price.) Surpluses cause the price to fall. Tutors will undercut one another's price to get some business, and the price will fall until it reaches the $3 equilibrium. As the price decreases, quantity demanded will increase, quantity supplied will decrease, and the surplus will disappear. This process is illustrated in Figure 1-9. The process comes to a halt when equilibrium is reached. The falling price has rationed away the surplus.

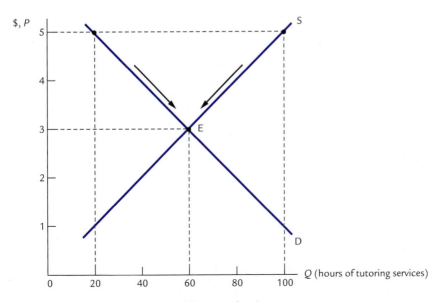

Figure 1-9 • Response to a Surplus of Tutoring Services
At a price of $5, quantity supplied exceeds quantity demanded by 80 hours. This 80-hour surplus will cause price to fall to the equilibrium price of $3.

© Cengage Learning

Shifts in Demand and Supply

The market for tutoring services will remain in equilibrium at point E unless some other factor affecting the market changes. Because things rarely remain unchanged, it is important to consider what might happen if the variables affecting either the demand for or the supply of tutoring services were to change.

Consider our earlier example in which an increase in student incomes caused an increase in the demand for tutoring services. The only thing that we are doing differently now is considering this shift in demand in the context of demand, supply, and equilibrium. The demand curve will shift forward to D′, as illustrated in Figure 1-10. *Note that the supply curve will not shift.* The old demand curve D becomes irrelevant, and a new equilibrium E′ exists at the intersection of the new demand curve D′ and the old supply curve S. By reading the new equilibrium price and quantity off the respective axes, we see that price has increased to $4 an hour and quantity has increased to 80 hours per week. Because demand has increased, the market price has increased, and suppliers have moved up their supply curve and increased the amount that they are willing to offer for sale (the quantity supplied). The increased demand curve and the unchanged supply curve have thus caused an increase in both equilibrium price and equilibrium quantity.

The opposite phenomenon would have occurred if there had been a decrease in demand. If student incomes had decreased, causing a decrease in demand, the demand curve would have shifted backward. The new equilibrium point would show that both price and quantity would have decreased.

Now consider the supply side of the tutoring market. Recall that a decrease in babysitting costs causes an increase in the supply of tutoring. If this increase occurs, the supply curve will shift forward *but the demand curve will not shift.* This phenomenon is illustrated by the shift of supply from S to S′ in Figure 1-11.

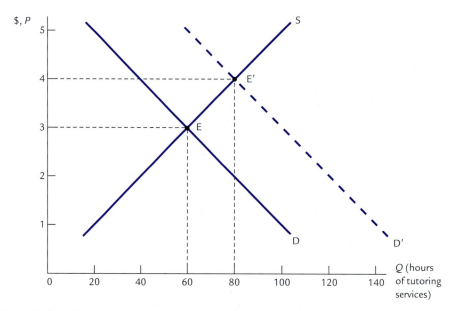

Figure 1-10 • Effects of Increased Demand for Tutoring Services
The increase in demand from D to D′ causes equilibrium price to increase from $3 to $4 and equilibrium quantity to increase from 60 to 80 hours.

© Cengage Learning

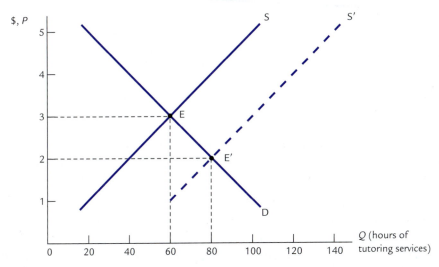

Figure 1-11 • Effects of an Increased Supply of Tutoring Services
The increase in supply from S to S′ will increase equilibrium quantity from 60 to 80 hours but decrease equilibrium price from $3 to $2.

The new equilibrium E′ is found at the intersection of the original demand curve D and the new supply curve S′. We see that the price has decreased to $2 an hour, while the quantity has increased to 80 hours per week. As a result of an increase in supply, the market price went down, so students (consumers) moved down along their demand curve, increasing the amount of tutoring services that they were willing and able to buy. Because supply increased, price decreased and the quantity exchanged increased. The increased supply curve and the unchanged demand curve have caused a decrease in the equilibrium price and an increase in the equilibrium quantity.

If supply had decreased because babysitting costs had increased, causing tutors to desire a higher price for tutoring services, the opposite phenomenon would have occurred. The supply curve would have shifted backward, resulting in a new equilibrium. The market price would be higher, but the equilibrium quantity would be lower.

The Real World

Whew! What a lot of graphs! But you now have learned the basic tools to answer many of life's economic questions. All markets have a demand (buyer's) side and a supply (seller's) side. And the things that affect supply and demand are the commonsense sorts of things described in the tutoring market example.

Demand curves shift if the number of buyers changes, if consumers' tastes change, or if the prices of other goods that the consumers regard as substitutes or complements change. In our tutoring example, a substitute for tutoring might be buying and using a study guide that goes along with a textbook. Substitute relationships occur when the consumer substitutes one good for the other good. A classic example of substitutes is butter and margarine. Complements are the opposite of substitutes. If the consumer uses more of one good, he or she will also use more of the other. A good example of complementary goods is digital cameras and memory cards. If the price of digital cameras goes down, all other things constant, more digital cameras will be purchased. With more digital cameras in the hands of consumers, there will be a greater demand for memory cards. Another example of a situation causing a shift in demand would be an increase in consumer incomes. While we normally expect an increase in income to cause an increase in demand, this is not always the case. Consider flat screen televisions, for example. A rise in consumer income will most likely cause a decrease in demand for flat screen televisions (whose price is now fairly low), but an increase in the demand for three-dimensional TV sets (still quite expensive).

A final example of a circumstance causing a shift in demand might be an expectation of the future. So if you read in the newspapers that a large increase in the price of toilet paper is expected next month, you and others may run out to buy toilet paper today, with the increased current demand actually causing a rise in its price (a self-fulfilling prophesy that is not uncommon in economics).

Supply curves shift if the number of sellers changes or if the factors that affect the producers' (sellers') costs change. So, a rise in the energy costs of a manufacturer will decrease the supply of manufactured goods. If businesses must pay higher wage rates to produce the same amount of output, the supply of output will decrease. On the other hand, if the price of raw materials goes down, the supply of the product for which the materials are used will increase. If technology improves, such that it becomes cheaper and easier to produce a product, supply of the product will increase. If the government taxes the production of a good or service or imposes costly regulations on the supplier, the supply of output will decrease; if the government provides subsidies (which lowers costs), however, the supply of the product will increase. Because these examples involve costs of production, we can think of higher costs of production as squeezing a supplier's profit margin, and thereby reducing incentives to supply the product. This would ultimately increase the price of the final product. Lower costs of production would do the opposite.

Figure 1-12 shows the factors that commonly cause real-world demand or supply curves to shift. Assume that you wake up some morning and read the following newspaper headlines: "Dramatic rise in energy prices causes increased production costs of

Factors That Cause Real-World Demand Curves to Shift

1. Changes in the number of consumers who wish to purchase the product.
2. Changes in the tastes of the consumers in the market.
3. Changes in the prices of complements or substitutes.
4. Changes in consumers' incomes.
5. Changes in consumers' expectations about the product's future price or availability.

Factors That Cause Real-World Supply Curves to Shift

1. Changes in the number of sellers in the market.
2. Changes in the prices of resources used to produce the product.
3. Changes in the technology used to produce the product.
4. Changes in the prices of other products that could be produced with the same resources.
5. Changes in government taxes or subsidies.
6. Changes in sellers' expectations about the product's future price.

Figure 1-12 • Factors That Cause Real-World Demand and Supply Curves to Shift

automobiles. Car prices rise." "New Children's Harry Potter book is released. Price of Harry Potter toys soar!" "Boycott of chocolate drives chocolate prices down. Chocolate growers dismayed."[1] "Great weather results in bumper crop of pumpkins. Pumpkin prices plummet!" How would you explain these price changes?

If you follow a step-by-step procedure, it is not hard to answer this question. (1) Draw a graph showing the particular market (cars, toys, chocolate, pumpkins) in equilibrium. Always label your equilibrium price *along the vertical axis* (label it P) and equilibrium quantity *along the quantity axis* (label it Q). (2) Consider the situation that is occurring. Decide whether its first and primary effect is on consumers or suppliers. Your answer will determine whether the demand or supply curve will shift. *You will shift only one curve in each graph!* Determine whether this curve should increase or decrease, and shift the curve forward or backward accordingly. (3) Find the new point of equilibrium and label the new equilibrium price and quantity *along their respective axes.* (4) Finally, compare the new quantity with the old quantity and the new price with the old price. It's as easy as pumpkin pie when there is a bumper crop of pumpkins! See Figure 1-13 for the analysis of these newspaper headlines.

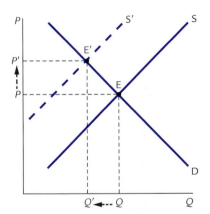

Rising costs of producing cars causes their prices to rise.

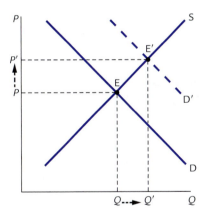

New Harry Potter book causes increased demand for Harry Potter toys, thereby raising their price.

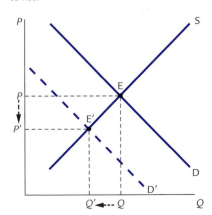

Boycott of chocolate decreases demand for chocolate, causing chocolate prices to fall.

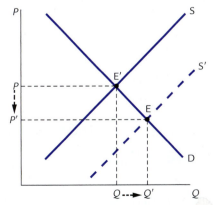

Great weather causes an increase in the supply of pumpkins, causing a decrease in their price.

Figure 1-13 • Newspaper Headlines: Demand and Supply

Which Comes First?

Which came first, the chicken or the egg? Which comes first, the price or the quantity? We know that price determines both, quantity demanded and quantity supplied. Yet demand and supply together determine the market price of the product. In a market economy, it is the simultaneous interaction of all prices, quantities, demands, and supplies that ultimately determines the final market price and the market quantity exchanged. And, of course, in the real world, demand and supply may both continually shift backward and forward, causing prices to continually change as well. Often, however, one curve will have a dominant shift in one direction, and this can explain much of the fluctuation that we see in real-world prices. In this text, we will keep things straightforward by generally shifting only one curve per graph.

Efficiency and Equity

Understanding demand and supply gives us greater insight into the working of the market economy and its production possibilities, because demand and supply determine how much of each particular good or service is produced. High prices encourage frugality. Only those most willing (with the greatest desire) or most able (with the greatest income) will purchase the product at high prices. The marketplace sifts out those with lesser preferences or lesser ability to afford the product, and the market thus serves as an allocating mechanism. High prices also encourage producers to offer more for sale.

In many ways, this function of market prices is desirable. Prices encourage thrift and careful choices among competing goods. Goods and services are allocated to those most willing to pay. Thus, the market is an effective allocative device. Without prices, products might go to people who do not strongly desire them and thus be wasted. Shortages of highly desirable goods and surpluses of less desirable ones might occur. But in the market, prices ration away these shortages and surpluses, suggesting that the marketplace is very **efficient** as a means of allocation and distribution.

Efficient
Using resources in such a way as to maximize the desired output.

Equity
Fairness.

On the other hand, the distribution of goods and services may not be equitable. **Equity** is a value-laden concept, and economists cannot say whether a particular distribution is fair. But certain results of market activity may not seem fair to some of us. A student may truly need tutoring services but not be able to afford them and thus fail the course. Children may go without milk, the homeless without shelter, and poor pregnant women without prenatal care because their low incomes render them unable to pay the prices that the market determines for these products. We might summarize by saying that the market entails both positive and negative aspects. **The market place is often efficient, but not necessarily equitable.**

Market Failures and a Glimpse of the Future

Most economists agree that the marketplace performs many useful functions. In addition to efficiency, a market-based economy provides economic incentives and tends to be highly productive. The combination of competition and proper price signals encourages efficient production of the products desired by consumers in the least costly manner.

Despite the benefits of a market economy, most economists recognize that the marketplace can also fail. The existence of many market failures does not necessarily imply that the marketplace itself is a failure. Rather, it points to ways that the government may become involved in the marketplace to assure that all societal needs are met. The following list of market failures also provides a glimpse into the chapters yet to come in this textbook.

Public Goods and Services

Public goods and services have unique characteristics that make it unlikely that the market will provide enough of them. As a result, the government often provides them. Public goods and services include national defense, public libraries, highway construction, crime prevention, public education, and others. At least to some point, the use of public goods and services by some of us does not keep others from using them. Your driving on a country road does not keep others from driving along it. Public goods and services are unlikely to be provided by the marketplace because they cannot be divided into small segments and offered for sale. For example, it doesn't make sense for each individual consumer to purchase one mile of the country road. Furthermore, if a private consumer *does* buy such a good or service, it is difficult to keep people who do not pay for the product from using it. Am I going to stand all day to make sure you do not drive on my own personal mile of the road? The entire notion of a private market for this country road takes on ridiculous proportions. It makes far more sense for the local government to provide the road and ensure its repair. Most economists agree that the provision of public goods and services is an appropriate role for government. Our disagreement concerns just what goods and services these will be, and how much of them we want. These disagreements are not trivial; they are taken up in Chapter 2 on crime prevention activities and drug control. They are also addressed in topics involving education, health care, and others.

Spillovers

Neither economic efficiency nor equity occurs when spillovers exist. Economic **spillovers** occur when some cost (or benefit) related to production or consumption "spills over" onto people not involved in the production or consumption of the good. Pollution of our environment is the most obvious example. If a manufacturer pollutes our air and water in the process of production, we will bear the costs of this pollution even if we don't own the company, acquire its profits, or buy its products. We bear the costs of pollution in terms of greater risk of illness, less aesthetic beauty, and lower-quality environment. The manufacturer has based its decisions on the profit motive, and has shifted part of the costs of production to society at large. Our natural resources are not being used appropriately, and our economy is not addressing our real needs and concerns. Our own dissatisfaction with the degraded environment will not remedy the problem unless collectively we are able to channel our concern through active government involvement. Issues surrounding pollution and government response are addressed in Chapter 3. Other goods and services provide spillover benefits to society. Education, discussed in Chapter 4, provides significant spillover benefits to society. The educated person is likely to provide innovation and creativity in the production process, and is more likely to vote and otherwise participate in government and public affairs. The educated person is less likely to be chronically unemployed or to commit a violent crime. He or she is more likely t pay taxes and less likely to be on welfare. The market will not, by itself, provide suf ient

Spillover

A costs or benefit of a private market activity that is shifted onto society at large. Alternatively called an externality.

levels of education, nor does it adequately compensate students for acquiring (and paying for) education, because the market place alone does not reflect these spillover benefits.

Inequity

We've already noted that the marketplace is not necessarily equitable. Discrimination is an issue of equity and is addressed in Chapter 5. Poverty and inequality of income distribution are also issues of equity. We may argue that the inability of low-income people to meet their basic needs is unfair. We may also argue that the extreme inequality of income distribution within the U.S. economy is unfair. These issues are addressed in Chapter 6 on U.S. poverty. Topics in other chapters, such as housing, health care, and social security also raise issues of equity. The problem of poverty at the global level is addressed in Chapter 10.

Market Power

Pure competition
A market in which many producers sell a standardized (identical) product to many buyers.

Our example of the demand and supply of tutoring services at a large university is one that approximates **pure competition**. There were many suppliers of tutoring services so that no single tutor could dictate the market price. If one of 100 tutors were to charge an exorbitant price, students would seek the services of the other 99. Competition protects us from unreasonable prices. We would not be protected if there were only one tutor. This monopoly supplier of tutoring services could charge a high price and consumers desiring the service would be forced to pay it. Even if there were a few more tutors available, this small group could hold back-alley meetings and fix the price of their services at a very high level.

Market power
The ability of an individual firm to influence the market price of its product.

Without competition, we would be at the mercy of this group. We would say that the single supplier and/or the price-fixing group possess **market power**, which is the ability of a supplier to influence the market price of its product. It is only with a large number of tutors—so many that it is unrealistic for them all to come to agreement about prices and so many that no individual supplier produces for a large share of the market—that market power is absent. To the extent that many U.S. industries consist of just a few dominant producers (examples are the automobile, steel, and breakfast cereal industries), competition is reduced and society's well-being suffers. Examples of firms charged with abusing their market power include Microsoft and Apple. Because market power arises when a small number of suppliers influence the market price of their product, it is reasonable to conclude that a larger number of suppliers, whether these are domestic or foreign producers, will serve to reduce market power. Many people are unaware of the important contribution of international trade in enhancing competition and reducing market power. This problem of market power is discussed in Chapter 13 and international trade is discussed in Chapter 12.

Instability

Finally, we return to the topic of production possibilities and employment. The factors that determine whether our nation will be on the production possibilities curve (operating at full employment) or *below* the production possibilities curve (with unemployed resources) are very volatile. Thus, at times we may have very low employment, and at other times we may have high employment. Closely related are the factors affecting the average level of prices throughout our economy. When the average price level rises, we say that we have **inflation**. Because prices and employment tend to fluctuate, many say that our market economy is inherently unstable. We address these issues in Chapter 14 on unemployment and inflation, Chapter 15 on government macroeconomic policy, and

Inflation
A rise in the average price level in the economy.

Chapter 16 on taxes and borrowing. In the process, we discover how our government and our central banking system can intervene in many ways to ensure greater stability of prices and employment.

Some Final Comments to Students

We've examined the production possibilities curve as a means of discussing scarcity. And we've studied the graphs of demand and supply to understand distribution. We will use these models throughout the text to analyze a variety of microeconomic and macroeconomic issues. **Microeconomics** deals with individual activity within the economy, whereas **macroeconomics** deals with the economy as a whole. Microeconomics covers topics such as the distribution of income within the country and the nature of individual markets such as agriculture, whereas macroeconomics covers topics such as total income and total output in the economy. When we speak of total output, we are really referring to gross domestic product. More specifically, **gross domestic product (GDP)** is the value of an economy's total output of goods and services produced within a particular year. GDP will be a very useful concept throughout the textbook because we often use it as a frame of reference. For example, it is somewhat meaningless to talk of the millions of dollars spent on health care when a more meaningful topic of discussion is the expenditure on health care relative to GDP. This is because GDP is really the nation's capacity to generate income that can be spent on health care or on any other good or service.

The terms *private* and *public* are also used throughout the text. The term **private** refers to individual people and businesses. It relates to *private* markets, which reflect consumer demand and producer supply. We speak of *private* spending (by people and businesses) and *private* ownership (by people and businesses). On the other hand, the term **public** refers to the government. Thus, we can speak *of public* spending and *public* ownership. Recall that we have already used these terms as we considered private and public goods.

As our world becomes increasingly internationalized, awareness of the economics of domestic social issues is insufficient. We must also be aware of our international economy. We must enter into the exciting world of international trade and finance, the devastating presence of international poverty, the important issues of world hunger and global agriculture, and the fascinating set of international issues addressed in Chapter 17. The world is alive on our TV sets and computer screens, in our travels and contacts with international students and faculty, and in our jobs of the future. We must be aware of our global world!

You, the Student

And now we've come back to the topic we started with: that is, you, the student. How do you fit into this world of economic problems? What do these problems mean for your life? And how can you affect the world around you? The Epilogue tackles these questions, as do the sections on "You, the Student" and "Discussion and Action Questions" at the end of each chapter. *Please read them! Also, read the ViewPoint sections in each chapter and begin to discover and formulate your own viewpoints within the framework of the economic left or right (or in-between) on each issue.* The definitions to the right will help you. The first step in making changes is to educate ourselves. And once we educate ourselves, we can make a positive difference in our world. With that in mind, let's begin the journey to understanding economic issues and policy!

Microeconomics
The study of individual areas of activity within the total economy.

Macroeconomics
The study of the total economy.

Gross domestic product (GDP)
Total output of an economy.

Private
Individual people and businesses.

Public
Government.

Economic liberal (economic left)
A person who believes in high levels of government involvement in the economy.

Economic conservative (economic right)
A person who believes in very low levels of government involvement in the economy.

View*Point*   The Economic Left and the Economic Right

The Economic Left	The Economic Right
(Liberal)	(Conservative)
The Extreme Left: Pure Socialism	The Extreme Right: Pure Capitalism
Characteristics of Socialism:	Characteristics of Capitalism:
Government Ownership of Land and Capital	Private Ownership of Land and Capital
Government Economic Decision Making	Private Economic Decision Making
Values of the Left: Equity	Values of the Right: Efficiency
Goal: More Government in the Economy	Goal: Less Government in the Economy

This book is intended to get you to think. As you acquire a basic understanding of economics, you also acquire a basic framework within which to form and justify your personal opinions about economic issues. Are you an economic conservative or an economic liberal? Are you conservative on some economic issues and liberal on others? Do you even know what these terms mean in the context of economics? From a U.S. perspective, being an **economic conservative** generally means believing in only a limited role for government in the economy. In the conservative view, the free market operates relatively well by itself, so that little government intervention in the form of regulations, taxes, and programs is needed. Indeed, economic conservatives believe that if left alone, the market will solve most economic problems. The conservative view exists on the right end of the economic philosophical spectrum. Being an **economic liberal**, on the other hand, generally means supporting far greater government involvement in the economy. In the liberal view, the marketplace entails many shortcomings, or market failures. These shortcomings can be rectified by government involvement. The liberal view is on the left end of the economic philosophical spectrum. Please keep in mind the economic spectrum throughout the textbook! We have already discovered that although the marketplace tends to be efficient, it is not necessarily equitable. We've recognized that many market failures exist. All of these suggest some proper role for government in the economy. Nevertheless, there is probably no

debate more contentious within societies than the ideal degree of government involvement in the economy.

The ViewPoint boxes at the end of each chapter clarify the positions of both economic liberals and economic conservatives to help you formulate your own beliefs. Keep in mind that while this section is intended to show opposite viewpoints, economists and policymakers often find themselves closer to the middle. On many issues, agreement among economists is widespread. Also keep in mind that an economic conservative or liberal is different from a social conservative or liberal. Social conservatives, for example, may oppose gun control and support prayer in schools. A social conservative (or liberal) may be entirely different from an economic conservative (or liberal). We will make this distinction in some of the chapters to come. Furthermore, the extreme ends of the economic spectrum, socialism and capitalism, do not tell us anything about the political systems of a country. Many countries, such as Chile in the early 2000s, have socialist economic systems along with democratic political systems, whereas Chile had a capitalist economic system ruled by a military dictator from 1973 to 1990. The conclusion is that you should not necessarily associate capitalism with democracy, or socialism with a dictatorship. Please make sure to read the ViewPoint sections! They are an essential feature of this book and will help you assess your own opinions. You may find that you are an economic liberal, or an economic conservative, or that your opinions vary with the particular issue.

SUMMARY

Economics deals primarily with scarcity: how shall we allocate our limited world resources to satisfy our seemingly unlimited human wants? Limited resources translate into limited production possibilities. The production possibilities curve shows us the alternative combinations of the maximum amounts of two different goods that can be produced during any particular time period, assuming full use of our technology and resources. Unemployment of resources results in production levels lower than those possible. Economic growth over time results in increasingly higher levels of production of all goods.

Our output and distribution decisions are mostly made in the markets for individual goods and services. Demand for a product by consumers and supply of a product by producers both hinge on the prices that must be paid or received. Demand and supply together determine the market

equilibrium, establishing the going market price and the quantity exchanged. Our market economy ensures that goods and services are distributed only to those most willing and able to pay the market price. Markets are often considered to be efficient, but not necessarily equitable.

Market failures include the problem of public goods and services, the existence of spillovers, problems of inequity, the presence of market power, and the lack of stability in our economy. An important issue is the role of government versus the free market. Economic liberals prefer a large role for government in the economy, and economic conservatives prefer a small role. As you continue your reading, you will make your own decisions about whether you are liberal or conservative on certain issues. Finally, you will consider your role within our world economy.

DISCUSSION AND ACTION QUESTIONS

1. Suppose your friend is strong on defense and insists that we must bolster our national defense, whatever the cost. How can you use economic logic to make him or her aware of the opportunity costs associated with his or her objective?

2. Unemployment imposes serious hardship on out-of-work individuals and their families. What are the costs of unemployment to society as a whole? (Keep in mind the production possibilities curve.)

3. Why, in a rich nation, is it important that we fully use our resources and technology to maximize our nation's output? Is it only the level of total output that is important, or are the types of output that we produce also important? Do you think that the distribution of this output is just as important as its total amount?

4. Do you think our nation's output should be distributed according to income or according to some other standard (such as basic human need)?

5. Equilibrium implies that quantity demanded equals quantity supplied at a particular price. Must consumers and producers actually sit down to discuss and decide on an equilibrium market price? Is a farmers' market or a flea market a competitive market? Why or why not?

6. Does the efficiency of the price mechanism ensure that our market-based economy is an equitable one? Why or why not?

7. The following schedules are for bushels of apples in a local market. Graph the supply and demand curves. What are the equilibrium price and quantity?

Price	Quantity Demanded	Quantity Supplied
$20	200	1,000
18	400	800
16	600	600
14	800	400
12	1,000	200

Now assume that an early freeze has decreased the apple harvest, and the new supply schedule is as follows. Has supply increased or decreased? What are the new equilibrium price and quantity? (Note that the demand curve is unchanged.)

Price	Quantity Supplied
$20	600
18	400
16	200
14	0

8. Go to the Web site at http://netec.mcc.ac.uk/JokEc, find a good economics joke, and share it with your teacher!

9. One additional source that may be useful if you need to do research on economics topics is the Web site of the British periodical, *The Economist*. Its articles on various topics can usually be understood by beginning students of economics. You can find this site at http://www.economist.com.

Note

1. Many activists are encouraging a boycott of chocolate that has been produced with cocoa beans from West Africa, where people are virtual slaves to the cocoa companies. Other activists are encouraging people to purchase "fair trade cocoa" (and other fair trade products, such as coffee and tea). The situation of "cocoa slavery" and "fair trade" products will be discussed more in Chapter 12 on international trade. (This is mentioned in Chapter 12 on international trade, where the citation refers the reader to www.corpwatch.org, a Web site for CorpWatch. Another site is www.globalslaveryindex.org, of the anti-slavery organization Walk Free Foundation.)

Appendix 1-1
Increasing Opportunity Costs

The production possibilities curve that we've considered is actually a simplified representation of the real world. Recall that for each additional 20 units of roses that were produced, society had to give up the production of 30 units of bread. This ratio of 20 units of roses to 30 units of bread remained constant, regardless of how much bread and roses were actually produced. In the real world, this ratio usually is not constant, but rather it is increasing. In other words, as we produce larger quantities of roses, we must usually give up increasingly larger quantities of bread. This is another way of saying that the opportunity cost increases as we produce more of one particular good. It increases because we ultimately use resources that are less well suited to producing more of this particular good. In our example, we might begin production by using those resources that are best suited for each product. As we produce more roses, we would eventually need to use resources that are more suitable for bread production (such as farmers who know little about roses and land not well suited to rose production), so that we would need to use larger and larger quantities of these resources to make up for their lower productivity. In other words, we must give up increasingly larger amounts of bread production to produce additional roses. And this means that the opportunity cost of rose production increases as we produce more and more of it. The same would be true for the production of bread.

Table 1-7 shows the production possibilities for bread and roses, under the more realistic assumption that opportunity costs are increasing. We note that if we begin with alternative A, 150 tons of bread and 0 tons of roses are produced. If we increase rose production by 20 tons, we will give up 5 tons of bread. If we produce 20 more tons of roses, we will give up 15 tons of bread. And if we produce 20 more tons of roses, we will give up 20 tons of bread. **In other words, we have increasing opportunity costs: as more and more of one good is produced, society must continually sacrifice increasingly larger amounts of the other good.**

Increasing opportunity costs
As more of one good is produced, society must give up increasingly larger amounts of the alternative good.

TABLE 1-7 • Production Possibilities Table With Increasing Opportunity Cost

Alternative	Bread (tons)	Roses (tons)
A	150	0
B	145	20
C	130	40
D	110	60
E	70	80
F	0	100

ROAD MAP

Chapter 2
Crime and Drugs

Chapter 5
Discrimination
Drug laws may result in discriminatory incarceration

Chapter 7
Housing
Public housing concentrates poverty and leads to dysfunctions such as drug use

Chapter 8
Health Care
Drugs have public health consequences and so would the legalization of drugs

Chapter 10
World Poverty
U.S. efforts to fumigate drug sources worsen health and poverty in developing countries

Chapter 14
Unemployment and Inflation
Does crime worsen during periods of recession and high unemployment?

Chapter 2

The Economic Toolbox

- Public goods and services
- Free-rider
- Cost-benefit analysis
- Production possibilities
- Elasticity of demand
- Excise tax

Crime and Drugs

D o these words of former secretary of state Hillary Rodham Clinton sound rather trite to you—just a little bit obvious? In fact, they are startling, because they represent, first of all, unusually blunt language from a secretary of state. Second, they represent a first major acknowledgement by a high-level U.S. government official that the U.S. *demand* for illegal drugs is the key factor in the illegal drug market. Ironically, as we shall see, by far most U.S. expenditures to control the illegal drug market are focused on the *supply* of drugs, and not the demand.

And, as we will see, the illegal drug trade, to which we will return, is just one example of crime in the United States. In discussing these topics, you will have the chance to put to use your knowledge of demand and supply graphs and production possibilities and to consider the economic concepts of public goods and services, cost-benefit analysis, the effect of excise taxes, and the elasticity of demand. And finally, as in all chapters, there is a ViewPoint section and there are suggestions for you to engage in various activities in the section, "You, the Student," and in the "Discussion and Action Questions" at the end of the chapter.

Crime, broadly defined, imposes huge costs on the United States each year. These costs include both the damage to property and to people, as well as the cost of policies undertaken by government to prevent and punish criminal activity. Not all these costs can easily be assigned a monetary value. We can calculate the replacement cost of a building destroyed by arson, but what is the cost for an assault victim? We can measure the person's medical bills and even the value of their lost productivity on the job, but how do we measure their trauma and pain? One element of these costs that is relatively easy to measure is the cost of administering the criminal justice system, which consists of police, courts, and prisons. This system, intended to prevent and punish crime, is responsible for expenditures of hundreds of billions of dollars annually by federal, state, and local governments.[1] Indeed, expenditures for the criminal justice system have been an increasingly important item in state government budgets over time. Recall our discussion of opportunity costs in Chapter 1. Resources absorbed by the criminal justice system cannot be used for education, poverty reduction, housing, health care, or any other worthwhile purpose, so it is important that these resources be used wisely. Economics will help us to analyze the effectiveness of our policies to combat crime.

When we think of crime, we usually think of violent crimes such as murder and assault. Perhaps we also include various offenses against property, such as arson and theft. However, by definition, a crime is any action that is forbidden by law and carries

Our insatiable demand for illegal drugs fuels the drug trade.

—SECRETARY OF STATE HILLARY RODHAM CLINTON, ON A VISIT TO MEXICO, MARCH 26, 2009

criminal penalties, which often include imprisonment. Among other crimes in the United States are identity theft, gambling, prostitution, possession of and trafficking in drugs, driving while under the influence of alcohol, and sales of pornography. These are crimes because society as a whole, or a significant portion of society, thinks they are wrongful actions and has prohibited them by law.

The Federal Bureau of Investigation (FBI) reports the number of violent crimes that occur per 100,000 people in the country. Violent crime is defined to include murder, forcible rape, robbery, and aggravated assault. These crime rates are shown in Table 2-1 for selected years from 1990 to 2011; using the most recently available data as this text is being written. *We see that violent crime rates have fallen since 1990, despite our recent recession and more recent less than robust economy.* Experts no longer see a necessary link between violent crime rates and the state of the economy that they once suspected. However, preliminary data suggest an increase in the violent crime rate in 2012, up to about 391, an increase of 1.2 percent from 2011. If this holds up, it may be an aberration, or it may mean a reversal of the downward trend. We will need to watch for further statistics.

Additional data are cited in Table 2-2, showing the number of the various types of violent crime, as well as less serious property crime. Despite falling violent crime rates, the number of crimes still seems high, and people indicate in opinion surveys that they do not feel safer.

TABLE 2-1 • Violent Crime Rates in the United States (Number of Crimes per 100,000 Inhabitants), Selected Years 1990–2011

Year	Violent Crime Rate[a]
1990	730
1995	685
2000	507
2005	477
2010	404
2011	386

[a]Violent crime includes murder and nonnegligent manslaughter, forcible rape, robbery, and aggravated assault; and by definition it involves force or threat of force.

Source: Department of Justice, Federal Bureau of Investigation, *Uniform Crime Report,* 2012, http://www.fbi.gov.

TABLE 2-2 • Number of Crimes, by Type of Violent Crime and by Property Crime, 2011, in Thousands

	Number of Crimes
Violent Crime[a]	1,204
Murder[b]	15
Forcible rape	83
Robbery	354
Aggravated assault	751
Property Crime[c]	9,063

[a]Violent crime includes murder and nonnegligent manslaughter, forcible rape, robbery, and aggravated assault; and by definition it involves force or threat of force.
[b]Includes nonnegligent manslaughter.
[c]Property crime includes burglary, larceny/theft, and motor vehicle theft, and by definition does not involve force or threat of force.

Source: Department of Justice, Federal Bureau of Investigation, *Uniform Crime Report,* 2012, http://www.fbi.gov.

In this chapter, we will look at several issues involving crime and economics. We will begin by examining the economic characteristics of crime prevention and a cost-benefit analysis of our criminal justice system. Then, we will consider the issues of white-collar crime, diversity and crime, and global dimensions of crime. We will then consider issues surrounding illegal drugs, especially the economic impact of their legalization. Finally, we will consider other so-called victimless crimes. In our analysis, we will practice using the tools you have already learned in Chapter 1: production possibilities and demand and supply, plus the new concept of cost-benefit analysis and the elasticity of demand.

Crime Prevention

Crime Prevention as a Public Good

Police activity and other crime prevention measures are examples of **public goods and services**. These goods and services, first discussed as market failures in Chapter 1, have characteristics that make private market production of them inefficient. First of all, public goods are **indivisible**, which means that they cannot be divided reasonably into small enough units to be sold in a market to individual consumers. (It doesn't make sense for each of us to purchase 1/100 of a criminal justice system, for example.) Second, up to a point, public goods and services are **nonrivalrous**. This means that the protection afforded to one citizen by a police officer on patrol, for example, does not "use up" the benefits of police protection and prevent other citizens from receiving the same benefits. (Most goods are rivalrous. Consider a hamburger: if you eat it, no one else can.) Finally, public goods are **nonexcludable** in that we cannot prevent specific citizens from deriving benefits from crime prevention activity. This last characteristic of public goods means that they are subject to the **free-rider problem**—for example, if police protection was provided by the private market, we would be unable to withhold the benefits of safer streets from those who refuse to pay. (Most goods, on the other hand, are excludable, so no free-rider problem exists. A good example is a theater seat; you can't get one if you don't pay for a ticket.)

The private market is extremely efficient in providing hamburgers and theater seats and many other goods that are divisible, rivalrous, and excludable. The intersection of demand and supply at the equilibrium price results in neither shortages nor surpluses, and both buyers and sellers agree that the value of the product is the equilibrium price. **However, the private market is not efficient in providing public goods.** Therefore, the government usually provides public goods and services and finances them with tax revenues.

There are many examples of public goods and services besides crime prevention. Examples of these include fire protection, public libraries, public schools and universities, national defense, the space program, highway construction, and public parks. Can you think of other examples?

Crime Prevention Measures

Crime prevention measures are undertaken by the police, the criminal courts, and our prison system. Police cars patrolling our neighborhoods, police-sponsored activities for young people, the support of neighborhood watch programs, and the investigation of crimes are among the duties of police. The courts are responsible for bringing to trial those who have been accused of violating criminal law and who have been apprehended by the police. The prison system exists to incarcerate, punish, and sometimes rehabilitate those convicted of crimes. Some practices, such as the operation of programs for disadvantaged youth, are preventive in that they may keep crime from occurring. Other

Public goods and services
Goods and services often provided by the government because their unique characteristics make it unlikely that the private market will provide them in sufficient quantity.

Indivisible
A characteristic of public goods in that they are impossible to divide into units sufficiently small to be sold in private markets.

Nonrivalrous
A characteristic of public goods in that use by one person does not prevent use by others.

Nonexcludable
A characteristic of public goods in that their benefits cannot be kept from persons who do not pay for the goods' provision in a private market.

Free-rider problem
A situation in which individuals that do not pay their share for a good or service nevertheless enjoy its benefits.

activities involving the investigation of crimes, trial of suspects, and sentencing of those found guilty are crime prevention measures because they may have a deterrent effect.

Evaluation by Cost-Benefit Analysis

Cost-benefit analysis

A study that compares the costs and benefits of a policy, program, or activity.

Net benefits

The excess of benefits over costs.

An appropriate method to evaluate government policy is cost-benefit analysis. Using this method, we add up the benefits from a particular course of action and compare them to the costs. The activity is justified only if the benefits are greater than the costs. Furthermore, if two policies have greater benefits to society than their costs, the one with the larger **net benefits**, or excess of benefits over cost, should generally be adopted. Cost-benefit analysis is also discussed in the context of environmental protection policies in Chapter 3 and higher education in Chapter 4.

Benefits and Costs of Crime Prevention Activities

In the context of anticrime policy, the benefits of crime prevention activities include the value of property damage that is prevented, as well as the medical expenses, psychological trauma, loss of income, and other expenses that are not incurred when criminal assaults are prevented. Costs of anticrime activity include the costs of equipment, such as squad cars and prison cells; the salaries and fringe benefits of police, court, and corrections personnel; and the costs of administering the system. Can you think of other costs?

Our direct expenditures on the criminal justice system are high and have been increasing rapidly over recent decades. Among police protection, the judicial system, and the correctional system, corrections have increased most rapidly. State governments are heavily responsible for prisons, and since state governments also fund public education, health care, and other important services, it is appropriate to examine the production possibilities curve introduced in Chapter 1. Resources used for corrections are not available for other uses. Figure 2-1 shows a production possibilities curve with corrections on the vertical axis. The curve illustrates that resources used for corrections are not available for other uses such as education and health care. Furthermore, we have moved from a point such as A to one such as B, which indicates increased criminal justice activity relative to other goods and services over the past quarter century or so.

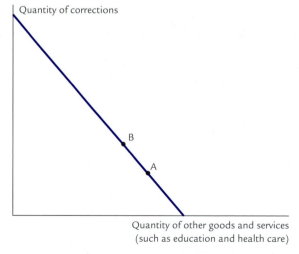

Figure 2-1 • Production Possibilities Curve for State Corrections
Resources used for state corrections are not available for other uses. Over time, states in the United States have moved from points such as A to point B on the curve.

© Cengage Learning

Increased Costs of Our Prison System

We've noted that among crime prevention activities, spending on corrections has increased most rapidly. This increase in resources devoted to our prison system mainly reflects a change in the thrust of our crime control policies. We now lock up in prison, or incarcerate, far more people than we did in the past. In 2011, there were 1.5 million inmates in our nation's prisons and jails.[2]

What do we notice about the incarceration rates in Table 2-3? First, the term *incarceration rate* is defined as the number of people in prison for every 100,000 residents in the country. We also note that with an incarceration rate of 716, the United States has the highest incarceration rate in the world. We've only fairly recently surpassed Russia, which formerly had the highest rate. The incarceration rate in Russia is 486. If we arbitrarily use an incarceration rate of 200 as a cutoff, then we see that the countries with the highest and middle level rates include several former Soviet republics (Russia, Belarus, Azerbaijan, and Kazakhstan) as well as an assortment of developing countries. (As for the Bahamas—let's just say you should avoid criminal activity if your spring break takes you to the sun and beaches of this country!) Lastly, what really stands out in the table is the fact that Western industrialized countries, as well as Canada, South Korea, and Japan, have very low incarceration rates, especially when compared with the United States.

Higher levels of incarceration and longer prison sentences are supposed to reduce crime primarily in two ways. They supposedly deter would-be offenders from committing crimes because of the increased likelihood of a prison sentence. And they physically prevent convicts from committing new crimes while they are in prison.

This movement toward prison expansion and greater incarceration has been one of the most controversial aspects of our crime prevention activities. It costs enormous amounts of money that might be put to better uses by cash-strapped state governments, including the education and health programs already mentioned. It might also be diverted to more successful policies of the "war on drugs," which might focus more heavily on education and rehabilitation (as discussed shortly). As a result, there has been significant effort to rationally evaluate this policy by cost-benefit analysis. The results of the studies, however, are not conclusive. Let's see why.

TABLE 2-3 • Incarceration Rates (Number of Incarcerated People per 100,000 Inhabitants), Most Recently Available, 20 Selected Countries Including Highest and Lowest[a]

Country	Incarceration Rate	Country	Incarceration Rate
High Rates		*Low Rates*	
United States	716	Tajikistan	130
Cuba	510	China	121
Russia	486	Canada	114
Belarus	438	South Korea	92
Azerbaijan	413	Germany	80
Middle Rates		Norway	71
Thailand	373	Sweden	67
Bahamas	371	Japan	54
Kazakhstan	316	Iceland	47
South Africa	286	Timor-Leste	22
Mexico	209	San Marino	6

[a]Year 2011.

Source: International Centre for Prison Studies (ICPA): A Partner of the University of Essex, *ICPS World Prison Brief*, www .prisonstudies.org/info/worldbrief. Data are continually updated as information becomes available.

Empirical Studies of the Trend Toward Higher Incarceration Rates

The discussion of our imprisonment policy is usually couched in terms of (1) decreasing violent crimes against persons or (2) prison overcrowding and the nature of the prison population. We all agree that we want to prevent rapes, murders, and muggings. Whether harsher sentences and more prisons prevent these and other crimes is the question.

Decreasing Violent Crimes Against Persons

Some researchers have indicated that the violent crime rate has indeed gone down as a result of our tougher policy; others have disagreed. These conflicting conclusions are the result of differences in research methods. Specifically, some studies control for age of criminals, whereas others do not.

The ages of 15 to 29 are violence-prone years in our society. As people mature, they are less likely to commit violent acts. The average age of the U.S. population is increasing, which in itself should cause a decrease in our violent crime rate. Age adjustment of data takes into account this changing demographic characteristic of the population in an attempt to rid the data of age bias. When the data are adjusted for the age distribution of the population, results indicate that a relatively small amount of crime is reduced by "get-tough" policies. When the data are not adjusted, the results indicate a larger reduction in crime.

In terms of cost-benefit analysis, studies that use age-adjusted data tend to find few benefits and great costs associated with higher incarceration rates. Studies without age adjustments find that the benefits of increased incarceration greatly exceed the costs. Thus, conflicting research methods lead to uncertain conclusions.

Prison Overcrowding and the Nature of the Prison Population

The second aspect of our incarceration policy concerns prison overcrowding and the need to continually build more prisons to accommodate the increasing number of prisoners. This need will, of course, lead to a still greater allocation of resources to corrections. *Although violent crime rates have fallen since 1990, the prison population has soared since then.* A number of factors have contributed to this increase. Let's consider three of these.

First, mandatory minimum sentences have been established for drug violations and other offenses, and now almost half of federal prisoners are drug offenders. These laws were established in response to the epidemic use of illegal drugs in the 1970s and 1980s in an effort to "get-tough" with drug offenders. The outcome, though, is that judges exercise less discretion in individual situations. Many people also believe that nonviolent drug offenders are a drain on our prison funding and risk becoming "hardened criminals" while in prison. Some commentators believe that the population most harmed by mandatory sentences has been women. Often, these women become involved in relationships with criminal men, and they may become peripherally involved with drugs as a result. Although these women may not be serious offenders, they and their children suffer from the women's long incarcerations. Indeed, research by the Department of Justice and other agencies has documented that many prisoners with mandatory sentences are low-level offenders whose continued imprisonment is extremely costly and wasteful of prison space.

The second factor in rising imprisonment is the 1994 federal crime bill, which contained a Truth in Sentencing provision. Under this law, over half of all states have qualified for federal prison funding by changing their sentencing laws to require that certain offenders serve at least 85 percent of their prison sentence before being considered for parole.

Third, the federal government and half the states have passed "three strikes and you're out" laws that require sentences of life for a third conviction of certain crimes. This movement originated in California, where a three-strikes law was passed several years ago after the kidnapping and murder of a 12-year-old California child. Other states have passed similar laws as a result of public outrage over repeat offenders. However, despite good intentions, these laws have resulted in life imprisonment of many people for relatively minor crimes. For example, one man whose third crime was stealing videocassettes and another man whose third offense was stealing golf clubs were both given life sentences in prison. The third "strike" of more than half of the prisoners is for a nonviolent offense such as drug possession.

Partially as a result of all three of these policies, the state and local prison population, along with prisoners in local jails is still large. Nevertheless, incarceration rates are decreasing. This is due to the fact that over half of the states have initiated sentencing reforms in the last several years. For example, Kansas and Washington have reduced the length of low-level drug terms, and Connecticut has granted judges more discretion in school-drug zone cases. Michigan has scaled back mandatory minimum sentences. New York State, which led the nation with harsh drug sentences decades ago, is now loosening these laws and increasingly relying on drug treatment.

The economic context is changing. Our economy worsened in the early 2000s, and by late 2007 we were officially in a recession (though our economy has improved since then, as we will see in Chapter 14). In a recession, people lose their jobs and incomes. With falling incomes, state governments receive falling tax revenues. If nothing else will curtail public spending on prisons, a deteriorating economy will. States as varied as Colorado, Kansas, Kentucky, and New Jersey have been closing prisons, reducing sentences as a result.

Another related effect of the economy concerns the death penalty. Most notably, in March of 2009, Governor Bill Richardson of New Mexico signed legislation to repeal the death penalty, which was seen as too costly. Similarly, in February 2009, Maryland governor Martin O'Malley, a Roman Catholic who has cited his religious opposition to the death penalty in the past, began arguing that capital cases cost three times as much as homicide cases where the death penalty is not sought. "And," he said, "We can't afford that."

Thus it seems that drug penalties, incarceration rates, and even death penalty cases may actually fall during times of a worsening economy. The latter case warrants further attention.

Cost-Benefit Analysis of the Death Penalty

Although many people assume that a sentence of life in prison must be more expensive than imposing the death penalty, several studies have shown that the death penalty in fact costs taxpayers far more. For example, over the times covered by these studies, the death penalty in California cost $114 million per year *beyond* the cost of lifetime imprisonment. In Kansas, the cost of capital cases was 70 percent more expensive than comparable noncapital cases. In North Carolina, the death penalty cost was $2.16 million more *per execution* than the lifetime imprisonment of convicted murderers. In Texas, a single death penalty case cost an average of $2.3 million, which was about three times the cost of imprisoning someone in a single cell at the highest security level for 40 years. Finally, in Florida, the death penalty costs $51 million per year *above* what it would cost to punish all first-degree murderers with life in prison without parole. Many of these costs occur at the trial level.[3]

Death penalty cases are expensive because the trials tend to take longer, they typically require more lawyers and more costly expert witnesses, and they are far more likely to lead to multiple appeals. Yet death penalty proponents maintain that repealing the death penalty to reduce costs is shortsighted; they argue that the death penalty is the greatest possible deterrent of capital crimes. Others disagree. According to a survey of the former and current presidents of the country's top academic criminological societies, 84 percent of these experts rejected the idea that the death penalty is an effective deterrent to murder.[4] These studies suggest that in terms of cost-benefit analysis, the costs of the death penalty far exceed any benefits.

White-Collar Crime

Our economy is badly weakened, a consequence of greed and irresponsibility ...
—President Barack Obama, Address to Joint Session of Congress, February 24, 2009

The president's harsh words about white-collar crime have not gone unnoticed. Indeed, the publicity surrounding corporate crime and high-level thievery suggests that this form of crime has reached all-time highs. The term *white-collar crime* is generally used to describe crime by business managers, as well as their supporting structure of boards of directors, accountants, investment bankers, lawyers, and other professionals who engage in dishonest practices for financial gain. White-collar criminals can also include corrupt politicians and lobbyists. Since they are nonviolent crimes, many people are less concerned about white-collar crime than some of the other crimes we've discussed. **Nevertheless, white-collar crime is real and seems to be growing in epidemic proportions.**

Certainly, individuals and businesses that are victims of white-collar crime experience as great a monetary loss as those who are victims of outright thievery. Many people have lost their retirement savings, and consequently their homes and health care. The ability of our federal, state, and local governments to provide basic services is threatened by the tax evasion that is often part of the white-collar criminal activity. Finally, campaign financing has been exploited by corporate financiers in a manner that threatens the very meaning of democracy. We can't even begin to measure the outcomes of government policies distorted by bribery and corruption among our elected officials.

The early 2000s arose as banner years for white-collar crime, with revelations of outrageous compensation packages for managers, loss of pensions and savings funds for employees, and allegations of abuse by large corporations, including Enron, WorldCom, Tyco, Global Crossing, and others. In the midst of his second year in office, President George W. Bush signed a corporate responsibility law that he vowed would improve oversight over business practices and create sanctions for white-collar criminals. Yet inadequate regulations and lax enforcement of laws that did exist brought the maligned names of additional CEOs, bankers, and administrators to the fore and helped usher in the financial crisis and global recession of late 2007. White-collar crime is certainly not of trivial consequence!

Diversity and Crime

Consider the following examples are actual crimes, both described in the *New York Times*.

Two brothers were walking home from a church party late at night. They were walking arm-in-arm, a common practice for Latin American brothers such as these. Romal was 38 years old and was visiting his brother, Jose, who was 31 years old. Jose was described as a kind and generous man and father of two. Suddenly, a car drove up and three men began shouting ugly anti-gay and anti-Latino vulgarities at the brothers. "Jose went down hard when a beer bottle was broken over the back of his head. A second assailant began beating Jose with an aluminum baseball bat, hitting him repeatedly on the head and body. The first assailant joined him and continued beating and kicking Jose well after he was comatose."[5]

On another day in 2009, 18-year-old Angie Zapata was beaten to death with a fire extinguisher. Angie was transgender. Her assailant had waited in her apartment and ambushed her when she returned home. Angie's brother broke down and said that "Only a monster can look at a beautiful 18-year-old and beat her to death." Her mother spoke as well, saying that "The only thing he can never take away is the love and memories that me and my children will have of my baby, my beautiful, beautiful baby."[6]

These two examples represent "hate crimes." They are one dimension of the topic of diversity and crime. The FBI began reporting statistics on hate crimes after passage of a 1990 law requiring the collection of data on crimes of prejudice based on race, ethnicity, religion, and sexual orientation. In 1994, crimes of prejudice based on disability were added to the list. The FBI defines a hate crime as a criminal offense committed against someone that is motivated, in whole or in part, by the offender's bias against people in terms of these categories. Figure 2-2 shows the shares of total hate crimes that are based on various types of prejudice. Note that race refers to African-American, Asian-American, Native American, white (Caucasian), and others. Ethnicity refers to Hispanic and other ethnicities and national origins.

Additional data not shown here reveal that among single-bias incidents, the largest racial bias (72 percent) is toward African-Americans; and among religious bias, 62 percent is toward Jewish people and 13 percent is toward Islamic people (a 44 percent increase since 2007). One controversial example of a crime occurred in early 2015, when a white male killed three Muslim students - a man, his wife, and her sister. As this text is written, investigations are under way to determine if this was a hate crime. Nevertheless, it is a contentious matter. The president of Turkey criticized President Obama and other top U.S. officials for not speaking out on this matter. The social media also picked up on the controversy, complaining that the U.S. news was too little and too late in reporting this event. One twitter comment noted that if a Muslim is at the back of a gun, it is widely publicized; but that if the Muslim is at the front, there is very little coverage.

Finally, the largest disability bias is toward the mentally ill.[7] As will be noted in Chapter 7, efforts are underway to add homeless people to the list of targets of hate crimes.

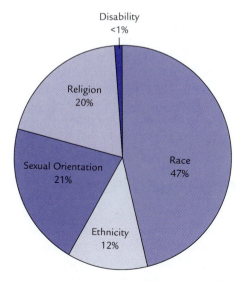

Figure 2-2 • Share of Each Factor Involved in Uniform Crime Report Hate Crime Statistics, 2011

Note: The above statistics refer to single bias crimes.

Source: The U.S. Department of Justice, Federal Bureau of Investigation (FBI), http://www.fbi.gov/.

Hate crimes are one dimension of the topic of diversity and crime. We have also already noted that many women are now being incarcerated, and while many are not serious offenders, they and their children suffer from their incarcerations. According to the Sentencing Project, the number of women in state and federal prisons has increased enormously. Nationally, the 104,000 women in prison is more than eight times the number in 1980. (The rate of prison incarceration for African-American women is 2.5 times higher than the rate for white women, and the rate for Hispanic women is 1.4 times higher.) The war on drugs has been the primary factor in this growth, with about one-quarter of women prisoners incarcerated for a nonviolent drug offense. Female incarceration for nonviolent property crimes represents close to one-third of women prisoners. The Sentencing Project also estimates that 62 percent of mothers in state prisons have minor children, and that 1 in 25 women in state prisons and 1 in 33 federal prisons are pregnant when admitted to prison (with most of these infants immediately separated from their mothers). Clearly, children suffer from their mother's incarceration and the loss of family ties.[8] Concerns are also raised about the fact that many women prisoners have histories as victims of physical and sexual abuse, and high rates of HIV infection.

We have also noted a racial dimension to incarceration. The majority of the people in prison are of racial and ethnic minorities. The Sentencing Project attributes much of this to the war on drugs, with drug offenders who are persons of color far outreaching their share of drug users in society. Some people point to racism as a cause for the disparity, and will be discussed further in the section on drugs.[9]

Women are frequently the victims of the crime of domestic violence. According a major recent review of violence against women, a series of reports found that about a third of women worldwide have been physically or sexually assaulted by a former or current partner. The head of the World Health Organization, Dr. Margaret Chan, called it "a global health problem of epidemic proportions." The rate of domestic violence against women was highest in Africa, the Middle East, and Southeast Asia, where 37 percent of women were assaulted in their lifetimes; the rate was 30 percent in Latin America; and in Europe and Asia, it was 25 percent. Sadly, the rate was 23 percent in North America.[10]

Women in the United States may fare even worse than North America as a whole. Earlier studies by the U.S. Centers for Disease Control and Prevention have found that about 25 percent of interviewed women said that they had been physically or sexually assaulted by a spouse, partner, or date.[11] Crime in the United States has indeed taken on a diverse and gendered form.

One final aspect of diversity is the massive recent reaction to police killings of unarmed afarican americans. Whether these killings were justified or not, depending on each case, there has been a loud cry for changes in police training and techniques to prevent these types of situations. In Ferguson, Missouri, for example, the justice department ruled that the police officer who shot an unarmed black 18-year old was justified. However, a scathing report by the justice departmentof the ferguson police department revealed outrageous racist practices and attitudes.

Global Dimensions of Crime

We have already noted that the United States has the highest incarceration rate in the world. It is interesting to consider another global dimension of crime as well. The impact of crime on the global business environment is an important consideration for the opening markets in Eastern Europe as well as the developing countries of the world. Survey data in Table 2-4 addresses white-collar crime in the form of what we can refer to as "bribery rate." These bribery rates are itemized on business surveys as "the percentage of firms expected to make informal payments to public officials to 'get things done'

TABLE 2-4 • Business Bribery Rates[a], Business Survey Responses, Selected Reporting Eastern European and Developing Countries, in Descending Order

Country	Bribery Rate[a]
Syria	83.8%
Congo, Rep.	81.8%
Congo, Dem. Rep.	65.7%
Yemen	68.2%
Uzbekistan	59.5%
Liberia	55.4%
Benin	54.5%
Azerbaijan	52.2%
Cameroon	51.2%
Angola	48.9%
Kyrgyzstan	47.8%
Iraq	31.8%

[a]As measured by the percent of firms making informal payments to public officials.

Source: World Bank, *World Development Indicators 2012* (Washington, DC: The World Bank, 2012). Data from 2008 to 2011.

with regard to customs, taxes, licenses, regulations, services, and the like." In the United States, we would certainly refer to these payments as bribes. We can see that many developing countries, especially in Africa and the Middle East, as well as several of the newly independent (formerly Soviet) republics such as Uzbekistan, Azerbaijan, and Kyrgyzstan, have high bribery rates. Note shown here is a bribery rate of 19.1 percent in the Bahamas, which might interest you if you end up incarcerated on your spring break as suggested earlier in this chapter (this is a joke—please do not commit a crime ☺).

Keep in mind that many countries may have improved their business climates since these surveys were completed, and are probably subject to more statistical error than usual. Nevertheless, both crime and corruption are serious problems, undoubtedly serving as impediments to business investment.

Should Drugs Be Legalized?

The Substance Abuse and Mental Health Services Administration (SAMHSA) of the U.S. Department of Health and Human Services regularly conducts a national survey on drug abuse. This survey asks people age 12 or older (and other age groups) about their drug use during their lifetime or more recent periods during their lives. The results of one of these surveys are shown in Table 2-5 (on page 40). *We see that over 22 percent of this population admits to using some illicit drug within the last month.* A large share of respondents (over 18 percent) admitted to using marijuana within the last month. Perhaps this is frightening to you. Perhaps not.

One of the most controversial topics in the issue of drug use, and in the entire field of crime and criminology today, is the legalization or decriminalization of illegal drugs. If we were to legalize these drugs, we would simply repeal the laws that make possessing and selling drugs a crime. If we were to decriminalize the possession or selling of drugs, we would reduce the severity of the laws against these offenses, making them misdemeanors punishable by modest fines. Economic theory can add another dimension to the discussion of this emotionally charged subject. Furthermore, the economic analysis we use here can be extended to other related topics. Let's begin by discussing the possibility of legalizing drugs.

TABLE 2-5 • Survey Results Showing Share of Respondents Age 12 and Older Acknowledging Illicit Drug Use Within the Last Month, 2011

Drug	% of Respondents
Any Illicit Drugs Use	22.5%
Marijuana	18.1%
Psychotherapeutics	6.1%
Cocaine	1.4%
Hallucinogens	1.0%
Inhalants	0.6%
Heroin	0.3%

Source: U.S. Department of Health and Human Services, Substance Abuse and Mental Health Services Administration (SAMHSA), Center for Behavioral Health Services and Quality, *National Survey on Drug Use*, Use of data averaged over 2010 and 2011, Revised March 2012, http://www.samhsa.gov.

Background on the Legal Status of Drugs

The United States has a history of prohibiting or regulating the use of mind-altering substances. Laws and public policy concerning these substances do, however, change over time. Opiates have been illegal since 1914 and marijuana since 1937. Alcohol was entirely prohibited between 1920 and 1933. Currently, alcohol and tobacco are legal but cannot be sold legally to minors. All of these substances are at least somewhat addictive, and our dominant attitude is that, at a minimum, they should be regulated. Legalization of drugs is therefore unlikely, but at least partial decriminalization might be politically feasible.

Despite widespread opposition to legalization of drugs in the United States, drug laws and policy have been much more relaxed in many European countries. These countries may provide better evidence of whether legalization of drug use is beneficial.

The War on Drugs: U.S. Antidrug Policy

In the last half of the twentieth century, two U.S. presidents have declared a war on drugs: Richard Nixon in 1971 and Ronald Reagan in 1982. The drug war has been one of the most popular of our recent conflicts, and our more recent presidents have supported it as well. With the possible exception of marijuana use, the majority of the populace supports the war on drugs as well. **In economic terms, the so-called war on drugs involves measures to decrease both the supply of and the demand for drugs.**

Decreasing the Supply of Drugs

Among the measures designed to decrease the supply of drugs have been (1) efforts to prevent drugs from entering the country and (2) increases in the severity of the punishment for selling drugs. We have hired more personnel: federal agents for the FBI and Drug Enforcement Administration (DEA), U.S. attorneys to prosecute drug cases, and clerical staff. We have given drug enforcement agencies more money with which to operate, and we have redirected dollars formerly allocated to drug treatment programs and research into law enforcement programs. We have built more prison cells to accommodate more people with sale of drug convictions. We have passed stricter laws and cut through bureaucracy in the attempt to decrease the supply of illegal drugs on the streets of our cities.

Since the 1980s, efforts to stem the supply of drugs coming into this country from abroad have involved the U.S. military. The century-old Posse Comitatus Act, which prohibited the military from enforcing civil laws, was amended in 1982 to permit the war chest of the U.S. military to be used for drug enforcement. As a result, the military is now involved in drug enforcement training, intelligence gathering, and detection.

Military personnel operate navy, army, and Marine Corps equipment for these purposes under the direction of civilian agencies.

By far, most of the money spent on the war on drugs has been directed toward activities designed to decrease supply (some suggest about 95 percent); the remainder has targeted programs to decrease demand.

Decreasing the Demand for Drugs

To decrease demand, we have instituted drug awareness and education programs for our youth. To deter our citizens from experimenting with drugs, we have increased the penalties for the possession of illegal drugs. Some of our prisons have drug treatment programs for offenders. Any education, treatment, or deterrent program is designed to act on the demand side of the drug market.

In 1988, the White House policy of zero tolerance of drug use was announced. Although this policy was initiated under Republican presidents, the "war on drugs" is bipartisan. Then-senator Joe Biden was the first to use the term *drug czar* in 1982, and since then, every administration has had a so-called drug czar.

The Argument Against Legalization of Drugs

The argument against the legalization of drugs is based mainly on (1) the adverse personal health consequences of drugs, (2) the expected increase in drug-related social problems if drugs were to be legalized, and (3) the successes of the war on drugs.

Personal Health Consequences

Proponents of continued drug prohibition argue that there is solid evidence that the legalization of drugs would have great personal health consequences. Some studies indicate that marijuana is at least as harmful to the lungs as tobacco—maybe more harmful—because it delivers more concentrated tar than do filter-tipped cigarettes. Moreover, the potency of marijuana has increased in recent years, so its effects persist longer. Marijuana is thought to inhibit personal growth and effective coping with personal problems.

A recent study reveals that heavy, long-term marijuana use beginning in the teens can possibly lead to a much lower IQ in later years. The decline was not seen in users who started smoking pot later in life. This study is among the first to assess IQ before and after the onset of marijuana use. Some suggest that it may also explain marijuana dependency, as many participants indicated that they had become dependent on marijuana, meaning that they continued to use it despite its causing significant health, social, or legal problems. An even larger number reported dependence starting at a later age.[12]

Marijuana may or may not be physically addictive, but many believe that marijuana may serve as a "gateway drug" from which the inexperienced user advances to more harmful substances that *are* addictive. Opponents of legalization believe that drug use would soar if we were to legalize drugs.

Drug-Related Social Problems

Opponents of legalization also argue that because more people would use drugs if they were legal, we would have more drug-related social problems. Like alcohol use, drug use contributes to higher worker absenteeism and lower productivity. Driving under the influence of alcohol contributes to car wrecks, injuries, and loss of life, and so would driving under the influence of legalized drugs. And like alcohol, drug use may contribute to birth defects or miscarriages. Alcohol currently contributes to many antisocial behavior patterns, including domestic abuse and other crimes; legalized drugs would contribute to such patterns as well.

A recent study conducted by the office of the White House Director of National Drug Control Policy for President Obama has established a strong link between drug use and crime, citing that 80 percent of the adult males arrested for crimes in Sacramento, California, in 2012 tested positive for at least one illegal drug. Marijuana was the most commonly detected drug, found in 54 percent of those arrested. Similar results were found in other cities as well, where cocaine ranked as the second most commonly found drug in those arrested. Of course, a link between drug use and crime *does not establish a cause and effect.* Nevertheless, the drug czar used this study to continue his opposition to legalization of marijuana and to call for more drug treatment.[13]

Successes of the War on Drugs

The war on drugs is certainly not an unqualified success, but it assuredly has had some limited victories. The fact that drugs are illegal has presumably reduced their usage. Use of marijuana and cocaine in the United States fell during the 1980s, as did the use of most other drugs. Opponents of drug legalization argue that we certainly should not adopt any policies that would conflict with any trend toward less drug use.

The Argument for Legalization of Drugs

The argument in favor of drug legalization is based on the following: (1) efforts to restrict the supply of drugs have largely failed, (2) there is a link between illegal drugs and crime, (3) drugs may contribute to corruption, (4) drug law enforcement may be discriminatory, (5) drug enforcement may violate our constitutional rights, (6) there are financial and opportunity costs of drug enforcement, (7) there are health consequences of our drug policies, and (8) there are many benefits of the legalization of drugs.

The Failure of Controlling the International Drug Supply

Many U.S. experts on drug control have emphasized international drug control efforts, because domestic efforts to control the supply have been virtually futile. Marijuana and opium can be grown almost anywhere, and the coca plant (from which cocaine is produced) is now grown in environments that were once thought inhospitable to it. Whenever supply from one area of the globe is disrupted, other areas rush to fill the void. It has been likened to pushing in on a balloon. For example, successful eradication of marijuana from Mexico in the 1970s led to greater importation of marijuana from the South American country of Colombia and expanded marijuana production in the United States. The United States has had some success in helping to shrink the production of the coca crop in Colombia, but this has coincided with an expanding coca cultivation in Bolivia and Peru.

Controlling the drug supply at the source faces many other obstacles. In some of the developing countries that export drugs, political parties are involved in the production and sale of these commodities. In others, drug cartels have power rivaling that of the government. Low-income peasants producing raw drugs cannot switch to legal crops and make nearly as high a profit. In some cases, growing and using the products are cultural: some Andean natives, for example, grow and chew coca leaves. While processed cocaine is dangerous, chewing the coca leaf might not be and the peasants who grow the product do not perceive themselves as criminals. While the United States has attempted to halt the production of coca and poppies by encouraging alternative crops, these efforts have often been expensive and unsuccessful programs. Furthermore, U.S. fumigation programs have caused health problems and have rendered some food crops inedible.

Stopping the foreign supply of drugs is clearly a challenge. As alluded to by Hillary Rodham Clinton at the beginning of the chapter, as long as Americans demand drugs, producers will try to meet that demand.

Illegal Drugs and Crime

Proponents of drug legalization argue that our current drug laws not only are ineffective in controlling supply, but they also have links to crime. We've already noted a possible link of drug use to crime. Furthermore, because drugs are illegal, they are provided by an illegal, or underground, economy. Therefore, the major beneficiary of drug prohibition is organized crime. Organized crime is the major source of illegal drugs, and sales of illegal drugs account for a large share of the revenues of organized crime in the United States. Drugs command a high price on the street, but this price is not based on high costs of manufacture. Instead, the price is largely attributable to the risks that traffickers take—risks for which they charge a high premium. These risk premiums are like an illegality tax that swells the coffers of organized crime.

Drug prohibition may contribute to crime in other ways. Since their illegality results in very high street prices, addicts may commit crimes to buy their drugs. Furthermore, much violent crime results from turf wars among drug dealers. A real victim of drug prohibition may be the law-abiding citizen hurt in the crossfire of a drug turf war. Finally, as mentioned, low-level nonviolent drug offenders may become more "hardened criminals" while in prison.

Contribution to Corruption

Proponents of legalization also argue that another cost of drug prohibition is its contribution to the corruption of the police and others in the criminal justice system. All vice-control efforts are particularly susceptible to bribes, and bribes are difficult to detect because there is no victim of bribery to file a complaint. Police may be disillusioned by the widespread use of illegal drugs and difficulties in ensuring convictions and the financial temptations may be enormous.

Discrimination and Drugs

Furthermore, drug laws may result in discriminatory incarceration. The mandatory sentence for possession of crack cocaine, often used by African-Americans, is higher than the mandatory sentence for powdered cocaine, which is more often used by whites. President Barack Obama has called for an end to this disparity, as have other Justice Department officials. (So too has former radical Sara Jane Olson, who once spent 25 years as a fugitive after joining the Symbionese Liberation Army, was captured and imprisoned in 1999, and has since been released.)

In addition, incarceration rates are generally high for racial and ethnic minorities, out of proportion with their drug use. A recent study utilizing federal data revealed that African-Americans were nearly four times as likely as whites to be arrested on charges of marijuana possession even though the two groups used the drug at similar rates, and that this disparity between black and white arrest rates has been increasing.[14] Finally, we've noted that women have increasingly been incarcerated for nonviolent drug-related issues, causing severe problems for their children.

Violation of Constitutional Rights

Another cost of drug prohibition may be the violation of our constitutional rights. Proponents of legalization argue that roadblocks and random searches of automobiles are violations of constitutional rights. The same may be true of exclusionary rule exceptions that allow authorities to use illegally seized evidence in court and of random drug testing. These actions are, however, accepted by society because public opinion so greatly favors drug law enforcement.

Another problem may be more serious. We frequently hear about prisoners who are brutalized while in prison, often by other prisoners. The issue of prison rape is a case in point, and the 2003 Prison Rape Elimination Act charged the Bureau of Justice Statistics with collecting data on sexual victimization in prisons and jails. Most recently, this agency estimated that about 4 percent of adult inmates in state and federal prisons nationwide experienced some form of sexual victimization within 12 months of arriving, either carried out by another inmate or a staff member. The rate among younger prisoners was higher, but not significantly different. Certainly these statistics represent a violation of these prisoners' constitutional rights. What is encouraging is that there is a lot of variation among prisons and jails, suggesting that active policy within these institutions can reduce the incidence of sexual assault.[15]

Financial and Opportunity Costs

Taxpayers bear the burden of the criminal justice system. The war on drugs has increased both the absolute dollar expenditures on the criminal justice system and the percentage of our resources devoted to drug violations. We already know that a very large share of convicts in state and federal prisons is there for drug law violations. The more effective our current drug laws are, the more prison cells we will need. The burden on taxpayers will escalate as we build and equip more prisons to accommodate drug violators.

We have also considered the opportunity costs of our criminal justice system. Resources used in the war on drugs cannot be used in alternative activities, such as investigating violent crimes and crimes against property. Nor can they be used for other useful social services, including public education, health care, and environmental protection. Similarly, if we pay high taxes for enforcing our drug laws, we as taxpayers are giving up alternative consumer goods. We can't have more of everything. **The war on drugs means that we give up alternative goods and services.**

Health Consequences

Proponents of legalization argue that although drugs may have adverse personal health consequences, so does drug prohibition. Because drugs are illegal, we cannot regulate their safety. Users cannot tell if the drugs are pure or adulterated or what their strength is. Marijuana may have been sprayed with the dangerous herbicide parquat or grown with dangerous fertilizers that are more hazardous to the user than the marijuana. Some argue that drug prohibition also keeps us from adopting rational policies to combat the spread of AIDS and other diseases through the use of shared needles. Although some governments of the world have instituted policies to exchange needles as a means of controlling the spread of AIDS, our federal government has not. The prevailing belief is that to support needle exchange programs is to support, or at least to condone, the use of illegal substances.

Benefits of Legalization

Proponents of legalization argue that repealing drug prohibition laws would provide many advantages. First, net financial benefits to the government from legalization would be considerable. We could tax the producers of the formerly illegal substances, generating many tax dollars for the government. Second, drugs would be safer if they were legal. We could regulate quality and institute needle exchange programs in good conscience. Third, the risk premium that stems from the illegality of drugs would disappear. As a result, drugs would not be such a profitable business for organized crime. Organized crime syndicates might exit the drug industry and be supplanted by legal pharmaceutical firms. Fourth, we would expect less criminal activity on the part of users who engaged in crime to finance their expensive drug habits when drugs were illegal. Potentially lower prices through legalization might reduce this crime. Finally, some of the resources saved could be directed toward education and treatment programs. This emphasis on the demand side of the drug market may well be more effective than the historical emphasis on supply-side programs.

The Economics of Prohibition or Legalization

Having laid out the cases for and against legalization, let's now add careful economic analysis to this discussion. The tool we will use is supply and demand analysis. Let's initially focus our attention on the demand for drugs. Figure 2-3 analyzes the effect of legalization on the demand for drugs. The graph shows supply and demand in a market for a particular drug, where D and S are the demand and supply curves if drugs are illegal. When drugs are prohibited by law, some potential users are deterred from using the drugs by the drug law penalties. Others simply prefer to act legally regardless of penalties. In these cases, demand for the drug might increase if drugs became legalized. The increase in demand is shown in Figure 2-3. When demand increases from D to D′, price and quantity increase to P′, and Q′, respectively.

How much the use of the drugs would change when the price changes depends on an important characteristic of the demand for the drug. The demand for highly addictive drugs is

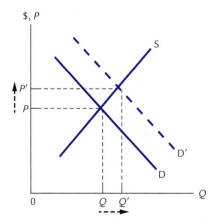

Figure 2-3 • Effect of Legalization of Drugs on the Demand for Drugs
Legalization would increase demand from D to D′, which would increase price to P′ and quantity to Q′.

Inelastic demand
Demand in which
buyers are relatively
unresponsive to changes
in price.

Elastic demand
Demand in which buyers
are relatively responsive
to changes in price.

said to be inelastic. An **inelastic demand** means that consumers are relatively unresponsive to changes in price: when prices go either up or down, quantity demanded doesn't change very much. This is certainly the case for a user who is physically addicted to a drug such as cocaine. For even large increases in the price of this drug, the user will scarcely reduce his or her usage. **We represent an inelastic demand with a relatively steep demand curve.**

Figure 2-4 shows both an inelastic demand curve and a flatter (elastic) demand curve. **Elastic demand** means that buyers are relatively *responsive* to changes in price. Thus, quantity demanded changes a lot for even small changes in price. This might be the case for less physically addictive drugs, such as marijuana. (Elasticity of demand is discussed in greater detail in the appendix to this chapter.)

Now let's consider the effects of legalization on supply. Note that the original supply curve S incorporates a risk premium to the drug traffickers, as well as the high costs of efforts to bribe local police. (It is pushed backward because of these higher costs of supplying the product when the product is illegal.) With legalization of this drug, supply will increase (shift forward) because the higher costs of production (bribery and risk premium) would no longer exist. This is shown in both graphs in Figure 2-4. As a result, the price of the drug would decrease and the equilibrium quantity would increase.

Note that equilibrium quantity (use) of the drug increases in both cases when supply increases. **However, drug usage increases just a little when demand is inelastic and supply increases, but it increases significantly when demand is elastic.** (The supply curve is shifted forward by the same amount in both graphs. It only *looks* like a larger shift in the second graph because demand is so flat.)

The fact of the matter is that we do not know whether the demand for most drugs is inelastic or elastic. Because drug markets are illegal, we lack information about price–quantity combinations in the real world. Although we would expect those addicted to a narcotic to have a highly inelastic demand, we really don't have good information about the responsiveness of casual users to changes in the price of controlled substances. What

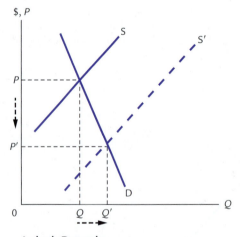

Inelastic Demand
In the case of the inelastic demand for drugs, the same increase in supply resulting from legalization would result in a smaller increase in drug usage.

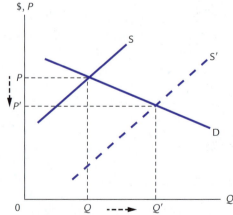

Elastic Demand
In the case of an elastic demand for drugs, legalization would shift the supply curve forward and result in a larger increase in drug usage.

Figure 2-4 • Effects of the Legalization of Drugs on the Supply of Drugs
Legalization of drugs would increase supply from S to S′, which would decrease price to P′ and increase quantity to Q′. The size of the effect on price and quantity depends on the elasticity of demand.

© Cengage Learning

little experimental knowledge we might someday have will come from the legalization of marijuana by several U.S. states and the legalization or decriminalization by countries such as the Netherlands and Mexico. As of 2015, several states have passed laws that allow and regulate the recreational use of marijuana and many more states allow it for medicinal use. While pot remains illegal under federal law, the Justice Department announced in 2013 that it will not interfere with the implementation of state legalization laws.

The Netherlands represents an interesting case. This country has the most lenient of Europe's soft-drug laws (marijuana and hashish) and legalization was not initially accompanied by greatly increased drug use by local inhabitants. However, it has attracted "drug tourism" by foreigners, raising a variety of problems. The city of Maastricht, for example, turned into a hub for foreign smokers and dealers, creating a multitude of problems, the most serious of which was a multimillion-dollar drug trade with a supply chain of illicit growers and underground traders. Many people came to the city not just to buy the small legal amounts, but to buy large amounts from dealers operating underground. Drug tourism also attracted pushers of hard drugs.[16]

In 2011, the Dutch government announced that sales to nonresidents would be prohibited nationwide on January 1, 2013. Only Dutch residents who registered with a coffee shop would be allowed to go legally to the coffee shops, which were to be turned into members-only clubs. As of late 2012, Amsterdam's mayor announced that the city's 220 coffee shops selling marijuana would remain open the following year and that he made the decision after considering the unintended consequences that would arise from a ban on marijuana sales, including a revival of black market trade. He also noted that the current system allows the government to monitor the quality of "soft" drugs and limit access to the coffee shops to those ages 18 and older, something that would be impossible if the trade were again to become clandestine.[17]

In 2008, the Mexican legislature voted quietly to decriminalize the possession of small amounts of pot, cocaine, methamphetamine, and other drugs, thereby easing the punishment for these offences. Users were to be advised of available clinics and encouraged to enter rehabilitation programs. Although there has been a great deal of criticism of this change, former Mexican president Felipe Calderon sought to distinguish between smalltime users and big-time dealers, targeting major crime-fighting resources toward the dealers and their drug lord bosses. It remains to be seen whether Mexico becomes another Netherlands in terms of the problems that may result, especially with a new president now in Mexico. Clearly, legalization of marijuana has not been without difficulty, either in the United States or elsewhere, and it is certainly likely that increased drug use has resulted from legalization.

Note that the increase in demand (shown in Figure 2-3) increases the price of drugs and the increase in supply (shown in Figure 2-4) decreases their equilibrium price. The changes are offsetting, so the effect on equilibrium price is really quite difficult to predict. Most experts, however, predict that the price of drugs would go down at least somewhat with legalization. **But note, however, that both the increase in supply and the increase in demand would increase equilibrium quantity, so that it is quite clear that drug use would increase with legalization.**

Regulation Through Economic Policies

Economists who favor drug legalization or decriminalization often also suggest the economic means of influencing the legal markets for drugs. First, they argue that a much greater percentage of the government's expenditures on drug-related programs should be directed toward demand-side treatment and education programs. As we have already noted, only a small share of drug-related expenditures are directed to demand-side policies. By decreasing demand, we can decrease use.

Excise tax

A tax applied to the sale of a specific good or service.

Second, a system of excise taxes can be levied on the legal drugs. (An **excise tax** is like a sales tax, except that it is imposed on only specific goods and services such as cigarettes, alcohol, and gasoline.) The effect of these excise taxes would be to decrease the supply of the drug, since we view the excise tax as an additional cost of production to the supplier. This is the case since it is the supplier of the drug who pays the tax dollars to the government. (Remember that an increase in the cost of production shifts the supply curve backward.)

Figure 2-5 shows a hypothetical market for a legalized drug with a public health excise tax levied on suppliers. **The decrease in supply caused by the excise tax causes an increase in the drug's price and a decrease in its use.** Thus, the increase in usage that results from legalization can be reversed through the use of the excise tax.

The level of tax on each drug should be correlated with the drug's harmful public health effects. If the clinical evidence indicates that the consequences of using cocaine are more severe than the consequences of using marijuana, the tax levied on cocaine should be higher. (Of course, the higher cocaine price may result in criminal behavior by users to support their drug habit.) Furthermore, revenues from the excise tax could be earmarked for treatment and education programs. In addition to the excise taxes, the substances would be regulated and kept out of the hands of minors, as we currently attempt to keep both alcohol and tobacco from being purchased by teenagers. Furthermore, drivers under the influence of any drug could be arrested, as should drivers under the influence of alcohol. So, legalization and the imposition of taxes would not eliminate the need for policing the market for drugs entirely. The policing burden would, however, be far lighter than it is under prohibition.

Illegal Use of Legal Drugs

Although our discussion in this chapter has focused on illegal drugs, another issue is the illegal use of *legal* drugs. For example, many people have become addicted to prescription drugs, such as the pain relievers OxyContin and oxycodone. Others abuse these drugs to get an artificial "high." Both Brett Favre (former quarterback for the Green Bay Packers) and Rush Limbaugh (conservative radio and TV host) have admitted addiction to prescription drugs, as have many more celebrities. Proper treatment is essential for

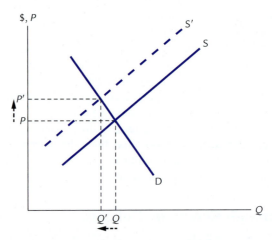

Figure 2-5 • How an Excise Tax Can Decrease the Use of a Legalized Drug
The excise tax causes a backward shift in the supply of the drug, resulting in a higher price and lower quantity (usage).

Source: The U.S. Department of Justice, Federal Bureau of Investigation (FBI), http://www.fbi.gov.

all drug abusers, whether the drugs are illegal themselves, or are legal drugs being used illegally, since both of these can be very dangerous to the user and others.

A Final Note on Drug Use

Economics can provide one perspective on a social issue such as drug use. It can provide very useful information and insights. But, in the final analysis, people may base their opinions about social issues and policy on other criteria, such as moral and ethical concerns. Economics can nevertheless provide an important dimension to the discussion.

The Legalization of Other Victimless Crimes

The economic analysis (and many of the noneconomic arguments) we have used to examine the controversy over the legalization of drugs can also be applied to arguments about the legal status of other so-called victimless crimes such as pornography and prostitution. These are considered crimes not because of violence against persons or property, but because of public censure and disapproval. It can be argued that, like drug use, the purchase of pornography or the services of a prostitute are a consensual transaction. That is, both buyer and seller consent to the trade. Thus, there is no victim.

Other people disagree. Studies show that most women in prostitution, for example, have been sexually abused as children. According to one expert in prostitution research, "Incest sets young women up for prostitution—by letting them know what they're worth and what's expected of them."[18] Other factors that direct women into prostitution are economic hardship and racism. The experience of being prostituted causes these women immense psychological and physical harm.

Others argue that pornography encourages the attitude that women are available for men's pleasure. "They like it, they want it, and men are free to take it." It's not possible to know how much violence and rape of women results from these types of attitudes. Finally, child pornography is clearly beyond the realm of a "victimless crime," since a child, by definition, cannot give mature and free consent.

Policing by the vice squad for victimless crimes is difficult because there is no "victim" to file a complaint. Corruption of police working the vice squad is thought to be higher than of police working details such as robbery.

If some crimes are truly "victimless," then the same arguments for legalization, regulation, and taxation therefore might be made for these offenses. **As with drugs, the equilibrium quantity would undoubtedly increase with legalization, but regulation and taxation might well be more efficient than prohibition (and might, in turn, reduce the equilibrium quantity).** But as with drugs, social and ethical issues related to legalization may outweigh the economic issues.

You, the Student

If you or a friend has a problem with drugs or alcohol, click on "Treatment Locator" on the U.S. Department of Health and Human Services Web site to find maps for locating drug and alcohol treatment programs (http://www.drugabusestatistics.samhsa.gov). You would be performing an important service for yourself or for this person, and being a real friend to this person by guiding them toward help.

View**Point**   Conservative versus Liberal

When discussing emotionally charged social issues such as the control of drugs, pornography, and prostitution, it is especially important to apply care in the way we use the terms *liberal* and *conservative*. These terms often have opposite meanings when we are considering government involvement in our daily lives (social liberals and conservatives) versus government involvement in the economy (economic liberals and conservatives). Let's try to understand the distinction. Economic conservatives support less government involvement in economic realms. They favor a market-oriented approach to most situations. Thus, economic conservatives would support the legalization of drugs and other victimless crimes. (Note that social conservatives would not support such legalization.) The economic conservative would value the efficiencies attained when market forces shift demand and supply curves if legalization occurs. Furthermore, they would prefer excise taxes and other market approaches (that involve incentives, demand, and supply) to account for the harmful community effects of drugs and other victimless crimes, instead of prohibition of the activity itself.

Economic liberals, on the other hand, favor greater government intervention in the marketplace. They would favor the criminalization and prohibition of drug use and other so-called victimless crimes. (Note that social liberals are more likely to support legalization of drugs.) We should note, however, that economists, like the rest of our society, usually hold opinions about the legalization of drugs and other crimes that are not based solely on economic principles. And, both economic and social conservatives and liberals may be conservative on some issues and liberal on others.

Summary

A crime is any activity forbidden by law and punishable by criminal penalty. Crime prevention is an example of a public good, which is characterized as being indivisible, nonrivalrous, and nonexcludable. Expenditures on our criminal justice system, which includes police, courts, and prisons, have increased greatly over recent decades. The greatest increase has occurred in the prison system.

An appropriate methodology to evaluate crime prevention is cost-benefit analysis. A policy should be adopted only if its benefits are greater than its costs. The results of cost-benefit studies on our prison expansion are contradictory and inconclusive.

Rising incarceration rates among women and minorities are cause for concern. So are the hate crimes toward minorities and domestic violence. International dimensions of crime and corruption include their negative effect on global business investment. And, as we all know, white-collar crime has become a serious problem in the United States.

Some crimes may be victimless because they are the result of consensual transactions between two free and mature parties. These crimes are illegal only because society, or a significant group in society, disapproves of them on moral,

health, or other grounds. Therefore, we have passed laws prohibiting them. Some consider drug use to be one such example of a victimless crime. Legalizing victimless crimes may be more efficient than prohibiting them. Legalization of drugs would result in an increased demand and supply. When demand and supply increase, the net effect on price is unclear, but equilibrium quantity will increase. If victimless crimes were made legal, we could regulate them, in part through taxation. This would serve to reduce their quantity. The elasticity of demand is an important factor in policy regarding drug use, as discussed in the appendix. The demand for highly addictive drugs, such as cocaine, is probably inelastic. The demand for a less-addictive drug may be elastic.

This entire discussion of drugs must be moderated by the fact that many people believe that drug use, as well as other "victimless" crimes are not truly victimless. This would change the nature of the discussion as other considerations would become relevant. We must also keep in mind that economics is only one factor regarding policy choices; people's moral values and ethics can and should also come into play.

DISCUSSION AND ACTION QUESTIONS

1. What is the definition of a public good or service? Name some other public goods and services besides crime prevention.

2. What is the free-rider problem? Why does it exist? What are examples of free riders?

3. What is meant when we say that a public good is indivisible, nonrivalrous, and nonexcludable?

4. Discuss cost-benefit analysis. What are the benefits of crime prevention? What are the costs? Are all the benefits and costs easily measurable? What should we do when costs or benefits are not quantifiable? Should we base all of our decisions on cost-benefit analysis?

5. (Appendix question) Of what significance is the elasticity of demand for drugs in the debate about legalization of presently illegal substances?

6. (Appendix question) How could taxes be used to regulate legal drug markets? How are excise taxes on drugs similar to excise taxes on cigarettes? Why are excise taxes on cigarettes and alcohol sometimes called "sin taxes"? Do we tax them solely because they are "sins"?

7. Is it possible to be a social liberal and an economic conservative (or vice versa) with regard to drugs and so-called victimless crimes? Be sure that you've read the ViewPoint section carefully.

8. Go to the Federal Bureau of Investigation Web site (http://www.fbi.gov), locate the Uniform Crime Report, and find the latest statistics on violent crime. Has violent crime increased or decreased in the latest year available?

9. Go to the Web site for the National Center for Victims of Crime at http://www.ncvc.org. How might this Web site be used by someone who has been a victim of crime?

10. The Sentencing Project has a Web site at http://www.sentencingproject.org. Try to discover the underlying view of the Sentencing Project toward expansion of prisons and incarceration in the United States. What is its view toward gender and racial issues?

11. The Bureau of Justice Statistics of the Department of Justice has a Web site at http://www.ojp.usdoj.gov/bjs. Try to find information on the number of prisons and prisoners in the United States.

12. Do you know any children with an incarcerated parent? A University of Minnesota researcher, Rebecca Shlafer, is promoting materials called "Little Children, Big Challenges: Incarceration," developed by Sesame Street, to be used to help children of incarcerated parents. Perhaps you can acquire the materials by contacting Shlafer or Sesame Street.

NOTES

1. U.S. Department of Justice, Criminal Division, Report to the U.S. Sentencing commission, July 23, 2012, www.doj.gov.

2. The Sentencing Project, http://www.sentencingproject.org, 2012–2013.

3. The Death Penalty Information Center; citing *The Los Angeles Times,* March 6, 2005; the Kansas Performance Audit Report, December 2003; the Indiana Criminal Law Study Commission, January 10, 2002; Duke University, May 1993; *The Palm Beach Post,* January 4, 2000; and *The Dallas Morning News,* March 8, 1992; reported in "Facts About the Death Penalty," January 19, 2007; http://www.deathpenaltyinfo.org.

4. The Death Penalty Information Center; citing Radelet and Akers, 1996; in "Facts About the Death Penalty," January 19, 2007; http://www.deathpenaltyinfo.org.

5. Robert D. McFadden (also reporting by Al Baker, David W. Chen, Kareem Fahim, Ann Farmer, Karen Zraick), "Attack on Ecuadorean Brothers Investigated as Hate Crime," *The New York Times.*

6. Dan Frosch, "Murder and Hate Verdict in Transgender Women's Death," *The New York Times,* April 23, 2009.

7. U.S. Department of Justice, Office of Justice Programs, Bureau of Justice Statistics, *Uniform Crime Report: Hate Crime Statistics* 2011, http://www.ojp.usdoj.gov/bjs.

8. The Sentencing Project, *Women and the Criminal Justice System, Facts about Prisons and Prisoners, Racial Disparity*, and other reports, http://www.sentencingproject.org, 2012–2013.

9. The Sentencing Project, *Racial Disparity*, http://www.sentencingproject.org, 2012–2013.

10. Maria Cheng, Associated Press, June 21, 2013.

11. Elizabeth Rosenthal, *The New York Times* (from *The International Herald Tribune*), "Women Face Greatest Threat of Violence at Home, Study Finds," October 6, 2006 (citing *The Lancet*, October 6, 2006, and the U.S. Centers for Disease Control and Prevention).

12. Madeline Meier, Duke University, and Richie Poulton, University of Otago, New Zealand, *Proceedings of the*

National Academy of Sciences Early Edition, August 27, 2012.

13. Rob Hotakainen, *McClatchy Newspapers*, May 24, 2013.

14. Ezekiel Edwards, lead author and Director of the American Civil Liberties Union Criminal Law Reform Project, *The New York Times*, June 4, 2013.

15. Erica Goode, *The New York Times*, May 17, 2013.

16. Marlise Simons, "Cannabis Cafes Get Nudge to Fringes of a Dutch City," *The New York Times*, August 20, 2006.

17. *The New York Times*, November 2, 2012.

18. Melissa Farley and Victor Malarek, "The Myth of the Victimless Crime," *The New York Times*, March 12, 2008.

Elasticity of demand is the responsiveness of consumers (in terms of their buying decisions) to changes in the price of the product. When buyers are relatively responsive to changes in price, we say that demand is elastic. When buyers are relatively unresponsive to changes in price, we say that demand is inelastic, as described earlier in the chapter.

When we say that buyers are relatively unresponsive to a change in price, we mean that a change in price has little effect on the quantity that consumers are willing to buy. If demand is elastic, and buyers are more responsive to changes in price, a change in price has a significant effect on quantity demanded. Economists frequently describe elasticity by calculating an elasticity coefficient. The formula for the **coefficient for the price elasticity of demand** is stated as the percentage change in quantity demanded divided by a percentage change in price.

If demand is elastic, the coefficient will have an absolute value greater than 1, indicating that any percentage change in price causes a larger percentage change in quantity demanded. However, if demand is inelastic, the coefficient's absolute value will be some fraction less than 1, indicating that any percentage change in price causes a smaller percentage change in quantity demanded. (Since a rise in price causes a reduction in quantity demanded and vice versa, the elasticity coefficient always has a negative value. However, in order to avoid confusion, we express the coefficient in absolute value; that is, we ignore the minus sign.)

The graphs in Figure 2-6 show the theoretical extremes of elasticity: perfect inelasticity and perfect elasticity. The demand in the graph on the left is perfectly

Coefficient for the price elasticity of demand

The percentage change in quantity demanded divided by a percentage change in price.

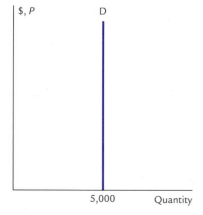

Perfectly Inelastic Demand
A perfectly inelastic demand is a vertical line.

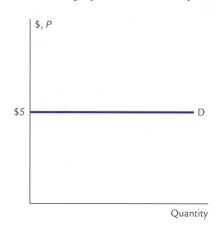

Perfectly Elastic Demand
A perfectly elastic demand is a horizontal line.

Figure 2-6 • The Extremes of Elasticity

inelastic. Regardless of any price change, quantity demanded does not change, but remains at 5,000. Since there is *no* response to a change in price, we say that demand is *perfectly* inelastic. Perfectly inelastic demand curves are always drawn as vertical lines, and they have an elasticity coefficient equal to zero. (The numerator would equal zero regardless of the size of the denominator.) The graph on the right in Figure 2-6 is a perfectly elastic demand curve. Perfectly elastic demand curves are always horizontal lines. Although price does not vary from $5, quantity demanded varies infinitely. This is the ultimate in responsiveness, with an elasticity coefficient equal to infinity.

Most demand curves are neither perfectly elastic nor perfectly inelastic. The more typical case of elasticity is related to both the location of the curve on the graph and its slope. If two demand curves intersect so that their location on the graph is very close, we can compare their elasticity in the region near their intersection by comparing their slopes. The flatter (closer to horizontal) curve will be more elastic. The steeper (closer to vertical) curve will be more inelastic.

Figure 2-7 shows two demand curves that intersect at $4 and a quantity of 200 units. Demand curve D_1 is more inelastic at prices near $4 and quantities near 200 than is D_2, which is flatter.

Elasticity has interesting implications when an excise tax is imposed on the sale of a good or service. In the case of a physically addictive drug, such as cocaine, demand is inelastic (though not perfectly so). In the case of a less physically addicting drug, such as marijuana, demand is elastic (though not perfectly so). Figure 2-8 represents these differing elasticities by the slopes of the two demand curves. If supply decreases (shifts to the left) by the same amount in both cases because of the imposition of an identical excise tax, equilibrium quantity of the drug changes very little in the case of inelastic demand, and it changes much more in the case of elastic demand. In addition, the equilibrium price of the drug increases by a larger amount in the case of the addictive drug with inelastic demand and a smaller amount in the case of the less-addictive drug with elastic demand. Since the amount of the excise tax is the vertical distance between the two supply curves, we see that the price of the drug increases by almost the full amount of the

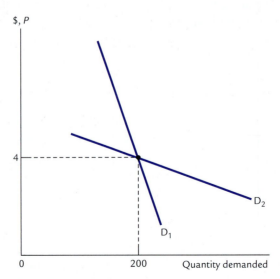

Figure 2-7 • Two Demand Curves of Varying Elasticity
D_1 is less elastic than demand curve D_2 at prices near their $4 intersection.

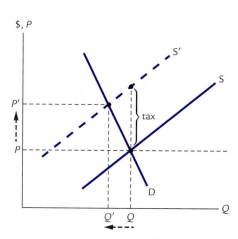

A relatively inelastic demand will have a large increase in price if supply is reduced because of the imposition of an excise tax. The greater burden of the tax falls upon consumers.

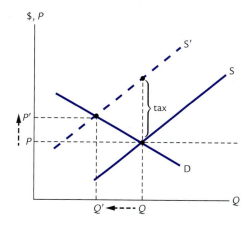

A relatively elastic demand will have a small increase in price if supply is reduced because of the imposition of an excise tax. The greater burden of the tax falls upon suppliers.

Figure 2-8 • Two Demand Curves of Varying Elasticity With the Imposition of an Excise Tax

tax in the case of inelastic demand. This means that the greater burden of the tax falls upon the consumer in the form of the higher price of the drug. In the case of elastic demand, the price of the drug rises very little. This means that the greater burden of the tax falls upon the supplier of the drug in the form of lower profits. **In general, we say that the burden of the tax falls most heavily on that group (consumers or suppliers) with the more inelastic curve.**

Can you explain the relative burden of an excise tax in the case of the perfectly inelastic demand curve and the perfectly elastic demand curves of Figure 2-6? In both cases, simply add a normal upward-sloping supply curve and then shift the supply curve backward. In the first case, the price of the drug increases by the full vertical distance between the two supply curves. In other words, the entire burden of the tax falls upon consumers of the drug. In the second case, the price does not increase at all. In other words, the entire burden of the tax falls upon suppliers of the drug. These are the extreme cases of the general observation that the burden of the tax falls most heavily on that group with the more inelastic curve. The phenomenon of elasticity and excise taxes is revisited in the appendices to Chapters 11 and 16.

Chapter 3

ROAD MAP

Chapter 3
The Environment

Chapter 10
World Poverty
Environmental protection is a luxury good that is not affordable in poor countries. Environmental issues are increasingly important as poor countries seek economic development.

Chapter 11
Global Agriculture
Chemical runoff from farms is a source of pollution. Some of our agricultural policies foster environmental harm.

Chapter 12
International Trade
Much pollution is global in nature. The different environmental regulations of different countries can distort trade. Trade agreements and polices can encourage either environmental destruction or protection.

Chapter 17
Globally Free Markets for the Twenty-First Century?
Do free markets and less government regulation have environmental consequences?

The Economic Toolbox

- Externalities
- Spillover costs and benefits
- Social costs of production
- Over- and under-allocation of resources
- Luxury goods
- Marketable pollution permits
- Cost-benefit analysis
- Subsidies

The Environment

The opening quotation to this chapter suggests change—change involving energy and our environment. Obama stressed at the outset of his presidency that investment in three areas of our economy are critical to our future: energy, health care, and education. And, he said at that time, "It begins with energy."

Most (probably all) of us are concerned to some degree about energy and environmental issues. In this chapter, we will consider the economics of environmental protection and environmental damage. Let's start by saying that economic activity affects the environment, often in a harmful manner. Production of goods often causes pollution. Consumption of goods can also cause pollution. We often use our scarce resources inefficiently and unwisely.

In this chapter, we will discuss the pollution created as a by-product of production, as well as policies to deal with this pollution. We will continue our use of demand and supply, and will be introduced to the concept of externalities and reintroduced to cost-benefit analysis. We will also focus particular attention on the topics of global warming (also referred to as climate change), finite energy sources (particularly petroleum), and other international environmental issues. We will consider the environmental effects of consumption, conservation, and recycling, with an eye to our own role in becoming more environmentally conscious. We will conclude with a discussion of the global environment, and, as always, we will consider various liberal and conservative viewpoints on the matter of pollution control. Finally, there are suggestions for you to engage in various activities in the section, *You, the Student*, and in the *Discussion and Action Questions* at the end of the chapter.

The Problem of Pollution

Let's consider the global problem of pollution. We will define **pollution** as waste that is not recycled. Motor vehicles and industrial plants emit carbon monoxide, sulfur oxides, nitrogen oxides, and other hazardous compounds into the atmosphere, thereby polluting our air. The burning of fossil fuels releases carbon dioxide, which, along with other greenhouse gases, traps heat within the earth's atmosphere, thereby contributing to global warming. Deforestation contributes to global warming and causes other problems for developing countries and the rest of the globe. The release of certain chemicals, primarily chlorofluorocarbons (CFCs), damages the ozone layer of our atmosphere, thereby allowing in dangerous levels of ultraviolet radiation from the sun. Industrial wastes, leaking septic tanks and landfills, and pesticides contaminate aquifers and threaten our water supply. We will consider the history of policy to control pollution shortly, as well as in Appendix 3-1.

Americans across the country are already paying the price of inaction [on climate change] … As a president, as a father and as an American, I am here to say, we need to act … I refuse to condemn your generation and future generations to a planet that is beyond saving.

—PRESIDENT BARACK OBAMA, ADDRESS AT GEORGETOWN UNIVERSITY, JUNE 25, 2013

Pollution
Waste that is not recycled.

In all of these cases, environmental damage is a harmful by-product of economic activity. The problem caused by pollution is that of spillover costs, and the results are twofold: inequity and inefficient resource allocation. These topics are discussed in the sections that follow.

Spillover Costs and Benefits

Externality

The cost or benefit of an economic activity that spills over onto the rest of society.

Pollution is the classic example of an economic externality. An **externality** is simply a cost or benefit of an economic activity that spills over onto the rest of society. Externalities can be positive or negative. Pollution represents a negative externality, or a **spillover cost**. Although firms that pollute incur the private costs of production such as wages and energy costs, they do not bear the entire cost of production. A portion of the production costs, specifically the pollution, spills over onto society. The accounting books of the polluting firm do not take into account the effects of pollution. Instead, society bears the burden of this pollution cost in the form of poorer health and productivity, higher health care expenses, greater cleaning costs, damage to buildings and forests, aesthetic displeasure, loss of nonrenewable resources, and so on. Other businesses bear the burden of the pollution cost in the form of damage to capital structures and machinery, harm to crops and needed resources, and so forth. **All negative externalities involve costs created by an economic activity that are shifted to other firms or individuals (or society at large); this situation is neither an equitable one nor an efficient one.**

Spillover cost

A negative externality; the cost of an economic activity that is shifted onto society.

Pollution is not the only negative externality that is common in our lives. Consider your dismay if you live near a newly constructed airport or highway. You will bear the burden of the noise pollution that results. Or imagine living in a heavily populated area, driving on heavily congested streets and freeways, and experiencing time delays and a greater probability of accidents. You would bear costs of congestion. These, too, are negative externalities.

Not all spillover costs are caused by businesses. We consumers also create negative externalities. A good example is our use of the automobile. As you know, Americans love their cars and as a result are reluctant to carpool or take public transportation. We incur private costs associated with driving: car payments, insurance, gas, oil, maintenance costs, taxes and license fees, and parking expenses. Society, however, bears a portion of the total costs in the form of the air pollution caused by auto emissions. Another example might be our use of throw away bottles and cans. We consumers pay for the product, but society bears a burden in the form of litter, solid waste, and an inefficient use of scarce resources. All negative externalities involve costs imposed on others who do not benefit from the production or consumption of the product.

Spillover benefit

A positive externality; the benefit of an economic activity that is shifted onto society.

Externalities can also be positive. We call positive externalities **spillover benefits**. Education is a classic example of a service that yields spillover benefits. You, the student, will benefit most directly from your education. You are likely to earn a higher income, to have a job you enjoy, and to have a richer intellectual life if you are educated. But society also benefits. College graduates tend to be better-informed citizens. They are less likely to be chronically unemployed. They are more likely to vote. They are less likely to commit crimes, or at least violent crimes. They often are more productive workers. So, spillover benefits are conferred on society. Because society receives these benefits, most people feel that society is justified in bearing part of the costs of education through tax revenues. We will address this issue of education in greater detail in the next chapter.

Another spillover benefit comes to society through immunization of children against common childhood diseases. Families pay for the shots and vaccinations and receive most of the benefits in the form of decreased risk of measles, smallpox, and polio. Others in society benefit as well, however. Other children, even if not immunized, are less likely to contract these diseases because the diseases will not be so prevalent. The families of nonimmunized children benefit without bearing any of the cost. Society benefits in terms of lower medical expenses. The burden of costs is inequitable if the responsible family is not in some way compensated for the benefits provided to society.

Let's begin our analysis by recognizing that the existence of an externality causes both inequity and inefficiency.

Inequity and Inefficiency

Inequity

Recall that we've defined inequity as simply unfairness. Externalities shift costs to groups that did not cause them and benefits to groups that did not earn them. As we have noted, pollution causes a spillover cost onto society at large, including other businesses. We, as a society, either tolerate the environmental degradation or clean up someone else's mess with our tax dollars. **This inequitable burden of costs is one of the chief economic characteristics of pollution.**

Inefficiency

In addition to inequity, externalities can cause resources to be inefficiently allocated. Simply put, we produce and consume too much of a product (overallocate resources to its production) if negative externalities are present, and we produce and consume too little of a product (underallocate resources to its production) if positive externalities are present. Let's consider a hypothetical case of resource allocation between two industries, the paper industry and the beer industry, in order to envision a concrete set of circumstance under which resources are inefficiently allocated as a result of an externality.

To simplify, the demand and supply curves for the two industries are drawn identically in Figure 3-1. Initially, we assume no pollution and therefore no spillover costs. The market equilibrium price P and quantity Q in each market is the socially desirable price and quantity because, as we would imagine, society likes to balance the costs and benefits of economic activities.

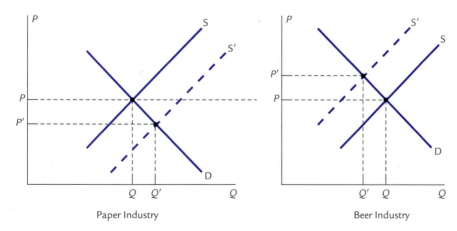

Paper Industry   Beer Industry

© Cengage Learning

Figure 3-1 • Effects of Water Pollution in the Hypothetical Markets for Paper and Beer
Pollution causes an overallocation of resources to the polluting industry (here, the paper industry). As a result, resources are underallocated to other industries (here, the beer industry).

Now suppose that firms in the paper industry decide it is too expensive to prevent pollution, and it is in their best interests to dump their by-products and waste into the adjacent river. They save on production costs, but cause water pollution. Decreased private costs of production in the paper industry will shift the firms' supply curve forward to S′ (since the firms' private costs of production will no longer include the costs of preventing pollution and lower costs of production result in an increase—forward shift—in supply). The market equilibrium price and quantity are now P′ and Q′, respectively. Too much paper is being produced and consumed at a price that does not reflect the costs of pollution. Society is no longer balancing the *full costs* of producing paper with its benefits.

The beer industry, which uses water as an input to beer production, will be adversely affected by the paper companies' actions. Assume that the beer industry has breweries located downstream on the same river. Because polluted water will not produce beer that is safe and good-tasting, beer producing firms in the formerly land of sky blue waters (a phrase used before most of you were born) have to clean up the water before they use it for brewing. The beer industry therefore incurs additional private costs of purifying the water, which shifts the beer industry's supply curve back to S′. This decrease in the supply of beer causes an increase in equilibrium price to P′ and a decrease in equilibrium quantity to Q′. Society consumes less beer and pays higher prices.

Underallocation of resources

The production of less than the socially optimum amount of a good or service.

Overallocation of resources

The production of more than the socially optimum amount of a good or service.

Thus, the externality in the paper market not only causes inequity, but also causes a distortion of resource allocation to the two markets, namely, the **underallocation of resources** to the beer market and the **overallocation of resources** to the paper market. Society consumes more paper and less beer than it would if not for the pollution. To most economists, an essential problem with pollution (or any other externality for that matter) is that it causes resource allocation to be distorted away from what is optimal for society. **We can summarize the discussion so far by stating that externalities cause both problems of inequity (unfairness) and inefficiency (improper allocation of resources).**

The paper and beer example just considered provides a concrete analysis of how over-allocating resources to one industry results in underallocating resources to another. However, it is also important to consider how negative externalities befall *society at large* and misallocate resources such that *society as a whole* fails to properly balance *social* costs and benefits of an economic activity. Since this situation is important, but quite a bit more theoretical, it will be addressed in Appendix 3-2 to this chapter.

U.S. Environmental Policies and Politics

The U.S. Environmental Movement

Air and water pollution are certainly not new phenomena. We tend to romanticize the past as a cleaner, better environment, but this view ignores much of our environmental history. The horse-drawn carriage left its own brand of pollution behind it.

Widespread concern about environmental quality is a recent phenomenon, despite our history of environmental problems. It began in the 1960s and was confined mainly to the United States and other economically advanced countries. Why did environmental concern occur so late, and why was it localized in these countries? First, growth in population, accompanied by increases in output, has greatly increased the amount of pollutants released into the air and water. Inevitably, the quantity of these pollutants has exceeded the natural cleansing abilities of the earth. And the effects are pervasive. The cities of the industrial revolution may have been grimy, unpleasant, and possibly hazardous to inhabitants' health, but the middle and upper classes could easily avoid these effects by moving to the pleasant, agrarian countryside. This strategy no longer works. Pollution follows us to our rural hideaways.

Second, the degree of peril occasioned by pollutants is greater today than it was in preceding centuries. Nuclear wastes and polychlorinated biphenyls (PCBs) are significantly different from the pollutants that plagued our great grandparents. Complex technologies have produced pollutants of which they never dreamed. The news that the polar ice cap is melting and there is a very real threat of global warming are problems of a different magnitude than those experienced by previous generations.

Finally, we have become more affluent, and the demand for environmental quality has increased markedly. Environmental quality is a **luxury good**, or a commodity with a demand extremely sensitive to increases in income. Once society's basic needs for food, clothing, and shelter have been met, citizens begin expecting other things, such as a healthier and higher-quality environment. **These three factors of population growth, increasing magnitude of problem, and higher incomes explain why the environmental movement is both recent and a product of affluent, economically advanced countries.**

Luxury good
A commodity for which demand is highly sensitive to changes in income.

History of U.S. Policies and Programs

Environmental legislation is based on the fact that spillover costs and misallocation of resources result from externalities unless the government takes an active role in controlling the situation. Business firms, which are primarily motivated by profit maximization, will not likely take a strong stand against pollution if they are not compelled to do so through government regulation or encouraged to do so by economic incentives. Nor will most consumers make major efforts to reduce their pollution unless forced to do so or provided with economic incentives.

Environmental regulation grew out of a grassroots movement, and therefore many initiatives were at the local level. Chicago and Cincinnati enacted laws to control smoke emissions from factories and power plants in the 1880s, before there was an environmental movement as such. Many other cities subsequently followed their lead. In fact, the federal government did not become involved in controlling air pollution until the 1950s. The Air Pollution Act of 1955 was merely a federal call for research into the problem.

It wasn't until the 1960s and subsequent years that the U.S. federal government sought to control pollution through legislation, executive orders, and action by the Environmental Protection Agency (EPA). References will be made throughout the chapter to various ups and downs in efforts to protect of the environment; partially because of Supreme Court rulings, legislative stalemate, and the views held by the executive branch. As mentioned, a history of many other efforts are detailed in Appendix 3-1 at the end of this chapter.

In response to the failure of Congress to come together in recent passage of an effective environmental bill, President Obama used his executive authority to advance a series of mandates, one in 2012 and several in 2013 and beyond. These are described in the following sections.

Present U.S. Policies and Programs

In 2012, President Obama established new rules to double the fuel economy for cars and light-duty trucks by 2025. More recently, in 2013, President Obama used his executive office authority to call for protections against climate change, including, for the first time, solid regulations affecting power plants. He established these orders at the time of the quotation that opens this chapter, and they include the following: (1) to launch federal regulations on carbon dioxide emissions from power plants; (2) to provide federal loan guarantees to spur investment in efficiency projects and advanced fossil energy; (3) to expand permission for renewable energy projects, including wind and solar; (4) to establish the goal of installing renewable energy projects on federally assisted housing projects; (5) to use more aggressive steps to increase efficiency for appliances and federal buildings; (6) to develop new fuel-economy standards for heavy-duty vehicles; (7) to create a national Drought Resilience Partnership to help communities prepare for droughts and wildfires; (8) to promote climate change preparedness for local governments, businesses, and hospitals; (9) to update flood risk reduction standards; (10) to work with China, India, and other major polluting countries to cut emissions; and (11) to end U.S. public financing for new coal-fired power plants in other countries. These will be referred to as "mandates" throughout this chapter. As you can see, these steps to reduce pollution and manage climate change include efforts both in the United States and the rest of the world.[1]

In 2013, the Supreme Court allowed the EPA's ability to regulate carbon dioxide emissions stand. However, controversy will undoubtedly continue, as several groups including the oil and chemical industry will challenge the EPA's regulatory authority.

A particularly contentious situation arose in 2015 involving the proposed Keystone Pipeline, a pipeline that would bring oil down from Canada to the U.S. gulf. Republicans asserted it would bring jobs, while Democrats cited environmental concerns. President Obama pledged to veto legislation approving the pipeline if Congress passed it. Congress did, and the president vetoed it. Congress failed to get enough votes to overcome the veto, the veto stood, and the pipeline failed.

The Proper Level of Government for Pollution Control

Because the federal government as well as state and local governments have been involved in regulation for environmental protection, it is important to address the issue of the *proper* level of government to handle environmental regulation. Some people argue that the federal government is characterized by a huge bureaucracy that is far from the people it governs and is unresponsive to the people's needs. The federal EPA, they argue, is slow to respond to local needs and is insensitive to local opinion. They feel that local, state, or regional, regulation would be more sensitive and responsive. Conservative representatives to Congress have generally taken a strong stand against federal regulations, including those that protect the environment. The George W. Bush administration opposed federal regulations and active regulation by the Environmental Protection Agency.

President Bush also favored giving states a larger role in environmental regulation. Ironically, he also opposed efforts by California, which had taken a lead on addressing global warming, from using more stringent air pollution rules than required by the federal government. We will return to discussion of California shortly. For now, note that it wasn't until 2009 under the new Obama administration that the EPA granted California's request to use the more stringent regulations. California felt forced to undertake control of greenhouse gases in part because it felt the federal government response had not been adequate. Within a few years of embracing California's rules for automobile emissions and mileage standards, President Obama announced the nationwide rules in that we've referred to, and, as is clear from his mandates, he supports a strong federal role in pollution reduction.

Although local regulation keeps government closer to the governed, the federal level may be the more appropriate level of government to regulate the environment. One reason is that whatever the source of air and water pollution, the problem affects neighboring communities, states, and even countries. Acid rain originating in the United States but damaging property in Canada has become a heated issue between the two nations. Global warming, ozone depletion, and loss of biodiversity are also global phenomena, as we will discuss shortly.

At the same time, local communities, acting in their own perceived self-interest, may be lax in setting standards to control air and water pollution. By tolerating pollution, they may attract industry and increase the jobs available for their citizens. As long as some pollution affects other jurisdictions, localities have an incentive to underregulate their own pollution sources. Indeed, a major cause of acid rain is the sulfur dioxide emitted into the atmosphere by the tall smokestacks of coal-burning electric utilities. The smokestacks were built to conform to local standards for air pollution, and they protect the local community but emit pollutants that damage distant communities. They were (and are) considerably less expensive than scrubbers, which are designed to eliminate most of the pollutants at the source. The localities export the problem rather than solve it. Adequately enforced federal legislation would help minimize both the disparity of pollution standards and the lax pollution standards that would exist if regulation were left to individual localities and states.

Furthermore, the states have widely differing resources. The federal government has a larger tax base than any state, and it has greater ability to finance pollution control activities. It can also mitigate the burden of pollution control by transferring income from affluent states to poorer states.

We define pollution as an externality, spilling from producer and consumer onto society at large. But we've also identified a secondary form of externality, which is geographical. **Since pollution can spread from one locality to another, or to the world for that matter, there will be an underallocation of resources devoted to pollution control unless it is addressed at a geographical level that incorporates the full extent of the pollution.** This means that while pollution control policy might be administered at a variety of government levels, the appropriate jurisdiction for setting pollution control standards should be large enough to capture all the negative spillovers. Thus, decisions about pollution control are most appropriately made at the national, or even international, level. (We will address international efforts shortly.)

Methods of Regulation

Government agencies, at any level, use the following methods to limit adverse environmental effects: (1) standards, (2) pollution fees, and (3) marketable pollution permits.

The Standards Approach

Let's look at the standards approach to pollution control first. This approach is the easiest to understand and the one originally used by environmental agencies.

With the **standards** approach, maximum acceptable levels of pollutants are established, and firms that exceed these levels are punished, usually by fines. Firms can thus be forced into compliance with the standard.

The logic of the standards approach is clear, and the process appears simple. But this approach is more complex than it at first appears. The agency must first set the standards and then enforce them. In addition, it should continually explore new technical possibilities and evaluate its programs.

Standards may be classified as performance standards or design standards. A **performance standard** specifies a certain level of performance or compliance that must be met. It does not specify the means by which that level must be reached. The regulating agency might require the firm to reduce the pollutants emitted in a combustion process by 10 percent, without specifying the means by which this standard will be met. A **design standard**, on the other hand, specifies not only the required level of performance but also the means to reach that level. Control of auto emissions by the installation of catalytic converters is an

Standards
Maximum levels of pollutants that are acceptable by law.

Performance standard
A regulation that specifies the required level of performance but not the means of compliance.

Design standard
A regulation that specifies both the required level of performance and the means of compliance.

example of a design standard. A performance standard leaves the compliance method up to the regulated firm. It is more flexible than the design standard and may encourage research into new technologies and lower-cost methods by business firms to meet pollution reduction goals. In practice, both types of standards are used.

The requirement of the catalytic converter, our example of a design standard, has been criticized by many. Catalytic converters are expensive. Old cars (that cause most of the pollution) are often exempt from the requirement. Poorly maintained converters fail, and not enough inspection takes place. Automakers have no incentive to design alternative engines or other technology that could cut emissions. Consumers have no incentive to drive less, better maintain their automobiles, or use less-polluting fuel sources. Since car emission standards require the use of catalytic converters, research into other emissions control methods has been stymied. The general problem with **technology forcing** is that methods that could control pollution more cheaply are not being encouraged, developed, or used.

Given the very real problems with the standards approach to environmental regulation, many economists propose that we use pollution fees or pollution permits instead. Both methods are more flexible than standards and rely on the marketplace to control pollution more efficiently than standards regulation can. Let's look now at how these types of policies can achieve our environmental goals at a lower cost than standards regulation can.

Pollution Fees

The two types of pollution fees are effluent fees and emissions fees. **Effluent fees** are taxes on production that causes water pollution, whereas **emissions fees** are taxes on production that causes air pollution. If the amount of the pollution fee is at least equal to the social spillover cost, the imposition of the tax will correct the overallocation of resources that results from pollution. It does this by giving firms an incentive to change their behavior. They can either pay the fee or find a new process of production that is less harmful to the environment.

Refer back to the polluting paper company in Figure 3-1. If the company continues to pollute, the government can impose an effluent fee, which can be viewed as an additional cost of production (since the supplier hands the fee over to the government). Supply will decrease in the direction of the original curve. Consumers will pay a higher price for the polluters' products because of the effluent fee. They will also consume less. In these ways, they will bear some of the burden of pollution control. This might be viewed as appropriate. If the company chooses to eliminate its pollution, the higher costs of doing so will also cause supply to decrease. The important point is that fees do not force technology. Instead, they give firms an incentive to look for least-cost techniques to cut pollution and fees. From the view of enforcement and administration, pollution fees are easier to administer than are standards. From society's view, they result in least-cost—and thus more efficient—pollution control.

Marketable Pollution Permits

Under the **marketable pollution permits** approach, also referred to as "cap and trade," the maximum level of pollution acceptable to society is divided into units, and the government issues permits that allow business firms to produce these units of pollution in their production process. These permits can be bought and sold. They will eventually wind up in the hands of firms for whom the costs of reducing pollution are the highest. This will result in the lowest cost to society (producers and consumers) of pollution control.

Let's consider an example. Suppose two farms are located along a river in a small rural locality. One farm is located on a hill, and the other farm is in a valley. The river

---

Technology forcing
Standards that force firms to use specific pollution control technologies.

Effluent fees
Taxes on production causing water pollution.

Emissions fees
Taxes on production causing air pollution.

Marketable pollution permits
Tradable permits that allow the owners of the permits to produce a given amount of pollution.

flows between them. We will assume it is costly for the farmer on the hill to contain the runoff of chemical fertilizers and pesticides into the river (since gravity must be overcome). Let's say it costs $100 for this farmer to prevent each unit of runoff from entering the river. (One unit could be a pound or a ton or any other way we have of identifying an amount of pollution.) Let's assume it is relatively cheap and easy for the farmer in the valley to control its runoff, perhaps $10 per unit. Now suppose, perhaps in response to citizen demands, the local government decides to allow only a total of four units of agricultural runoff into the river, and each pollution permit that it grants "permits" the recipient to produce two units of pollution. Each farmer is thus allocated two pollution permits, meaning that each farmer is permitted to pollute two units of pollution into the river. Let's assume that previously each farm would cause four units of water pollution.

One alternative is for the government to forbid each farmer from causing more than two units of pollution. This means that *each* farmer would have to eliminate two units of pollution, at a cost of $200 for the farmer on the hill and a cost of $20 for the farmer in the valley. Society will end up with four units of water pollution (instead of the former eight units) and a total cost of $220 for pollution control (remember that the two farmers are part of society). These farmers will presumably pass at least some of their pollution-prevention costs onto consumers of their products in the form of higher prices (consumers are also part of society).

The other alternative is for the local government to issue the same two pollution permits to each farmer, but allow the farmers to buy and sell their permits (that is, the permits are *marketable*). The two farmers may agree on a price of $50 per permit. The farmer on the hill will find it advantageous to purchase the two pollution permits from the farmer in the valley, paying a total of $100 for the right to continue to cause its four units of water pollution. The farmer in the valley will find it advantageous to sell its two pollution permits to the farmer on the hill, receiving $100 from this farmer but incurring $40 to eliminate its entire four units of pollution. Society once again ends up with only four units of water pollution (instead of the original eight units), but incurs a total cost of pollution control of only $40 (the actual amount of money spent in stopping the pollution, and not the money that is merely changing hands but doing nothing for the environment). By allowing pollution permits to be marketable, the same amount of pollution will be prevented, but the total cost of pollution control will be minimized.

We've already noted the lead taken by the state of California to reduce pollution, and this initiative included the innovative step of introducing marketable pollution permits for the emissions of greenhouse gases. Calling it the California Global Warming Solutions Act, this state (with a Republican governor and a Democratic legislature and the sixth largest economy *in the world*) took the unprecedented initiative to plan to reduce its emission of carbon dioxide by 25 percent by 2020. Low pollution control cost companies are permitted to sell their pollution permits to high pollution control cost companies, creating an incentive for firms to find the most efficient ways to control pollution and to reward them for doing so. The additional benefit is that California's initiatives are estimated to increase statewide income by billions of dollars while providing thousands of new jobs. This growth would come from the creation of green technologies and lower energy costs.[2]

The federal government has been less successful in extending marketable pollution permits with respect to air pollution. There have been efforts, however. In 1979, the Environmental Protection Agency established its first marketable pollution permits on an experimental basis. The earliest experiments focused on individual firms that caused pollution at various stages in each of their production processes. Amendments made to the Clean Air Act in 1990 extended the concept industry-wide, creating pollution permits for coal-burning utilities and addressing the issue of pollution caused by one state but drifting downwind to other states. However, this policy essentially ended in 2010 when the EPA issued a ruling against it. Efforts to revive it were squelched when, in August 2012, a U.S. Appeals Court issued a decision not to restore it but to send the issue back to the EPA for further consideration. Thus, up until the recent Obama mandates, EPA policies utilizing pollution permits have made limited strides.

Methods of Regulation and the Marketplace

Pollution permits and pollution fees are incentive-based regulation schemes, utilizing the efficiencies of the marketplace. Studies indicate that these schemes do work. They are less expensive than standards regulation and do not stifle technological change. Instead, they encourage research and the development of new pollution control technologies. And, marketable pollution permits are now more likely than previously to take on a vital role in the context of state and national policies. They have also become an important element of international agreements and policies, as we will see shortly. But first, let's consider two important global aspects of pollution in greater detail: global warming, also called climate change, and world petroleum use.

Global Aspects of Pollution

Let's consider two of the most significant aspects of the global environment, climate change (of which we've already begun our discussion) and world petroleum use.

Climate Change

> *Right now it seems that the glaciers are moving faster than the negotiators.*
> —John Coequyt, Greenpeace Energy Policy Analyst, November 4, 2006[3]

Many experts believe that the major environmental issue of the twenty-first century is global warming, also referred to as climate change. Scientists have long since concluded that global warming is a serious phenomenon that is caused by human activity. In fact, the United Nations World Meteorological Organization reported that the decade of 2001–2010 was the hottest decade in history. Similarly, the National Climatic Data Center reported that 2012 was the hottest year on record in the United States.

We also know that whatever efforts are now made to address global warming are too late to reverse future catastrophic results, although action now can prevent additional catastrophes from occurring.

Scientists have identified the emissions that contribute to global warming and made dire predictions of what will come true if the production of greenhouse gases is not reduced. Despite awareness of the problem, society has been reluctant to deal with it. While the term "moving at glacial speed" has traditionally meant "moving very slowly," the Greenpeace analyst, quoted above on the eve of the twelfth international global warming conference, suggests that the glaciers are moving much more rapidly. We can only hope that the United States and the rest of the world are now taking responsibility for the problem much more seriously.

The Data

Carbon dioxide is one of the principal greenhouse gases. Global production of carbon dioxide is addressed in Table 3-1, which displays the amount of carbon dioxide produced by the top 10 emitting countries of the world. Note that China has surpassed the United States as the world's largest emitter of carbon dioxide. China produces close to 9,000 million

TABLE 3-1 • Carbon Dioxide Emissions, Top 10 Emitting Countries, Million Metric Tons per Year, 2011

Country	Million Metric Tons of Carbon Dioxide Emissions	Country	Million Metric Tons of Carbon Dioxide Emissions
China	8,715	Canada	777
United States	5,491	Germany	748
Russia	1,788	Iran	625
India	1,726	Korea, Rep.	611
Japan	1,181	Saudi Arabia	513

Source: U.S. Energy Information Administration, Department of Energy, Posted June 27, 2013, http://www.eia.doe.gov/.

(9 billion) metric tons per year, whereas the United States produces about five and one-half billion metric tons. Both China and the United States exceed the emissions of any other country by far, each emitting about three or five times the emissions of the next highest country (Russia). We should note that the poorest countries of the world cause very little by way of carbon dioxide emissions. Nevertheless, the impact of climate change falls most heavily on the poorest countries of the world, including those in Africa and southern Asia. For example, while Vietnam causes very little carbon dioxide emissions, scientists are concerned that up to one-third or more of the Mekong Delta, where tens of millions of people live and nearly half the country's rice is grown, could be submerged if sea levels rise by three feet in decades to come as a result of global warming affecting this poor country. Storm surges related to climate change would create an intrusion of salt water that could contaminate much of the remaining delta area, rising temperatures in the Central Highlands of the country could put the coffee crop at risk, and large areas near the capital city of Hanoi could become inundated with water. Yet environmental protection is a luxury good for the poor people of this country, and the governments of the greatest carbon dioxide emitting countries are less concerned about geographical areas outside of their own proximity.[4]

Since the United States is the second largest emitter of carbon dioxide in the world, it is interesting to see how our emissions have changed over time. Table 3-2 shows these data for selected years from 1980 to 2012. Note that our emissions have grown considerably since 1980. However, they have not increased steadily—we see that they declined from 1980 to 1985 and from 2000 to 2005. More significant is the decline from 2007 to 2012. Perhaps we can continue this trend. Keep in mind that in addition to industrial pollution, we produce carbon dioxide emissions whenever we heat our homes, drive our cars, and purchase electricity and consumer goods made by carbon dioxide emitting businesses.

TABLE 3-2 • U.S. Carbon Dioxide Emissions,[a] Selected Years 1980 to 2012

Year	Million Metric Tons of Carbon Dioxide	Year	Million Metric Tons of Carbon Dioxide
1980	4,755	2000	5,816
1985	4,585	2005	5,776
1990	5,013	2007	5,903
1995	5,293	2012	5,300

[a]From the consumption and flaring of fossil fuels.

Source: U.S. Energy Information Administration, Department of Energy, Posted June 27, 2013, http://www.eia.doe.gov/.

U.S. and International Policies

An international summit dedicated to reducing global warming and other environmental problems was held in Kyoto, Japan, in 1997. The result of the Kyoto summit was a treaty designed to reduce global warming. This Kyoto Accord required industrial countries to substantially reduce greenhouse gases that cause global warming, with implementation beginning in 2005 and covering a commitment period of 2008 through 2012. At the time of the Kyoto Summit, President Bill Clinton signaled his support for the treaty. However, President George W. Bush opposed the Kyoto treaty and refused to sign it, calling instead for voluntary restraint among U.S. companies.

Upon entering office, President Obama made an immediate call for legislation to limit carbon dioxide emissions. The first Congress under his administration entered the fray with the 2009 House of Representatives Climate Control Act. The Climate Control Act explicitly made use of the term "cap and trade." As a form of marketable pollution permits, cap and trade would require polluters to acquire "pollution credits" (or permits) equal to the amount of their pollution. These pollution credits could be bought and sold in the marketplace, and as in our previous discussion of pollution permits, could be sold by firms for whom pollution reduction is relatively easy and cheap, to firms for whom pollution reduction is relatively difficult and expensive. Pollution would be reduced in the most efficient and costless manner. Other aspects of this Climate Bill included requirements that power plants, factories, and automobiles cut emissions and that electricity producers get at least 15 percent of their energy from renewable sources by 2020.

The 2009 Climate Bill was rejected by the U.S. Senate. Nevertheless, the attempt was historic—or in the words of Mark Shields of the Jim Lehrer show, "it is epic."[5] It was the first bill ever to embody the principle of reducing carbon dioxide emissions by law. Despite the failures of Congress to unite on a climate control bill, President Obama did usher in many of the same objectives in the 2013 mandates that we've already considered.

Finally, the European Union Emissions Trading System (EU ETS) was the first and largest international organization using pollution permits to address climate change. It was initiated in 2005 and of January 2013, it covers 31 countries (all European Union members plus Croatia, Iceland, Norway, and Liechtenstein).

Just as global warming is one particular environmental issue that we face, another is the consumption of the earth's finite supply of petroleum. As an international environmental issue, it is useful to focus a bit of attention on petroleum in particular and energy in general.

World Petroleum Use

Petroleum is a finite resource. If for no other reason than that, we must find a way to move beyond a petroleum-based economy. The United States has also been highly dependent upon imports of petroleum, including imports from the Middle East. Because of these concerns, environmentalists and others have paid attention to our petroleum use and have begun to recommend alternatives.

The Data

Table 3-3 displays global consumption of petroleum for the top 10 consuming countries of the world. We see that the United States uses by far more petroleum than any other country in the world. This is almost twice the amount of petroleum consumed by China, which consumes the second largest amount of petroleum in the world. Below China, the remaining top 10 consumers are considerably smaller. We also know that except for South Africa, most of Africa and countries in other poor regions consume very little petroleum.

With the United States being the largest user of petroleum, we should consider how our consumption of petroleum has changed over time. Table 3-4 reveals these data for

TABLE 3-3 • World Petroleum Consumption, Top 10 Using Countries in Descending Order, 2012

Country	Million Barrels per Day	Country	Million Barrels per Day
United States	18.6	South Africa	3.0
China	10.2	Brazil	2.6
Japan	4.7	Canada	2.3
India	3.4	Germany	2.3
Russia	3.2	Korea, Rep.	2.3

Source: U.S. Energy Information Administration, Department of Energy, Posted June 27, 2013, http://www.eia.doe.gov/.

TABLE 3-4 • U.S. Petroleum Consumption, Selected Years 1980 to 2007

Year	Million Barrels per Day	Year	Million Barrels per Day
1980	17.1	2000	19.7
1985	15.7	2007	20.7
1990	17.0	2012	18.6
1995	17.7		

Source: U.S. Energy Information Administration, Department of Energy, Posted May 20, 2013, www.eia.doe.gov.

the time period 1980–2012. We note that petroleum consumption has largely increased over time, though it has fallen most recently.

The demand and supply of petroleum naturally affects the price of this resource. Various factors influence demand and supply in this market. The market power held by the Organization of Petroleum Exporting Countries (OPEC) was strong in the 1970s, when this organization of 13 oil-exporting countries had the ability to greatly influence the market price. (OPEC is discussed in more detail in Chapter 13 on market power, which is defined as the ability to influence the market price of the product.) OPEC wielded its market power by controlling its supply of petroleum. By setting quotas on the oil exports of each member country, OPEC was able to restrict the supply of oil when it deemed preferable. This is shown in Figure 3-2.

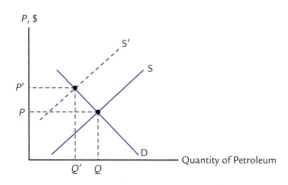

Figure 3-2 • A Decrease in the World Supply of Petroleum by OPEC
When OPEC decreases the international supply of oil, quantity falls to Q′ and price rises to P′.

International demand for petroleum is expressed by curve D in Figure 3-2, whereas the international supply is shown by curve S. Assuming that OPEC supplies a sizeable amount of the world's petroleum exports, this organization is able to reduce the global supply to S′ by reducing its members' exports. This decrease in supply will raise the market price of petroleum to P′ and reduce the internationally sold quantity to Q′. Today, supply fluctuations are more likely to be caused by instability in the Middle East, rather than a unified effort on the part of OPEC.

The U.S. government also maintains stocks of petroleum that it releases to the market when oil prices rise to high levels. This release of oil stocks would be tantamount to shifting the supply curve in Figure 3-2 forward once again, thereby reducing the price. Other factors also affect the price of oil. For example, in the summer of 2006, BP Amoco Oil Company announced that it was shutting down a sizeable portion of its oil fields along the northern coast of Alaska to correct a problem of corrosion in its pipelines. This caused a temporary reduction in the supply of oil. Similarly, Hurricane Katrina reduced the oil-producing capacity of our nation's Gulf states, just as the war in Iraq reduced its oil-producing capacity. Shifts in the demand for oil affect the market price for oil. Rising demand because of higher population levels and higher standards of living can be offset by deliberate measures by consumers to conserve their use of petroleum.

Petroleum prices in the United States are shown in Table 3-5 for selected years over the time period 1970–2012. Notice the very low price of $3.40 per barrel in 1970. By 1974, the 1973–74 Arab Oil Boycott (in response to U.S. support of Israel in the Arab-Israeli wars) caused the price to jump threefold, to $10.38 per barrel. By 1980, when the 1979 Iranian Revolution resulted in a cutoff of oil to the United States, prices nearly tripled again. And while oil prices have varied in the 1980s and 1990s, we see a distinctly rising trend in the 2000s. At $100.93 per barrel in 2012, we can say that oil prices have increased to about 30 times what they were in 1970. Can you think of factors that might have contributed to this long-term increase?

While not shown in the table, petroleum prices plunged by 2014 and beyond. They were cut in half from the summer of 2014 to the summer of 2015! A number of factors contributed. Certainly the demand for oil has recently been increasing more slowly, especially as consumers began buying more fuel efficient cars. And supply has been steadily increasing, including from the United States. Do you think this new trend will continue?

Gasoline Prices and Policies

Prices of petroleum are, of course, reflected in prices at the gas pumps, and these are the prices that probably hit most of you where it hurts. Table 3-6 shows these prices in the United States for the time period 1995–2012. We see a rising trend throughout, and as

TABLE 3-5 • Crude Oil Prices[a] (U.S. Dollars per Barrel), Selected Years 1970 to 2012

Year	Price	Year	Price
1970	$3.40	2000	$28.26
1974	$10.38	2005	$50.24
1980	$28.07	2010	$76.69
1985	$26.75	2012	$100.93
1990	$22.22		
1995	$17.23		

[a]U.S. crude oil composite acquisition cost by refiner.

Source: U.S. Energy Information Administration, Department of Energy, http://www.eia.doe.gov/, released June 3, 2013.

TABLE 3-6 • U.S. Retail Motor Gasoline Prices (Nominal U.S. Dollars per Gallon), Regular Unleaded, 1995 to 2012

Year	Price
1995	$1.11
2000	$1.48
2005	$2.27
2010	$2.72
2011	$3.52
2012	$3.62

Source: U.S. Energy Information Administration, Department of Energy, http://www.eia.doe.gov/, released June 3, 2013.

you perhaps know, gas prices have sporadically reached over $4 per gallon in some geographical locations within the United States during this time period. Since 2012, gasoline prices have fallen, in line with the fall in petroleum prices. The price of gas was was below $2.50 per gallon by early 2015. Again, do you think these low prices will continue?

You may think that the obvious solution to high gasoline prices, when they occur, is to impose price controls (also called price ceilings). While we will consider this option of price ceilings in Chapter 7 on Housing and Chapter 10 on World Poverty, we will note for now that this type of government effort to outlaw high prices doesn't work as well as we might wish. Prices may be kept artificially low, but shortages are the automatic result. These were the outcomes of well-intentioned but poorly thought-out price ceilings on gasoline and other energy products in the 1970s (discussed in the appendix to Chapter 7). We will consider alternative policies shortly.

Evaluation of Environmental Policies

Pollution affects our lives. And policies to prevent or reduce pollution also affect our lives. Whatever the method used by regulators, regulation raises the firm's production costs and increases the price we pay for the products we buy. These policies also, of course, result in air, water, and soil of higher quality. Such policies must be efficient. One framework for evaluating public policies of all types is cost-benefit analysis, already introduced in Chapter 2 in the context of crime prevention.

Cost-benefit analysis is the systematic comparison of all the costs of a program with all the benefits. The program should be undertaken only if the benefits are greater than the costs. From the perspective of the environment, let's look at the costs and benefits of environmental protection programs. The costs of these programs are the costs incurred by government in regulating business, in running public recycling programs, and in any other activity that cuts down on or cleans up pollution. Business firms also incur costs of environmental protection. If they adopt a more expensive but less-polluting process, their increase in cost is an environmental protection cost. If they use less-polluting but more costly raw materials, the difference in cost is also an environmental protection cost. If they install and maintain pollution control equipment, such as scrubbers in smokestacks, they incur an environmental protection cost. Consumers can also incur environmental protection costs if they install high-efficiency, less-polluting furnaces and other appliances, or if they incur the expense and inconvenience of recycling. The environmental protection costs are the total of all these costs, whether incurred by government, businesses, or households.

Cost-benefit analysis
A study that compares the costs and benefits of a policy or program.

The benefits of environmental protection are the improvements in our environmental quality that result. Some of these benefits are quantifiable. We save on cleaning costs if air pollution is reduced. Businesses save on repair costs when acid rain no longer damages their structures. We save on medical costs when people no longer suffer the ill health that results from pollution.

However, many of the benefits of environmental programs cannot be calculated in monetary terms. The personal benefits of improved health and longevity go far beyond the savings on medical costs. The biodiversity of our rain forests is expected to yield yet undiscovered products to benefit humankind. And there is no way to place a price on a stream used for trout fishing or a lake used for swimming that might otherwise be too polluted for use.

In reconciling the costs with the benefits of environmental protection, we must take a wide view and a long view. We must consider the monetary and nonmonetary benefits of environmental protection, and we must consider the benefits to future as well as current generations. Indeed, we've hit upon another type of externality. We've defined pollution as a negative externality that spills costs onto society at large. We've also noted a secondary form of externality, which is geographical. One locality spills pollution onto other localities and even onto the world as a whole. There is still this final form of externality that occurs, which is an intertemporal one. Pollution caused by one generation spills costs onto future generations. **Unless citizens of the present time period address the needs of future generations, an underallocation of resources devoted to pollution control in the present will fail to meet the needs of our children and grandchildren.**

Conservation and Recycling

Pollution by producers is an important facet of our environmental problem, but consumers also contribute to the problem. We exhaust nonrenewable resources such as petroleum at an increasing rate. We cause emissions of greenhouse gases, and we consume ever larger amounts of goods and services.

While many people point to overpopulation in the developing world, in fact it is the developed world that strains the environment the most. The United States plays an inordinate role. With about 4.5 percent of the world's population, the U.S. consumption of petroleum represents 22 percent of global petroleum consumption and its consumption of energy represents 20 percent of global electricity consumption.[6] Compared to the least developed countries of the world, with 0.3 metric tons of carbon dioxide emissions per person, the United States emits 17.3 metric tons per capita (compared to 4.7 metric tons per capita for the world as a whole).[7] *Given its consumerism, U.S. society stresses the environment far more than does an overpopulated poor country.* We live in a society characterized by a throwaway mentality, planned obsolescence, and the production of unnecessary and ecologically harmful products. The antithesis of this attitude is one of conservation and recycling. Let's look first at the economics of conservation, then that of recycling. Then let's examine a few innovative policies to reduce pollution by consumers.

Economics of Recycling

It is also possible to save and reuse some of our natural resources. Many communities and business firms have established recycling programs in an effort to reduce the strain on our landfills and resources. Recycling has many dimensions and many economic aspects.

Recycling programs vary throughout the nation. Communities commonly recycle aluminum and newspapers. Some communities also recycle cardboard, magazines, tin cans, glass, plastics, scrap metal, and used oil. You can also recycle your used printer ink cartridges through the U.S. Postal Service. Recycling keeps these commodities out of landfills. As our population has grown, so have the wastes we produce. Landfills have filled up. Old landfills, in which everything (including hazardous waste) has been dumped, are recognized as environmental hazards that pollute the land and water supply.

Although modern, state-of-the-art landfills are environmentally safe if located and monitored properly, their use is nevertheless controversial. If you have ever followed the local political wrangling over the site of a proposed new landfill, you are aware of this. No one wants the landfill anywhere near his or her property, and citizens' groups form to fight landfill siting projects. Reducing the bulk of our garbage through recycling is therefore a popular alternative to landfilling.

The two most pressing problems faced by recycling programs are (1) motivating consumers and businesses to recycle and (2) developing markets for recyclable goods.

Motivation to Recycle

Studies have found that people are more willing to recycle if it is convenient for them to do so. Collecting recyclables at consumers' homes (curbside recycling) or establishing numerous neighborhood (or campus) drop-off points makes recycling easier and more convenient for people.

Although some people recycle because they are environmentally conscious, others are willing to do so only if they are given sufficient economic incentives. These incentives can take a variety of forms.

Many households pay for waste disposal services by a fixed fee to a public or private garbage collection service. A family might pay $10 a month to have its garbage collected. The charge is the same whether the family has 1 bag or 12 bags of garbage per week. There is no incentive to reduce the amount of waste that is collected.

On the other hand, some communities charge households for each bag or can of garbage they discard. A charge of $2 per bag of garbage provides an incentive to decrease the number of garbage bags. Households can save money by buying products with less packaging or by recycling or composting their waste. Although such programs hold much promise for motivating consumers to recycle, they also may create some less desirable effects. They may motivate some people to dispose of their garbage illegally by dumping it in vacant lots or along country roads or by burning it themselves.

Under another type of incentive system, the government sets a target for recycling a product, and *producers* are responsible for ensuring that their product is recycled. Producers are required to buy "credits" from firms that recycle their type of product. For example, if a 50 percent recycling target were set for newspaper, the local newspaper company would be required to buy 500 pounds of credits for every 1,000 pounds of newspapers it produces. It would buy its credits from firms such as cardboard box producers that can use old newspapers in producing their product. Because the box producer is paid for using old newspapers, it has an incentive to use recycled newsprint instead of new paper pulp.

The price of the recycling credit is set by market forces. If the box manufacturer can use the newspapers at low cost, the price of the credit will be low. If a second firm can use old newsprint at a still lower cost, it will sell the credits to the newspaper at a still lower price. The old newspaper will go to the firm with the lowest use costs, and society's recycling costs will be minimized. As with taxes and subsidies, recycling credits are most appropriate for particularly troublesome items in our waste stream.

A final example of an economic incentive to reduce waste by recycling is the beverage container deposit, which is legally required in several states. Consumers pay a deposit of 5 or 10 cents per can or bottle when they buy beer or soda pop. Their money is returned when they bring the containers back to the store or a redemption center. A similar situation exists for plastic milk and water containers. Studies have shown that states with beverage deposit laws recycled far more containers than nondeposit states. **The bottom line is that economic incentives can motivate us to recycle and reuse materials, which extends the life of our resources and landfills.**

Markets for Recyclable Products

A serious problem faced by recycling programs is lack of markets for recyclable materials. Old newspapers can be used to make paper or cardboard, or they can be shredded for animal bedding. Glass can be used as an additive for asphalt paving. Other recyclable materials have similar uses. But the firms that produce recycled products often face an uncertain demand. They may therefore suspend the purchase of the recyclable materials, and recycling centers will build up inventories of these articles. When we drop off our recyclables at the recycling collection point, we assume that these articles will be put to some appropriate use. In fact, they sometimes go to landfills because there is no user for them. The EPA has awarded numerous grants to local governments so they can develop additional markets for recyclables. Further uses of recycled products must be found, and consumers, governmental units, and business firms must be given incentives to choose products made with recycled material, if such a choice is available. Many people are averse to buying products made with recycled materials (for example, retreaded tires) because they view the products as inferior to those made with new materials. (Your author is sometimes reluctant to purchase fair trade writing journals made out of elephant dung, even though the paper has been completely sanitized and the profits benefit low-income producers in developing countries—more on fair trade in Chapter 12.) If there are real or perceived quality differences between recycled products and new ones, market forces will result in price differences that are consistent with the quality differences. Last, we must also raise the issue that sometimes recycling is simply not an efficient choice in the context of the resources used in recycling, the negative by-products created in the process, or the possible lack of safety of recycled products.

Economics of Conservation

This section is especially targeted to you, the student, in an effort to see how you and I and others can personally address the problem of pollution. As a starting point, let's review the law of demand from Chapter 1. Price and quantity demanded are negatively related. Consumers will buy more at low prices than at high ones. It therefore follows that raising the price of a product will result in less consumption of it, whereas lowering the price will cause greater consumption. The market can act as a mechanism to encourage conservation. And the government can influence the market by taxes or by **subsidies**, which are payments to producers or consumers of the product.

Let's look at a few examples of such policies, beginning with a hypothetical market for gasoline. The United States is castigated by environmentalists for being the world's largest consumer of oil. Much of the oil we consume is in the form of gasoline to power cars, sport utility vehicles, and light trucks. The price per gallon of gasoline in the United

Subsidies

Payments from the government for some given action, such as recycling.

States is unrealistically low because it is not fully adjusted to account for pollution costs and depletion of natural resources (the negative spillovers). Gas prices in the United States are much lower than in much of the rest of the industrialized world, where countries impose gasoline taxes higher than those in the United States. Such taxes increase the price of a gallon of fuel, giving consumers an incentive to conserve gas. And *incentives* is what economics is all about!

Let's consider two hypothetical countries, illustrated in Figure 3-3. Let's assume identical demand and supply curves for gasoline in each hypothetical market. These identical curves result in an initial equilibrium price of $2 per gallon, and an initial equilibrium quantity of 4 million gallons in each country (corresponding to point E in each graph).

Recall that an excise tax is an additional cost of production that must be paid to the government *by the sellers* of the product. The tax will thereby cause a decrease (backward shift) in supply.

Now suppose that the first country (the low-tax country) imposes a gasoline tax of $1 per gallon, and the second country (the high-tax country) imposes a tax of $2 per gallon. The supply curve in the low-tax country shifts back (upward) by $1 per gallon to S′ (the vertical distance between the two supply curves is the amount of the tax). The new equilibrium price to consumers is $2.50 per gallon, and the new equilibrium quantity is 3 million gallons (corresponding to point E′). The imposition of the tax has increased price slightly and resulted in a decrease in consumption of 1 million gallons of gasoline.

In the case of the high-tax country, the supply curve shifts back (upward) by $2 per gallon to S″ (again, the vertical distance between the two supply curves is the amount of the tax).

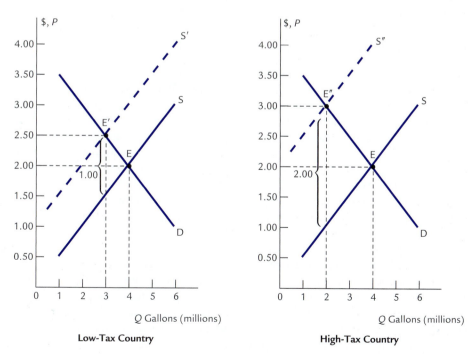

Figure 3-3 • Effects of Hypothetical Gasoline Taxes on the Price and Sale of Gasoline
The higher ($2 per gallon) gasoline tax results in the consumption of only 2 million gallons of gas and thus encourages greater conservation than the lower ($1 per gallon) tax.

© Cengage Learning

The new equilibrium price is $3 per gallon, and the new equilibrium quantity is 2 million gallons (corresponding to point E″). The imposition of the tax has increased price greatly and has resulted in a decrease in consumption of 2 million gallons of gasoline. In both cases, consumption decreases, but far more significantly where gasoline taxes are higher.

How does this conservation occur? In many ways. Drivers are less likely to make unnecessary trips. They are more likely to take public transportation if it is available. They carpool. When purchasing a car, they compare the fuel efficiency of various models and weigh this information heavily in their decision to buy. **Higher gasoline prices give individuals an incentive to make many independent decisions that result in conservation of oil supplies.** Conversely, a low price encourages us to waste gasoline. However, Americans do not vote for politicians who campaign on the promise to raise gasoline taxes, although it might be in our long-run best interest to do so.

Let's realize that the tax will also raise an issue of equity. A gasoline tax will raise the price of gasoline to consumers, rich and poor alike. However, poor Americans tend to spend a higher share of their income on gasoline (richer Americans purchase a lot of other things besides gasoline, and they save or invest a significant share of their incomes). Lower-income consumers also tend to drive older cars with poorer gas mileage. They don't trade them in as often as higher-income people do, and they can't afford hybrids or new models that are more fuel efficient. Commutes are often longer as well, as people in inner cities drive to jobs in the suburbs. Raising gasoline taxes would exacerbate this negative impact of high gas prices on low-income Americans. Tax credits for the poor may be one way to modify the impact.

The bottom line with regard to conservation is that taxes increase market prices and therefore lead to efforts to conserve. **The marketplace, combined with taxes (or subsidies), is an effective tool for implementing conservation policy.**

Innovative Policies

Beginning in 2003, motorists driving into central London were charged $8 per day for the privilege. By 2013, the fee was over $15 per day. While controversial, the goal of the policy is to reduce the volume of traffic in the area, ease congestion, and raise money for investing in public transportation. Another example is Oslo, Norway. High taxes make gasoline expensive, the government requires that cars must be checked every other year for safety and emissions, there are road tolls and annual automobile fees, and parking and auto insurance are extremely expensive. Mass transportation, on the other hand, is very cheap and convenient for those who wish to get around town and even into the countryside. Those who support these policies believed that the costs of pollution should be placed back on those who cause the pollution, thereby giving them an incentive to change their ways.

Even though these types of policies are controversial, they suggest some policy measures that might encourage U.S. automobile drivers to reduce downtown congestion. The gasoline tax already discussed is one example. What are some others? What if, instead of constructing more parking ramps and charging minimal prices for parking, cities placed a moratorium on parking construction and raised the fee for parking? What if, instead of widening city roads and building new ones, cities placed a moratorium on road construction as well, perhaps even expanding pedestrian malls that are open to pedestrians and bicyclists but not automobiles? What if, instead of expecting that city buses and subways be self-supporting, the city government recognized their positive externalities in the form of reduced congestion, pollution, and resource depletion and subsidized them instead (thereby making them cheaper or free and thereby more attractive to commuters)? What if other cities followed the lead of Los Angeles, which recently became the most populous U.S. city to outlaw plastic shopping bags (paper bags will be sold for 10 cents)? Some of these ideas may not be feasible, but they do make us question whether cheap gasoline prices, more parking ramps, and high fees for mass transit are self-defeating and create more congestion rather than less. All are ideas using incentives to reduce reliance on the automobile.

Have you read the book by Al Gore that is a companion to his global warming movie, *An Inconvenient Truth*?[8] The book uses recycled paper and claims to be "carbon neutral." This means that its publisher, Rodale, used a system of carbon offsets to make up for the energy sources used in production of the book. In other words, the publisher helped finance the production of clean energy sources to make up for the "less clean" energy used in producing, printing, and transporting the book.

How does this affect you? Well, you can become "carbon neutral" as well! More and more consumers, feeling guilty about use of their SUVs and other polluting consumer items, go to the Internet to purchase carbon offsets. By using a carbon offset Web site, you can calculate the amount of carbon dioxide produced when you drive (or fly, or use air conditioning or home heating) and buy an offset that goes toward the production of the same amount of nonpolluting energy. Depending on the organization, offsets may go to subsidizing existing clean power production or toward financing new wind turbines or solar collectors. You will be in good company. Ben & Jerry's buys offsets to cover its manufacturing and retail operations, and the Rolling Stones have purchased offsets to make their concerts carbon neutral. Some people argue that carbon offsets are a trick to make polluting consumers feel less guilty about their pollution, and others claim that this is a real opportunity to make a difference. Those who use carbon offsets in the context of an overall environment friendly lifestyle are, of course, the most consistent and effective conservationists. (See the Discussion and Action Questions at the end of the chapter for a list of suggested carbon offset Web sites,[9] as well as other conservation-related activities you can engage in.)

The Effects of Environmental Policy on the U.S. Economy

The environmental movement and our environmental policies are not uncontroversial. Environmental regulation has increased the costs of American business and has therefore been accused of the following adverse effects on the U.S. economy. Critics argue that by increasing costs, environmental regulation has contributed to inflation, which is a general increase in the average level of prices. (Nevertheless, inflation has not been a serious problem in the United States for many years.) They also argue that environmental regulation has reduced national output, since increased costs of production because of regulation cause the supply curves of producers to shift backward. Lower output implies increased unemployment, since fewer workers are needed to produce lower output levels. Critics also argue that because output is lower, economic growth, which is the increase in national production, will slow down. U.S. firms will be less competitive than their international counterparts because they face stricter environmental regulations than many firms abroad. This was certainly the concern in the controversy associated with the 1994 North American Free Trade Agreement (NAFTA), which we will consider shortly.

Others argue that employment has actually increased as a result of environmental regulations because the decrease in jobs in polluting firms has been offset by an increase in jobs at firms formerly harmed by pollution (remember the paper and beer industries?).

Furthermore, jobs have been created in pollution control and in new technology development. Jobs are also created at solar, wind, geothermal, and other renewable energy companies. Moreover, continued reliance on our finite resources will ultimately only raise the cost of using these resources. Keep in mind the production possibilities curve introduced in Chapter 1. Although there may be some short-run cost of environmental protection on our economy, over the long run, we know that without environmental protection, the production curve would actually shrink inward as our resources are depleted. This would be the opposite of economic growth. Hence, the long- and short-run benefits of environmental protection must be considered along with the short-run costs.

International Aspects of Pollution Control

Global Issues

Aside from global warming and use of finite petroleum supplies, other global issues include ozone depletion, acid rain, deforestation, loss of biodiversity, and desertification. In contrast to the problem of global warming, efforts to reduce ozone depletion have been viewed as one of the greatest environmental success stories over the past few decades. Nations have largely been able to agree on reductions in the use of chlorofluorocarbons that damage the ozone.

Less success has been achieved in other areas, however, including those dealing with problems in the developing world. These involve deforestation, loss of biodiversity, and desertification, all of which have both local and global implications. As a result of the international debt crisis (discussed in greater detail in Chapter 17) and other financial difficulties, many developing countries have been forced to undertake policies that maximize their earnings of internationally accepted currencies (such as U.S. dollars). These policies have emphasized exports and indiscriminate foreign investment. While used to acquire export earnings, unmanaged timber operations and expanded agricultural plantations have resulted in deforestation, which is the loss of trees and other vegetation. Multinational corporations, seeking grazing land for cattle, profits from mining operations, expanded energy infrastructure, and other ventures, have also contributed to the destruction of developing country forests. Deforestation impacts global warming by reducing the vegetation that naturally absorbs carbon dioxide and by creating carbon dioxide emissions when forests are burned.

Deforestation, however, also has other negative effects. It results in the loss of precious biodiversity through the extinction of species of animals and plants that live in our rainforest environments. It also reduces the fertility of once-productive agricultural land by eliminating the vegetation that protects against wind and rain-caused soil erosion. This is especially true in the case of desertification, which is the shifting of desert sands across previously fertile land that occurs when forested windbreaks are removed. Desertification and the loss of fertile land are serious problems in many sub-Saharan African countries that rely on land for food production.

Since the rest of the world has a stake in practices affecting global warming and biodiversity, it seems that the rest of the world should assist the developing countries in ways that reduce the necessity of engaging in practices that cause deforestation.

Deforestation is not the only environmental issue in the developing world. In an effort to attract foreign investment, environmental regulations are often deliberately lax. Indeed, this is one of the reasons that developed country corporations often flock to developing countries, attracted to the lower costs of production arising from minimal environmental laws and worker protections. NAFTA is a case in point. Even though "side agreements" that would supposedly equalize environmental laws and worker protections were built into the NAFTA accord, these regulations have often not been enforced. There are also concerns about pesticides that are banned by the United States but are exported by U.S. corporations to Central American countries, where the chemicals contaminate groundwater and harm the health of farm workers. Similarly, U.S. waste and environmentally harmful products are often shipped to other countries.

Industrial pollution is also a problem. One of the most notorious global examples of industrial pollution occurred in 1984, when a Union Carbide subsidiary plant accidentally released toxic emissions in Bhopal, India. More than 1,000 people were killed, and more than 200,000 were injured. It was the worst industrial accident ever recorded until then. Other horrific accidents have occurred elsewhere in the world. Two years after Bhopal, the official death toll of the 1986 Chernobyl nuclear accident in Ukraine (then a Soviet republic) was 3,576, though some estimates suggest that many more people were killed, many more were injured, many more experienced cancer, women are still bearing deformed children, and contamination in the Ukraine and neighboring countries continues to this day. Another nightmare catastrophe occurred in Fukushima, Japan, when a combination of tsunami and earthquake resulted in a major nuclear accident, with an unknown numbers of lost lives and serious problems involving relocation and mental health among residents.

These examples are striking in their losses of life, but many more examples of commercial pollution affect global consumers and workers day after day. Clearly, the global pollution problem has many aspects.

Global Policies

Just as local governments do not effectively control local pollution that affects the nation, individual nations do not effectively control national pollution that affects the world. As we have seen, environmental policy should be made by decision-making groups that represent all those affected by negative spillovers. Environmental problems such as loss of biodiversity, ozone depletion, and global warming are international issues. International action is therefore necessary.

Major international environmental summits have been held to try to deal with some of these problems. Participants have sought environmental treaties modeled after our international trade treaties and have tried to reform and strengthen the United Nations' powers with regard to the environment. The first international environmental summit was the Rio Earth Summit in Brazil in 1992. Two outcomes of this summit were the Climate Change Convention, designed to address global warming, and the Biodiversity Convention, intended to protect vulnerable species and protect the natural environment. At the time, President George H. W. Bush refused to sign the Biodiversity Convention, but he did endorse the Climate Change Convention.

Another major international summit took place in Johannesburg, South Africa, in 2002, 10 years after the first summit. This latter summit, entitled the World Summit on Sustainable Development, presented an opportunity for governments, United Nations agencies, global financial institutions, nongovernment organizations, and others to work to achieve sustainable development in the developing world. Tens of thousands of people from all over the world attended this summit, which set new targets on poverty and development aid. A subsequent resolution adopted by the General Assembly of the United Nations in late 2005 reaffirmed its commitment to sustainable development, stating that "development is a central goal in itself and that sustainable development in its economic, social and environmental aspects constitutes a key element of the overarching framework of United Nations activities."[10]

Other international environmental agreements have been made, including the 2005 European Union Emissions Trading System and the 1997 Kyoto Protocol, both already mentioned. In December 2012, the Doha Amendments to the Kyoto Protocol were approved to cover the new time period of 2013 through 2020. Nevertheless, as of this writing, the United States has not signed on (as it is not a signatory of the original accord) and the amendments have not yet been put into legal force.

The first Annual World Student Environmental Summit took place in Kyoto in 2008, and involved over 50 student representatives from several countries around the world. The student summit has taken place every year since then, and you can check Facebook for updates for the current year. (This site is listed in the Discussion and Action Questions at the end of the chapter.)

Finally, the Millennium Development Goals incorporate a strong global stand for ensuring environmental sustainability. The eight Millennium Development Goals (MDGs) were adapted by the 189 members of the United Nations in 2000. These goals embody a commitment to making substantial progress toward the eradication of poverty and the achievement of other human development goals by 2015. They are the strongest statement yet of an international commitment to ending world poverty, and they rightly incorporate the important concept of sustainability. Specifically, MDG Number 7 includes the words "Integrate the principles of sustainable development into country policies and programs" and "reverse loss of environmental resources."

One measure that we, as global citizens, can take is to encourage our government's support of international initiatives to protect our global environment, and at the same time, to lift the world's poorest out of poverty through sustainable development.

You, the Student

Do you have a conservation or environmental student organization on campus? If not, would you like to start up one? Possibilities are endless, but you might consider initiating a campus recycling project. In addition to recycling paper and cardboard, your group could place containers for collection of glass, metal, and used computer ink cartridges.

View*Point*   Conservative versus Liberal

Economists often make decisions about environmental matters on noneconomic grounds, as they do with certain other issues (such as drugs) discussed in this book. It is possible for both liberal and conservative economists to care deeply about the environment.

Because liberals are not necessarily averse to government intervention in the economy and the regulation of private businesses, they generally wish to see government take an active role in protecting the environment. As such, liberals may well favor standards regulation, as well as policies drafted at the national and international levels. Liberals may well take the position that we should do whatever it takes to get the job done and not worry about the government's expanding role in the economy. As you know, President Barack Obama has taken a strong stand in favor of pollution control (though he does support policies that utilize the market place, including marketable pollution permits and carbon offsets).

Conservatives, on the other hand, want to limit the role of government in the economy. They are consequently more likely than liberals to oppose environmental regulation. They will be more likely to favor pollution control policies that utilize market forces rather than other methods. Thus, they favor pollution fees and marketable pollution permits over the regulation of pollution by means of standards. Conservatives may also prefer state and local solutions to environmental problems over policies developed at the federal and international levels. They, like former president George W. Bush, may also prefer voluntary compliance of industry over forced compliance.

SUMMARY

Economic activity causes pollution. Pollution is a spillover cost of production that causes inequity and distorts the allocation of resources in the economy. Pollution causes resources to be overallocated to the market in which it occurs and underallocated to other affected markets, thereby creating inefficiency. Government therefore regulates private business by the standards approach, pollution fees, and marketable pollution permits.

The standards approach has been criticized, especially when it forces certain types of technology on producers of the product. Conservation and recycling programs also reduce pollution. Such programs are most effective when they give individuals and businesses some economic incentives for participation. Environmental programs can be evaluated by

cost-benefit analysis, and these programs should be used only if benefits are greater than costs. Benefits must be broadly considered and include the monetary and nonmonetary benefits to current and future generations, locally and globally.

Many environmental problems are, in fact, international in nature. These include the emission of greenhouse gases and the consumption of finite petroleum resources. The United States is a major emitter of carbon dioxide and user of petroleum. Other global environmental issues include deforestation, loss of biodiversity, and desertification. Since resources will be underallocated to pollution control unless the decision-making entity is large enough to incorporate all of the effects of pollution, international cooperation will be necessary to solve our international environmental problems.

DISCUSSION AND ACTION QUESTIONS

1. Why do polluters pollute? Consider various reasons for both individuals and businesses.

2. How does pollution distort resource allocation in the economy? Consider both over- and under-allocation of resources.

3. What are some of the costs of pollution control? Should we be willing to pay anything and sacrifice everything to eliminate all pollution?

4. What do you think is the appropriate level of government to deal with pollution? Does it matter what type of pollution we are considering? Why?

5. Can you think of examples of negative or positive externalities not mentioned in the text?

6. Compare the various incentive-based environmental policies to the standards approach. What are the strengths and weaknesses of each?

7. Do you think it is appropriate that the consumer bears part of the burden of effluent or emission fees in the form of higher prices? Why or why not?

8. Explain cost-benefit analysis. Would the results of cost-benefit analysis ever be different in the short run than in the long run? Why or why not?

9. Do you think that we are a throwaway society? Are your attitudes toward consumption the same as your parents'? Your grandparents'?

10. Is it efficient to convert food (corn) into ethanol to burn in our cars and trucks? Would this be economical if the government taxed the use of gasoline and subsidized the use of ethanol? How might the government justify these taxes and subsidies?

11. Keeping in mind that environmental regulation is a luxury good, would you expect American attitudes to be the same as attitudes of poor citizens of developing countries?

12. Consider pollution, congestion, and other problems in our large cities. People often demand additional roads and parking structures to handle these problems. How might these measures be self-defeating? What are other (incentive-based) policies that might be used to reduce automobile use and/or increase the use of mass transit?

13. Consider the parking situation on your own campus. (I've never been on a campus where students didn't complain about parking.) Is the parking adequate? Do you have to walk quite a distance if you park your car? Should the school or city build additional parking structures? What are the implications of these for gasoline use? Are there better alternatives?

14. Does your campus recycle? If not, what can you do to initiate a recycling program?

15. Are you a liberal or a conservative on issues of environmental protection? Why?

16. Check out the Web sites http://www.carbonfund.org, http://www.terrapass.com, http://www.nativeenergy.com, http://www.self.org, or similar sites to learn how to purchase carbon offsets for the carbon dioxide you emit when driving your car.

17. The U.S. Environmental Protection Agency (EPA) provides information about EPA policies and environmental issues. Check out its Web site at http://www.epa.gov and report on some of the information that pertains to human health.

18. Go again to the Environmental Protection Agency Web site (http://www.epa.gov). Click "Where You Live," go to "Search Your Community," enter your zip code, and find current environmental issues in your geographical area.

19. The Web site for the World Business Council for Sustainable Development is http://www.wbcsd.ch. Go to this Web site to discover information on the coalition of hundreds of international companies that are united by a shared commitment to sustainable development through economic growth, ecological balance, and social progress. It concerns itself with poverty and other social justice issues, and it provides an extensive list of publications. After surfing, do you find yourself to be in general agreement with the World Business Council, or do you find that you largely disagree?

20. The World Summit on Sustainable Development in Johannesburg was mentioned in the text of this chapter. The Web site for the summit, http://www.johannesburgsummit.org, provides much information, including surveys, documents, publications, and summaries of the summit. What were some of the major accomplishments of the summit?

21. The Web site for Resources for the Future, an environmental research group, is http://www.rff.org. Use this Web site to browse for information on research topics such as the environment, natural resources, and methods of environmental protection. Are there any environmental protection tools or techniques that seem particularly useful to you?

22. The Environmental News Service has up-to-date information on environmental issues at its Web site, www.ens-news.com. Use this Web site to find examples of the latest news on environmental issues.

23. Check out the Facebook page for the latest World Student Environmental Summit at https://www.facebook.com/WorldStudentEnvironmentalSummit. If you are interested, why don't you talk to your teachers or advisor about possible scholarships or independent study credits for attending the summit?

Notes

1. Mark Landler and John M. Broder, *The New York Times*, June 26, 2013.

2. John Doerr, "California's Global-Warming Solution," *Time Magazine*, September 11, 2006, p. 55.

3. Andrew C. Revkin, "Talks to Start on Climate Amid Split on Warming," *The New York Times*, November 5, 2006.

4. Seth Mydans, "Vietnam Finds Itself Vulnerable if Sea Rises," *The New York Times*, September 24, 2009.

5. Jim Lehrer Show, June 26, 2009.

6. Based on calculations from data of the U.S. CIA Factbook, www.cia.gov. Population data are July 2013 estimates, world electricity consumption data are 2009 and 2010 estimates, and consumption of refined petroleum products data are 2011 estimates.

7. Based on calculations from data of the World Bank, *World Development Indicators 2012*. Washington, DC: 2013.

8. Rachael Donadio, "Saving the Planet, One Book at a Time," *New York Times Book Review*, July 9, 2006.

9. Much of this information is from Anthony DePalma, "Gas Guzzlers Find the Price of Forgiveness," *The New York Times*, April 22, 2006.

10. Resolution adopted by the General Assembly of the United Nations: 2005 World Summit Outcome, October 24, 2005.

Appendix 3-1
History of Federal Efforts to Limit U.S. Pollution

The 1955 Air Pollution Act was the first piece of federal legislation to deal with the issue of pollution by calling for research into the problem of air pollution. This appeal was followed by the Clean Air Act of 1963 to control air pollution and the subsequent Clean Air Act of 1970 to enforce national clean air standards. Also in 1970, the Environmental Protection Agency (EPA) was formed by executive order to administer all the environmental laws. The Federal Water Pollution Act of 1972 further mandated that the EPA reduce discharges into the nation's waterways, and the EPA's mission was subsequently amended to add protection of land and other environmental issues to its jurisdiction.

Of special concern in the early 1970s were automobile emissions, which contributed greatly to the smog plaguing the nation's cities. The Clean Air Act was further amended and strengthened in 1977 and again in 1990, and in the latter case, many polluters (with the exception of power plants) were forced to reduce emissions of toxic material such as mercury, arsenic, and lead. Before leaving office, the Clinton administration declared that power plants should be subject to the controls under the Clean Air Act, but the Bush administration reversed that opinion. Indeed, it wasn't until 2002 that President George W. Bush acknowledged for the first time that human activity causes global warming. However, in 2003, the Bush Administration Environmental Protection Agency ruled that carbon dioxide was not a pollutant, thereby eliminating the opportunity for the EPA to regulate carbon dioxide.

The federal government and the Environmental Protection Agency acquired greater authority when the Supreme Court ruled in 2006 that greenhouse gases are indeed forms of pollution, and a 2007 ruling gave the executive branch the authority to control the greenhouse gas emissions of existing power plants. These were major victories for environmental groups. Despite an absence of effective action over the next few years during the Bush administration, President Obama made an immediate call for legislation to limit carbon dioxide emissions upon entering office. As we've noted, the House of Representatives responded with the 2009 epic Climate Bill, which was not supported by the Senate and thereby not set into law.

Nevertheless, as we've seen in the text, various rulings extended and then reversed the ability of the federal government to control greenhouse gas emissions. These led to the Obama mandates of 2012 and beyond that are addressed within the chapter.

Appendix 3-2

The Effects of a Negative Externality on Society in the Case of a Single Market

L et's consider a more general analysis of pollution as a by-product of production and its effect on society as a whole. For this hypothetical example, we will examine one specific market, the market for spring vacation air travel to the Bahamas during one week in March. We will consider pollution caused by this market and its effects on efficiency and resource allocation for society at large.

Remember that we defined pollution as waste that is not recycled. We will assume that the amount of pollutants emitted by firms will increase proportionately with output. However, low levels of output will not result in spillover costs, because the natural processes of the earth can absorb and reprocess a certain amount of waste (pollutants). If production increases beyond the level that natural processes can handle, we incur pollution and therefore spillover costs. As we will see, an essential difference between the economist's view of the market and the environmentalist's is that some level of pollution will be acceptable, even optimal.

First let's consider the supply of air transportation to the Bahamas. Let's assume that natural processes can absorb the hypothetical air pollutants that we create if we provide 2,000 units of output (passenger tickets); but that if we provide more than 2,000, we exceed the earth's capacity to cleanse itself. (Let's keep it simple by pretending that college students flying to the Bahamas during this particular week in March represent the only people traveling to the Bahamas by air.) After the production of 2,000 units of output, we have a negative externality (the pollution that is not absorbed naturally by the earth).

Curve S^P in Figure 3-4 is the hypothetical private market supply curve. This curve is based on the firms' (airlines') private costs of production but does not reflect the full **social costs of production** when pollution occurs. **These social costs of production include both the private costs to the producer (since the producer is part of society) and the spillover costs borne by the rest of society.** Curve S^S is the hypothetical social supply curve. This curve is higher in the graph (in terms of the dollar axis) than the private supply curve, reflecting the higher social costs of production. The vertical distance between S^P and S^S at each level of output is the hypothetical amount of the spillover cost.

Now let's consider the hypothetical market demand curve for air travel to the Bahamas. Remember that demand reflects the value of the product to consumers in society, because it represents the prices that consumers are willing to pay for a ticket to the Bahamas. D is the market demand curve in Figure 3-4.

The private market supply curve intersects with the demand curve at a quantity of 5,000 units (tickets to the Bahamas) and a price of $400 per person. Note, however, that the social supply curve intersects with demand at only 4,000 units and a price of $500. The private market supply curve results in output that is too high, because it is based on a cost that is too low. When markets base their output decisions on their costs of production, they do so

Social costs of production

The total costs of production, including private costs and spillover costs.

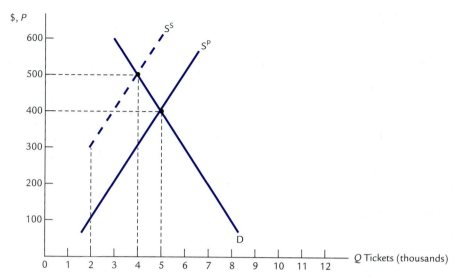

Figure 3-4 • Allocative Effects of Pollution in a Hypothetical Market for Spring Vacation Air Travel to the Bahamas
Hypothetical air and noise pollution means that the social costs are above the private costs of providing air travel. The higher social costs means that the private market equilibrium price is too low, resulting in the overallocation of resources to air travel.

© Cengage Learning

on the basis of private costs of production only, and not on the full social costs of production. However, the socially optimal level of output is based on the full social costs of production. This is because we wish to balance our desire for the product with the *full* social costs of production. Because the free market results in too much output, we say there is an overallocation of resources to the production of this product. Too much output may not sound like a problem, but remember that society has scarce resources. Too much production of a product that society doesn't want (especially when it causes pollution) means we end up with too little production of products that society *does* want. Inefficient allocation of resources means that society's preferences are not being met.

The socially correct quantity in Figure 3-4 is 4,000 units, and at this quantity, we will have some pollution. The environmentalist's goal would be to eliminate all pollution, but if we do that we have to cut production to 2,000 units. **Most economists believe that if all costs are accurately reflected in the supply curve, and society's values are accurately reflected in the demand curve, the market output is efficient and desirable.** Society values those extra 2,000 units enough to be willing to bear the cost of the pollution that accompanies them. In the region between 2,000 units (no pollution) and 4,000 units (socially desirable output), the demand curve is above the social supply curve, indicating that society values these units of the good more than it costs to manufacture them, including the costs of pollution. Thus, economists would not recommend cutting back production to 2,000 units to eliminate all pollution. (And students heading for the Bahamas during spring break can breathe a collective sigh of relief!)

Chapter 4

The Economic Toolbox

- Externalities
- Private and public education
- Spillover costs and benefits
- Inefficiency
- Overallocation and underallocation of resources
- Property tax financing
- Tax base
- Tax rate
- Charters, magnets, and vouchers
- Subsidy
- Investment in human capital
- Direct and indirect (opportunity) costs
- Cost-benefit analysis
- Affirmative action

Education

A mong the promises made by President Obama in his Inaugural Address is a commitment to the transformation of our nation's education system. This is smart policy, because if we wish to be competitive internationally, and if we wish to reduce unemployment (much of which is structural, meaning that we have jobs or the potential for jobs, but they are in areas in which we currently do not have enough qualified workers), education for a new age is essential. Jobs for the future include data analysis and marketing, computer engineering, counseling and therapy, scientific research, including biotechnology, biomedicine, nanotechnology, and many others. And, historically, the United States has valued education highly. We provide public primary and secondary education (kindergarten through high school, or K–12) free to the student and the student's family. Higher education (postsecondary) public colleges, universities, vocational-technical colleges, and community colleges are partly financed by tax revenues so that tuition is more affordable for the average student. Public education is viewed as the force that levels the playing field and ensures that all Americans have an equal opportunity to succeed in our society. Education has been one of our most important antipoverty policies. Furthermore, our economy reaps the benefits of education in the form of literate, productive workers. Education is the classic example of a good or service that creates positive externalities, as we will discuss shortly.

In this chapter, we will look at the U.S. education system. First, we will discuss the spillover benefits (positive externalities) of education, including both K–12 and higher education. Second, we will consider global comparisons of educational "inputs" and "outputs." Third, we will look at educational attainment in the United States. Fourth, we will focus on K–12 education and pay special attention to the financing of K–12 education, the quality of K–12 education, and various proposals for improving K–12 education. We will consider both public schools and private schools. **Public schools** are those that are financed by taxes and operated in part by government. **Private schools** are not owned and operated by government but by churches, businesses, or other groups in the private sector. They are largely financed by tuition and endowments, which we will discuss shortly. And finally, we will focus on higher education, including both public and private universities. We will discuss higher education as an investment in human capital, as well as other issues in higher education.

We will discover, in the process of discussing these issues, that neither K–12 nor higher education has achieved the outcomes we so optimistically embrace as a nation. The transformation that Obama speaks of will require some improvements—which, of course, will entail some controversy.

We will transform our schools and colleges and universities to meet the demands of a new age.

—*PRESIDENT BARACK OBAMA, INAUGURAL ADDRESS, JANUARY 19, 2009*

Public schools
Schools that are operated by the government and are financed by tax revenue.

Private schools
Schools that are not operated by the government and that are mainly financed by student tuition and endowments.

Education's Spillover Benefits

The provision of education creates private benefits that go to the student and the student's family. The educated individual is able to earn higher wages than the uneducated worker. The educated worker is less likely to be frequently unemployed and is more likely to find a job that is intellectually rewarding. He or she may be exposed to a wider variety of aesthetic experiences that enrich life. These are the private benefits of education that the student receives. You and your family probably considered many of these factors while you were deciding whether to go on to college.

The provision of education also creates benefits for society. Educated citizens are more likely to vote and otherwise participate in public life. They tend to be more innovative and contribute more to the economy's output. They earn more and therefore may pay more income taxes. They are less likely to be chronically unemployed than are uneducated workers. They are less likely to go on welfare and less likely to commit crimes, or at least violent crimes. **Therefore, society receives spillover benefits from education, and the educated person receives private benefits.**

These spillover benefits to society are examples of externalities. As discussed in Chapter 3 on the environment, **externalities** are benefits or costs of an economic activity that spill onto society as a whole. These externalities can be either negative or positive. A positive externality provides a benefit to society and is called a **spillover benefit**. A negative externality imposes a cost on society and is called a spillover cost. The classic example of a **spillover cost** is pollution. The classic example of a spillover benefit is education. Externalities create some degree of **inequity**, which has been defined as unfairness. In the case of education, it wouldn't be fair to you if you had to pay the entire cost of your education, since many of the benefits of your education spillover onto society. Externalities also cause society's resources to be inefficiently allocated. Our economy will produce either too much (overallocate resources) or produce too little (underallocate resources) when externalities occur. This improper allocation of resources is an example of **inefficiency**. **Externalities thereby create inequity and inefficiency.**

Figure 4-1 shows the underallocation of resources that results from education's spillover benefits. D^P is the demand for education in the private market. The benefits that students and their families expect to receive determine this demand. It shows how much

Externalities
The costs or benefits of an economic activity that spill over onto the rest of society.

Spillover benefit
A positive externality; the benefit of an economic activity that is shifted onto society.

Spillover cost
A negative externality; the cost of an economic activity that is shifted onto society.

Inequity
Unfairness.

Inefficiency
Using resources in such a way as not to maximize the desired output from them.

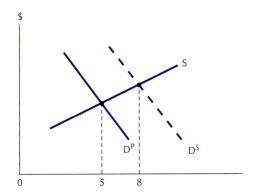

Quantity (number of students enrolled), millions

Figure 4-1 • Effects of the Spillover Benefits of Education
Because the private market does not reflect the spillover benefits of education, the number of students enrolled (5 million) is less than the socially optimum number (8 million).

they value (are willing to pay for) education. The supply curve intersects this demand curve at an equilibrium quantity of 5 million. Thus, 5 million students would enroll.

But the private market demand curve is not the socially correct demand curve, because it does not reflect the benefits gained by society from education. If we take the spillover benefits into account, demand would be greater. So, the true socially correct demand curve, based on the benefits received by students *and* by the rest of society, is D^S, where D^S (the social demand curve) reflects how much students *and* the rest of society value education. D^S intersects supply at an equilibrium quantity of 8 million, which is the socially optimal amount. Because the private market demand does not reflect the positive externalities, the market will produce too little education. **We say that the market underallocates resources whenever spillover benefits exist.** The market equilibrium is not efficient, or optimum for society, when this occurs.

The spillover benefits justify the government's provision of K–12 education, subsidization of college education through grants and financial aid to students, and establishment of public colleges and universities. These policies correct the underallocation of resources. If the government's contribution toward the student's education is just equal to the spillover benefits that society receives from education, the socially optimum amount of education will be produced and consumed in our economy.

Different levels and types of education yield different amounts of private and spillover benefits. Most people agree that the spillover benefits of K–12 education are tremendous, because basic literacy is developed through such education. The provision of primary and secondary education free to the student is therefore justified by the societal spillover benefits. Some argue, however, that most of the benefits of postsecondary education are private and that spillover benefits from college education are few. They therefore feel that the primary burden of college costs should be borne by the student and the student's family. What do you think?

Global Comparisons of Educational Inputs and Outputs

There are two ways to look at educational data. We can consider inputs, such as educational spending or number of teachers per pupil; or we can consider outputs, such as literacy rates and test results. Let's first consider our spending on education, and compare it with the other countries of the world.

Spending on Education

Our country incurs large government expense for our nation's educational system, spending 5.4 percent of gross domestic product (GDP) on education. However, this places the United States in a tie for thirteenth and fourteenth among the 18 Western industrialized countries shown in Table 4-1. Clearly, most of these countries spend a higher share of GDP on education, and some countries (such as Denmark, Cyprus, Norway, and Sweden), spend a much higher share. Data from the same source (but not shown here) reveal that even very poor countries manage to spend higher shares of GDP on education than the United States. For example, Cuba spends 12.9 percent, Vietnam spends 6.6 percent, and Costa Rica spends 6.3 percent of GDP.

TABLE 4-1 • Global Comparisons of Public Direct Expenditures on Education as a Percent of Gross Domestic Product (GDP), from Highest to Lowest; for Western Industrialized Countries, Most Recently Available Data from 2009 to 2010

Country	Spending as Percent of GDP
Denmark	8.7
Cyprus	7.9
Norway	7.3
Sweden	7.3
Finland	6.8
Belgium	6.6
Ireland	6.5
Austria	6.0
France	5.9
Netherlands	5.9
Portugal	5.8
U.K.	5.6
U.S.	5.4
Switzerland	5.4
Germany	5.1
Canada	5.0
Spain	5.0
Italy	4.7

Source: World Bank, *World Development Indicators 2012* (Washington, DC: World Bank, 2012).

Pupil to Teacher Ratios

Another input into our educational system is teachers, and we will see a correlation between pupil/teacher ratios and government spending on education. Thus, one concern is overcrowding. Overcrowding is one concern in a number of our nation's schools. *A lower pupil to teacher ratio suggests more time the teacher can spend on each child, presumably providing a higher quality of education.* For elementary schools, the average number of students per teacher is 14 in the United States (toward the higher, or worse, end among the 13 Western industrialized countries in Table 4-2 for which data are available). Several such countries, notably Luxembourg and Sweden, have much lower (better) numbers. Among selected Eastern industrialized countries, countries such as Georgia, Montenegro, and Poland have even far superior numbers. And finally, we can see a correlation between government spending and relatively low pupil to teacher ratios in some poor developing countries (Cuba, Costa Rica, and Vietnam), with Cuba having a ratio well below that of the United States. On the other hand, the poorest African countries rank at the bottom of the list. The 10 countries in the world with the highest pupil to teacher ratios are in African countries.

Literacy Rates

One way to measure an *outcome* of educational systems is with the adult literacy rate. For purposes of definition, people age 15 and older are considered adults. We see from the data in Table 4-3 on page 92 that literacy rates range as high as (approximately) 100 percent in the Western industrialized world and Eastern industrialized world. (Only a few of the countries in these regions with 100 percent literacy rates are shown in the table.)

TABLE 4-2 • Global Comparisons of Primary Education Pupil per Teacher Ratios, Western Industrialized Countries, Selected Eastern Industrialized Countries, and Selected Developing Countries, Most Recently Available Data from 2009 to 2012

Country	Ratio
Western Industrialized Countries[a]	
Luxembourg	9
Sweden	10
Austria	11
Belgium	11
Portugal	11
Spain	12
Germany	13
Cyprus	14
Finland	14
U.S.	14
Ireland	16
France	18
U.K.	18
Selected Eastern Industrialized Countries[b]	
Georgia	8
Montenegro	8
Poland	9
Russia	18
Albania	20
Kyrgyzstan	25
Selected Developing Countries[c]	
Cuba	9
Thailand	16
China	17
Costa Rica	17
Vietnam	20
Ghana	33
Congo, Rep.	49
Guinea-Bissau	52
Burkina Faso	53
Ethiopia	55
Mozambique	55
Rwanda	58
Chad	63
Zambia	63
Malawi	76
Central African Republic	81

[a]All Western industrialized countries for which data are available.
[b]Lowest, highest, and selected Eastern industrialized countries in between.
[c]Lowest, highest 10, and selected developing countries in between.

Source: World Bank, *World Development Indicators 2012* (Washington, DC: World Bank, 2012).

TABLE 4-3 • Adult Literacy Rates,[a] for Selected Western Industrialized Countries, Eastern Industrialized Countries, and Developing Countries, Most Recently Available Data from 2009 to 2011

Country	Literacy Rate
Western Industrialized Countries[b]	
U.S.	100%
Italy	99%
Spain	98%
Cyprus	98%
Greece	97%
Eastern Industrialized Countries[c]	
Russia	100%
Poland	100%
Kyrgyzstan	99%
Croatia	99%
Uzbekistan	99%
Moldova	99%
Hungary	99%
Montenegro	98%
Bosnia & Herzegovina	98%
Bulgaria	98%
Romania	98%
Macedonia	97%
Developing Countries[d]	
Cuba	100%
Costa Rica	96%
China	96%
Vietnam	93%
El Salvador	84%
Iraq	78%
Bangladesh	57%
Guinea-Bissau	54%
Gambia	50%
Sierra Leone	42%
Benin	42%
Guinea	41%
Chad	34%
Mali	31%

[a]Age 15 and over.
[b]Most Western industrialized countries have literacy rates approximating 100%. Other than the United States, only those with lower literacy rates are shown here.
[c]Most Eastern European industrialized countries have literacy rates approximating 100%. Aside from Russia and Poland, only those with lower literacy rates are shown here.
[d]Selected developing countries ranging from highest to lowest.

Source: World Bank, *World Development Indicators 2012* (Washington, DC: The World Bank, 2012).

Literacy rates vary considerably among the developing countries. The priority placed on education in Cuba is revealed by the 100 percent literacy rates, as well as the relatively high literacy rates in the poor countries of Costa Rica and Vietnam. We've already noted the commitment to education in these countries. We also note a high literacy rate in China. However, quite disconcerting is the fact that literacy rates fall to extremely low levels in many very poor countries. We've noted that circumstances in many African countries are very poor and the lowest seven literacy rates in the world (which are shown in the table) are in Africa. Just as in the developed countries, improvement in education is critical for development to proceed.

Educational Attainment in the United States

The U.S. Census Bureau computes data on the highest levels of educational attainment achieved by the U.S. population age 25 years or older. Out of about 205 million people in that age category, over 25 million people have attained less than a high school education, 62 million have achieved a high school diploma, 34 million attained some college but no degree, almost 20 million received an associate's degree, close to 41 million received a bachelor's degree, over 16 million received a master's degree, 3 million obtained a professional degree, and over 3 million received a Ph.D.[1] Figure 4-2 displays rounded-off percentages of the population in this age group. Sadly, 30 percent of this population does not have a high school diploma.

Clearly, high school dropout rates are part of this picture. The high school dropout rate is defined by the Department of Education as the percent of 16- through 24-year-olds who are not enrolled in school and have not earned a high school degree. While the national high school dropout rate seems high at 7 percent in 2011, it has improved from 12 percent in 1990. Unfortunately, there is a large divergence between

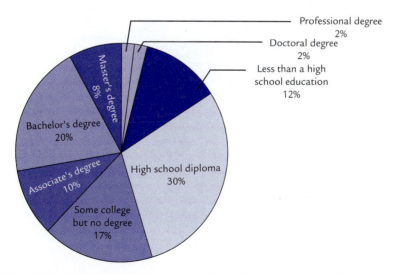

Figure 4-2 • Highest Educational Attainment in the United States Among People Age 25 or over as a Percent of the Total, 2012

Source: U.S. Census Bureau, *Current Population Survey, Annual Sociology and Economic Supplement,* 2012, http://www.census.gov.

low-income families and higher-income families. The 2011 dropout rate for low-income students was the highest of all income levels, at 13 percent (well above the national average). There is also a gap in dropout rates for students of different race and ethnicity. In 2011, the dropout rate for white Caucasians was 5 percent, 7 percent for African-Americans, and 14 percent for Hispanics. The gaps between whites and Hispanics narrowed from 1990 to 2011, though the gaps between whites and African-Americans were not measurably different.[2]

We will continue to assess the U.S. educational system, beginning with K–12 education, and then higher education.

Kindergarten Through Grade 12 (K–12) Education

Primary and secondary education in the United States may be free to the student, but the government incurs great expense for them. Let's consider this funding of K–12 education.

The Funding of K–12 Education

In academic year 2010 (the most recent year for which data are available), spending for public K–12 education was divided among local, state, and the federal governments as shown in Figure 4-3. *Note that the federal government contributes a very small share, whereas local and state governments bear the principal burden for funding primary and secondary education.* Not shown in the figure is the fact that the federal share has risen since 2005, up from 9 percent up to 13 percent. The local government share has remained about the same, indicating that the state share has fallen (from about 47 percent to 43 percent). Indeed, spending for the local public school system is the largest item in

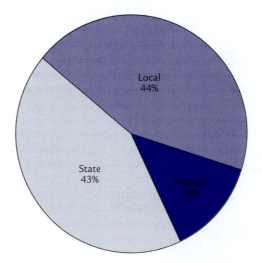

Figure 4-3 • Financing Public K–12 Education, 2010
The above chart shows the percentages of funds provided by each level of government to public elementary and secondary schools in the United States.

Source: U.S. Department of Education, *Digest of Education Statistics*, National Center for Education Statistics, http://www.nces.ed.gov/, as reported by the New American Foundation, http://www.newamericafoundation.org, published June 30, 2013.

most local budgets.[3] As we shall see, the financing of K–12 education raises difficult issues.

Local government spending on K–12 education is heavily financed by the local property tax, and this creates the problem of many schools being underfunded, resulting in poor education in many of these schools. The amount of property taxes that can be collected to support the schools depends on the **tax base** and the **tax rate**. The tax base is the value of taxable property (land, homes, other buildings, and so on) in the school district, whereas the tax rate is the percentage of the tax base that is collected as property tax. Property in the suburbs has a high value. Industrial plants, stylish shopping centers, and $1,500,000 homes add up to a large tax base. But decaying inner-city slums have little value. Moreover, a large percentage of inner-city property is exempt from the property tax. Tax is not collected on municipal buildings, colleges, hospitals, and art museums. The tax base to support inner-city schools is thus usually relatively small compared with tax bases in the suburbs. If the tax rate is the same, the suburbs will collect many more tax dollars per student. In fact, tax rates are often higher in the cities, but because of their inadequate tax bases, inner cities cannot come close to matching the suburbs in educational spending per student.

The state government's contribution toward public K–12 education is meant to enrich and equalize education within a particular state. Since there are rich and poor communities in every state, and since local property tax revenues vary greatly, state aid is often intended to provide more equal funding and educational opportunities among rich and poor communities. Naturally, this creates controversy in higher-income school districts.

Nevertheless, the heavy reliance on the local property tax to fund K–12 education creates inequities too great to be resolved just by state aid. This is especially the case when state aid distribution formulas provide aid to all, not only poor school districts. Some rural school districts are severely underfunded, as are most inner-city school districts. Spending per student varies widely. Low spending often means shoddy facilities, inadequate supplies, and understaffed classrooms. In turn, these conditions contribute to high dropout rates and functional illiteracy. Another problem occurs if the state itself is poor, with a distressed population as a whole and a low tax base. The state then has little ability to assist low-income school districts.

Tax base
Value of income, earnings, property, sales, or other variables to which a tax rate is applied.

Tax rate
Percentage of the tax base that must be paid to the government as tax.

The Quality of K–12 Education

Early Studies

The first shock to our country about the quality of education took place in 1983, when a commission appointed by President Ronald Reagan released its report titled *A Nation at Risk*. The commission reported, "The educational foundations of our society are presently being eroded by a rising tide of mediocrity that threatens our very future as a Nation and a people." The report noted that test scores were falling, schools were asking less and less of their students, and U.S. pupils were performing worse than their European counterparts. *A Nation at Risk* catapulted the discussion about the quality of education into the national arena.[4]

The second shock took place when social critic Jonathan Kozol reported on the terrible conditions in six inner-city school systems in 1992. He described these inner-city schools in his book, *Savage Inequalities: Children in America's Schools*. In each case, the physical facilities were dreadful. He observed schools with holes in their roofs, vocational classes in which young people were being taught typing on old manual typewriters in the age of computers, libraries converted to classrooms because schools housed half again as many students as they were built to house, and classes in which students had to share the few books available. Such basics as working toilets, toilet paper, soap, and chalk were in chronically short supply.

Teachers' salaries were lower in these underfunded school districts than in other school districts. Young teachers tended to burn out and quit, either to find teaching jobs in better-paying, better-supplied suburban districts or to leave teaching altogether. To cut costs, the inner-city school districts often hired "permanent subs" at still lower salaries and without benefits. Even that measure was not enough to stretch the budget to cover the entire year, and some classes simply went unstaffed, especially in the spring when funds were exhausted.

Many students observed in Kozol's study were chronic truants by the time they reached eighth grade. In effect, they had dropped out before they even reached high school. Dropout rates were in the neighborhood of 50 percent to 60 percent in the schools Kozol visited. Nor did graduation mean much. The quality of education was so poor that a high school diploma did not guarantee literacy. Kozol noted that in Chicago, 27 percent of high school graduates read at the eighth-grade level or below. At the city's community colleges, which received most of their students from the Chicago public schools, the noncompletion rate was 97 percent.[5]

We know that at least some of the circumstances reported in *A Nation at Risk* and *Savage Inequalities* have improved. For example, some states have been forced to address the issue of school funding. In a landmark state Supreme Court ruling in 1989, the school funding system of the state of Texas was found to be unconstitutional. Spending per pupil ranged from $2,112 in the poorest district to $19,333 in the richest. The property tax base in the poorest district was only $20,000 per pupil, whereas in the richest district it was $14,000,000. The primary problem was the extremely low tax bases in the poorest school districts.

Other areas of the country were also found to have significant differences in property tax bases and spending per student. For example, the tax base per student in Camden, New Jersey, was only 10 percent of the state average. In 1989–1990, the property tax base per pupil ranged from $39,000 to more than $340,000 in Kentucky. In Kentucky, however, some of the poorest districts were rural.[6] These disparities in spending per pupil led to numerous court cases in which low-property-value school districts challenged their state's school-financing system. Several of these cases, such as the one in Kentucky, resulted in changes in the way that state governments finance K–12 education. Many states have revised the formulas by which they distribute funds to equalize spending per student. Federal funds have also been designated to improve education in our poorest school districts. Although some terribly underfunded inner-city school districts remain, the picture is brighter than it was in the early 1990s.

Newer Studies

Despite this difficult history, achievement scores of students have improved over time. Beginning in 1971, the National Assessment of Educational progress has monitored the academic performance of 9-, 13-, and 17-year-old students in the areas of reading and mathematics. Using the most recently available data from 2012, both 9- and 13-year-olds scored higher in reading and math in 2012 than students their age in the early 1970s. Scores were 8 to 25 points higher in 2012 than in the first assessment year. However, 17-year-olds did not show significantly different scores from the first assessment. Perhaps it is also notable that since the previous administration of the assessments in 2008, only 13-year-olds made gains, and in both reading and mathematics. Thus, despite some gains, there is also some stagnancy.[7]

Another problem in U.S. K–12 education is the disparity in achievement between students of different gender and students of different race and ethnicity. This is especially the case as many white Caucasians have moved from inner cities to the suburbs, leaving behind racial and ethnic minorities in the inner cities. As we've discussed, these school districts may well be underfunded. If minority children receive inferior education because they must attend poor schools, they will emerge inadequately prepared to enter our labor markets or to go on to college.

There is some indication of improvement in the achievement statistics, however. Using the same source as above, the 2012 data suggest that the gaps between students of different gender and race and ethnicity have been narrowing. This is the result of larger improvements by African-American and Hispanic students than white students. Only the gap in mathematics at age nine has not shown a significant change from 1971. Furthermore, while female students scored higher in reading than male students at all three ages, the 2012 results show nine-year-old males making larger reading gains than females, leading to a narrowing of the gender gap for this group. Furthermore, in mathematics, male 17-year-olds scored higher than female students. However, the gender gap for this group narrowed because female students made gains but the male students did not.

Finally, high school dropout rates signify concerns about the quality of education, as well as other factors. While dropout rates have fallen quite consistently for non-Hispanic white students (from 11.4 percent in 1980 to 5.3 percent in 2007), they have fluctuated somewhat for non-Hispanic black and for Hispanic students. The 2007 dropout rates are relatively high for each group of students, at 8.4 percent for non-Hispanic blacks and an astounding 21.4 percent for Hispanics.[8] While many factors may contribute to dropout rates, the quality of education is undoubtedly one of these.

We'll return to the issue of diversity at the end of this chapter and will analyze it as a form of discrimination in Chapter 5.

Using a different set of data, one of the most recent international studies of U.S. student achievement in comparison with students from Organization for Economic Cooperation and Development (OECD) countries measures 15-year-olds' average scores on reading, mathematics, and science literacy every three years. (The OECD consists of 34 largely European and other developed countries.) The 2009 results revealed that U.S. students' average score in reading literacy was 500, which was not measurably different from the OECD average of 493. In mathematics literacy, U.S. 15-year-olds' average score of 487 was somewhat lower than the OECD average score of 496. Finally, the U.S. average science literacy score was 502, not measurably different than the average score of 501 in other OECD countries.[9] This is encouraging, as previous studies have shown U.S. students lagging.

As a result of less than ideal test results, high dropout rates, differential access to quality schools, and disparities in the funding of suburban versus inner-city schools, our nation has been debating the issue of education. President George W. Bush made educational "reform" a centerpiece of his domestic policy. Indeed, he referred to the *No Child Left Behind Act* of 2001 as "the cornerstone of my administration." Since most of you are probably familiar with this program, we will look at it briefly and then consider objections and the Democratic response to the program. Then we will consider proposals that focus on (1) an increase in competition among schools (including the use of vouchers), (2) reform of the tax system that funds K–12 education, and (3) President Obama's proposals for improving K–12 education and Congress's reaction to them.

Proposals and Policies for Improving K–12 Education

No Child Left Behind

As we noted, President George W. Bush touted the *No Child Left Behind* program. This legislation embodied four key principles: (1) stronger accountability for results; (2) greater flexibility for states, school districts, and schools in the use of federal funds; (3) more choices for parents of children from disadvantaged backgrounds; and (4) an emphasis on teaching methods that have been demonstrated to work. All third through eighth grade, students are required to take tests in reading and math. These tests allow the public to track the performance of every school in the country. Data are disaggregated for students by economic disadvantage, disability, and limited English proficiency to ensure that no child, regardless of background, is left behind. This disaggregation means that even if the school as a whole has good test results, it will also be evaluated on the test results of any disadvantaged groups. Schools that do poorly are targeted for assistance and then become subject to corrective action and ultimately restructuring. Students in poor-quality schools are then given a new range of options, including a transfer to better public schools and additional educational services such as tutoring, after-school services, and summer school. This program is similar to the charters, magnets, and vouchers insofar as it seeks to enhance competition and accountability in education. If schools do poorly, the consequence is that students would go to alternative schools.

As with other initiatives, *No Child Left Behind* raised many concerns. One problem is that while focusing almost exclusively on reading and math, schools are forced to neglect other areas of learning, including those that foster creative thinking and fine arts appreciation. And, as you know, one important objective of school is to stimulate a love of learning. "Studying for the test," which is what opponents of *No Child Left Behind* say it amounts to, doesn't epitomize the ranges of learning that many people believe are important. Others assert that *No Child Left Behind* offers penalties to poorly performing schools when it should be offering funding to help them improve. Under the Obama administration, the president and legislators have been discussing ways of improving *No Child Left Behind*, including providing funding for poorly performing schools to improve their outcomes.

Federal education law has been due for congressional reauthorization since 2007. As a result of legislative inaction and President Obama's dissatisfaction with *No Child Left Behind*, Obama announced in 2011 that his administration would grant waivers from *No Child Left Behind* to qualified states. States must offer an approved plan to prepare all students for college and career, focus aid on the neediest students, and support effective teaching and leadership. As of the time this is written, waivers have been approved for almost all states in the union.

On a similar note, state leaders have come together to develop a group of standard learning outcomes in English and math, referred to as Common Core. While only recently implemented, Common Core testing has come under the same types of opposition to testing under *No Child Left Behind*, including less time available for other forms of learning and the issue of "studying for the test".

Increase Competition: Charters, Magnets, and Vouchers

Advocates of policies designed to increase competition among schools note that competition in markets for goods and services results in greater efficiency in the production and allocation of resources. They argue, therefore, that measures to increase the competition among a city's schools can be expected to improve performance and simultaneously cut costs. Competition presupposes that consumers can choose among various suppliers. However, public education has traditionally operated on a take-it-or-leave-it basis: a student could either attend the public school in his or her school district or attend a private or (religion-based) parochial school. Traditionally, there have not been choices among public schools for students, and frequently private or parochial schools are expensive or inaccessible. **Proposals to increase competition therefore aim to increase choice.** Three types of programs to provide such choice are charter schools, magnet schools, and school vouchers.

Charter Schools. Charter schools are public schools that operate with freedom from many of the regulations that apply to traditional public schools. According to the U.S. Charter Schools organization, "The charter that establishes each such school is a performance contract detailing the school's mission, program, goals, students served, methods of assessment, and ways to measure success."[10] The length of time for which charters are granted varies, but many are granted for three to five years (renewable at the end of the contract). Charter schools are typically sponsored by state governments or local school boards. The basic concept underlying charter schools is that they have greater autonomy in exchange for accountability.

Charter schools offer an alternative to public schools. Those who favor competition in education argue that charter schools can provide such competition. Just like market demand and supply for any other good or service, the demand for education by good schools will be high, with students and their families willing to pay the cost of the school. Schools that provide a poor service will lose their "customers" and will eventually fail unless they decide to improve their quality. Hence, competition among schools theoretically assures that the outcome is high-quality education for all.

A recent study found that charter schools benefit students from poor families, African-American and Hispanic students, and English-language learners more than their peers in other groups. These students are doing better than they were four years ago, surpassing traditional public schools in reading gains and keeping pace in math. Nevertheless, some have disputed these results and argue for greater focus on improving traditional public schools instead.[11]

The Bush administration supported charter schools, and President Obama has voiced his support as well.

Magnet Schools. Another means through which cities have increased the choices of students and their families is the establishment of so-called magnet schools. Magnet schools are public schools that focus on some particular type of curriculum in an attempt to excel in that aspect of education. The city of St. Paul, Minnesota, offers magnet schools that focus on international business, the sciences, and the fine arts. Parents and students can choose any one of them, regardless of the school district in which they reside.

The major argument in favor of magnet schools is that if a school's specialty is desired by families and if it does a good job of providing an education, the school's enrollment will grow; conversely, if a magnet school's specialization is in low demand or it does a poor job of educating, its enrollment will decline. Money for running the schools depends on enrollment. The school with increasing enrollment will be allocated more resources. The budget of the school with decreasing enrollment will decrease. Just as with charter schools, the competition provided through magnet schools will theoretically improve the quality of education for all.

Vouchers. Another means to increase consumer choice is the tuition voucher. In such a program, each student is given a voucher for some particular amount of money to apply toward tuition in qualified public or private schools. The student's family chooses the school it likes best. If parents are satisfied with their child's public school, they use their voucher to keep their child in that school. Parents who are dissatisfied with the local public schools can enroll their children in private schools, including parochial schools, and part or all of the tuition can be paid with the voucher. Funding is thus withdrawn from the poorer-quality schools and transferred to the better schools through the vouchers. Proponents of vouchers argue that the increased competition is healthy for our educational system. We can tear down the financial barriers between public and private schools. Good schools have been advocated by President Bush and Republicans in general.

In 2002, the U.S. Supreme Court ruled that an Ohio school voucher program was constitutional. In Cleveland, Ohio, thousands of students now receive a voucher toward tuition at private schools. Since then, support for similar programs in other states has spread. More recently, in Wisconsin, conservative governor Scott Walker has supported the use of vouchers in Milwaukee and Racine, and has been attempting to expand their use statewide. Since there would be caps on enrollment and size of vouchers, opponents are concerned that many needy students will be left out of superior schools, but also that future increases in the size of vouchers will substantially **privatize** the state school system, to the detriment of public schools.

Privatization

The transfer of government enterprises or responsibilities to the private sector.

Opposition to Charters, Magnets, and Vouchers. Many people oppose the types of policies just discussed. Despite the argument that these alternatives provide more competition in our nation's schools, many believe that these programs will in fact endanger our existing public school system. The concern is that our poorest school districts simply cannot compete with the better-off charter, magnet, and private schools and that many students will be relegated to poorer-quality schools. For one thing, popular charters, magnets, and private schools must often close enrollment early because they run out of space, so that students who want to enroll in them often cannot do so. Second, the better schools may be located some distance from the student's home, making it difficult or impossible to arrange transportation. Third, consumers of education (students and their parents) may not be sufficiently informed about educational options for any of these programs to result in an efficient market. Fourth, many opponents argue that vouchers for private religious schools violate our nation's separation of church and state. Fifth and most important, these programs shift funds from public schools to private ones. Poor public schools receive fewer resources and become even poorer. With respect to vouchers, a major concern is that the size of the voucher will not cover the entire tuition at an alternative school. This means that low-income students will be forced to remain in even poorer-quality public schools, from which funding is transferred in the form of vouchers for higher-income students to the better schools. As indicated, enrollment caps are a related problem. One educator refers to vouchers as "financial aid for the rich." She states, "When those who *can* make 'choices' in school choice movements are gone, those who are left in public school are those who need help the most."[12] Because of these objections, we must also consider the alternatives.

Proposals for Financing Reform

As we noted in our earlier discussion of inner-city schools, property tax financing of public education results in unequal spending per student. The redistributing of funds through state equalization measures and federal grants to poor school districts is one way to alleviate this problem, though this would need to be expanded in order to fully reduce inequity. Tax reform is another option. Let's first address the issue of property tax reform.

Property Tax Reform: The Michigan Experiment. In 1993, the state of Michigan changed the way it finances education, perhaps offering an innovative solution that other states would like to emulate. Here's how the Michigan experiment evolved.

Although Michigan was a national leader in economic growth and high living standards in the 1960s, it became an economic laggard in the decades thereafter. The primary reasons were the restructuring of the U.S. economy and profound changes in the automobile industry, on which Detroit's economy is based. High-paying jobs in manufacturing disappeared, while lower-paying service sector jobs were created. It was argued that Michigan's high average property tax rate was one reason causing businesses to locate in other states.[13]

Michigan's average property tax rate was about 30 percent above the national average, but the actual property tax rates of school districts in the state varied. Businesses tended to locate in districts with low property tax rates, because lower taxes meant lower costs of doing business. These districts spent considerable sums per pupil on education, but their large tax bases enabled them to do so at low tax rates. At the same time, Detroit, which in 1990 had a high property tax rate of 4.40 percent (compared with the national average rate of 1.67 percent), could not attract new business investment and was forced to postpone government expenditures of all types. (As you probably know, the situation in Detroit has deteriorated much more since then, with the city declaring bankruptcy in 2013.) Local spending per Michigan student ranged from $3,000 in property-poor districts, such as Detroit, to $11,000 in property-rich districts. The state needed to reform its tax laws to encourage economic development as well as to provide more equality in educational opportunity throughout the state.

Michigan's new tax plan replaced the local property tax with a blend of tax sources to finance education. More specifically, the new law raised the state sales tax by 2 percent, increased the tax on cigarettes by 50 cents, and levied a new real estate transfer tax and a new 6 percent tax on out-of-state telephone calls.

This new tax scheme involved some redistribution of funds from rich to poor districts. Revenues raised from local property taxes were pooled and distributed to the schools by the state. Minimum per-student funding was increased from $3,000 to $4,200 the first year. High-spending districts could increase their spending per pupil only by a local referendum in which the citizens of the district voted to increase spending.

Property taxes to finance education were not fully eliminated, but locally determined rates were replaced by statewide tax rates that varied for different types of property. The new tax rates were, on average, lower than the property tax rate on businesses. Because the rates were the same throughout the state, businesses' locational decisions within the state would not be distorted.

Critics of the Michigan plan argued that it threatened local autonomy. Local school boards have traditionally controlled public education. Critics feared that state funding will inhibit local choice. Proponents argued that something had to be done to attract business and equalize education throughout the state. Because the property tax burden is high and educational opportunities are unequal in many other states, these same arguments are heard elsewhere. If the Michigan experiment is viewed as a success, other states are more likely to revise their tax systems.

Federal and State Corrective Funding. An alternative to property tax reform is to shift the major burden of financing public education to the state and federal government levels. This can be done through state equalization measures and federal grants to poor school districts. Property taxes would provide little if any financing for public schools and the problem of differential property tax bases would disappear. This approach has many merits. First, unequal funding between poorer and richer school districts would be eliminated. Children would be treated more equally throughout the state and throughout the country. Second, larger expenditures for disadvantaged children could be used to address their needs for the highest possible corrective educational efforts. Finally, as we will see in Chapter 16, the property tax is extremely regressive (meaning that its heaviest burden falls on low-income people). Reductions in property taxes would address this issue as well.

This approach has two obvious problems. One is that state governments throughout the country have been experiencing worsening budget crises. Partly as a result of the recently poor national economy and partly because of reduced federal transfers to state governments, most states are in poor shape to expand their funding of public education. Also, as we've noted in Chapter 2, many state governments have been spending increasingly larger amounts on crime prevention, especially on prisons, leaving a smaller share of funding available for public education. Alleviating this problem would require higher state taxes or greater federal expenditures on public education and assistance to state governments. The other problem involves the common view that local citizens and their school boards should be making decisions involving their schools. The fear is that if the federal and state governments finance a larger share of public education, the autonomy of local decision making will be lost. Although there is no automatic relationship between funding and autonomy, enough people believe there is and will object to a shift in funding away from local school districts. Nevertheless, expanded federal government spending would be a viable option, overcoming the problem of disparate funding abilities of rich versus poor states.

President Obama's Proposals for K–12 Education

In the second month of his presidency, President Obama stressed the importance of education in America in his address to the joint session of Congress.[14] He said,

> *Right now, three-quarters of the fastest-growing occupations require more than a high school diploma. And yet ... we have one of the highest high school dropout rates of any industrialized nation.... This is a prescription for economic decline, because we know the countries that out-teach us today will outcompete us tomorrow. That is why it will be the goal of this administration to ensure that every child has access to a complete a competitive education— from the day they are born to the day they begin a career.*

He also spoke directly to parents:

> *In the end, there is no program or policy that can substitute for a mother or father who will attend those parent/teacher conferences, or help with homework after dinner, or turn off the TV, put away the video games, and read to their child. I speak to you not just as a president but as a father when I say that responsibility for our children's education must begin at home.*

These were not just words. In the first phase of the economic recovery plan, President Obama dramatically expanded early childhood education and improved its quality. He expanded funding for Headstart, which is significant due to the disparities in early cognitive abilities in disadvantaged children, including minorities, before they even reach kindergarten. He also provided resources necessary to prevent severe cuts and teacher layoffs that would have harmed our K–12 educational system, and his proposals included incentives for teacher performance and a commitment to charter schools. But he also called for future reform.

Again in 2013, President Obama announced plans to further expand preschool. In doing so, he reiterated his State of the Union pledge to make high-quality preschool available to all children. According to the President, "Study after study shows that the earlier a child begins learning, the better he or she does down the road. We are not doing enough to give all of our kids that chance." While many educators have noted that expansion of preschool programs would be the greatest advance of U.S. education in many years, the president's plans are controversial. Opponents are concerned about the cost of the program and the role of "big government."

The Issue of Poverty

The financing of education has been a major part of our discussion of public K–12 education. However, some research has indicated that increased spending per student does not *by itself* improve average student performance by very much. Instead, the research shows that the best predictor of student performance is the poverty rate among the school's students. Simply put, students in localities with high poverty rates generally do not perform as well on standardized tests as students from schools in more affluent areas. The issue may not only be the spending per student on education, but also whether the student lives in a poverty-stricken area. As we discuss in Chapter 7 on housing, residential segregation creates inner-city ghettoes, concentrates poverty, and contributes to the creation of a distressed population. The poor performance of students from these areas reflects a host of economic and cultural factors outside of school. *Increased spending on schools is one step toward greater educational opportunity for low-income students, but many researchers now believe that programs to alleviate poverty and the social dysfunction that accompanies poverty are also needed to improve the academic performance of inner-city students.*[15] Thus, we can say that fundamental improvements in our nation's economy and poverty programs are necessary for achieving real reforms in our educational outcomes.

Final Words on Public K–12 Education

As a nation, we pride ourselves on the equal opportunity we offer our citizens. One of the most important means of ensuring equal opportunity is through our public school system. The public schools are meant to give all students the tools to survive and compete in our highly technological economy. If differences in spending per student are vast because of the way we finance our public schools, then we do not have equal educational opportunities. And, if we do nothing about the underlying poverty that affects student performance in our inner cities, then we still will not have equal educational outcomes.

Higher Education

We've already noted that only about 42 percent of Americans receive a degree in higher education, whether it is an associate degree, a bachelor's degree, or beyond. Studies also show that having a degree in higher education offers at least some protection from downturns in our economy, including our recent recession. And, of course, higher education is a difficult undertaking for lower income students, students who have been inadequately prepared as a result of poor K–12 education, and as we will see, students of minority race and ethnicity.

At the present time, higher education *is* plagued by many economic problems. Costs have risen. State governments, which provide the greatest support for higher education, have suffered from a low tax base due to the recent recession, as well as due to competing uses of limited state funds. Federal support has stagnated at about one-third of total government spending on higher education. Local governments contribute very little. As a result, tuition in public institutions of higher education has increased greatly. The recent poor economy, along with a decline in stock values, has reduced the **endowments** of private institutions. Financial aid rules have changed, and the value of Pell grants (for low-income students) is limited. Colleges and universities have adopted various policies to cope with these problems, and students (especially, but not exclusively, students from low-income families) have had to cope with problems of access to our nation's public colleges.

Endowments
Income-earning investments of a school or other institution.

Let's look at some issues related to higher education. First, we will consider the two types of higher education: public and private. Second, we will look at the notion of higher education as an investment in human capital. Third, we will examine the justification for and role of government in supporting higher education, as well as who really benefits from government support of public universities. Fourth, we will consider the trend toward decreasing government support of higher education. We will look at financial aid programs, including the Pell grants intended to extend educational opportunity to poor students. And finally, we will consider affirmative action in higher education; the role of you, the student; and the left and right positions on education.

Public and Private Higher Education

Subsidize
The payment of some of the costs of an economic activity by the government.

U.S. postsecondary (higher) education consists of colleges, universities, community (junior) colleges, and technical-vocational schools. Some are private schools, not operated by the government. Many others are public schools run by state governments and occasionally by municipalities. Virtually none of these schools, private or public, is free to the student, as is K–12 education. Costs to the students and their families vary widely, however. A College Board Advocacy and Policy Center study reports that the average in-state total of tuition and fees was $8,655 for public four-year colleges and universities in 2012/13. Another $9,205 would be added for room and board for students living on campus.[16] The cost of a private institution can easily be as high as twice the average cost of a public institution. Realize, however, that there is considerable variation around the averages. Public schools generally have lower tuition than private schools because state governments **subsidize** the public universities. By far, most American postsecondary students attend public institutions.

Higher Education as an Investment in Human Capital

Investment in human capital
Spending that is designed to improve the productivity of people.

Education, as well as other services (such as health care and job training), are often referred to as an investments in human capital. An **investment in human capital** is any spending designed to increase the productivity of people. Through education, students can improve their skills and productivity and thereby also increase their earnings. Government data show that earnings increase as education increases, regardless of the worker's race, ethnic group, or gender, although large disparities in earnings among these groups exist. Table 4-4 shows the **median (middle)** weekly earnings for workers age 25 or older. *Note the systematic increase in earnings as the level of education rises.* (Unfortunately, we will see in Chapter 5 that while earnings increase with education for all gender and racial and ethnic groups, the earnings themselves will be much lower for women and most minorities at all educational levels.) However, you can readily see that one of the smartest things you've done in your life is complete high school, followed by your decision to attend college.

Median (middle)
If there is a series of numbers from low to high, the median would be the one exactly in the middle.

Direct cost
Actual paid expenses.

Indirect cost
The opportunity cost of forgone alternatives.

Obtaining an education costs money, as you know. In considering an educational investment, you analyze the expected benefits and costs. The benefits are increased earnings throughout your working life subsequent to your graduation. The costs are both direct and indirect. **Direct cost** refers to the tuition and fee payments, costs of books and supplies, and all the other expenditures you make to obtain a degree. **Indirect cost** is the opportunity cost of forgone earnings. (Recall from Chapter 1 that opportunity costs are forgone alternatives.) Because you are in school, you do not work—at least most of you do not work full time—so you give up earnings. Like your tuition payments, these forgone earnings are a cost of your education. You will theoretically make the investment only if the expected increased earnings justify the total direct and indirect costs.

TABLE 4-4 • Median Weekly Earnings, People Age 25 and Older, by Educational Level, 2011

Educational Levels	Earnings
All	$815
Less than High School Degree	$471
High School Degree	$652
Some College, No Degree	$727
Associate's Degree	$785
Bachelor's Degree	$1,066
Master's Degree	$1,300
Ph.D. Degree	$1,624
Professional Degree	$1,735

Source: Bureau of Labor Statistics, *Current Population Survey,* www.bls.gov, last modified May 22, 2013.

Appendix 4-1 to this chapter provides a numerical and graphical example of a **cost-benefit analysis** of attending college. For simplicity here, let's just consider the factors that a student would consider. Suppose that this student is you, and that you graduate from high school at age 18 and expect to retire at age 66. You may take time off for child-rearing, but let's ignore that possibility for simplicity. Let's assume that you will either attend college full time until the age of 22 and then graduate, or you will not attend college at all. Let's further assume that you will not work while you are a college student, which is not the case for many students but which simplifies the discussion greatly. If you do not attend college, you will go to work in a relatively low-wage job after graduating from high school. Therefore, annual earnings will be relatively low and increase only modestly as you gain job experience throughout your working life. Some earnings will occur, however, during the four years subsequent to high school graduation.

If you attend college instead of working, those first four years' earnings will be given up, so they are part of your opportunity cost of obtaining a college education. The earnings given up to attend college are the "indirect costs" of your education. Direct costs will also be incurred. You (or your family) must pay tuition and fees, buy supplies and books, and pay room and board (or at least the amount in excess of what you would incur by living elsewhere).

However, if you obtained a college degree, you will be more promotable. Employers put more-educated employees into positions of greater responsibility. Furthermore, employers may invest in more on-the-job training for educated workers than they do for uneducated workers. On-the-job training makes you a more valuable employee. You can reasonably expect your earnings to increase substantially as you establish yourself in your field. The possibilities are much greater if you graduate from college than if you do not. Therefore, your annual earnings will be greater and the difference between what you earn and what you would have earned without the degree will increase over time.

For your cost-benefit analysis you would compare your earnings without college over your working life with your net earnings with college over your working life (your earnings minus total costs of education). You will undoubtedly be better-off having gone to college.

The preceding discussion is based on the assumption that you are a traditional student who entered college right after high school. In fact, you may be a nontraditional, older student, and you may be a part-time rather than a full-time student. Increasing numbers of students fit in these categories. For those of you over age 25, the decision may be more complex because you probably have greater responsibilities and greater indirect costs, but it will be made on much the same basis.

Cost-benefit analysis
A study that compares the costs and benefits of a policy or program.

Investment in human capital theory has been criticized for being overly simplistic and for its implicit assumption that the only reason we obtain an education is to increase our lifetime earnings. Many of us obtain an education because we simply like to learn. We know that our life will be fuller and more intellectually rewarding if we are educated. In some disciplines, we may not necessarily expect to earn a great deal more money with our degree, but we do hope to have a job that is more rewarding in its nonmonetary aspects or that it contributes to the greater good of society. In short, our decisions have more dimensions than the theory incorporates.

More recently, commentators have called into question the results of our cost-benefit for many students. Specifically, for those students who do not graduate, those students who fail to find full-time and adequately-paying jobs, and those students who become saddled with student debt, the decision to attend a four-year college is called into question.

Investment in human capital theory does have considerable explanatory power, however. It offers an explanation for the young age of most people in college. First, young people have many years to earn the higher salaries that result from their education. The increased earnings over their lifetimes are therefore greater. Second, young people will have smaller opportunity costs than older workers who have some labor market skills and who probably earn at least slightly higher wages.

This theory also helps us explain the effects of financial aid to students on enrollment in our colleges and universities. Financial aid decreases the students' direct costs, which makes the investment (and enrollment) more likely. Nevertheless, as we will see, the indirect costs for low-income students are often too large for them to justify a college education.

Justification for Government Support of Public Higher Education

In most states, the public postsecondary education system consists of one major research institution (the flagship), a number of comprehensive (four-year) universities, and a number of community (junior) colleges. The flagship institution is a major, doctoral degree-granting institution, whereas the comprehensive schools are principally four-year teaching institutions that may offer a few master's degree programs. The two-year community colleges offer associate's degree programs and serve as feeder institutions to the comprehensive schools. These two-year schools also offer remedial programs, and their cost is significantly lower than the cost of four-year schools. In most states, vocational and technical schools are financed separately and are governed by a different board than is the university and community college system.

As you will recall, state taxes are a major source of income for these public higher education systems. Because the states contribute to the cost of operating these schools, tuition is lower than the full cost of educating a student. In other words, education is subsidized by the state government. Historically, the subsidy has been justified with two reasons. First, the existence of spillover benefits to the state of having an educated citizenry means that higher education will be provided at less than efficient levels if government does not intervene. (Recall that in the case of positive externalities, too few resources are allocated to the good or service. Government subsidies will encourage a larger, more efficient outcome.) Similarly, it may not be perceived to be equitable if people pay the entire cost of their education while society in general receives part of the benefits. Government subsidies can correct this inequity. **Our economic theory of positive externalities can therefore be used as a justification for government subsidies of higher education as a means of achieving greater equity and efficiency.** Second, Americans believe in the concept of equal access to education. Although we don't necessarily believe that all people should receive equal benefits of a market economy, we do generally believe that all citizens should have an equal opportunity to be educated and thereby have a chance at higher incomes.

Although, the first of these two justifications (the spillover effects) is warranted, the second one is not. This is because when we examine financial aid records, we learn that most of the students in our public colleges and universities come from high- or middle-income families. This means that if our purpose is to improve access to higher education for low-income students, our state subsidies for higher education are a very inefficient way to do it. We may still justify the government subsidy of education by its social spill-over benefits, but we must recognize that most of the students we are subsidizing are not from poor families. We will revisit this issue shortly.

Limited Government Support for Public Higher Education

As we've already noted, state support of public higher education has been limited. This represents a change in social values and spending priorities, as well as limited budgets and calls for reduced taxes. At the state level, higher education has been squeezed out by increased spending on prisons and health care, which are discussed further in Chapters 2 and 8, respectively.

With limited government support, U.S. public universities and colleges have reacted in various ways. First, virtually all of our states have increased tuition significantly. Second, many schools have established enrollment caps. And finally, some schools are experimenting with differential tuition. Let's look at each of these policies.

Responses to Limited Government Support for Higher Education

Raising Tuition

When state tax funds decrease, an obvious reaction is to increase the tuition charged to all students to make up the missing funds. Over time, tuition revenues must cover a larger share of the costs of public institutions. As a result, tuition has increased substantially.

Quite obviously, tuition levels affect access to the university system. Some students simply cannot afford the higher tuition unless they can obtain greater financial aid to off-set their higher educational costs. Equally as obvious, the students who feel the negative effects most are from low- and middle-income families.

Enrollment Caps

An **enrollment cap** is a maximum limit on the number of students allowed to enroll in a school. In order to maintain relatively high faculty/student ratios, reasonably small class sizes, and other widely accepted measures of quality in a time of declining state educa-tion budgets, many state college systems have instituted enrollment caps.

Once established, enrollment caps will generally decrease enrollment to some speci-fied level over time, necessitating rationing of openings. A common way to accomplish this task is to increase admission standards. Raising the cutoff score on the American College Test (ACT) or the Standard Achievement Test (SAT) college entry test or increasing the minimum high school class rank for entry into the college system will eliminate a number of students who would have been admitted in the past. This measure has the advantage of eliminating students who might have been poor risks for completion of college, rather than simply excluding students at random. On the other hand, it might eliminate "late bloomers," who achieve mature study habits in college instead of in high school. It may also eliminate students of low-income and/or diverse backgrounds who

Enrollment cap
A maximum limit on the number of students allowed to enroll in a school.

have received poor-quality K–12 education. At any rate, enrollment caps serve to reduce access of the general public to publicly supported education.

As more students graduate from high schools and seek to enter the public university system, there is pressure on the system to become more efficient and to move students speedily through the educational pipeline. In some schools, this pressure is contributing to new policies that raise tuition for students who have already achieved some number of credits beyond the number required to graduate. Students would be charged normal tuition rates for some maximum number of credits, and then charged higher rates for credits taken beyond the acceptable norm. There is also pressure on specific popular programs. After a certain level of class overcrowding in these programs is reached, schools tend also to limit entry into these particular programs because they simply do not have the resources to allow students into them. They might also charge differential tuition rates for different programs, as we will consider now.

Differential Tuition

One other avenue being explored by some universities is to utilize differential tuition, which entails charging higher tuition for majors and programs in high demand by students and charging lower tuition for those programs with lower demand. Since this provides us with a fascinating discussion utilizing the demand and supply analysis that you are familiar with, you may be interested in exploring the topic in Appendix 4-2 to this chapter.

Financial Aid: What About Low-Income Students?

In addition to state support for public higher education, financial aid is available through many sources to help low-, middle-, and upper-income students bear the costs of education. Some aid comes directly from the federal government, some from states, and some from the college or university directly. This aid comes in many forms: scholarships and fellowships, employer assistance, veterans' assistance, college work study, loans, and Pell grants.

The Pell Grant is a federal grant that is targeted to low-income undergraduate students. In fact, this grant represents almost all federal grant money dispersed to college students. Many students mistakenly assume, however, that this grant provides a free ride to low-income students. This is not the case. The Pell Grant was never intended to cover the full costs of a college education. But, it is heartening to know that federal disbursements of Pell grants have increased over time. Using constant 2011–2012 dollars (that is, adjusting for inflation), the amount of federal grants has increased almost four times in the last decade, from $10 billion in 2000 to nearly $38 billion in 2010. During the same time, the number of recipients of federal grants increased from 4 million students to 11 million.[17]

Finally, while government support for higher education and financial aid packages for students help them meet the direct costs of higher education, these do not address the *indirect costs* of higher education. Recall that the indirect cost is the opportunity cost; that is, the income forgone while attending school rather than working in a full-time job. Low- to middle-income students may not be able to afford the opportunity cost of these forgone earnings, because they and their families count on this income for survival.

All this means is that not all students have equal access to our institutions of higher education. First, you need to graduate from high school before attending college, and not all Americans have an equal opportunity for a quality K–12 education. Income is the major factor in determining who goes to a good high school with a high graduation rate, and low-income students are more likely to attend poor high schools with high dropout rates. Second, the state subsidizes tuition by financing a large share of the construction and operation of public postsecondary schools, but this benefits all students who attend public postsecondary schools, most of whom are not students from low-income families. Third, the value of Pell is not always adequate to enable students from very low-income families to afford college. Finally, the opportunity cost of education in the form of forgone earnings while attending school prevents many low-income and even middle-income persons from obtaining higher education.

Financial Aid: New Proposals

President Barack Obama has begun making some wide-ranging proposals for restructuring financial aid. Among these is one to link federal financial aid and high educational ranking among colleges and universities. School rankings would hinge on tuition costs, graduation rates, student debt, graduate earnings, and the percentage of low-income students they serve, among others. Many feel that these rankings would increase the transparency of school outcomes, as well as create greater accountability by rewarding better performing schools. Ideally, competition would encourage other schools to improve their outcomes as well.

The President made other suggestions as well, including the expansion of so-called massive open online courses (MOOCs) (that students can take for free) and competency-based degrees (where students can earn credits by showing what they know rather than taking classes). The President has also proposed funding the tuition and supplies for students attending two-year colleges, as long as they meet certain requirements (including at least half-time participation). As this text goes to print, these proposals have not yet been taken up by Congress. Based on what you know about opportunity costs, what do you think might be a major problem for low-income or single-parent students in the latter proposal?

Affirmative Action: What About Underrepresented Groups?

First, we know that K–12 educational attainment and quality varies considerably by race and ethnicity. Achievement scores and high school graduation rates tend to be much lower for racial and ethnic minorities than for the white Caucasian population. High school dropout rates are higher. Educational attainment varies considerably. Table 4-5 displays educational attainment for whites, African-Americans, Hispanics, and Asian-Americans; in terms of the percent of each group that achieves various educational levels. It is interesting to note that in each category, higher percentages of Asian-Americans achieve the higher education degrees. Whites are far more likely than African-Americans and Hispanics to achieve the various higher education degrees.

TABLE 4-5 • Educational Attainment by Race and Ethnicity, Share of Total Group (%), Age 25 Years or over, 2010

Race or Ethnicity	Educational Attainment	
	High School Degree or Higher	Bachelor's Degree or Higher
All	87.1%	29.9%
White	87.6%	30.3%
African-American	84.2%	19.8%
Asian/Pacific Islander	88.9%	52.4%
Hispanic	62.9%	13.9%

Note: Since educational attainment is expressed as high school degree or higher and bachelor's degree or higher, the former column includes students with bachelor's degrees, associate's degrees, and higher level degrees; and the latter column includes master's degrees, professional degrees, and Ph.D. degrees.

Source: U.S. Census Bureau, U.S. Census of Population, *Current Population Reports* and "Educational Attainment," www .census.gov, released September 30, 2011.

Finally, as mentioned, we will discover in Chapter 5 that people of minority racial and ethnic groups have lower earnings than white Caucasians when we compare people with *identical levels of education*. We will see that several types of labor market discrimination lie at the root of these earnings differentials.

While this discussion of race and ethnicity has taken place on a negative note, this is not entirely the case with respect to affirmative action. As we will also see in Chapter 5, the U.S. Supreme Court has recently ruled that affirmative action is constitutional in the case of graduate admissions to the law school at the University of Michigan. **The Court stated that race can be used as a factor in university admission decisions, and that indeed "a diverse student body has its own benefits."** Still, the issue of affirmative action is controversial. President George W. Bush opposed the University of Michigan affirmative action program, despite support from certain members of his administration. Nevertheless, the Obama administration supports it, and the Michigan standard was reaffirmed by the Supreme Court in 2013. It continues to guide the admission policies of colleges and universities today, though controversy dictates that it will continue to be challenged.

As the diversity of our population continues to increase, we must continually seek broader exposure to other cultures. As such, the movement toward multiculturalism in our schools and colleges is a positive one. Beyond merely spreading greater knowledge of other cultures, our multicultural educational opportunities will spread greater appreciation of all people within our society.

A Final Note

In 2012, 15-year old Malala Yousafzai (Yoo'-saf-zhen) was shot by the Taliban in northwest Pakistan for her vocal support of girls' education. She recovered, became a global advocate for girls' education, and was the youngest recipient of the Nobel Peace Prize in 2014. Education is the most important factor in alleviating poverty in developing

View*Point*   Conservative versus Liberal

Conservatives favor policies to increase competition in our public K–12 system, whereas liberals emphasize tax reform, the redistribution of tax dollars from rich to poor districts to equalize educational opportunities, and programs such as Head Start. Therefore, conservatives favor school voucher systems to give parents and students more choices of schools and curricula. They also like to see more competition among schools in the form of private schools, charter schools, and magnet schools. Liberals, on the other hand, fear that widespread use of school vouchers would endanger our public school system by transferring funds away from the poor schools (and poor students) that need them most.

Both liberals and conservatives usually believe that providing universal education in the K–12 level is a legitimate government role, given primary and secondary education's demonstrated spillover benefits to society. Conservatives generally support spending on K–12 education by local governments, whereas liberals are more willing to support expanded state and federal spending. Conservatives do not, in general, favor extensive tuition subsidies or financial aid for students in higher education unless spillover benefits can be shown to result from this postsecondary education. Liberals are more likely to favor expanded financial aid to low-income students, as well as tax credits for educational purposes. Liberals are also more likely to support remedies for inequity in education for racial and ethnic minority students, including affirmative action.

countries, and the education of girls in particular has widespread positive externalities. We know that if a mother has been educated, she there is a higher chance of her children's survival and a greater likelihood that her children, including her girl children, will go to school. Thus, the education cycle becomes intergenerational. You can Google her name to learn more about her or to find out about her book entitled, *I Am Malala*.

You, the Student

We know that disadvantaged children, including those living in poverty, those who are homeless, those with single parents, children of migrants, and those facing other disadvantages, do not have equal opportunity in our society. They do not receive the full benefits of education that other children enjoy. If you are concerned about this, you might want to consider joining Americorps. This organization fits individuals such as you with programs to help the needy within the United States, including needy children. Go to http://www.americorps.gov to learn about the program and the benefits for those who choose to serve in it, including a modest living allowance, student-loan forbearance, health coverage, and child care; as well as an education award that can be used to pay off qualified student loans or to finance further education at eligible institutions. You might also want to visit the Big Brother/Big Sister Web site at http://www.bbbs.org to see if you could offer your friendship and role model to a disadvantaged child.

SUMMARY

Education is the classic example of a positive externality, spilling benefits over onto society. This provides a justification for government support for public education to assure greater efficiency and equity. However, funding our public elementary and high schools primarily from local property taxes results in extremely unequal spending per student. As a result, underfunded schools have inadequate facilities, high student/teacher ratios, poorly staffed classrooms, and various other inadequacies. Underfunded high schools have higher dropout rates, and their graduates receive a poorer education. A number of proposals have been put forth to improve our public schools. These include efforts to increase competition in education through charter schools, magnet schools, and vouchers. Others prefer to equalize education between poor and rich school districts through state or federal funding, along with property tax reform. We also know that increasing funding to schools in areas of concentrated high poverty will not be effective in

itself in improving student outcomes. It is also necessary to alleviate poverty in these areas.

Our postsecondary school system consists of vocational-technical schools, community colleges, four-year colleges, and universities, both public and private. Public schools have lower tuition than private schools, because state governments subsidize them. By far, most American postsecondary students attend public institutions. While cost-benefit analysis justifies the investment in human capital associated with higher education, our public higher education system benefits mainly upper- and middle-income families, not low-income families. Decreasing state support, rising tuition, and the limited value of Pell grants have made it difficult for low-income students, who already may face untenable circumstances with opportunity costs (foregone income), to access higher education.

Finally, diversity is an important component of a multicultural education. Among other things, it fosters greater appreciation of all people within our society.

DISCUSSION AND ACTION QUESTIONS

1. How do spillover benefits distort the allocation of resources to education? Can you think of other examples of goods with spillover benefits?

2. Draw a graph indicating how negative externalities (spillover costs) would (1) result in a lower price of a

good when its production creates the spillovers and (2) cause overallocation of resources. (*Hint:* Refer to Chapter 3.)

3. Draw a graph indicating how positive externalities (spillover benefits) would (1) result in a higher price of a good or service when its consumption creates spillovers and (2) cause underallocation of resources. (*Hint:* Refer to Figure 4-1.)

4. How does property tax funding of K–12 education create inequality? Consider your response in terms of both the tax rate and the tax base. What can be done to create greater equality?

5. What could be done to help inner-city schools other than providing them with more funding?

6. What do you think of the *No Child Left Behind Act,* especially its requirements that schools test their students annually? Have you ever taken these tests? Do you think these tests are accurate indicators of school quality? Do you see any problems associated with the testing programs?

7. What do you hope to gain by your attendance at institutions of higher education? Is it primarily a higher income, as suggested by human capital theory, or do you have other objectives in mind?

8. (Appendix question) How would charging different tuition for different majors improve the allocation of a school's resources? Do you think this measure would be a good one? Can you think of any problems that might arise?

9. Who are the most likely beneficiaries of higher education? Why do low-income students encounter problems as they seek access to higher education (and often middle-income students as well)?

10. Consider the following. Joe is deciding whether to go to college full time. If he does not attend college, he will continue to work at his present job. Joe earns $14,000 annually. He estimates that tuition and fees at the local public college will be about $10,000 per year and that he can graduate in four years if he does not work. The starting salary in the field he hopes to enter is about $30,000, and he estimates that he will earn about $600,000 more in his working lifetime with a college degree than without one. What will be Joe's opportunity cost of four years of college? What will be his net benefits (benefits minus costs)? Should he make the investment in education?

11. Do you think you received a good quality K–12 education? Why or why not?

12. Go to the Census Bureau Web site (http://www.census .gov). Click E for *education* in the A–Z option. Find the latest data for the percentage of the population that has a high school degree only and the percentage of the population with a bachelor's degree.

13. Go to the Department of Education's home page at http:// www.ed.gov and seek out information about your possible eligibility for financial aid. Who is the current education secretary of the United States?

14. Check out the Cato Institute Web site at http://www.cato .org. This research institute has a reputation of supporting conservative causes. What examples can you find at this Web site for conservative opinions on school vouchers, *No Child Left Behind,* or other educational issues? Why would you say these are conservative?

15. Go to the home page of the Brookings Institution at http://www.brook.edu. This research institute has a reputation of supporting liberal causes. Can you find examples of liberal opinions on school vouchers, *No Child Left Behind,* or other educational issues? Why would you describe these as liberal?

16. Supporters of charter schools have a Web site at http:// www.uscharterschools.org. This Web site seeks to support families choosing charter schools for their children by providing information about charter school startup and assistance, resources, calendars of events, and other topics pertaining to charter schools. Can you use the Web site to find out whether there are any charter schools in your geographical area?

17. Check out the College Results page of the Education Trust Web site to find information on college graduation rates and college records on graduating diverse groups of students (http://www.collegeresults.org/).

18. Go to the White House Web site at http://www .whitehouse.gov and search for recent speeches given by the president about education in the United States.

19. Look up information on Headstart. Recent information suggests that minority children fall behind in cognitive abilities even before they enter kindergarten. Can this type of program help children who, for various reasons, fall behind their peers even before entering kindergarten?

NOTES

1. U.S. Census Bureau, *Current Population Survey, Annual Social and Economic Supplement,* 2012, http://www .census.gov.

2. U.S. Department of commerce, Census Bureau, *Current Population Survey,* www.census.gov.

3. New America Foundation, http://www .newamericafoundation.org, published June 30, 2013.

4. *A Nation at Risk: The Imperative for Educational Reform,* Report of American President Ronald Reagan's National Commission on Excellence in Education, 1983.

5. This discussion is taken from Jonathan Kozol, *Savage Inequalities: Children in America's Schools* (New York: HarperCollins, 1992). See specifically pages 58–59, 69, and 225.

6. Margaret E. Goertz, "The Finances of Poor School Districts," *Clearing House* (November–December 1994), pp. 74–77.

7. *The National Assessment of Educational Progress*, June 2013, http://www.nces.ed.gov/nationsreportcard/pubs/main2012/2013/2013456.aspx.

8. National Center for Education Statistics, nces.ed.gov/programs/coe/.

9. National Center for Education Statistics, Institute of Education Sciences, *Trends in International Math and Science Studies*, nces.ed.gov/fastfacts/.

10. The U.S. Charter Schools organization, http://www.uscharterschools.org.

11. Margaret Raymond, Director, Center for Research on Education Outcomes, *National Charter School Study*, June 2013.

12. This educator was a long-time public high school principal who had, along with her children, been students at a parochial school. Despite her strong support for private education, she nevertheless opposes the use of vouchers due to the negative impact it has on low-income children in public schools.

13. The principal source for the material is this section is the *Chicago Fed Letter* (Chicago: Federal Reserve Bank of Chicago, May 1994).

14. President Barack Obama, Address to Joint Session of Congress, February 24, 2009, http://www.whitehouse.gov.

15. See James Traub, "What No School Can Do," *The New York Times,* Jan. 16, 2000, and Denise C. Morgan, "The Less Polite Questions: Race, Place, Poverty and Public Education," in the *Annual Survey of American Law* (New York: New York University School of Law, 1998).

16. Sandy Baum and Jennifer Ma, "Trends in College Pricing," 2012, in *The Trends in Higher Education Series*, College Board Advocacy and Policy Center, http://advocacy.collegeboard.org.

17. Condition of education—2013 Spotlights—*Financing Postsecondary Education*, http://www.nces.ed.gov/programs/coe/indicator_tua.asp.

Appendix 4-1

Cost-Benefit Analysis of Higher Education as an Investment in Human Capital

L et's consider a specific numerical example of the cost-benefit analysis of a college degree that was discussed in the chapter. We can then consider a figure that displays the important variables.

Let's assume that you graduate from high school at the age of 18 and can expect to retire at age 66. We assume that you will either attend college full time until the age of 22 and then graduate, or you will not attend college at all. We further assume that you will not work while you are a college student, which is not the case for many students but which simplifies the discussion greatly. If you do not attend college, you will go to work in a relatively low-wage job after graduating from high school. Therefore, annual earnings will be relatively low and increase only modestly as you gain job experience throughout your working life. Some earnings will occur, however, during the four years subsequent to high school graduation. Let's assume that those earnings will be $20,800 for the first year if you work at a wage of $10 per hour ($10 per hour multiplied by 40 hours per week multiplied by 52 weeks per year = $20,800). Let's assume your wage increases by $.20 per hour (or $400 per year) over each of the next three years (as well as over your remaining 44 years of working. Let's simplify by not factoring in taxes. If you attend college instead of working, those first four years' earnings will be given up, so they are part of your opportunity cost of obtaining a college education. The earnings given up to attend college are the "indirect costs" of your education and equal $20,800 during the first year, $21,200 during the second year, $21,600 during the third year, and $22,000 during the fourth year, or $85,600 over the four years. Direct costs will also be incurred. You (or your family) must pay tuition and fees, buy supplies and books, and pay room and board (or at least the amount in excess of what you would incur by living elsewhere). Let's assume these direct costs amount to $5,000 per year, or $20,000 over the four-year period. The total cost of your education then is ($85,600 + $20,000).

If you do not attend college, your lifetime earnings will include the $85,600 of the first four years, plus your earnings for the remaining 44 years of working, for a total of $1,339,000. This was calculated by adding on $.20 per hour for each year over your working life (i.e. $20,800 + $21,200 + $21,600 + $22,000 + $22,400 + $22,800 + ….).

However, if you obtained a college degree, you will be more promotable. Employers put more-educated employees into positions of greater responsibility. Furthermore, employers may invest in more on-the-job training for educated workers than they do for uneducated workers. On-the-job training makes you a more valuable employee. You can reasonably expect your earnings to increase substantially as you establish yourself in your field (far more than $.20 per hour per year). Therefore, your annual earnings will be greater and the difference between what you earn and what you would have earned without the degree will increase over time. Let's assume that your total earnings for your 44 years on the job market (48 years minus the 4 years in college) equal $4,000,000.

For your cost-benefit analysis you would compare your earnings without college ($1,339,000) with your net earnings with college (your earnings minus total costs of education, or $4,000,000 minus $40,800), which is $3,959,200. Clearly you are better-off having gone to college.

Figure 4-4 describes the decision variables in our cost-benefit analysis of attending college. The horizontal axis represents your expected working life if you graduate from high school at the age of 18 and can expect to work until retirement at 66 years. We continue to assume that you will either attend college full time until the age of 22 and then graduate, or you will not attend college at all. We further assume that you will not work while you are a college student, as we previously assumed. If you do not attend college, you will go to work in a relatively low-wage job after graduating from high school. Therefore, annual earnings will be relatively low and increase only modestly as you gain job experience throughout your working life. Some earnings will occur, however, during the four years subsequent to high school graduation.

If you attend college instead of working, those first four years' earnings will be given up, so they are part of your opportunity cost of obtaining a college education. The earnings given up to attend college are labeled "indirect cost" in Figure 4-4. Direct costs will also be incurred. You (or your family) must pay tuition and fees, buy supplies and books, and pay room and board (or at least the amount in excess of what you would incur by living elsewhere). The direct costs are shown by the area below the horizontal axis because they are negative amounts (money paid out).

After you graduate from college, you may go to work for only slightly higher earnings than you would receive had you simply worked since high school. But because you obtained your education, you will be more promotable. You can reasonably expect your

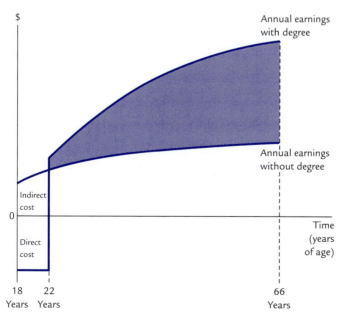

Figure 4-4 • The Decision to Invest in College Education
The investment will be made only if the increase in lifetime earnings justifies the direct and indirect costs of education.

earnings to increase substantially over time. The possibilities are much greater if you graduate from college than if you do not. Therefore, your annual earnings will be greater and the difference between what you earn and what you would have earned without the degree will increase over time. The total increased earnings over your working life are represented by the shaded area in Figure 4-4. Your cost-benefit analysis displays the positive net benefits of attending college.

Another way to conduct your analysis is to compare the increased earnings from college attendance to other earnings that you might have accrued if you had invested your college costs in some other way, such as in an apprenticeship program or a vocational school. Notice that either way, you are using a form of cost-benefit analysis, much as we did in Chapter 3 on Environmental Protection and Chapter 2 on Crime Prevention. If you are a very sophisticated decision maker, you compute a rate of return on your investment, which is your net benefit (benefit minus cost), divided by the amount of your investment. Then you compare the **rate of return** on your college education to the rates of return on other investments you could have made.

Rate of return
The "benefit rate," computed by dividing the net benefit by the amount invested.

Appendix 4-2

Differential Tuition

U.S. universities and colleges are under tremendous pressure to become more efficient. Greater efficiency would enable schools to meet student needs at lower cost and therefore hold down tuition to an affordable level. One suggestion has been to charge different tuition for different programs to increase efficiency. This would mean higher tuition in programs with heavy demand by students and lower tuition for those with lower demand.

One problem that universities face is that they are slow to react to changing demands for programs. To attract quality faculty to the university, the institution has made a commitment to tenured faculty in particular disciplines. The school has acquired physical facilities that are needed for a particular program and may be inappropriate for most other uses. Yet, demand for particular programs varies over time. Schools' adjustments to these changes in demand take time, and while the adjustment is taking place, efficiency decreases. Either surpluses or shortages of class sections may occur in particular majors.

A number of years ago, there was a great deal of discussion in higher education about charging higher tuition for very popular, growing majors and lower tuition for declining majors. You will probably recognize this discussion as an exercise in demand and supply analysis, and you are right. Consider the following hypothetical situation. A school has a pre-law program, which is growing rapidly. Influenced by the popular television shows *The Good Wife* and *How to Get Away With Murder*, many freshmen are declaring pre-law majors. At the same time, interest in the school's philosophy major is declining. Tuition and fees are the same whether you major in pre-law or philosophy. Figure 4-5 illustrates this situation.

Assume that the school's tuition is $6,000 and that the school would like to supply classes for 300 majors in each program at that tuition (price). But the number of students demanding the pre-law major (quantity demanded) at that tuition is 600. So, there is a shortage of 300 slots for pre-law majors at the $6,000 tuition. In fact, the shortage is not so obvious, but it is felt in greatly increased class size in the pre-law major. It is observed in closed classes and bottlenecks in students' programs. Students cannot graduate in four years, because they cannot get the classes they need. The demand is simply beyond the school's capacity to meet it.

Now look at the graph for the philosophy program. Here again, the school would like to supply classes for 300 students at the uniform $6,000 tuition. But demand is so low that only 100 philosophy students enroll. A surplus of philosophy classes is available. This surplus will be felt in very small classes and inefficient use of university resources. To help alleviate the problem, some philosophy professors may become part-time administrators or participate in a program to advise students who have not yet decided on majors.

Now assume that the school increases the tuition in the pre-law program to $8,000, the equilibrium price. The shortage will be eliminated, and the school will have an

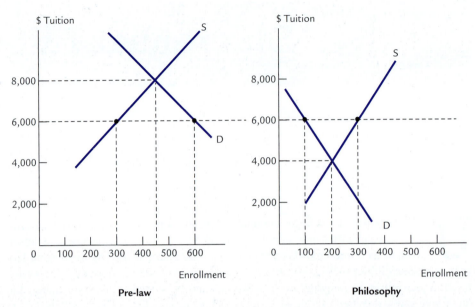

Figure 4-5 • Improving Resource Allocation by Charging Different Tuition for Different Programs
At uniform tuition ($6,000), there will be a shortage for pre-law students and a surplus for philosophy students. Different tuition ($8,000 and $4,000) eliminates the shortage and surplus and improves resource allocation.

© Cengage Learning

equilibrium number of 450 pre-law majors. Because the school receives extra tuition, it can hire part-time faculty to teach more sections of pre-law courses, and pre-law students will encounter fewer bottlenecks.

Simultaneously, the school lowers the tuition to $4,000 for philosophy majors. At $4,000, philosophy attracts 200 majors (quantity demanded), and the surplus is eliminated. Classes are a reasonable size, and resources are used more efficiently. Differential tuition has greatly decreased the school's resource allocation problems.

You may be somewhat skeptical. You might wonder why a student would change majors just because the tuition was lower. Or you might think it is unfair to charge different tuition for different programs. You might not believe that schools could adjust tuition precisely enough to achieve a really efficient allocation of resources. And, indeed, the educational community has had the same reservations, so there has been little experimentation with different tuition for different programs.

Some experimentation with user fees has been done, however. As state funding has decreased, schools have instituted various fees in an attempt to increase their revenues. Some fees are, in fact, surcharges designed to discourage students from entering overcrowded majors or to cover the costs of providing majors that require expensive supplies and equipment. Science and art are two areas in which this might occur.

Part II

The Economics
of Social Issues

Ryan McVay/Digital Vision/Thinkstock

Chapter 5

ROAD MAP

Chapter 5
Discrimination

Chapter 2
Crime and Drugs
Various groups of minorities experience hate crimes.

Chapter 4
Education
Property tax funding results in underfunded innercity public schools that are attended by minority children. Human capital discrimination causes disparities in earnings and income.

Chapter 6
U.S. Poverty
Discrimination is one cause of poverty in the United States.

Chapter 7
Housing
Minorities were frequent victims of sub-prime mortgage lending. Residential housing segregation concentrates poverty and leads to discrimination in education and employment. Public housing also concentrates poverty and leads to discriminatory outcomes.

Chapter 14
Unemployment and Inflation
U.S. minorities have higher unemployment rates than do whites. Discrimination results in unemployment and inefficient use of labor, moving our economy from a point on the production possibilities curve to a point below the curve.

Chapter 8
Health Care
Minorities are more likely to be uninsured than are whites. Infant mortality rates are higher for minorities than for whites.

The Economic Toolbox

- Diversity
- Earnings differentials
- Discrimination
- Statistical discrimination
- Occupational crowding
- Rational choice
- Affirmative action
- Residential segregation
- Educational segregation

Discrimination

Over 45 years have elapsed since President Lyndon Johnson's Kerner Commission submitted its shocking 1968 report blaming racism and discrimination, poverty, and unemployment for the riots that had besieged the nation's central cities during the 1960s. And over five decades have passed since Dr. Martin Luther King, Jr., delivered his celebrated "I Have a Dream" speech at the foot of the Lincoln Memorial, climaxing the historic August 1963 March on Washington for Civil Rights.

Still, it was late 2002 when Senate Majority Leader Trent Lott, a Republican from Mississippi, stated publicly at a Senate party for Senator Strom Thurmond, "I want to say this about my state: When Strom Thurmond ran for president, we voted for him. We're proud of it. And if the rest of the country had followed our lead, we wouldn't have had all these problems over all these years, either." As your author read this quotation to a class of students similar to you, there was an audible gasp. These students and the rest of the American public knew that in 1948, when Thurmond ran for president, he was running as the nominee of the Dixiecrats, a racist renegade party organized for only one purpose: to oppose civil rights for African-Americans. During that campaign, Thurmond stated, "All the laws of Washington and all the bayonets of the Army cannot force the Negro into our homes, our schools, our churches." Lott subsequently apologized and resigned as majority leader.

Racism continues all around us. Following the singing of the national anthem at a National Basketball Association Finals game in 2013 by a young Hispanic American man, tweets followed: "This lil Mexican snuck into the country like 4 hours ago now he singing the anthem", "Can't believe they have the nerve to have a beaner sing the national Anthem of AMERICA", "Nine out of ten chances that kid is illegal". The news director for a television station made this Facebook post about a stranger he found in his yard one night, "Add drunk, homeless, Native American man to the list of animals that have wandered into my yard." The Justice Department report on the Ferguson, Missouri police department mentioned in Chapter 2 found racist emails stating that Obama would not be president for very long because "what black man holds a steady job for four years"; a photo of bare-chested dancing women, apparently in Africa, captioned as "Michelle Obama's High School Reunion"; and President Obama depicted as a chimpanzee. And, a chant by the Sigma Alpha Epsilon fraternity at the University of Oklahoma was discovered in 2015, chanting a song excluding African Americans from joining the group and including the n-word and a reference to a lynching. "There'll never be a n***. You can hang him from a tree. But he'll never sign with me."

Our nation is moving toward two societies, one black, one white— separate and unequal.

—REPORT OF THE PRESIDENT'S NATIONAL ADVISORY COMMISSION ON CIVIL DISORDERS (THE KERNER COMMISSION), MARCH 1, 1968

These comments make us wonder if much has changed since the Dixiecrats, since Dr. King, or since the Kerner report. This chapter opens with the Kerner Commission's dire prediction. Was it accurate? The ensuing years have been full of controversy and change. Have we come any closer to realizing Dr. King's dream? Have African-Americans and other ethnic and racial minorities in America attained equal access to the prerequisites of our affluent society? Or, are doors still closed to some people on arbitrary bases such as race, religion, ethnicity, and gender?

The answers to these questions are not easy. Let's begin by looking at the composition of the U.S. population according to the U.S. Census Bureau. Then we will look at the sociological meaning of the word *minority* and discuss the concepts of prejudice and discrimination. We will also examine the available data on the socioeconomic position of U.S. minorities, particularly in relation to labor market discrimination and earnings. After discussing discrimination in detail, we will consider the various policies with which we try to eliminate prejudice and discrimination. Finally, we will consider other forms of discrimination, including residential and educational segregation.

The Diversity of the U.S. Population

The United States is becoming more diverse. Yet, our national heritage has *always* been one of diversity of race, ethnicity, and nationality. The Native American Indian population had developed a rich and varied culture before the first nonnative populations journeyed to this country. In the fifteenth and sixteenth centuries, white European settlers began arriving in the United States. They came in search of freedom and a better way of life. More recent immigrants have come for the same reasons. The preponderance of the most recent waves of immigrants has been from Asia and Latin America, but immigrants come from everywhere on the globe.

The data in Table 5-1 illustrate some of this rich diversity. The percentage of people belonging to various racial and ethnic groups is shown for the years 2000 and 2013. Bear in mind that the term *Hispanic* refers to people of Latin American ancestry and to an ethnicity as opposed to a race. In fact, Hispanics may be of any race, though the vast majority is white. For this reason, when we add up the shares of all racial groups in the population, we do not add on Hispanics, as this would take the total over 100 percent. In addition, we

TABLE 5-1 • Resident Population, Percent of Total Population, by Race and Hispanic Origin, July 2000 and July 2011

	2000[a]	2013[a]
Total	100%	100%
White	81.1%	77.7%
Non-Hispanic White	69.5%	62.6%
Hispanic[b]	12.5%	17.1%
African-American	12.7%	13.2%
Asian-American[c]	3.8%	5.5%
Native American[d]	0.9%	1.2%
Two or more races	1.4%	2.4%

[a]Percents do not add up to 100 because of rounding and the inclusion of Hispanics, which is not a racial group. All percents except for the last row are for people of one race only.
[b]Persons of Hispanic origin may be of any race.
[c]Asian-Americans include Native Hawaiian and other Pacific Islanders.
[d]Native Americans include Alaska natives.

Source: U.S. Department of Commerce, Census Bureau, Population Division, http://www.census.gov, 2015.

sometimes wish to know characteristics of the non-Hispanic white population, so that statistics are often given for all whites and for non-Hispanic whites separately.

The largest group of people is white, also called Caucasian, representing about 78 percent of the population in 2013. *The percentage of whites decreased substantially since 2000, indicating growing diversity in the population.*

Hispanics

By 2000, the Hispanic population rose to nearly tie with African-Americans as the largest minority group in our nation, as shown in Table 5-1. Their share of the population had literally exploded by 2013, when 17.1 percent of our population was Hispanic. (Many prefer the term *Latino* or *Latina* instead of *Hispanic*.) Census Bureau data indicate that by far the largest share is of Mexican origin. Many others are Puerto Rican, Cuban, and people with roots in Central and South America and the Caribbean Islands. The Hispanic population is highly concentrated in the southwestern states, with large shares living in Texas and California. Other states with high concentrations of Hispanic people include New Mexico, Arizona, New York, and Florida.[1]

African-Americans

African-Americans represent the largest *racial* minority in the United States. Their share of the total population is about 13 percent, an increase since 2000. Census Bureau information notes that the locations with the largest shares of African-Americans are the District of Columbia Mississippi, Louisiana, Georgia, Maryland, and South Carolina.

Asian-Americans

Asian-Americans represent 5.5 percent of the U.S. population, up substantially from 3.8 percent in 2000. Census Bureau information reveals that the largest share is Chinese. Other major groups are Asian-Indian, Filipino (from the Philippines), Vietnamese, Korean, and Japanese. The diversity among Asian-Americans is significant, since some groups (such as Chinese and Japanese) have been in the United States for a long time, and others (such as those from the Southeast Asian nations of Vietnam, Laos, and Thailand) have arrived more recently. The states with the highest shares of Asian-Americans are Hawaii, California, New Jersey, New York, Washington, and Nevada.

Native Americans

Native Americans make up the smallest of any racial group in Table 5-1, with 1.2 percent of the U.S. population. The share has increased slightly since 2000. The largest tribal groupings are the Cherokees, the Navajos, the Chippewa's, and the Sioux. The states with the largest shares of Native Americans are Alaska, New Mexico, South Dakota, Oklahoma, Montana, North Dakota, and Arizona.

Note that all of the racial groupings are for people of single race only. We also see that 2.4 percent of the U.S. population consists of people of two or more races. The shares of the U.S. population belonging to the various racial groups are displayed in Figure 5-1 on page 124. (Note that the figure does not include Hispanics, who represent an ethnicity.)

The Census Bureau provides other information on diversity, including fascinating information on the place of birth of our population (born in the United States vs. foreign born). You can discover the regions of the world from which our foreign-born populations come, and you can find out the ancestry of our population, from Arab to Welsh. The notes at the end of this chapter provide information on the Census Bureau Web site.

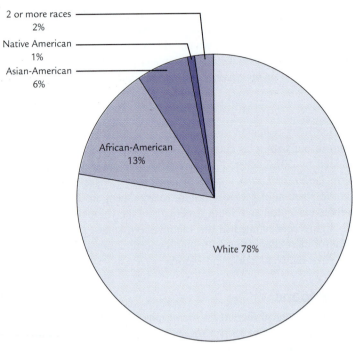

Figure 5-1 • Population of Racial Groups as a Share of the Total Population, 2013[a]

[a]Hispanics are not a racial group.

What Is a Minority?

Quite obviously, we are a racially and ethnically diverse population, even though white people outnumber any other group. Indeed, they outnumber all other groups added together. Numerically, nonwhite groups are minorities. But when we are speaking of racism, prejudice, and discrimination, it is perhaps wiser to use the sociological definition of the word minority, because we are speaking of a phenomenon that is central to that discipline. A **minority** is a group that has lesser access to positions of power, prestige, and status in a society. The term has little to do with numbers and everything to do with power. From this perspective, females, who outnumber males by several million, are a minority because they do not have equal access to positions of power.

Let's define a few other terms before we go on. **Prejudice** is the prejudgment of individuals or groups on the basis of stereotypes and hearsay, plus the refusal to acknowledge evidence that conflicts with such prejudgment. Prejudiced people might believe, for example, that all Hispanics are lazy; even though they may meet Latinos who are ambitious and conscientious workers, they hold fast to that belief by rationalizing that these ambitious people are the exceptions.

Prejudice is an internal attitude, but discrimination involves actions. **Discrimination** means treating people differently for arbitrary, often prejudicial, reasons. We discriminate if we do not rent to a Hmong family because they are Asian immigrants. We discriminate if we refuse to hire a qualified woman to fill a job formerly held by a man. Sociologists and psychologists have much to say about the types of prejudice and discrimination that exist in our world. They can explain the many causes of prejudice to us. I recommend that you take their courses to learn about these things. But some of the causes and many of the effects of

Minority
A group with less access to higher positions in society.

Prejudice
A prejudgment on the basis of stereotypes and hearsay, plus the refusal to consider evidence that conflicts with the prejudgment.

Discrimination
Action that treats individuals differently on the basis of some arbitrary characteristic.

discrimination are economic. Lower incomes, inferior education, higher rates of unemployment, poorer housing, and inadequate medical care may be consequences of discrimination. These are the things we wish to examine in this chapter.

Earnings and Income

Earnings and income are two different concepts. **Earnings** refer to income received in the form of wages and salaries from labor market activities (that is, from working). **Income**, on the other hand, is money received from all sources. It includes not only earnings, but also interest on savings accounts, dividends received on stock shares, rents received from ownership of property and land, welfare cash benefits, and so forth. By far, the largest share of total income in the United States is in the form of wages and salaries, and earnings are the principal source of income for most American families. We will focus our attention on earnings in the pages that follow. But let's first note that families and individuals with high earnings are more likely to save and make investments that will provide other forms of income than are low-earnings workers. In other words, high-income people are more likely than low-income people to receive income in other forms besides earnings from working.

Earnings
Money received from labor market activities.

Income
Money received from all sources.

Earnings Differentials and Discrimination

Earnings from labor markets depend on both the wage rate that the worker receives and the number of hours that the worker works. Your earnings are your wage rate times the hours you work. If your family (household) has two, or even three, persons working full time, you will have more earnings than a family with only one person working full time at the same wage rate. So, let's look at the earnings of full-time workers to eliminate both the effect of part-time workers and the effect of different numbers of workers in the household. Table 5-2 compares the median weekly earnings of full-time workers age 16 and older. (*Median* means middle, so that if we have a list of people's earnings from highest to lowest, median earnings are right in the middle of the list.) *Note that full-time working women earn less than that of full-time working men (83 percent), and full-time working African-Americans and Hispanics earn far less than full-time working white Caucasians.* (Asian-Americans earn *more* than white Caucasians.) The earnings differences are not proof of discrimination, although the pattern certainly makes one wonder what the causes of such large differences are.

TABLE 5-2 • Median Weekly Earnings of Full-Time Workers by Gender and Race and Ethnicity, Age 16 and Older, 2014

All	$791
Men	$871
Women	$719
White	$816
African-American	$639
Hispanic	$594
Asian-American	$953

Note: Based on these statistics, women earn 83 percent that of men; and African Americans earn 78 percent, Hispanics earn 73 percent, and Asian Americans earn 117 percent that of whites.

Source: Bureau of Labor Statistics, www.bls.gov/cps/cpsaat37.htm, 2015.

Several types of discrimination can affect labor market activities. Technically, labor market discrimination occurs when *like* workers are treated unequally on the basis of some arbitrary characteristic such as race, gender, or ethnicity. In the context of the labor market, *like* means "equally productive." It is not discrimination when college graduates earn more than high school graduates if the college graduates are more productive because they have developed job-related abilities to a greater extent than the high school graduates. It is not discrimination if a concert violinist has greater innate ability than the rest of us, and the labor market compensates her by paying her a premium for her talent. It *is* discrimination if two equally productive workers are treated differently because one is African-American and the other white or because one is female and the other male.

Workers can be treated differently in at least four ways that may affect their earnings. First, they may be paid different wage rates solely on the basis of some arbitrary characteristic. This practice is called **wage discrimination**. Second, they may be last hired and first fired in an economic downturn; hence, they will be unemployed more than other groups. This practice is called **employment discrimination**. (Employment discrimination can also include discriminatory promotion practices.) Third, workers may be prevented, or at least discouraged, from working in some fields and encouraged to work in others, resulting in separate white and nonwhite occupations and/or separate men's and women's occupations. This practice is called **occupational discrimination**. All of these types of discrimination directly affect earnings, and they all occur after the worker has entered the labor market. (One enters the labor market as soon as he or she begins to actively seek employment.)

The fourth type of discrimination is more indirect. It occurs before the worker's entry into the labor market, but it certainly influences how he or she fares in the labor market. This discrimination is **human capital discrimination**, or discrimination with respect to education or training. If some groups receive more education or better quality education than do others, members of these groups will be rewarded by the labor market for the skills and abilities that they have developed through education and they will have higher earnings than workers who are less educated.

Earnings and Education

Let's pose a related question. To what extent do earnings differences reflect differences in education? Let's consider earnings differentials for men and women first, and then for different racial and ethnic groups. Table 5-3 displays data showing average annual

Wage discrimination
Paying equally productive workers different wages on the basis of some arbitrary characteristic.

Employment discrimination
Not hiring certain workers on the basis of some arbitrary characteristic.

Occupational discrimination
Not hiring some groups of workers for particular jobs, resulting, for example, in men's jobs and women's jobs or minority jobs and white jobs.

Human capital discrimination
Anything that prevents certain groups from acquiring the level or quality of education or training to which other groups have access.

TABLE 5-3 • Average Annual Earnings of Full-Time Workers Age 25 Years and Older, by Highest Educational Attainment and Gender, in 2014

Attainment	Educational		
	Men	Women	Women/Men[a]
No high school diploma	$517	$409	79%
High school graduate	$751	$578	77%
Associate's degree or some college	$872	$661	76%
Bachelor's degree or higher	$1,385	$1,049	76%

[a]Women's average earnings as a share of men's average earnings.

Source: Bureau of Labor Statistics, www.bls.gov, 2015.

earnings of full-time workers age 25 years old and older, by highest educational attainment, in 2014. (Notice that Census Bureau data in this table are *average annual earnings* for workers age 25 and above, whereas in the previous table, statistics were *median weekly earnings* for people age 16 and above.) It is significant that we are comparing only full-time workers; otherwise earnings differentials might be because of women being more likely to work part time than men. In addition to earnings, the table shows the share of women's earnings relative to men's. First, we note that as was discussed in Chapter 4 on education, average annual earnings do increase along with educational attainment. This is true for men and women (as well as all racial and ethnic groups in Table 5-4). Second, we notice that women who receive a bachelor's degree or higher, for example, can be expected to receive annual earnings that are 76 percent of that of white men. Does this shock you? In fact, women at all levels of educational attainment earn considerably less than men.

When we compare earnings differentials for people of different races and ethnicities, as shown in Table 5-4, we see that for every educational level, African-Americans and Hispanics earn a smaller share of the earnings of white Caucasians. For example, African-Americans with a bachelor's degree receive on average only 79 percent of the earnings of white Caucasians. The disparity is smaller between

TABLE 5-4 • Median Weekly Earnings of Full Time Workers Age 25 Years and Older, by Highest Educational Attainment and Race and Ethnicity, in 2014

Educational Attainment	White	
No high school diploma	$493	
High school graduate	$696	
Some college or associate's degree	$791	
Bachelor's degree	$1,132	
	African-American	**African-American/White**
No high school diploma	$440	89%
High school graduate	$579	83%
Some college or associate's degree	$637	81%
Bachelor's degree	$895	79%
	Hispanic	**Hispanic/White**
No high school diploma	$466	95%
High school graduate	$595	85%
Some college or associate's degree	$689	87%
Bachelor's degree	$937	83%
	Asian-American	**Asian-American/White**
No high school diploma	$477	97%
High school graduate	$604	87%
Some college or associate's degree	$748	95%
Bachelor's degree	$1,149	101.5%

Source: Bureau of Labor Statistics, www.bls.gov, 2015.

Hispanics and whites. The disparity almost disappears when comparing Asian-Americans and whites, and Asian-Americans with an bachelor's degree actually earn more than whites.

Earnings and Unemployment

Your earnings will be lower if you have frequent periods of involuntary unemployment than if you are employed continually. To be considered unemployed, a person must be actively looking for work. The government then calculates the unemployment rate, which is the number of unemployed people as a percentage of the total number of people who are either working or actively seeking employment. Let's look at unemployment rates for African-Americans, Hispanics, Asian-Americans, and whites and for men and women. Table 5-5 shows these data for 2014. The overall unemployment rate for men (6.3 percent) is higher than for women (6.1 percent). This is not always the case, and they are frequently equal. However, some economists believe that subsequent to a recession (as is the case with these data), women experience less unemployment. Asian-Americans experience the lowest unemployment rates among all races. *But note especially that Hispanics experience higher rates of unemployment and African-Americans experience far higher rates of unemployment than do whites.* Year after year, the African-American unemployment rate is almost twice the white unemployment rate, and the Hispanic rate falls somewhere between the other two. Keep in mind that to be considered unemployed, you must be actively seeking employment. So, for one reason or other, these people are not being hired. One reason may be discrimination.

Earnings and Experience

More difficult to assess is the effect of experience on earnings. For example, even if we were to compare the earnings of full-time year-round working women and men with identical levels of education, it is likely that women will on average have less experience in the labor market. This is because women in our society may still be more likely to take time off from work to care for infants and young children. As a result, they may receive lower earnings than men.

TABLE 5-5 • Unemployment Rates by Gender, Race, and Hispanic Origin, Age 16 and Older, 2014, in Percent

	Male 2014	Female 2014
Total population	6.3	6.1
White	5.4	5.2
African-American	12.2	10.5
Hispanic	6.8	8.2
Asian-American	5.3	4.6

Source: U.S. Bureau of Labor Statistics, www.bls.gov/CPS, 2015.

Some Explanations of Discrimination

Some discrimination may be the result of prejudice, but it is also possible for some labor market discrimination to occur without any prejudice in the personal, malicious sense. Let's look at the issues of statistical discrimination and occupational crowding.

Statistical Discrimination

If an employer judges a prospective employee on the basis of the characteristics of the group she belongs to rather than on her own characteristics, the employer is practicing **statistical discrimination**. You will recognize this to be an example of employment discrimination as was just defined. For example, the employer might believe that a young woman is more likely to take a parental leave than a man is. Or the employer might believe that married women with children are absent more often than men because they will be the ones to stay home with sick children who cannot be taken to day care. He might believe that women are more likely than men to quit their jobs because their spouses are being transferred. And he might be right on average. He would not be right in each case, however, because individuals do not fit the characteristics of their group in every way. Many men take time off work to care for young children, and they often quit jobs to accompany wives who have been transferred.

But if the employer hires only men, he will on average avoid the characteristics to which he objects in the group. He will save money in the hiring process because screening individual applicants is expensive. So, he may see it as simply a good business decision to hire men for the position. Indeed, if the perceived differences between men and women are accurate, the discriminator's costs will be lower than a nondiscriminator's. Young women who would have been equally productive, or even more productive, than the men who are hired in the job are therefore discriminated against. The discriminating employer may pass over extremely productive women workers. Furthermore, if the average labor market characteristics of men and women converge over time, the cost savings from statistical discrimination will disappear.

Can you think of other examples of statistical discrimination? One example on the minds of young adults is the fact that many auto insurance companies charge higher premiums for young men than young women and for students with lower grade point averages than students with higher ones. This is because young men and students with lower grades can be shown statistically to have more automobile accidents. Nevertheless, the situation doesn't seem fair to you if you are a perfectly responsible and careful young man who receives poorer grades. And it *isn't* fair, but it still persists. Even though this isn't an example of job-related discrimination, it does demonstrate the idea of statistical discrimination.

Occupational Crowding

Occupational crowding occurs when there are white people's jobs and non-white people's jobs, or men's jobs and women's jobs in the economy. Let's focus on men and women. Refer again to Table 5-2. As we've noted, the data for men and women are striking. Why do women earn 83 percent that of men? In Table 5-3, why do we see that women with a bachelor's degree or higher earn 76 percent of men? The answer to these questions is, at least in part, that in the U.S. economy, some occupations are dominated by men and other occupations are dominated by women, and that men's occupations are more highly paid than women's. Although this is slowly changing, women are crowded into relatively few occupations, whereas men have more occupational choices. Women are a high percentage of our college-educated elementary schoolteachers and social workers. They dominate retail sales and the clerical fields. The reasons for this occupational segregation are complex. Some

Statistical discrimination
Judging an individual on the average characteristics of his or her group.

Occupational crowding
Crowding some groups of workers into a limited number of jobs.

women are in so-called women's fields because they have made a rational choice to take these jobs. It's what they have always wanted to do. Others are in such occupations because these traditional women's fields are the only ones they ever really considered working in or the only ones they have been encouraged to enter. Still others wind up in these fields because of discrimination against them in the fields in which they would rather work or because they lack the specific education to enter other vocations that they would prefer.

Figure 5-2 illustrates the effects of occupational crowding. Each graph represents a labor market that is similar to other markets we have examined. Instead of the quantity of tutors or drugs or education, the horizontal axis shows the quantity of labor (number of workers). The vertical axis shows the price of labor (the wage rate). The supply of labor shows the number of workers willing to work at various wage rates. The demand for labor shows the number of workers that employers are willing to hire at various wage rates.

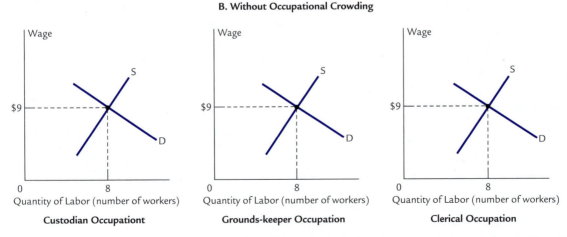

A. With Occupational Crowding

Custodian Occupationt — Quantity of Labor (number of workers) — $10, 100

Grounds-keeper Occupation — Quantity of Labor (number of workers) — $10, 100

Clerical Occupation — Quantity of Labor (number of workers) — $7, 200

If the 200 female workers are crowded into the clerical occupation, while the 200 male workers divided themselves between the custodian and grounds-keeper occupations, women will earn lower wages ($7) than men ($10).

B. Without Occupational Crowding

Custodian Occupationt — Quantity of Labor (number of workers) — $9, 8

Grounds-keeper Occupation — Quantity of Labor (number of workers) — $9, 8

Clerical Occupation — Quantity of Labor (number of workers) — $9, 8

If occupational crowding is eliminated, the 400 workers will be randomly distributed among the three occupations and they will earn the same wage ($9).

Figure 5-2 • Labor Markets With and Without Occupational Crowding

Assume that there are 400 workers in an economy consisting of your college and that one-half are men and one-half are women. Furthermore, there are three occupations at which the workers may work. Two of the occupations are traditionally men's jobs; let's assume they are custodians and grounds-keepers. One is traditionally a women's job, let's say clerical workers. If there is equal demand for workers in all three occupations, the demand curves will look like the ones in Figure 5-2. In the top panel (A) of Figure 5-2, we have occupational crowding, and all the women are crammed into the clerical positions, whereas the men are divided custodians and grounds-keepers. As a result, men earn higher wages than women. The disparity in earnings is because of women choosing (or being pushed into?) the clerical positions. In the bottom panel (B) of the figure, occupational crowding has been eliminated, and there are no men's or women's jobs. The 200 workers are randomly distributed throughout the labor markets, and because there is equal demand, there will be equal numbers in each of them. The wage rates will be equal.

Effects of Labor Market Discrimination

Some of the effects of discrimination are obvious; others are not. With discrimination, there are always gainers and losers. The groups with higher employment and higher earnings (whites and males) are obvious gainers. The groups with lower employment and earnings (minorities, including women) are losers. But there is another, less obvious loser, and that is our economy as a whole.

Effects on the Economy

Our national output will be reduced by discrimination because we are not using our labor force in the most efficient way possible. Hiring on the basis of arbitrary characteristics does not achieve maximum productivity. Figure 5-3 illustrates this concept using the same production possibilities curve that we developed in Chapter 1.

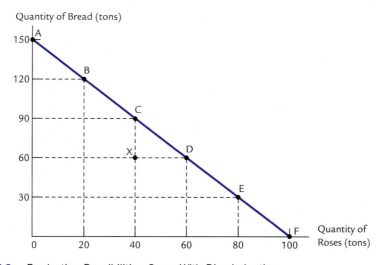

Figure 5-3 • Production Possibilities Curve With Discrimination
With discrimination, labor is not utilized as efficiently as possible, and the nation's output of bread and roses is at point X, below the production possibilities curve.

© Cengage Learning

As we discussed in Chapter 1, we are on the production possibilities curve only if we have full and efficient employment of society's resources. With discrimination, we are at some point such as X below the production possibilities curve. We are not achieving our maximum potential national output of bread and roses because we are inefficiently utilizing the labor of the economy. Qualified workers are unemployed or working below their potential. Failure to fully employ women and minorities to their potential results in billions of dollars of lost gross domestic product each year. Thus, discrimination hurts our economy as well as individuals within it.

Effects on Individuals

The effects of labor market discrimination on the employment and earnings of women and other minorities can be extensive. For example, if we look at various measures of socioeconomic well-being, we can see that the same groups that are discriminated against in labor markets occupy an inferior position with respect to other aspects of their lives. For example, racial and ethnic minorities, families headed by single women, and older women have much higher poverty rates than non-minorities, families headed by single men, and older men. As we will see in Chapter 6, African-Americans and Hispanics have a poverty rate two and one-half to almost three times that of the white non-Hispanic population, and single-female-headed families have a poverty rate almost two times the poverty rate for single-male-headed families. We will also see that minority groups of people face restricted home ownership housing and segregation (Chapter 7) and less access to adequate health care (Chapter 8). As a result, for example, African-Americans and Native Americans have much higher infant death rates than whites. We have also seen in Chapter 4 that minority groups have fewer opportunities for quality education in the United States. These are the very inequities warned about in the 1968 Kerner report.

Problems in Measuring Labor Market Discrimination

Such systematic patterns as those revealed by the statistics presented earlier certainly raise questions about the presence of discrimination on the basis of gender, race, and ethnicity. But some of the disparities may be attributed to alternative factors. Some economists argue that many of the differences are the result of rational choice, not discrimination. Let us look at this viewpoint before we go on.

Rational Individual Choice

Some economists and sociologists argue that women choose so-called women's occupations because these are complementary to their primary roles as mothers and wives. The skills learned to teach other people's children to read can be utilized within one's own family. The same is true of nursing skills. Therefore, the selection of a traditional women's occupation may be the result of rational choice, not discrimination. In the same way, some women may choose to take the "mommy track" within the corporate structure, avoiding the high-level promotions that take too much time away from family. Of course, men may choose the "daddy track" as well.

Moreover, the decision not to finish high school may consign a minority worker to low-wage, dead-end jobs throughout his or her life, but it can be argued that this decision was a conscious choice that he or she made. (It can also be argued that this was not wholly a deliberate choice.) Lower earnings caused by unfortunate past choices might not be categorized by all as discrimination. In all of these cases, it is difficult, if not impossible, to determine how much of the earnings differential is the result of rational choices and how much is because of discrimination.

Choice, Discrimination, and Culture Intermingled

Other people question whether either women or minorities make truly independent choices. Culture and tradition play a large part in our lives. We give little girls dolls and dollhouses and we give boys building sets. Children still appear to leave elementary school believing that boys are good at math and girls are good at English. How much truly individual choice do young women have?

Furthermore, discrimination may be a cause of decisions that, having been made, affect earnings and incomes. If a minority youth sees that his older relatives who finished high school are frequently unemployed and appear to find jobs only near the minimum wage, he will have less incentive to finish high school. If a young woman believes that she will be discriminated against if she trains for the sciences, she will be far more likely to train as an elementary schoolteacher. In short, discrimination can be both a cause and an effect.

Keep in mind, though, that much of this discussion has assumed that women and men continue to undertake traditional roles and values, when in fact these traditions are changing. It is more and more common to find men caring for children, staying home when the children are sick, seeking out jobs as nurses and elementary school teachers, and so on. And, of course, many women are choosing the opposite. To place too much emphasis on traditional expectations for women and men would be a mistake.

Individual choice, discrimination, and culture are intermingled to produce the results we have discussed. All the disparities are not attributable to discrimination, but some portion of them is. The controversy revolves around how large this portion is.

Policies to Eliminate Labor Market Discrimination

The government can, and does, act to reduce discrimination. Some policies involve direct intervention in markets, whereas others involve indirect intervention. Let's begin with direct labor market policies. Many such policies are a legacy of the civil rights movement of the 1960s. Among these are the following notable pieces of legislation.

The Equal Pay Act of 1963

This landmark antidiscrimination law made it illegal for an employer to pay men and women different wage rates for doing the same job. The law was therefore an important policy against gender discrimination. Prior to its passing, the practice of paying women less than men who did the same job was common; it was justified on the traditional basis that men were the breadwinners of families, whereas women were mainly secondary earners in the family.

Although this important piece of legislation ended the practice of unequal pay, it clearly did not end all gender discrimination. It certainly had no impact on the occupational segregation that persists in the United States. As long as a hospital pays all its licensed practical nurses, male and female, the same wage rate for doing the same job, it is behaving in a lawful manner. But if employees in this traditionally female occupation are poorly paid in comparison to automobile mechanics, the Equal Pay Act will not address that issue.

The Civil Rights Act of 1964

This law is the most important antidiscrimination statute we have. It not only makes discriminatory compensation (including fringe benefits) illegal, but it also forbids discrimination in hiring, promoting, and firing. Furthermore, it is broader in coverage than the Equal Pay Act. It forbids discrimination on the basis of race, gender, color, religion, or national origin. The law applies to all employers with 15 or more workers engaged in interstate commerce, to all labor unions with 15 or more members, and to all workers employed by educational institutions and by state, local, and federal government. The Civil Rights Act created the Equal Employment Opportunity Commission (EEOC), which administers it.

Affirmative Action in Employment

Affirmative action
Efforts to provide equal opportunities in terms of employment and education to underrepresented groups of people.

In 1965 and 1968, executive orders intended to stop discrimination by firms that do business with the federal government were issued. These orders require that all federal contractors whose contracts exceed a specified dollar level develop **affirmative action** programs. The term implies that firms should be able to demonstrate that they are not discriminating. If, on examination, it is found that a firm under-employs women and minorities, numerical goals to increase the representation of these groups must be established. The objective is for the firm's workforce to reflect the demographics of the available labor force. If the firm is a law practice and 25 percent of the lawyers in the area are women, the firm should strive to hire so that eventually 25 percent of its lawyers are female. However, if there is a lack of qualified applicants, the law is waived.

Quotas
Rigid numerical requirements in hiring.

Affirmative action programs have been controversial since their inception. Critics argue that they have resulted in **quotas**, or rigid numerical proportions of jobs held for minorities and women. These jobs, they argue, are filled with little regard for the workers' qualifications. This criticism is not valid, however, since the Supreme court outlawed quotas a long time ago. Still others argue that affirmative action has resulted in **tokenism**, or the hiring of certain workers solely to demonstrate an attempt to comply with affirmative action. These critics regard affirmative action as a system of preferences that results in **reverse discrimination** against white males. This is not the intent of affirmative action, however, and it misleads people into unwarranted opposition to affirmative action.

Tokenism
Hiring minorities to comply with affirmative action, not for their abilities.

Reverse discrimination
Discrimination against white males.

On the other hand, affirmative action proponents argue that affirmative action is the only way to end historical patterns of discrimination, and that it is justifiable to give preference now to groups that have historically been discriminated against. They point out the disparities in earnings of various ethnic, racial, and gender groups and maintain that affirmative action is necessary to narrow these gaps over time. They also maintain that diversity in the workforce is a positive thing in and of itself.

As you undoubtedly know, the Supreme Court interprets our laws. All laws must conform to the U.S. Constitution. The Supreme Court upheld the constitutionality of job-related affirmative action programs in a series of important decisions in the mid-1980s. More recently, however, Supreme Court decisions have seemed to chip away at affirmative action. The Court declared illegal a program to set aside a portion of the construction work of the city of Richmond, Virginia, for minority-owned firms. It also permitted certain public employees to challenge existing affirmative action programs on the basis of reverse discrimination. Affirmative action appears to be under legal attack as you read this.

Some economists argue that direct government intervention in labor markets, such as affirmative action, is unnecessary, or even harmful. Nobel laureates Milton Friedman and Gary Becker both argued that the employer who hires on any basis other than efficiency, which means finding the most productive worker for the job, will be at a competitive disadvantage compared with other employers. They argue that discriminating employers have higher costs than non-discriminators, so eventually they will be driven from the market. Direct intervention in labor markets, they argue, is therefore unnecessary.

Thomas Sowell, a conservative African-American economist, goes still further. He argues that government intervention in favor of disadvantaged groups actually hurts these groups. He cites as an example the Native American. Sowell states that Native Americans have the longest relationship (as a ward of the state) with the federal government of any of our minorities, and Native Americans are consistently at the very bottom of our economic ladder. Sowell argues that minorities such as Japanese-Americans, who were not favored by the government, have succeeded far better than the recipients of the government's largesse.

Other economists argue that labor markets clearly have neither solved the problem of discrimination nor, for that matter, even made substantial progress toward eliminating discrimination. Nor do they believe that discriminators are necessarily at a cost disadvantage. Instead, they note that statistical discrimination probably results in short-run cost savings. Therefore, they argue that we need programs such as affirmative action. They propose that programs directed at the supply side of the labor market are especially needed. Affirmative action is now directed at the demand side of the market, or at the business firm that hires and promotes. Supply-side efforts would attempt to supply these employers with workers who have the proper education and skills for the positions available. What, they ask, is the advantage of an employer's willingness to hire female auditors if none are available? Therefore, training women and minorities so that they can supply the needed skills is important. They argue, for example, that we need more female economics majors to fill opening economic positions and that we should be concerned about women's access to such education.

Affirmative action is the subject of extensive political debate. Opponents argue that a "system of preferences" is no longer necessary because our national values, as well as our laws, have changed so as to prevent discrimination from occurring. Others disagree. Still others feel that affirmative action programs should be targeted more carefully toward disadvantaged groups. It is quite likely that the debate over affirmative action programs will continue well into the future.

Indirect Labor Market Policies

The government can also work in less direct ways to reduce labor market discrimination. For example, improving educational opportunities for racial and ethnic minorities and women will put them in a better position vis-à-vis the labor market. We will discuss this momentarily. Furthermore, many low-income workers with families have child-care problems, which can be alleviated by subsidized day care programs. Many families also lack reliable transportation, and mass transit is often inconvenient or unavailable. Since many jobs have shifted from central cities to the suburbs, central-city residents without adequate transportation may remain unemployed as a result. Indeed, Dr. Martin Luther King, Jr., maintained that public transportation was a civil rights issue.

Maintaining a healthy economy through appropriate fiscal and monetary policies also can be construed as an antidiscrimination policy. A healthy economy implies job opportunities. If there is a relative surplus of job openings compared to workers, employers cannot afford to discriminate. The truly tight labor markets during World War II opened windows of opportunity for many female and minority workers.

Finally, other government policies can indirectly affect labor markets. For example, recent welfare reform that focuses on work requirements has made it extremely difficult for low-income single mothers to acquire college degrees. This often means that these women will remain in low-skilled, low-wage occupations indefinitely.

Other Forms of Discrimination

Although our discussion has focused primarily on labor market discrimination and its effects, there are certainly other forms of discrimination that are equally onerous and are, in fact, linked to labor market discrimination. These forms of discrimination include residential and educational segregation.

Recall from Chapter 4 that the quality of public schools varies considerably, in large part because of the way that public education is financed in our country. In short, low-income residential areas often end up with poorer-quality schools. Insofar as these schools are typically located in racially segregated central-city neighborhoods, minority children often receive a poorer-quality education than nonminority children. Thus, residential and educational segregation lead to lower-wage-paying jobs, higher unemployment rates, and unequal opportunities for minorities. Some children bear additional problems linked to education and residence, and sometimes to poverty. These include children of immigrants, children of migrant farm workers, children in homeless families, children of parents with addictive disorders, and children in violent situations. The instability in these families makes education difficult, at best.

Residential Segregation

Residential segregation institutionalizes discrimination. As nonminority populations have fled to the suburbs, minority residents often remain trapped in central cities. Still, many large urban areas of the South have had metropolitan-wide desegregation plans since the early 1970s. For example, two Supreme Court orders in the 1970s created mandatory desegregation across the entire metropolitan areas of Wilmington, Delaware, and Louisville, Kentucky. These orders have produced much higher levels of integration throughout the two states.

In contrast, the Supreme Court's 1974 Detroit decision in *Milliken v. Bradley* blocked desegregation across Detroit's metropolitan population. The central city was to desegregate separately from the suburban fringe. The ruling prevented effective desegregation, and Detroit became one of the nation's most segregated metropolitan areas. With a high concentration of racial minorities within many of our country's central cities, and a high concentration of whites in the suburbs, desegregation must be carried out at the metropolitan level. As a result of the precedent set, as well as a failure of political action on the issue, little or no progress has been made toward residential desegregation since 1974.

A Harvard study based on the 2000 census indicates that people still live in largely segregated neighborhoods.[2] The researchers found that between 1990 and 2000, whites, African-Americans, Asians, and Hispanics still tend to live apart. In particular, the average white person living in a metropolitan area (including central cities and suburbs) lives in a neighborhood that is about 80 percent white. Recent Census Bureau data indicate that very segregated metropolitan areas for African-Americans and whites include Detroit, Cleveland, St. Louis, and Newark. Highly segregated metropolitan areas for Hispanics and whites include New York, Newark, Los Angeles, Chicago, and Philadelphia. One factor that may help to reduce segregation is the recent renovation of some central cities, which is expected to draw more white people into the inner cities. Residential segregation is discussed in more detail in Chapter 8 on housing.

Educational Segregation

It has been over 50 years since the U.S. Supreme Court struck down the "separate but equal" doctrine in *Brown v. Topeka Board of Education* (1954). In that case, the Court ruled that segregated schools were in fact unequal and did irreparable harm to minority children. Since then, our country has proceeded to integrate its schools at a pace that varies by state and region.

Evidence indicates that large-scale school desegregation works not only to improve objective measures of achievement such as test scores but also to increase the probability of college attendance. It also positively affects type of college, college major, and types of employment as an adult. Research by the University of Chicago's Metropolitan Opportunity Project, however, shows an extremely strong pattern of continued educational segregation for African-Americans and increasing segregation for Hispanics in our central cities. Furthermore, minority high schools in almost all cases have large numbers of low-income students. There are strong positive correlations between predominantly minority schools, high proportions of poor children, and low educational achievement. Far too many African-American and Hispanic students are trapped in schools where dropout rates are high and opportunities for success minimal.[3]

Certainly, residential and educational segregation are linked. People living in segregated neighborhoods are likely to attend segregated neighborhood schools. In turn, students who attend poor-quality segregated schools are more likely to eventually receive lower wages and experience higher unemployment rates. Furthermore, these people are more likely to live in poverty. **What this all means is that equal opportunity in education is essential for overcoming decades of disadvantage.** As discussed in Chapter 4, a better way of financing our nation's public primary and secondary education must be found, and segregation must be eliminated. In addition, the issue of affirmative action in higher education must be addressed.

Affirmative Action in Education

The issue of affirmative action in college and university admissions has been a politically volatile one, particularly during the administration of President George W. Bush. Early in 2003, the Bush administration argued in a brief to the Supreme Court that the University of Michigan gives unconstitutional preferences to African-American, Hispanic, and Native American applicants. The Bush administration argued, "At the core, the Michigan policies amount to a quota system that unfairly rewards or penalizes prospective students based solely on their race." This statement drew immediate criticism from higher education officials and civil rights leaders. Even Colin Powell, Bush's secretary of state at the time, disagreed with him on the matter. Dozens of large Fortune 500 businesses, including Microsoft, Intel, American Airlines, and Proctor & Gamble, also disagreed with the president. According to James Hackett, chief executive officer of Steelcase Corporation, "If you're going to be a global company and you're going to attract and retain the best people, then the mirror you have to present is that you're a very diverse company."

In mid-2003, the U.S. Supreme Court ruled simultaneously on two University of Michigan cases, one for graduate admissions (the law school) and the other for undergraduate admissions. In the case of the law school, the Supreme Court stated that race can be used as a factor in university admission decisions, and that indeed "a diverse student body has its own benefits." However, the Court also ruled that in the undergraduate case, a more rigid system relying on specific points given to students based on their race and ethnicity is not constitutional. The University of Michigan cases were the first tests of affirmative action in college admissions since the famous 1978 *Bakke* decision, which invalidated racial quotas. As mentioned in Chapter 4, the constitutionality of the Michigan case allowing diversity to be used as a factor in school admissions was affirmed by the Supreme Court in 2013. In other words, they affirmed the concept of affirmative action in college admissions. Continued controversy, however, means that the Supreme Court will again address affirmative action.

As the diversity of our population increases, we will naturally turn our faces toward a broader exposure to other cultures. The movement toward multiculturalism in our schools and colleges reflects the changes in our broader society. Schools attempt to reflect the diversity of the population in their faculty and students. The purpose of the multicultural teaching methods and materials is to spread greater knowledge of other cultures. An important objective of multiculturalism is to increase the respect with which we treat people of all races, genders, and ethnicities.

A Final Note

In June 2013, the Supreme Court struck down a section of the Voting Rights Act that had established a formula for the federal government to use in blocking state voting laws that the Department of Justice thought were racially discriminatory. This ruling was unexpected and shocked many people—many of whom believe that states will use the ruling to establish discriminatory voting legislation. It remains to be seen how states will respond and whether Congress will pass legislation to prevent such discrimination from taking place.

You, the Student

Do you think you have ever been a victim of discrimination? If so, you can check out the Equal Employment Opportunity Commission home page at http://www.eeoc.gov. This Web site provides information on how to charge an employer with violation of equal opportunities laws. What is the basis for your view that you have been discriminated against (age, gender, race, etc.)?

In addition, we can reduce racism and intolerance in more personal ways. After the publicity surrounding the Sigma Alpha Epsilon video mentioned earlier, the University of Oklahoma's president called on all people to have zero-tolerance towards racism. Any time you see or hear such a video, tweet, Facebook entry, or racist joke or comment, challenge it. It is only on this personal level that people learn that racism, and indeed all forms of intolerance and bullying, are unacceptable.

View*Point*   Conservative versus Liberal

Many conservatives argue that the remaining disparities between the earnings of minorities and whites and between those of women and men are the result of rational choice, not discrimination. They point out that gaps between these groups have narrowed somewhat since the 1960s. Conservatives oppose government intervention in markets, including labor markets. They see affirmative action as misguided and a source of great inefficiency. They believe that changing social values and the passage of antidiscrimination laws have alleviated the problem of discrimination and that affirmative action is no longer needed.

Liberals believe that government programs have done some good but that they have not completely solved the problem of discrimination. Therefore, they see a need to continue affirmative action programs. They see great value in diversity of the workplace and educational institutions, and they are committed to overcoming the results of decades of unequal treatment of minorities. In addition, they often propose alternatives to property tax financing of public education, which creates inequality in education and thereby denies equal opportunity to all residents of our nation.

Summary

The United States has a rich diversity of people of different races and ethnicities, including those who are Hispanic, African-American, Asian-American, and Native American. This diversity will continue to grow in the near future. The quality of life for people of minority races, however, may be substantially below that of white Americans. Furthermore, women are in a position similar to most racial and ethnic minorities. All face lower earnings and a greater likelihood of poverty, with all the implications that lower income and poverty have for health, housing, and education.

Labor market discrimination consists of wage discrimination, employment discrimination, occupational discrimination, and human capital discrimination. All of these can result in earnings differentials between minority and nonminority groups even when educational levels are constant. Some of the wage differentials may be caused by statistical discrimination and occupational choice. Besides labor market discrimination, discrimination exists in the form of residential and educational segregation. Affirmative action has become an important though controversial tool to reduce labor market and educational discrimination.

The past 50 years have seen changes in our legal environment. Many overtly discriminatory practices are now illegal. But the relative positions of minorities and whites are still greatly unequal. Reduced discrimination and segregation in our society would increase our economy's efficiency and benefit us all. Multiculturalism enhances the richness of our society and experience.

Discussion and Action Questions

1. Go to the Census Bureau Web site (http://www.census.gov), scroll to "Population Finder," and type in your home town to find out its population size. Continue to navigate the Web site to see if you can find recent data on the diversity of the U.S. population. Has it changed much from the data in this textbook?

2. Is it possible to be a member of a minority when, in fact, your group has greater numbers than another group? Can you think of any examples besides the one from the text?

3. What factors explain the disparities in earnings between men and women? Minorities and whites? Are the factors different for race and gender?

4. What is the relationship between education and earnings? Does this relationship explain all the earnings differences among various groups? Why or why not?

5. Explain statistical discrimination. Do you think such discrimination is widespread? Can you think of any examples besides the ones mentioned in the text?

6. Do you think occupational crowding is widespread? Is the pressure for young women to enter traditional women's fields as great as it used to be? If you are a young woman, will you be entering a traditional women's field when you graduate? Did your mother work in a traditional field?

7. Affirmative action began in the late 1960s. It has been accused of amounting to reverse discrimination. Do the data in the chapter support this view?

8. Do you believe in affirmative action? Can you support your opinion with rational analysis and explanation?

9. In the nineteenth century, secretaries were generally male, and the occupation was prestigious and well paid. Is this true today? Can you explain the change in attitudes?

10. Why is measuring the extent of discrimination in our culture so difficult?

11. Visit the Web site for the Bureau of Labor statistics at http://www.bls.gov. How do the statistics on unemployment rates vary for people of different gender, race, and ethnicity? What are some reasons for the differences? Is it possible that some of the people who are classified as unemployed are simply too lazy to search for a job? (*Hint:* Keep in mind how the Bureau of Labor defines unemployment.)

12. Can you find information on the 2003 U.S. Supreme Court decisions about affirmative action on the Web site at http://www.affirmativeaction.org? How do the rulings distinguish between the University of Michigan Law School and its undergraduate program?

13. What are the goals and philosophy of the American Association for Affirmative Action (http://www.affirmativeaction.org).

Notes

1. All data in this section are from the U.S. Department of Commerce, Census Bureau, http://www.census.gov. Unless otherwise indicated, other data in this chapter are from the same source.

2. The Civil Rights Project, Harvard University, http://www.law.harvard.edu.

3. Much of this material is taken from Gary Orfield, "Have the Kerner Warnings Come True?" in *Quiet Riots*, ed. Fred R. Harris and Roger W. Wilkins (New York: Pantheon, 1988).

Chapter 6

ROAD MAP

Chapter 4
Education
The financing of elementary and secondary education results in less access to and poorer quality of education for the poor

Chapter 5
Discrimination
People of racial, ethnic, and gender groups that are subject to discrimination face higher poverty rates

Chapter 7
Housing
The poor are more likely to be homeless or live in substandard overcrowded housing

Chapter 6
U.S. Poverty

Chapter 8
Health Care
The poor are more likely to lack health care and to experience poor health

Chapter 14
Unemployment and Inflation
Those groups with higher unemployment rates are more likely to be poor

Chapter 10
World Poverty
The poor in the United States and in the rest of the world face some similar problems

The Economic Toolbox

- Relative poverty
- Absolute poverty
- Income distribution
- Poverty line
- Poverty rates
- Incidence of poverty
- Feminization of poverty

- Recession
- Investment in human capital
- Universal entitlements
- Negative income tax
- Economic disincentives
- Trickle-down philosophy
- Lorenz curve (appendix)

U.S. Poverty

Most of us are concerned about the poor, but we tend to think that poverty is not a problem that will ever affect us personally. We picture the poor as people in central cities, possibly women with too many children or people whose families have always been dependent on welfare. The poor live on the reservations or in the hills of Appalachia or on the urban streets. We imagine that the poor are drug addicts or alcoholics. They are mentally or physically ill or disabled. They are the very old or the very young. But they are never one of us.

These stereotypes are misleading. Many poor adults are people much like us. They are people who never imagined they would some day be poor. They are people like the single mother in the chapter introduction. They are people who have become poor as a result of some life crisis: the loss of a job, the death or desertion of a spouse, an unplanned pregnancy, or an unexpected illness. These are normal events that could alter the lives of any of us.

As of 2013, 14.5 percent of the total U.S. population, were poor by government definition.[2] This means that they lived in a household with total cash income falling below some level that is considered necessary to satisfy their basic needs. Poverty in the midst of plenty is an issue of equity. Recall from Chapter 1 that our market-based economy tends to be efficient, though not necessarily equitable. The poverty statistics appear large for one of the richest countries of the world. But what do the numbers mean? Who are these poor? And what can be done about the problem of poverty in the United States?

There are two ways to look at poverty. One is by considering **relative poverty**—a situation in which people are poor in comparison to other people. The other is by considering **absolute poverty**—a situation in which people experience actual hardship according to some objective criterion. We will consider both of these in turn, beginning with relative poverty.

Relative Poverty

Because relative poverty focuses on comparisons among people in different income classes, the standard measure of relative poverty is income distribution.

I went to college so that I can earn a living wage for my children and me. I want my children to play safely and have an opportunity to be educated. I want to raise socially responsible, morally responsible and psychologically sound children who are capable of coping and dealing with society and its ills. They must have a mother who isn't totally stressed out over every penny so that when clothes are accidentally ruined I don't flip out over how I am going to provide for that expense and rip unjustly on the unfortunate child. This comes with a livable income.

—FROM IN OUR OWN WORDS: MOTHERS' PERSPECTIVES ON WELFARE REFORM[1]

Relative poverty
A situation in which
people are poor in
comparison to other
people.

Absolute poverty
A situation in which
people experience the
hardship of poverty
according to some
objective criterion.

Income distribution
The division of total
income in an economy
among people of different
income groups.

Money income
All household income
from any source,
including income
transfers, calculated
before taxes.

Income transfer
A cash transfer from
the government to an
individual for which
no good or service is
provided to the
government in return.

In-kind transfers
Transfers of goods or
services (or access to
goods or services) from
the government to an
individual for which
no good or service is
provided to the
government in return.

Measuring Relative Poverty

Income distribution refers to the division of total income in the economy among different income groups. Statistics on income distribution are based on the U.S. Census Bureau concept of **money income**: that is, all household income received from working, interest, rent, dividends, or any other source before payment of taxes. Included as money income is any government **income transfers**, such as Social Security payments, veterans' cash benefits, and unemployment compensation. Not counted as part of money income, however, are **in-kind transfers**, which are government transfers of goods or services (or direct access to these goods or services) such as food stamps, health care, housing assistance, and free legal aid.

For the purpose of analyzing income distribution, the total population of the country is ranked according to income and then divided into fifths. That is, the percentage of total money income going to the poorest 20 percent of the population is determined, as well as that going to the second-poorest 20 percent of the population, and so on. If income was distributed perfectly equally, each 20 percent of the population would receive 20 percent of total money income. Table 6-1 indicates that income distribution in the United States is far from equal, with the richest one-fifth of the American population receiving over one-half of all money income in the country in the latest year for which data are available (2013). The poorest group received only 3.5 percent of the total. Income distribution is also displayed for the year 1981.

Trend in the U.S. Distribution of Income

Income distribution in the United States is becoming increasingly unequal. Comparisons between 1981 and 2013 in Table 6-1 indicate that the poorest four-fifths of the population have seen their share of total money income decrease, whereas the richest one-fifth has enjoyed an increased income share. In a relative sense, the rich are becoming richer, while the poor are becoming poorer. The year 1981 was chosen as a comparison year, as this year began a series of policy changes put into effect by the Reagan administration and subsequently the George W. Bush administration that had the effect of creating a less equal income distribution

It is important to point out that a perfectly equal income distribution is not necessarily the ideal. Most people, economists included, argue that some degree of income inequality is essential to preserve incentives. If you didn't think you would eventually have a higher income, you might have no incentive to work hard, study well, invest wisely, take necessary risks in business, and so on. Productivity and economic efficiency would suffer. On the other hand, many people also argue that income distribution can be too unequal. Poor

TABLE 6-1 • Distribution of Total Money Income in the United States by Fifths of the Total Population, 1981 and 2013

Fraction of Total Households	Percentage of Total Money Income Received (%)	
	1981	**2013**
Poorest fifth	5.0	3.5
Second fifth	11.3	9.1
Third fifth	17.4	14.9
Fourth fifth	24.4	22.9
Richest fifth	41.9	49.6

Source: U.S. Department of Commerce, Census Bureau, Economics and Statistics Administration, http://www.census.gov, 2015.

people may have very little incentive to try to move up the income ladder when their income is so low and the odds of reaching the top are so poor. Poverty also results in poor health and nutrition, which may sap energy and harm labor productivity. We've also noted that poverty is associated with poorer quality education, which also harms productivity. Finally, the argument goes, inequality of income to the degree experienced in the United States is hardly necessary to provide adequate incentives to work and produce.

As we begin to think of the reasons why income distribution has become less equal since 1981, we need to recognize that certain factors *have not* played a direct role. Important changes in our nation's tax system since 1981, for example, served to place more income into the hands of upper-income people. This is especially true of the major tax cuts under President Ronald Reagan in the 1980s and President George W. Bush in the 2000s. These changes in the nation's tax system do not directly affect the Census Bureau statistics on income distribution, however, because these statistics are based on money income. (Recall that money income is calculated *before* payment of taxes.) Similarly, changes in certain government in-kind transfers since 1981 do not alter statistics on the income distribution because the value of food stamps and other such transfers are also excluded from the calculation of money income. Thus, although changes in taxes and government in-kind transfers to the poor will indeed alter the well-being of people, they will not directly affect the statistics on income distribution.

Other factors must account for the changes in income distribution observed in these data. One of these factors would be the *indirect* effect of tax cuts for the rich. **Although the higher after-tax income that results from the tax cuts does not show up in the income statistics, certainly higher incomes permit greater financial investment by the rich, thereby indirectly raising their future incomes.** One other obvious factor affecting the changes in income distribution is structural change in the economy. The loss of blue-collar manufacturing jobs and the creation of low-wage service-sector jobs characterize such change. We will consider these matters shortly when we turn to the topic of absolute poverty. But first let's compare income distributions across different countries.

International Comparisons

It is interesting to compare statistics on income distributions across different countries. The task is complicated, however, by the fact that data are not always accurate or comparable. Furthermore, statistics on income distribution for other countries of the world are often not calculated as frequently as for the United States. Nevertheless, the World Bank does provide some such information. *These numbers suggest that the United States has the least-equal income distribution of all the Western industrialized nations for which data are available.* (Of the remaining nations, including the developing countries, many have greater equality and many have less equality of income distribution than the United States.)[3]

Finally, graphs can be used to compare the income distribution in one country over different time periods or to compare income distributions of two countries. These graphs are discussed in the appendix to this chapter.

Absolute Poverty

Because the poor are on the lower rungs of the income distribution ladder, the concepts of relative poverty and absolute poverty are intricately linked. Recall that absolute poverty refers to a situation in which people experience actual hardship according to some objective criterion.

Measuring Absolute Poverty in the United States

Poverty line
A level of income below which a household is considered poor.

The **poverty line** is the official criterion for determining absolute poverty. The poverty line is simply a level of household income that delineates an amount considered adequate to cover basic needs for survival: food, clothing, housing, and so on. The concept of money income that was used in the statistics on income distribution is used in calculating poverty statistics as well. The poverty line is adjusted for family size. Larger families have a higher poverty line. If household money income falls below the poverty line, all members of the household are considered poor.

Meaning of the Poverty Line

It is important to realize that the concept of official poverty is not a measure of those who would be poor in the absence of government income transfers, because money income *does* include these cash transfers. Rather, the official poverty statistics include all of those people who are poor *despite* these transfers. It is equally important to realize that official poverty does not necessarily confer eligibility for government programs, either now or in the past. States may require that families have income much lower than the federal poverty line to qualify for certain welfare programs. Official poverty reflects a statistical measure only.

Life at the Poverty Line

Consider the implications of life at the poverty line. Imagine that you live in a family of four, and household money income is at the 2013 poverty line of $23,834. Assuming that your family spends one-seventh of its income on food, your family would have $3,405 for food and the remaining $20,429 for all other expenditures for the year. Each person would have an average of $16.37 per week, or $2.34 per day for food. Have you tried to live on that? The family as a whole would have $1,702 per month to cover rent, fuel, utilities, insurance, transportation (including auto maintenance), clothing, medical and dental needs, educational expenses, entertainment, and taxes. Existence at the poverty line is frugal, to say the least.

Trends in Poverty Statistics

Poverty rate
The percentage of the population that is poor.

A comparison of poverty statistics over recent years shows fairly dramatic trends. When measuring the number of poor people as a percentage of the total population, poverty was very extensive up until 1960, when the **poverty rate** was 22.2 percent (see Table 6-2). (Certainly, the nostalgia that many people have for the 1950s is misguided. The "wonder years" were not so wonderful for the fifth of our population that was poor.) However, this poverty rate declined substantially throughout the 1960s and the early

TABLE 6-2 • Poverty Rates: The Percentage of the Population Living Below the Poverty Line, Selected Years 1960–2013

Date	Poverty Rate (%)	Date	Poverty Rate (%)
1960	22.2	2000	11.3
1970	12.6	2005	12.6
1973	11.1	2010	15.0
1980	13.0	2011	15.0
1983	15.2	2012	15.0
1990	13.5	2013	14.5

Source: U.S. Department of Commerce, Census Bureau, http://www.census.gov, 2015.

1970s with the economic prosperity of the period, as well as the antipoverty programs that began with the Kennedy and Johnson administrations. The national poverty rate reached a low of 11.1 percent of the total population in 1973, and then climbed to 13.0 percent in 1980. The poverty rate rose to 15.2 percent by 1983, reflecting the poor economy of the early 1980s and the Reagan-era budget cuts. Poverty rates declined since 1990, reaching a recent low of 11.3 percent in 2000. The latter period corresponds to one of the longest periods of steady economic growth in U.S. history. Unfortunately, as a result of the subsequent poor economy, the U.S. poverty rate rose to 15 percent in 2010 through 2012. As the economy began recovering, the poverty rate fell to 14.5 percent in 2013 and will presumably continue to fall. *A national poverty rate close to 15 percent is certainly very troublesome.*

The Incidence of Poverty

Equally important to consider is the **incidence of poverty**. That is, what is the distribution of poverty within the country? There are two ways to look at statistics in describing the poor. Both are correct, but they reflect very different perceptions of the poverty problem. We can examine who the poor are (telling us what share of our nation's poor are represented by various groups of people), or we can look at the share of each group of people that is poor (telling us the likelihood that someone within each group will be poor). The former refers to the **composition of poverty**, and the latter refers to poverty rates. We will consider both approaches to the statistics and analyze their implications.

Incidence of poverty
The distribution of poverty within the country.

Composition of poverty
The number of poor people in each group of the population as a share of the number of poor in the nation.

Who Are the Poor?

First, of the millions of people in the country who are poor, by far most of them are white. Does this surprise you? It shouldn't, since most of the people in the United States are white. Second, over a third of the poor are children. To be a poor child means to live in a family with income below the poverty line, *despite* any cash assistance that the family may receive from the government.

Although statistics such as these show who the poor are in the United States, they do not adequately show which groups bear a greater likelihood of being poor. To identify these groups, we must approach the statistics from the other perspective of poverty; that is, we must analyze which groups in the United States have higher poverty rates.

Which Groups Have Higher Poverty Rates?

The proportion of all persons in the United States who were poor in 2013 was 14.5 percent (see Table 6-3). However, if we make comparisons among different racial and ethnic groups, we see enormous disparity. At 12.3 percent, the poverty rate for white people is well below the national average. Perhaps more significantly, the poverty rate for non-Hispanic whites (recall that Hispanics may be of any race) is only 9.6 percent. The poverty rate for African-Americans is almost three times this rate, at 27.2 percent. The poverty rate for Hispanics is just slightly lower than that for African-Americans, at 23.5 percent. Asian-Americans have a relatively low poverty rate of 10.5 percent. Thus, although most of the poor in the United States are white, an African-American or Hispanic person has a far greater likelihood of being poor than does a white Caucasian person.

What is surprising to many is that older people (age 65 and over) have a poverty rate of 9.5 percent, which is below the national average. This relatively low rate is caused in large part by the Social Security program, which is discussed in Chapter 9. The war on poverty among older people has not been won, however. According to recent Census

TABLE 6-3 • Poverty Status of Persons and Families, by Race and Ethnicity, Age, Geographical Area, and Type of Family, 2013

Characteristic	Poverty Rate (share of each group that is poor, %)
Persons	14.5
Race and Ethnicity	
White	12.3
Non-Hispanic White	9.6
African-American	27.2
Hispanic	23.5
Asian-American	10.5
Age	
Under 18	19.9
18–64	13.6
65 and older	9.5
Geography	
Central City	19.1
Suburb	11.1
Rural	16.1
Families	11.2
Type of Family	11.8
Married couple	5.8
Male householder (no spouse present)	15.9
Female householder (no spouse present)	30.6

Source: Based on information from the U.S. Department of Commerce, Census Bureau, http://www.census.gov, 2015.

Bureau data, women aged 65 or older have a poverty rate close to twice (1.7 times) the poverty rate of men aged 65 or older! A number of factors contribute to this disparity between older men and women, including the longer life expectancies of women, the lower lifetime earnings that we noted in Chapter 5, and the way the Social Security System operates (see Chapter 9).

Equally disconcerting is the fact that children have a greater likelihood of being poor than any other age group in the United States. Children under the age of 18 have a poverty rate of almost 20 percent. We've already noted that over one-third of all the poor people in the country are children. It is very sad that in a prosperous country such as ours, where we pride ourselves on the notion of equal opportunity, so many children begin life disadvantaged by poverty. Consider the words of one woman in poverty:

> *[I am concerned] that my children will be strong healthy people, and not have to go through what I have; my daughter to be able to think clearly about things; my son to never abuse any woman in his life. For me—just to provide what my kids and I need and a little extra to survive; that I finish school someday—to be able to work where I want to work—because the way that I see it is if you're not happy doing what you're doing, it won't last long. I hope my kids will not inherit my poverty; they deserve much more.*[4]

Also note the higher poverty rate for people living in central cities, as opposed to the suburbs. Rural poverty rates are also relatively high. The high poverty rate in central cities confirms the discussion in Chapter 4 concerning the low property tax base resulting in poor funding levels for inner-city schools.

Finally, we see that families with a female householder and no spouse present have a 30.6 percent chance of being poor. In contrast, families with a male householder and no spouse present have a 15.9 percent chance of being poor (about one-half the likelihood of the female-headed families). While we might expect single-headed families to be more likely to be poor than those headed by married couples, the high poverty rate among female-headed families is alarming. *All of these statistics imply quite clearly that poverty in our country is a children's issue; it is also a women's issue, and it is a race and ethnicity issue.*

The Implications of Poverty

It has been said that poverty statistics are just people with the tears washed off. What is the real meaning of poverty as it affects people's lives? Certainly, hunger is a problem for the poor. Bread for the World, a national citizens' lobby on hunger issues, reports that 11.1 percent of households in the United States are food insecure, meaning that they are at risk of hunger.[5] They regularly have to skip meals, rely on emergency food, eat less, or eat less-nutritional food because their families cannot buy the food they need.

Homelessness is also an implication of poverty and is discussed in more detail in Chapter 7. In addition, adequate health care is often not available to our nation's poor. As we will see in Chapter 8, many of the poor are not covered by **Medicaid** (the government medical program for low-income Americans). Also, despite the presence of **Medicare** (the government medical program for the elderly), many poor older people find themselves unable to afford the costs of medications, Medicare premiums and deductibles, and uncovered medical expenses (though Medicaid will sometimes pay some of these expenses).

Medicaid
A government program providing medical coverage for eligible low-income people.

Medicare
A government program providing medical coverage largely to elderly people.

The Feminization of Poverty

The statistics show that women bear the greatest burden of poverty. Many have suggested possible reasons for this feminization of poverty.[6] Reasons include the growth in the number of female-headed households, teenage pregnancies, discrimination in the labor market, and domestic violence toward women. Racial and age discrimination may exacerbate the gender discrimination faced by these women. In particular, teenage girls who drop out of school for the birth and care of a child find it difficult to complete their education and eventually find remunerative employment. For those who do manage, additional factors may complicate their lives. For example, in the words of one woman:

> *"I think I did things right even at the time I was only sixteen, ... I married, finished high school, went on to college, and worked, got divorced ... but haven't received one child support payment."[7]*

Insufficient child care, inadequate educational and training programs, limited assistance, and insufficient or nonexistent child support prevent many single mothers, and especially teenage mothers, from participating successfully in our economy and achieving independence from the forces of poverty. Other women have forgone educational and career opportunities to remain at home to care for children and family. They frequently find themselves in poverty if their husbands die or desert them. Finally, many women are victims of domestic violence. This threat to safety and well-being can prevent many women from entering the labor force, retaining jobs, and supporting their families.

Causes of Poverty

As already indicated, national poverty rate rose were quite high in 2010 and 2011. This is largely due to the poor economy, which while improving, still leaves behind large numbers of unemployed and poor people until recover is well at hand. These and other factors contribute to poverty.

Recession

As mentioned, rising poverty rates can be outcomes of a poor economy. Recession was an important factor in the high poverty rates of the early 1980s, the early 1990s, and the first years of the new millennium. The years 2007–2009 encompassed our most recent recession. A **recession** is a reduction in our nation's output. When businesses are producing lower output levels, the need to hire workers lessens, and lower employment levels result. (Recession is discussed in more detail in Chapter 15, which examines macroeconomic policy.) With unemployment at 25-year highs by 2009, one would expect a high incidence of poverty as income decreases for laid-off workers and as new entrants to the labor force are unable to find jobs. Furthermore, many employed workers find their hours of employment reduced during a recession. Wages also tend to fall during periods of rising unemployment. However, national unemployment rates are only part of the explanation of poverty. Other factors must be considered, especially insofar as poverty rates have not declined as much as one might expect as the nation has been recovering from the recent recession. These other factors include labor productivity, structural changes in our economy, personal factors, demographic trends, and budget cuts for antipoverty programs.

Recession

A decline in a nation's gross domestic product (output) associated with a rise in unemployment. Technically, there must be a decline in real gross domestic product (GDP) for at least two consecutive quarters.

Poor Labor Productivity

People with few skills, limited experience, and little education often have a difficult time finding employment at a satisfactory wage because their labor productivity is considered to be low. As a result, these people are more likely to be poor than are those who are better trained and educated. Many of you are still in school because you expect that your higher education will enhance your productivity and therefore your future income. Low labor productivity also ties in closely with structural changes in the economy as a cause of poverty.

Structural Changes in Our Economy

Changes in the structure of our economy contribute to unemployment and poverty. Technological change (such as robotics in the automobile industry) has enabled machines to replace workers. Furthermore, the lower-wage service sector (child care, restaurant service, and so on) has grown at the expense of the higher-wage manufacturing sector. Finally, the flight of businesses and jobs to the suburbs has left poverty-stricken inner cities in its wake.

These structural changes relate directly to the issue of labor productivity. The point is that the number of good, high-wage, blue-collar jobs has decreased greatly, and the economic gap between high school graduates and workers with higher education has widened. There are simply few well-paying jobs with stable employment left for relatively unskilled and uneducated people.

Personal Factors

People without adequate skills and education are more likely to be poor. But these are not the only factors constraining their incomes. Many individuals lack what can be referred to as "job readiness," or the capacity to show up ready to work, on time, on a daily basis. This lack of readiness may be caused by mental disability, inexperience, immaturity, or other factors. Many families, especially single-parent families, lack adequate child care that would enable parents to work. If parents do work, they must miss work when their child is sick, their child-care provider is on vacation, or other circumstances exist that make for spotty attendance at work. Still other workers lack adequate transportation to their job sites. Poorer individuals tend to have less reliable cars, and when their cars break down, they may not be able to afford repairs. At the same time, public transportation may be time consuming or unavailable in the locations where workers need to travel to work and to take their children to child care. Many poor families experience all of these difficulties. Clearly, the oft-quoted query, "Why don't they just get a job?" reflects a vast oversimplification of the problem.

Demographic Trends

Demographic statistics indicate that the number of births to unmarried mothers as a percent of all births increased over 1960 to 2010, as revealed in Table 6-4. In addition, all racial and ethnic groups shown in Table 6-4 had rising percentages from 1960 to 2010. The increasing percentages of births to unmarried mothers certainly represent one factor that may contribute to poverty. It is interesting to note that between 2010 and 2011, however, these statistics fell slightly for total births, whites, non-Hispanic whites, and African-Americans. The drops are very small and may or may not reveal a new trend that will be interesting to watch.

Perhaps even more important with respect to poverty is the number of births taking place by teenagers. According to the Centers for Disease Control and Prevention (CDC), in 2011, a total of 329,797 babies were born to women aged 15 to 19 years, for a live birth rate of 31.3 per 1,000 women in this age group. **This is a record low birth rate for U.S. teens in this age group, and a drop of 8 percent from 2010.** This is certainly good news, and the CDC suggests that teens seem to be less sexually active and those who are active are more likely to use birth control than in previous years. The decline in teen birth rates holds for women of all races and ethnicity, and was the greatest

TABLE 6-4 • The Percentage of All Births That Were to Unmarried Mothers, By Race and Ethnicity, Selected Years 1960 to 2011

	1960	1970	1980	1990	2000	2010	2011
Total Births	5.3	10.7	18.4	28.0	33.2	40.8	40.7
White	2.3	5.7	11.2	20.4	27.1	35.9	35.7
Non-Hispanic White	Na	Na	9.6	16.9	22.1	29.3	29.0
African-American	Na	37.6	56.1	66.5	68.5	72.1	71.8
Hispanic	Na	Na	23.6	36.7	42.7	52.8	53.3
Asian-American[a]	Na	Na	7.3	13.3	14.8	17.0	17.2
Native American[b]	Na	22.4	39.2	53.6	58.4	65.6	66.2

[a]Asian or Pacific Islander.
[b]American Indian or Alaskan Native.

Note: Na means data not available.

Source: Child Trends Data Bank, www.childtrends.org/?indicators=births-to-unmarried-women.

for Hispanic teens (with a drop of 11 percent from 2010). Still, non-Hispanic African-Americans, Hispanics, and Native Americans experience the highest rates of teen pregnancy and childbirth. Together, African-American and Hispanic teens comprised 57 percent of U.S. teen births in 2011.[8]

For those teen births that do occur, we know that just as the term *feminization of poverty* suggests, it is especially difficult for young single mothers to complete high school and to provide adequate incomes for their families when they lack access to good jobs and quality child care is unavailable or unaffordable. The high unemployment rate faced by young unskilled fathers is a contributing factor in their absence from the family and their limited support.

Budget Cuts

Many people mistakenly believe that our government spends an enormous amount of money on programs designed to improve conditions for the poor. Many of these same people believe that these programs are ineffective, at best. As a result of these attitudes, support for cuts in government programs for the poor has been widespread since the early 1980s. The budget cuts that took place early in the Reagan administration (1981–1983) were a case in point and were particularly harmful to the poor. Many families, particularly those headed by single mothers, lost eligibility for or received lower benefits from government cash assistance programs. Their children also lost food stamps, access to Medicaid health coverage, eligibility for government school lunch and breakfast programs, and the benefits of a host of other services. These expenditure cuts occurred during a period when unemployment and poverty rates in the country were high and increasing.

Controversy over government poverty programs continued throughout the 1980s and the 1990s, culminating in the welfare reform of 1996. The new welfare program has created its own controversy, including its limitations in periods of high unemployment. We will return to the topic of welfare reform shortly.

Additional Causes of Poverty

Additional causes of poverty are related to specific aspects of the labor market within our economy. Having a job does not necessarily preclude poverty. A person working for the 2014 federal minimum wage of $7.25 per hour for 40 hours per week and 52 weeks per year will earn only $15,080 annually, well below the $23,834 poverty line for a family of four, as noted earlier. A minimum wage job clearly does not pull these families out of poverty!

We also know that women, on average, earn far less than men do, at least in part because of labor market discrimination. This topic was discussed more extensively in Chapter 5. Racial and age discrimination also serve to lower the earnings of various minority groups, older people, and teenagers. In addition, poverty-stricken individuals include those who for various reasons could not work even if adequately paying jobs were available. These people include the very old, parents of the very young, and the mentally and physically ill and handicapped.

Solutions to Poverty

Solutions to poverty are subject to considerable controversy: witness the continual stream of editorials and letters to the editor in your daily newspaper concerning welfare reform, welfare abuse, government spending, and the like. Let's analyze various solutions that might be used to confront the problem of poverty.

Macroeconomic Policies to Relieve National Unemployment

Given that recession is a cause of poverty, it is useful to know that the government and Federal Reserve System can undertake various fiscal and monetary policies designed to increase national employment. These policies are discussed more fully in Chapter 15. **For the moment, it should suffice to say that although national economic prosperity cannot alleviate all poverty, it *can* work hand in hand with other poverty reduction programs.** Certainly, it makes little sense to train, educate, and provide work-support services to the hard-core poor and unemployed in an attempt to help them obtain gainful employment, only to find that national unemployment rates dictate that jobs will be unavailable. *Requiring* the poor to work when jobs do not exist, as mandated by our cash welfare programs, makes even less sense!

Microeconomic Policies to Improve Labor Productivity

We can address the problems of poverty associated with low labor productivity, structural changes in the economy, and some of the personal factors mentioned previously by investing in people. We often think about business firms investing in various forms of capital, such as factories and machinery. We can also talk about investment in *human* capital. An **investment in human capital** is any spending that improves the productivity of people. Obviously, spending on education and job training can improve the skills and abilities of people and make them more productive, enhancing their ability to get good jobs and their likelihood of receiving higher incomes.

Investment in human capital
Spending that is designed to improve the productivity of people.

In addition to job training and education, various programs can improve the job readiness of workers who have difficulty finding or keeping jobs. Transportation and child care needs must also be addressed. During periods of low unemployment rates, businesses might be desperate to find workers. As a result, these businesses might realize that they need to provide training, child care, and transportation for their workers. Unfortunately, when the economy shifts to a position of scarcity of jobs rather than scarcity of workers, businesses tend to cut back on provision of these services.

Universal Entitlements

Many of those concerned about poverty have called for expanded systems of **universal entitlements**. These types of programs are not necessarily directed toward the poor. They are targeted to all people who meet various types of criteria. All school-age children in our country, for example, are entitled to a public education. Thus, certain standards of education are ensured for all children, regardless of income. Many would expand these types of provisions and guarantees to other areas of importance: child care, medical coverage, maternity and paternity leaves, and child or family allowances. In Norway, homemakers are even paid for their essential work in the home! These types of programs are taken for granted in many other Western industrialized countries, and they certainly would address some of the problems associated with the feminization of poverty.

Universal entitlements
Payments (or programs) to which eligible citizens have a right by law.

The arguments against universal entitlements center on their expense and their potential for disincentives. Opponents ask, for example, why the government should fund child care for all people within some category, rather than just for low-income families in need. And if child allowances provide cash income based on the number of children per family, won't the allowances cause the birthrate to increase?

Proponents reject these claims. They argue that the political likelihood of enacting and maintaining programs and policies is much greater if such programs benefit all, rather than just the poor. (Social Security, a politically popular program, is a case in point.) Furthermore, only if programs providing benefits such as medical care and child care are targeted to all will quality be ensured; programs for only the poor have often been of substandard quality. (Low-income housing is sometimes an example of this.) Finally, universal entitlements would avoid the stigmatizing of the poor and the pitting of various groups of citizens against one another in their quest for important services.

A Negative Income Tax

Negative income tax
A taxation system that taxes people with incomes above a certain level and pays people with incomes below that level.

A **negative income tax** has been proposed by politicians and economists in a variety of forms but would typically tax income earners at various positive rates as long as income lies above some specified level—for example, the poverty line. At this specified level, income would not be taxed. Below this level, people would actually receive payments from the government, amounting to a negative tax. Payments could be automatic, work through our current income tax system, and depend on family size.

Proposals vary considerably as to the size of payments as well as the overall intent of the program. For some proponents, the negative income tax would entirely replace all current government programs, including farm price supports, student loans, Social Security, and so on. For others, it would replace only government poverty programs; other programs would remain intact. Milton Friedman, an economist who was an early advocate of the negative income tax, believed that it should replace a large number of government programs. Other proponents have suggested that the tax be used in conjunction with various other government poverty programs; indeed, they suggest that the beauty of the negative income tax is that it would free up funds and personnel currently involved in the bureaucracy of our cash assistance programs. These resources could be put to work meeting the various social needs of low-income clients.

The proposal has a number of other attractive elements. It is simple and probably efficient. It could be designed to cover the cash needs of all Americans, not just those in specific categories. And, if properly run, it could minimize disincentives for work effort. As long as individuals receive at least some substantial portion of each additional work dollar and always are better off working than not, the incentive to work will remain. The actual feasibility and desirability of any such negative income tax proposal will depend on actual payment levels, the types of government programs that complement it, and the minimization of any potential work disincentives.

Earned Income Tax Credit (EITC)
A federal tax credit for low-income workers and families. The credit is available whether or not the worker pays federal personal income taxes.

Despite the many positive aspects of the negative income tax, few politicians have been willing to consider it seriously. However, the 1986 tax reform took some steps toward the goals envisioned in the negative income tax plan. Various exemptions, deductions, and credits have virtually eliminated the obligation of very-low-income families to pay federal income taxes. Furthermore, increases in the federal **Earned Income Tax Credit (EITC)**, a tax credit originally geared to low-income working families with children, has reduced the tax burden of these poor families. The EITC is actually a limited form of the negative income tax insofar as it returns money to low-income working families even if they paid no federal income taxes. President Bill Clinton increased the EITC and expanded it to low-income single individuals and couples without children in 1993. If eligible people pay no income taxes, they simply receive a check from the government for the amount of the credit. If they have already paid taxes, they are reimbursed by the appropriate amount and potentially receive an additional payment. Benefits can amount to thousands of dollars per family, depending on the number of children that they have. People without children must be at least age 25 by the end of the year. Families with both single and married parents are eligible.

However, people must work and must file a federal personal income tax form to be eligible. Widespread ignorance about the program and the need to file a return keeps many eligible people from benefiting from the EITC.

According to the Center on Budget and Policy Priorities, the EITC lifts millions of people, many of them children, out of poverty each year, making it the nation's most effective antipoverty program for working families. Research shows that the credit has contributed to a significant increase in labor force participation among single mothers. Because the EITC works so well to help low-income working families without diminishing their incentive to work, many states and even cities have established a statewide or citywide EITC, and others have argued for expanded use of the credit at both the federal and state government levels.[9]

Miscellaneous Solutions

Because discrimination plays a role in poverty, it is important that our nation strive to provide equal opportunities to all people in the areas of education, housing, and employment. Equal opportunity legislation and affirmative action were discussed in more detail in Chapter 5. In addition, the financing of public education must be addressed to ensure quality schools for all children. This topic was thoroughly covered in Chapter 4. Our nation's housing programs and health care system must also address the needs of the poor, as we will see in Chapters 7 and 8. Finally, we need to consider an increase in the minimum wage. Because there are costs and benefits associated with the minimum wage, we will carefully consider this topic in Chapter 14 on unemployment and inflation.

Welfare and Other Government Programs

Several government programs are designed to help the poor. These programs include food stamps (now called SNAP, or the Supplemental Nutrition Assistance Program); general assistance; Medicaid; the State Children's Health Insurance Program (SCHIP); Supplemental Security Income (SSI); the Special Supplemental Nutrition Program for Women, Infants, and Children (WIC); the Earned Income Tax Credit (EITC); and Temporary Assistance for Needy Families (TANF). These programs are described as **public assistance** programs in Table 6-5 on page 154.

Although **Social Security** has removed many people from poverty, it is not considered an antipoverty program because it is available to all who are eligible, regardless of income. Social Security is an example of a **social insurance** program into which workers pay while they work and from which they receive benefits when they become eligible. **Thus, the public assistance programs in Table 6-5 are targeted to low-income people, whereas social insurance programs are not.** Other social insurance programs include Medicare and unemployment compensation.

Temporary Assistance for Needy Families (TANF) is a **block grant** from the federal government to state governments for use in state welfare programs. (TANF is pronounced TAN-EF.) It is the public assistance program that we will consider in detail momentarily. It replaces **Aid to Families with Dependent Children (AFDC)**, which was our nation's most important public assistance program for many years. The AFDC program provided cash assistance to poor families with children. This program generated controversy in the United States for decades and was revised many times. The controversy culminated in the passage of legislation that eliminated AFDC and replaced it with TANF. The issues that motivated this action are discussed in the next section.

Public assistance
Any government program that is targeted to aid low-income people.

Social security
A federal program that provides income transfers to retired workers, the survivors of deceased workers, and disabled workers.

Social insurance
Any government program funded by payroll taxes on employers, employees, or both. It is targeted to aid certain eligible groups of people, and a person need not have low income in order to be eligible.

Temporary Assistance for Needy Families (TANF)
A block grant from the federal government to state governments to be used in state welfare programs in compliance with federal guidelines. (Pronounced TAN-EF.)

Block grant
A lump sum of money given by the federal government to state governments to use as they wish within broad federal guidelines to develop programs to meet a broad category of need.

Aid to Families with Dependent Children (AFDC)
Our nation's former welfare program that provided cash assistance to eligible low-income families with children.

TABLE 6-5 • Explanation of Government Programs

Program	Explanation
Public Assistance Programs	
Food stamps (SNAP)	Federal government program providing vouchers (coupons) to low-income people, which are accepted as payment by stores for food. Now called the Supplemental Nutrition Assistance Program.
General assistance	Local government assistance designed to meet local needs and fill gaps in state and federal government programs.
Medicaid	Combined federal and state government program providing medical coverage for eligible low-income people.
State Children's Health Insurance Program (SCHIP)	Combined federal and state government program providing medical coverage for eligible low-income children.
Supplemental Security Income (SSI)	Combined federal and state government program providing cash income to low-income aged, blind, and disabled people.
Special Supplemental Nutrition Program for Women, Infants, and Children (WIC)	Federal government program providing nutritious food to needy pregnant women and young children when special health needs exist.
Earned Income Tax Credit (EITC)	Federal tax credit for low-income working people.
Temporary Assistance for Needy Families (TANF)	Block grants from the federal government to state governments for use in state welfare programs that comply with broad federal guidelines.
Social Insurance Programs	
Social security	Federal government program providing cash benefits to retired workers, survivors of deceased workers, and the disabled.
Unemployment compensation	Combined federal and state government program providing benefits to eligible unemployed workers.
Medicare	Federal government program providing medical coverage largely to elderly people.

Welfare Reform

Both conservatives and moderates agreed on the need for welfare reform, as was evident in the Republican "Contract with America" (the 1990s blueprint guiding conservative proposals for our nation's economy) and in Democratic President Bill Clinton's election promise to "end welfare as we know it." Dialogue culminated in the passage of a major welfare reform bill. This legislation, signed into law by President Clinton in 1996, called for the phase-out of the AFDC program and the phase-in of the new TANF program. It is useful to examine the controversy that created the call for welfare reform.

Controversy over Welfare

The following controversy concerned many Americans. The issues raised are also the types of issues that concern economists, including disincentives, dependency, and expense.

Economic Disincentives

Many people were concerned about possible disincentives built into the AFDC program. Although individual state programs varied, the federal program was such that if a recipient (usually a mother) took a job and began earning income, she lost AFDC benefits dollar for dollar of the income earned. Although she may have received benefits to cover the additional costs of working (transportation, child care, and so on), often these were inadequate. If income rose and Medicaid benefits were lost (as well as eligibility for child nutrition programs and other services), the family may well have been placed in a far more precarious situation than before the mother went to work. Furthermore, severe restrictions on benefits had often been placed on families with a father present in the home. In many cases, these restrictions may have encouraged the father to leave the family so that the mother and children could receive benefits. Others argued that the program encouraged illegitimacy. **Thus, economic disincentives were said to exist for work effort and family stability.**

Welfare Dependency

Another concern was that government programs encouraged people to develop long-term dependence on welfare. Research results on this issue were mixed. Various studies reported different percentages of families remaining dependent on welfare. Despite the discrepancies in findings, the data suggested that most people did not become persistently dependent on welfare but used such assistance to get through a difficult financial period resulting from a divorce, an unplanned birth, an illness or death, a lost job, or other factors. Even though the percentage of families persistently dependent on welfare may have been small, it was significant. The dependent recipient was the stereotype in the minds of people as they railed against AFDC.

Welfare Expense

Finally, people were concerned about the expense of welfare programs. Here, it is important to maintain a correct perspective. Census Bureau data reveal that in the last several years of the AFDC program, federal spending on this program represented only about 1 percent of the federal budget. (Food stamps and other nutrition programs combined represented only about 2 percent.) *Although it is always important to use funds wisely, many people held the mistaken opinion that welfare was draining the federal budget.*

Temporary Assistance for Needy Families (TANF)

The 1996 legislation phased out the AFDC program and replaced it with TANF block grants to individual states for use in their welfare programs, with the ostensible goal of assisting families in moving from welfare to employment. The TANF program allows the states wide discretion in determining their programs, eligibility standards, and benefit levels. States must comply, however, with some broad federal guidelines. These guidelines specify that states very much (1) provide assistance to needy families so that children may be cared for in their own home or in the homes of relatives, (2) end the dependence of needy parents on government benefits by promoting job preparation, work, and marriage, (3) prevent and reduce the incidence of out-of-wedlock pregnancies and establish annual numerical goals for preventing and reducing the incidence of these pregnancies, and (4) encourage the formation and maintenance of two-parent families.

In addition to these restrictions, states may add their own stipulations. They may require, for example, that minor, unmarried parents live with an adult and attend school in order to be eligible for child care benefits. They may deny additional assistance to children born to mothers already receiving benefits. They may also provide lower benefits to people moving to their state if the previous state's benefits were lower. In addition to these changes, the 1996 legislation eliminated welfare benefits for most legal immigrants. (Illegal immigrants were already ineligible for most programs.)

Despite the references to marriage and families (with results on child and maternal welfare being mixed), most of the attention to TANF focuses on the work requirements and time limits. With few exceptions, recipients must work (or participate in work activities, such as completing high school, community service, and so on) no later than two years after coming on assistance. Single parents must participate in work activities for at least 30 hours per week and two-parent families must participate in work activities 35 or 55 hours per week, depending on the circumstances. Failure to participate in work requirements can result in a reduction or termination of benefits to the family. Recipients of TANF are limited to a total of five years of eligibility in their lifetimes.

It is widely known that welfare caseloads have fallen dramatically in almost every state in the first several years since 1996 and by more than half nationally as a result of the new legislation. The reduction in caseloads was initially touted as a sign of the program's success. Even President Bush referred to this success in his 2006 State of the Union Address. However, the fact is that much of this early decline in the number of families receiving assistance was due to the decline in the proportion of families *eligible* for assistance. And this occurred *despite* the rise in national poverty rates in the 2000s. Very poor families that do not receive TANF miss out not only on the income assistance that could help them financially but also on programs that could help them prepare to find employment.

In addition, studies show that most of the program beneficiaries who successfully found jobs during this time period ended up in very low-wage-paying jobs with little or no opportunity for advancement or they experienced periods of joblessness. Even though large numbers of single mothers around the country did enter the workforce, many of them did not escape poverty. Studies also show that many of the families that had been unable to move from TANF to work have serious barriers to employment, including significant physical and mental disabilities.[10]

Declining caseloads are a misleading indicator of TANF's success. Caseload reductions indicate less reliance on government assistance, but they do not account for the well-being of poor families and children. Other factors must be taken into account. While employment among TANF recipients increased in the early years of reform (while the economy was experiencing a period of growth), employment declined over a later period since 2000. About 20 percent of welfare leavers are not working, without a spouse, and without any public assistance.[11] Furthermore, many of those who left TANF for a job have been concentrated in low-wage occupations, increasing the numbers of the working poor.

Although many of these results to date are discouraging, there are grounds for optimism in terms of improving that program. Within the context of the broad federal guidelines, states have had considerable discretion and flexibility in developing their own welfare programs. *In an ideal situation, each state would take into account the complexity of poverty among its citizens and seek to provide solutions that incorporate training and education, child care, health care, nutrition, transportation, counseling, and other forms of assistance.* They might also provide state EITCs and subsidies to employers to cover the costs of hiring welfare clients. In many situations, unfortunately, states put forth only the minimal effort needed to comply with federal law. Furthermore, the current fiscal crises of many state governments, resulting from limited tax revenues and inadequate federal revenue sharing with states, have made it very difficult for states to improve their programs. Additionally, those states with the most distressed populations and high poverty and unemployment rates are also the states with the most limited tax base. Only expanded federal funding can overcome these disadvantages and assure adequate welfare programs for all people in the United States.

Concerns About Welfare

Financing

Many controversial issues surround the TANF program. As mentioned, a major issue is the level of federal funding. In the reauthorization of TANF in 2005, The Deficit

Reduction Act (responding to the hundreds of billions of dollars of spending on the war in Iraq and tax cuts for high-income individuals, with soaring federal government budget deficits as the result) raised work participation rates, limited that activities that could be counted as work, and so on. The Deficit Reduction Act sought to reduce these deficits through reduced federal spending on several poverty programs, including TANF. With the economy worsening and turning to recession at the end of 2007, new leadership in 2009 sought to assure an adequate safety net for people suffering from unemployment, declining incomes, and foreclosure of their homes. President Obama's recovery package (stimulus bill) increased funding for TANF by $5 billion and created a Contingency Fund, funded at another $2 billion. This contingency fund ran out of money by 2010, and the program has continued underfunded.

What About Recession?

Another serious problem with a welfare system that is centered on work responsibility involves the problem of business cycles. Our economy alternates between periods of growth and decline in GDP, or in other words, between expansion and recession. Our new welfare system was initiated during a period of steady economic growth and prosperity, and optimism was high for the success of the program. What happens to the program when recession hits, as it hit hard in late 2007? The program became inadequate, with millions of people losing their jobs over the course of the recession. Expansions in unemployment insurance helped many, but most unemployed people are not eligible for this. (For example, first-time job seekers and many of the lowest-paid workers are left out from unemployment compensation, as is discussed in Chapter 14 on unemployment and inflation.) What to do when we have a work-based welfare system but no work is a major problem with our welfare system.

Difficult Caseloads

Up until the recent recession, during which all types of workers lost their jobs, welfare advocates had argued that their "easy" clients had already been placed in jobs and the remaining "difficult" clients were those with one or several serious impediments to work, including mental retardation, physical and mental illness, addiction disorders, and seriously ill children. Even in a high-growth economy with plenty of jobs, a work-based welfare program with a five-year limit on cash assistance is not adequate for many of these people. Some people, in every culture and country, will never be able to work and will need assistance indefinitely. Others may be able to work in certain settings if their work impediments are addressed. One positive feature of the TANF program is that individual states may allow certain activities to meet the TANF work requirement, thereby allowing the welfare client to receive cash assistance. These activities might include parenting classes, budgeting tutoring, skills workshops, and so on.

What Fulfills the TANF Work Requirement?

This issue of fulfilling the work requirement can be addressed in many ways. The original TANF legislation permitted participation in vocational education to count toward a state's work participation requirement for up to 12 months for any individual, but for no more than 30 percent of a state's welfare recipients. Beyond this, some states have permitted higher education to count for the work requirement, though tighter federal restrictions have limited the ability of states to allow education and training to count for the work requirement. According to welfare advocates, this means that many women with children will not be able to work toward higher skills and education that would permit them to take adequate wage-paying jobs with benefits, eliminate their welfare dependence, and contribute tax revenue many times over the value of any TANF benefits they would have otherwise received. A single parent of young children who is working full time has little if any free time. As one single woman explained at the beginning of the TANF program:

> *I will complete the higher education degree I am currently seeking. ... I am told that as of next semester, I will no longer be eligible for childcare assistance and will also be forced to work a minimum of thirty hours per week. School will no longer be a consideration in my case. My sons are three and one-half, and four and one-half, and will need to be in daycare for another year and a half at least. I am eligible for student loans, which will cover the cost. However, my main concern is the work requirement. It will be extremely difficult to keep up a good grade point, work, and still be able to be a mother to my children. This will mean that we will be together as a family less than we are now. That's what frightens me.[12]*

How are Children Cared For?

This young woman raises a second controversial element of welfare reform, which is whether mothers of young children should be required to work outside of the home. Many feel that work is better for mother and child. Others believe that the choice to work should reside with the parents, as it does for higher-income families. A critical issue is child care. Child care is often unavailable for infants and prohibitively expensive for other children. When funds are insufficient for child care, children may be poorly cared for by an older sibling or by neighbors or relatives already overworked with children of their own. Regardless of whether children are cared for by parents or child care workers, child care should be perceived as a valuable form of work in our society and needs to be addressed by any welfare program.

The Role of Economic Growth versus Government Programs

Because recession—which is a decline in national output—causes unemployment rates to go up, we might expect that economic growth—which is an increase in national output—would cause unemployment rates to go down. Higher output levels means more people working, which means fewer people in poverty. **This is, in fact, the essence of trickle-down philosophy: the benefits of economic growth and prosperity eventually trickle down to all.** Support for this view has been a hallmark of both the Ronald Reagan and George W. Bush administrations.

Certainly, greater national prosperity does reduce poverty and is one reason for the falling poverty rates we observed during the 1990s. However, there are three particular problems with the trickle-down philosophy. First, some of the policies that supposedly generate economic growth may directly increase absolute and relative poverty, as well as worsen the standards of living of the poor. This phenomenon is discussed in greater length in the section on supply-side policy in Chapter 15, which describes the issues of cuts in government programs that affect low-income people and cuts in taxes that primarily benefit

Trickle-down philosophy
The view that the benefits of economic growth and prosperity will "trickle down" to all.

higher-income people. Second, the newly created jobs that result from economic growth benefit those who are hired into these jobs. Remember that many others are left behind in the labor market, including those who are ill or disabled, the elderly, the young, victims of discrimination, and single parents of young children, as well as people without adequate job skills, education, experience, and transportation. The benefits of economic growth fail to trickle down to these people. Finally, a job does not guarantee a living wage. Recall that the minimum wage may well leave a family below the poverty line. One final issue involves greater reliance on private charities to deal with the problems of poverty. Indeed, a hallmark of President George W. Bush's administration was the creation of "faith-based initiatives." Others argue that although the use of faith-based initiatives may help alleviate the poverty problem, the ability of private charities in funding antipoverty programs will be inadequate (especially in times of recession when charitable contributions fall off). **Government programs will always be necessary to help those who cannot achieve success through economic growth alone.**

Complexity of Poverty

The problem of poverty is very complex and without simple solutions. If there were only one cause and one type of poverty, solutions would be readily found. Instead, a variety of circumstances affect different individuals. The solutions to poverty among elderly women will be far different from the solutions to poverty among unskilled and uneducated 18-year-olds. The needs of single women with children will be far different from the needs of the disabled. The problems of poverty in inner-city ghettoes are far different from the problems in the suburbs and the countryside.

Many students who work hard to finance their education find it difficult to be sympathetic to the poor. They work hard, so why don't the poor? We must remember that it is one thing to be successful at work, but it is another thing to be successful at work while caring for young children, coping with a disability, or lacking transportation or opportunities for employment. Many of the poor experience multiple problems that limit their successful employment. Some Americans have adopted a punitive attitude toward the poor, but many others are sincere in their concern for the poor, though they have different views about how to approach the issue of poverty. What we must do is try to understand the complexities of poverty and avoid stigmatizing and stereotyping the poor. At the same time, we must seek common ground for solutions to poverty that work. We cannot expect these solutions to be simple.

You, the Student

Are you concerned about the problem of poverty in the United States? If so, there are many organizations such as Bread for the World that lobby our government on behalf of the poor in the United States and the rest of the world. The Web site at http://www.bread.org can fill you in on current legislative issues involving the poor and provides Web links to other organizations concerned about similar issues. What legislative issues involving poverty are currently being discussed in Congress? Would you like to contact your legislators about these? (Go to http://www.senate.gov and http://www.house.gov. if you wish to find your legislators' names and addresses. You don't even need a stamp – just email them as shown on their Web sites!)

View*Point*   Conservative versus Liberal

People generally adopt either a liberal or a conservative approach to the poverty issue. Liberals are more inclined to stress the need for government involvement in antipoverty efforts; they believe there are equity issues that are not dealt with by the market economy. Conservatives are much more leery of government involvement and are concerned that too many programs or too much assistance creates inefficiencies and disincentives for work effort. Liberals tend to prefer extensive federal involvement in poverty programs, whereas conservatives prefer greater responsibility by private charities and by state governments. Liberals favor a direct approach to dealing with the problem of poverty; conservatives often favor an indirect, trickle-down approach (that we will consider in Chapter 15 on macroeconomic policy).

On the other hand, many economists believe that solutions to poverty should not be viewed as alternative courses of action. Indeed, an effective solution might combine elements of each alternative. A prosperous economy with high employment is an important—but only a partial—solution. Universal entitlements may ensure more adequate standards for many, as would a negative income tax (or expansion of the EITC). Efforts to improve the productivity and job readiness of workers are lauded by liberals and conservatives alike. Given the complexity of poverty and the individual needs of people, many economists believe that solutions to poverty must be varied and individualized.

SUMMARY

Relative poverty is a situation in which people are poor in comparison with other people. Relative poverty is measured by the distribution of total money income to different income groups. Recent U.S. statistics on income distribution indicate that the poorest fifth of the population receives 3.2 percent of total income, whereas the richest fifth of the population receives over 51 percent. Income distribution in the United States has become considerably less equal since 1981. The United States has the least-equal income distribution of all the Western industrialized nations.

Absolute poverty is defined through the use of the poverty line. If a family's money income falls below the poverty line, all members of that family are defined by the government as being poor. The poverty line varies depending on family size and is adjusted annually for inflation. The 2011 poverty line for a family of four is $23,021.

The U.S. poverty rate exceeded 20 percent in 1960. This rate fell dramatically during the 1960s and 1970s, reaching a low of approximately 11 percent in 1973. Poverty rates were high in 1980 and 1990 as a result of recession, and they currently amount to 15.0 percent as a result of the struggling economy. Although most poor people in the United States are white, African-Americans and Hispanics have considerably higher poverty rates. Households with single female parents have higher poverty rates than other households, and children have the highest poverty rate of all age groups. The implications of poverty include hunger, homelessness, and poor health.

Causes of poverty include recession, low labor productivity, structural changes in our economy, personal factors, demographic trends, and cuts in government programs that assist the poor. Proposals to reduce poverty have taken a variety of approaches and include macroeconomic policies to reduce national unemployment, microeconomic policies to improve worker productivity, a system of universal entitlements, a negative income tax and expanded earned income tax credit, antidiscrimination policies, a higher minimum wage, and welfare. The debate over welfare reform culminated in the passage of legislation in 1996, which eliminated Aid to Families with Dependent Children (AFDC) and replaced it with Temporary Assistance for Needy Families (TANF). The new program emphasizes work and time limits for assistance. One thing that we know is that poverty is complex; the causes of poverty vary per person and the solutions do as well.

DISCUSSION AND ACTION QUESTIONS

1. Should incomes in the United States be distributed equally? If not, should there be at least a greater degree of equality than we presently have? What are the advantages and disadvantages of greater equality? How might greater equality be achieved?

2. Were you surprised to learn that the United States has the greatest inequality of income distribution among the Western industrialized countries? What do you think are some reasons for this?

3. (Appendix Question) Is the official government definition of poverty an adequate one? Does it understate the true extent of poverty? Does it overstate it? How might the measure of poverty be improved? The Census Bureau (http://www.census.gov) has begun recording poverty statistics with alternative definitions of poverty. Check out the Web site.

4. Many people would be surprised by the information on declining teenage births as a percentage of overall births. Does this information surprise you? What do you think are some reasons for the decline in teenage births as a share of the total? Do you think it is a permanent or temporary phenomenon?

5. Are you eligible for the Earned Income Tax Credit? Find out if you're eligible by going to the Internal Revenue Service Web site at http://www.irs.gov. If you find yourself eligible, be sure to file your income tax returns even if you are not required to do so because of low earnings. Otherwise, you will not benefit from the EITC.

6. Should mothers of young children be required to work in return for government assistance? Does the age of the child make a difference? What about the number of children? What are the issues involved?

7. Should states or the federal government be given more responsibility for poverty programs? What are the implications of placing greater responsibility for these programs on the states? Think about the financing of programs, the extent of poverty in different states, and problems relating to different eligibility criteria and benefit levels across different states.

8. Which do you feel is more effective in reducing poverty: government poverty programs or economic growth of the nation? How do private charities fit in? Are you conservative or liberal when it comes to addressing poverty?

9. This textbook uses 2011 statistics for poverty rates and income distribution. Update these figures by using the Census Bureau Web site (http://www.census.gov). Search under Income and Poverty.

10. Check the Web site for the Center on Budget and Policy Priorities (http://www.cbpp.org) to discover a wealth of information on government programs and their effects on people. What are some of the topics that are of interest to you?

11. Go to http://www.cbpp.org to search for suggestions by the Center on Budget and Policy Priorities about how state governments can improve their welfare programs. How do these suggestions address poverty-related issues, such as housing, health care, and nutrition?

12. Browse through the Web site for the Center on Budget and Policy Priorities once again at http://www.cbpp.org. Do you think this is a liberal or a conservative research institute? Why?

13. Browse through the Web site of the Heritage Foundation at http://www.heritage.org. Do you think this is a liberal or a conservative research institute? Why?

14. The Center for Disease Control explores many health topics and issues, mostly discussed from a noneconomic perspective. Check out the Web site at http://www.cdc.gov to discover health care problems associated with poverty.

NOTES

1. These words, and the words of other women throughout the text, are actual quotations of women who were involved in a project of the Women and Poverty Public Education Initiative, funded by the Charles Stewart Mott Foundation. These quotes are taken from *In Our Own Words: Mothers' Perspectives on Welfare Reform*, the Women and Poverty Public Education Initiative, 1997 Women's Studies Consortium Outreach Program, University of Wisconsin-Parkside, Kenosha, Wisconsin. Major portions of the report were prepared by Laura Wittmann, Anne Statham, and Katherine Rhoades, as well as Loretta Williams, Jean Verber, Julie Elliott, Selina Vasquez, Kathe Johnson, Nancy Bayne, Ethel Quisler, May Kay Schleiter, Diana Garcia, Iredia Seiler,

Mary Ellen Lemke, Michelle Graf, Bets Reedy, Jean Radtke, Kim Noyd, Susan Taylor Campbell, and Davida Alperin. (Quotations may contain slight grammatical alterations made by the authors.)

2. U.S. Department of Commerce, Census Bureau, http://www.census.gov. Unless otherwise stated, all statistics in this chapter are from this source.

3. World Bank, *World Development Indicators 2013* (Washington, DC: The World Bank, 2013). Comparisons are based on the Gini coefficient, a measure of distribution of income or consumption expenditures, for the most recent year available.

4. Laura Wittmann et al., *In Our Own Words*.

5. Bread for the World, *Hunger 2009: Global Development: Charting a New Course* (Washington, DC: Bread for the World Institute, 2009), citing *Household Food Security in the United States 2007* (2008), U.S. Department of Agriculture.

6. The phrase *feminization of poverty* was first used by sociologist Diana Pearce in "The Feminization of Poverty: Women, Work, and Welfare," *Urban and Social Change Review* (February 1978). It also appears, along with an extensive discussion of the feminization of poverty and its causes in Ruth Sidel, *Women and Children Last: The Plight of Poor Women in Affluent America* (New York: Viking, 1986). In her book, Sidel emphasizes the point made in the introduction to this book, namely, that women are often just one normal life crisis away from poverty. She also makes the arguments in favor of universal entitlements that are discussed subsequently under the section in the chapter entitled "Solutions to Poverty."

7. Laura Wittmann et al., *In Our Own Words*.

8. The Centers for Disease Control and Prevention, "CDC 24/7: Saving Lives. Protecting People," *About Teen Pregnancy*, www.cdc.gov/teenpregnancy/aboutteenpreg.htm.

9. The 2006 information is from the Center on Budget and Policy Priorities, Ami Nagle and Nicholas Johnson in *A Hand Up: How State Earned Income Tax Credits Help Working Families Escape Poverty in 2006*, http://www.cbpp.org.

10. Much of the information on the federal TANF program is from Sharon Parrott, director of Welfare Reform and Income Support Policy at the Center on Budget and Policy Priorities, before the Committee on Ways and Means in the House of Representatives, July 19, 2006, http://www.cbpp.org/r7-19-06tanf-testimony.htm.

11. Acs, Gregory and Pamela Loprest, 2007, "TANF Caseload Composition and Leavers Synthesis Report." The Urban Institute.

12. Laura Wittmann et al., *In Our Own Words*.

Graphing the Data on Income Distribution

I t is useful to have a "picture" of income distribution that can readily be used to compare different time periods or different countries. In other words, we need to be able to graph the data on income distribution.

We will first compare the United States for the year 1981 and 2013, using the data from Table 6-1 in the text to compile the numbers for the graphs. We display these data in Figure 6-1. These graphs show the percentage of population on the horizontal axis and the percentage of total money income on the vertical axis. The 45-degree diagonal lines are hypothetical lines that exactly cut the graphs in half and would indicate perfect equality of income among the various income groups if they were to represent actual income distribution. For example, the poorest 20 percent of the population would receive 20 percent of total money income, the next 20 percent of the population would receive 20 percent of total money income, and so on. This 45-degree line is useful as a reference line.

Whereas the diagonal line shows hypothetical perfect equality of income, the Lorenz curve shows the actual income distribution. Note that the Lorenz curve is based on *cumulative* distributions derived from numbers in Table 6-1. Let's consider the top graph, which is based on the 2013 data. First, the poorest 20 percent of the U.S. population received 3.5 percent of total money income. The poorest 40 percent of the population (the two bottom income groups) received 12.6 percent of total money income (3.5 percent to the poorest 20 percent of the population plus 9.1 percent to the next poorest 20 percent of the population). The poorest 60 percent of the population (the three bottom income groups) received 27.5 percent of total money income (3.5 percent plus 9.1 percent plus 14.9 percent). Continuing this process completes the Lorenz curve.

Compare the bottom graph in Figure 6-1 with the top graph. The bottom graph is based on 1981 data from Table 6-1 in the text and was compiled in a manner similar to the top graph. We can see at a glance that the bottom graph shows more equality of income distribution. The Lorenz curve in the lower graph is closer to the 45-degree line. Since a hypothetical Lorenz curve lying directly on the 45-degree line would indicate perfect equality of income distribution, then the closer the actual Lorenz curve lies to the 45-degree line, the more equality of income distribution.

Lorenz Curve
A graph that displays the income distribution.

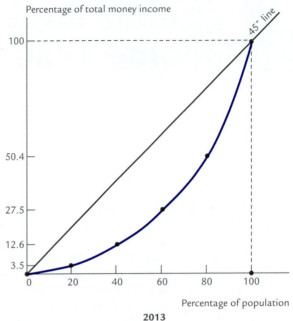

2013

The Lorenz Curve shows the cumulative distributions of income (along the vertical axis) for the poorest 20 percent of the population, the poorest 40 percent of the population, the poorest 60 percent of the population, and so on, up to the entire 100 percent of the population. Since the Lorenz curve lies relatively far from the 45-degree line, we know that income distribution is relatively unequal.

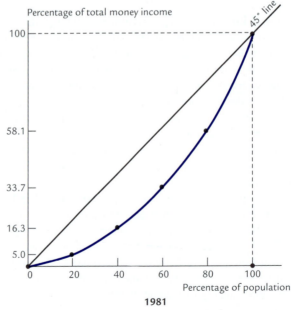

1981

The Lorenz Curve shows the cumulative distributions of income (along the vertical axis) for the poorest 20 percent of the population, the poorest 40 percent of the population, the poorest 60 percent of the population, and so on, up to the entire 100 percent of the population. Since the Lorenz curve lies relatively close to the 45-degree line, we know that income distribution is relatively equal.

Figure 6-1 • Lorenz Curves for the United States, 2013 and 1981

Let's also compare income distribution between the United States and an arbitrary European country. We'll use Norway as an example of a Western industrialized country with a relatively high degree of income equality. Unfortunately, the year 2010 is the most recently available year for data from the World Bank for most countries. Table 6-6 shows the information on income distribution for Norway.

TABLE 6-6 • Distribution of Total Money Income in Norway by Fifths of the Total Population, 2010

Fraction of Total Households	Percentage of Total Money Income Received (%) 2010
Poorest fifth	9.0
Second fifth	14.5
Third fifth	18.0
Fourth fifth	22.6
Richest fifth	36.0

Source: World Bank, World Development Indicators 2014, @worldbank.org, 2014.

Figure 6-2 once again displays the United States (2013) on the top graph, and the information for Norway on the lower graph. Cumulative distributions for Norway are calculated as before, resulting in 9.0 percent of total money income going to the poorest twenty percent of the population, 23.5 going to the poorest 40 percent, 41.5 percent going to the poorest 60 percent, and so on, up to 100 percent going to 100 percent of the population. Since the Lorenz curve is farther from the 45-degree line than in the graph for the United States above, we can see that income distribution is more equal in Norway.

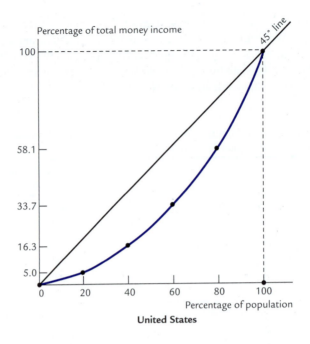

United States

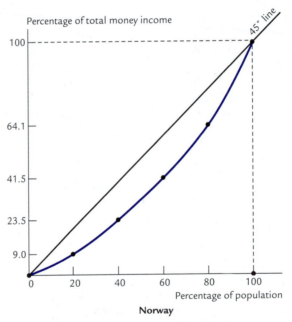

Norway

Figure 6-2 • Lorenz Curves for the United States and Norway
The Lorenz Curves above for the United States and Norway show that income is
distributed more equally in Norway than the United States (since the Lorenz Curve
is closer to the 45-degree line for Norway than the United States).

Appendix 6-2
Measurement Problems with the Poverty Line

The poverty line was initially based on the Department of Agriculture's 1961 "Economy Food Plan," later refined and renamed the "Thrifty Food Plan." A minimum food budget was determined and multiplied by three, because the cost of food was considered to represent about one-third of consumer expenditures, according to studies of consumer spending patterns in the 1950s. In each subsequent year, the poverty line has been adjusted upward to reflect inflation, which is a rise in the average price level.

This measure of official poverty has been the target of much controversy. Some economists and politicians have argued that this indicator exaggerates the true extent of poverty in the country because it ignores the receipt of in-kind transfers. Because these benefits are ignored in calculating a family's money income, the family may be classified as officially poor, even though its actual well-being is enhanced by transfers such as food stamps and Medicaid health coverage.

Another problem arises when adjusting the poverty line for inflation. Many economists believe that the Consumer Price Index, which is used to measure inflation, actually overstates the extent of inflation. (This issue is discussed in Chapter 14.) In this case, inflation adjustments would result in an artificially high poverty line and an overstatement of the extent of poverty.

Others have argued that official poverty statistics do not exaggerate the actual extent of poverty in this country, but rather underestimate it. They argue that the concept of household income used to measure poverty ought to be after-tax income because this is the income that can actually be used by households for their personal needs. (As a case in point, the poor pay a very large share of their income in the form of Social Security taxes.) They also argue that the poverty line is inadequate. The threshold was established when food expenses actually were one-third of a consumer's budget; since then, increases in fuel, housing, and health care costs have increased the importance of these items relative to food expenditures in a typical budget. Recent studies indicate that U.S. families spend about one-seventh of their incomes on food, rather than one-third. This statistic would suggest that food expenses perhaps ought to be multiplied by some number larger than three (such as seven) to arrive at an official poverty line. Furthermore, the Department of Agriculture's minimum food budget was never intended to represent a long-term adequate diet.

Chapter 7

ROAD MAP

Chapter 2
Crime and Drugs
Public housing concentrates poverty and its dysfunctions

Chapter 4
Education
Property tax funding and residential segregation contribute to low-quality inner-city schools

Chapter 5
Discrimination
Residential segregation still exists. Minorities were especially harmed by sub-prime mortgage lending

Chapter 6
U.S. Poverty
Public housing and residential segregation concentrate poverty. Property taxes place the heaviest burden on low income people

Chapter 7
Housing

Chapter 10
World Poverty
Price ceilings in poor countries work similarly to rental ceilings

Chapter 16
Taxes, Borrowing, and the National Debt
Tax breaks for homeowners and property taxes on home values are significant elements of our tax system

Chapter 15
Government Macroeconomic Policy
The housing crisis contributed to recent U.S. recession and the fiscal stimulus was designed in part to help overcome the housing crisis

The Economic Toolbox

- Housing markets
- Housing prices
- Rental ceilings
- Public housing
- Subsidies
- Fair market rent

- Housing vouchers
- Housing segregation
- Index of dissimilarity
- Homelessness
- Price ceilings (appendix)
- Perfect inelasticity (appendix)

Housing

The President's remarks in March 2009 refer to a housing crisis that traces back to well before the onset of the U.S. recession in December 2007 and extends beyond the problem of homelessness alone. Many economists believe that this particular housing crisis and the factors associated with it were among the major causes of the recession *and* that the housing crisis itself has been worsened by the recession. The causes of the crisis involved sincere and valiant efforts to achieve the American dream of homeownership, greed and corruption on the part of some lenders and investors, subprime mortgage lending, lax regulations, reckless borrowing and heartbreaking foreclosures—all of which hit the middle class hard, and, as is usually the case, the poverty class even harder. Although the housing sector is now improving, there are still many problems, as we shall see. In the process, we will utilize demand and supply analysis, and introduce a graphical discussion of price ceilings.

Housing, like food, is a commodity that has special connotations for many of us. Shelter from the elements is a basic biological need, and most of us see adequate housing (however defined) as a fundamental right. We are concerned, and often confused, about the homeless. We worry that low-income families cannot afford to rent houses or apartments in our cities. We realize that the single largest investment most U.S. families ever make is the purchase of their home. And, we watch as our friends and neighbors lose their homes while many of us wonder if we will be next. Others simply wonder if they will ever be able to afford a home.

We will begin this chapter by looking at issues involving homeownership and affordability, which are topics that pertain to the period before, concurrent with, and since the housing crisis. We will consider the subprime mortgage crisis and will look at government policy with regard to homeownership. We will then turn our attention to low-income rental housing and measures that are intended to assist poor families in acquiring adequate housing. We will also look at the economic consequences of housing segregation. Finally, we will return to the problem of the homeless that was alluded to by our president in the introductory quote.

One of the changes in attitudes that I want to see here in Washington and across the country is that it is unacceptable for children and families to be without a roof over their heads in a country as wealthy as ours.

—PRESIDENT BARACK OBAMA, SPEAKING TO REPORTERS ON MARCH 24, 2009

Homeownership: The American Dream

Although we speak of *the* housing market in the United States, a great many markets for housing exist within our country. There are markets for rental housing, owner-occupied housing, single-family dwellings, duplexes, and multifamily dwellings such as cooperatives and condominiums. If you live in a college dormitory, that building is part of the broader housing market. Market conditions vary greatly with geography and the socioeconomic characteristics of different locations. These markets are subject to the forces of supply and demand, as are other markets. Thus, the price of the average residence, as well as its size and other characteristics, varies with the location of the house. **Homes in areas with healthy economies and growing populations tend to gain in value over time, whereas the value of houses in depressed regions with declining populations tends to decline.** As realtors like to remind us, the three most important factors about housing are location, location, and location!

Figure 7-1 illustrates this concept. Assume that the two graphs are for houses with the same size and quality characteristics in two cities, Detroit and Boston. Detroit, part of the so-called Rust Belt, is a city in decline. Factories and jobs have moved out of Detroit to other cities and countries. Unemployment is high, and many workers have left the area. Boston, on the other hand, is a more dynamic city, attracting many residents and potential homebuyers. The declining population in Detroit has resulted in a decreasing demand for housing in Detroit, whereas the growing population in Boston has caused an increased demand for housing in Boston. Thus, the two cities are subject to opposite shifts in the demand for housing, as shown in each graph as a shift from D to D′. As a result of the demand shifts, the equilibrium market price of housing will change to P′ in each of the diagrams. The price of housing in Detroit will be lower than in Boston.

Really large differentials in housing prices can occur as the result of long-term economic growth trends in particular areas. The economy and population of the southern California region grew rapidly following World War II, creating an increase in the demand for housing. Housing prices escalated until, in the 1980s, houses in southern California cost three or four times as much as similar houses in the Midwest. With the post–Cold War defense cuts of the early 1990s, which threw the California economy into a severe recession, the regional housing demand slackened and housing prices began to decline. Housing prices then rose again, and by late 2007, Fresno, California, hit the news when a Depression-era-type tent city popped up on a railroad lot to provide "housing" for those

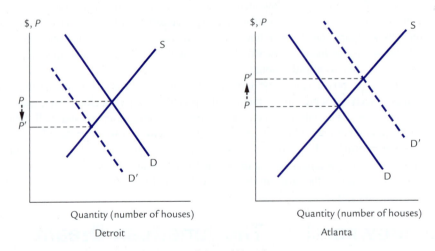

Quantity (number of houses)

Detroit   Atlanta

Figure 7-1 • Regional Differences in the Price of Housing
The decreased demand for housing over time in Detroit caused the price of housing to fall, whereas the increased demand in Boston caused housing prices to rise.

© Cengage Learning

who couldn't afford California's high housing prices. Tent cities like this prompted President Obama to make the statement about homelessness that introduces this chapter.

Trends in Homeownership

In 1960, 57 percent of housing units were occupied by their owners and 37 percent were occupied by renters. (A remaining category, called "other," refers to housing units held off the market or used seasonally and accounts for numbers not adding to 100 percent.) As we see in Table 7-1, the share of owner-occupied housing increased substantially from 1960 to 2010. In the United States, as noted, homeownership represents the *American dream*, whereas renting is often viewed as less desirable. To the extent that this is true, it appears that a small majority of Americans are indeed experiencing the American dream.

Before we go on to address other aspects of the current homeownership picture, let's note that the rates of homeownership vary greatly among different racial and ethnic groups. These data are presented in Table 7-2, and we see that non-Hispanic whites have the highest homeownership rate, with 74 percent of this population owning their own homes. The homeownership rates for other groups of Americans are much lower. The group with the lowest homeownership rate is African-Americans, with a rate of 45 percent. Hispanics are just ahead, with 47 percent. Many reasons account for the disparities, including the lower incomes of minority people that we noted in Chapter 5. Discrimination may also be a factor. Racial disparities in mortgage (housing) lending have been debated and studied for decades. One charge has been that mortgages have been unfairly denied in certain minority neighborhoods, a practice called **redlining**. Also, some localities refuse to provide low or moderately priced housing, which effectively keeps lower income minorities out of the area. We will study the matter of

Redlining
The practice of denying mortgages in certain minority neighborhoods.

TABLE 7-1 • Share of Total Housing Units That is Owner- and Renter-Occupied, Selected Years from 1960 to 2010

	1960	1990	2000	2010
Owner-occupied	57%	58%	61%	65%
Renter-occupied	37%	35%	32%	35%

Source: U.S. Department of Commerce, Census Bureau, Housing and Household Economics Statistics Division, *Housing Vacancies and Homeownership,* http://www.census.gov.

TABLE 7-2 • Homeownership Rates by Race and Ethnicity of Householder,[a] 2010

Group	Rate (%)
All	**67**
White	71
Non-Hispanic white	74
African-American	45
Native American	52
Asian-American	59
Hispanic	47

[a]For persons of single race. Hispanics may be of any race.

Source: U.S. Department of Commerce, Census Bureau, Housing and Household Economics Statistics Division, *Homeownership Rates by Race and Ethnicity of Householder,* http://www.census.gov.

TABLE 7-3 • Vacancy Rates for Homeowner Housing Units, Percent of Units Vacant, Selected Years, 2000–2012

2000	2005	2007	2008	2009	2010	2011	2012
1.6%	1.9%	2.7%	2.8%	2.6%	2.5%	2.4%	2.0%

Source: U.S. Department of Commerce, Census Bureau, http://www.census.gov.

segregation in housing later in this chapter, as well as the subprime market in relation to minority homeownership.

In addition to homeownership rates, statistics on vacancy rates can be very informative. As we look at the data in Table 7-3 on vacancy rates, we get a better glimpse at the housing crisis and recent recession. The table shows that with the housing crisis beginning in 2007, the vacancy rate for owner-occupied housing had increased from 1.9 percent in 2005 to 2.7 percent in 2007. The vacancy rate continued to rise through 2008, until it began to fall along with recovery in the housing sector and as of 2012, it was at a relatively low rate of 2.0 percent. The higher vacancy rate during the housing crisis suggests that people were having difficulty selling their homes or had lost them through foreclosures. A foreclosure takes place when homeowners are unable to meet their monthly mortgage loan repayments and the lender takes ownership of the home. We will discuss this in more detail shortly.

The Price of Housing

We've traced some of the history on homeownership and vacancy rates. These and other variables relate to demand and supply in the overall housing market, which of course determines housing prices. We can pose a few interesting questions about housing prices. First, what has been the long-term trend in housing prices and has this served to make housing more or less affordable to our nation's homebuyers? And second, what is the nature of housing prices in relation to what we referred to as the housing crisis? Both of these questions, we shall see, determine whether ordinary Americans can achieve the American dream of owning their own home.

The Long-Term Trend in Housing Prices

First, let's consider the long-term trend in housing prices for selected years from 1990 to 2010. We see in Table 7-4 that the median sales price of a new house has been rising

TABLE 7-4 • Median Sales Price of a New House, Median Household Income (Annual), and Median Price Relative to Median Household Income, Selected Years 1990 to 2010

Year	Median Sales Price of New Homes Sold	Median Household Income	Median Sales Price/Median Income
1990	$122,900	$29,900	4.1
1995	$133,900	$34,100	3.9
2000	$169,000	$42,000	4.0
2005	$240,900	$46,300	5.2
2006	$246,500	$48,200	5.1
2007	$277,900	$50,200	5.5
2008	$232,100	$50,300	4.6
2009	$216,700	$49,800	4.4
2010	$221,800	$49,300	4.5

Source: U.S. Department of Commerce, Census Bureau, http://www.census.gov.

from 1990 to 2007. (Recall that the term *median* means middle. If we had a list of housing prices from highest to lowest, the median value would be the one in the middle of the list.) The median price reached almost $278,000 in 2007, representing the peak of the "housing bubble" in terms of its rising prices. (Some geographical regions had housing prices peaking in 2006.) Nevertheless, the median price, by itself, does not tell us enough about the affordability of housing. We can adjust for inflation and assess the affordability of housing by considering the median price of a home relative to median household income. Table 7-4 shows that after making this calculation, the median price of a house relative to median income (the fourth column in the table) is rising from 1995 to 2007 (though it dips temporarily from 2005 to 2006). This suggests that houses had indeed become less affordable over this time period, though prices fell substantially in both nominal values (column 2) and income-adjusted values (column 4) in 2008 and 2009. They rose again somewhat in 2010.

Before we consider the second question with respect to housing prices, let's consider the alternative that exists for people for whom homeownership is unaffordable. Renting is the obvious alternative. Table 7-5 shows median rent relative to median income in the fourth column. Note that rent relative to income is shown as a percentage, since in any given month, rent will be lower than income. (In Table 7-4, the final column displays numbers greater than one, merely demonstrating that housing prices are *multiples* of annual incomes.) Table 7-5 reveals that, since 1995, median rent relative to income fluctuated somewhat until the year 2000, whereupon it rose steadily until 2009 and remained at approximately that level mostly thereafter. Thus, rental housing has mostly become less affordable. *This will be an important factor as we consider the problem of homelessness toward the end of this chapter.*

Many factors contributed to the rising price of housing during the first half of the 2000s. Rising incomes and population size served to increase the demand for housing, thereby pushing up its price. However, there were also other factors at work. Credit was readily available, in part because of considerable foreign investment in U.S. financial markets. Abundant credit (referred to as a "credit bubble") encouraged lenders, including mortgage lenders, to charge low interest rates and to avoid the normal careful screening of borrowers to assure their credit-worthiness. (Misperceptions among mortgage lenders about the management of risks contributed to the loose screening of borrowers.[1])

TABLE 7-5 • Median Asking Rent (per month), Median Household Income (per month), and Median Rent Relative to Median Household Income, Selected Years 1990–2012

Year	Median Asking Rent per Month	Median Household Income per Month	Median Rent/ Median Income
1990	$371	$2,495	14.9%
1995	$438	$2,840	15.4%
2000	$483	$3,499	13.8%
2005	$605	$3,861	15.7%
2006	$633	$4,017	15.8%
2007	$665	$4,187	15.9%
2008	$696	$4,192	16.6%
2009	$708	$4,148	17.1%
2010	$698	$4,106	17.0%
2011	$694	$4,171	16.6%
2012	$724	$4,251	17.0%

Source: U.S. Department of Commerce, Census Bureau, http://www.census.gov.

The U.S. government also encouraged mortgage lending. Among administrators in the Clinton and Bush administrations were politicians who genuinely wanted to help more Americans, including low-income people who couldn't obtain traditional mortgages, fulfill the American dream of owning a home. Henry Cicnero, the Director of the Department of Housing and Development under Clinton, wanted to spread homeownership not just to white Caucasians, who, as we know, have much higher homeownership rates than minorities; he wanted to expand homeownership to other racial and ethnic groups as well. Consumers responded to the various inducements (as well as their belief that housing values would only continue to climb) and increased their demand for housing. This, of course, increased housing prices.

Housing Prices and the Housing Crisis

The credit boom became a housing boom. People who never could have afforded a conventional mortgage were being offered easy terms and incentives. These unconventional mortgages are referred to as *subprime mortgages,* because the borrowers did not meet the higher credit-worthiness standards of "prime" borrowers. Many people borrowed. Many banks lent. Homes were purchased like never before. But then, the bubble burst. Credit dried up. As we saw in Table 7-4, housing prices plummeted after 2007. Homeowners defaulted on loans. Lenders foreclosed (and took ownership of) their customers' homes. The subprime crisis became a housing crisis, which, as we will see, spread crisis well beyond the housing market.

Before we consider the subprime market, it may be useful to comment on traditional mortgage lending.

Traditional Mortgage Lending

The traditional mortgage lending market has institutional safeguards built into it. Borrowers are carefully screened. Lenders are careful to examine a number of elements to assure that the borrower can make timely payments and ultimately repay the mortgage. **The elements that must be considered are (1) the down payment, (2) the monthly mortgage payments, and (3) the buyer's income and debt.** We will look at these much more carefully in Appendix 7-1 of this chapter, as they will undoubtedly be important to you if you are considering someday purchasing a home.

The Subprime Mortgage Crisis

Subprime mortgage
A mortgage loan made to a borrower with less than "prime" borrowing characteristics.

Thus, we see that when people wish to buy a house and take out a traditional mortgage, there are built-in safety features to ensure that the person can afford the house and the mortgage payments. These features were relaxed with **subprime mortgages**. Again, subprime means below prime. In other words, the person who is borrowing (taking out a mortgage) doesn't meet the conditions of a "prime" borrower. He or she has too little income or too much debt. Lenders are normally reluctant to lend money to such a borrower. If given incentives or directives by the government and its agencies (or if the degree of risk of the mortgage is masked by the way mortgage risks are managed in financial markets), the lender will overlook the subprime conditions of the borrower and make the loan anyway, though frequently with an adjustable-rate mortgage (ARM). An ARM means that mortgage interest rates do not stay constant and fluctuate with market rates. Even higher income homebuyers who could qualify for a conventional mortgage frequently entered the subprime market, borrowing with ARMs, and often buying well over their heads.

Both borrowers and lenders had reason to be involved in the subprime mortgage market. Borrowers frequently signed onto adjustable-rate mortgages, knowing that interest rates were currently low and believing that if interest rates started to rise, he or she could refinance on the basis of the rising value of his or her home. Lenders also anticipated that if the borrower defaulted on the loan, the high-valued home used as collateral would accrue to the lender. Neither borrower nor lender anticipated the burst in the housing bubble. When it did burst, housing values plummeted, interest rates rose, monthly adjustable-rate mortgage payments became unaffordable, and borrowers defaulted on their payments. Lenders foreclosed on the homeowner, taking ownership of the home. Indeed, borrowers have plenty of incentive to let foreclosure take place. If you owe $200,000 on what is now a $100,000 valued home, continued investment in the form of monthly mortgage payments doesn't make financial sense. And, of course, as foreclosed homes flood the market, housing prices are pushed down further.

We know that many middle-class and lower-income class homeowners suffered bankruptcy and/or the foreclosure of their homes. To the extent that racial and ethnic minorities were especially encouraged to participate in subprime mortgages, they suffered as well. Yet the upper class is also suffering, though that may not arouse the same degree of sympathy. An example are the residents of elegant Summit Street in St. Paul, Minnesota, a beautiful tree-lined boulevard on a bluff overlooking St. Paul's Cathedral, the Minnesota River, and the city of St. Paul. Elegant mansions are interspersed with prestigious colleges and churches, bordered by rivers, and surrounded by the elegance befitting the capital city of Minnesota. But, as of 2009, the mansions of Summit Street were in danger, with many homes on the market and no one buying. Potential buyers had experienced investment losses and economic insecurity, and the large easy-credit mortgages used to purchase upper-bracket homes were no longer available. Even luxurious Summit Street was not immune to the housing crisis.[2]

As we will see in subsequent chapters, the subprime mortgage crisis has not been isolated from the rest of the economy. Increasingly, investors bought financial securities that were backed by mortgage debt. These were called **mortgage-backed securities**, or MBSs. Less conventional (and less regulated) lenders, as well as conventional lenders, were investing more and more in these unconventional mortgaged-backed securities. Not only was regulation lax, but the government encouraged expanded trade in these securities as well. Foreign as well as domestic investors purchased them in record numbers, in part, because they were unaware of the degree of risk. When housing values fell, along with the value of the mortgages, the value of the MBSs collapsed as well. Representing a significant part of the financial sector in the United States, as well as several other countries that invested heavily in MBSs, this collapse led to a collapse of our overall economy (and other economies) and recession set in by late 2007. The spiral continued as the recession triggered job loss across the country, with high U.S. unemployment rates and lower incomes for homeowners and buyers. People became even less able to pay their mortgages or make new home purchases, and the housing crisis continued. Our cities and suburbs were filled with empty foreclosed homes, as well as homes that their owners are trying to sell, but only as of 2013 are people buying in significant numbers. Thus what began as a subprime mortgage crisis had turned into a full-fledged global recession, spiraling back and further harming the housing market.

You may have heard of Fannie Mae and Freddie Mac. These institutions are called government-sponsored enterprises, or GSEs, and they purchase mortgages and mortgage-backed securities. In 1995, Fannie Mae and Freddie Mac began receiving government tax incentives for purchasing mortgage-backed securities that included loans to low-income borrowers in the subprime market. In 1996, the government set a goal that at

Mortgage-backed security (MBS)
A financial security that is backed by mortgage debt.

least 42 percent of the mortgages purchased by these GSEs be issued to low-income bor-rowers. This target was increased to 50 percent in 2000 and 52 percent in 2005. As the housing crisis hit and the value of mortgages and mortgage-backed securities plummeted, it was feared that Fannie Mae and Freddie Mac could not make good on their mortgage obligations, and the Federal government was forced to place them into a conservatorship, effectively nationalizing them at the taxpayers' expense. Private investment banks were in trouble as well, and in 2008, the crisis peaked for the nation's five largest investment banks. Lehman Brothers went bankrupt, Bear Stearns and Merill Lynch were taken over by other companies, and the government bailed out Goldman Sachs and Morgan Stanley. Many other financial institutions went bankrupt, were taken over by the government, or received government assistance and bailout money. Thus the government was heavily involved in the financial sector, including the growth of the subprime market and the cri-sis that resulted.

The government ultimately began to help homeowners avoid foreclosure. In early 2009, President Obama announced a $75 billion program for homeowners and an addi-tional $200 billion for Fannie Mae and Freddie Mac to purchase and refinance mortgages.

Government Policy Toward Homeownership

A number of state and federal policies promote homeownership. We've already noted that government housing agencies had been encouraging the use of the subprime market to expand housing loans for some time. This policy, along with too little regulation, con-tributed to the problems of the subprime market that we've been considering. However, there are other important federal housing policies, the most significant of which involves the federal personal income tax.

Federal tax policy promotes homeownership by permitting the deduction of mortgage interest payments from income before personal income taxes are calculated. This deduc-tion benefits mainly middle- and higher-income households, however, because higher-income households, on average, buy more expensive homes and also pay personal income taxes at higher tax rates. Conversely, low-income households buy less expensive homes and are far more likely to rent than to own, in which case they receive no interest deduction on their federal income taxes.

The income tax deduction is a huge housing subsidy for middle- and upper-income classes, but not for the poor. The total value of the mortgage interest deduction and direct housing assistance for households in the top fifth of the income distribution by far exceeds any housing subsidies provided for our lowest income households.

Rental Housing for Low-Income Families

Some families cannot afford, or may not want, to buy a house. The availability of low-cost, adequate quality rental housing for low-income families is therefore important. We've already noted that rent as a share of income has increased since 2000, making rental housing less affordable. In addition, low-cost rental housing has become scarcer than it has been in the past.

Demand and Supply

The high price of rental housing results from the interaction of demand and supply. Figure 7-2 shows the changes that have taken place over time in the market for relatively low-cost rental housing. The shift of supply from S to S′ is a decrease in supply. Some

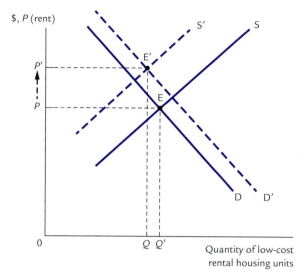

Figure 7-2 • Trends in the Market for Low-Cost Rental Housing Units
The reduced supply of low-cost rental housing and increased demand for it have resulted in less and higher-priced rental housing for low-income families.

© Cengage Learning

people trace the decrease in the supply of affordable housing units to the development of superhighways and urban renewal in the 1950s. Both of these programs destroyed thousands of low- and moderate-cost rental units in the name of urban development. Indeed, some pundits renamed the phenomenon of urban renewal "urban removal," because the poor tenants who had formerly lived in the "renewed" areas could no longer afford to live there. More recently, the process of **gentrification** has further reduced the supply of low-cost housing as traditional low-cost rental units have been restored and converted into middle- and upper-middle-class properties. Frequently, Wall Street institutional buyers purchase cheap housing, fix it up, and rent it out at high prices for high profits. The conversion of apartment buildings into condominiums throughout our cities has further decreased the supply of rental housing. In addition, some of our cities are experiencing a process of disintegration. Housing units have been abandoned and vandalized. Public housing stands vacant because of a lack of funds for upkeep and modernization. All of these factors have reduced the supply of adequate, low-cost housing.

The demand for low-cost rental housing has also increased over time. Part of the increase is the result of population growth. Part results from the growth in the number of poor and near-poor families as income distribution has become more unequal, as we discussed in Chapter 6. Both the increase in demand and the decrease in supply have caused the price (rent) for so-called low-cost rental housing to increase, as is shown in Figure 7-2 with points E and E′. **The final result is a housing affordability crisis for poor families—a crisis that is worse in some regions than in others.**

The search for affordable rental housing has become more difficult for poor families. The high rental prices obviously harm the well-being of low-income families, because when families spend a large percentage of their incomes on housing, little remains for food, clothing, and other necessities. One result is that low-income families are often crowded into older housing units that have physical problems. Another result is an increase in homelessness.

One measure used to assist low-income households is **rental ceilings** (also called **rent controls**), by which the government establishes a maximum rent for certain housing units. Other programs to help the poor obtain affordable rental housing can be divided

Gentrification
The conversion of low-cost apartments into middle- and upper-middle-class housing.

Rental ceilings (rent controls)
Legally imposed maximum rents on rental housing.

into programs to increase the supply of low-cost housing and programs to increase the demand for housing by enabling poor tenants to acquire (demand) adequate housing. Let us look at all three options individually.

Rental Ceilings

During World War II, the United States had a national system of rental ceilings. After the war, only New York City retained its rental ceilings, but during the 1970s, a number of other cities, many of them "university towns," adopted such measures. Some cities considered, but did not adopt, rental ceilings.

   Suppose that your school is located in College Town, which has adopted rental ceilings. Many college students are low-income people, and there is often a great demand in college towns for reasonably priced off-campus student housing of acceptable quality. At the same time, towns dominated by colleges often have landlords who buy up old houses and rent them to groups of college students, charging extremely high rents. Therefore, you might initially be much in favor of controlling the rents that landlords could charge you. But let us consider the consequences of rental ceilings.

Price ceilings
Legally imposed maximum prices of a good or service.

   Rental ceilings are a specific example of **price ceilings**, which are legally imposed maximum prices (rents) of a good or service. Price ceilings are discussed in Chapter 10 in the context of food price ceilings in developing countries. (Other examples of price ceilings are discussed in Appendix 7-2 to this chapter.) To be effective (which means to have an effect on the market), price ceilings must be below market equilibrium prices. Because prices are not free to rise above some specified maximum, price ceilings interfere with the rationing function of price. As we discussed in Chapter 1, markets tend to clear at an equilibrium price and quantity, and in the process, shortages and surpluses are rationed away. This is the rationing function of price in a competitive market. Because rent prices cannot rise above the rental ceiling to the equilibrium price, they cannot perform a rationing function. Therefore, they actually create a shortage.

   Figure 7-3 shows the effects of the rental ceiling on the hypothetical rental market in College Town. Before the rent controls are imposed, the equilibrium rental market price is $700 per month and the equilibrium quantity of apartments is 1,000. The local government establishes a rental ceiling of $500 to help poor tenants, including struggling students. Initially, nothing much happens except that tenants pay lower rents and landlords receive lower rents. But as time passes, both prospective tenants and landlords

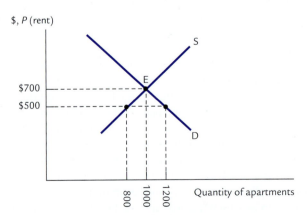

Figure 7-3 • The Effect of a Rental Ceiling in College Town
The rental ceiling of $500 creates a shortage of 400 apartments in College Town.

adjust to the rental ceiling. Because they are receiving lower rents, landlords have less incentive to provide rental housing, and they move down their supply curve until they are supplying only 800 units at the rental rate of $500. They do this by abandoning units that need repairs, demolishing some units so the land can be used for commercial purposes, and converting some units to other uses such as condominiums. Meanwhile, the quantity demanded of these apartments increases to 1,200, because at the low rent, more people desire to live in rental housing. Young adults may move out of their parents' houses, students may move off campus, and people living with roommates may seek their own apartments. There is a shortage of 400 rental units in College Town. And it is a shortage that the market cannot ration away, because the rental price cannot rise above $500 to reach the market equilibrium. **Note that in the graph of rental ceilings (or any price ceiling), we do not shift either the demand or supply curve).** Rather, we consider where along the original demand and supply curves the rental ceiling will hit, and determine the quantity demanded and quantity supplied at that rental price.

Rental ceilings produce some gainers and some losers. Obviously, the original tenants in the rent-controlled units gain. They stay there and pay lower rents. Those who move into rent-controlled units also gain, because their rents are lower than they would be without the controls. But people that cannot find an apartment in College Town because of the rental ceilings lose. And the landlords lose in two ways. They receive lower-than-market equilibrium rents; and if they sell their buildings, they will receive lower prices, reflecting the lower income generated by the properties.

Over time, rental ceilings have other effects. Landlords do less routine maintenance, and the properties deteriorate more rapidly. In effect, landlords let the apartments deteriorate until they are worth only the lower rent.

The rent-controlled units that are in good repair are a real bargain, encouraging development of illegal markets. Units might be subleased at rates higher than the rental ceilings. Alternatively, landlords may require large payments, perhaps in the form of huge damage (security) deposits, before they rent out their property. Both the sub-leasers and the prospective tenants who make upfront payments to obtain the rent-controlled apartments are usually middle-class families, rather than the poor. A program to help low-income households afford decent rental housing has become a program that subsidizes the middle class.

Rental ceilings are generally intended to help the poor, which certainly include many college students. **In the end, however, the poor are probably the group harmed the most by rent controls.** They have fewer choices. They cannot afford to buy homes. They cannot afford to move out to the suburbs. They cannot afford the huge security deposits needed to move into a rent-controlled apartment in good repair. They are likely to be crowded into substandard, overpriced housing or to become part of our nation's homeless.

Rental ceilings may also encourage discrimination. Because of the housing shortage, each landlord has many people who wish to rent. Landlords can afford to be selective about who they accept as tenants. Although many of these examples are illegal, the landlord may decide to discriminate on the basis of race or ethnicity, age of renters (and whether they have children), religion, sexual orientation, disability, or even student status!

Rental ceilings are attractive on the surface, but they cause shortages and a deteriorating stock of affordable housing. Because these rental ceilings do not benefit the poor households for which they were intended, but instead benefit higher-income people, rental ceilings are a very inefficient method for providing affordable rental housing to low-income families. Appendix 7-2 to this chapter shows similar effects from other examples of price ceilings.

Public Housing: A Program to Increase the Supply of Rental Housing

Public housing

Housing units owned and operated by a local public housing authority but federally subsidized and often federally regulated.

The oldest and perhaps best-known program to supply low-income housing is called **public housing**, which began in 1937. Constructing public housing was justified initially as a means to create employment during the Great Depression of the 1930s. Public housing units are owned and operated by a local public housing authority, but the units are federally subsidized and often federally regulated. The federal government establishes the eligibility requirements for tenants and the ratio of rent relative to income that will determine what the individual tenant will pay for housing. Currently, there are about 1.2 million households living in public housing units.[3]

The public housing program is criticized because it often concentrates poor and distressed populations into particular areas (though there are also single-family public housing units spread throughout some cities). It may also segregate people both racially and by income level. *Life in the "projects" has often become synonymous with poverty, social dysfunction, and high crime rates.*

Much of the political support for public housing over the years has come from the construction industry. Indeed, the whole program was terminated under President Richard Nixon's administration in 1973, which was a boom year in the construction industry. The program was then reactivated in 1976, when the bottom had fallen out of the construction market. Moreover, several studies have shown that public housing is an expensive method to house the poor. Public housing units cost more than either new private housing units or used low-income housing. Therefore, the availability of public housing is limited. Many eligible families remain on waiting lists for years; some large cities have reported waiting periods of up to 10 years.

Furthermore, some economists argue that public housing displaces private housing, causing the latter to be abandoned or converted to other purposes because the supply of public housing units causes the market price of available private housing units to fall. (As you know, an increase in supply causes a decrease in price, or in this case, rent.) The private landlords then either retire some of their units or use them for other purposes, thereby shifting the supply curve back again. Public housing is an increasingly controversial policy, so let us look at one other method to house the poor.

Rental Housing: A Program to Increase the Demand for Rental Housing

Supply-side policies help the poor by providing more low-income housing in the rental market. Another way to help low-income households would be to give them subsidies (vouchers) and to let them choose their own housing. These subsidies increase the poor families' ability to express their demand for housing in the private housing market.

Housing (Rent) Vouchers

Housing voucher

Housing subsidies in the amount of the difference between the fair market rent and 30 percent of a poor family's income.

Fair market rent

An amount determined by HUD to be reasonable rent for low-income housing in that area.

The principal demand-side housing program is the housing vouchers program, which is part of the Section 8 housing program. Most **housing vouchers** go to very poor families. Recipients must occupy a dwelling that meets minimum government standards. The housing vouchers are based on the difference between the **fair market rent** for the locality and 30 percent of the tenant's income. If the fair market rent for an apartment is $700 and the family's income is $1,000, the voucher will be in the amount of $400 ($700 minus 30 percent of $1,000).

As with public housing, this program serves only a modest fraction of eligible households because of its underfunding. Even the Department of Housing and Urban Development's Web site states that there may be a long wait for assistance under the housing voucher program. Many cities have even stopped adding names to their waiting lists for housing vouchers, since the wait time has become so long as to almost become irrelevant. For example, in the college town where your author lives, no names are being added because the wait times are currently too long (15 years!). Minneapolis and St. Paul had not added new names to their lists in almost a decade, and then announced a brief period during which they would add 2,000 additional names by lottery. The Twin Cities expected that some 60,000 residents were to apply. These long waiting lists for voucher assistance will grow even longer unless additional dollars are appropriated.

In terms of economics, demand-side housing subsidies initially cause the price of low-cost housing to increase, because the demand for such housing increases. However, over time, we can expect landlords to supply more units. They increase maintenance on their dwellings and upgrade lower-quality housing in order to participate in this housing submarket, thereby increasing (shifting forward) the supply of available housing.

Many economists prefer demand-side subsidies to the supply-side methods of aiding low-income families to obtain housing. As we noted, demand-side subsidies not only increase the demand for housing but may also increase the private supply of low-cost housing units (whereas public housing appears to decrease that supply). **The demand-side subsidies are paid directly to low-income households rather than to developers or construction firms, and some argue that the benefits are thus more certain to go to the intended group, our low-income families.**

Do Our Housing Policies Meet the Needs of the Poor?

Although many U.S. families are helped by public housing or housing vouchers, housing activists maintain, and government officials acknowledge, that there is simply not enough money allocated to provide adequate housing for all our ill-housed poor and near-poor families. Many families eligible for housing assistance receive no aid because budget constraints do not permit assistance for all qualifying families. Across-the-board cuts in federal government spending over the last few years have cut expenditures on housing programs for the poor and have increased homelessness.

In addition to the problem of housing for low-income people are the issues relating to housing for the aged, the disabled, those with AIDS, the mentally ill and chemically addicted, and ex-offenders. Programs for these people require funding and specific assistance to meet their varied needs.

Finally, let's address the problems of homelessness and segregation.

Homelessness in the United States

By the very nature of homelessness, the homeless are difficult to count, so estimates of their number vary widely. Traditional methodology for counting the homeless has been to count the people who are in shelters or on the streets. This approach may be useful for determining how many people need services such as shelter and soup kitchens. However, these counts often fail to find the "hidden" homeless, those who sleep in automobiles, campgrounds, boxes, caves, or boxcars. These counts also ignore other people in "homeless situations" who are forced to live with relatives and friends in overcrowded or substandard temporary conditions. They also miss the point that the number of homeless at any one point in time does not address the complexity and extent of the problem whereby many people are homeless at some point *over time*. Nevertheless, Move for Hunger, a hunger and homelessness advocacy organization, reports that the number of homeless on any given night exceeds 640,000 in the United States.[4]

The number of homeless is increasing. The U.S. Conference of Mayors collects survey data on homelessness in 29 U.S. cities. According to their 2011 report, the number of people experiencing homelessness increased by 6 percent over the previous year. The number of *families* that experienced homelessness increased by 16 percent. Among households with children, unemployment was the leading cause of homelessness. This was followed by a lack of affordable housing and by poverty. Among individuals, unemployment was also the primary cause of homelessness, followed by a lack of affordable housing, mental illness and a lack of needed services, and substance abuse and a lack of needed services. In about two-thirds of the cities, shelters had to turn away both families with children and individuals because of a lack of available beds.[5] Although these surveys are done in cities, keep in mind that there are few or no rural homeless shelters, despite significant levels of rural homelessness.

Who Are the Homeless?

The homeless population is certainly diverse, and includes many families with children. Some homeless people are women and children fleeing abusive relationships. (The same survey of cities just cited reports that 13 percent of homeless adults are homeless as a result of domestic violence.) Also among homeless adults, 16 percent have physical disabilities, 13 percent are veterans, and 4 percent are HIV positive. Twenty-six percent of the homeless adults are severely mentally ill, with their homelessness partially resulting from government policy. Since the 1970s, this policy has been to deinstitutionalize mental health care, meaning that many patients with mental illness have been released from public mental hospitals. At the same time, the government has not allocated adequate funds needed to support community-based mental health services such as halfway houses, and as a result, many deinstitutionalized patients have joined the ranks of the homeless. Others come to be homeless because their substance abuse is so severe that they simply cannot hold a job or pay rent on an apartment. Some homeless people are teenagers running away from dysfunctional families.

However, the rest of the people who are homeless are very much like us, only poorer. The survey of cities revealed that 15 percent of homeless adults are employed. Nevertheless, many of these homeless work at the minimum wage rate, which provides inadequate income for paying rents. Furthermore, many of our nation's families are just one or two paychecks away from homelessness. If an emergency (such as the death or desertion of a spouse or a serious illness) occurs, their savings may not be adequate to pay the rent or the mortgage. Homelessness is also a consequence of unemployment. Losing a job and the income it represents can cause a poverty-level family to lose housing because it can no longer pay the rent. Unemployment may also be a consequence of homelessness, because holding down a job when you are primarily concerned about where you and your family will sleep is very difficult.

Solutions to Homelessness

Certainly, given the various reasons for homelessness and the variety of homeless people, the causes of homelessness are diverse and complex. The solutions to homelessness may be complex as well. Probably the most desirable way of leaving the ranks of the homeless is to find a job that pays enough for rent on a housing unit. But searching for employment is difficult, if not impossible, for homeless people. It is hard to present yourself well if you do not have bathroom facilities available to you, let alone washing machines and ironing boards. The homeless also have neither an address nor a phone number by which prospective employers can contact them.

Homelessness compounds the problems of poverty. Homeless children often do not attend school, or they attend school sporadically. Homeless parents have difficulty keeping their children clean and appropriately dressed for school. The children are often malnourished as well as homeless, and malnourishment leads to difficulty in learning. Studying and doing homework while being homeless are obviously far more difficult than studying and doing homework in a stable home environment. Thus, homeless children face great burdens that keep many from succeeding in school, a prerequisite to rising out of poverty as an adult.

Homeless advocates argue that we need coherent long-term policy concerning the homeless, rather than reacting in ad hoc ways to emergencies. We need a comprehensive housing policy that includes both emergency shelters and permanent low-cost housing. Our reactive policies, such as shelters and short-term placement in hotels, are both inadequate and wasteful. One program begun by President Bush and continued by President Obama that seeks to place the homeless into apartments has been found to be of foremost importance in terms of reducing the problems faced by the homeless, as well as cost-effective by reducing spending on incarceration and shelters. *We must continue to devise policies such as these that promote permanent housing arrangements, rather than using so-called Band-Aid treatments once the problem occurs.*

One Final Comment

One final comment on homelessness: We noted in Chapter 2 that the government is required to tabulate and publicize the number of hate crimes that are targeted toward people due to their race or ethnicity, religion, sexual orientation, or disability. The National Coalition for the Homeless also calls on the government to track the number of hate crimes committed against people on the basis of their homelessness. Unfortunately, hate crimes are just another example of the many problems faced by homeless people in America.

Housing and Segregation

The problem of racial segregation in U.S. housing is serious. Studies show that housing discrimination still exists. For example, a 2012 study by the Department of Housing and Urban Development sent out pairs of testers, one white and one minority in each pair. Conducting over 8,000 tests separately across 28 metropolitan areas, the Department used testers of the same gender and age who presented themselves as equally qualified to rent or buy a unit of housing. The study revealed that blacks and Asian-Americans were treated differently than their white counterparts and often given fewer options. Hispanics were also treated differently when renting, but experienced about equal treatment as whites when seeking to buy a home. This type of discrimination is one reason why racial segregation is so extensive.

The census data reveal that large shares of African-Americans and Hispanics live in our central cities, yet they make up very small shares of the population in the suburban areas surrounding these cities. Many metropolitan areas that have countywide desegregation plans, especially in the south, have slowly become more racially integrated. But inner cities that are heavily populated by minorities and surrounded by a ring of white suburbs display persistent racial segregation.

Segregation occurs not only between the central city and its suburbs but also within central cities as well. Several indexes have been developed to measure the extent of segregation within central cities. The one most commonly used is the **index of dissimilarity**. For a city with two districts and two races (white and African-American), this index is calculated by adding together the differences between the percentage of African-Americans and the percentage of whites living within each district of the city and dividing this sum by two. The reason we divide by two is that if segregation were to be reduced, a two-way move would have to take place. A white person would have to move into an African-American area, replacing an African-American person who would move into a white district.

To illustrate the calculation of the index of dissimilarity, assume for simplicity that a city consists of two equal-size districts. In District 1 live 80 percent of all African-Americans and

Index of dissimilarity
A measure of segregation.

20 percent of all whites. The difference in the district is 60 percent, or 60. In District 2 live 20 percent of all African-Americans and 80 percent of all whites. Again the difference is 60. To calculate the index, add together the differences and divide by two, as follows:

$$\text{Difference in District 1} = 60$$
$$\text{Difference in District 2} = 60$$
$$\text{Sum of Differences} = 120$$
$$120 \text{ divided by 2} = 60$$

If there were no segregation, 50 percent of both African-Americans and whites would live in District 1, so its difference would be 0. The same would be true of District 2, in which the remaining 50 percent of each race would live. The index of dissimilarity would therefore be 0. On the other hand, if we had total segregation, with 100 percent of African-Americans in District 1 and 100 percent of whites in District 2, the index would be 100. The index of dissimilarity will vary between 0 and 100, and the higher it is, the greater is residential segregation. Of course, this calculation would be more complicated if we considered a larger number of segregated groups of people.

The Census Bureau has calculated a weighted-average index of dissimilarity for all U.S. metropolitan areas every 10 years recently up until the year 2000. Table 7-6 displays this index for 1980, 1990, and 2000. As we can see, the index has fallen over time, revealing less segregation. However, the decline is not very large. In addition, these calculations are made for whites and African-Americans only and do not measure segregation with respect to Hispanics, Asian-Americans, Native Americans, and so on. Finally, the index for U.S. metropolitan areas overall disguises the high degree of segregation that occurs in certain metropolitan areas. For example, Detroit, Milwaukee, and Cleveland are examples of metropolitan areas that have had much higher than average levels of segregation.

Housing segregation, in combination with the labor market discrimination discussed in Chapter 5, serves to isolate minorities, especially African-Americans, who are among the most strictly segregated of all minorities. Isolation puts African-Americans at an economic disadvantage. They live in the ghetto, and the jobs are usually in the suburbs. They have neither information about who is hiring nor easy access to work sites by means of public transportation. We have seen that African-American poverty rates are significantly higher than the poverty rates of whites. Therefore, poverty is concentrated in the ghetto. These circumstances guarantee that poor African-Americans have a markedly inferior economic environment than do poor whites. Concentrated poverty often leads to family instability, crime, welfare dependency, housing abandonment, and low educational attainment. The housing stock of the inner cities deteriorates. The public schools are seriously underfunded, as explained in Chapter 4, and the quality of the public education is exceedingly poor.

TABLE 7-6 • Weighted-Average Index of Dissimilarity for African-Americans and White Caucasians for All U.S. Metropolitan Areas in 1980, 1990, and 2000

Year	Index of Dissimilarity
1980	73
1990	68
2000	64

Note: The index of dissimilarity shows the degree of segregation between African-Americans and white Caucasians, and ranges between 0 and 100. The larger the number, the more segregation exists.

Source: U.S. Department of Commerce, Census Bureau, http://www.census.gov/hhes/www/housing.

View*Point*   Conservative versus Liberal

Housing policy is one area in which the conservative and liberal viewpoints are quite clearly delineated. The conservative position is that government participation in housing markets should be eliminated, or at least minimized. Thus, conservatives would encourage the transfer of public housing units to the private sector (private tenants or landlords). If they were consistent, conservative economists would also eliminate the mortgage interest deduction, although many conservative politicians regard this deduction as the equivalent of a sacred cow. (Politicians who argue for the repeal of cherished middle- and upper-class tax breaks seldom get re-elected.) If it is necessary to aid poor families to obtain shelter, conservatives favor such measures as rent vouchers, which allow poor families

to afford housing in the private sector. Their principal argument is that the market is more efficient in solving housing problems than is the government, and they view this as a market-oriented solution.

Like conservatives, many liberals favor rent vouchers to help the poor. Unlike conservatives, however, liberals are more likely to stress government's role in solving housing problems. They see homelessness as a problem that government should solve by assuring permanent housing and in some cases providing temporary shelters as well. Liberals are not unconcerned with efficiency, but they stress that government's involvement in housing markets may be necessary to increase poor people's access to housing and to provide greater equity within our economy.

You, the Student

Are there any homeless students on your campus or community? Are there any campus activities you or student organizations could initiate to raise awareness of homelessness? You can find information about both of these issues by googling "homelessness" and "colleges or universities."

SUMMARY

The housing market is in fact many markets, which differ by region, type of housing, and other characteristics. The cost of both owner- and renter-occupied housing has increased more rapidly than family income over recent years, leading to concern about the affordability of housing. White Caucasians are more likely to live in their own home than are racial and ethnic minorities.

Policies to aid low-income households in obtaining shelter include rental ceilings, supply-side policies such as public housing, and demand-side policies such as housing vouchers. Rental ceilings create shortages of housing. Public housing benefits both the construction industry and low-income households. Demand-side policies appear to benefit low-income

families and to encourage the provision of low- and moderate-cost housing units by the private sector. Funding for both programs has been inadequate to meet the housing needs of low-income people and will remain insufficient in the foreseeable future.

Residential segregation remains a problem in the United States. It leads to a disadvantaged economic environment for minorities in this country. In addition, the problem of homelessness is complex and only partially related to a scarcity of low-cost housing. Housing advocates argue that we need a cohesive, long-term strategy to attack the problem, instead of the reactive strategies we now have.

DISCUSSION AND ACTION QUESTIONS

1. (Appendix 7-1) What factors affect a family's ability to afford housing? Will you satisfy the "American Dream" by becoming a homeowner in the near future (if you are not already)?

2. Describe the effects of rental ceilings. Who benefits from rental ceilings? Who suffers? What are the long-term effects of rental ceilings? How can landlords and tenants cheat on rental ceilings? Do you think that rental

ceilings might lead to more discrimination against certain groups?

3. What is the housing situation in your college town? Do you believe that rents are unjustly too high? What is the quality of housing? Are you aware of situations in which students were discriminated against or students were unfairly denied the recovery of their security deposits? Do you think you have ever been discriminated against or treated unfairly in terms of housing?

4. Which two groups are the primary beneficiaries of public housing?

5. How do housing vouchers work? If we had only so much money for housing assistance, what would be the best way to assist low-income families?

6. Should we subsidize housing for each of the following groups?
   a. Homeless families
   b. Low-income families
   c. Middle- and upper-income families
   d. Do we subsidize these groups? How so?

7. Do you take the conservative or liberal position on the issue of housing?

8. How many paychecks away from homelessness is your household? What would you do if disaster struck and you (or your family) lost your income? Would you rely on savings, relatives, or friends? What if none of these resources were available to you?

9. Go to the Web site of the National Association of Realtors (http://www.realtor.com) and find the most recent value of the average existing home.

10. Go to the following Web site: http://www.hud.gov. This Department of Housing and Urban Development Web page provides links to other research and sources of data on housing for low-income families. How does this Web site compare with the Web site of the National Coalition for the Homeless in terms of being liberal versus conservative? Why do you feel this way?

11. Go to the Web site of the Center on Budget and Policy Priorities (http://www.cbpp.org) and search for current information on housing programs and proposals. Is this a liberal or conservative organization?

12. What do you and the general public know about discriminatory practices and the fair housing law? Go to the HUD Web site and take the survey at http://www.huduser.org/publications/hsgfin/FairHsngSurvey.html. A representative sample of adults took the survey in 2000–2001 and in 2005, and results did not improve over the time period, with average Americans failing to recognize two out of eight scenarios as violations of the antidiscrimination law. Although more people supported the fair housing law in 2005 than in the earlier year, still one-quarter of respondents were unsympathetic to the law.

NOTES

1. Mortgage lenders often misunderstood and underestimated the risks involved with subprime lending by assuming that risks of nonpayment were minimized through the bundling of large groups of mortgages together and then hedging the risk with complex financial derivatives. This gave them greater willingness to lend to subprime borrowers.

2. Christopher Snowbeck, "A Grand Glut," *St. Paul Pioneer Press* (July 12, 2009).

3. Department on Housing and Urban Development, http://www.hud.gov.

4. Move for Hunger, moveforhunger.org, citing the National Alliance to End Homelessness.

5. U.S. Conference of Mayors 2011 Status Report on Hunger and Homelessness in America's Cities: A 29-City Survey, December 2011, conferenceofmayors.org/housing. Unless otherwise indicated, all data in this section are from this source.

Appendix 7-1
Traditional Mortgage Lending

W ill you be able to afford a house when you are ready to buy one? Will you be able to get a loan (mortgage) to buy the house? **The elements that must be considered in analyzing the affordability of homeownership and the ability to obtain a mortgage are (1) the down payment, (2) the monthly mortgage payments, and (3) the buyer's income and debt.** Let's look at each of these elements.

The Down Payment and Other Expenses at the Time of Purchase

The **down payment** is the amount of the buyer's own money that must be paid at the time of the purchase. A standard mortgage often requires a 20 percent down payment, which means that the buyer must "put down" 20 percent of the purchase price at the time of the purchase. For those eligible, a housing loan from the Federal Housing Administration may require a smaller down payment. Finally, some new houses are sold with only 5 percent down payments. These homes are seen as good investments, and the lender assumes that they can easily be resold if it is necessary to foreclose on the loan. Older housing usually is sold with traditional mortgages that require the higher down payments. As a general rule, lenders require buyers who pay lower than normal percentages down to purchase **mortgage insurance**. Mortgage insurance protects the lender if the buyer defaults on the loan.

In addition to the down payment, the buyer must make other payments at the time of purchase. These payments include mortgage **points**, which are fees charged by lenders at the time they grant mortgages. Points are like interest in that they are a charge for borrowing money. One point equals 1 percent of the amount borrowed, so if you were to pay one point on $100,000 borrowed, you would pay $1,000.

Lenders typically use both the interest rate and points to establish their charges for lending you money. Lenders might be willing to give you a lower interest rate if you pay more points, or they might charge more points if you make a smaller down payment. In some localities, laws have been passed that establish a legal maximum interest rate above which the financial institution is legally prohibited from charging. These laws are called **usury laws** and were discussed in more detail in the previous appendix to this chapter. In these localities, points are often used to offset the low interest rates that can legally be charged.

Closing costs refer to the total expenses, including points, that buyers pay at the time that the loan is finalized and the title to the property is conveyed to them. The closing cost is money you must come up with if you are to buy a house. Closing costs include

Down payment
The amount of a homebuyer's own money required by the lender for the purchase of a home.

Mortgage insurance
Insurance that pays off a mortgage if the borrower defaults.

Points
Fees charged by a lender at the time it grants a mortgage.

Usury laws
Laws establishing a maximum legal interest rate.

Closing costs
The total amount of money paid at the time a person purchases a house.

the down payment, loan application fees, points, title search fees, title insurance, attorney's fees, appraisal fees, and other miscellaneous charges.

Monthly Mortgage Payments

The monthly mortgage payment is made up of payments on the principal (unpaid balance) of the loan plus interest payments. For most of the life of the loan, more of the monthly payment goes to pay interest charges than to repay principal. The amount of interest paid over the life of the loan is extremely sensitive to the length of the loan. Table 7-7 illustrates this fact. The table shows the monthly payments for an 8 percent conventional mortgage loan of $50,000 to be paid over 10 years, 15 years, 20 years, and 30 years. The borrower will pay 8 percent annually on the unpaid balance of the loan, and the amount by which the unpaid balance is reduced is much smaller if the payments are stretched out over a longer period of time. The monthly payment is the amount that the buyer must pay if the $50,000, plus 8 percent interest, is to be paid in the stated number of years. The total amount paid is the monthly payment multiplied by the number of payments, and the interest paid is the difference between the total payments and the $50,000. Note that a 30-year conventional mortgage involves the payment of nearly four times as much interest as a 10-year conventional mortgage.

The mortgage payment increases with the amount borrowed and with the interest rate charged by the lender. Therefore, an increase in the average price of housing units or in the interest rates charged by lenders will increase the homebuyer's monthly payments.

In the late 1970s, we experienced an extremely high rate of inflation, which is a rise in the average level of prices in our economy. Both housing prices and the interest rates charged by lenders for long-term loans increased markedly. The housing market was stifled by the high interest rates. Many potential buyers could not afford the monthly payments at the high rates of interest. Lenders did not want to tie up funds for 30 years because the interest rate they could receive on other loans or investments might increase significantly in that time period. Lenders therefore began issuing **adjustable-rate mortgages (ARMs)**. On an adjustable-rate mortgage loan, a rate is established for a period of time, such as two or four years. When the time is up, the buyer can either continue the mortgage at market interest rates, refinance, or pay off the remainder of the loan. As we will see, a final option is to default on the loan.

Property taxes and homeowner's insurance are sometimes part of the monthly payment of the borrower. **Property taxes** are levied by local governments to fund services such as education and police protection. These taxes are generally a given percentage of the approximate market value of property (land and buildings), so more expensive houses will bear more property taxes. **Homeowner's insurance**, which covers the replacement cost of the house and its contents, may be required by the lender to protect itself in the event of natural disaster. Monthly payments toward insurance and property taxes are

Adjustable-rate mortgages (ARMs)
Mortgage loans on which interest rates are adjusted to market levels.

Property taxes
Taxes levied by local governments to fund services such as education and police protection.

Homeowner's insurance
Insurance that covers the replacement cost of a house and its contents.

TABLE 7-7 • Monthly Payments on a $50,000 Mortgage, Various Lengths of Loan

Loan Terms	10 Years	15 Years	20 Years	30 Years
Monthly payment	$606.65	$472.85	$418.25	$384.50
Number of payments	120	180	240	360
Total amount paid	$72,798	$86,013	$100,380	$138,420
Principal	$50,000	$50,000	$50,000	$50,000
Interest paid	$22,798	$36,013	$50,380	$88,420

© Cengage Learning

sometimes required by the lender. These payments are placed in a temporary escrow account from which insurance and taxes are paid when due.

The Income and Debt of the Buyer

Most lenders require that prospective borrowers satisfy affordability guidelines. The most common affordability criterion is that monthly mortgage payments not exceed a particular percent of the borrower's before-tax income. Furthermore, total monthly installment payments such as auto loans and charge card payments cannot exceed some percent of before-tax income. The prospective homebuyer's monthly income is therefore an important factor in determining whether the family can afford to buy a particular home.

In addition to income, debt is an important factor in a family's ability to purchase a house. Credit cards "maxed out" or other consumer debts may prevent a buyer from meeting mortgage lenders' guidelines.

Thus, we can see that traditional precautions benefit both lender and borrower. The lower likelihood of foreclosure benefits both.

© iStockphoto.com/bjdlzx

Appendix 7-2

Price Ceilings

You may never have lived in rent-controlled housing, but some real-world examples of price ceilings have almost certainly affected you and your family. Let's consider some of these price ceilings.

A Price Ceiling on Football Tickets

Your school probably has a football (or basketball, hockey, or baseball) team that you, your fellow students, and even college alumni follow. Imagine that your team is having an exceptional year. All seating is filled to capacity. In fact, many fans who want to attend games cannot get tickets. To obtain tickets, you either have to stand in line for hours or have some "connection" allowing you to receive preferential treatment.

Such a situation is shown in Figure 7-4. Note first that the supply curve is vertical (*perfectly inelastic*). The football stadium has 20,000 seats, so regardless of the price of football tickets, just 20,000 tickets will be available. Quantity supplied will not change, no matter what happens to price. The demand curve for tickets, however, has the usual downward slope, implying that more people are willing and able to buy tickets when the price is low. If the market was allowed to operate by itself, an equilibrium would occur at a price of $9 and the quantity 20,000. There would be no shortage of football tickets at the equilibrium price.

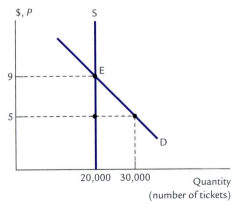

Figure 7-4 • The Effect of a Price Ceiling on Football Tickets
The $5 price ceiling for football tickets results in a shortage of 10,000 tickets.

© Cengage Learning

But let's assume that the school administration sets a price for football tickets of $5, which administrators believe to be a fair and appropriate price for sports tickets. After all, the administrators do not want to unduly burden students and alumni with high ticket prices. They want only to bring in enough ticket revenue to cover the team's costs.

The $5 price operates like a price ceiling, because the price is set below the equilibrium level. Thirty thousand fans demand the $5 tickets. Only 20,000 seats are available, so only 20,000 fans will be able to obtain tickets. The market has a shortage of 10,000 tickets.

Without intending to do so, the school administration created an inefficient market. Fans were given an over incentive to buy a football ticket, and a shortage was the natural result. In addition, people wasted hours standing in line. If the price of tickets were allowed to rise to the $9 level, these conditions could have been avoided.

Have you ever tried to purchase tickets to hear your favorite rock band? Maybe one reason you love this band is their effort to be fair to fans by charging relatively low prices. But almost as soon as the concert is announced, you discover that the tickets are sold out. Without intending it, the pricing decision creates a shortage in the same way as the pricing decision for football tickets. The low price ceiling and limited number of seats create a shortage.

A Price Ceiling on Gasoline

If you did not drive in the 1970s, ask your parents or grandparents about the gasoline short- age that occurred. They will undoubtedly tell you about long lines of cars trying to reach gas pumps and about gas stations closing early because they had sold all their gasoline. Some gas stations sold only to their established customers and turned away strangers. Many customers were unable to purchase gasoline. Other customers continually "topped off" their almost-full tanks whenever they had a chance. People got up early to wait in line, spent a lot of time looking for gas, worried about shortages of gas, and were extremely frustrated by the situation. If ever a market were inefficient, it was the 1970s U.S. gasoline market.

Problems in the gasoline market were closely related to problems in the market for petroleum. In the early 1970s, many Arab governments initiated a boycott on petroleum products sold to the United States. This was known as the Arab Oil Embargo. It effectively reduced oil supplies headed toward the United States. At almost the same time, the 13-member Organization of Petroleum Exporting Countries (OPEC) flexed its economic muscles by reducing the world supply of crude oil. The natural result of these actions was a dramatic increase in the price of crude oil. Prices went from $2.50 per barrel in the fall of 1973 to $10 per barrel in the spring of 1974. Consequently, prices of petroleum products, including gasoline, also skyrocketed. Because oil-based inputs are central to many production processes, the higher prices for oil products translated into higher costs of production and caused the supplies of virtually all manufactured and agricultural products that use petroleum products in their production to decrease. These declining supplies caused prices in general to rise, resulting in inflation.

Again in 1979, oil supplies were reduced as Iran cut off its supplies to the United States. Petroleum prices jumped again, and gasoline prices rose as well. Gas shortages became acute. Once again, inflation was the political and economic problem of the day.

The restricted supplies and resulting high prices of petroleum did not cause the gasoline shortages. If price is free to increase, equilibrium will occur at the point at which quantity demanded equals quantity supplied, and there will be no shortage.

A shortage will result only if price is prevented from rising to the equilibrium level, as shown in Figure 7-5 on page 192. This phenomenon is exactly what occurred in

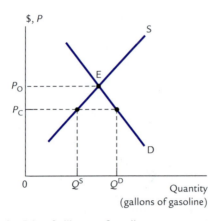

Figure 7-5 • The Effect of a Price Ceiling on Gasoline
The market equilibrium price is labeled P_O, whereas the price ceiling is labeled P_C. The price ceiling on gasoline results in a shortage of gasoline.

1973–1974 and again in 1979. Price ceilings on petroleum and petroleum products existed throughout this period. These ceilings became effective (that is, had an effect on the market), however, only when the market prices of petroleum products rose above them. (As long as the market price remains below a price ceiling, the government prohibition against charging prices too high cannot have an impact. Price simply remains at the equilibrium level.) When gasoline prices skyrocketed in 1973–1974 and again in 1979, the price ceilings became effective and encouraged suppliers to undersupply at the same time they encouraged consumers to over-demand. The shortage depicted in Figure 7-5 was the result.

Would it have been better to simply allow the higher gasoline prices to exist? Certainly, the market would have been more efficient; quantity demanded would have equaled quantity supplied, and no shortages would have been created. But the high gasoline prices might have created problems for low-income consumers. Gasoline is a necessity to those who must drive to work. Can you think of any better (more direct) ways to ensure that low-income commuters could afford the necessary gasoline?

A Price Ceiling on Interest Rates

Do you recall the mention of usury laws near the beginning of this chapter? Usury laws are price ceilings on interest rates (that is, interest rate ceilings). Often, governments put these interest rate ceilings into effect to prevent interest rates from rising too high. The outcome is the same as the other price ceilings that we have considered. The graph is shown in Figure 7-6, with the quantity of loanable funds on the horizontal axis (the amount of funds to be borrowed and lent) and the price of loanable funds (the interest rate) on the vertical axis. The demand for loanable funds represents all people who would like to borrow money. The supply of loanable funds represents all people who would like to lend money. (Lenders are also often savers: If you place your money in a savings account, you are lending your money to the bank, which is lending the money to other borrowers.) Equilibrium would exist at point E, with an equilibrium quantity of $3 million and an equilibrium interest rate of 8 percent. If, however, the government places an interest rate ceiling at 6 percent, we can see that the quantity demanded of

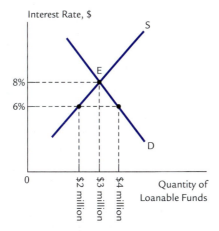

Figure 7-6 • The Effect of an Interest Rate Ceiling
The interest rate ceiling on loanable funds results in a shortage of loanable funds.

loanable funds will be $4 million and the quantity supplied will be $2 million. A shortage of $2 million is created.

Other Examples

In Chapter 10, we will consider price ceilings on foods, such as rice, in developing countries. Even though farmers in the rural sector tend to be poorer than consumers in the urban sector, developing country governments often impose price ceilings on staple foods (such as cereal grains) to keep urban residents happy. As is often the case, people riot in the cities when food prices rise too high, creating political instability for governments. The price ceilings create the typical problem of food shortages, as well as artificially low prices received by farmers, who in turn face lower incomes and less incentive to produce food. Partly because of pressure from international organizations, many developing countries are now removing their price ceilings. Similar price ceilings have existed in socialist countries such as the former Soviet Union. As these countries are now engaged in economic reforms, they are decontrolling these prices. The trade-off: consumers now pay high prices for food, but there are no shortages. Governments are wise to use market prices to provide appropriate incentives, but they still must find programs that directly assist low-income farmers and consumers.

One more example: We discuss pharmaceutical prices in Chapter 9 on health care. Because pharmaceutical prices are often very high and rapidly rising, many people are calling for price ceilings on these medications to keep their prices more affordable. Like housing and food, health care is a "special market" that often calls for government involvement. The outcomes of price ceilings would be typical, however: lower prices but at the cost of creating shortages. Do you have any ideas about better (more direct) ways to deal with the fact that many people cannot afford pharmaceutical drugs?

Chapter 8

ROAD MAP

Chapter 5
Discrimination
Minorities are more likely to be uninsured than are whites. Minorities have lower life expectancies and higher infant mortality rates.

Chapter 6
U.S. Poverty
Poor people often lack access to quality health care. Medicaid is subsidized health care for low-income people. Poverty can lead to poor health.

Chapter 7
Housing
Residential segregation concentrates poverty and contributes to lack of access to quality health care.

Chapter 8
Health Care

Chapter 9
Social Security
Medicare provides health insurance for most elderly Social Security recipients. Social Security provides income for disabled workers.

Chapter 14
Unemployment and Inflation
Health coverage is often dependent on having a full-time job.

Chapter 10
World Poverty
Poverty in poor countries leads to poor standards of health.

The Economic Toolbox

- Life expectancy
- Infant mortality rate
- Physician sovereignty
- Defensive medicine
- Third-party payment
- Cost shifting
- Medicaid
- Medicare
- Means tested
- Affordable Care Act (ACA)
- Health insurance exchange (marketplace)
- Privatization
- Medical savings accounts
- National health insurance
- Socialized medicine

Health Care

President Barack Obama has made health reform his signature policy change throughout his eight-year administration, culminating in the Affordable Care Act—ACA (otherwise referred to as Obamacare). We will be professionals and refer to it as the Affordable Care Act or the ACA, rather than the more common Obamacare. The results of the act are rather staggering. In his same speech, he noted more than 3 million Americans under age 26 have gained coverage under their parents' plans. As this book is being written, more than 8 million Americans have signed up for private health insurance through government sponsored Web sites, and many others have become eligible for Medicaid coverage. And because of this law, no American can ever again be dropped or denied coverage for a pre-existing condition.

There are many more aspects of the ACA that we will consider in this chapter. Most of all, we will see that the act is controversial, especially among Republicans in Congress and economic conservatives in general. But first we need to consider the circumstances that made many come to believe that the law was necessary. We like to think that the U.S. health care system is the best in the world. For some Americans it is. Overall it is not. Certainly there are problems with the Canadian and European systems. We can talk about some of them. Yet the fact remains, as we will see in this chapter, that we spend the greatest amount of money on health care and achieve the poorest health care outcomes of all the Western industrialized world.

President Obama speaks in terms of ideal standards: comprehensive reform, universal coverage, and affordability. As we examine our current system, and as we imagine health care reforms, we can consider where we stand with respect to these three goals.

In this chapter, we first examine data on health care in the United States. We look at our expenditures and examine where we rank relative to other countries in terms of these expenditures and the quality of our health. We then look at the unique characteristics of health care that contribute to a more costly and poorer quality of health care than we would like. Finally, we look at proposals for reform of our health care system, especially the ACA. Let's begin by looking at health care expenditures in the United States.

Health insurance reform is all about—the peace of mind that if misfortune strikes, you don't have to lose everything.... That's why, tonight, I ask every American who knows someone without health insurance to help them get covered by March 31st. Moms, get on your kids to sign up. Kids, call your mom and walk her through the application. It will give her some peace of mind—plus, she'll appreciate hearing from you.

—PRESIDENT BARACK OBAMA, STATE OF THE UNION ADDRESS, JANUARY 28, 2014

U.S. Health Care Expenditures and Outcomes

Estimates of total health care expenditures in the United States are shown in Table 8-1 for selected years of the time period 1960–2011. We see that total health care expenditures in the United States are projected at $2.7 trillion in 2011, a huge increase over 1960. Although these expenditures are not adjusted for **inflation**, they have clearly increased far more rapidly than the average level of prices in our economy.

Furthermore, Table 8-2 shows how the United States compares with other Western industrialized countries and Japan in terms of health care expenditures as a share of

Inflation

A rise in the average price level.

TABLE 8-1 • National Health Expenditure Estimates, Selected Years, 1960 to 2011 (current dollar amounts in trillions)

Year	Expenditures
1960	$0.1
1970	$0.1
1980	$0.3
1990	$0.7
2000	$1.4
2005	$2.0
2006	$2.0
2007	$2.2
2008	$2.4
2009	$2.6
2010	$2.6
2011	$2.7

Sources: U.S. Department of Commerce, Census Bureau, *Statistical Abstract of the United States,* http://www.census.gov; and The Centers for Medicare and Medicaid Services, http://www.cms.gov.

TABLE 8-2 • National Health Care Expenditures as a Percent of GDP of the Western Industrialized Countries and Japan, 2013

Country	Percent	Country	Percent
Austria	11.5	Japan	10.1
Belgium	10.8	Luxembourg	6.9[a]
Canada	10.9	Netherlands	12.4
Denmark	11.5	Norway	9.0
Finland	9.1	Portugal	9.4
France	11.7	Spain	9.6
Germany	11.3	Sweden	9.6
Greece	9.3	Switzerland	11.3
Ireland	8.1	United Kingdom	9.4
Italy	9.2	United States	17.9[b]

[a]Lowest
[b]Highest

Source: World Bank, *World Development Indicators 2013* (Washington, DC: World Bank, 2013).

gross domestic product (GDP). Of the 20 countries listed, the United States ranks the highest by far, over two and one-half times that of Luxembourg (which spends the lowest as a share of GDP). The table shows that the United States spends almost 18 percent of GDP on health care!

Regardless of how you put it, we are spending a large percentage of GDP on health care, and these health care expenditures have risen enormously over time. Simply put, we are spending much more on health care, as a society and as individuals, than we have in previous years.

Social Significance of Increased Expenditures

Financial costs are a claim on the nation's resources. When health care expenditure as a percentage of our national output increases, it means that we are allocating more of our resources to health care. Therefore, we are giving up other goods and services to acquire medical care. Recall the production possibilities curve from Chapter 1. Over any given time period, assuming full employment and a fixed quantity and quality of resources and technology, our nation is capable of producing only a limited amount of goods and services. If we choose to have more of one good, such as health care, we must necessarily produce less of something else. Figure 8-1 shows a production possibilities curve for medical care and all other goods and services. We have moved from point A in 1960 to point B today. As a result, we are sacrificing the production of other goods.

Outcomes of Health Expenditures

Since we are spending so much on health care, we want to know whether these expenditures are resulting in a high standard of health for our nation's citizens. The two most commonly used health care indicators are life expectancy at birth and infant mortality rates. **Life expectancy** is the average number of years that a child born in a particular year is expected to live. The **infant mortality rate** measures the number of infant deaths

> **Gross domestic product (GDP)**
> A measure of the total output (and income) produced in a nation in one year.

> **Life expectancy**
> The age to which a baby born in a particular year can be expected to live on average.

> **Infant mortality rate**
> The number of babies who die within their first year of life per every 1,000 live births.

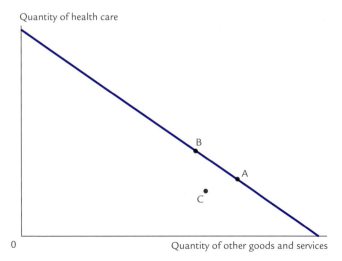

Figure 8-1 • Production Possibilities Curve for Health Care
As we have moved from point A to point B, we have obtained more health care, but we have given up other goods and services. At point C, we are using our resources inefficiently.

© Cengage Learning

(deaths of children under 1 year of age) per 1,000 live births. These measures are shown in Table 8-3 for the United States and for the other countries we considered in Table 8-2.

Note that the United States has the lowest life expectancy, and it has the highest infant mortality rate among all of the countries. Japan, which has a medium range level of health care expenditures as a share of GDP (Table 8-2) has the best health outcomes among all listed countries if we consider both life expectancy and infant mortality rates combined. *Tables 8-2 and 8-3 suggest that nations that spend less than the United States on health care as a share of GDP perform better than the United States on health outcomes.* Although other factors certainly affect these health indicators, as we'll discuss momentarily, the data displayed in this table show cause for concern.

Furthermore, statistics reveal that the quality of health care in the United States varies enormously among racial and ethnic groups. Somewhat dated statistics from the Statistical Abstract of the United States show that while the national average for infant mortality rates was 6.8 in 2007, it was 5.6 for white infants and 13.2 for African-Americans. The 2008 national average life expectancy was 78.0, whereas the white life expectancy was 78.4 in comparison with the African-American life expectancy of 74.3.[1] These high infant mortality rates and low life expectancies for African-Americans are on par with many developing countries.

Although nutritional, cultural, and other lifestyle characteristics influence these statistics, the statistics also depend on income and discrimination. We noted in the poverty statistics in Chapter 6 that African-American people have poverty rates much higher

TABLE 8-3 • Life Expectancies and Infant Mortality Rates for the Western Industrialized Countries and Japan, 2012

Country	Life Expectancy	Infant Mortality Rate
Austria	81	3
Belgium	80	3
Canada	81	5
Denmark	80	3
Finland	81	2[a]
France	83	3
Germany	81	3
Greece	81	4
Ireland	81	3
Italy	83[a]	3
Japan	83[a]	2[a]
Luxembourg	81	2[a]
Netherlands	81	3
Norway	81	2[a]
Portugal	80	3
Spain	82	4
Sweden	82	2[a]
Switzerland	83[a]	4
United Kingdom	82	4
United States	79[b]	6[b]

[a]Best
[b]Worst

Source: World Bank, *World Development Indicators 2013* (Washington, DC: World Bank, 2013).

than Caucasians. The same is true of Native Americans and Hispanics. These groups are also more likely to experience discrimination, as we discussed in Chapter 5. At the same time, an unequal *quality* of health care and unequal *access* to health care are certainly important factors. Pregnant women with limited access to quality prenatal care, for example, are more likely to die from complications of pregnancy and delivery, and their babies are more likely to be premature or in poor health. As the director of the World Health Organization stated in the year 2000, there are three Americas. There is high-quality health care for the rich and mediocre health care for the middle-income class. However, he notes that "it's the bottom 5 percent or 10 percent, made up of Native Americans living on reservations, the inner-city poor, rural blacks and Appalachia that is a third America. They have health conditions as bad as those in sub-Saharan Africa." Based on our statistics, his comments are still relevant today.

In summary, we have seen high and increasing health care expenditures in the United States, and yet our health indicators are below those of other Western industrialized countries. We've also seen that health indicators vary enormously by race within our country. What are the reasons for these negative outcomes? *Why do we spend so much on health care, yet we have relatively poor outcomes?* Let's explore two reasons for this inconsistency in the next section on health care problems. These problems include rising health care costs and a lack of access to health care.

U.S. Health Care Problems

Let's focus on two specific problems in U.S. health care. These are escalating health care costs and lack of access to health care.

Escalating Health Care Costs

The reasons why we as a nation spend so much on health care are twofold: (1) a growing demand for health care and (2) waste and inefficiency. Both of these factors have to do with unique characteristics of the health care market, a market that is quite unlike the market for hamburgers, pajamas, or mystery novels. Let's consider a number of these characteristics, especially as they pertain to a rising demand for health care.

Physician Sovereignty

Physician sovereignty means that it is the doctor (or other health care professional) that controls the demand for medical care. We do not shop around for the most appropriate medical care, comparing price and quality characteristics of numerous models, as we would if we went to the hardware store to buy a hammer. Instead, we accept that we need the tests, drugs, and treatments that the doctor prescribes. Medical care requires expert knowledge; we are not capable of making sophisticated diagnoses on our own. Instead, we rely on the physician. The doctor may take cost considerations into account, but they are clearly secondary. Decisions are made on the basis of accepted medical practice and the assurance of good medical care. The normal frugality of a shopper who compares prices carefully and budgets wisely is not present in medical care. While this is not necessarily bad, it does contribute to a higher demand for, and therefore rising costs of, health care. Furthermore, under traditional **fee-for-service** insurance, the more services that are recommended the more income the doctor or medical clinic receives. **All of these can cause an increased demand for health care.**

Physician sovereignty
A medical doctor's control over the demand for medical procedures.

Fee-for-service
The charging of a specific fee for provision of a specific health care service.

Defensive Medicine

Malpractice insurance
Insurance carried by health care professionals to protect themselves from large malpractice damage awards.

Medical malpractice suits are expensive. In addition to the rising cost of **malpractice insurance**, which helps drive up medical costs, the threat of malpractice suits causes physicians to practice **defensive medicine**, which also drives up health care costs. Rather than be found guilty of carelessness, doctors prescribe tests and procedures that are virtually certain to be unnecessary. For example, it has been estimated that one-half of the caesarean-section deliveries performed in the United States each year are unnecessary, but malpractice awards are so large when babies are injured in the birth process that caesareans are done at the first sign of any irregularity, despite their high cost. (Caesarean operations cost about twice what vaginal deliveries cost.) **For these reasons, defensive medicine leads to a higher overall demand for medical care, the potential for waste, and higher medical costs.**

Defensive medicine
The ordering of unnecessary tests and services by health care professionals solely to protect themselves from charges of malpractice.

Third-Party Payment

Third-party payment
A health care payment made by someone other than the patient or the patient's family.

Third-party payment means that most medical expenditures are paid for by either government programs or private insurance. This phenomenon makes patients less cost conscious than they would be if they had to pay directly for medical services. The indirect link between insurance premiums and our medical costs is tenuous—our insurance premiums do not appear to be directly linked to the number of visits we make to the doctor's office or to the number of trips we make to the hospital emergency room. When a third party pays for our medical care, we are more willing and able to ask for additional medical services. Again, this is not necessarily bad. **However, like physician sovereignty and defensive medicine, third-party payment increases the demand for medical care and therefore its price.**

Rapid Technological Change

We see rapid technological change in kidney dialysis machines, magnetic resonance imaging, transplant techniques, nuclear medicine, and many others. These are expensive and when hospitals invest in highly specialized equipment, hospital costs soar.

Medical experts and their patients often judge hospitals by the quality of physicians who are on their staffs. And reputable medical doctors often choose to practice at hospitals that have all the latest technology. This means that hospitals competing for first-class medical specialists must have it all. Thus, expensive machinery is duplicated in the several hospitals of our cities. Doctors must use the technology to justify its installation. Their demand for expensive tests and treatments for their patients increases, representing a rise in the overall demand for health care. Many experts believe that expensive and rapidly changing technology is the major force driving hospital costs.

One of the fastest growing elements in health technology spending today is prescription drugs. New pharmaceutical products can increase the quality and length of life. While they are often very cost-effective (in comparison with treating outcomes that could have been prevented with pharmaceuticals), many of these new drugs are extremely expensive. Some of the drugs may also bring new patients into the health care system. (Experts estimate that a large portion of Viagra sales was to men who had not previously been treated for impotence.) **Thus, spending on prescription drugs has increased rapidly, and demand for these drugs, along with other forms of medical technology, is part of the overall increase in demand for medical care.**

Cost Shifting

Cost shifting
The practice of recovering the unpaid costs of some patients by charging higher prices to other patients.

Hospitals and physicians routinely engage in **cost shifting**, which is the transfer of the unpaid costs of some patients to well-insured patients through the raising of fees.

Third-party payment makes the patient and the patient's family less concerned about costs. Hospital administrators find it relatively easy to pass along cost increases for needed treatments. Furthermore, the hospital reimbursement procedures of Medicaid and Medicare often leave a portion of a patient's costs uncovered, and some hospitals treat urgent cases even if payment is unlikely. They then cover these uncompensated costs by raising their rates and collecting more from insurance companies for the treatment of patients who have good insurance (or from affluent patients with no insurance). Cost shifting distorts decisions made about health care and makes calculation of the costs of a given treatment difficult.

Attitudes of Patients

Americans' attitudes toward medical care affect our health care system in several ways. We believe in our high-tech medical system. We hear on the television and read on the Internet about new treatments and studies, and we believe that virtually any treatment should be available to us. We believe that more tests are better than less, that aggressive medical treatment can cure virtually anything, and that we do not need to take much responsibility for our own health. **This belief leads us to demand excessive care without much regard for cost.**

Consequences of These Characteristics

These characteristics of the market for medical care have helped to cause medical costs to skyrocket over time, as shown in Figure 8-2. Physician sovereignty, defensive medicine, third-party payment, cost shifting, and the increase in tests and treatments caused by rapid technological change all imply increases in the demand for health care. Our attitudes as patients also create larger demands for medical care. These are all shown by the increase in demand in Figure 8-2. **This means we now consume more medical care and we pay higher prices.**

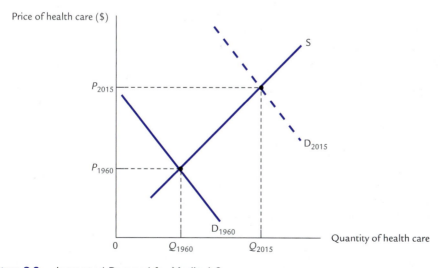

Figure 8-2 • Increased Demand for Medical Care
Because demand has increased since 1960, medical care prices have risen as we have consumed a greater quantity of health care.

© Cengage Learning

Waste and Inefficiency

In addition, consumer advocates maintain that hundreds of billions of dollars of our health care expenditures are wasted. These wasted dollars represent the unnecessary tests and medical procedures already discussed and unnecessary surgeries and drugs. As noted, many hospitals each operate extremely expensive equipment instead of sharing identical million-dollar machines. This duplication leads to both higher costs and more unnecessary tests, because use justifies the investment in the machines in the first place. Furthermore, paperwork costs are tremendous. Every private insurance company and the government have their own forms to be filled out. The maze is more complicated for those who have more than one health insurer or require referrals. Hospitals and clinics hire numerous employees who handle billings, referrals, and appeals. If you have a friend who works for a physician or hospital, ask about the paper maze. The paperwork adds greatly to health care costs. These types of administrative costs alone have been estimated at almost $200 billion per year. Finally, for reasons we will consider shortly, many patients forgo cost-effective preventative health care interventions, such as prenatal care, blood pressure checks, and child immunizations. As a result, costly interventions, such as surgeries, emergency room visits, and preventable illnesses, rather than preventative care, take place.

Refer again to Figure 8-1 on page 197. In terms of the production possibilities curve, we are probably neither at point A nor at point B, but at a point such as point C, inside the curve. By cutting some of the waste and inefficiency now present in U.S. medical care, as well as shifting resources into preventative measures, we could move toward the curve and clearly be better off.

One Additional Thought

While many of our nation's hospitals are not-for-profit, many of them, along with our clinics and other medical facilities are for-profit businesses. Certainly, our insurance companies and pharmaceutical firms are out to make a profit. This is the American way. However, are these profits higher than they should be? Or to push the point, should health care even *be* part of a for-profit industry? There are those who suggest that it should not be—that health care (like food and basic housing) should be a fundamental right. Those who feel this way argue that profits in the health care industry are a large source of health care costs. Those who go further and argue for a single-payer system (the government or a form of cooperative) believe that such a system could eliminate the expenses due to overlapping bureaucracy as well as profits. Estimates suggest that we could save hundreds of billions of dollars per year with a single-payer system, representing some 15–20 percent of health care costs. We will consider this shortly.

Lack of Access to Health Care

The second problem in U.S. health care has been the lack of access of many people to our health care system. Unless we have unlimited wealth, we all depend on some form of health insurance or program. Otherwise, we may well incur unaffordable medical costs, or we go without health care. Some of us have private insurance that we purchase from a private insurance company, either directly or now on the health care exchange (more about this shortly). One problem we've had with private insurance is that companies could turn you down or charge exorbitant premiums if you had a pre-existing condition. Often these conditions were very minor, but became serious impediments to obtaining health insurance coverage. Insurance companies could also drop you once you acquired a serious medical problem, and they could place lifetime limits on medical expenses covered.

These are no longer problems, as they are forbidden by the Affordable Care Act. Many other people have insurance coverage through their place of employment. Employees of large firms are much more likely to have such a fringe benefit than are employees of small firms. Other people benefit from public health coverage that is provided by the government, primarily in the form of Medicaid or Medicare. However, as shown in Table 8-4, over 15 percent of our nation's population was without any health coverage in 2011. This percent has gone down somewhat since 2011, and if we consider actual numbers of people (not shown), there were 260.2 million people *with* health insurance in 2011, up to 263.2 million people covered in 2012. The number has been rising since then.

We also note that coverage varies considerably among different groups of people in the United States. People of racial or ethnic minority are more likely to be without any health care coverage, with Hispanics and African-Americans being far more likely to be without coverage than non-Hispanic whites. Nevertheless, we see considerable improvement for these groups over the time period 2011 to 2012. While it is too early to see all of the effects of the ACA, it certainly is a factor in the improvement in coverage from 2011 to 2012.

Thus, we see that financial access to medical care depends on private health insurance coverage or eligibility for government health programs, such as Medicaid or Medicare. Private insurance, whether purchased directly by the subscriber or provided by employers, can be complicated. We will leave the discussion of the intricacies of private insurance for Appendix 8-1. to this chapter. Nevertheless, we should recognize that private insurance may still be expensive for the consumer. These expenses may be lessened by the subsidies awarded by the ACA, as we shall see shortly.

Medicaid is subsidized health care for poor people and the medically indigent, and **Medicare** is a system of subsidized health insurance for the aged. Let's consider each of these programs separately.

Medicaid

One of the keys to understanding why large percentages of the poor are without health coverage has to do with the way that Medicaid is administered. Medicaid (as opposed to Medicare) is a program designed to pay for medical services for the nation's poor and for medically indigent persons. (Medically indigent people have such high medical expenses that, whatever their income, they cannot afford their medical care.) Since eligibility depends on the family's income, we say that Medicaid is **means-tested**.

Although Medicaid is national in scope, it is administered by the individual states, and states are free to establish their own eligibility requirements and benefit levels within

Medicaid
A government program providing medical coverage for eligible low-income people.

Medicare
A government program providing medical coverage largely to elderly people.

Means-tested
A way of determining who is eligible for a program, based on the person's low-income status and possibly low asset ownership.

TABLE 8-4 • Percent of People Without Health Insurance Coverage, by Race and Ethnicity, 2011, 2012

Group	% Without Government or Private Health Insurance Coverage	
	2011	2012
All	15.7	15.4
White	14.9	14.7
Non-Hispanic White	11.1	11.1
African-American	19.5	19.0
Hispanic[a]	30.1	20.1
Asian-American	16.8	15.1

[a]Hispanics may be of any race.

Source: U.S. Department of Commerce, Census Bureau, http://www.census.gov.

certain federal guidelines. This type of flexibility has been increasing over time and was greatly expanded as a result of the 1996 welfare reform discussed in Chapter 6 on U.S. poverty. Individual states also have the option of supplementing federal financing with state revenues. As a result, Medicaid eligibility and coverage varies considerably by state. In many cases, eligibility for Medicaid depends on factors in addition to income, such as age, disability, and assets. In many states, a person must not only be poor, but must be extremely poor before receiving health assistance. Some states also require that to be eligible, a family must include children. *As a result, poor single individuals and couples, including the working poor, are often ineligible for Medicaid.* Furthermore, eligibility for Medicaid does not guarantee access to quality medical care. Medicaid recipients may find it hard to find physicians who will treat Medicaid patients, because the government reimburses only a portion of the average physician's fee. Some states require that a co-payment be paid for some medical services. Finally, one problem with our national welfare program, entitled TANF (discussed in Chapter 6), is that once people find a job and leave the TANF program, they often lose their Medicaid coverage. Since studies reveal that many of those leaving welfare for work have ended up in low-wage jobs without health insurance coverage, these people end up worse off than they were while receiving Medicaid. This is a real problem for the working poor.

President Obama intended a vast increase in the number of people eligible for Medicaid through an expansion of federal government financial infusions to individual states for this purpose. However, the Supreme Court ruled that states need not accept the expansion and the dollars that came with it, and over half of all states chose to reject the expansion. This eliminated opportunities for health care for many poor residents of conservative states.

In addition to the standard Medicaid program, the **State Children's Health Insurance Program (SCHIP)** became available in 1997. The intention of the program is to provide health care to children in families whose income is too high for the children to qualify for Medicaid, but too low for the family to afford private insurance. Like Medicaid, this program is jointly financed by the federal and state governments and is administered by the states. Not all states provide the same benefits, but all do include immunizations and care for healthy babies at no cost. This program has greatly improved access to health care by our nation's children who would be otherwise ineligible for Medicaid. In addition, many state Medicaid programs now have coverage for low-income pregnant women. Note that many state programs use other names for their Medicaid and State Children's Health Insurance programs. President Obama expanded federal funding for SCHIP within the first few weeks of his presidency.[2]

State Children's Health Insurance Program (SCHIP)
A federal program providing health care coverage for children in low-income working families.

Medicare

The Medicare program was established in 1965 when it became evident that many aged Americans could not afford the health care that they needed. Medicare is an insurance program sponsored by the federal government. Medicare hospital insurance (Part A) is financed by required payroll taxes on workers and employers. This benefit includes inpatient care in hospitals, as well as some hospice care and some home health care. Optional Medicare medical insurance (Part B) for physicians' services, certain treatments, and other medical services and supplies is financed through monthly premiums, co-payments, and deductibles paid by the insured person (these terms are discussed in Appendix 8). Because these payments never cover the full amount of the covered services received by Medicare patients, the federal government finances the largest share of the costs. In addition, optional prescription drug coverage (Part D) began in 2006. Like Part B, the recipient pays a monthly premium for the drug coverage, but in this case, the insurance is provided entirely by private companies. In addition to the premium, most recipients also pay a deductible and a fee (co-pay) for their prescription medications. Almost all elderly persons over the age of 65 years are eligible for Medicare, as well as certain categories of disabled people. Medicare is not means-tested—that is, benefits do not depend on a person's having few assets and low income. Both rich and poor are covered alike.

Medicare does not cover all of older people's medical care. Many older Americans who can afford it also carry expensive "Medigap" insurance, which covers the medical expenses not covered by Medicare.

Because of both rising medical costs and the increasing proportion of elderly people in our population, Medicare has become an increasingly expensive program. As costs have increased, the government has sought to reduce its role in paying for these additional costs. The government has limited its payments to health care providers. Medicare payroll taxes on workers and employers have increased. Finally, premiums paid by Medicare recipients have increased, deductibles have increased, and certain benefits have been cut. As a consequence of government austerity measures, Medicare recipients are now paying larger out-of-pocket amounts of their nonpharmaceutical health care costs than they formerly did.

Thus, many issues with Medicare are similar to the issues of medical care in general. *High and escalating costs, affordability of care, and access to care concern the elderly who rely on this program.* Even though Medicaid will sometimes pay Medicare premiums and other out-of-pocket expenses for some eligible low-income Medicare beneficiaries, other low-income elderly people refrain from using medical services because they cannot afford certain related expenses or they skip the optional portions of Medicare because they cannot afford the monthly premiums. Furthermore, some important medical services and supplies are not covered at all.

To summarize this section: *We see that the lack of access to health care coverage, whether it be private or governmental, is a problem for many people. And, even when people do have access, they may still face restricted coverage and incur high out-of-pocket expenses, or they may go without health care as a result.* The high cost of health care is certainly a problem for many people without adequate health care coverage.

There have been a number of proposals to improve our health care system, both on the economic left and right, but by far the most extensive reform is that of the Affordable Health Care Act. It has been immensely controversial and some of its difficulties are the fault of both republicans and democrats. Let's consider the ACA in detail, including some of its controversies.

The Affordable Health Care Act

In an effort to overcome the types of problems that we have been discussing in U.S. healthcare, the Affordable Health Care Act was initiated by President Obama and passed by Congress in 2010. The ACA is the most significant piece of health care legislation in the United States today. The primary goal of the ACA is to achieve universal health coverage (or nearly so), while at the same time containing costs and applying certain mandates. The principal mandates are (1) all people are required to have health insurance coverage or pay a fine; (2) insurance companies cannot turn away, drop, or increase the premiums of their subscribers with pre-existing or new conditions; nor can they place a lifetime limit on benefits; (3) insurance policies must include a broad range of preventative health care; and (4) young people can remain on their parents' health care coverage until age 25.

The ACA is intended to extend health care to the uninsured and to make it more affordable to many. It is important to understand its most significant features, especially since these directly involve economics. In particular, we will consider cost containment and universal coverage.

Cost Containment

Two elements of the ACA are particularly important for cost containment. One of these is the assurance of coverage of preventative care. As we've noted, preventative care is far more cost-effective than doing without. It is much cheaper to our health care system if a child receives childhood immunizations rather than infecting other children with childhood diseases, if a pregnant woman receives good prenatal care rather than having a premature low-birth-weight baby spending weeks in a neonatal intensive care unit; and an elderly person receives regular blood pressure checks rather than suffering a stroke or heart attack. In these ways, preventative care is not only better for the individual, for our health care system as a whole.

Similar to this is the requirement that all people have some form of health insurance coverage. A person without coverage is less likely to receive preventative care. Beyond this, people often make the claim that if an insured person experiences a medical emergency, emergency rooms and hospitals are required to take them. While this may be true, it doesn't address the problem that this emergency may end up costing huge health care dollars, and the person may die or suffer serious medical consequences despite a tardy intervention. The health care expenses end up being covered by someone, as we considered with respect to cost shifting. Finally, people without access to health care cost society in terms of missed work and school. These types of health care expenses can be avoided.

Universal Coverage

The other major goal of the ACA is to assure that all citizens of the United States, or at least a very large share of them, have access to health care coverage. Universal health care is important on equity grounds, but also grounds of efficiency. People who are not covered by health care insurance cost society a lot of money, as described in the previous paragraph.

Furthermore, it is important that all citizens, including those who are relatively young and healthy, have health insurance. This is for their own good, but also for the viability of the health care system. We need low-risk citizens combined with older or sicker high-risk citizens to balance out costs and make health insurance affordable for the health insurance company, its members (in terms of premiums and other out-of-pocket costs), and government.

While universal health care makes good economic sense, we know there has been considerable controversy about the ACA, especially the requirement that all people have insurance or pay a fine to the government. This coverage may be in the form of (1) private insurance coverage, including health care plans that citizens currently subscribe to; (2) health insurance coverage through their place of employment; (3) government health insurance in the form of Medicare and an expanded Medicaid program; or (4) new health care programs set up and placed on a web-based health care exchange (marketplace) for citizens to choose from. Let's consider each of the four possibilities for health care coverage and discover the controversy.

Keeping Current Health Care Policies

At the onset of the ACA, President Obama promised that Americans could keep their current insurance policy if they were happy with it. While this is true, controversy arose when people discovered the obvious: if insurance companies were to follow federal government mandates to expand preventative care and accept subscribers with pre-existing conditions, they were going to want to raise their premiums. At this time, this issue has not yet been resolved, and has created a lot of animosity toward the program.

Health Care Policies Through Employment

The ACA requires large companies (with over 50 full-time employees) to offer health insurance to their employees. While costs to businesses are one issue, another controversy is that certain institutions do not want to offer their employees coverage that includes medical care they do not believe in. For example, a Catholic church may not want to offer coverage of contraceptives to its employees, especially those that may be abortifacient. While modifications have been made for these institutions, Catholic owners of other businesses are not exempt from this. This issue has yet to be resolved.

Expansion of Medicaid

President Obama intended a large expansion of the Medicaid programs of all states in the country by infusing federal funds into state government programs. Governors of many conservative states opposed this expansion of government, and a Supreme Court ruling eventually gave states the choice to accept or reject the expansion. Some states even chose to reduce their Medicaid programs. It is difficult to see why certain states would reject the opportunity to provide more insurance coverage to their citizens when the opportunity comes without cost, other than perhaps an overall opposition to the ACA.

The Health Care Exchange (Marketplace)

Individual states are given the option of using a federal government Web site or devising their own. The Web site would show a range of options of insurance programs, with the user choosing the one most appropriate for his or her family. Low-income people are offered subsidies for subscribing, which occur in the form of federal tax breaks. Once choosing an option, subscribers can simply apply online and be enrolled. One main problem with the marketplace was the technical difficulty with its rollout. Another problem seemed to be people's confusion about the exchange and whether they should even bother to purchase insurance when up until now they knew they could not afford it. The marketplace was not well publicized and many people were unaware that they could very well be eligible for subsidies, making their contributions to health insurance coverage relatively small. Part of the problem rested with conservative governors, however. Some spread misinformation about the marketplace, discouraged people from signing up, and refused to cooperate with federal coordinators assisting people with the Web sites. While the difficulties for people to subscribe are subsiding, people initially have huge time-consuming delays in accessing information and subscribing to policies.

Conservative opposition to the ACA has had important impacts on our economy. This opposition was a fundamental demand by Republicans in the fall of 2013 when Congress failed to extend the government budget and threatened to avoid raising the debt ceiling. After several weeks of government shutdown, Congress was able to overcome its disagreement while leaving the Affordable Care Act largely intact. Nevertheless, it demonstrates the heated opposition that has arisen over the act.

As such, many Republican governors and state legislators have fought against the ACA. There have been over 40 efforts by Congress to overthrow or defund the ACA. About half of all states have rejected the opportunity to establish their own Web sites for health care marketplaces and chose to rely on the federal site instead. Most of the same states have turned down the federal dollars for Medicaid expansion. Certainly those with a conservative bent see the programs offered on the health care exchange and the government mandates as intrusions by government in our economy. They also disapprove of the expansion of Medicaid, presumably for similar reasons. Some are furious with the government requirement that all people have some health coverage or else pay a fine.

A new challenge to the health care exchanges involves the subsidies to low-income subscribers. Several conservative politicians have filed a case with the U.S. Supreme Court, arguing that the ACA should provide such subsidies only in states that have established their own exchanges, and not in ones using the federal exchange. As the text goes to print, the Supreme Court has not yet ruled.

Other Options for Health Care in the United States

Given the controversy over the ACA and the problematic history of health care in the United States, it is appropriate to consider some of the many other programs that have been proposed. Some of these alternatives move in the direction of a more market-based (conservative) approach; other alternatives rely on greater government involvement in the health care industry, a more liberal approach. Let's briefly consider some of these.

Approaches on the Economic Right (Conservative)
Increased Competition on the Supply Side of Health Care

Some conservative economists argue that the government has too large of an influence on health care in this country. They desire the elimination or a sharp reduction in the government's participation in health care. Recall that the strength of competitive free markets is their efficiency in equating private demand and supply. This consideration fosters arguments in favor of a return to free markets on both the demand and supply sides of the health care market.

In terms of the supply side of health care, conservatives argue that a more privatized, profit-oriented, and competitive supply of health care services would result in lower costs. As we've noted, many hospitals are not run on a "for-profit" basis; other goals, such as offering quality overall care, utilizing the most advanced technology, or specializing in particular services, are paramount. The **privatization** of government-owned and government-run hospitals and other reforms to increase competition among hospitals, it is argued, would force them to pay more attention to the bottom line, thus eliminating a great deal of inefficiency. (On the other hand, supporters of public hospitals attack for-profit hospitals specifically for this "bottom line" mentality: their specialization in high-profit services, their neglect of other less profitable but important services, their cost-cutting measures that can dangerously decrease the quality and safety of patient care, and their highly publicized turning away of uninsured and low-income patients.)

Advertising within the health care industry, which can improve competition among suppliers by improving consumer awareness of the alternatives, was long considered unethical. However, since optical firms have begun to advertise, for example, we have seen lower prices for glasses and contact lenses. If prices charged by physicians, clinics, and hospitals

Privatization
The transfer of government enterprises or responsibilities to the private sector.

were advertised, as well as the prices of various services and medications, perhaps competition among suppliers would increase, keeping prices lower. It should be noted, however, that the sort of nonprice television and magazine advertising in which the large pharmaceutical firms are now engaging will not make prices lower. Advertising of Ambien and Lipitor, for example, is aimed at increasing patient demand, increasing both price and quantity. And, of course, the advertising campaigns drive up the drug companies' costs, putting even more upward pressure on prices. Furthermore, advertising by large companies may drive away business for generic products, in this way reducing competition.

Increased Competition on the Demand Side of Health Care

Closely related to advertising is the notion of a well-informed consumer, able to use information wisely in the context of perfect competition. President George W. Bush once heralded this idea, stating that "Health care policy ought to be aimed at bolstering the consumer—empowering individuals to be responsible for health care decisions." However, while good information is always important, it cannot always be put to best use in the context of health care. People's choices are constrained by their insurance coverage, the availability of providers accepting Medicaid, and other factors. For example, the *St. Paul Pioneer Press* reviewed rankings provided by Minnesota Community Measurement (a nonprofit formed by the state's doctors and health plans) that showed the worst quality health care clinics are in urban centers and the best are in wealthy suburbs, often inaccessible to poor inner-city residents. For example, the top three clinics in the Twin Cities metropolitan area have 27 locations in the metro area, but 40 percent of these aren't on regular bus routes and the remainder require average bus rides from downtown Minneapolis of an hour and a half—not counting multiple transfers, higher costs for suburban express fares, and the time involved in walking to the clinics. In addition, measurement of quality can often be very difficult.[3] Once again, the market for health care doesn't function in the same way as the market for used cars, jeans, or other goods and services.

Curtailment or Elimination of Medicare and Medicaid

Conservatives also note that rising health care costs are at least partly the result of demand that is not tempered by the usual norms of frugality and concern for price. Certainly, the existence of Medicare and Medicaid is of consideration here. Conservatives argue that people abuse these programs, and that Medicaid discourages people from working. However, without these programs, many people who could otherwise not afford medical care presumably would not receive such care, or at least not the type and degree of care that they now receive. Because health care for these people is reflected in the total demand for medical care, the demand for medical care would decrease without these programs, and health care prices would go down. (Despite the conservative argument, this withdrawal of medical care from the poor and the elderly would be deemed unfair by others in society. A fairly significant portion of Americans view basic medical care as a fundamental right.)

Medical Savings Accounts

Medical savings account
A type of insurance in which the purchaser makes payments into an account that can be drawn against in times of illness.

A related conservative demand-side proposal would replace current health insurance programs with the **medical savings account**. Some proponents of this proposal view it as a possible way to eventually reform Medicare. The medical savings account is a type of insurance. The purchaser—whether employer, government, or insured—makes regular payments into a medical expenses account, which the insured can draw against if he or she becomes ill. The insured party controls how the funds in the account are spent: what tests are performed, what procedures are done, and by whom they are done. Monies not spent for medical care are returned to the insured person, giving him or her a stake in minimizing the costs of treatment. Proponents of medical savings accounts believe that the accounts would eliminate the perverse incentives built into other third-party payment systems (incentives that increase demand for too much medical care). Critics believe that they would benefit only relatively healthy people, who would save money on health care. Seriously ill people, they argue, would find that their insurance was inadequate for any high level of sophisticated care.

We do currently have a form of medical savings accounts referred to as health savings accounts. These were established under the 2003 Medicare drug legislation. Individuals who have a high-deductible private health insurance policy can place money into savings for use in paying out-of-pocket health expenses. Contributions to health savings accounts are tax deductible and may be placed in stocks, bonds, or other investment (savings) vehicles, with the earnings accruing on a tax-free basis. Withdrawals from the health savings accounts also are tax exempt as long as they are used for out-of-pocket medical costs. Some employers also offer this form of service.

Some have proposed substantial new tax incentives and subsidies for health savings accounts, including new tax credits and deductions. Critics argue that this proposal, and health savings accounts in general, would weaken the existing health insurance system, strain the federal budget, and provide the largest tax breaks to higher income people.

Approaches on the Economic Left (Liberal)

Competition

Competition in health care provision took on a liberal perspective with President Obama's original proposal for health care reform. Arguing that health insurance companies need competition in order to "keep them honest," the president proposed a public option that would compete with private plans. Consumers would have a choice between the private plans and the public plan. Met with charges by extremists on the right that this amounts to socialism, the proposal was mired in congressional debate and the proposal was eventually dropped. It is not a form of socialism, though it does increase government involvement in health care. Let's consider the real meaning of socialized medicine, and examine a range of socialist and other forms of national health insurance systems throughout the Western industrialized world.

National health insurance
Health care systems that involve government assurance of universal coverage of the population.

National health insurance represents the opposite alternative to privatized market-based care and is more likely to be supported by liberal economists. National health insurance of one kind or another is common throughout the Western industrialized world. The goal of national health insurance is universal coverage. Under such coverage, everyone would have health insurance and people would not fall between the cracks, as they have in the U.S. system.

Canada has a system of national health insurance. The Canadian system stands midway between the United States' free enterprise system and many European systems of socialized medicine, in which doctors are salaried government employees. Canadian doctors are paid by the government according to a negotiated schedule of fees for services. The tax-supported Canadian program pays all hospital and medical bills. The system is thus an example of a single-payer health insurance system, and the single payer is the government. A single-payer system is much less expensive to administer than is a multi-payer system, such as we have in the United States. And, all people, whether rich or poor, employed or unemployed, have access to medical services.

The system is not perfect, however, and its costs are rising as new technologies are adopted. Although most Canadian citizens and physicians are happy (on balance) with the system, a common criticism is that elective medical interventions are often postponed (and sometimes more critical interventions are delayed) because of shortages of health care. Indeed, one way the Canadian system contains costs is the deliberate slowdown of the adoption of new technologies, and it is not considered necessary for all hospitals to have all the latest technology. Thus, rationing takes place in the sense that some people must wait for services and others must travel for service. A recent Ipsos/McClatchy non-scientific online poll found that 52 percent of patients in Canada stated that they could see their family doctor quickly when they needed to (compared to 59 percent of Americans), but that only 26 percent of Canadians said they could see specialists without long waits (compared to 47 percent of Americans). It appears there is a trade-off in these countries between greater access to health care by low-income people and shorter waits to see a specialist.[4]

As a budding economist, how would you improve the Canadian system? If people must wait to receive medical care, how can we induce more health care to be forthcoming? In other words, how can we increase the quantity supplied of medical care? You're right—you increase the price. If medical providers are in short supply such that patients must endure long waiting periods for health care, the government needs to increase its payments to providers. This, of course, increases the expense of the program.

The Canadian health care system underwent a significant change in 2005. The Canadian Supreme Court ruled that it was permissible for the province of Quebec to allow the purchase and sale of private medical services and insurance. This was a highly controversial move, and other provinces have since debated the merits of adopting a similar practice. The Quebec system now amounts to a two-tiered one (two options for medical coverage, public and private), and some are concerned that the quality of the public system will deteriorate relative to the private one.

Socialized Medicine

Socialized medicine is a specific form of national health insurance, and it involves extensive government intervention in health care. Great Britain has a system of socialized medicine. As in Canada, providers are salaried employees of the government and hospitals and clinics are government owned. The system is cost-effective insofar as it eliminates the bureaucracy associated with a multi-payer system. The system is nonprofit, though doctors receive very large bonuses for keeping people healthy, hence an emphasis on preventative care. Waiting periods for health care had been a problem, but more recently the waits were reduced by paying more money to providers and allowing people their choice of hospitals (thereby creating competition among hospitals, though they compete to survive and not for profits).

Other advanced countries contain some similar elements to Great Britain without being entirely socialized. For example, Taiwan's government is the single payer and citizens carry a "smart card" that simultaneously serves to contain the patient's medical history and medications and to act as a "credit card" charging the government for medical services. Germany has a two-tiered system of private and public provision of national health care, though by far most people choose the public option. Insurance companies compete, but are not allowed to earn profits. The government pays the premium for the poor and jobless. Switzerland requires all people to have health insurance, but the government pays the premium for the poor.

Other Approaches
Group Practices and Managed Care

While not necessarily conservative or liberal, many believe that various forms of group practices increase efficiency and lower costs. For example, physicians operating in a clinic may have lower costs per service than a doctor in solo practice. Expensive technology and equipment can be more efficiently utilized (as can office staff), and physicians can specialize in various fields. Specific forms of group practices may yield additional efficiencies.

Health maintenance organizations (HMOs) are a form of group practice. They utilize the services of group physicians either working within or for the organization. The organization contracts with insurance companies to care for the insured person's medical need for a given rate. A patient's care is coordinated by a medical clinic or primary care physician. The patient needs a referral from the primary care physician to be treated by a doctor who is not in the organization. A similar form of group practice is the **preferred provider organization (PPO)**, which contracts with health insurance companies to provide health services at a reduced rate. Together, these organizations are what is meant by "managed care."

Managed care is rapidly replacing traditional fee-for-service insurance in the United States. The major reason is the high cost of providing fee-for-service coverage. Managed care is simply a less expensive way of obtaining medical care. As medical care costs rise, driving up the cost of standard fee-for-service insurance, many people have elected to become members of managed care organizations, and these organizations are becoming larger.

As with the Medicare program, there is an incentive for the managed care provider to be cost-efficient in its provision of medical services. Service costs that "go over contract" would be costly to an HMO. Costs below the contracted price would benefit the HMO. As a result, services that cut costs in the long run, such as health screening, nutrition, and exercise classes are often provided by HMOs. There is a healthy emphasis on preventive medicine. Still, some people complain that they cannot get a referral for coverage of a visit to an outside specialist, and others worry about the quality of care when the emphasis is on cost control. Managed care is thus controversial.

Health maintenance organizations (HMOs)
Health insurance plans under which the covered care is limited to designated providers and the use of services is coordinated by a patient's primary care physician. HMOs often encourage preventative care.

Preferred provider organization (PPO)
A health insurance plan under which a group of medical providers contract to provide the insured patient's medical care at discounted rates.

Compromise?

With opinions about health care so strong and divergent, it is clear that there must be some sort of compromise. Economists generally recognize the benefits of universal coverage and comprehensive care that includes preventative measures. Even without the equity (fairness) argument, there are strong efficiency arguments for this. Nevertheless, we don't have to move so far to the left that the government is the single payer and sole provider of health care. While there may be room for legitimate changes and improvements in the Affordable Care Act, it does strike a compromise between the left and the right. Its success in achieving its goals remains to be seen.

You, the Student

Check out the Web site of the World Health Organization (WHO) at http://www.who.int and find and read about a global health issue that interests you. Note that health problems facing the poor in the developing countries of the world are often quite different from those facing people in the United States. For example, your author's Kenyan son-in-law's brother is currently suffering from cerebral malaria, a condition that can be

View**Point**   Conservative versus Liberal

Conservatives, who believe in limited government, strongly oppose national health programs on the basis that such programs signify an expansion of the government's role. They favor privatization and increased competition, the trimming of Medicare and Medicaid, the development of medical savings accounts, and a stronger role for the unregulated market. This is the position of many conservatives in Congress.

Liberals, on the other hand, believe that the market has done a poor job of allocating medical care. They argue that the special characteristics of health care make it unlikely that the market will ever reach an equitable and efficient solution. They therefore favor policy ranging from bolstering Medicaid and Medicare to developing national health programs on the order of those in other industrialized countries.

life-threatening. A young Ugandan friend suffers an intestinal problem that occurs in the United States, but his lack of access to treatment and supplies has rendered him an outsider among schoolmates and he was forced to leave school as a result. Other examples include tropical diseases and a far greater incidence of HIV/AIDS (especially in Africa). You can also find country-specific health information on this site and decide whether you would like to be an advocate for poor country health care on your campus. One exceptional book you may wish to read is *Never Give Up: Vignettes from Sub-Saharan Africa in the Age of AIDS*, by Kevin Winge.

SUMMARY

The United States spends large and increasing amounts of money on health care, both in absolute dollars and as a percentage of gross domestic product. Despite these expenditures, the United States has the worst life expectancies and infant mortality rates in the Western industrialized world. Furthermore, racial differences in these statistics are pronounced.

The market for health care is different from other markets in ways that cause demand to be inflated and costs to be poorly constrained. As a result, we face escalating health care costs, inefficiency and waste, and unequal access to health care. Public and private health insurance have recently left over 15 percent of Americans uncovered. This number has begun to improve with the Affordable Care Act and the future universality of coverage remains to be seen.

The ACA was proposed by President Obama and approved by Congress in an effort to achieve universal health coverage (or nearly so), while at the same time containing costs and applying certain mandates. The ACA has been enormously controversial, with conservatives attacking its expansion of government involvement in health care.

Alternative proposals for health care in the United States include an increase in privatization and competition, expansion of managed care practices and medical savings accounts, development of national health insurance, and the revision of existing Medicaid and Medicare programs. The choice among these proposals is controversial, as is the direction of new policy approaches by the president and Congress.

DISCUSSION AND ACTION QUESTIONS

1. Go to the *World Development Indicators* on the World Bank Web site (http://www.worldbank.org) and find the latest figures on health care expenditures for industrialized countries. How does the United States compare with other countries in the latest year?

2. How do life expectancies and infant mortality rates in the United States compare with those of other industrialized countries? How do they compare with the developing countries discussed in Chapter 10?

3. Which other factors besides health care enter into the statistics on life expectancy and infant mortality rates?

4. Define each of the following terms and explain how each affects the demand for medical care: (1) physician sovereignty, (2) third-party payment, (3) defensive medicine, and (4) attitudes of patients.

5. Do you agree that it is possible to overallocate resources to health care, or do you believe that the reasons for a high demand for health care (mentioned in question 4) are appropriate?

6. How does cost shifting make the calculation of the cost of particular medical treatments difficult?

7. Go to the Centers for Medicare & Medicaid Services at the Department of Health and Human Services Web site at http://www.cms.hhs.gov. Use the information on this Web site to understand the differences between Medicare and Medicaid.

8. Go to the White House Web site (http://www.white-house. gov) and click speeches given by President Obama on health care. Do you agree with his statements?

9. How does managed care result in a decrease of health care costs?

10. Do you believe that basic medical care is a right of citizenship? What features do you think a national health plan should have? (This does not necessarily mean socialized medicine.)

11. What is the conservative position on national health insurance? What is the liberal position? What is your view toward national health insurance? Justify your answer. Visit the Web site of the Physicians for a National Health Program (http://www.pnhp.org) for more information on national health insurance. Is this a liberal or a conservative organization?

12. Go to the Census Bureau at http://www.census.gov. Click H for *health* in the A–Z option, and see what types of U.S. statistics are available at this site.

13. Go to the U.S. Senate homepage at http://www.senate. gov and find the Web site for your U.S. senators. Search for any statements or proposals they have made on the topic of health care reform.

Notes

1. U.S. Department of commerce, Census Bureau, Statistical Abstract of the United States 2012, http://www.census.gov.

2. More specific information on benefits and eligibility for these government programs, see the Health and Human Services Web site, including the document entitled "Medicaid at a Glance" (http://www.hhs.gov /MedicaidAtAGlance).

3. Becky Jungbauer, "Health Care Choice Limited for Inner-City Communities," *St. Paul Pioneer Press* (December 2006).

4. Steven Thomma, McClatchy Newspapers, *St. Paul Pioneer Press* (July 15, 2009).

Appendix 8-1

Private Insurance

With private insurance, the patient pays a portion of the cost through an array of premiums, deductibles, and coinsurance payments. A **premium** is a payment (usually made on a monthly basis) to own an insurance policy and to be eligible for its benefits. Many people with job-related insurance coverage contribute monthly premiums along with their employers. A **deductible** is an amount of health care charges that the patient must pay before receiving insurance payments on the remainder of health care charges. It is usually a given amount specified for a time period or on a per-service basis. A **coinsurance payment** is some percentage of medical care charges over and above the deductible that the subscriber must pay.

If your insurance company requires a $200 deductible annually and 10 percent coinsurance, and your yearly covered medical expenses are $1,000, you will pay the $200 deductible plus 10 percent of the remaining $800 ($80) for a total of $280. The insurance company will pay the remaining $720. Most health care policies have maximum amounts that they will cover as well, either on an annual basis or a lifetime basis. In addition to the $280 that you must pay, you will pay a premium (unless it is fully paid by your employer) and you will be responsible for any expenses that go beyond the maximum amount covered by your insurance program.

Deductibles and coinsurance keep costs to the insurer down, as well as discourage excessive use of medical services. If subscribers are required to pay some amount per service, they will be less inclined to use unnecessary services frivolously. On the other hand, the expense to the subscribers may actually deter them from seeking important services. Furthermore, the financing, including premiums, becomes regressive for subscribers. Even if a low-income and a high-income family pay the same dollar payments of premiums, deductibles, and coinsurance, the low-income family is paying a larger percentage of its income in these payments. Thus, the poorer family has a greater burden in paying these expenses. This **regressivity** could be eliminated if premiums and other payments were tied to income. *All this means that even if you have health insurance, your out-of-pocket expenses may still be high. This can result in patients skimping on medical care or reducing needed expenditures on other items (such as food and energy).*

Premium
A payment to purchase and keep in force an insurance policy.

Deductible
A payment on an annual or per-service basis that must be made by the insured person before the insurance company's payments begin.

Coinsurance payment
A percentage of medical expenses that the insured person must pay over and above the deductible.

Regressivity
A situation in which a larger percentage of income is taken from low-income people than high-income people.

ROAD MAP

The Economic Toolbox

- Privatization
- Social insurance
- Pay-as-you-go
- Social adequacy
- Tax base
- Tax rate

- Regressive versus progressive taxes
- Adverse selection
- Social Security wealth effect
- Early retirement effect
- Widows' income gap

Social Security

Hmmm...aside from the joke about his father, the former president raised an important issue. The baby boom generation is stressing the Social Security program, which will present us with difficult choices. Yet his comments are notable for what he left out. Specifically, he did not reiterate his previous requests for partial privatization of the Social Security program. As we shall discover again in Chapter 17, **privatization** means the transfer of assets or responsibility from the government to the private sector. In the case of Social Security, the *political unpopularity* of partial privatization is likely the cause of its omission from the former president's latest speech and its absences from the speeches of President Barack Obama.

As you probably know, the U.S. Social Security system and the associated Medicare health insurance system affect us all. If we work, we pay Social Security and Medicare taxes. If we become disabled, we will be able to collect benefits from the Social Security Administration (SSA). If our spouse dies, we may be able to receive benefits for ourselves and our surviving children from Social Security. When we retire, we will collect retirement benefits and health benefits from the SSA. Retirement probably seems impossibly far away for most of you, but you undoubtedly have relatives who are retired, and they receive Social Security checks on the third of each month (unless their Social Security is automatically deposited to their bank account). You may sometimes worry about the future of the Social Security system and whether it will be there for you when you finally retire.

A Social Security payment is an entitlement, or a payment that eligible citizens have a right to receive based on U.S. law. Recall the discussion of universal entitlements in Chapter 6. Entitlements are a huge share of the federal budget; because these payments are mandated by law, they are outside the discretionary control of Congress. The only way payments can be decreased is to change the law that entitles citizens to them. In the current political atmosphere, in which cutting federal government expenditures appears to be of paramount importance, discussion of entitlements and the laws that govern entitlements is both loud and emotional. Social Security and Medicare are therefore controversial. And, they are expensive. Because Social Security receives so much media coverage, it is one of those programs about which most of us have an opinion but often little knowledge to back it up.

In this chapter, we consider the Social Security program as it now exists and look at some of the problems and controversial issues that surround it. We also consider the probable future for the program.

This year, the first of about 78 million baby boomers turn 60, including two of my Dad's favorite people—me and President Clinton.:-) This milestone is more than a personal crisis—it is a national challenge. The retirement of the baby boom generation will put unprecedented strains on the federal government.

—*PRESIDENT GEORGE W. BUSH, STATE OF THE UNION ADDRESS, 2006*

Privatization
The transfer of government enterprises or responsibilities to the private sector.

Entitlement
A payment that eligible citizens have a right to receive by law.

Social Security: A Social Insurance Program

The Social Security Act of 1935 established the Social Security program. Widespread unemployment, hunger, poverty, and wasted human resources during the Great Depression of the 1930s had focused the nation's attention on the economic insecurity that resulted. The Social Security Act was seen as a solution to these problems. The original law provided only retirement benefits at age 65 for most workers in industry and commerce. Since then, the law has been amended many times. Social Security now has provisions for disabled workers and their dependents and for survivors of deceased workers. It covers virtually the entire working population, including the self-employed, and benefits are tied to the consumer price index so that they increase automatically with inflation in the economy. Therefore, the purchasing power of retirees' benefits remains the same even when the average price level goes up. (You often hear about older people living on a "fixed income," meaning that income does not adjust for inflation. In fact, older people are in the age group that is *least likely* to be living on a fixed income!) Medicare, an associated program that provides highly subsidized medical insurance for aged and disabled Social Security beneficiaries, was established in 1965, and prescription drug benefits were added in 2006.

Social insurance

Any government program funded by payroll taxes on employers, employees, or both. It is targeted to aid certain eligible groups of people, and a person *need not* have low income in order to be eligible.

Private insurance

A private program provided by for-profit insurance companies and funded by premiums. Its purpose is the pooling of risk of losses.

Social Security is a good example of social insurance. **A social insurance program is like a private insurance program, except that benefits are provided by the government instead of by private companies.** Like your private life or private health insurance, the purpose of social insurance programs is to pool risk of losses from such occurrences as death or illness. This means that combining high- and low-risk individuals enables us to manage the consequences better. Because the concept of social insurance is sophisticated and difficult to explain by itself, let's contrast social insurance with two other types of programs that contribute to the economic security of the population. These are private insurance and public (social) assistance. First, **private insurance** is provided by for-profit insurance companies, not the government. Its purpose is like that of social insurance, the pooling of risk of losses. Table 9-1 compares social insurance with private insurance programs.

Although the basic purpose of the two kinds of insurance is the same, they differ in most other characteristics. Social insurance is compulsory, whereas private insurance is voluntary. If you are a covered worker, you must pay Social Security taxes and participate in the program, whereas no one requires that you purchase a private insurance policy. The reason that social insurance is compulsory is obvious. Many people might

TABLE 9-1 • Characteristics of Social Insurance and Private Insurance

Social Insurance	Private Insurance
1. Purpose is pooling of risk	1. Purpose is pooling of risk
2. Compulsory	2. Voluntary[1]
3. Government monopoly	3. Competition among private insurers
4. Financed by tax payments	4. Financed by insurance premiums
5. Pay-as-you-go	5. Fully funded
6. Statutory (legal) right of beneficiaries	6. Contractual right of beneficiaries
7. Operates under principles of social adequacy and individual equity	7. Operates under principle of individual equity

© Cengage Learning

choose to postpone participation until they neared retirement or choose not to participate at all if the decision were left up to them. Then the cost of the program for other covered workers would increase.

The private insurance industry is composed of a large number of competing firms, although it is dominated by a much smaller number of large firms. The SSA is the sole provider of this social insurance, and it is therefore a government monopoly.

Revenue for social insurance programs is provided by taxes that are earmarked for providing benefits to those who qualify. Since the funds are taken directly from your paycheck, they are referred to as **payroll taxes**. In the case of Social Security and Medicare, the payroll tax is a matching tax with equal amounts paid by employees and their employers. This financing mechanism contrasts with private insurance, in which funds are generated from premium payments made by policyholders.

By law, private insurers must operate on a **fully funded** basis—that is, they must have reserves sufficient to pay all the claims likely to be made on them. Social insurance, such as Social Security, is not fully funded. Instead, it is a **pay-as-you-go system**. The taxes collected from current workers and employers are used to pay benefits to current retirees and other current beneficiaries. The decision to make Social Security a pay-as-you-go program, rather than a fully funded one, came about in the 1930s. It was reasoned that there would always be new workers coming into the compulsory program to pay taxes to support beneficiaries, so a fully funded program was unnecessary. Contingency funds intended to cover six months' to one year's benefits were established, but the program's current taxes were intended to pay current benefits.

Your right to benefits under Social Security is a **statutory right**—that is, this right is defined by the current Social Security law. If Congress changes the law to make benefits either more or less generous, your right to benefits will change with the law. On the other hand, you have a **contractual right** to payments as specified in a policy purchased from a private insurer. The company cannot unilaterally change the terms of your policy.

Finally, private insurance is based on the principle of **individual equity**. You get back benefits proportional to what you paid in. If you purchased a larger policy, paying more premiums to do so, you will get back larger payments (or your heirs will). Social insurance is based on the principles of individual equity *and* social adequacy, or the need to provide a minimum floor of economic security to the population as a whole. Furthermore, the emphasis of the program is more on **social adequacy** than individual equity. Low-wage workers will therefore receive benefits that are proportionally larger in comparison to the taxes they paid in than will high-wage workers.

Social insurance shares some characteristics with private insurance, but it shares other characteristics with public (social) assistance. **Public assistance** programs are needs-based welfare programs of the government. Table 9-2 contrasts social insurance with public assistance programs.

Payroll taxes
Taxes based on earnings from work, usually deducted directly from workers' paychecks.

Fully funded
Having sufficient reserves to pay all expected liabilities; it is a legal requirement of private insurance.

Pay-as-you-go system
A program in which current taxes pay current benefits.

Statutory right
A right that is specified by law.

Contractual right
A right that is specified in contract between parties.

Individual equity
The principle that benefits received are proportional to amounts paid in.

Social adequacy
The principle that benefits are sufficient to provide a minimum level of economic security to the population as a whole.

Public assistance
Any government program that is targeted to aid low-income people.

TABLE 9-2 • Characteristics of Social Insurance and Public Assistance

Social Insurance	Public Assistance
1. Covers entire eligible population	1. Covers needy
2. Financed by earmarked payroll taxes	2. Financed from general government revenues
3. Operates under principles of social adequacy and individual equity	3. Operates under principle of social adequacy
4. No stigma attached to receipt of benefits	4. Stigma attached to receipt of benefits

© Cengage Learning

We noted that public assistance programs are needs-based. This means that to receive benefits from these welfare programs, a person must demonstrate that he or she is poor or that assets and income are below a certain level. Benefits are paid not from earmarked taxes, but from the government's general revenues. There is no relationship between taxes paid in, currently or in the past, and the benefits received by recipients. Public assistance programs are pure welfare programs. Because every worker is eligible for Social Security and Medicare, but only the poor receive welfare, a stigma is often attached to welfare that is not present for social insurance programs.

Social Security Taxes and Benefits

Social Security and Medicare taxes account for about a third of all federal taxes collected. Moreover, Social Security's share of the budget has increased greatly over time. Let's first discuss taxes and benefits separately; then we will look at the total program.

Social Security Taxes

Tax base
The value of income, earnings, property, sales, or other valued items to which a tax rate is applied. In the case of the Social Security tax, the tax base is earnings through working.

Tax rate
The percentage of the tax base that must be paid to the government as tax.

Regressive taxes
Taxes that take a larger percentage of income from low-income people than from high-income people.

Progressive taxes
Taxes that take a larger percentage of income from high-income people than from low-income people.

Proportional taxes
Taxes that take the same percentage of income from people at all income levels.

The Social Security tax you pay is determined by the tax base and the tax rate. The **tax base** for Social Security is the maximum amount of an individual worker's earnings that is subject to the tax. The **tax rate** is the percentage of the tax base that will be collected for Social Security.

As of 2013, the tax rate was 6.2 percent for Social Security and 1.45 percent for Medicare, so we often speak of a total payroll tax rate of 7.65 percent. Because employees and employers pay equal amounts of these payroll taxes, the combined tax rate of both workers and employers for both taxes is 15.3 percent. Self-employed persons paid 15.3 percent after some adjustments have been made to their earned income.[2]

The Social Security and Medicare tax bases are also different. As of 2013, the Social Security tax base was only the first $113,700 of each worker's annual earnings, whereas all of the worker's earnings were taxable for Medicare.

Let's examine how the tax has increased during the life of the Social Security program. In 1937, the tax base was $3,000, and the tax rate was 1 percent. (At that time, the program only covered retirement benefits for those over 65 years of age.) The average worker pays a much larger share of his or her earnings in Social Security taxes now than at the inception of the program.

The Social Security tax is often criticized because it is regressive. Taxes may be regressive, proportional, or progressive. **Regressive taxes** take a larger percentage of income from low-income people than from high-income people, whereas **progressive taxes** take a larger percentage of income from high-income people than from low-income people. **Proportional taxes** take the same percentage of income from all people. There is certainly room for discussion about whether proportional or progressive taxes are fairer, but not very many people would argue that regressive taxes are equitable. This issue is discussed in greater detail in Chapter 16.

The Social Security tax is regressive for two reasons. First, only the tax base is taxed in any given year. So, in 2013, only the first $113,700 earned by each worker was taxable. Therefore, the entire wages and salaries of most workers were subject to the tax, but only a portion of the earnings of workers who earned more than $117,000 was taxable. So, low-earnings workers paid Social Security taxes equal to 6.2 percent of their total earnings, and high-earnings workers paid a lower percentage of taxes on their total earnings. (Think how much of Johnny Depp's earnings was exempt from the Social Security tax!)

Second, only earnings from working are taxable for Social Security and Medicare. Other forms of income, such as rents, interest, capital gains, and stock dividends, are not subject to these taxes. Because higher-income people have more income from sources other than wages and salaries, they also have more income that is not taxable for these social insurance programs. **Thus, Social Security and Medicare taxes are rightly characterized as regressive, with their greatest burden on low-income people.** We shall see shortly, however, that the payment of benefits is progressive.

Social Security Benefits

Social Security benefits are mainly in the form of checks mailed by the U.S. Treasury to beneficiaries at the beginning of each month. Most recipients receive their checks on the third of the month if the benefits are not automatically deposited into their bank account. Medicare benefits are in the form of payments to hospitals, doctors, and others for medical care. Medicare's effects on our health care system have been discussed in Chapter 8. Here, we concentrate on the discussion of Social Security retirement benefits.

To qualify for Social Security benefits, the recipient must be a fully insured worker or the dependent of a fully insured worker. That is, the worker must have paid Social Security taxes on a minimum amount of earnings for a minimum period of time.

Benefit amounts are based on the retired worker's prior Social Security tax contributions. A complex formula that takes into account the worker's highest 35 years of earnings (adjusted for inflation) determines the amount of the worker's monthly check. The benefits are progressive in the sense that low-earnings workers receive a higher replacement rate than high-earnings workers do. The **replacement rate** is the percentage of the final working year's earnings that is replaced by Social Security benefits. Thus, although Social Security taxes are regressive, the benefit schedule is progressive. **Higher-income earners will generally receive higher Social Security benefits, but these will be a smaller percentage of their prior year's earnings.**

Replacement rate
The percentage of the worker's last working year's earnings that is replaced by Social Security retirement benefits.

The Problem and the Response

Let's consider the principal problem with Social Security, which is the aging population of our country. Then we will consider some actions that have been taken to address it, as well as the long-run viability of the program.

The Long-Run Problem: An Aging Population

The long-term problem of Social Security is demographics. The average age of the U.S. population is increasing, which implies that we have fewer workers paying taxes and more retirees receiving benefits. Life expectancy in the United States has increased since the beginning of the Social Security program. In 1940, life expectancy at birth 63 years; in 2013, it is projected to be 79 years.[3] The percentage of the population that is over 65 years of age is increasing. Increased life expectancy means that there will be more older people collecting retirement benefits. [Note that life expectancies represent average life spans for males and females. But keep in mind that the increase in life expectancies of 16 years, respectively, does not mean that citizens will live 16 years longer on average. Instead, it means that child and infant deaths are falling, thereby raising the average life expectancy for the population as a whole. Thus, beneficiaries will receive benefits for somewhat longer periods of time, but they will not

TABLE 9-3 • The Ratio of Workers Paying Social Security Taxes to Each Social Security Beneficiary, Selected Years from 1950 to 2040[a]

Year	Worker to Beneficiary Ratio
1950	16.5
1960	5.1
2008	3.3
2014	2.8
2033	2.1[a]

[a]Projection.

Source: The Social Security Administration, http://www.ssa.gov, 2014.

receive benefits for the full 16 years longer that is indicated by the changes in life expectancies. It also means that a larger fraction of infants now born will live to collect Social Security benefits.]

In addition to longer life expectancies, many workers are retiring at earlier ages, and early retirements imply longer periods of retirement during which workers do not pay Social Security taxes but do receive benefits. Moreover, the baby boomers, that post–World War II demographic bubble, are expected to begin retiring in the first decade of the twenty-first century. This group has a higher life expectancy and a lower birthrate than previous generations and will swell the ranks of the retired still more.

Because Social Security is a pay-as-you-go system, it is sensitive to such demographic changes. In 1950, 16.5 workers paid Social Security taxes for every Social Security beneficiary. This ratio has fallen dramatically since then, down to 2.8 in 2014. It is projected to fall to 2.1 in 2033. (See Table 9-3.) The implications of this for taxpayers, retirees, and the financial viability of the system are substantial. Let's look at these implications.

First, if fewer taxpayers are going to provide the same benefits to Social Security retirees on a pay-as-you-go basis, then these taxpayers individually must pay higher taxes. On the other hand, if more taxes are not collected per worker, then benefits must be cut or a source of funding other than the payroll tax must be found. If nothing is done, the financial viability of the system is in doubt.

Efforts to Address the Problem

Congress first wrestled with the problem of the aging population in the early 1980s, and the result was an amendment to the Social Security Act in 1983. Major provisions of the amendment are (1) to raise the normal retirement age, (2) to begin building up trust fund accounts to take care of the increase in benefits expected when the baby boomers retire, and (3) to begin to tax a portion of Social Security retirement benefits for income tax purposes. Let's consider these in turn.

Increasing the Normal Retirement Age

Normal retirement age

The minimum age at which workers can retire with full Social Security benefits.

The **normal retirement age** is the minimum age at which covered workers can retire and still receive full benefits from Social Security. The 1983 amendment to the Social Security Act gradually raised the normal retirement age. The normal retirement age was initially 65 years for those born in or before 1937, and proceeded to increase by incremental months until the normal retirement age was 66 years for those born in 1943. Again, the normal retirement age proceeded to increase by incremental months until the normal retirement age was 67 for those born in 1960 or later. Workers can also retire at 62 years of age, but their retirement benefits are proportionally reduced if they do so. At the present time, many workers choose to retire earlier and receive smaller benefits. The closer to the normal retirement age that they are when they retire, the smaller the reduction in benefits that they will incur.

The increase in the normal retirement age means that many workers will pay taxes for two years longer, and they will collect retirement benefits for two years fewer. Because we are living longer on average, working longer on average may make sense.

Building up Trust Fund Balances for Baby Boomer Benefits

The second change begun in 1983 was a partial departure from the pay-as-you-go philosophy of Social Security. Taxes were established to increase trust fund balances to pay benefits to baby boomers. The baby boomers were born between the end of World War II and about 1965, a period during which the economy was booming and the birthrate increased. As this exceptionally large cohort of similarly aged Americans has advanced through life, they have made a difference. When they began school, they overcrowded the nation's schools and put stress on our public education system. When they reached maturity, they began families of their own and strained the nation's housing resources. They began retiring in about 2010, stressing the Social Security system.

To accommodate the baby boomers, trust fund balances are being built up. That is, the government is now collecting more taxes than are needed to pay benefits to current retirees. The surplus taxes are invested in U.S. government securities and therefore earn interest that is also credited to the trust funds. The intention is to have the funds available to pay benefits to baby boomers. These trust funds are estimated at $2,760.3 billion in 2013, and the 2013 Trustees Report estimates that the trust fund reserves will be exhausted by 2033.[4] This is because, as more and more baby boomers retire, the trust fund balances will be drawn down, because more benefits will be paid out than will be collected in taxes. At the point the trust funds are exhausted, the system will revert to a strictly pay-as-you-go system. Unless additional funds flow into the program, only about 75 percent of current program costs will be covered.

> **Trust fund**
> Taxes collected and invested specifically to pay future Social Security benefits.

Taxing Social Security Retirement Benefits

Originally, Social Security retirement benefits were exempt from income taxation. **In 1984, retirees first began to pay federal income tax on their Social Security benefits.** The taxes paid are credited to Social Security trust funds and are invested in U.S. securities. This taxation of benefits is somewhat controversial, but it has resulted in substantial revenues and contributed to the financial viability of the system. Individual federal tax return filers usually pay a tax on 50 percent of their benefits if their "combined income" is more than $25,000. Combined income is defined as total gross income plus one-half of Social Security benefits. They may pay taxes on 85 percent of their benefits if their "combined income" is over $34,000. Since our income tax system is progressive, people with very little income pay little or no taxes. People with other sources of income or very high Social Security benefits pay taxes on Social Security benefits just as they do on income from investments.

Long-Run Financial Viability of Social Security

We've noted that once the Social Security trust funds are exhausted, the system will return to a pay-as-you-go system. Given the increasing proportion of older people in the population, this change could lead to either higher Social Security taxes, decreased or delayed retirement benefits, or an increase in the payroll tax or other sources of income.

What does this mean for you? If you are, for example, a 20-year-old student, you will not receive benefits until you are at least 67 years old, and your benefits will likely be taxed. And unless other sources of financing are made available, your benefits will be less than 75 percent of current beneficiaries or your payroll taxes will be raised.

In the short term, the Social Security program is solvent, but in the long run, the program is not expected to be financially sound. **Although more steps will be needed to ensure the financial viability of the Social Security retirement system in the future, it is currently not in any danger of collapsing.**

The same cannot be said of Medicare. This social health insurance system reflects the problems of all health care in the United States. Outlays on a per-patient basis are rising rapidly. The outlays on current beneficiaries are increasing more rapidly than are the payroll taxes collected to fund Part A, the compulsory portion of the program. Part B, voluntary supplemental Medicare coverage, is financed by premiums paid by beneficiaries and by the general revenues of the federal government. Each year, premiums are inadequate to cover increasing costs, and the government contributes from its revenues to cover the program's shortfall. Part D, the new prescription drug program, is also voluntary and is funded by monthly premiums of enrollees and Medicare. The financial future of Medicare is uncertain at best.

Other Issues and Problems

Let's discuss some of the other issues and problems connected with the Social Security program. First, we discuss the issue of making the Social Security system voluntary rather than compulsory. Second, we analyze whether Social Security is a "bad buy" for younger workers. Third, we discuss the controversy over Social Security's effect on private savings. Fourth, we look at the system's treatment of women. Fifth, we consider Social Security, immigrants, and racial and ethnic groups. Finally, we consider whether other countries are faced with similar Social Security challenges.

Should Social Security Be Made Voluntary?

U.S. citizens are independent souls, and they tend to dislike being forced to do anything. The compulsory nature of Social Security therefore has been controversial since the program's beginnings. Many conservatives argue that Social Security should be made voluntary, rather than compulsory. Their arguments are based on principles of greater economic freedom and limitation of the role of government in our lives. A related question concerns the fairness of the Social Security system to younger workers (a complex issue we examine in detail in the next section).

A voluntary system implies that individuals would have the option of participating or not participating in Social Security. If they choose not to participate, they could buy private insurance to satisfy their needs for economic security, they could choose to provide for their needs through other means, or they could decide not to provide for these needs at all.

The arguments for a compulsory Social Security program are (1) that a voluntary program would make provision of a minimum level of economic security to the entire population more difficult, (2) that the poor could not afford to purchase

private insurance or save to provide for their own economic security, and (3) that a voluntary system would be subject to greater adverse selection. Let's look at these arguments more closely.

First, social insurance is intended to provide a minimum level of income to the entire population. Carrying out this intention through a voluntary program would be far more difficult. Some people simply would choose not to participate in any program and not to provide for their retirement. Others might purchase retirement income insurance through private firms but let the insurance lapse if they encounter hard times. Because society does not want our elderly population to starve or go homeless, we might find ourselves taking care of these individuals through welfare programs instead of social insurance. Indeed, it is the Social Security system, though not a public assistance program, that reduces poverty rates among elderly people, as mentioned in Chapter 6 on U.S. poverty.

Second, low-income workers who work at or near the minimum wage simply may not be able to afford to buy private insurance that provides benefits similar to those provided by Social Security. Remember that lower-income workers have a higher replacement rate (benefits as a percentage of earnings) than higher-income workers. Premiums necessary to purchase similar coverage from private insurers would be beyond the financial capability of this group. Nor would these low-earnings workers be able to save enough to provide for their families' economic security.

Finally, a voluntary system would increase the probability of adverse selection. **Adverse selection** is a problem for both social and private insurance. Adverse selection is any process by which the choices made by insured persons lead to higher-than-average loss levels for the program. (If healthy people do not purchase health insurance but sick people do, for example, the insurance companies will have higher average loss ratios and receive fewer premium payments.) Remember that the benefits of social insurance are based more on social adequacy than on individual equity. Therefore, some workers receive a higher return on their tax contributions than do others. If the program were made voluntary, the workers receiving the lower returns (younger workers, healthier workers, and workers with fewer dependents) might well decide to withdraw from the program and purchase private insurance in which the returns are based only on the principle of individual equity. If they were to withdraw from the Social Security program, the program would cover a greater proportion of high-risk people (workers slated to retire soon and workers likely to become disabled) and a smaller proportion of low-risk people. Loss levels and the cost per covered worker of the program would rise. Taxes for those who chose to participate would need to be increased, and more workers would find private insurance a desirable option. Social Security might eventually be reduced to an expensive program covering mainly those who are poor risks.

During the congressional debate that led to the passage of the Social Security Act of 1935, an alternative proposal for a voluntary system was made. It was not adopted, because the arguments for a compulsory system were more compelling. As we have seen, the issue is controversial to this day.

Adverse selection
A process by which insured people's choices lead to higher-than-average loss levels for the program's sponsor.

The "Bad Buy" Issue: Is Social Security Unfair to Younger Workers?

One of the concerns you may have about Social Security is its fairness to you and your generation. Social Security is quite generous to current retirees. But will it be as generous to you? Would you be able to provide better for your old age if you could just use your current Social Security taxes to invest any way you want? Is Social Security a bad buy for young workers?

One of the most complex issues involved in the Social Security program is whether young workers will receive their money's worth from Social Security. These workers pay Social Security taxes to support currently retired persons, survivors, and disabled persons. The value of the taxes paid by younger workers and their employers exceeds the value of the benefits that they can expect to receive. Thus, some critics of Social Security argue that younger workers are being cheated and that they should be allowed to opt out of Social Security and purchase private insurance protection. They argue that young people will get a fairer deal from buying private insurance than they get from Social Security. This is, of course, an argument for a voluntary Social Security program. Let's look at the bad buy argument carefully.

Most of the studies indicating that the young worker is cheated under Social Security make the assumption that the individual employee is entitled to all of his or her employer's tax contribution. This assumption is based on the belief that firms pay lower wages to their workers in order to compensate themselves for the Social Security taxes they pay on behalf of their employees. If this assumption is not valid, and workers *do not* receive lower wages because of their employers' Social Security contributions, then the belief that the system is unfair to younger workers is not justified. It all depends on how much money we assume the worker places into an alternative program. The alternative program looks good if we assume the worker puts in the entire amount otherwise paid by employer and employee into Social Security; the alternative program does not look so good if the worker only puts in the amount paid by the worker into Social Security.

The employer's matching half of the Social Security tax was never intended to be credited to an individual worker's account. Its purpose is to benefit all covered persons rather than a specific person. At the beginning of the program, it was necessary to provide benefits to many workers who worked a relatively few years in employment that was covered by Social Security. When they retired and began collecting Social Security benefits, the employer's portion of the tax was intended to make that possible. Moreover, the employer's contributions make redistribution of income from high- to low-income workers possible. **The employer's share of the tax provides for social adequacy, not individual equity.**

In addition, many of the studies supporting the bad buy argument consider only survivor and retirement benefits. Researchers make the assumption that if the individual worker were given the taxes paid by both the employer and the employee, the worker could purchase life insurance and a retirement annuity more cheaply than he or she could acquire the same coverage through the Social Security program. This assumption does not account for all the benefits provided by Social Security. Social Security is a unique social insurance program that also provides disability coverage and medical insurance through Medicare. If we adjust for these benefits by removing taxes paid to support them, the results of the studies change greatly. **It is far less clear that Social Security is a bad buy for younger workers when these benefits are taken into consideration.**

Does Social Security Decrease Savings?

Critics of the Social Security program argue that it has decreased private savings in the United States. They argue that the need to save for retirement privately is decreased because the Social Security program exists. This phenomenon is called the **Social Security wealth effect**. The wealth effect causes us to spend more during our working years on consumer goods, because we do not feel the need to save. Indeed, the United States has one of the developed world's lowest private savings rates, as we shall see in Chapter 17.

Others argue that Social Security actually increases private savings by encouraging earlier retirements. This effect is called the **early retirement effect**. Workers who retire earlier must provide for a longer period of retirement and therefore must save more during their working years. If the wealth effect is greater than the early retirement effect, then Social Security decreases private savings. If the early retirement effect exceeds the wealth effect, then Social Security increases private savings.

Social Security's effect on private savings is an issue for empirical research, and many studies have been done on the issue. Trying to measure the portion of savings that is affected by Social Security as opposed to the portion of savings that is not affected by Social Security is difficult, and the results of the studies are inconclusive. Many of the studies do not take into account that workers may save for purposes other than retirement. For example, many workers save for vacations, down payments on houses, their children's education, or other purposes. Nor do the studies consider that children might have to support their aged parents if Social Security did not exist. The question is truly complex, and we simply do not know the effect of Social Security on savings.

Social Security's Treatment of Women

Social Security is meant to be gender-neutral; it is supposed to treat men and women equally. But, largely because our society and culture do not treat the sexes equally, men and women are not treated equally under Social Security. We discuss two of the women's issues in Social Security. They are the widow's income gap and the possible unfair treatment of working wives under the program.

The Widow's Income Gap

Widows (or widowers) of covered workers can collect monthly survivorship benefits based on the earnings record of the deceased spouse. Surviving children are also entitled to benefits until they reach the age of 18. The surviving spouse's benefits are paid only until the youngest child reaches the age of 16. Then, at the age of 60, the surviving spouse can again collect benefits on the earnings record of the deceased worker. The benefits will be lost if the surviving spouse remarries before reaching the age of 60.

Consider the following case. Tom and Mandy are a young couple with three small children. Mandy worked before their second child was born but hasn't worked outside the home since that time. Tom suddenly dies. Mandy is 28 years old. Her youngest child is three years old. Mandy can receive survivorship benefits, as can the three children. Her benefits will end, however, when the three-year-old reaches 16 years of age. Mandy will be only 41 years old. She cannot again collect benefits on Tom's earnings record until she reaches the age of 60. If she has stayed home with the children, she will probably have few marketable skills with which to support herself.

Mandy will face a gap in survivor's benefits of 19 years. So will many middle-aged widows (women) who are under 60 years of age but who have grown children when their husbands die. It should be noted that widowers (men) face the same problem as widows.

Social Security wealth effect
The tendency of the population to substitute Social Security for private saving, thus decreasing private saving.

Early retirement effect
Social Security's effect of increasing private savings by encouraging earlier retirements.

If the wife was the primary (or even an equal) wage earner in the marriage, a surviving widower will face the same situation. Since, however, there are still a great many so-called traditional marriages in the United States, and since men on average earn more than women, and since women tend to live longer than men, the coverage gap is primarily a women's issue.

Unfair Treatment of Working Wives

A wife can receive retirement benefits based on her own earnings record, or she can receive retirement benefits based on her husband's record as his spouse. As a matter of course, the SSA will pay her the highest retirement benefits after calculating the benefits using her own record and her husband's. Usually, her spousal benefits will be one-half of what her husband receives. Wives who have never worked outside the home, or who did not work enough to be fully covered for retirement benefits, are entitled to the same spousal benefits as are wives who worked throughout their married lives.

Many wives, on applying for Social Security retirement benefits, discover that they are entitled to larger spousal benefits than they would be entitled to if they were to receive benefits based on their own earnings record. It therefore appears as if their tax contributions are lost, and, at least for Social Security retirement purposes, that their years of working do not matter.

Why is this the case? Remember from Chapter 5 that women make significantly less on average than do men. If the couple is typical in this way, the man will have compiled a larger earnings record. Furthermore, women are in and out of the labor market because of family responsibilities more than men are. This, too, will contribute to a lower earnings record. Thus, the one-half of her husband's retirement benefit is more than the benefits based on her own earnings. It appears as if her years of working and paying payroll taxes are wasted.

Again, it should be noted that husbands might find themselves in the same situation if their earnings record is much smaller than their wives'. They might find that their spousal benefits are larger than benefits paid on their own records. The Social Security law treats spouses of either gender the same. *But the labor market institutions of the United States treat men and women differently, and this differential treatment is reflected in treatment for Social Security.* All of this contributes to the great disparity in poverty rates between older men and older women, with women about twice as likely as men to be classified as poor.

Social Security, Immigrants, and Racial and Ethnic Groups

The SSA welcomes immigrants to the United States on its immigration home page (http://www.socialsecurity.gov/immigration/)! This site provides Social Security and other information to different groups of immigrants, including students, refugees, and asylum seekers. It also provides written and Internet content in Spanish; the SSA states that "we offer this service as a courtesy to our customers who pay into Social Security and do not speak the English language." In addition, the SSA provides Social Security information in Arabic, Armenian, Chinese, Farsi, French, Greek, Haitian-Creole, Italian, Korean, Polish, Portuguese, Russian, Tagalog, and Vietnamese.

The SSA also provides a specific Internet site to American Indians and Alaska Natives (http://www.socialsecurity.gov/aian/), Asian-Americans and Pacific Islanders (http://www.socialsecurity.gov/aapi/), and others. The mission statement on the American Indian Web site includes the goal of "including outreach to those living in remote areas," and provides information on how individuals and tribes or nations can acquire various Social Security and other information. The Asian-American Web site points out that by 2050, approximately 1 out of every 10 Americans will be of Asian or Pacific Islander descent. It also points out that Filipino World War II veterans who served in the organized military forces of the Philippines whereas the forces were in the service of the U.S. armed forces are eligible for special benefits.

Do Other Countries Face Similar Problems with Social Security?

The problems with Social Security are not unique to the United States. The world's 65-and-older population will triple by midcentury to 1 in 6 people, according to the U.S. Census Bureau. The world's population has been aging for many years because of declining births and medical advances that increase life spans.

According to the SSA, most countries in Europe, as well as Japan and China, have more serious challenges than the United States. More than 30 of these countries, including Great Britain, Australia, and Sweden, have established their own versions of personal (privatized) saving accounts. Some developing countries are also beginning to confront problems facing their aging populations and are responding with government or privatized programs.

The South American country of Chile is notable as a developing country with a privatized Social Security program. This program began under the conservative right-wing military dictatorship of Augusta Pinochet over 1973–1990, when the government Social Security program was supplanted with a plan for Chilean workers to save 10 percent of their salaries in private accounts. Yet today, about half of Chile's workforce has either not participated or has not accumulated enough to provide an adequate monthly benefit. The privatization program failed, and the new leftist government announced in 2006 that it would pursue far-reaching reforms that would increase the government's role in Social Security. One thing is clear: the problem of caring for elderly citizens is not unique to the United States.

What Does the Future Hold for the Social Security System?

Americans have long been skeptical about the promise of Social Security. Each generation has applauded the system's support of their parents and grandparents but has doubted that Social Security will "be there for them." Each generation fears the collapse of the system before that generation reaches retirement. In opinion poll after opinion poll, Americans express their uneasiness. This skepticism was only briefly allayed by the changes made by Congress in 1983.

In part, workers' renewed doubts are the result of Social Security's worsening financial position. It is now obvious that trust fund balances will be drawn down more rapidly than once predicted. But part of the skepticism arises because most

Americans simply do not understand the system. And inaccurate reporting in the media contributes to both their uneasiness and their lack of understanding. When, for example, the Social Security board of trustees reported in 1999 that the retirement trust fund balances were to be exhausted by 2037 (we know this number has changed by now), newspaper headlines throughout the country read "Social Security Bankrupt by 2037." Although the exhaustion of trust fund balances is not exactly good news, the return to a pay-as-you-go system is not the same as bankruptcy. As we've already noted, after 2033, the system will continue to pay benefits at a level of about 75 percent of today's benefit level, even without our making changes to increase its financial stability. But benefits will have to be paid from current tax collections after that date.

Nevertheless, issues of financing and financial soundness remain. Trust fund balances are now predicted to be drawn down more rapidly than previously expected. The Medicare hospital insurance trust fund is in really poor condition. The state of the new prescription drug plan is questionable. There is cause for concern in the context of politically unpopular budget deficits that crowd out spending options. Without doubt, changes will be made to the Social Security system. Because the system offers a measure of economic security to us all, we should be concerned about whether these changes reflect the underlying principles and values of the social insurance system. If we allow the system to deteriorate until it reaches a crisis situation, changes made at that point may not be consistent with these values. Let's look at some of the changes that might be made in the future.

Altering the Social Security Tax

Some are concerned about the heavy burden of Social Security taxes on low-income workers in our economy. We have noted that the tax is highly regressive and that this regressive tax has increased in size over time. There has been little outcry about the regressivity of this tax, perhaps because most people do not fully understand its implications. On the other hand, recent cuts in capital gains taxes, dividend taxes, and personal income taxes have primarily benefited high-income people. We address the issue of the effects of taxes on income distribution in greater detail in Chapter 16.

For now, let's just think about how we might reduce the regressivity of the Social Security tax. It may not be as hard as we think. Instead of placing a ceiling on the amount of our earnings that is taxed each year (currently $113,700), we might put a floor in place instead. That is, we might say something along the lines that your earnings below $113,700 are not taxed but your earnings above this level are. In this way, very-high-income earners would be taxed more heavily than low-income earners, and the regressivity of the current system is reversed in a simple way.

Cutting Current Social Security Benefits

Various proposals have been made to cut current Social Security benefits, either across the board or for high-income recipients. Some proposals would tinker with the benefits formula to decrease the benefits of particular earnings classes. Others would eliminate adjustments for inflation, either temporarily or permanently. Eliminating such cost-of-living adjustments is, in fact, a form of benefits reduction. Obviously, cutting current benefits would make the trust funds last longer.

A proposal introduced in Congress in 1999 would have cut current benefits. The proposal was to revise the cost-of-living adjustment (COLA) of current Social Security recipients. Social Security benefits are adjusted each January to cover the inflation that occurred in the preceding year. The inflation is measured using the consumer price index (CPI). Economists generally agree that the CPI somewhat overstates inflation but they disagree about how much. (This issue is discussed in Chapter 14.) The legislative proposal would have adjusted the COLA and decreased the annual increase in benefits of current beneficiaries. The proposal was defeated in Congress.

Proponents of cutting the benefits specifically of high-earner retirees point out that not all Social Security recipients are poor. People who earned more while working are also more likely to have received private pensions and have investment income than low earners. In other words, they do not need the Social Security check as much as lower earners. Eliminating or cutting their benefits would make the system more progressive, keep a minimum floor of income under the lower and average earners, and cut the costs of the Social Security program.

On the other hand, cutting the benefits of high earners might threaten the individual equity principle that makes Social Security a social insurance program instead of a welfare program. As a social insurance program, Social Security has enjoyed widespread acceptance and a lack of stigma. As a wise person once said, "Programs for the poor tend to be poor programs." Social Security has always been perceived as a program for everyone. Eliminating the benefits of high earners might lead people to view Social Security as a welfare program, and welfare programs are more vulnerable to political maneuvering than are social insurance programs.

Increasing Retirement Ages

As mentioned previously, the so-called normal retirement age will increase over time to 67 years under our current law. Another suggestion to strengthen the system is to raise both the normal retirement age *and* the early retirement age.

Proponents of an additional increase in the normal retirement age point out that the U.S. economy is evolving from a manufacturing economy to a service and information economy. Jobs are therefore less physically demanding, on average. Furthermore, advances in health care have made U.S. workers healthier in their fifties and sixties. Therefore, they argue, it will not be a disservice to increase the normal retirement age further.

Over time, U.S. workers have retired at younger ages. Many argue that Social Security has contributed to this trend. When workers retire at earlier ages (such as age 62), they still receive a large percent of the monthly Social Security benefits they would have received at the normal retirement age. Those who propose an increase in the earliest age that a worker can retire and still receive Social Security benefits argue that workers who choose early retirement at reduced benefits often do so without realizing how long they will need to provide for themselves in retirement. As their other assets are exhausted, their reduced Social Security benefits may not be adequate to provide for their needs, or certainly not enough to keep them comfortably. Raising the early retirement age would encourage workers to continue working—and paying Social Security taxes—longer. Because their monthly benefits would be greater when they retire, they would be better off, and so would the Social Security system.

Investing Social Security Taxes in the Stock Market

Social Security trust funds are invested to earn interest until they are needed to pay benefits. The trust funds must, by law, be invested only in government securities, which are the safest possible investment because the full faith and credit of the federal government stands behind them. But stocks in America's corporations often pay investors far higher rates of return than do government bonds. Many critics of the system argue that allowing the managers of the Social Security trust funds to invest a portion of the tax revenue in the stock market would greatly increase the investment earnings of the funds. Others point out that investment in the stock market is more risky than investing in government securities, as we've certainly seen in the 2008 stock market crash. Nevertheless, a portion of the trust funds will probably be invested in stocks at some point in the future.

Partial Privatization

As we have noted, President Bush once proposed that portions of the Social Security program be privatized. His proposal was that 2 percent of a worker's earnings be put into investment accounts selected by the worker. The Social Security tax rate would be reduced by the same amount. Thus, instead of the SSA investing all Social Security tax revenue in government securities, the individual worker would direct a portion to be invested in stocks or mutual funds. The worker would then retain control over this portion of his or her retirement funds. Allowing workers to direct the investment of tax contributions is quite different from simply allowing the managers of the Social Security trust funds to invest in corporate stocks. Critics argue that high-wage earners would receive more sophisticated investment advice than would low-income workers. Thus, they argue, the proposal would increase the retirement income of high earners and decrease the retirement income of low-income earners.

Whether this change in the Social Security system takes place remains to be seen. In the current environment of corporate scandals and public mistrust of these institutions, it seems unlikely that the system will change in this direction in the very near future. It also seems unlikely that a Democratic president and Democrats in Congress would look with favor upon privatizing a portion of Social Security.

What happens to the future of Social Security is critical. It represents economic security to some people and an undue tax burden to others. One thing is certain: Social Security *will* change over time. And it is highly unlikely that the system will be as generous to us as it is to today's retirees. What does this mean to you as you begin your career? It means that you should save for your retirement, on a personal basis and through employer-sponsored or other retirement plans, if you wish to maintain your living standard. Social Security may supplement your savings, but you should not expect to be able to retire comfortably on Social Security benefits alone.

You, the Student

Do you know any elderly people, maybe a grandmother, or neighbor, or landlady? Are you close enough to her to ask her about her Social Security benefits? Does she feel these benefits are adequate for her lifestyle? Does she feel she suffers from the "widows' income gap" or is otherwise treated unfairly? Do you agree with her?

View*Point* Conservative versus Liberal

Conservatives believe that Social Security represents big government. They argue that we would be better off if we did not have to pay Social Security taxes but were encouraged by some measure, such as a tax break, to provide for ourselves in retirement or disability through private investments. Many conservatives therefore favor partial or total privatization of the system. They also, of course, would favor making Social Security voluntary.

Liberals, on the other hand, tend to support the principle of social, not private, insurance to provide a minimum floor of income support under the total population. Liberals worry about the regressivity of the Social Security payroll tax and want to make changes to ensure the continued financial viability of the system. They do not worry about the size of the system. Nor do they worry that the system represents big government.

SUMMARY

Social Security is a social insurance system. Although Social Security taxes are regressive, the program's benefits are progressive. The purpose of the system is to provide a minimum floor of economic security to U.S. workers. The size and tax burden of the system have increased over time.

Social Security is headed for difficulty. Its long-run problem is that fewer workers pay taxes to support each recipient as time passes; hence an issue is the long run viability of the system. Trust fund balances are now being built up to pay benefits to the baby boomers. Other issues include the system's fairness to women and to younger workers, the effect of Social Security on private savings and the desirability of making the system voluntary. Changes likely in the future are a decrease in benefits, an increase in the normal and early retirement ages, and the full taxation of benefits.

DISCUSSION AND ACTION QUESTIONS

1. Do you believe that Social Security is unfair to women? To younger workers? Why or why not? If you think that Social Security is unfair, what could be done to make it more fair? What other problems might these measures cause?

2. Explain how Social Security taxes are regressive. Remember that regressivity does not mean that the low-income person pays more actual tax, but that he or she pays more tax as a percentage of his or her income. How could the tax be made less regressive?

3. Compare and contrast social insurance with private insurance. Can you think of other examples of social insurance programs?

4. Compare and contrast social insurance programs with public assistance programs. Can you think of other examples of public assistance programs?

5. Do you believe that Social Security should be made fully funded? What would the advantages and disadvantages be?

6. What changes do you feel are likely to be made to Social Security in the next 15 to 20 years? Why? Go to the SSA Web site at http://www.ssa.gov. Click About Social Security's Future to see some frequently asked questions about the future of Social Security, as well as the answers supplied by the SSA.

7. Again, go to the home page of the SSA at http://www.ssa.gov and notice many other links, both serious and light-hearted. For example, click on the link for the most popular baby names for a recent year.

8. What is the long-run problem with Social Security? Do you feel that the steps taken in 1983 to solve the problem were adequate?

9. For a conservative view of the Social Security system, go to http://www.cato.org, the home page of the Cato Institute, a conservative research institute. The site has links to papers arguing for privatization of Social Security.

10. For a more liberal view of the Social Security system, go to the Center on Budget and Policy Priorities

at http://www.cbpp.org, and look for recent discussions of voluntary Social Security accounts and/or privatization of Social Security. What is the difference between the liberal and conservative views?

11. Go to the White House Web site at http://www.white house.gov to find information about a variety of policies and reports, including many speeches by the president. Search for speeches that include comments about Social Security.

NOTES

1. Under the Affordable Care Act (Obamacare), people are required to have one or another form of health insurance or pay a penalty.

2. The SSA, http://www.ssa.gov, 2014. Unless otherwise stated, all statistics in this chapter are from this source.

3. The World Bank, *World Development Indicators*, www .worldbank.org, 2014.

4. The SSA, http://www.ssa.gov, 2014.

Global Poverty, Agriculture, and Trade

Chapter 10

ROAD MAP

Chapter 3
The Environment
Many environmental issues are global and some apply specifically to poor countries.

Chapter 6
U.S. Poverty
There are some similarities between poverty and income distribution in the United States and poor countries.

Chapter 10
World Poverty

Chapter 11
Global Agriculture
Agricultural development is important in poor countries. Commodity markets in poor countries are similar to U.S. agricultural markets. Poor countries suffer from U.S. agricultural policies.

Chapter 12
International Trade
Some aspects of trade have negative impacts on poor countries.

Chapter 14
Unemployment and Inflation
These are two frequent problems in poor countries.

Chapter 17
Globally Free Markets for the Twenty-First Century?
International debt is the source of much poverty in poor countries. Developing countries have engaged in economic reforms that have harmed the health and education of the poor.

The Economic Toolbox

- Gross national income (GNI)
- GNI per capita
- Economic growth
- Composition of gross domestic product
- Distribution of income
- Economic development
- Newly industrializing countries
- Capital-intensive technology
- Labor-intensive technology
- Infrastructure
- Price ceiling
- Export cropping
- Investment in human capital
- Underemployment
- Informal employment sector
- Millennium development goals

World Poverty

I n Chapter 6, we considered the problem of poverty in the United States. Although U.S. poverty is a very serious matter, we must remember that the problem of poverty is far more serious for the "marginal people" in many other parts of our globe. Consider the boy in the Brazilian *favela* (slum) described in the quotation that opens this chapter. The poor countries of the world go by a variety of terms: developing countries, less-developed countries (LDCs), low-income countries, and Third World countries are but a few. Throughout this discussion, the term developing countries will generally be used.

Most of the developing countries are located in three geographical regions of the world: Latin America, Africa, and Asia. Table 10-1 lists most of these developing countries by region. As the name of a country appears in our discussion, you should reinforce your knowledge of geography by checking the region to which it belongs.

The World Bank recently published statistics indicating the enormous poverty of many people around the world. More than 1 billion people still live in deep poverty, while at the same time, rising inequality and social exclusion seems to accompany rising prosperity in many countries. Forty-nine percent of people in sub-Saharan African and 31 percent of people in South Asia (including India, Pakistan, Bangladesh, Myanmar, and others) are classified as living in extreme poverty. The least developed countries have an average life expectancy of 61, partly as a result of extremely high infant death rates. For many countries, the statistics have worsened over the last few years.[2]

GNI per Capita

Economists have traditionally measured the prosperity of a country according to its gross domestic product (GDP) or gross national product (GNP), where both of these terms vary somewhat in their measurement of production (output) of a country. More recently, the World Bank has begun reporting data for **gross national income (GNI)**. GNI is identical to GNP in value and can be thought of as the income generated from the production of the nation's output. Gross national income is the broadest of all income concepts and allows us to focus on the more concrete idea of people's incomes rather than a nation's production.

One day I was collecting scrap when I stopped at Bom Jardim Avenue. Someone had thrown meat into the garbage, and he was picking out the pieces. He told me: "Take some, Carolina. It's still fit to eat." He gave me some, and so as not to hurt his feelings, I accepted. I tried to convince him not to eat that meat, or the hard bread gnawed by the rats. He told me no, because it was two days since he had eaten. He made a fire, and roasted the meat. His hunger was so great that he couldn't wait for the meat to cook. He heated it and ate. So as not to remember that scene, I left thinking: I'm going to pretend I wasn't there. This can't be real in a rich country like mine. I was disgusted with that Social Service that had been created to readjust the maladjusted, but took no notice of we marginal people. I sold the scrap at Zinho and returned to Sao Paulo's back yard, the favela. The next day I found that little black boy dead. His toes were spread apart. The space must have been eight inches between them. He had blown up as if made out of rubber. His toes looked like a fan. He had no documents. He was buried like any other "Joe." Nobody tried to find out his name. The marginal people don't have names.

—CAROLINA MARIA DE JESUS, IN CHILD OF THE DARK[1]

TABLE 10-1 • The Developing Countries of the World, by Region

Latin America and the Caribbean	Africa		Asia
Argentina	Algeria	Liberia	Afghanistan
Barbados	Angola	Libya	Bangladesh
Belize	Benin	Madagascar	Bhutan
Bolivia	Botswana	Malawi	Cambodia
Brazil	Burkina Faso	Mali	China
Chile	Burundi	Mauritania	Timor–Leste
Colombia	Cameroon	Mauritius	India
Costa Rica	Central African Rep.	Morocco	Indonesia
Cuba	Cape Verde	Mozambique	Iran
Dominican Rep	Chad	Namibia	Iraq
Ecuador	Comoros	Niger	Jordan
El Salvador	Congo, Dem. Rep. of	Nigeria	Korea, Rep. of
Grenada	Congo, Rep. of	Rwanda	Laos
Guadeloupe	Cote d'Ivoire	Senegal	Lebanon
Guatemala	Djibouti	Sierra Leone	Malaysia
Guyana	Egypt	Somalia	Mongolia
Haiti	Equatorial Guinea	South Africa	Myanmar
Honduras	Eritrea	Sudan	Nepal
Jamaica	Ethiopia	South Sudan	Oman
Mexico	Gabon	Swaziland	Pakistan
Nicaragua	Gambia	Tanzania	Papua New Guinea
Panama	Ghana	Togo	Philippines
Paraguay	Guinea	Tunisia	Qatar
Peru	Guinea-Bissau	Uganda	Saudi Arabia
Suriname	Kenya	Zambia	Singapore
Uruguay	Lesotho	Zimbabwe	Sri Lanka
Venezuela			Syrian Arab Republic
			Thailand
			United Arab Emirates
			Vietnam
			West Bank and Gaza
			Yemen

© Cengage Learning

Gross national income (GNI)
The income generated from the production of a nation's output. Gross national income is the broadest of all income concepts.

GNI per capita
Gross national income per person on average. Calculated by dividing total gross national income by total population.

The phrase *per capita* simply means "per person." Thus, **GNI per capita** means "gross national income per person on average," and it is calculated as follows:

$$\text{GNI per Capita} = \frac{\text{Total GNI}}{\text{Total Population}}$$

Thus, GNI per capita can be thought of as income per person on average. The phrase *on average* is important. It refers to the *typical* person in the country, if (and this is a big if) this income is distributed to all people equally. As we will see, income is never distributed equally. In the extreme, most income flows to a select few, while the masses live in abysmal poverty.

If GNI per capita is used to measure the prosperity *of a country*, then it is interesting to compare the prosperity of different countries throughout the world. In doing so, we are struck by the enormous differences and the incredible lack of prosperity of the poorest countries. Table 10-2 shows comparisons of GNI per capita for the richest and poorest countries of the world and for a few selected countries in between.

Notice that Norway has the highest GNI per capita of almost $100,000. (Remember that this is income per *person*, not per family!) The United States ranks considerably lower, with GNI per capita of just over $52,000. Having a relatively low GNI per capita, but still much higher than the very poorest countries, are countries such as Saudi Arabia and Brazil. And while there are some very poor countries in Asia and Latin America, the 20 poorest countries of the world are listed at the end of the table. They are all in Africa, and Burundi is the world's poorest, with GNI per capita of $240.

As you examine the poorest countries on the list, refer back to Table 10-1 to identify the regional location of each. We noted that most of the *poorest countries* of the world are located in Africa. Ironically, most of the *world's poor* live in Asia, because of the huge populations of poor people living in Asian countries such as China, India, Indonesia, Pakistan, and Bangladesh.

Economic Growth

Even though economists look at GNI per capita as a measure of a country's prosperity, they often look at the growth in GDP as a measure of **economic growth**. This correlates with how rapidly GNI is growing and enables us to think about whether GNI per person on average is growing as well. Let's define economic growth as an increase in GDP over

Economic growth
Growth rate of GDP over time, sometimes averaged over several years.

TABLE 10-2 • Gross National Income (GNI) per Capita for the Richest, Poorest, and Selected Countries in Between, 2012

Country	GNI per Capita ($)	Country	GNI per Capita ($)
Norway	98,780	Burkina Faso	670
Switzerland	80,970	Mali	660
Denmark	59,870	Zimbabwe	650
United States	52,340	Rwanda	600
Canada	51,570	Sierra Leone	580
Saudi Arabia	24,310	Tanzania	570
Brazil	11,630	Gambia	510
Costa Rica	8,820	Guinea-Bissau	510
Panama	8,510	Central African Rep	510
South Africa	7,460	Mozambique	510
China	5,720	Togo	500
Indonesia	3,420	Uganda	480
Swaziland	2,860	Eritrea	450
India	1,550	Guinea	440
Vietnam	1,550	Madagascar	430
Zambia	1,350	Niger	390
Pakistan	1,260	Ethiopia	380
Cambodia	880	Liberia	370
Bangladesh	840	Malawi	320
Haiti	760	Burundi	240

Source: World Bank, *World Development Indicators 2014* (Washington, DC: World Bank, 2014).

some time period. Table 10-3 shows the growth in GDP in 2012 for selected developing countries. The countries are listed in order from higher economic growth to lower.

Note that it would be preferable to consider the growth in GDP over a longer time period, such as four years. Then, for example, if we were considering the time period 2009–2013, we would be looking at the growth of GDP over this entire time period and dividing through by the four years. This would give us the *average annual* (yearly) growth of GDP over this time period. It would avoid the problem of focusing on only one year, which may be an aberration caused by especially high commodity prices or some other temporary factor affecting the value of production.

Also notice that these economic growth rates may be positive, negative, or zero. The first 10 countries listed have high or extremely high growth rates of GDP. Some of these country's growth rates may be transient, reflecting discoveries of oil and precious minerals. Other countries have rapid growth results that result from carefully adopted economic reforms that have enhanced productivity and efficiency. Finally, some countries have had such horribly low levels of GDP in the recent past that any kinds of improvements can make the growth of GDP appear large.

On the other hand, the growth rates of some of the listed countries are zero or negative, indicating that conditions in the country may well be worsening. Realize that our real interest is whether GDP (or income) *per person* is increasing, and not just GDP alone. For example, even though population growth rates are high in the cases of Sierra Leone and Niger (not shown, but averaging 3 percent and 4 percent per year on average over 2000 to 2012, respectively), the extremely high growth rates of GDP by far surpass population growth, allowing a sizeable increase in income per person on average. However, in the case of Barbados, a 0 percent GDP growth rate coupled with a population growth rate of 0 percent over 2000 to 2012 (not shown) means that income per person

TABLE 10-3 • Average Annual Growth Rates of GDP, Selected Developing Countries, From Higher to Lower Growth, 2013

Country	2013 Growth of GDP (%)
Sierra Leone	15.2
Afghanistan	14.4
Mongolia	12.3
Niger	10.8
Panama	10.7
Liberia	10.2
Bhutan	9.4
Ghana	7.9
Vietnam	5.2
Cameroon	4.6
Barbados	0.0
Swaziland	−1.5
Bermuda	−4.9
Guinea-Bissau	−6.7
Sudan	−10.1
South Sudan	−47.6

Source: World Bank, *World Development Indicators 2014* (Washington, DC: World Bank, 2014).

on average is actually unchanging. Finally, in a country such as Swaziland, with a negative GDP growth and even a low population growth rate of 1 percent (not shown), income per person on average will be falling. *Thus, both high GDP growth and low population growth help determine the prosperity or lack thereof of the country.* As a final note and in comparison to the countries listed in the table, the 2013 growth rate of GDP in the United States was 2.8 percent, somewhat below our historical average.

As we will see later in the book, GDP falls during a period of recession. But for GDP to fall in such high numbers, such as we see for Sudan and South Sudan, greatly disruptive circumstances must be occurring. War and the instability that accompanies it is a common reason. Inefficient and unstable governments is another factor. These factors are common in many African countries, and the instability in the Middle East that has restricted the movement of people and goods in and out of Palestine has crippled the economy of this impoverished country.

Negative growth rates sound abominable, and positive growth rates sound so good. And they are! But before we can address the problem of poverty in developing countries, we must ask an important question. Whereas economists have traditionally viewed the per capita income or output of a country as an indicator of a *nation's prosperity*, and they have viewed economic growth as an indication that matters are improving, we must ask whether these income and output statistics are adequate measures of the economic well-being *of people* (as opposed *to countries*). As we shall see, they are not!

Problems in Measuring Well-Being

Two problems with GDP and GNI involve the composition of output and the distribution of income.

Composition of Output

One problem with the use of aggregate (total) output data is that it does not address the composition of GDP. That is, of what does gross domestic product actually consist? Certainly, it makes a great deal of difference whether a country produces quality health care, education, housing, and food for its people or whether it produces large amounts of military hardware for regional warfare, nonessential luxury goods for a few, and grandiose skyscrapers and structures that fail to serve the needs of most. Compare Saudi Arabia and Costa Rica in Table 10-2 as examples. The 2012 GNI per capita for Saudi Arabia is $24,310, over two-and-a-half times the GNI per capita of $8,820 of Costa Rica, yet Saudi Arabia has a significantly lower average life expectancy. **Average life expectancy** is the age to which a baby born in a particular year can be expected to live. As we shall see shortly, the average life expectancy in Saudi Arabia is only 75, whereas the average life expectancy in Costa Rica is 80 years. (The life expectancy of the developing country of Costa Rica is even higher than that in the United States!) One explanation for these differences is that 8 percent of GDP in Saudi Arabia is allocated for national defense, whereas Costa Rica spends next to nothing on the military. (Its constitution prohibits any armed forces.) This frees up resources that can be devoted to health care, education, and other life-saving measures. As we will see shortly, life expectancies and infant mortality rates in Costa Rica are similar to those of much more prosperous countries because Costa Rica chooses to produce more goods and services that benefit its people. This is but one example. Many countries divert even far greater shares of GDP to military production than does Saudi Arabia.

Composition of GDP
The items of production of which GDP consists.

Average life expectancy
The age to which a baby born in a particular year can be expected to live.

Distribution of Income

Distribution of income

The distribution of income between different income groups.

An even more serious problem concerns the **distribution of income**. The distribution of the income was discussed in Chapter 6 on U.S. poverty. We know that GNI per capita tells us the income per person *on average*. This is the income received by a typical person, *if* we assume that income is distributed equally to all. We know, in fact, that neither in prosperous countries, such as the United States, nor in poor countries, such as Zambia, is income distributed equally. To the extent that a small, well-to-do elite of any particular country may receive the bulk of the nation's income, the masses of people may live very poorly indeed. *A high value of GNI per capita really tells us nothing about the standard of living of most of the country's residents, because it tells us nothing about the distribution of this income.*

One way of examining income distribution is with the Lorenz curve introduced in Appendix 6.1. You may recall that this curve is based on data showing the share of total income in a country that goes to each fifth of the population. Another measure of income distribution is the share of total income that goes to the poorest 20 percent of the population. We can say that those countries with higher shares of income going to the poorest 20 percent of the people have the greatest equality of income distribution, and those countries with lower shares going to the poorest 20 percent have the least equality of income distribution. Statistics for selected developing countries are presented in Table 10-4. Even though differences may appear small, they have a great impact on the income distribution. Notice that many of the lowest-income countries—Bangladesh and Ethiopia, for example—have more equal income distributions than do higher-income countries such as Brazil and Panama. (Recall that in Chapter 6, we observed that the share of income that goes to the poorest 20 percent of the U.S. population was 3.2 percent, meaning that the poorest 20 percent of people in countries such as Egypt and the Philippines receive a higher *share* of the country's total income than the poorest 20 percent in the United States.)

TABLE 10-4 • Share of Total Income to the Poorest 20 Percent of the Population, From Lower Share to Higher Share, Selected Developing Countries, 2012

Country	Share (%)[a]
Bolivia	2
Haiti	2
Brazil	3
Panama	3
South Africa	3
Zambia	4
Zimbabwe	5
Philippines	6
Vietnam	7
Ethiopia	8
Bangladesh	9
Egypt	9

[a]Several countries use expenditure data rather than income. This generally understates income inequality.

Source: World Bank, *World Development Indicators 2014* (Washington, DC: The World Bank, 2014).

South Africa provides a good example of a relatively prosperous country with an income distribution that is severely distorted in favor of the rich. According to Table 10-4, only 3 percent of total income is distributed to the poorest 20 percent of the South African population. Despite a per capita GNI of $7,460, South Africa has an average life expectancy of 56 years and an infant mortality rate of 33. The **infant mortality rate** is the number of children who die within their first year of life, per 1,000 live births. It is sometimes used as an alternative measure to average life expectancies. The fact that much poorer countries are superior in these measures attests to the significance of income distribution. Contrast South Africa with Vietnam, which has a per capita GNI of only $1,550 (about one-fifth of South Africa's) but an average life expectancy of 76 (as opposed to South Africa's 56) and an infant mortality rate of 18 (as opposed to South Africa's 33). Table 10-4 shows that the poorest 20 percent of people in Vietnam receive 7 percent of total income, one explanation of the higher standards of living in relatively poorer Vietnam.

Mechanisms to improve the equality of the income distribution are almost always controversial, at least in the short run, because some individuals must lose while other individuals gain. Raising taxes on the rich and redistributing the income to the poor may be politically difficult, especially when a country's leader depends on the support of the rich. Other methods might prove more successful, such as eliminating price distortions to ensure that certain groups of people receive more adequate incomes. For example, raising agricultural prices would lead to higher incomes for low-income farmers. (This measure will be discussed in greater detail shortly.) Shifting government resources to adequate nutrition, health care, and education to the poor could go a long way to improve their well-being, and may be politically easier than explicitly taxing the rich and giving to the poor. Finally, government policies might include a redistribution of **assets** (the most notable of which is land), because greater equality in ownership of income-earning assets is often fundamental to ensuring greater equality of incomes. The unequal distribution of land is the source of the highly unequal income distribution that we observed in South Africa.

One of the problems facing many countries with an **indigenous** population is the loss of ownership of native-owned land. The situation in Chiapas State in Mexico is a case in point. The 1990s brought forth a series of changes designed to move Mexico toward a more market-based economy. One of these changes was an alteration of the Mexican constitution to allow commercial sales of indigenous land. The native Indian people traditionally maintained communal ownership of their land, and rights to use the land were allocated to individual people and families within the community. As more and more indigenous land is now being sold, Indian farmers are losing their livelihoods, as well as their cultural ties to the land. This and other issues culminated in 1994, when the people of Chiapas rose up in demonstration against the Mexican government. The Mexican army responded by destroying farms, killing livestock, confiscating property, and taking the lives of many Chiapas residents. The January date of the uprising corresponded with the date that the North American Free Trade Agreement (NAFTA) was implemented. This treaty, which is seen by many Mexicans to epitomize their country's disdained market-oriented economic reforms, is discussed in Chapter 12.

The issue of land ownership also came to a controversial test in the east-central African nation of Zimbabwe, which is one of the poorest countries in the world and has an unequal income distribution (the poorest 20 percent of the population receives 5 percent of the income). The cause of the unequal income distribution is the fact that a tiny white minority has owned about one-third of the productive land in the country, leaving very little remaining for each of the vast majority of black farmers. In 2000, squatters began occupying white-owned farms with the support of President Robert Mugabe, who

Infant mortality rate
The number of babies who die within their first year of life per every 1,000 live births.

Assets
Property that is owned, such as land.

Indigenous
People who are of native-born ancestry in a country.

called the occupation a legitimate protest against unfair ownership. Legitimate or not, some of the occupations have become violent, and people were killed. With government plans to confiscate more than half of white-owned farming land becoming increasingly controversial at the international level, the extent of a stable and peaceful reform in Zimbabwe's land distribution remains to be seen. A major complication is the instability of the Zimbabwean government and economy. At the present time, the occupations have devastated the agricultural production of the country, which is suffering from food insecurity as a result. It is no surprise that Zimbabwe is listed in Table 10-2 as having an extremely low level of GNI per capita.

Economic Development and Standards of Living

Economic development

A multifaceted process that involves improvements in standards of living, reductions in poverty, and growth in GDP per capita.

Largely because of the issue of distribution, we cannot say that growth in GDP is synonymous with economic development. This notion bears repeating: **economic development is not the same as economic growth**. Indeed, we can define **economic development** as a multifaceted process that improves the living conditions of the masses. It entails improvements in standards of living and reductions in poverty, as well as growth in GDP per capita. Economic development also incorporates the idea of liberation from any economic or political oppression. Although growth in GDP per capita is one element of the definition of economic development, it is clearly not the whole story.

Many economists use measures that directly indicate the actual well-being of people of developing countries rather than relying on income or output data alone. Some of the best indicators of living standards are the average life expectancies and infant mortality rates already mentioned. These measures avoid the distribution problem mentioned previously with respect to GNI per capita. Although life expectancies tend to be higher for the very elite of a country, they will not differ by multiples of thousands, as income levels often do. A high-income person may have an income of 1,000 times the income of a low-income person, but the rich person's life expectancy will not be 1,000 times the life expectancy of the poor person.

Moreover, indicators such as life expectancies and mortality rates avoid the measurement problems inherent in income and output statistics. Life expectancies, for example, do not need to be adjusted for inflation, exchange rates, market prices, and so on. These measurement problems sometimes distort comparisons of income and output between different countries.

In addition, life expectancies and mortality rates measure *end results* of government programs and the state of the economy. Other measures sometimes used to reflect standards of living, such as calories per capita, number of doctors per person, or school enrollment figures, actually measure inputs into the development process. They do not tell us the quality of calories, health care, or education; and they do not tell us the outcome of these measures. Life expectancies and mortality rates, on the other hand, measure the outcomes of all such policies and programs. Finally, life expectancies and mortality rates are easily conceptualized by policymakers and the populace alike, and they overcome the discrepancies associated with the composition of GDP.

Life expectancies are shown in Table 10-5 for selected developing countries, ranging from Costa Rica with the highest life expectancy (80 years) to Sierra Leone with the lowest (45 years). Botswana, Swaziland, and Central African Republic also have extremely low life expectancies (47 and 49 years). (Although not shown in the table, the countries with the highest life expectancy *in the world* are Japan, France, Iceland, Italy, and

TABLE 10-5 • Life Expectancy at Birth and Infant Mortality Rate,[3] Selected Developing Countries, in Order of Highest Life Expectancy to Lowest, 2012

Country	Life Expectancy	Infant Mortality Rate
Costa Rica	80	9
Cuba	79	4
Vietnam	76	18
Saudi Arabia	75	7
Ethiopia	63	47
Haiti	63	57
Zimbabwe	58	56
South Africa	56	33
South Sudan	55	67
Burundi	54	67
Central African Republic	49	91
Swaziland	49	56
Botswana	47	41
Sierra Leone	45	117

Source: World Bank, *World Development Indicators 2014* (Washington, DC: The World Bank, 2014).

Switzerland; with life expectancies of 83 years. The United States ranks thirty-second, with an average life expectancy of 79 years.) It is important to realize that a life expectancy of 49 in Swaziland, for example, does not mean that a typical person will die at age 49. What it means is that a very large number of infants and children die, bringing down the *average* life expectancy for the country as a whole. Furthermore, countries in southern Africa, such as Swaziland, Botswana, South Africa, and others have been especially hard hit by HIV/AIDS (Acquired Immunodeficiency Syndrome). It is startling to realize that the life expectancy in Botswana was 63 in 1990 and now it is 47. As a result of AIDS and other factors, such as unequal income distribution, life expectancy dropped by 16 years. Other countries with AIDS-related drops in life expectancies include South Africa (62 to 56 years between 1990 and 2012) and Zimbabwe (61 to 58). These changes are *astounding*, and we will return to the discussion of AIDS again shortly.

Table 10-5 also displays infant mortality rates for the developing countries. Worldwide statistics for infant mortality rates range from a high of 117 in Sierra Leone (meaning that 117 of every 1,000 babies, or roughly 12 of every 100, will die before their first birthdays) to a low of 4 in Cuba. The United States (not shown) has an infant mortality rate of 7.

All of these statistics suggest both enormous divergence between the standards of living in poor countries and those in prosperous countries and the appallingly miserable conditions in the very poorest countries. With this understanding of standards of living in mind, as well as the definitions of economic growth and development, we need to address the most important question of all: how can economic development be achieved to improve the economic well-being of all? The sections that follow will address this issue.

Issues in Economic Development

Development economists and developing country governments have traditionally favored development theories and practices patterned after the Western industrialized world. This preference has led to policies directed toward the urban and industrial sectors. This strategy has proved successful for countries such as Singapore, South Korea, Taiwan, and

Newly industrializing countries (NICs)
Singapore, South Korea, Taiwan, and other countries achieving rapid growth through industrialization.

Capital-intensive technology
Technology utilizing large amounts of capital.

Labor-intensive technology
Technology utilizing large amounts of labor.

Hong Kong. (Hong Kong is no longer considered a country separate from China.) These countries are classified as **newly industrializing countries**, or NICs. They've had many characteristics contributing to the success of their industrialization strategies, including a well-educated labor force; a fairly homogeneous, entrepreneurial culture; and international conditions conducive to their success at the time of their early development. Nevertheless, industrialization strategies failed to produce the same results in many other countries. One major reason is that industrialization emphasized **capital-intensive technology** (technology utilizing large amounts of physical capital), as well as mechanisms to squeeze savings for investment from low-income residents. Agriculture was viewed only as a means of acquiring cheap food and tax revenue with which to develop the industrial sector and support the urban population. Only more recently have economists and policymakers begun to see that other policies may be more appropriate for many developing countries. We are discovering that the key to development often lies in the agricultural sector. We are recognizing the importance of **labor-intensive technology** (as opposed to capital-intensive technology), which can utilize large numbers of people who would otherwise be unemployed. At the same time, we are beginning to acknowledge the important role of women—indeed, all people—in development.

Agricultural Development

The specter of famine was rising on the horizon.... The rice drooped, then wilted, and finally died.... He saw tears on his mother's cheeks. His father came and put an arm around his wife's shoulders. "Mother of my sons," he said, "we shall both go without food for ourselves so that the rice lasts longer. The children must not suffer." The summer passed almost without a single downpour and once again it was time for the winter sowing. Without water, however, there would be no winter sowing.... It was then that he realized that all the livestock was going to perish. November went by. The departure of the cattle had cut off the peasants' only fuel supply.... Gone was the sound of the children's laughter. Their small stomachs swelled up like balloons and several of them died, the victims of worms, diarrhea, and fever—yet in reality victims of hunger.... the women wept in silence.[3]

Development of the agricultural sector in most developing countries is now recognized as extremely important for several reasons. First, most of the world's poor live in the agricultural sector; hence, efforts to benefit this sector will most directly benefit the needy as well. Second, the agricultural sector typically offers the greatest potential for development. In a society with scarce technology and capital, the fruits of investment come most easily from agriculture. Techniques also tend to be far more labor-intensive in agriculture than in modern industry, thereby offering employment for larger numbers of people. And finally, the agricultural sector most directly addresses the most vital need of all people, that of food security. With careful planning and policy, the Indian famine described in the preceding passage needn't occur.

Access to Inputs, Extension, and Markets

For agricultural development to occur and food security to be achieved, both the government of the developing country and the international community must fulfill important roles. The local government must recognize that although appropriate policies can dramatically improve agricultural productivity and the lives of the poor, inappropriate agricultural policy can do far more harm than good. Policies aimed at land reform are often vital. In many countries (especially in parts of Asia and Latin America), a select few control large landholdings, resulting in severely distorted income distributions, as well as inefficiencies in agricultural production. Land must be redistributed in a manner that allows more appropriate income distribution and maximum incentives for agricultural production. In addition to land, other agricultural inputs are important. Farmers must have access to the necessary seeds, fertilizer, irrigation, animals, structures, and vehicles. Perhaps the most important input is agricultural credit; unless financing can be arranged for the masses of poor farmers, access to the other inputs will probably also be denied. We'll return to this latter important input momentarily.

Adequate inputs are not enough. Farmers will require extension services if they are to use increasingly complex but more productive farming techniques and inputs. They will also require reliable transport and market facilities. Poor farmers frequently must travel long distances over poor-quality roads, and without any form of transport other than their own labor, to reach areas to market their products. Even when transport vehicles are available, there may be serious problems. Consider this Kenyan farmer's story:

> One Friday afternoon, Mwangi Muchai, 50, ... climbed into his Toyota pick-up bound for Nairobi, 100 kilometers away. He had loaded over a ton of cabbages from his farm onto the pick-up, hoping to sell them in the capital's ... wholesale market. "I never made it to Nairobi," he says sadly. "I was barely 15 minutes on my way when it started raining and the earth road became slippery."... The pick-up skidded into a ditch, and that was the end of his journey. Mr. Muchai says he and some neighbors tried to push the vehicle out of the ditch, but it proved too heavy.... In any case, the road was altogether too slippery to drive on even if the pick-up had been rescued. "As I walked back to my house and abandoned the pick- up," Mr. Muchai remembers, "I felt the greatest disappointment of my life and, for a while, regretted ever becoming a farmer. I felt anxious about facing my wives and telling them that a whole season's sweat for the family would go down the drain as the vegetables rotted in that ditch." Before the time the rains ended, Mr. Muchai had lost his entire load of cabbages.[4]

Economists recognize that governments must take responsibility for providing adequate **infrastructure**, such as the extension services, roads, and market facilities just discussed, lest agricultural productivity break down at any of these points. This undertaking is difficult for governments strapped for financial resources.

Export Cropping

In relation to food security, the issue of export cropping must also be addressed. **Export cropping** refers to a pattern of agricultural production for export, rather than production of food for local consumption. Many countries choose to produce products such as coffee, tea, rubber, and cocoa to export and thereby obtain foreign currency. Although the theory of international trade tells us that a country should specialize in products it is "good at," as we will see in Chapter 13, it is also true that export cropping can trigger food insecurity and inequality in the income distribution in low-income countries. We will see in Chapter 17 that the international debt crisis has increased developing country dependence on export cropping, as developing country governments are forced to earn foreign currency to pay off their debts. This practice has often been at the expense of the food security needs of local residents. It has also often contributed to environmental problems.

Infrastructure
Social overhead capital, including facilities for transportation, communication, marketing, and extension services.

Export cropping
Agricultural production for export, rather than production of food for local consumption.

Agricultural Prices

Price ceilings
Legalized maximum prices for goods or services.

Beyond ensuring access to inputs, extension, and markets, government policy must focus on appropriate agricultural prices. Economists and international agencies have recently promoted market-based prices to revitalize the agricultural sector. Far too often, developing country governments have established **price ceilings** in order to maintain low food prices and placate the end consumer, who is typically a resident of an urban area. One goal of price ceilings is to keep prices of basic necessities low for poor consumers. Although many urban people may be poor, urban dwellers tend to have higher incomes and lower poverty rates than rural residents do. In the process of holding down prices for this better-off—but politically more vocal—group, price ceilings also keep prices low for the products sold by farmers. This practice results in two serious problems. First, rural incomes fall and poor farmers become poorer. Second, incentives for agricultural production are reduced; those with other options will seek to produce in sectors where the incentives are greater. These problems are illustrated in Figure 10-1, using the market for rice as an example. A similar example, using the market for rental housing, is discussed in Chapter 7 on housing. (Additional examples are discussed in the appendix to chapter 7.)

The demand for rice is indicated by D. The supply curve is indicated by S. If the market operates freely, an equilibrium will occur at the point at which the price of rice is $2 per bushel and the quantity is 1,000 bushels. If the government places a price ceiling on rice, however, the price may be held down at a level such as $1 per bushel (representing the price ceiling). The rice cannot legally be sold at a price above this price ceiling. The artificially low price causes consumers to move down along their demand curve, as they try to buy larger quantities of rice at the attractive low price. Consumers will wish to purchase 1,500 bushels (quantity demanded). Suppliers, on the other hand, will have less incentive to produce and sell rice. They will move down along their supply curve, reducing the quantity supplied to 500 bushels (they may produce other products instead). Quantity demanded exceeds quantity supplied. A shortage of rice is the result. Consumers have been encouraged to "over-consume." Suppliers have been encouraged to "under-supply." Despite the lower prices, many consumers have become worse off,

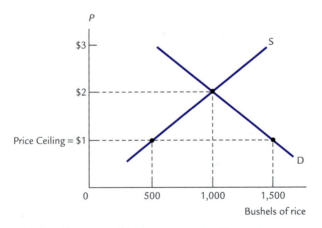

Figure 10-1 • Developing Country Price Ceilings on Rice
At the market equilibrium price of $2 per bushel, quantity demanded equals quantity supplied at 1,000 bushels of rice. When a price ceiling of $1 per bushel is imposed, quantity demanded increases to 1,500 bushels, while quantity supplied falls to 500 bushels. A shortage of rice results, and the producer incomes fall.

© Cengage Learning

particularly those who are unable to buy the rice due to the shortage. Incomes to many poor agricultural workers have fallen as well.

Many developing countries have adopted market-determined agricultural prices, including the communist country of Vietnam. As part of the economic reforms designed to move the Vietnamese economy closer to a market-based economy, the government of Vietnam has raised rice prices to market-determined levels. Previously, as in many other countries, the government had kept the price of staple food artificially low to please urban consumers. As a result of the price decontrol, Vietnam's status changed in just a few short years from a rice importer to one of the world's largest rice exporters. Rising incomes in the rural sector have come far in reducing previously high rural poverty rates.

Although agricultural prices are often found to be too low, care must be taken when governments promote market-based prices. Poor urban residents, who must purchase their food, will suffer from higher prices. We are also becoming aware that even rural residents are often net buyers of food, selling their agricultural produce at harvest and buying food and other agricultural products throughout the year. Rising food prices will hurt these farmers as well. In the face of rising agricultural prices, government assistance must be targeted directly to low-income purchasers of food. In addition, poor farmers may require special assistance to ensure their access to inputs, infrastructure, credit, and markets. The benefits that result from these forms of targeted assistance in the form of productivity improvements and rising rural incomes would outweigh the increased prices that farmers would pay for any purchases of food. These examples of targeted assistance are quite different from price ceilings, which lower prices for all consumers and producers, rich and poor alike, and cause the market distortions that we've discussed. *Economists generally prefer the targeted assistance to needy citizens to the government manipulation of prices that we see with price ceilings.*

International Role

The international community must assist low-income countries to meet their agricultural development and food security needs. We must develop systems to ensure that adequate and timely food aid will be available to countries in emergency situations, as well as to particularly vulnerable populations such as orphans, AIDS victims, and so on. At the same time, we must be cautious about continuing to provide food aid to non-vulnerable people in non-emergency situations, a practice that can often do more harm than good. As will be discussed in Chapter 12 on agriculture, ongoing food aid leads to dependence by developing countries and pushes down food prices, thereby lowering incentives for local food production. Nevertheless, it is vital that food aid be available in emergency situations and other times when it is appropriate.

The international community might also enact measures to ensure the greater stability of world food prices. One suggested measure is the establishment of an international **buffer stock** of cereal grains, whereby managers can buy up grain in years of high production (thereby pushing up low market prices) and sell off grain in years of low production (thereby pushing down high market prices). In this manner, prices are stabilized within a medium range rather than allowed to fluctuate wildly. Greater price stability would ensure that low-income food-importing countries are not left unable to buy when world shortage conditions might send prices skyrocketing, as they did in the early 1970s. This practice would also help overcome the reluctance of large food-producing countries such as the United States from holding back food aid in times of global shortages.

The international community can also undertake efforts to ensure that the bottlenecks of inadequate transport, shipping, ports, and storage facilities are resolved. We can offer

Buffer stock
A mechanism for stabilizing agricultural prices, whereby an agricultural product is purchased and placed in storage during years of high production and released from storage and sold during years of low production.

technical assistance in terms of improved production methods and agricultural extension services. Most important, we must recognize that hunger is caused by poverty. *If we assist agricultural development and help alleviate rural poverty, we will go a long way toward reducing the travesty of hunger in a world of plenty.*

Efforts to provide technical assistance, improved seeds and fertilizers, food aid, and other forms of assistance have often had mixed results and are therefore complex. It is important that assistance be targeted to small farmers and poor consumers. Often, governments, nongovernmental organizations, and private businesses can make positive contributions to world food security, but these efforts must be carefully implemented. A recent report put out by the U.S. Agency for International Development concludes that despite the complexity and the need for carefully thought-out programs, combined efforts by these various players, along with poor farmers groups, can enhance food security. However, they warn that care must be taken to assure benefits to small farmers and other poor groups of people. This will be discussed in greater detail in Chapter 11 on global agriculture.[5]

Human and Natural Resource Development

Investment in human capital

Spending that is designed to improve the productivity of people.

Regardless of emphasis on industrial or agricultural development, investment must also be made in each nation's most precious resource: people. Economists sometimes refer to this as an **investment in human capital**, likening it to an investment in physical capital. This concept is discussed in Chapter 6 on U.S. poverty and Chapter 4 on education. Human investment programs have not only an immediate benefit, namely, the improved standard of living of the beneficiary, but also a long-term payoff, just as other forms of investment do. The long-term benefit is the development of a more productive labor force and a better-educated citizenry.

Human investment programs include those designed to improve health, sanitation, education, and skills. Again, it is important that we abandon some of our Western notions about the form of these programs. Many poor developing countries can derive far more benefit from village-level health practitioners providing basic health care, immunizations, and prenatal care than from expensive high-tech hospitals located in capital cities, out of reach of the masses of people. Most countries will benefit more from the spread of primary education to school-age children and basic literacy training to adults than from expensive doctoral universities located in major cities. Just as with income distribution, benefits that spread to large masses of people rather than to an elite few are most likely to foster positive development.

Education probably holds the greatest promise. Numerous studies have linked education (primarily of women) to widespread benefits: reduced infant mortality rates, improved child nutrition, later age at marriage, lower birthrates, and greater likelihood that their children will be educated. *The cycle is thus self-perpetuating and intergenerational, as children (including girls) become educated.*

Increasingly, development economists are also recognizing the need for a safe and convenient water supply. Many women and children have the task of spending several hours every day walking long distances to retrieve water, carrying it home in the exhausting fashion of head-loading. Often, the water carries bacteria and waterborne diseases. Fresh wells located in villages would improve the health of the people and free the time of women and children for other activities.

Women also spend considerable time gathering firewood, especially as wood becomes increasingly scarce. Wood is the primary source of fuel, and cooking is its primary use, especially in Africa. The clearing of forests for expansion of farming and commercial timber operations is causing a serious problem of **deforestation** in many countries. As trees are depleted, soil and wind erosion increase. **Desertification** may follow, as desert areas are left with no natural barriers to their continual encroachment on cropland. The ultimate effect is the depletion of soil fertility. Villages and organizations have begun the search for solutions to this problem, ranging from the production of woodlots for village fuel use to the invention of simple, fuel-efficient cooking stoves. Natural resource development as such should improve the well-being of people and at the same time preserve the environment.

Deforestation
The clearing of forested areas in an unmanaged fashion.

Desertification
The encroachment of desert on previously fertile land.

Women's Role in Development

In the workplace, women are at the bottom of the pyramid inside the country. They are also the poorest people in the country. They are the people who lose their jobs first. They're the people who are taken off of agricultural farms when these farms are turned into cash crop farms. They ultimately decide whether or not a child is fed. They cry when their boys or husbands are detained, arrested, or made refugees, or die.[6]

As the previous discussion suggests, women play an important role in economic development. And in the words of the South African woman quoted here by the lobbying group Bread for the World, we see that women face the greatest obstacles. For a long time, government and international policies alike have neglected women in developing countries. Women have therefore been treated unfairly.

Women in developing countries also have lower standards of living than their male counterparts. Women typically have **literacy rates** far below those of men. In Niger, for example, only 15 percent of women can read and write, whereas 43 percent of men are literate. In Nepal, the literacy rate is 47 percent for women, but is 71 percent for men. The reason for this disparity in many developing countries is simply that fewer girls go to school than do boys, often for cultural reasons and economic reasons, including the fact that girls are needed to help their mothers on their farms. Furthermore, because families often must pay expensive school fees, they choose to invest in the boy child instead of the girl child. The boy will often remain responsible for his family of origin, whereas the girl will often go to live with the family of her husband. Where adult education programs exist, women are frequently unable to participate for the same types of reasons that girls don't participate. Childcare, farm work, and homemaking leave little time for the "extravagance" of education.

Literacy rates
The percentages of populations that can read and write.

Since society receives so many benefits from the primary education of its citizens, and especially the education of girls, creative ideas should be used by governments and international agencies to promote the primary education of all children. Aside from eliminating tuition, uniform costs, costs of supplies, and other school fees, one policy measure might be to reward the child's family by providing free breakfast and lunch for the child at school and sending home additional food or small amounts of money for the family of the child in school. (Recall the discussion of positive externalities in Chapter 4 on education. The social spillovers derived from education justify government or international spending.)

High maternal mortality rates are another serious problem. The **maternal mortality rate** is the number of deaths of women for pregnancy-related reasons per 100,000 live births. In Afghanistan, for example, the rate of 400 tells us that 400 of every 100,000, or almost one out of every 250 live births are associated with the death of the mother. Because women in Afghanistan have an average of over five children in their lifetimes, the average Afghani woman has almost a 2 percent chance (1/250 times five) of dying

Maternal mortality rate
The number of deaths of women for pregnancy-related reasons per 100,000 live births.

for pregnancy-related reasons. These statistics are alarming, especially when we consider the children left behind when their mothers die.

The problems of women in developing countries go far beyond unfairness, however. Although women are primarily responsible for producing most **subsistence food crops** in much of the developing world, and although they produce and market many other agricultural crops and processed items, they are least likely to receive agricultural extension services, agricultural credit, and access to agricultural inputs such as quality land. Women also tend to be primarily responsible for food preparation and homemaking; fuel and water acquisition; safeguarding of the family's nutrition, hygiene, and health care; and oversight of the children's education. *As long as policy measures that provide education, credit, agricultural extension, technology, and agricultural inputs are targeted toward men, neither the agricultural productivity of the country nor the well-being of the family will be adequately served.*

Microenterprise Credit

While availability of credit is important to men and women, we will focus our discussion on microenterprise credit for women, as they are least likely to have access to credit. This is because (1) they generally do not own collateral (assets such as livestock or land are typically in the husband's name), (2) they often require basic literacy and numeracy, which we've noted that women are less likely than men to acquire, (3) they must often be the head of the family, a status normally given to men unless the woman is single, and (4) rural women have great difficulty traveling to credit agencies located in cities. And, of course, a woman's workday is extremely busy, making it all the more difficult to take time out of the day to seek a loan.

Microenterprise credit refers to small loans to be used for small entrepreneurial purposes. In other words, they are loans intended to assist people in starting up their small businesses. A woman may sew clothing for a living. But imagine if she were able to borrow $100 with which to purchase a sewing machine—she could multiply her productivity many times over and create a far better income for herself and her family. Banks are generally reluctant to be in the business of making small loans due to high transactions costs. For example, they would much prefer to loan $1,000 to one person than to make ten $100 loans to 10 people. They also generally insist on collateral to lower the risk of default. Both of these problems can be overcome when people, and in particular women, form groups in which the group leader takes out a relatively large loan.

Your author has interviewed with large numbers of women's groups that are involved with microcredit in Kenya and Uganda. These include groups that are rural, urban, and slum; large and small; at various stages of progress toward their business activities; and with various forms of structures. Some do not borrow from a credit source at all, but each member makes regular payments to the group leader, who then lends the money to group members. Each woman takes turns borrowing until all have had this opportunity. Other groups are much more complicated, consisting of several women's groups that are part of larger cooperatives that borrow and lend the money. The group format has many benefits. It lowers transactions costs for banks willing to lend, thereby eliminating the need to charge higher than normal interest rates. Furthermore, the group dynamic ensures that the lender will be repaid, as the group will do whatever it takes to avoid default, which would cause lenders to cut off their source of loan funds. In this fashion, there is no need for collateral to assure repayment of the loan.

One important result that your author discovered is that in virtually every case where a woman responded, she expressed her intention to use the income generated by her new

Subsistence food crops
Crops grown primarily as food for the family. A small amount may be marketed.

Microenterprise credit
Small loans that are used for small entrepreneurial purposes.

business to pay for her children's education. Given what we know of the significance of education in developing countries, this is indeed an important discovery.

Population Issues

The preceding discussion of the role of women in developing countries returns us to the issue of population growth. We will consider other population-related issues as well.

Population Growth

Many people believe that high population growth is a problem in many low-income countries because more people means more sharing of already limited resources. Other people, including many in the developing countries, do not believe that population growth is a problem. If we consider population to be a problem only relative to resources, then we must realize that outside of China, the United States consumes the most petroleum and emits the most carbon dioxide in the world (see Chapter 3). Except for South Africa, there are no African countries listed among the top 10 countries in both of these lists. In this respect, the poorest people in the world consume very few resources and cause very little environmental damage. One could further argue that the problem isn't even that there are too many people living in the developed world, but that our consumption levels of petroleum and other products is too high.

To the extent that rapid population growth is a problem in the developing world, intense controversy attends possible solutions. One thing we know: merely passing out contraceptives to the world's low-income women is ineffective. This simple strategy does not address cultural and religious factors, nor does it get at the issue of the motivation to have children. Clearly, people have important reasons for having the children that they do. In agricultural societies, children are necessary to provide labor on the farm and assist their mothers in gathering water and fuel. Because poor countries lack formal social security systems, and because poor people are often unable to accumulate savings, having children is usually the only means that parents have to ensure that they will be cared for in their old age. And finally, as long as women expect that a certain number of their children will die (recall the high infant mortality rates), they will have "extra" children to ensure the survival of a desired number. Consider the words of a woman farmer in Africa:

> *"My first child died at the age of two,"* says Hamza Amadou, a farmer in Niger who wants to have at least eight children. *"The second caught malaria and died at the age of seven. At this rate, how can I think of practicing contraception? If I don't have any children, who will help me to produce food and feed my family, and who will take over when I die?"*[7]

On a more optimistic note, we also know that as development proceeds, population growth rates naturally tend to fall because women become motivated to have fewer children, and they gain a greater sense of control over their lives. As women receive greater income-earning alternatives to the bearing of children, as they have greater expectations that their children will survive, as agricultural productivity improves, and as schools and better futures become available to themselves and their children, women naturally tend to have fewer children and are better able to provide for the ones they do have. An important element in all of this change is a sense of empowerment. Once women are able to ensure their children's survival as well as control the economic aspects of their family's well-being, they have a greater sense of control over their entire lives and take a more active role in structuring them. To talk about limiting births to the Nigerian woman whose first two children died is to ignore the root of her problems. The other important

Opportunity cost
The best alternative forgone in order to produce or consume something else; what you give up to get something else.

element is our economic concept of **opportunity costs**. As long as the best thing a woman can do for her family is to bear additional children, she will do so. On the other hand, if she can acquire an education and/or engage in remunerative activities, the opportunity cost of bearing additional children will be high, and she will have motivation to engage in family planning.

If we view development as a process of liberation from oppression, population policy should not be oppressive. Any policies to limit births should take into account the religious and cultural values of the people involved. In an area of devout Roman Catholics, for example, research on and promotion of effective natural family-planning techniques would perhaps be appropriate (when AIDS is not an issue). Policies that intrude on the morals and human rights of individuals, particularly policies that are coercive, are not elements of true development.

It is also important to keep in mind that real development is necessary for birthrates to fall. That is, a rise in GDP per capita alone may not achieve the desired results. The benefits of economic development must accrue to the masses of people, including women, before a substantial impact on birthrates can be expected. **The fundamental problem underlying rapid population growth is poverty. The fundamental solution is economic development.** A narrow focus on birthrates alone will not be effective.

Urbanization and Rural–Urban Migration

The problem of a highly concentrated population is particularly evident in many developing country cities. In fact, 7 of the 10 largest cities of the world are in developing countries. Seven of the 10 cities are in Asia, 2 are in Latin America, and 1 is in the United States. None are in Africa. (See Table 10-6.)

Along with high concentrations of people is the concentration of poverty in many developing country cities. Large shares of the entire developing world metropolitan population live in slums or shantytowns. In some cities, such as Mexico City (Mexico), Kolkata (India), Mumbai (India), Nairobi (Kenya), and Casablanca (Morocco), the proportion of people dwelling in slums is extremely high. Most of these slum dwellers lack adequate water supplies, sewerage, plumbing, electricity, and even shelter. Many inhabitants are forced to live in makeshift shacks of cardboard, tin, or plastic sheeting; many simply live on the sidewalk.

Underemployment
A situation in which people work limited hours or with low productivity.

Informal employment sector
An employment sector consisting primarily of service occupations in an unofficial setting.

One of the causes of urban poverty is a high level of unemployment and **underemployment**. Underemployment refers to situations in which people work limited hours or with low productivity. Much underemployment occurs in the urban **informal employment sector**. The informal sector consists primarily of service occupations: shoe shining, drug dealing, prostitution, collection of paper and metal scraps for sale, bicycle transportation, and street sales. The latter include the sale of virtually everything: cigarettes, used

TABLE 10-6 • Population of the World's Ten Largest Cities, 2012

City	Population	City	Population
Tokyo, Japan	37,126,000	Manila, Philippines	20,767,000
Jakarta, Indonesia	26,063,000	Karachi, Pakistan	20,711,000
Seoul, South Korea	22,547,000	New York, USA	20,464,000
Delhi, India	22,242,000	Sao Paulo, Brazil	20,186,000
Shanghai, China	20,860,000	Mexico City, Mexico	19,463,000

Source: Based on 2012 Census, numbers include population within the recognized metro area of the city, and they also include people living in the immediate surrounding area outside of the established border of the city (the immediate suburbs). Information is not yet available in some parts of Africa and Asia. *World Atlas,* http://www.worldatlas.com/citypops.htm.

clothing, charcoal, blood, sticks for starting fires, food, and so on. Low productivity, low incomes, irregular work hours, and no benefits characterize many of these services. They do, however, provide work and income for people who might otherwise remain unemployed. Furthermore, some of these informal occupations provide important services to the community, such as carpentry, bricklaying, and sewing. Informal employment also enables poor women to simultaneously care for their children.

Although natural population increases can sometimes explain high urban population density, the other important factor is migration. **Rural–urban migration** brings in countless people from the countryside to the cities each day. These people are searching for better jobs, higher incomes, and the "glamour" of the city life. Thousands of migrants arrive daily in the cities listed in Table 10-6. Even on the African continent, several million migrants come to the cities each year.

An interesting problem may emerge when policymakers attempt to reduce the poverty and misery in many developing world cities. As better housing and services are provided and better employment opportunities are created, even larger numbers of migrants may be attracted to the cities. As migrant numbers swell, even more people may become homeless and unemployed. Efforts to reduce urban problems may turn out to be counterproductive!

This consideration returns us to our earlier focus on agricultural development. *Along with any policy efforts to improve urban standards of living must be policy measures to improve the well-being of people in the countryside. Only then can the incentives for rural–urban migration be reduced and the flow of urban migrants tempered.* Policy measures must focus on improving agricultural productivity and incomes. Health care, educational programs, infrastructure, and services must be provided in the rural sector as well as the urban sector. Price incentives for agricultural production and opportunities for small-scale, labor-intensive industries in rural areas must exist. Only then will the rural–urban balance be improved and urban problems reduced.

Rural–urban migration
The movement of people from the rural sector to the urban sector, often in search of better living conditions.

AIDS

One final challenge of many developing countries is that of AIDS. In 2012, there were 35.3 million people in the world living with HIV/AIDS (HIV is the virus that leads to AIDS), and there were 1.6 million deaths.[8] While HIV/AIDS is a serious problem in many countries around the world, it has reached epidemic proportions in many countries of Africa. Table 10-7 reveals the rates of HIV/AIDS for the nations with the 10 highest

TABLE 10-7 • Prevalence of HIV/AIDS, 2012

Rank	Country	% of Population Age 15–49 With HIV/AIDS
1	Swaziland	27
2	Botswana	23
3	Lesotho	23
4	South Africa	18
5	Zimbabwe	15
6	Zambia	13
7	Namibia	13
8	Mozambique	12
9	Malawi	11
10	Uganda	7

© 2015 Cengage Learning

rates. Ranging from 11 percent to 27 percent, these rates of infection are astounding. Notice that all of these countries are in the southern part of Africa. While relatively high rates of HIV/AIDS exist in other countries, such as Bahrain (3 percent), and Haiti and Jamaica (2 percent), these are low in comparison with the countries in the table. Most AIDS-related deaths are in sub-Saharan Africa. Many of these are children, acquiring AIDS from their mothers at birth. Women in Africa have higher rates of HIV/AIDS than men, and most HIV infections are spread through heterosexual relations. Many African children are now orphans. Aside from the direct impact of AIDS, the health systems of poor countries are overwhelmed in the face of the epidemic. Efforts to assist AIDS patients reduce the systems' capacity to deal with other important health problems, including preventative and primary care. We are seeing the stark effects of AIDS as life expectancies drop in afflicted countries.

The Millennium Development Goals

Many of the developmental objectives that we've considered—reducing maternal mortality rates, increasing basic literacy, lessening the AIDS epidemic, to name only a few—are embodied in the Millennium Development Goals (MDGs). We've already referred to the MDGs in the context of the goal for sustainable development in Chapter 3 on the environment. This entire set of objectives, to be achieved by the year 2015 (Table 10-8), has been broadly accepted by the international community as a focus for increased assistance to developing countries in the new millennium. The consensus of the world community to support the MDGs was relatively easy to obtain. The proof of real commitment toward achieving these goals is seen in the actual contributions by the developed countries.

The 2013 MDGs Report shows that many of the goals have been met or are within close reach, while accelerated progress and bolder action are needed in many areas. Those in the first category include the halving of the proportion of people living in

TABLE 10-8 • The Millennium Development Goals and Targets for 2015

Goals	Targets for 2015
1. Eradicate extreme poverty and hunger	–Reduce by half the proportion of people living on < $1 per day –Reduce by half the proportion of people who suffer from hunger
2. Achieve universal primary education	–Ensure that all boys and girls complete a full course of primary schooling
3. Promote gender equality and empower women	–Eliminate gender disparity in primary and secondary education, preferably by 2005, and at all levels by 2015
4. Reduce child mortality	–Reduce by two-thirds the mortality rate of children under 5
5. Improve maternal health	–Reduce by three-fourths the maternal mortality ratio
6. Combat HIV/AIDS, malaria, and other diseases	–Halt and begin to reduce the spread of HIV/AIDS –Halt and begin to reverse the incidence of malaria and other major diseases
7. Ensure environmental sustainability	–Integrate the principles of sustainable development into country policies and programs; reverse loss of environmental resources –Reduce by half the proportion of people without sustainable access to safe drinking water –Achieve significant improvement in lives of at least 100 million slum dwellers by 2020
8. Develop a global partnership for development	–Develop further an open, rule-based, predictable, nondiscriminatory trading and financial system; include a commitment to good governance, development, and poverty reduction—both nationally and internationally.[a]

[a]Goal 8 has additional targets that relate to debt relief, youth employment, pharmaceutical drugs, technology, and others.

Source: United Nations Development Program, *Millennium Development Goals*, http://www.undp.org/mdg/.

extreme poverty, a gain in the number of people gaining with improved sources of drinking water, gains in the fight against malaria and tuberculosis, a reduction in the proportion of slum dwellers in the cities of the developing world, a lower debt burden and improved climate for trade for developing counties, and a reduction in global hunger. The areas that still require significant new effort include environmental sustainability, improvements in child survival, progress in reducing maternal deaths, better access to antiretroviral therapy (to fight AIDS) and knowledge about HIV prevention, expanded primary education, improved sanitation, and a reversal in the reduction of aid money (especially to the world's poorest countries). The report further states that rural–urban gaps persist, the poorest children are most likely to be out of school, and gender-based inequalities in decision-making power persist.[9]

A People-Oriented Strategy

Many issues of development have been addressed. As we consider each issue, as well as any strategy to invoke change, we must be mindful of the needs and participation of developing country people. Empowerment of all residents of low-income countries is important, including the women, indigenous, and ethnic minorities who are often left out. Poverty and lack of opportunity undermine empowerment, preventing people from taking control of their lives and, in the process, improving their lives. *This consideration suggests that development strategists must listen to and ultimately meet the needs of all people if they are to be successful.*

You, the Student

World poverty seems to us to be an immense and far-away problem, and despite being concerned, we often feel powerless to make a difference. In fact, by living in a developed country democracy, we actually have far more power than we might think. The United States greatly affects the well-being of the people of developing countries through our policies on foreign aid, global agriculture, and international trade. Some of our policies can be beneficial, such as the use of development assistance, and some can be harmful, such as our agricultural subsidies to U.S. farmers and agribusiness and our trade restrictions against developing countries. We will examine the latter two issues in the two chapters that follow. For now, we must admit that the foreign aid issue is complicated, and even the best of intentions can go wrong.

However, as citizens of this democracy, we have the ability to learn about the issues and to contact and influence our legislators and president on matters such as foreign aid. *We can actually do more* as a citizen of this country than if we were living and working in a developing country. Bread for the World, a citizens' lobby on world food and poverty issues, has spent 40 years educating citizens and legislators about domestic and global problems of hunger and poverty, and continues to help write legislation and inform us on measures that can lessen the problem of world poverty. For example, Bread for the World has recommended that all U.S. foreign aid be redesigned and streamlined in order to become more effective. Foreign aid policy would be directed by a single cabinet-level director with responsibility for coordinating all aspects of foreign assistance. This would bring food aid, development assistance, technology transfer, and all other forms of aid; as well as the policies of the Department of Agriculture, the State Department, and all other government departments and agencies; under the umbrella of the foreign aid director. The director would also coordinate discussions with developing countries, as well as other foreign donors and institutions. Certainly this type of directorship could have very positive results for dealing with an issue as complex as world poverty.

ViewPoint   Conservative versus Liberal

Different economists have different views about how economic development should take place. Conservative economists prefer a growth-oriented strategy that focuses on increasing GDP per capita. The assumption is that all people will eventually benefit from the growing prosperity of the country. Issues such as income distribution and poverty do not receive primary attention because it is assumed that the incomes of all people will rise as economic growth proceeds. Indeed, conservative economists may argue in favor of an unequal income distribution on the grounds that high-income people save more than low-income people do. (Low-income people need to spend all of their income on food and basic consumer goods.) By placing more income in the hands of the rich, savings will increase, thereby enabling greater investment and ultimately increased national productivity and growth.

Liberal economists feel that economic growth by itself is not the panacea for underdevelopment. They note that although some people benefit from economic growth, notably the owners of large landholdings and businesses and those able-bodied and fortunate enough to take newly created jobs, many others do not benefit. In particular, workers with few skills and little education, those who are physically disabled, the very young and the very old, and farmers who grow crops on too little land with too few inputs will not be able to take advantage of benefits of economic growth. Strategies must be designed to focus on poverty and income distribution. Otherwise, it is argued, high-income groups will only become richer, while low-income people become poorer.

We can play a role by encouraging our legislators and president to consider this approach and support this type of legislation. Contact information for our politicians and for Bread for the World can be found in the Discussion and Actions Questions at the end of this chapter.

SUMMARY

Economists define economic growth as the increase in real gross domestic product per capita. GNI per capita reflects income accruing to each individual person, on average. In 2012, GNI per capita ranged from a high in Norway of almost $100,000 to a low in Burundi of $240. Other measures, such as infant mortality rates and life expectancies, are usually better indicators of standards of living, particularly because income and output per capita do not address the issues of composition and distribution.

Economic development is a multifaceted process involving growth in GDP per capita, improvement in standards of living, and reduction of poverty. Economic development must take into account the needs of agricultural development and food security, human and natural resource development, and the role of women and all residents of low-income countries, as well as the issues of population growth, AIDS, and rural–urban migration. Appropriate policies at the domestic and international level are vital to the development needs of low-income countries.

DISCUSSION AND ACTION QUESTIONS

1. Is GNI per capita an adequate indicator of the well-being of people in developing countries? Why or why not? Are there better indicators?

2. Consider the countries listed in Table 10-1, and choose one that interests you. Go to the World Bank Web site at http://www.worldbank.org, and choose the country from the country listing. What is the country's current GNI per capita and life expectancy? How do these statistics compare with those of other countries mentioned in this chapter? Is the life expectancy what you would expect, based on the level of GNI per capita?

3. Now choose the same or a different country, and look it up on the CIA Web site (http://www.cia.gov/). After locating the country, click "People," and find statistics

relating to standards of living. What is the infant mortality rate? Compare the statistics that are available for males and females. How do their life expectancies compare? How do their literacy rates compare?

4. How does the United States compare with the countries listed in Table 10-4 with respect to its share of income to the poorest 20 percent of the population? Does the comparison surprise you? Prosperous countries have greater means to ensure equitable income distribution, but this greater capacity does not mean that they choose to do so.

5. Why does hunger persist in a world of plenty? Is the problem one of underproduction, overpopulation, distribution of income, over consumption, or all of these factors? Explain.

6. How might land reform be achieved in developing countries? What issues are involved? What are the political and ethical implications?

7. Agricultural development has garnered much attention. Equally important is the development of human capital that is, improvement in the most important economic resource: people. How can better education, housing, health, hygiene, and nutrition develop human capital and thereby develop the country as well?

8. Why must women be targeted for assistance in the development process? Why is it important that all beneficiaries of development policies and programs be active participants in the design and operation of these programs?

9. What are some of the means used to control population growth in various parts of the world? Are these effective?

Are they appropriate? Are they ethical? Do the ends justify the means?

10. Why is microenterprise credit important for women? What are the benefits to the woman and her family? What are the benefits to society?

11. How can efforts to reduce unemployment and misery in developing country cities be counterproductive and actually increase urban problems? What are some alternative solutions?

12. What is the role of the developed countries in promoting development policies in the developing countries? What are the ways that we as individuals can become involved?

13. Go to the Web site of the United Nations AIDS Program at http://www.unaids.org. Choose a country and look up the prevalence of AIDS/HIV in that country. How does the country compare with other countries in the world?

14. Would you like to be able to make a difference in the lives of people in the developing world? One source of information is the organization Bread for the World. This national citizens' lobby has a Web site at http://www.bread.org that contains information on current U.S. legislation involving world hunger and poverty, as well as contact information for U.S. legislators so that interested citizens can contact them. This Web site also provides links to other similar organizations.

15. You can contact your representatives in the House of Representatives at http://www.house.gov, and your senators in the U.S. Senate at http://www.senate.gov. You can contact the president at President@whitehouse.gov.

NOTES

1. From *Child of the Dark* by Carolina Maria de Jesus, translated by David St. Clair, copyright © 1962 by E. P. Dutton & Co., Inc., New York, and Souvenir Press, Ltd., London. Used by permission of Dutton, a division of Penguin Group (USA) Inc.

2. The World Bank, *World Development Indicators 2012* (Washington, DC: The World Bank, 2014). Unless otherwise indicated, all data in this chapter are from the World Bank. (When 2012 data are unavailable, most recently available data are used.)

3. Dominique Lapierre, *The City of Joy* (New York: Warner Books, 1985), pp. 15–21. These words describe the despair of a family in famine-struck India.

4. John Araka, Wilfred Machua, Wainaina Bidan, Fanwell Zulu, Colleen Lowe Morna, Ben Ephson, Abdou Gninguc, and Methaetsile Leepile, "Getting Produce to Market," in *African Farmer* (New York: The Hunger Project, December 1989).

5. United States Association for International Development (UWAID), *Partnerships to Drive Agricultural Growth*, May 19, 2014.

6. Sharon Pauling, "She Speaks with Wisdom," in *BREAD* (Washington, DC: Bread for the World, Spring 1988).

7. Souleymane Anza, Shadrack Amokaye, Colleen Lowe Morna, and Pierre Pradervand, "Farmers and Family Planning," in *African Farmer* (New York: The Hunger Project, December 1989).

8. United Nations AIDS Program, "2006 Report on the Global AIDS Epidemic," http://www.unaids.org. Adults are defined as persons age 15 to 49 years. Children are of age less than 15.

9. United Nations, *2013 Millennium Development Goals Report*, www.un.org/millenniumgoals/.

ROAD MAP

Chapter 3
The Environment
Certain farming practices are a source of pollution. Policies such as removing highly erodible land from cultivation satisfy both environmental and agricultural policy goals.

Chapter 5
Discrimination
Immigrant farm workers and Native American populations work for low wages and/or lose their agricultural land

Chapter 11
Global Agriculture

Chapter 10
World Poverty
U.S. agricultural subsidy and export policies harm developing-country farmers. Agricultural development is essential to economic development in poor countries.

Chapter 13
Market Power
Concentration is increasing in farming

Chapter 12
International Trade
Agricultural products are a major U.S. export. Government policy toward U.S. agriculture affects our competitiveness in world markets. Developing countries produce and export primary commodities that face problems similar to those faced by U.S. agriculture.

The Economic Toolbox

- Inelastic demand
- Real price
- Agricultural subsidies
- Price supports (floors)
- Rationing function of price
- Dumping
- Concentration
- Biotechnology
- Target prices and deficiency payments (appendix)

Global Agriculture

D o you agree with the statement above? Should the goals of a global food system be to provide food for all people and a decent life to farmers and farmworkers? As we read through this chapter, we will find that while these goals are laudable and reasonable, they are not always what drive agriculture policy, in the United States or abroad. For example, we are now coming out of the Great Recession of the late part of the first decade of the 2000s. While jobs are returning, many of them are part-time and many pay very low wages. Poverty is high and along with it, so is hunger. To make a bad situation worse, a major outcome of the 2014 Farm Bill was a cut in SNAP, the Supplemental Nutrition Assistance Program (formerly called Food Stamps). The reduction in $8 billion to this program means a loss of $90 per month in food stamp benefits to 850,000 households. We will return to the farm bill shortly, but first we will first consider agriculture in the United States (though much of this discussion is relevant globally), and ultimately examine global agriculture as it affects the world's hungry people.

U.S. Agriculture

This land is your land. This land is my land. From California to the New York Island; from the red wood forest to the Gulf Stream waters. This land was made for you and me.
Words and lyrics by Woody Guthrie, 1956
Sung by Pete Seeger at the 2013 Farm Aid Concert[2]

Pete Seeger, age 94, sang his signature song in a surprise appearance at the 2013 Farm Aid Conference in Saratoga, New York. Farm Aid concerts have taken place every year since 1985, initially organized by John Mellencamp and joined by Willie Nelson, Neil Young, and others. The song reflects our nation's pride in our rural environment, which includes our natural resources, rural culture, and the agricultural sector; and the concerts have had the stated goals of supporting family farms, fighting against corporate agriculture, advocating for fair farm prices, and encouraging consumers to buy locally grown food. Clearly, there is concern for the small and family farmer. The 2014 concert is scheduled for Durham, North Carolina, and will feature the same latter set of artists, plus others. If you wish to attend Farm Aid concerts, just look up their schedule under Farm Aid Concert and go to Ticketmaster to purchase your tickets.

The primary goals of agricultural policies should be providing food for all people and providing a decent life for farmers and farmworkers in this country and abroad. A key measure of every agricultural program and legislative initiative is whether it helps the most vulnerable farmers, farmworkers and their families and whether it contributes to a global food system that provides basic nutrition for all.

—THE U.S. CONFERENCE OF CATHOLIC BISHOPS, FARM BILL, FEBRUARY 2009[1]

So, what *is* happening in U.S. agriculture? How does agricultural policy affect our farmers and our small and family farmers in particular? How does it affect consumers? And how does it affect producers and consumers around the globe? In this chapter, we will discuss the unique characteristics of the American rural and agricultural sectors; the types of government policy, recent farm bills, an evaluation of government policy, U.S. and world hunger, and the politics of agricultural policy. The appendices cover the elasticity of demand and target prices and deficiency payments.

Characteristics of the Rural Sector

First, *you probably know that the population of the U.S. rural sector is smaller than that of the urban sector.* About 46.2 million people, or 15 percent of the U.S. population, reside in rural counties, which spread across 72 percent of the nation's land area. We noted in Chapter 6 that the rural poverty rate is estimated at 17 percent, whereas the poverty rate in central cities is 20.0 percent and is 11.3 percent in the suburbs.[3] Hence, the rural sector shares some of the abysmal poverty that we see in some of our nation's central cities.

Clearly, in terms of these indicators, standards of living in our rural environments are poorer than those in our suburban areas. Nevertheless, the rural sector is not synonymous with agriculture, so let's consider the characteristics of the agricultural sector specifically.

Characteristics of Agriculture

Before we even consider agriculture in detail, you should be aware that in the most recent farm census, 14 percent of the total farms had women as principal family farm operators, whereas 86 percent of these principal farm operators were men. Many more women contribute to farming in important ways. We should be certain to think of the farmer as "she," as well as "he."

Furthermore, whereas over three-quarters of the general U.S. population is white, about 96 percent of farm operators are white and 2.5 percent are of Hispanic origin. (There is overlap in these numbers, since most Hispanics are white. Remember the discussion of Hispanic and non-Hispanic whites in Chapter 5 on discrimination.) African-Americans represent 1.4 percent, Native Americans represent 1.7 percent, and Asian-Americans represent 0.5 percent of principal farm operators. Except for Native Americans, all minority groups represent smaller shares of principal farm operators than their share of the population would suggest, and white farmers represent a far greater share. It is interesting that while Native Americans, the first farmers of our nation, represent 1.2 percent of the U.S. population, they represent a somewhat higher share of farm operators. (You can see the population shares of all of these groups in Table 5-1.)

Certain characteristics of agriculture distinguish the farm sector from the remainder of the economy. Some of this discussion involves the short run (one year to the next) and some involves the long run (over several years). The characteristics are as follows:

- An inelastic demand and fluctuating supply for farm products in the short run
- Extensive technological advance in the past three-quarters century
- Immobile resources

Let's see how these characteristics affect farmers, especially those in the United States.

Inelastic Demand and Fluctuating Supply for Farm Products in the Short Run

Recall our discussion of inelastic demand when we considered the market for addictive drugs in Chapter 2. When we say that a product has an **inelastic demand**, we mean that its buyers are relatively unresponsive to changes in its price. This means that buyers show little variation in the quantity they buy when the price changes. This is the case for most farm commodities, as well as the many commodity exports from developing countries that we discussed in Chapter 10. As discussed in previous (and future) chapters, we represent inelastic demand with a relatively steep demand curve. And, as we shall see, the inelasticity of demand has considerable significance for farm prices and farmers' incomes, especially when we simultaneously consider short-run weather-related fluctuations in supply.

Inelastic demand
Demand in which buyers are relatively unresponsive to changes in price.

Price Instability

Let's begin by looking at the significance of the inelastic demand for farm products on the stability of farm prices in the short run. If demand is inelastic, the small fluctuations in supply that might result from either exceptionally good or exceptionally bad weather will have a resounding effect on the prices that farmers receive for their products. Figure 11-1 illustrates this effect. **The demand curve is shown to be relatively steep, reflecting the fact that any small percentage change on the horizontal (quantity) axis is associated with a large percentage change on the vertical axis (price).**

The graph in the figure shows a hypothetical demand curve for corn with an initial equilibrium price of $3 per bushel and an initial equilibrium quantity of 5 million bushels. This corresponds with equilibrium point A. Now consider an increase in supply from S to S′ caused by exceptionally good weather, creating a new equilibrium point B. The equilibrium quantity increases to 6 million bushels, which is a relatively small percentage increase (20 percent). Now consider the price change. Because of the inelastic demand, the effect of the supply shift on the market price is very large. The increase in supply causes

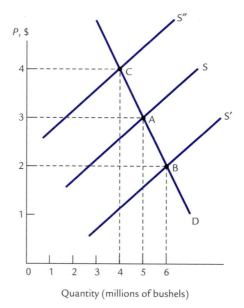

Figure 11-1 • The Effect of Inelasticity on Price in the Corn Market
Because the demand for farm products is inelastic, an increase in supply from S to S′ will cause a sharp decrease in price, whereas a decrease in supply to S″ will cause a sharp increase in price.

the price to fall all the way to $2 per bushel (a relatively large decrease of 33 percent). Similarly, a relatively small percentage decrease in supply caused by poor weather (from S to S″) would cause a relatively large percentage increase in price up to $4 per bushel (a 33 percent increase). **The combination of short-run weather-related supply fluctuations and inelastic demand results in large fluctuations in agricultural prices in the short run.** To convince yourself of the outcomes of inelastic demand, try drawing the same graph but with a flatter demand curve. When demand is not inelastic, identical fluctuations in supply will cause much less price variation than when demand is inelastic.

Farm Income

Bumper crop

An unexpectedly large crop resulting from good growing conditions.

Now let's consider how farmers' incomes are affected by this inelastic demand in the short run. If good weather causes an increase in supply (a **bumper crop**), which causes price to decrease, then overall farm income will also fall. This is because income from a corn crop is equal to the number of units sold times the price at which they are sold. Refer again to Figure 11-1. At the initial price of $3, farmers sold 5 million bushels, earning income of $15 million from their corn crop. (Five million bushels times $3 per bushel is $15 million.) After the increase in supply, farmers sold 6 million bushels at a price of $2 per bushel. They earned only $12 million for their corn crop. **Because consumers have an inelastic demand for agricultural products, a short-run decrease in price results in a short-run decrease in total farm incomes. Similarly, a short-run increase in price (from bad weather) results in a short-run increase in total farm incomes**.

Note that if demand were elastic, we would get entirely different results. In fact, they would be the opposite. Table 11-1 summarizes all results.

Note that these counterintuitive results are true for *total farm income*, not the income of an individual farmer. The farmer who has lost an entire crop will certainly not have higher income in the bad-weather year. Also note that these were short-run results. Demand is inelastic in the short run; and supply, price, and income fluctuate in the short run. These refer to year-to-year situations, as opposed to changes that occur over a long period of time. We now consider this long-run time period.

Extensive Technological Change in the Past Half Century

Real price

Price as adjusted for the effects of inflation. We do this when we consider price changes over time.

In the long run, rapid growth in supply due to technological change and slow growth in demand have caused the real prices of farm products to fall. (When we say **real price**, we mean the price as adjusted for inflation.) Commercial farmers have adopted new techniques and use new, efficient machinery. New high-yield crop varieties exist. Intensive use of fertilizers and pesticides increases yield per acre. Artificial insemination and other improved breeding techniques have resulted in more reliable growth in cattle herds. Irrigation has improved. And, as we discuss shortly, use of biotechnology is expanding rapidly, despite its controversy. In general, the results of these technological changes are a trend toward capital-intensive agriculture, large-scale farming enterprises, and a pronounced increase in the supply of farm products. Although the number of farmers is much smaller than a half century ago, the supply of farm products has increased markedly.

As a result of this technological advance, American agriculture is highly productive, though it is not the most productive in the world. Table 11-2 reveals the productivity of many countries, where productivity is defined in terms of agricultural value added

TABLE 11-1 • The Effects of Elastic and Inelastic Demand on Total Income

When demand is	Then a decrease in price will cause	And an increase in price will cause
Inelastic	Farm income to fall	Farm income to rise
Elastic	Farm income to rise	Farm income to fall

TABLE 11-2 • Agricultural Productivity; Value Added per Worker[a] in (Constant 2005) Dollars; for the Highest, Lowest,[b] and Selected Countries in 2012[c]

Country	Value ($)	Country	Value ($)	Country	Value ($)
France	75,178	Russia	5,969	Congo, D.R.	285
Norway	65,249	South Africa	5,967	Nepal	270
Netherlands	60,398	Mexico	4,103	Ethiopia	257
Canada	59,818	China	749	Gambia	249
Belgium	56,515	India	672	Zimbabwe	239
Australia	53,777	Afghanistan	413	Uganda	213
United States	49,817	Rwanda	294	Burundi	129
Japan	42,943				

[a]This refers to the additional value contributed per worker on average.
[b]This is the lowest among *reporting* countries.
[c]Most recently available data are used when 2012 data are not available.

Source: World Bank, *World Development Indicators 2014*, www.worldbank.org.

per worker. The most productive countries, in order, are France, Norway, and the Netherlands. The United States ranks seventh. In general, the countries with the highest agricultural productivity are in the Western industrialized world. Eastern European and Latin American countries tend to range in middle productivity, and the least productive countries tend to be in South Asia and Africa (with the exception of South Africa).

Compared with the large increase in supply, the increase in Americans' demand for food over time has been relatively small. That increase is attributable mainly to a small increase in our population. We have grown more affluent over time, but we have spent our additional income on things other than food.

The long-run increase in supply is shown in Figure 11-2, but the much smaller increase in demand is omitted for purposes of simplicity. **The combined effects of the**

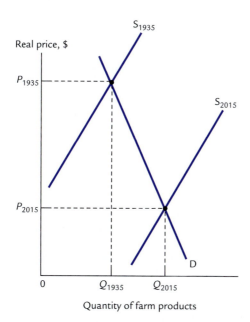

Figure 11-2 • Effects of a Large Increase in Supply in the Market for Farm Commodities in the Long Run
The large increase in supply, coupled with a relatively small increase in demand (not shown), has caused the real prices of agricultural commodities to fall in the past 80 years.

large long-run increase in supply and the modest increase in demand (not shown) have greatly decreased the real price of farm products. This change is not a year-to-year price fluctuation of the sort caused by agriculture's inelastic demand, but a long-run trend instead. We see that the equilibrium quantity of agricultural products is larger but that the real price has decreased.

If we were to consider a long-run graph of *global* agriculture, we would still have the large increase in supply that is shown in Figure 11-2, and until recently, a small increase in demand. However, incomes are increasing in populous countries such as China, India, Brazil, and others that have encouraged greater consumption of foodstuffs such as bread and meat (which use large amounts of food grain in production). This has the potential for a long-run rise in global food prices, though whether it is a long run change remains to be seen.

Immobile Farm Resources

The principal resource used in farming is, of course, land. With the exception of land near rapidly growing cities, which can be used for farming or development, most farmland has few alternative uses. So, although one farmer may leave farming and find a job in the city, land tends to remain in agriculture. Some other farmer buys the land and continues to farm it. If real prices fell as precipitously in other sectors as they have in farming, people and resources would rapidly flow out of these markets into other markets that are believed to be more profitable. But land is not removed from agriculture. Either farmland lies fallow or someone farms it. Agriculture's main resource is slow to respond to adverse industry conditions.

According to the USDA, there is some evidence of a fairly unchanging amount of farmland if we compare the number of acres in farmland between 2007 and 2012. The difference between the two years is insignificant, however.

Although the limited use to which farmland can be put undoubtedly contributes to this resource immobility, it can also be argued that the government's agricultural policies have kept agricultural resources *in* agriculture (or reserve) when they perhaps should have been transferred to other lines of production. Let's consider this policy.

U.S. Government Policy Toward Agriculture

The U.S. government has been extensively involved in agriculture since the Great Depression of the 1930s. The entire country (indeed, much of the world) was in distress during the 1930s, but agriculture suffered more than other sectors. Real farm prices fell, and farm income and profits plummeted. Furthermore, the prices that farmers received for their crops decreased more than the prices that they paid for their inputs.

Because the price of farm products was too low to cover farmers' costs, the government initiated a variety of policies to assist farmers. Congress passed the Agricultural Adjustment Act in 1933 to restore the standing of farm incomes relative to incomes in the rest of the economy. This was one of the first pieces of Franklin D. Roosevelt's New Deal legislation to be enacted. The government has been extensively involved in agriculture ever since.

The objectives of farm policy have been to stabilize conditions in farming and to increase real farm incomes. Accordingly, programs were devised to affect the supply of agricultural products, the demand for agricultural products, and the price received by farmers. Two policy instruments were used early on. These were price supports and programs to restrict supply. As time passed, target prices and deficiency payments also became important. All forms of government payments to farmers are generally referred to as **agricultural subsidies**. Our government has also attempted to increase the demand for agricultural products in order to raise prices. We now discuss the price supports, programs to restrict supply, and policies to increase demand, and we leave the discussion of target prices and deficiency payments for Appendix 11-1 of this chapter.

Agricultural subsidies
Government programs to assist agriculture.

Price Supports

Price supports are examples of **price floors**, which are government-imposed *minimum* prices for a good or service. These minimum prices set a "floor" below which the market price is not permitted to fall. To be effective, which means to have an effect on the market, these price floors must be above the market equilibrium price. (A price floor set below the market equilibrium would not have an effect on the market, since the market-determined price would take over. There is no law that says the prices cannot go *above* a certain level.) Agricultural prices are thereby prevented from falling below the price floor. As we discussed in Chapter 1, markets tend to clear at an equilibrium price and quantity. In the process, shortages and surpluses are rationed away. This is the rationing function of price in a competitive market. When agricultural prices are kept artificially high, they cannot perform the rationing function. Let's look at this problem through a hypothetical example of the U.S. wheat market in Table 11-3.

The equilibrium price is $3.50, at which both quantity demanded and quantity supplied equal 2,500 million bushels of wheat. At this equilibrium price, 2,500 million bushels will be exchanged and the market will clear. If price is temporarily above equilibrium, at $4, a surplus will exist in the market.

At the price of $4, farmers produce and offer 3,500 million bushels for sale, but consumers are willing to buy only 2,000 million, so only 2,000 million bushels are exchanged. The remaining 1,500 million bushels are an unsold surplus in the market. If the price is free to fall, the surplus will cause it to decrease. It will fall as long as there is a surplus to push it down. As price falls, a message is sent to buyers: increase the amount you buy, because price is falling. An opposite message is sent to sellers: decrease the amount you sell, because price is falling. Buyers and sellers each move down their respective demand or supply curve. When the equilibrium price ($3.50) is reached, quantity supplied equals quantity demanded, and there is no more surplus to drive the price down further. The falling price has rationed away the surplus. This process is what economists mean when they refer to the **rationing function of price**, which results in markets being an efficient means of allocating goods and services.

Price supports
Legally imposed minimum prices of goods or services. Price supports are specific examples of price floors.

Price floors
Legally imposed minimum prices of a good or service.

Rationing function of price
The ability of a flexible market price to clear the market of shortages and surpluses.

TABLE 11-3 • Demand and Supply of Wheat (Hypothetical Data)

Quantity Demanded Millions of Bushels	Price ($)	Quantity Supplied Millions of Bushels
1,500	4.50	4,500
2,000	4.00	3,500
2,500	3.50	2,500
3,000	3.00	1,500
3,500	2.50	500

© Cengage Learning®

Now assume that the government had set the legal minimum price at $4, so that price could not fall in response to the surplus. The surplus would not be rationed away. Instead, the market would have a persistent surplus of wheat. And that is what happens when the government supports the prices of farm commodities. The price supports actually create surpluses. Figure 11-3 shows the demand and supply data graphically, indicating the surplus that exists at a price of $4.

The method by which some U.S. farm prices are supported is indirect, but the result is the same as the price floor. Prices are supported by granting farmers loans on their stored commodities through the Commodity Credit Corporation (CCC), which was established in 1933 for this purpose. Farmers can get loans based on the value of their commodities at a rate established by the government (such as $4 per bushel). They put up their commodities as collateral. If the market price is above the loan rate, the farmer can withdraw the commodity from storage, sell the commodity, repay the loan, and keep the profits. On the other hand, if the market price is below the support price, the farmer simply surrenders the commodity to the government instead of repaying the loan. *The loan rate is therefore the effective price support.* The government is the buyer of the surplus, and it is the government (and taxpayers) that bear the losses.

By means of price supports, income is redistributed to the farm sector from taxpayers in general. Whenever income is redistributed, some groups gain and others lose. Let's look at the losers and the gainers. Taxpayers, who are also consumers, are obvious losers. Their taxes are used to buy and store the surplus at artificially high prices, and the higher prices lead to higher food prices.

Let's summarize the results of the agricultural price floors. Agricultural prices are held artificially high, which encourages excess production. Surplus crops result, which are costly for the government and taxpayers. At the same time that surplus crops are produced, consumers are discouraged from purchasing the crops because of the artificially high prices and low income consumers find it difficult to purchase nutritious food. Our agricultural system is inefficient, and it transfers benefits to our farm sector.

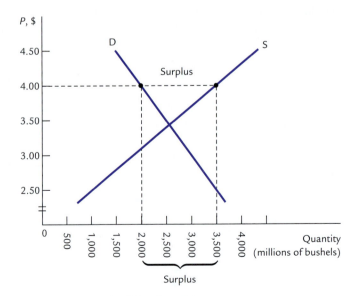

Figure 11-3 • Wheat Markets with Price Support
When a price support keeps the price of wheat from falling below $4, a surplus of 1,500 million bushels of wheat is created.

© Cengage Learning

The farm sector is the gainer, but in a manner that many taxpayers do not understand. *The lion's share of the support goes to large farmers, because the subsidy is paid on a per-unit-of-output basis.* Large-scale farmers produce more bushels (units of output), so they receive bigger subsidy payments from the government. (Some of our subsidy programs pay per unit of land, such as per acre. This also benefits larger farmers, since they have more acres under production.) This reality undoubtedly conflicts with our vision of government farm programs as helping small, struggling American farmers. Most of us picture small-scale production on the "family farm" when we think of farmers. Agricultural economists Willard W. Cochrane and C. Ford Runge refer to the average citizen's false image of agriculture as the "Little House on the Prairie" image.[4] Consider the following words of one farmer: "Nostalgically, many remember when farming was considered a comfortable, laid back, safe and healthy way of life. The farm was a 'good place to raise kids.' The hard work of farming was offset by a sense of independence, the joy of being your own boss."[5] This "nostalgic" view of farming does not apply to the bulk of agricultural production today.

The average voter is far more likely to support farm programs that he or she believes guarantee a decent living to the hard-pressed, hardworking small farmer than to support programs that offer huge subsidies to large farms. Government benefits also accrue to large agribusinesses like Cargill, Monsato, and others. We will explore these topics in more detail shortly.

Programs to Restrict Supply

Price supports have been combined with **programs to reduce supply**. Refer again to Figure 11-3. Assume that government analysts believe that a "fair" price for farm commodities is $4 per bushel. This price might cover the costs of production, including some level of wages for the average farmer. One way to ensure that farmers receive $4 per bushel is to support the price at $4 and create a surplus in the process, as we've just discussed. Another method would be to shift the supply curve back to the point at which supply intersects demand at $4. The effects of this method are shown in Figure 11-4.

Programs to reduce supply

Policies to decrease the amount produced and offered for sale.

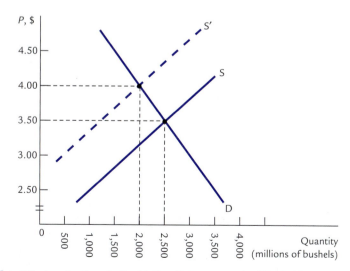

Figure 11-4 • Effects of a Supply Restriction Program on the Wheat Market
If the supply of wheat can be decreased from S to S′ by a government program, the market price will increase from $3.50 to $4.

© Cengage Learning

After the decrease in supply, the equilibrium price is $4, and the market clears with 2,000 million bushels of wheat being exchanged. No surplus results for which the government is the buyer of last resort. No storage charges will be incurred. No loss of the stored grain due to damage from rodents or simple deterioration with age will occur. Programs to reduce the supply of farm products appeared preferable to rigid price supports in the 1930s, and these programs continue to receive support.

Accordingly, the history of U.S. farm policy is filled with efforts to reduce supply, as we will see shortly. Early efforts were voluntary and often involved land rent payments on acres taken out of the production of specific crops coupled with support prices on crops grown on the individual farmer's remaining land. Despite these attempts to control supply, the surpluses grew. Commercial warehouses were filled. Abandoned schoolhouses and (in some cases) churches were used for storage. Consequently, efforts to restrict supply became more formal and far-reaching.

In 1956, the Soil Bank was instituted. It encouraged the long-term withdrawal of farmland from production of any crops and stricter compliance with acreage controls on specific crops. Farmers were paid for not farming. In subsequent legislation, supply restriction programs were continued under other names, such as the Set-Aside program, the Payment-in-Kind (PIK) program, and the "10-year plan," which encouraged farmers to put highly erodible acres in a long-term supply restriction program. Under the Set-Aside program, farmers were paid for setting aside and not farming a proportion of their total acres. They were guaranteed support prices on crops grown on their remaining acreage. Under the PIK program, they were given surplus commodities from the government's storehouses instead of cash, but PIK resembled the Set-Aside program in other respects. The 10-year government plan required a longer commitment of farmers not to farm their entire acreage, and it restricted alternative uses of land by more than the two prior programs, but otherwise the programs were similar. Programs such as Conservation Reserve Program (CRP) are used to protect low-productivity but environmentally vulnerable land.

These supply restriction programs have not always worked in terms of producing farm supplies. Acres were taken out of cultivation, but supply continued to increase, pushing down market prices. Why? Put yourself in the place of the American farmer. Would you put your best or your worst land in the Set-Aside program? Of course, you would put aside those swampy, poorly drained acres on which you get your tractor stuck every spring! You would be foolish to set aside well-drained, fertile acres in favor of your less-productive land. And that is what farmers have done: they have put their poorest land into supply restriction programs and then farmed the remaining acres more intensively. If rows of corn are planted closer together, and irrigation and fertilization of the crop is increased, the supply of corn increases despite acreage reduction programs. Simply by behaving in an economically rational way, the farmer dooms supply restriction programs to failure.

Like price supports, supply restriction programs favor large farms over small farms. The more acres put into the supply restriction program, the larger will be the payment to the farmer. And like price supports, supply restriction programs represent a redistribution of income from taxpayers at large to the agricultural sector.

While the CRS and other supply restriction programs may benefit conservation, the failures of price support and supply restriction policies to reduce oversupplies are evident in the large stockpiles of agricultural products that have existed in the United States.

These agricultural surpluses have pushed our government to experiment with demand-side programs in addition to supply restriction programs.

Efforts to Increase Demand

Efforts to decrease supply have been accompanied by various efforts to increase domestic and international demand for U.S. agricultural products. You are undoubtedly familiar with some of the programs used in an attempt to increase domestic demand. Surplus commodities are distributed to the public school system for use in the school lunch program. (This practice explains some of the strange menus you encountered as an elementary school student.) Food stamps are distributed to poor families so that they can purchase more food. (As we noted earlier, the food stamp program is now called SNAP, the Supplemental Nutrition Assistance Program.) Surplus commodities such as cheese and milk powder have been distributed directly to the poor through various welfare agencies and food banks. The objectives of these programs are both humanitarian and pragmatic. Feeding the poor and seeing that schoolchildren receive a free or subsidized lunch are worthy humanitarian aims, and the pragmatic purposes of these programs are to increase the demand for agricultural products and to get rid of our surpluses.

Foreign demand for U.S. farm commodities has been affected by two types of programs: foreign food assistance programs (such as Food for Peace) and export subsidies. The foreign food assistance programs have been a means of disposing of surplus commodities abroad. When U.S. surpluses accumulate, we distribute more food abroad. When our surpluses are smaller, we send less humanitarian food aid to developing countries. After the first war in Iraq, surplus milk powder was made available to citizens of that country. During the 1980s, when Congress restricted foreign aid funds to Ecuador because of its brutal government, administration officials deliberately sent far more surplus milk powder to the country than its residents could possibly consume so that Ecuadorian sales of the milk to other countries could bring in desired revenue. In the world food crisis of the early 1970s, millions died of famine while the United States cut off food aid because our surpluses were relatively low. In many cases, our food aid programs have done more harm than good to poor developing-country residents, as we will see shortly.

The U.S. government also pays export subsidies to U.S. agricultural exporters and agribusinesses, as well as the assistance to U.S. farmers that we've discussed. These serve to make our agricultural exports "more competitive" (cheaper) to foreign consumers. This causes an increase in foreign consumption of U.S. agricultural products because U.S. prices will be lower than those of other countries. Indeed, we have lowered the world price of some commodities so much that we have been accused of **dumping**, or selling our farm products abroad at prices well below cost. These types of subsidies have also been used to a large extent in much of Western Europe and Japan. The decrease in the price of U.S., European, and Japanese commodities has greatly upset the other grain-producing and grain-exporting countries of the world, such as Canada, and has triggered retaliation. They also have negative effects on developing countries, as we shall see. We will return to this issue shortly.

Efforts to increase the price of farm products by increasing demand have not been very effective. In most cases, we have merely disposed of accumulated surpluses.

Dumping
Exporting goods at low prices, even below the cost of production.

However, evidence indicates that some of the domestic programs meet their humanitarian objectives. For instance, SNAP increases poor families' access to food.

Recent Farm Bills

Congress supposedly passes a new comprehensive farm bill every five years, but disagreements within Congress and with the president have made this difficult, if not impossible. Gridlock in Congress has been most evident throughout the Obama administrations and has been manifest by an absence or major delay in a comprehensive budget bill, immigration bill, farm bill, and others. In some of the recent farm bills, Congress has attempted to coordinate and reevaluate the various farm programs. In 1990, for example, farmers were first required to put some of their acreage in a supply restriction program if they were to participate in the target price and deficiency payment programs. Then, in 1996, Congress passed the so-called *Freedom to Farm Bill*, which eliminated deficiency payments on some crops such as feed grains and wheat. It also assured income support payments based on acreage, which of course benefited larger farmers. Restrictions on what farmers could plant and remain eligible for government farm programs were virtually eliminated, an action that was viewed as a major step toward "getting the government out of farming." The income support payments were scheduled to last for seven years until passage of the new farm bill.

The effects of the *Freedom to Farm Act* were what you probably would have predicted from reading the previous sections. At first, many farmers were delighted to have less government interference with their decisions about what (and how much) to plant. However, farmers responded to the legislation by increasing supplies of corn and many other commodities, thereby causing international grain prices to fall to historically low levels. Many farmers' incomes did not cover their costs. More farmers left agriculture. And in response to a number of natural disasters, such as floods and droughts, as well as the adverse market conditions just mentioned, Congress passed emergency farm aid measures in 1998, 1999, and 2000.

In 2002, President Bush signed a new farm bill, entitled the *Farm Security and Rural Investment Act.* This bill covered the time period from 2002 to 2007, but specified expenditures for a 10-year time period. Once again, the benefits of the farm bill were heavily targeted to large U.S. farms and agribusinesses, and the bill eliminated many provisions that would have targeted assistance to small- and medium-sized farms. Little was done to alter the price distortions and commodity overproduction that resulted from previous farm bills. And, while the bill did expand programs for farmland conservation and rural development, it failed to address **concentration** in the U.S. farm industry or strengthen competition in rural America. Instead, the bill (along with a crop insurance bill) was slated to provide $191 billion in direct subsidies to farmers over the 10-year time period (which was more than what was expected to be spent on K-12 education and environmental protection combined over the same 10-year time period).[6]

In 2008, a new farm bill was passed, over President Bush's veto. This bill was called the *Food, Conservation, and Energy Act* and it covered the time period 2008 through 2012. Many church, consumer, farm, environmental, and social justice groups came together to address problems in U.S. farm policy and seek improvements in the 2008 bill along the lines of the quotation that opens this chapter. They achieved some, but not all, of their goals. Among the positive outcomes are the following:

Concentration
The domination of a market by a few large firms.

- An increase in spending on SNAP, the Emergency Food Assistance program, and the Fresh Fruits and Vegetable program (a snack program for low-income public schools)
- Improvements in food aid in countries with emergency food needs
- Lower benefits for highly profitable farmers and agribusinesses
- Additional funding for conservation programs
- Additional funding for small farmers and beginning and socially disadvantaged farmers

Although the farm bills failed to make the large-scale changes necessary to shift our agricultural supports away from large farms and agribusiness, it did make modest changes in that direction and provide support for other important programs.[7]

A new farm bill was scheduled to emerge five years later, in 2013. However, the tremendous gridlock in Congress stifled any efforts at substantial reform of our agriculture policy, and while a new farm bill was eventually passed in 2014, it left out important but controversial elements.

The 2014 farm bill, called the *Agriculture Act of 2014*, will remain in force through 2018, with some provisions extending beyond this time. Major elements of the bill include the following:

- It makes changes in agricultural commodity programs
- It adds new crop insurance options and spending
- It streamlines conservation programs
- It reduces funding for SNAP
- It expands programs for specialty crops, organic farmers, bioenergy, rural development, and beginning farmers and ranchers

In terms of the commodity programs, the bill reduces spending by $14.3 billion over the 10-year period, $3 billion to $4 billion less than under the House and Senate versions of the bill. Based on our earlier discussion of price supports, economists would generally prefer the larger reductions in this area.[8]

An Evaluation of U.S. Farm Policy

For 29 years, my family has made its living growing corn and soybeans in Mazon, Illinois—population 764. Most of my neighbors live on or near farms; they always have. Many of the people I worship with every Sunday at Mazon Congregational Church still work on farms, though they're not sure how long they'll keep going. Still, the personal satisfaction—the sense of fulfillment—that we all used to experience from working hard and bringing in a harvest has dwindled, and for some, disappeared. My first year in farming was 1973, and that year we sold corn for $3.90 per bushel; I was able to buy a new tractor for $12,500. Last year I sold corn for $1.90, and a similar new tractor cost $100,000.[9]

As is obvious to the farmer quoted here, government policies have not solved the core farm problem of declining real incomes to small- and medium-sized farmers, and they have had some unforeseen side effects. As we shall see, by treating a symptom (overallocation of resources to farming) rather than a cause, they have contributed to an increasingly concentrated agricultural sector. The benefits of our agricultural programs have gone largely to large and rich farmers and agribusinesses, thus promoting a negative income distribution. Our programs have also resulted in production techniques that have harmful environmental consequences. Additional issues involve biotechnology and diversity (farm workers and U.S. minority populations). Finally, issues involving U.S. and global hunger are probably most significant and will receive the most attention. As we consider each of these issues in turn, we will see that many of them are interrelated.

Treating a Symptom

The low price of farm products is a symptom of a resource allocation problem in the economy. We simply produce too many farm products in comparison with other goods. The solution to the problem is to decrease the resources devoted to farming. As long as prices are supported artificially high, there will be an incentive to continue to overproduce. Indeed, government policies are a part of the farm problem because they encourage the retention in agriculture of resources that would otherwise leave farming and be used for other purposes.

Still, there are times when agricultural resources are scarce or weather for agriculture is poor. Unintended shortfalls in agricultural products result in rising prices for food and other agricultural products. This is a short-run problem, but still is significant.

Increased Concentration in Agriculture

A market is said to be concentrated if it contains a relatively few large firms that dominate the market. We will discuss market concentration and its negative effects at great length in Chapter 13 on market power. For now let's just note that the current trend seems to be toward greater concentration in agriculture. As we discussed previously, the "Little House on the Prairie" image of American agriculture is a false one today, but it was a more accurate image in the 1930s, when government involvement in agriculture first began. Many more farmers were responsible for producing our nation's agricultural output, whereas now a much smaller number of farmers use far more modern techniques and larger farm size to produce much larger average output levels.

There is some evidence that concentration in agriculture has increased in just the last five years. Table 11-4 shows that the number of farms has decreased by 4.4 percent from 2007 to 2012. Over the same time period, the average size of farms has increased by 3.8 percent. *To the extent that concentration has increased over time, this raises concern over potential market power among these farms.*

Distribution of Benefits

We've noted that our agricultural programs largely benefit larger farms and agribusinesses, since subsidies are doled out per unit of output (or per unit of land under production). The more output or land, the more the subsidy.

The Environmental Working Group (EWG) records the value of agricultural subsidy payments that go to various recipients in the United States. It notes that 10 percent of the largest and richest U.S. farms collect almost three-quarters of all federal direct farm

TABLE 11-4 • Number of Farms (millions) and Farm Size (Acres), 2007 and 2012

FARMS	2012	2007	Change from 2007 to 2012
Number of Farms	2.109	2.205	−4.4%
Average Size of Farms	434	418	+3.8%

Source: U.S. Department of Agriculture (USDA), Economic Research Service, *2012 Agricultural Census,* www.ers.usda.gov, 2012.

subsidies. Out of a total of about $5 billion in direct payments in 2007, 149 recipients each received over $250,000. Furthermore, 1,234 recipients received over $120,000, and 5,125 recipients received over $60,000. This leaves less than $2,000 on average for each of the remaining 2 million farmers.[10]

If our goal is to serve small and medium size farmers and to ensure a living for low income farmers, as suggested in the opening quotation to this chapter, then our subsidy programs distort this goal. We need to restrict payments to the larger farms and firms and pay more attention to the smaller ones. This will simultaneously address the issue of concentration in agriculture, as well as support the many smaller farmers who are the backbones of many of our rural communities.

Harmful Environmental Effects

Another false image of American agriculture noted by Cochrane and Runge is that farmers are "stewards of the land" or protectors of the land and environment.[11] Farming is viewed as a healthy, wholesome way of life. In fact, modern farming has been reliant on chemical fertilizers to increase yield per acre to thereby obtain more government payments. It relies on pesticides to decrease insect damage and maximize yield. It creates nitrate pollution of water wells in farm states and other environmental problems.

As people have left farming, they have been replaced by machines that are both expensive and dangerous. Farming is now one of the most dangerous sectors of the economy as measured by workplace accidents and deaths. Irrigation in the lower Midwest has damaged aquifers (underground water supplies serving large areas) but increased bushels per acre on which deficiency payments are earned. Commodity programs have encouraged the production of crops that are particularly likely to cause erosion, because these crops often have had high target prices. Farm life is neither particularly healthy nor environmentally benign. And our government programs have contributed to these adverse effects.

Some economists argue that the increasing concentration of agriculture worsens the environmental problems associated with large-scale production. Huge cattle feedlots, factory hog farms, and dairies with 1,200 cows on relatively few acres create significant problems of odor and waste disposal. Realistically, we will never return to the idealized notion of small family farms. We can, however, preserve the small- and medium-sized farms that remain if we adjust our national farm policy so that it no longer favors the largest producers. Policies that promote the greatest possible yield have proved self-defeating because they worsen the resource allocation problem and, in the process, increase concentration. Policies that promote a more diverse and less chemical-dependent agriculture appear to make more sense.

Biotechnology

Production of genetically modified organisms (GMOs) has increased greatly over recent years. U.S. agricultural companies have taken the lead in developing biotechnology, in which seed varieties are genetically altered in order to increase yields. Farmers use the GMOs as a means of preventing crop disease and reducing pesticide use. Some people have characterized biotechnology as the means to solve the ever-present problem of world hunger, much as the Green Revolution was expected to relieve famine in earlier decades.[12] Opponents maintain that the environmental and health risks of biotechnology are severe and that technology will do little to help with world hunger reduction. They argue that the development of GMOs will primarily benefit large multinational corporations and farms. The debate over GMOs is expected to continue for some time and to create controversy between leaders of various governments. The effect of biotechnology, for better or worse, is probably most worrisome for poor farmers in developing countries, as we shall see shortly.

Diversity and Agriculture

We've already noted that whereas about three-quarters of the U.S. population is classified as white, a much larger share of the U.S. principal farmers are white (95.9 percent). Except for Native Americans, there is less diversity among principal farm operators than in the overall U.S. population. It is ironic that the original farmers and inhabitants of the land in the United States—that is, Native Americans—have consistently been at the bottom of the economic ladder, with extremely high rates of poverty and hunger.

Another particularly at-risk population includes farm workers (often Hispanic migrants from within the United States or across national borders). Many of these farm workers harvest fruit and vegetable crops, which are not covered by government agricultural subsidies, as well as assist with dairy production. Wages to farm workers are often very low and their housing and living conditions are often quite poor. Another issue involves pesticide poisoning. An estimated 10,000 to 20,000 hired farm workers are poisoned by pesticides on the job each year. For example, farm workers and their children have an increased risk of leukemia, non-Hodgkin's lymphoma, brain cancer, infertility, birth defects, and neurological disorders due to pesticide exposure. A recent study in Oregon found that migrant farm workers who had repeated exposures to neurotoxic pesticides scored far worse on tests of intellectual functioning, memory, and attention than did comparable immigrants who had no contact with pesticides. The problem is even more serious, given that poverty prevents many farm workers from receiving medical treatment when they are ill or injured and education for children is often poor or sporadic. Despite the risks, the federal government has very few pesticide safety regulations that could protect farm workers.[13]

A final diversity issue involves African-American farmers. In 1920, at the height of black farm ownership, 1 in 7 U.S. farms was operated by an African-American; by 1992, the number had fallen to 1 in 100. (The data just cited shows that this number has increased somewhat by 2007.) One reason for the startling decline until recently may well be U.S. Department of Agriculture (USDA) policy. According to an article published by the Environmental Working Group, the USDA had systematically discriminated against African-American farmers for decades, denying them access to crop loans that were made to "similarly situated" white farmers in their communities. In 1997, a historic civil rights class action suit, known as *Pigford v. Veneman*, was filed against the USDA. Two years later, the government admitted to wrongdoing and made a $2.3 billion settlement—the largest civil rights settlement in U.S. history. Implementation of the settlement was difficult, however, and nearly 9 out of 10 African-American farmers who sought restitution through the case were originally denied. In 2008, a coalition of organizations led by the National Black Farmers Association lobbied to win several important items for black farmers, including restitution in this civil rights case.[14] Presidents Clinton and Obama greatly expanded the numbers and speed in making payments, including payments for women and Hispanics who also claimed discrimination. Some say that the restitution payments went way too far in terms of what was appropriate.

U.S. Hunger

It is ironic that in the United States, which is one of the richest countries in the world and one of the largest food producers in the world, there is a serious problem of hunger. According to the Center on Budget and Policy Priorities, utilizing USDA data, some 17.6 million households, with 49 million people, lacked access to adequate food at some point in 2012 because they didn't have enough money or other resources to meet their basic food needs. These people are considered to be *food insecure*. Among these 49 million people, about 7 million had *very low food security*, meaning that household members skipped meals or took other steps to reduce what they ate because they lacked resources. Some 21.6 percent of U.S. children lived in food insecure households, with about half of them experiencing food insecurity themselves. The share of households with seniors who are food insecure appears to be trending upward. Food insecurity has been the greatest in Mississippi, Arkansas, Texas, Alabama, North Carolinas, Georgia, Missouri, and Nevada. Finally, the data likely understate food insecurity because they don't include homeless individuals or families.[15]

There are a number of reasons for hunger in the United States. First, we know that weather-related short-run fluctuations in supplies of agricultural products result in fluctuating prices, so that there are frequent years of rising food prices. To the extent that global warming causes greater fluctuation in weather patterns, we can expect to see more fluctuation in production, and therefore more fluctuation in prices. Second, we've noted that the long-run decline in food prices may be reversing as a result of the rising global demand for agricultural goods due to rising incomes in countries such as India, China, and others. These incomes and demand for food are expected to continue to rise. Third, U.S. price supports are designed to keep prices of certain agricultural commodities artificially high. Fourth, even though evidence suggests that the use of corn to produce fuel may actually increase energy use and the release of greenhouse gases, the use of agricultural products for biofuels is subsidized by the U.S. government. The increased demand for corn and other agricultural goods for this additional use have caused agricultural prices to rise. And, as farmers respond to rising corn prices, they divert their cropland out of other crops, such as wheat and soybeans, contributing to rising prices of these crops as well. And finally, we've noted the major cuts in SNAP resulting from the 2014 farm bill, with these cuts harming the food security of our nation's poorest citizens.

Global Agriculture and World Hunger

A final consideration is that our heavily subsidized agricultural sector produces commodities that compete unfairly with those of developing countries. The developing countries often rely on their own agricultural exports for much-needed foreign currency. If, for example, rice produced in Arkansas can be sold internationally at artificially low prices (due to U.S. government subsidies to U.S. suppliers), then Thailand's rice exports to the United States and to other trading partners will be diminished. This is an especially serious problem because the European countries and Japan, other potentially major markets for developing-country agricultural exports, have policies similar to our own. Bread for the World, an organization concerned about world and domestic hunger, recently reported that the annual subsidy payments received by farmers in the rich countries (the United Sates, the European Union, and Japan) amounted to about $280 billion, yet the total annual development assistance to the developing countries was about $60 billion, less than one-quarter of the subsidies.[16] Since U.S. and European farm subsidies, as well as the use of biotechnology, serve to increase food production, it is natural to assume that they will reduce world hunger and famine. Let's try to understand why this is probably not the case.

First, a lot of food is currently produced in the world. Overall, our world has been characterized as having abundant supplies and indeed surplus stocks of agricultural products that are never even consumed. The problem of world hunger has far less to do with global food production and a lot more to do with how this produce is distributed. Food, as well as other production, is distributed to people who have the incomes to buy it. Low-income people in poor countries cannot afford to buy enough food for themselves and their families, especially in years when food prices are relatively high. *Thus, hunger is a problem of poverty, not production.* In addition, civil war, political instability, bad weather, poor transportation, and lack of storage facilities can exacerbate problems of hunger.

Second, we must remember that most residents of developing countries live in the rural sector and earn their incomes through crop production. When U.S. and European subsidized agricultural products flood world markets—whether this is due to surplus production due to government policy or indiscriminate food aid—it causes low world agricultural prices. Poor farmers in developing countries who cannot match the output of large world farmers earn little income from their production of food and thus become poorer. They also have less incentive to produce food. They may seek employment in sectors that can more reliably provide for the needs of their families. Or they may swarm to cities in hopes of higher incomes, but in reality become unemployed and live in squalid conditions. *This is why, while famine conditions require emergency food aid, and poor consumers require targeted assistance, prolonged food aid and dumping of agricultural products by developed countries actually exacerbate the problem of world hunger.*

A third reason that developing countries are disadvantaged in agriculture has to do with the trade restrictions imposed by the wealthy countries. The developed countries, including the United States, impose import tariffs on products that developing-country farmers can produce cheaper than rich-country farmers, such as rice, sugar, and cotton. These trade restrictions prevent the agricultural commodities produced by developing countries from entering the United States and other prosperous countries, and cost developing countries billions of dollars in forgone sales. *Once again, this harm done to developing countries by developed country trade restrictions by far exceeds any amount of development assistance offered by rich countries to poor countries.* We will consider trade restrictions in more detail in Chapter 12.

Finally, the patents owned by U.S. multinational corporations and agribusinesses prevent outsiders from producing genetically modified food and allow these large U.S. corporations to flood the world market with their agricultural products. Or, if poor developing-country farmers have access to genetically modified seeds, these seeds only work if farmers also purchase expensive products sold by the multinational corporations, such as fertilizer. Just as Green Revolution technology wasn't made available to many poor farmers in low-income countries in the past, the new biotechnology is not available to all poor farmers throughout the world today. In addition to health and environmental concerns about biotechnology, *the most likely economic effects will be large increases in world food production, causing lower prices of agricultural products and preventing poor farmers from succeeding in agriculture.* And it is the latter outcome that may serve to increase, rather than decrease, world hunger.

The Complexity of World Hunger

World hunger is a complex issue. We've seen that, contrary to what we might think, food aid and technological advances that result in lower food prices can actually harm poor developing-country farmers (and benefit developing-country consumers, who may not be poor). However, there are also plenty of poor consumers in developing countries, and many poor farmers are actually net food purchasers (buying more food than they sell). These groups of people are harmed by high food prices. The problem is that U.S. food policies are usually not designed to assist the poor residents of the world. U.S. agricultural policies are designed to help U.S. farmers, and the richer ones at that. U.S. trade restrictions are also designed to help U.S. farmers and U.S. agribusiness. Genetically modified organisms are developed by agribusiness in order to increase their own profits, and food aid is often motivated by the benefits that accrue to U.S. food processing and shipping firms, as well as U.S. farmers. So how do we meet the admirable goals expressed in the opening quotation to this chapter? How do we establish a "global food system that provides basic nutrition for all"?

Although world hunger is a complex issue, some elements of policy are clear cut. First, emergency food aid is always important during a food emergency. This is a much different situation than ongoing food aid, which has more likelihood of creating rural poverty and food insecurity. Second, it is better to purchase food from neighboring regions and distribute it to those affected by the food emergency than it is to ship U.S. agricultural products as food aid. This is certainly cheaper, thereby enabling a greater provision of food. But it also has the benefit of bolstering food prices in the neighboring regions and thereby benefiting rural farmers rather than undercutting them by a flood of food aid into the region. For example, if there is a food emergency in the country of Zimbabwe (which we've noted elsewhere is in a state of crisis), it would be cheaper and more efficient to buy food from neighboring Zambia, and it would benefit Zambia's farmers as well. Third, if poor-country farmers are to benefit from expanding food technology, they will need access to inputs, including seed varieties, fertilizers, extension services, and so on. Otherwise, technological advances will lower global food prices, putting those poor farmers who cannot afford the technology out of business, and exacerbating rural poverty in poor countries. Fourth, direct assistance to poor consumers and poor farmers is almost always preferable to policies, such as price supports, that artificially manipulate market prices. Finally, U.S. and other developed-country agriculture subsidies and trade restrictions need to be modified in order to benefit, rather than harm, the developing countries of the world.

Bread for the World has made a number of recommendations to improve policy for hungry people. One major recent policy proposal is that all U.S. foreign aid policy be directed by a single cabinet-level director with responsibility for coordinating all aspects of foreign assistance. This would bring food aid and the policies of the Department of Agriculture, as well as various aspects of many other government departments and agencies, under the umbrella of the foreign aid director. The director would also coordinate discussions with developing countries, as well as other foreign donors and institutions. Certainly this type of directorship could have very positive results for dealing with an issue as complex as world hunger.

In 2010, President Obama's administration established a policy package that includes suggestions made by Bread for the World. Key aspects of the package include its comprehensive nature (targeting small- and medium-sized farms and firms, poor consumers, and many developing countries) and its broad base of players (U.S. universities, U.S. government agencies, foreign governments, farmers, private agribusinesses, and nongovernmental organizations). According to a 2014 report published by the U.S. Agency for International Development, the program has already contributed to rising incomes for farmers around the world and helped save millions of people from starvation. The program is controversial, perhaps especially in its inclusion of agribusinesses (which are presumably motivated by profits) and genetically modified organisms (which we've already noted are controversial). Often, private businesses and modern technology can make positive contributions to world food security, but these efforts must be carefully implemented.[17]

The Politics of Agricultural Policy

Given all the concerns we've raised in this chapter, it is no wonder that some people ask why our taxpayers, many of whom have low or medium incomes themselves, should shift their earnings to higher-income farms and agribusiness. And why do farm payments dwarf expenditures for other programs that we've discussed in this text, including programs for education, environmental protection, poverty reduction, health care, and housing? And finally, why should high-income farmers and corporations receive government benefits when smaller farmers and other small business owners receive little, if any? What are the politics behind all this, and how could our policy be improved?

If most Americans are concerned about small- to medium-sized family farmers, then most farm payments should not go to the wealthiest farmers and agribusinesses. The fact that they do is the effect of politics and economics. How many consumer groups band together and advocate against farm policy that raises the price of food purchased in supermarkets? If you said none, you are probably right. *But*—how do you think the U.S. farm lobby compares with this diffuse and uninformed consumer group? Farm lobbying groups have organized in virtually every state in our nation. These groups are well financed by the large commercial farmers who use their vast financial resources to seek, not just beneficial agricultural policies, but policies that particularly benefit them as opposed to smaller farmers. Unfortunately, the smaller farmers that need the government benefits are neither informed about the effect of policies nor powerful as a lobbying group.

In addition, almost all members of the U.S. House of Representatives have at least one crop in their states whose producers vote pro-farmer. Senators are overrepresented by rural populations that vote pro-farmer as well. It is difficult to be re-elected when ignoring this group of farmers. Typically, lobbying and voting do not emphasize the need to target benefits to the poorest farmers. Finally, many legislators are uninformed or uninterested in the effect of our agricultural subsidies and trade policies on poor farmers in developing countries. As this book is being written, the U.S. House of Representatives has just passed a bill that would keep 2 million people from receiving lifesaving food aid annually in order to increase subsidies to the world's largest shipping companies. The bill requires that food be shipped by these companies rather than purchased locally or regionally, which would be quicker, more efficient, more supportive of regional farmers, and enable more starving people to be served. This is a classic example of politics over people.

A Final Note

The world today is not meeting the goals expressed in the introduction to this chapter. In particular, we have still not achieved a "global food system that provides basic nutrition for all." A new "world food crisis" developed in response to the 2007–2008, 2012, and early 2014 rise in world food prices. Over a billion people in the world are hungry. Some 15.1 percent of children under age five are malnourished, contributing in part to an underage five mortality rate of 47.8 children per 1,000 live births. Not only does hunger cause child deaths, but it also leads to political instability, as exemplified by riots in the cities of Argentina, Cameroon, Haiti, India, and other countries around the world.[18]

You, the Student

If you've read this chapter and found yourself interested in the problems of world and domestic hunger and poverty, there are lots of things you can do about it. Some of these are suggested in the Discussion Questions at the end of this chapter. In addition, you may want to check out the organization, *Bread for the World*. This organization, referred to in Chapter 10, is a citizens' lobby that seeks to influence legislation regarding world and domestic hunger and poverty. It does this largely by informing people about the issues, pending legislation, and significant legislators. While it has a Christian perspective, it has links to a large number of other organizations of different faiths or no faith background that are involved in the same issues. You will find suggestions for how to make a difference. There are probably many other things that you and your friends can think of, including food drives, charity fundraisers, and letter-writing campaigns. You may especially want to contact your legislators to encourage their support for a revamping of foreign aid as was discussed in the section on the complexity of world hunger.

On a simpler, more entertaining level (a treat to yourself after performing the good works in the paragraph above), go to a Farm Aid concert. You can find the venue and the performers on the Internet under Farm Aid Concert or Ticketmaster.

View*Point*   Conservative versus Liberal

Conservative economists and politicians have argued for a long time that price supports, target prices, and supply restriction programs have contributed to our farm problem instead of solving it. Because of these programs, our country simply allocates too many resources to agriculture. Theoretically, conservatives would end virtually all farm programs and let market forces determine the outcomes for farmers. Also, by encouraging less government antitrust activity and fewer government environmental regulations (so that there is less government involvement in agricultural markets), the outcomes of conservative policy might be greater concentration in agricultural markets and unchecked environmental harm.

These conservative policies and outcomes might not actually take place, however, because politicians on both the left (liberal) and the right (conservative) face strong lobbying activity in favor of government programs that benefit farmers in their state. For example, conservative southern senators and representatives to Congress are under a great deal of pressure to support farm programs that benefit tobacco producers. There are other examples in almost every other state. And since large agribusinesses have more political power than do smaller farmers, the unequal distribution of the benefits of our farm programs has been accepted by many conservatives as a natural phenomenon.

Liberal economists and politicians, on the other hand, are more comfortable supporting agricultural programs. Liberals do not wholeheartedly endorse the programs, however, and many believe that they should be gradually phased out. Their major objection to the programs is that the bulk of government payments goes to large farms rather than small family farms. They would also like government efforts to reduce concentration in agricultural markets and to ensure environmental protection; and they would like greater diversity of input and output on these topics. Finally, globally minded economists and politicians are concerned about the effects of U.S. programs on the poor in developing countries.

SUMMARY

Agriculture is characterized by inelastic demand in the short run, fluctuations in short-run supply, immobile resources, and such rapid technological change that supply has increased far more rapidly than demand. Thus, despite high productivity, agriculture has long been a troubled sector of the U.S. economy. Since the 1930s, government policies aimed at the farm problem have promoted the over-allocation of resources to the agricultural sector. Furthermore, despite these policies, the proportion of our population engaged in farming has shrunk to about 1 percent. Supply restriction programs, price supports, and target prices have not saved the small American farm but instead have contributed to the farm problem. Concentration has increased in agriculture, in part because of our farm policies. Policies that promote the greatest possible yield have proved self-defeating because they worsen the resource allocation problem and in the process increase concentration, create environmental problems, and provide payments for our richest farmers and agribusinesses.

Finally, our farm policies affect the rest of the world. The policies of such a large and prosperous country can either help or hinder the development efforts of developing countries. Our agricultural subsidies and trade policies create harm. Food aid, development assistance, and biotechnology all become possible solutions or contributors to the problem of world hunger, depending on how they are managed.

DISCUSSION AND ACTION QUESTIONS

1. How does demand inelasticity affect farm prices and farmers' incomes? How does this issue compare between U.S. agricultural production and primary commodity production in developing countries (as will be discussed in Chapter 12 on international trade)?

2. What is the direction of the trend in concentration in farming? How have government programs contributed to this trend?

3. How do price floors interfere with the rationing function of price? Use price supports as an example. Can you think of any other examples of price floors in our economy? (*Hint:* Remember that there are markets for *services* as well as for goods!)

4. Why don't supply restriction programs work well in increasing farm prices and incomes?

5. Do you believe that the government should be involved in agriculture? What kinds of policies would you suggest? Do you think that direct benefits to low-income farmers might be a possible solution?

6. Go to the Census Bureau Web site (http://www.census.gov). Look for information under *agriculture*. Can you find the number of farms in your state?

7. Visit the official Web site of the Department of Agriculture at http://www.usda.gov. What information can you find about current agricultural policy? What other type of material is available there?

8. Check out the statistical arm of the Department of Agriculture at http://www.nass.usda.gov. This site contains the latest of the agricultural censuses. Look up some statistics that you have interest in.

9. Go to the Web site of the Farm Services Agency at http://www.fsa.usda.gov/pas/farmbill/. Read more about the latest Farm Bill, including the answers to frequently asked questions.

10. The Web site of the Food and Agriculture Organization of the United Nations (FAO) provides information about U.S. farm subsidies and how they affect the rest of the world. Go to the Web site at http://www.fao.org and investigate the effects of U.S. agricultural subsidies on the developing countries of the world. This site contains information about biotechnology, farm conservation, hazardous pesticides, and more.

11. Go to http://www.ewg.org to see the home page of the Environmental Working Group. This nonprofit organization has assembled the records of farm benefits that have been paid to farmers as well as other types of information. Do you think this is a liberal or conservative Web site?

12. The USDA provides information that is not just beneficial to farmers. For example, go to the USDA Web site (http://www.usda.gov) and find information you may need about current food recalls!

13. Farmworker Justice is an organization dedicated to helping migrant and seasonal farm workers improve their working conditions and wages, labor and immigration policy, health and safety, and access to justice. Go to its Web site at http://www.fwjustice.org and find out more about these issues. If you are concerned about the issue, you may want to seek information on this site about what you can do to make a difference.

14. Have you ever thought about writing to your legislators about farm policy? Probably not! Consider some of the issues: Farmworker Justice, the effects of U.S. agricultural subsidies on poor farmers in developing counties, inefficiencies in our food aid programs, inequities

in our farm programs, and so on. Have the issues raised in this chapter encouraged you to write such a letter? Do it! (You can find your senators at http://www.senate.gov and your representatives at http://www.house.gov.)

15. For which nonfarm products is demand likely to be inelastic? Why is this the case? For which types of products is demand more likely to be elastic?

16. How do target prices differ from price supports? Do different groups win or lose from these programs? (This topic is discussed in Appendix 11-1 of this chapter.)

NOTES

1. The U.S. Conference of Catholic Bishops, Department of Justice, Peace and Human Development, Office of Domestic Social Development, *Farm Bill*, February 2009, http://www.usccb.org.

2. Farm Aid Concert, www.farmaid.org/concert, 2014.

3. Poverty rates are for 2011, and are from the U.S. Department of Commerce, Census Bureau, Population division, www.census.gov, release date June 6, 2013. Population sizes are for 2012. All other data in this paragraph are from the U.S. Department of Agriculture, Economic Research Service, 2012 Census of Agriculture, www.ers.usda.gov, 2012 or 2007. (The USDA compiles a survey on agriculture every five years, and the last complete survey was in 2007. The 2012 survey was not complete as of early 2014 and some data still refer to 2007. Unless otherwise indicated, other statistics in this chapter are from the 2007 or 2012 source.)

4. Willard W. Cochrane and C. Ford Runge, *Reforming Farm Policy* (Ames: Iowa State University Press, 1992), p. 21.

5. Jon Evert quoted in *Agriculture in the Global Economy: Hunger 2003* (Washington, DC: Bread for the World Institute, 2003), p. 44.

6. The Environmental Working Group (EWG), 2003 (http://www.ewg.org/farm).

7. The U.S. Conference of Catholic Bishops, Department of Justice, Peace and Human Development, Office of Domestic Social Development, *Farm Bill*, February 2009, http://www.usccb.org/.

8. U.S. Department of Agriculture, Economic Research Service, *Agricultural Act of 2014: Highlights and Implications*, http://www.ers.usda.gov/agricultural-act-of-2014-highlights-and-implications.aspx

9. Doug Harford quoted in *Agricultural in the Global Economy: Hunger 2003* (Washington, DC: Bread for the World Institute, 2003), p. 38.

10. The Environmental Working Group (EWG), 2007 (http://www.ewg.org/farm).

11. Cochrane and Runge, *Reforming Farm Policy*, p. 22

12. The Green Revolution consisted of new high-yielding seed varieties that were designed to withstand climate and other conditions in developing countries. If used with proper (and expensive) chemical fertilizers, irrigation, and other inputs, they resulted in greatly increased yields of wheat, rice, and corn. Larger and wealthier farmers were able to adapt the new seeds and corresponding inputs, causing large increases in food production, consequent reductions in food prices, and increases in their own incomes. The problem was that most poor people in developing countries are farmers who were unable to adapt the new seeds and corollary inputs, and who produced low yields sold at the prevailing low prices. Their incomes and standards of living suffered.

13. Bread for the World, *Healthy Food, Farms & Families: Hunger 2007* (Washington, DC: Bread for the World Institute, 2007).

14. Information in this paragraph is from The Environmental Working Group, *The Last Plantation*, from *Color Lines Magazine*, Jessica Hoffman, http://www.ewg.org/node/, 2009.

15. Center for Budget and Policy Priorities, CBPP Statement: Stacy Dean, Vice President, Food Assistance Policy, on New USDA Report on "Food Insecurity," lachapelle@cbpp.org.

16. Bread for the World Institute, Per Pinstrup-Anderson, "About Us," from the *2005 Annual Report on the State of World Hunger: Strengthening Rural Communities* (Washington, DC: Bread for the World Institute, 2005), http://www.bread.org/about-us/institute/.

17. U.S. Agency for International Development, *Feed the Future: Partnerships to Drive Agricultural Growth*, www.feedthefuture.gov, 2014.

18. World Bank, *World Development Indicators*, www.wdi.worldbank.org, 2014.

Appendix 11-1
Target Prices with Deficiency Payments

By the 1960s, the government had acquired huge surpluses under the price support program. Something had to be done. In many commodity markets, rigid price supports were replaced by flexible price supports based on past market prices. These price supports (loan rates) were markedly lower than those used previously. They became a less important instrument of farm policy for most commodities, whereas **target prices** became a more important instrument. Under target pricing, farmers received direct payments. These payments are called **deficiency payments**. They cover the gap between the target price and the actual market price. Since the 1960s, U.S. farm bills have varied in terms of the significance of target prices and deficiencies in overall farm policy.

Figure 11-5 illustrates how target pricing works. Suppose that policymakers determine that a $4 target price is justified by the costs of producing cotton, but the market price is below $4. They establish $4 as the target price for cotton. At a target price of $4 corresponding to point A, farmers will offer 3,500 million bushels (quantity supplied) of cotton for sale.

The price at which buyers are willing to buy 3,500 million bushels (quantity demanded) is $2.50, corresponding to point B. So, the price will fall to $2.50, and the

Target prices

A program in which farmers are paid the difference between the target price and the market price.

Deficiency payments

The target price minus the market price, multiplied by the number of units sold.

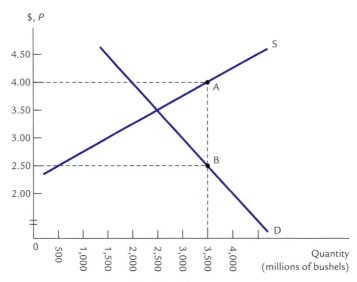

Figure 11-5 • Effects of Target Pricing on the Cotton Market
With target prices, price is allowed to fall to the level that clears the market ($2.50); farmers receive deficiency payments for the difference between the target price ($4) and the market price ($2.50).

© Cengage Learning

entire quantity supplied by farmers will be purchased. Farmers will receive $2.50 from the market for a bushel of cotton, but the government will send them a check for the difference between the target price ($4) and the market price ($2.50). So, for each bushel sold, the farmer will receive a government deficiency payment of $1.50. A farmer selling 10,000 bushels will receive a check for $15,000.

Target prices differ from the previously discussed price supports in a number of important ways. First, because the market price is much lower than the target price, the cost of farm commodities does not drive up the cost of food. Indeed, because target prices drive down the market price for farm products to below the free-market equilibrium, food is made cheaper for buyers. Second, because prices are lower for consumers whether they are in the U.S. or the export market, American farm products are more competitive on world markets at the lower prices. Of course, this causes the same problems for developing countries that we've already discussed. Third, the market is less distorted by target prices than by price supports, because no surplus is created. Finally, the costs to taxpayers of target prices and deficiency payments are easier to count because the costs associated with surpluses are not incurred.

Of course, some similarities occur between price supports, target prices, and supply restriction programs. They all result in a transfer of income from taxpayers to farmers. They all favor large-scale farmers over small farmers. And they all harm the exports of other nations, including the developing countries of the world.

Chapter 12

ROAD MAP

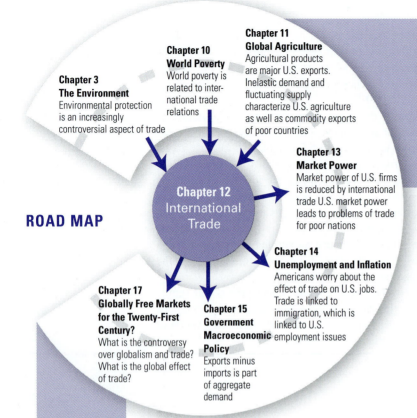

Chapter 3
The Environment
Environmental protection is an increasingly controversial aspect of trade

Chapter 10
World Poverty
World poverty is related to international trade relations

Chapter 11
Global Agriculture
Agricultural products are major U.S. exports. Inelastic demand and fluctuating supply characterize U.S. agriculture as well as commodity exports of poor countries

Chapter 12
International Trade

Chapter 13
Market Power
Market power of U.S. firms is reduced by international trade U.S. market power leads to problems of trade for poor nations

Chapter 14
Unemployment and Inflation
Americans worry about the effect of trade on U.S. jobs. Trade is linked to immigration, which is linked to U.S. employment issues

Chapter 15
Government Macroeconomic Policy
Exports minus imports is part of aggregate demand

Chapter 17
Globally Free Markets for the Twenty-First Century?
What is the controversy over globalism and trade? What is the global effect of trade?

The Economic Toolbox

- Trade balance
- Absolute advantage
- Comparative advantage
- Production possibilities curve
- Consumption possibilities curve
- Trade restrictions
- Declining terms of trade

- Inelastic demand
- Agricultural subsidies
- NAFTA
- Exchange rates (appendix)
- Group of eight (G-8)
- Group of twenty (G-20)

International Trade

I n 2007, the United States had experienced a financial crisis. It was followed by a national economic crisis. By now, you know all this. But what does it mean for the rest of the world? Everything! The world is so interconnected that, as they say, when the United States sneezes, the world catches pneumonia. What then happens when the United States is in economic crisis?

As we will see, the U.S. economic and financial downturn did have important implications for international trade and international finance. The economic downturn meant that many Americans lost their jobs—and their incomes. When our incomes fall, we buy fewer goods—fewer U.S. goods and fewer foreign-produced goods. When we buy fewer foreign goods, foreign companies are forced to cut back on production and they lay off their workers. With lower incomes, those workers buy fewer goods. The process spirals, and the impact of U.S. recession spreads to virtually every corner of the globe where people are buying and selling goods and services. By early 2009, the economic crisis was estimated by the World Bank to cause the largest annual decline in world trade in 80 years.[1]

Let's back up and reconsider the housing crisis. As described in more detail in Chapter 7 on housing, we ran into trouble when abundant funds and scarce regulations led financial institutions to overextend in lending money to homebuyers, who, for a variety of reasons, lacked the wherewithal to make good on their loan payments. Housing loans are called mortgages, and these mortgages lost their value when repayment became unlikely. However, U.S. financial institutions took on investments that were backed by these mortgages as collateral—mortgage-backed securities. These were purchased by many American business and individuals, as well as many foreign people and countries. When the value of mortgages fell, so too did the value of the mortgage-backed securities. Millions of investors lost the value of their investments. Just as economic crisis spread around the globe, the financial crisis did as well.

These sound like complex topics, and they are. But the economics behind them is pretty basic—supply and demand. By using these simple economic tools, we can understand the realm of international trade in this chapter, as well as the realm of international finance in the Appendix to this chapter.

We know that the world is becoming increasingly internationalized. As communications and transportation improve, we become more and more linked to other parts of the globe. Through imports, we consume products such as cocoa and bananas that we could never produce efficiently domestically. Through exports, as indicated in the remarks by President

When ninety-eight percent of our exporters are small businesses, new trade partnerships with Europe and the Asia-Pacific will help them create more jobs. We need to work together on tools like bipartisan trade promotion authority to protect our workers, protect our environment, and open new markets to new goods stamped "Made in the USA." China and Europe aren't standing on the sidelines. Neither should we.

—PRESIDENT BARACK OBAMA, STATE OF THE UNION ADDRESS, JANUARY 28, 2014.

Obama above, we create jobs for our citizens. The World Bank, the International Monetary Fund, and the World Trade Organization (WTO) are now becoming household words. International investment takes place at a frantic pace. Multinational corporations locate subsidiaries in remote parts of the world. Chances are good that you will one day work for a company involved in international business. On your own computer, you can communicate around the globe by electronic mail in a matter of seconds. On your own campus, international faculty members teach you and students from abroad share your classes. You are undoubtedly becoming aware of international issues.

Yet, many Americans seem reluctant to think "internationally." We see the world as complex and confusing and sometimes refuse to think of matters beyond our own backyard. Why is international economics so intimidating? Is it because it's so foreign: foreign countries, foreign currency, and foreign terminology? It's a mistake for us to retreat to the familiar, for the world will march on without us, and just as President Obama indicated, the rest of the world isn't standing on the sidelines. Neither should we, and international economics will grow increasingly important in our lives. And, as we noted, international economics is not as difficult as you might think. The next several pages will convince you of that. Last, you'll find that by inserting phrases like "the dollar traded high today" into your everyday conversation, you'll soon be impressing your friends and relatives!

The Importance of Trade

Exports
The value of goods and services sold to foreigners.

Imports
The value of goods and services purchased from foreigners.

Trade balance
The value of a nation's exports minus its imports.

Trade deficit
The amount by which a nation's trade balance is in deficit (imports exceed exports).

Trade surplus
The amount by which a nation's trade balance is in surplus (exports exceed imports).

Over time in the United States, we have seen the increasing importance of international trade in terms of the dollar size of our exports and imports. Our **exports** are the value of goods and services that we sell to foreigners, whereas our **imports** are the value of goods and services we buy from them. A good way to consider our exports and our imports is in terms of their share of gross domestic product (GDP). Recall that GDP is the value of our nation's production. As a share of GDP, our exports increased from 4 percent in 1960 to 14 percent in 2012. Our imports increased from 3 percent of GDP in 1960 to 17 percent in 2012. Our exports plus imports as a share of GDP is 31 percent. This number shows the importance of international trade in our economy. Our exports minus imports is our **trade balance**, valued at −6 percent of GDP (14% − 17% = −3%) in 2012. The negative number means that we have a **trade deficit** of 3 percent of GDP. If a country has more exports than imports, the trade balance is positive. We refer to this as a **trade surplus**.

Table 12-1 displays data for a diverse group of countries around the world. Column 3 reveals that international trade plays a very large role in some countries and a much smaller role in others. From the table, we can see that the importance of trade to the United States is much less than it is in many other countries. Large countries with a great deal of diversity in production, such as the United States, Brazil, Argentina, and Japan, often have fairly low levels of imports because they have little need for them. Other very poor countries, such as Sudan, South Sudan, Nepal, and Afghanistan, have low import levels because they cannot afford them. The great diversity of export levels is due to different reasons for different countries. Column 4 shows that many countries have a trade deficit, whereas others have a trade surplus.

Even though the ranking among countries is fairly low for the United States, the statistics do show that international trade is nevertheless important for the United States, and increasingly so. But is this situation good or bad? To answer this question, we must consider the benefits of trade.

TABLE 12-1 • Exports, Imports, Exports plus Imports, and Trade Balance (Exports minus Imports); Percent of GDP; in Order from Lower to Higher Exports plus Imports as a Percent of GDP, Selected Countries; 2012

Country	Exports (% of GDP)	Imports (% of GDP)	Exports + Imports (% of GDP)	Exports − Imports (% of GDP)
Sudan	18	6	24	12
Brazil	13	14	27	−1
United States	14	17	31	−3
Japan	17	15	32	2
Argentina	17	20	37	−3
Nepal	33	10	43	23
Afghanistan	39	6	45	33
China	25	27	52	−2
South Sudan	43	10	53	33
Canada	32	30	62	2
Mexico	34	33	67	1
Zimbabwe	76	44	120	32
Congo, D.R.	67	55	122	12
Vietnam	77	80	157	−3
Belarus	77	82	159	−5
Estonia	90	91	181	−1
Ireland	84	108	192	−24
Maldives	107	106	213	1
Luxembourg	148	177	325	−29
Singapore	178	201	379	−23

Note: The column labeled Exports plus Imports as a % of GDP signifies the importance of trade to the country. The column labeled Exports minus Imports as a % of GDP is the trade balance. A negative value indicates a trade deficit.

Source: World Bank, *World Development Indicators,* 2014 (Washington, DC: World Bank, 2014).

The Benefits of Trade

Forget about the international environment for a moment and think about yourself as a producer and consumer. Imagine: What would life be like if you tried to produce everything you need and want? You would grow your own food, build your own house, sew your own clothes, and teach yourself economics! Or you could try to specialize in something you're particularly good at, maybe accounting or computer programming, and then earn a living at this task. You could use your income to purchase all of the other things that you need and want.

Most of us would agree pretty quickly that we are better off specializing in what we are good at and exchanging our income for the things that we want to consume. Why? Because we are simply not very good at producing everything that we need. Some of us would spend so much time figuring out how to bake bread or fix the plumbing that we would never get around to any other activities. Far more efficient for me to teach economics, hire a plumber, and stop at the bakery!

This way of thinking is an appropriate analogy for individual countries trying to determine whether to engage in international trade. A country might try to be self-sufficient; that is, to produce everything that its people need and want. Indeed, politicians in many countries have advocated this goal from time to time. It sounds so strong and independent! But like an individual, a country can specialize in the production of a limited number of products that it is especially good at producing. It can then export these products and use the resulting income to import the other things that its people desire. Just like the individual, the country will gain from specialization and exchange.

More specifically, what is the source of these benefits? You now have some idea, but we need to be more precise than simply saying we ought to specialize in the activities at which we are good. Exactly what do we mean by being "good at it"? The answers lie in the concepts of absolute and comparative advantage.

Absolute Advantage

Absolute advantage
A situation whereby a country can produce a good at a lower resource cost than another country.

Absolute advantage is defined as a situation whereby a country can produce a good at a lower resource cost than another country. Resources include labor, land, capital, and so on. Note that we are comparing the resource cost of producing a good in one country with the resource cost of producing the good in another country. Consider the United States and Brazil as examples. Brazil has a climate and land type far more beneficial to the growing of coffee than does the United States. Someone might be able to devise a climate control system that would allow coffee to be produced in the United States, but it would be very difficult to do so, and it would entail a high resource cost. Brazil can produce coffee at a lower resource cost.

On the other hand, the United States is better suited for the growing of barley than is Brazil. Proper land, weather, machinery, and technology allow the United States to produce barley at a lower resource cost than Brazil. We say that Brazil has an absolute advantage in coffee production (compared with the United States), whereas the United States has an absolute advantage in barley production (compared with Brazil). It would be far more reasonable for the United States to devote its resources to barley production (rather than to produce both barley and coffee) and then exchange with Brazil to acquire coffee. With the United States specializing in barley and Brazil specializing in coffee, both countries are producing more total output than if each country tried to produce both goods. Larger total output means larger total consumption: each country could benefit from specialization and trade.

Comparative Advantage

The situation we just described presents a fairly obvious example of the benefits of trade. A country need not possess absolute advantage as described previously to garner these benefits, however. Consider a situation in which one country enjoys an absolute advantage in the production of two goods, and another country possesses an absolute advantage in none. Suppose, for example, that the United States can produce both digital video disks (DVDs) and shoes at a lower resource cost than Greenland. Should the United States produce both DVDs and shoes or specialize in production of one good and trade with Greenland for the other good? To answer this question, we need to consider the concept of comparative advantage.

Comparative advantage
A situation whereby a country can produce a good at a lower opportunity cost than another country.

Comparative advantage is defined as a situation whereby a country can produce a good at a lower opportunity cost than another country. Notice the similarity to absolute advantage. We are comparing two countries and two goods. However, the term *resource cost* is replaced with *opportunity cost*. This difference is important. Recall from Chapter 1 that opportunity cost refers to that which you give up in order to get something else. That is, to produce some amount of one good, a country must give up the opportunity for some production of another good. Resources are limited; when they are put into one use, they cannot be put into another. Let's be more specific.

Suppose that labor is the only resource used in producing DVDs and shoes and that workers receive identical daily wages (two simplifying assumptions). Let's assume that each worker in the United States can produce either eight DVDs or four pairs of shoes per day (or some combination in between), and that each worker in Greenland can produce either two DVDs or two pairs of shoes per day (or some combination in between). This information is displayed in Table 12-2.

Clearly, the United States has an absolute advantage in the production of both DVDs *and* shoes. Because each worker in the United States can produce more DVDs and more shoes than each worker in Greenland, the resource cost of producing both of these goods will be lowest in the United States.

According to the table, each worker in the United States can produce either eight DVDs or four pairs of shoes per day. Each worker in Greenland can produce either two DVDs or two pairs of shoes per day. This means that, compared with Greenland, the United States has an absolute advantage in the production of both DVDs and shoes.

But let's think in terms of comparative advantage. The opportunity cost of producing eight DVDs in the United States is the four pairs of shoes that will not be produced. Or put another way, the opportunity cost of producing each two DVDs in the United States is one pair of shoes (a 2:1 ratio). On the other hand, the opportunity cost of producing two DVDs in Greenland is the two pairs of shoes that will not be produced (a 1:1 ratio). In terms of forgone shoe production, the United States has a lower opportunity cost than Greenland for DVD production. One DVD requires that we give up only one-half pair of shoes, whereas Greenland gives up a whole pair of shoes for each DVD. Because the United States gives up fewer shoes when producing DVDs, it has the comparative advantage in DVD production.

Now consider the production of shoes. The opportunity cost of producing four pairs of shoes in the United States is the eight DVDs that will not be produced. Put another way, the opportunity cost of producing two pairs of shoes is four DVDs (a 1:2 ratio). On the other hand, the opportunity cost of producing two pairs of shoes in Greenland is only two DVDs (a 1:1 ratio). In terms of forgone DVD production, Greenland has the lower opportunity cost for shoe production. That is, Greenland has the comparative advantage in shoe production.

What this means is that if the United States specializes in DVD production, and Greenland specializes in shoe production, the two countries will be able to come up with a rate of exchange in trade that will be mutually beneficial. The rate of four DVDs in exchange for three pairs of shoes would benefit both countries, for example. Greenland could receive four DVDs from the United States by selling three pairs of shoes in exchange. This is a more effective strategy than Greenland trying to produce the four DVDs, for it would then have to give up four pairs of shoes in production (the 1:1 ratio). The United States could receive three pairs of shoes from Greenland by selling the four DVDs in exchange. This is a more effective strategy than the United States trying to produce the three pairs of shoes, for it would then have to give up six DVDs in production (the 1:2 ratio). Each country can trade at a rate of exchange that is superior to the opportunity costs associated with domestic production. (Notice that this discussion is theoretical, since Greenland can only produce two of either good in one year. It is realistic if we extend the time period to more than one year or consider more than two countries.)

TABLE 12-2 • United States and Greenland Production of DVDs or Shoes per Day, per Worker

Country	DVD Production	Shoe Production (pairs)
United States	8	4
Greenland	2	2

© Cengage Learning

Why shouldn't the United States produce both DVDs and shoes? After all, it can produce both goods at a lower resource cost than Greenland. But by specializing in DVD production, the United States can obtain more DVDs and shoes than if it tried to produce them both. This outcome can be easily illustrated by the production possibilities curve, a technique with which you are already familiar.

Recall from Chapter 1 that the production possibilities curve shows alternative combinations of the maximum amounts of two different products that can be produced by one economy, during a particular time period when resources are fully and efficiently utilized. Notice that the production possibilities curve in Figure 12-1 shows that each worker in the United States can produce either eight DVDs or four pairs of shoes (or some combination in between) per day. (We could multiply these numbers by the number of workers in the United States to obtain the total number of DVDs and shoes that the United States could produce and end up with a more conventional production possibilities curve.) In the absence of trade, the United States cannot consume more DVDs and shoes than it produces.

Now let's introduce the possibility of trade. Suppose the United States decides to specialize in DVD production because this is where it has its comparative advantage. Further, suppose that the United States agrees with Greenland to trade at the rate of exchange of four DVDs for three pairs of shoes. Again, this trade ratio is arbitrary but is chosen as representative of a ratio that will benefit each country. This situation is displayed in Figure 12-2, with the production possibilities curve of Figure 12-1 repeated for convenience. Note that if the United States produces at point A (reflecting specialization in the production of eight DVDs), it can move to alternative points along a new curve, which we might call a **consumption possibilities curve** with trade.

The United States, for example, may decide to sell four DVDs to Greenland (back up four DVDs from point A to A′) in exchange for three pairs of shoes (move up three pairs

Consumption possibilities curve

A curve that shows alternative combinations of the maximum amounts of two products that can be consumed within a country during a particular time period.

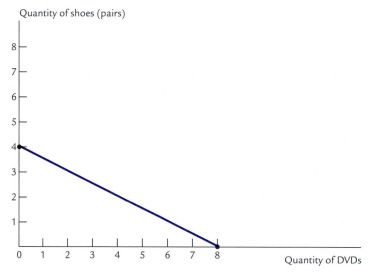

Figure 12-1 • Production Possibilities for Each U.S. Worker per Day, With No Trade
The production possibilities curve shows alternative combinations of the maximum amounts of two products that can be produced by one country (or one worker in a country) during a particular time period. This graph shows that each U.S. worker can produce either eight DVDs or four pairs of shoes (or some combination in between) per day.

© Cengage Learning

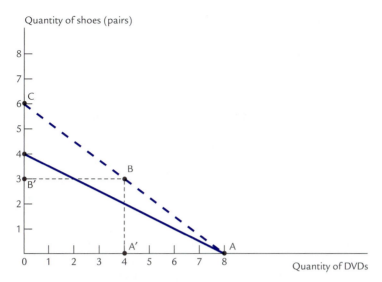

Figure 12-2 • Production Possibilities for Each U.S. Worker, and Consumption Possibilities with Trade, per Day, with Trade
This graph shows that each U.S. worker can produce either eight DVDs or four pairs of shoes (or some combination in between) per day. With no trade, the United States would be restricted to consuming amounts indicated along the production possibilities curve. With trade, and a trade ratio of four DVDs for three pairs of shoes, the United States can consume along the higher consumption possibilities curve.

© Cengage Learning

of shoes from A′), moving consumption back up along the consumption possibilities curve from point A to point B (at which the United States ends up with four DVDs and three pairs of shoes). Alternatively, the United States might sell another four DVDs (back up four more DVDs from point B to B′) in exchange for another three pairs of shoes (move up three more pairs of shoes from B′), moving its consumption point back up along the curve from point B′ to point C (at which the United States ends up with no DVDs and six pairs of shoes). With the exception of point A, the United States is better off at all points along the dashed consumption possibilities curve made possible through specialization and trade than along the production possibilities curve in the absence of trade. We could draw a similar graph for Greenland, indicating the same types of benefits through specialization in shoe production and trade with the United States for DVDs. **By specializing according to comparative advantage, both countries can benefit from trade.**

The Basis for Advantage

Why is one country better at producing a good than another country? Whether we're thinking in terms of absolute or comparative advantage, there are some basic reasons why one country will have the advantage. Some obvious factors are weather and climate. Sometimes, weather and climate can be overcome (through the use of greenhouses to produce tomatoes, for example), but extraordinary efforts to overcome natural factors may entail a high resource cost. This high cost will give the advantage to the country with the more favorable natural conditions.

Labor is another important factor in determining advantage. A country with higher labor productivity might have an advantage in producing goods that require a large amount of labor input. Factors that contribute to labor productivity include the obvious ones, such as labor training and education, but other factors may be even more important. Sophisticated capital equipment and technology used in conjunction with labor will greatly enhance labor productivity. *U.S. workers tend to be very productive because they are well trained and educated and because they often work with modern capital and technology.*

When considering labor costs, both productivity and wages are important. Suppose that one worker in Gambia is paid the equivalent of $5 per hour and can produce five baskets per hour. Suppose that one worker in the United States is paid twice the wage rate, or $10 per hour, but can produce twice the baskets, or 10 baskets per hour. Which country has the higher labor cost? Neither! The labor cost of producing each basket is identical in each country ($1 per basket). Labor costs in the United States and Gambia are identical because the U.S. worker receives twice the wage but is also twice as productive. Again, while skills and education are important determinants of labor productivity, even more important are the capital and technology that are used in conjunction with labor. As a result, U.S. workers are generally highly productive. This productivity factor is important to keep in mind when there is talk about cheap foreign labor. *Foreign labor is cheap only if productivity is high and wages are low.* People often complain about U.S. workers losing jobs to cheap foreign labor. Do you see now how this may be untrue?

Other factors determining advantage include the quality and availability of land, capital equipment, technology, and other resource inputs. Singapore, for example, has scarce land, hence extremely high land costs. Such a country would not have an advantage in the production of most agricultural products.

All of the Benefits of Trade

Whew! The most basic benefits of trade are the gains from specialization according to absolute or comparative advantage that we have just discussed. Such specialization leads to greater output from limited resources and to benefits to each trading nation and the world as a whole. Some additional benefits are also important. Consumers receive a greater diversity of products and more choice among competing brands than they would if purchasing only domestic goods. We all are choosy among brands when buying our DVD players or personal computers and our choices often include foreign products!

Furthermore, the increased competition among firms made possible by trade will reduce the likelihood and degree of market power, benefiting society. We will see in Chapter 13 that concentration and market power within an industry result in lower output levels (and lower employment), less efficient production, and higher prices to consumers. Increased international competition reduces the probability of these negative outcomes by reducing concentration within the industry. Instead of only three major automakers, many automobile companies sell to the U.S. market. Larger numbers of firms have less ability to restrict output and drive up prices.

The Distribution of Benefits

Economic theory clearly indicates that individual nations benefit from trade as they specialize according to their advantage, but we must realize that not all people within the country benefit from trade. Although the country as a whole becomes better off, there will be some gainers and some losers within the country. That is, the benefits of trade will not be distributed equally. This unequal distribution is one of the concerns about free trade.

We can see the distribution of benefits from trade if we consider a simple graph for a country as it moves from a no-trade situation to a situation in which it begins to import a product (the free trade situation). Let's consider the United States and the market for cotton cloth. The only assumptions we need to make to keep the analysis simple are that (1) all cotton cloth is identical whether produced in the United States or elsewhere, and (2) the United States is a large producer of cotton cloth. Consider the first graph in Figure 12-3, in which D and S represent the hypothetical domestic demand and supply curves, respectively, for cotton cloth in the United States. Equilibrium at point E (with the corresponding price of $1 per yard and the quantity of 1,000 yards) reflects the situation in which the United States engages in *no international trade* of cotton cloth.

Now suppose the United States begins importing cotton cloth into the country. The second graph in figure 12-3 shows this situation *with international trade*. D will continue to represent the domestic demand (that is, the demand for cotton cloth by U.S. consumers), and S will continue to represent the domestic supply (that is, the supply of cotton cloth by U.S. producers). But note the new supply curve S^T as well. S^T represents the total free trade supply curve for cotton cloth (the "T" can stand for *total* and/or free *trade*). It includes all of the supply represented by the domestic supply curve S, plus additional supply by foreign countries. (Hence, the curve is drawn by simply shifting the domestic supply curve forward; that is, by increasing it.) The new supply curve S^T now becomes the relevant curve for determining equilibrium price and quantity *consumed* under the free trade situation. At the new equilibrium point E^T, determined by the intersection of D and S^T, the new free trade price is $0.75 per yard, and the quantity consumed is 1,500 yards. This new price is lower, representing an improved situation for U.S. consumers of cotton cloth. The new quantity consumed is higher, indicating that consumers are now purchasing larger quantities of cloth. Clearly, consumers of cotton cloth gain from trade.

Consider U.S. producers of cotton cloth, however. *Although the new supply curve S^T is the relevant curve for determining equilibrium price and quantity consumed under free trade, the old supply curve S is still the relevant curve for representing the supply decisions of domestic suppliers.* At the new lower price of $0.75, domestic suppliers reduce the quantity they produce to 500 yards (the new domestic quantity supplied). Note that U.S. consumers are buying a quantity of 1,500 yards and U.S. suppliers are selling a

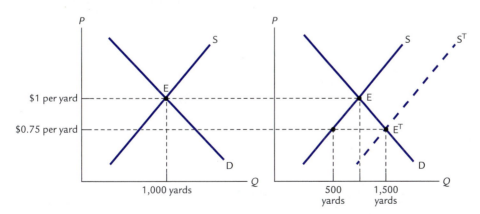

Figure 12-3 •
The first graph shows no trade, and corresponding equilibrium price of $1 per yard and equilibrium quantity of 1,000 years. The second graph shows the situation where the United States begins to import cotton cloth. D continues to represent domestic demand, while S^T represents the total free trade supply curve. The new equilibrium is E^T. Equilibrium price falls to $0.75 per yard, quantity consumed increases to 1,500 yards, and quantity produced domestically falls to 500 yards.

© Cengage Learning

quantity of 500 yards; the difference between them is made up by imports of cotton cloth into the country. U.S. producers of cotton cloth are harmed by free trade: they receive a lower price for their product, and they now sell a smaller quantity. Both the individual cloth companies and the workers for these companies (who may experience layoffs) lose as a result of trade.

Even though the benefits of trade accrue to the United States as a whole (the efficiency gains due to comparative advantage) and to U.S. consumers of cotton cloth in particular, U.S. producers of cotton cloth are harmed. The effects of free trade are summarized in Table 12-3. It is the U.S. producers of cotton cloth (firms and workers) who will argue most vehemently in favor of trade restrictions on foreign-produced cloth. To the extent that these producers are politically powerful (typically more powerful than unorganized consumers), the U.S. government may respond to their appeals with a variety of trade restrictions.

Restrictions to Free Trade

Quota

A restriction on the quantity of an imported good.

Tariff

A tax on an imported good.

Two common types of trade restrictions are quotas and tariffs. A **quota** is a restriction on the quantity of an imported good. A quota on sugar, for example, means that only a limited amount of sugar from other countries will be allowed to enter the United States. Once this quota is met, Americans will be forced to buy U.S.-produced sugar, or to go without. A **tariff** does not limit the quantity of an imported good but is simply a tax imposed on the imported product. A tariff on sugar coming into the United States would serve to raise the price of the product (in this case, sugar) to American consumers, making them more likely to purchase American-grown sugar.

The purpose of most U.S. trade restrictions is to force or encourage American consumers to buy more American-made products and fewer foreign counterparts. They are thus designed to protect American producers, despite the fact that the resulting trade barriers reduce the benefits of free trade that would otherwise accrue to our country. Trade restrictions on cotton cloth imports cause the price of cotton cloth in the United States to rise, thereby benefiting U.S. cloth producers (firms and workers) and hurting U.S. cloth consumers. (In the extreme case of a trade restriction that would totally prohibit imports of cotton cloth into the United States, we would revert back to the original type of demand and supply curves in Figure 12-3, a situation in which prices to consumers are higher, smaller quantities are consumed, and larger quantities are supplied domestically.) The fact that we have many trade restrictions means either that American producers are more powerful in protecting their interests than American consumers or that American consumers do not understand the consequences of trade restrictions for their own well-being. Both of these situations probably exist.

Trade restrictions have powerful effects beyond the ones discussed previously with respect to producers and consumers, as you would expect. The nation as a whole will

TABLE 12-3 • The Effects of Free Trade in Cotton Cloth Imports into the United States

Effects of Free Trade on:	Effect	Reason
The United States as a whole	Gain	Efficiency gain through specialization and exchange according to comparative advantage, greater diversity of product, reduced opportunity for market power
U.S. consumers of cotton cloth	Gain	Lower price and increased quantity consumed
U.S. firms producing cotton cloth	Lose	Lower price and decreased quantity supplied
U.S. workers producing cotton cloth	Lose	Jobs lost as cotton cloth production decreases

© Cengage Learning

lose the benefits of specialization and exchange according to advantage. Competition within protected industries will decrease because foreign competition among producers is lessened. Consequently, domestic producers will have more market power. (As we will learn in greater detail in Chapter 13 on market power, increased market power may cause output within the concentrated industry to fall. If firms produce less output, they may hire fewer workers, suggesting that workers within concentrated U.S. industries, such as the American automobile industry, may falsely be convinced that trade restrictions will protect their jobs. A graph like that of the cotton cloth industry in the second graph of Figure 12-3 may not accurately reflect workers' interests in the case of a concentrated industry with market power.)

And finally, producers within other industries, in particular our other export industries, will likely suffer as a result of trade restrictions. If the United States imposes quotas on imports of cotton cloth, U.S. producers of wheat and corn for export may see their foreign sales decline. This sales drop may occur for a variety of reasons. First, other countries may respond to U.S. trade restrictions with restrictions of their own. This action is called **retaliation**. If the United States limits imports of Sri Lankan cotton cloth, Sri Lanka may limit imports of U.S. corn. Moreover, incomes of foreign producers of cotton cloth may fall as the United States restricts its purchases. As the incomes of Sri Lankans fall, they will be less *able* to purchase U.S. corn. And finally, U.S. trade restrictions will affect the value of the U.S. dollar relative to foreign currencies. The change in this value will likely reduce U.S. exports, as indicated in the Appendix to this chapter. Table 12-4 summarizes the effects of U.S. trade restrictions on cotton cloth imports. It is entirely the opposite of Table 12-3.

Because U.S. producers (workers and firms) of cotton cloth are the only beneficiaries of trade restrictions and because the rest of the United States suffers, perhaps we should seek better ways to deal with the hardships suffered by these producers when we freely import cotton cloth. If other countries have the advantage in cotton cloth production, then by encouraging continued production by U.S. firms, we are supporting relatively inefficient U.S. industries. (We also harm the residents of poor countries such as Sri Lanka.) The United States does not really benefit in the long run. But, rather than leaving these U.S. firms and workers to suffer their losses through trade, we might seek solutions that improve the efficiency of U.S. industry (for example, through subsidies for research and development) or that retrain workers and redirect firms to production of more advantageous goods. The latter solution is pursued under the North American Free Trade Agreement, which is discussed shortly. **Do keep in mind the main point, however, that the United States as a whole benefits when importing products in which it does not have a comparative advantage.** If a reason for the lack of comparative advantage is cheap foreign labor, then the United States as a whole benefits from cheap foreign labor.

Retaliation

A situation in which one country responds to the trade restrictions of another country by imposing trade restrictions of its own.

TABLE 12-4 • Effects of Trade Restrictions on Imports of Cotton Cloth into the United States

Effects of Trade Restrictions on:	Effect	Reason
The United States as a whole	Lose	Efficiency loss through failure to specialize and exchange according to comparative advantage, less diversity of product, greater opportunity for market power
U.S. consumers of cotton cloth	Lose	Higher price and decreased quantity consumed
U.S. firms producing cotton cloth	Gain	Higher price and increased quantity supplied
U.S. workers producing cotton cloth	Gain	Jobs gained as cotton cloth production increases
U.S. producers of export goods	Lose	Loss of export sales

© Cengage Learning

The Rest of the Controversy

U.S. job and business loss is always one of the concerns regarding international trade, though most citizens do not fully understand the benefits of trade. It is not the only concern, however. Many of the issues are much broader and involve economic justice throughout the world. These global issues involve trade in developing countries, the economics and politics of trade, and international trade agreements.

Developing Countries

The year was 1999. The place was Seattle. Widespread protests broke out amid clouds of tear gas in the air and battalions of police in the streets. Environmentalists, human rights protesters, and labor activists were there. The target of the demonstrations? The World Trade Organization, on the occasion of its opening meeting to prepare for the policy discussions of the year.

The time, the place, and the setting were unusual. Now they have become commonplace. Rarely does a meeting of the **World Bank**, the **International Monetary Fund (IMF)**, or the **WTO** take place without its attendant protesters. Suddenly, demonstrations against these international organizations are on the nightly news, the daily newspapers, the *New York Times* and the *Wall Street Journal*, and the Internet. Demonstrators are protesting against sweatshops, environmental destruction, unsafe working conditions, child labor, unemployment, firm shutdowns, and a host of other problems perceived to be the result of the global economic system as "managed" by the international organizations responsible for the rules of the game across much of the globe.

Many of these problems are specific to the developing countries, which are frequently hurt by international trade. These poor countries of the world have experienced problems with trade, even when carefully following the economic theory of specialization according to comparative advantage. Let's consider some of the problems affecting developing countries.

Lack of Diversity in Exports

One trade-related problem for developing countries is the lack of diversity in exports. Costa Rica, for example, relies on coffee exports for a large share of its export earnings. Yet, if bad weather significantly harms the coffee crop, or if international prices of coffee fall dramatically, the Costa Rican economy could be devastated. It would be better not to specialize so completely. Greater diversity of exports would provide some insurance against problems that might beset one particular product. In the meantime, however, poor countries are vulnerable to national and international circumstances that are largely beyond their control.

Declining Terms of Trade

Another closely related problem concerns the reliance of many developing countries on primary commodities for export. **Primary commodities** are unprocessed raw materials or agricultural products, such as coffee, sugar, tea, cocoa, and rubber.

These types of products have experienced a problem known as **declining terms of trade**. Over time, the prices of poor-country exports (especially primary commodities) have declined relative to the prices of poor-country imports. Declining terms of trade is a long-term phenomenon. *Demand for poor-country exports has tapered off (and therefore the relative price of the exports has decreased), in part because of the development of synthetics and developed-country trade restrictions.* At the same time, the prices of manufactured goods and petroleum products imported into poor countries have generally increased (because of market power in developed-country industries and the market power of the Organization of Petroleum Exporting Countries). As a result, poor-country

---

World Bank
An international organization whose mission is to end extreme poverty and boost global prosperity by promoting leadership, scholarship, and loans to countries in need.

International Monetary Fund (IMF)
The global organization, established in 1944, with the goal of providing loans and reducing world financial instability.

World Trade Organization (WTO)
The global organization, established in 1995, with the goal of reducing barriers to trade among member countries.

Primary commodities
Unprocessed raw materials and agricultural products.

Declining terms of trade
A decline in the value of a country's exports relative to the value of its imports.

export earnings have declined relative to poor-country expenditures for imports. This situation has undermined poor developing countries' attempts to import needed products and repay international debt, as discussed in Chapter 17. It has also made it necessary for developing countries to exploit natural resources, such as timber, as a source of export earnings. This practice has led to environmental degradation.

Price Instability

Another problem related to primary commodities is their instability. Prices for these types of products are often very unstable. *This is a short-term phenomenon (one year or season to the next), whereas declining terms of trade is a long-term problem (over several years).* This short-run instability is related to two common characteristics of primary commodity markets. Consider the hypothetical market for coffee depicted in Figure 12-4. The demand curve is drawn fairly steep, suggesting that demand is inelastic. Recall from Chapter 2 that **inelastic demand** exists when consumers are relatively unresponsive to changes in price. That is, they do not alter the quantity they purchase very much when there is a price change. A steep demand curve reflects this small change in quantity demanded relative to price. Compare the percentage change in quantity demanded along the quantity axis corresponding to points A and B, for example, with the larger percentage change in price between these two points. Quantity demanded falls from 5,000 pounds to 4,000 pounds (a 20 percent reduction) when price rises from $1 to $2 per pound (a 100 percent increase).

> **Inelastic demand**
> Demand in which buyers are relatively unresponsive to changes in price.

Inelastic demand characterizes the markets for many primary commodities. It makes sense in the coffee market, for when coffee prices rise, the coffee drinkers among us will be reluctant to significantly reduce our consumption of coffee. We are creatures of habit, especially when it comes to our caffeine consumption. The same is true for other commodities, such as tea and tobacco.

The other characteristic of markets for primary commodities is a fluctuating supply. The supply of many primary commodities is heavily dependent on weather, and weather tends to fluctuate. **The combination of fluctuating supply and inelastic demand results in a large fluctuation in price, as is evident in Figure 12-4.**

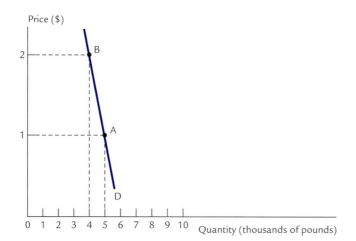

Figure 12-4 • The Demand for Coffee
In the coffee market, the demand curve D is drawn relatively steep. This reflects an inelastic demand for coffee. Notice that a large increase in price from $1 to $2 (a 100 percent increase) is associated with just a small decrease in quantity demanded from 5,000 to 4,000 pounds (a 20 percent decrease).

(Experiment a little: redraw the graph with a relatively flat demand curve, yet identical fluctuation in supply. You will see that the price will no longer fluctuate as much.) Prices fluctuate from year to year, just as weather fluctuates from year to year. (We addressed this same issue in Chapter 11 when we considered the markets for U.S. agricultural products.)

This fluctuation in price can be very detrimental for countries producing primary commodities for export. Although prices may average to an acceptable medium over the long run, the fluctuation is hard to deal with in the short run. A producer might go out of business entirely, and a country may have its export earnings plummet in a particularly bad year. These potential outcomes have led to some developing countries' attempts to join together in commodity agreements that seek to stabilize commodity prices. These agreements have met with mixed success.

Overreliance on Imports

An additional trade problem for poor countries is the possibility of overreliance on imports of important goods from other countries. According to the theory of comparative advantage, a country is better off importing a good in which it lacks an advantage, but what if the importation of an essential product becomes unreliable? When international food prices skyrocketed in the early 1970s, developing countries dependent on food imports found themselves priced out of the market. Hundreds of thousands of people starved to death throughout the developing world. When international oil prices quadrupled during the 1970s, many poor oil-importing countries could no longer afford basic energy inputs. Furthermore, imports may become unreliable for noneconomic reasons: supplies may be cut off for political reasons, or shipping and transportation systems may be disrupted because of adverse weather, civil unrest, or war. A village that specializes in tea production instead of rice, for example, might suffer from food insecurity when rice supplies to the village are cut off. We have repeatedly observed this type of dynamic in many African and other countries (Figure 12-5).

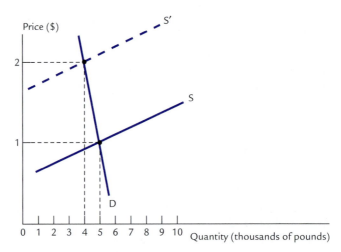

Figure 12-5 • The Market for Coffee
The demand for coffee D is inelastic, while supply fluctuates from S to S′ from one year to the next. The combination of inelastic demand and fluctuating supply results in large fluctuations in price, from $1 to $2 per pound (a 100 percent increase).

Exploitation

Finally, globalization has created opportunities for local and foreign companies to exploit local environments and local workers, including children, in the production of goods for export. This practice has especially been publicized in the garment and carpet industries. Most recently, the issue of "cocoa slavery" has arisen in the West African country of Côte d'Ivoire, where adults and children are in effect forced into slavery in the production of cocoa.

Slavery conditions have also been found, in the following order of prevalence (percent of population in slavery), in Mauritania, Haiti, Pakistan, India, Nepal, Moldova, Benin, Gabon, and Gambia; and in very high numbers in China, Russia, Congo, Bangladesh, and others. This slavery may take the form of human trafficking, debt bondage, forced marriage, kidnapping or sale of children, and others. Of course, poverty, war, and ignorance lie at the bottom of many of these problems, but many of us are also becoming aware of our role as consumers, when we purchase items produced in so-called sweatshops and slave conditions. Many of us seek out "fair trade" coffee, tea, fruit, and other products. Our buying decisions may indeed affect the practices of international companies.[2]

Exploitation has also been widely publicized in the carpet and garment industries. Children, for example, are often forced to use their small nimble fingers in looms producing carpets in parts of Asia. Garment factories have been notorious in their faulty construction and unsafe practices that have resulted in such highly publicized incidents as the horrific fire that killed 112 workers and the collapse of a group of factories that killed close to a thousand workers, both within 5 months of each other in 2012 and 2013, in Bangladesh. The factories in these examples produced clothing that was purchased by Wal-Mart in the first and possibly the second example and by other retailers. As we shall see in Chapter 13, Wal-Mart has since announced new practices intended to avoid these types of circumstances.

All of these issues suggest that poor nations must be very careful as they plan their development strategies. Comparative advantage ought to be an important element of such strategies, but attention must also be directed to proper diversification and processing of commodity exports because processed goods are less vulnerable to some of the problems that we've discussed. Issues of food security must also be addressed. Wealthier countries must ensure that trade is fair and that their own trade restrictions on poor countries are reduced. In addition, wealthy countries and companies must accept their share of responsibility when their policies and profits encourage environmental degradation and unjust labor conditions. You and I also play an important part in our role as consumers of internationally produced products.

Economics and Trade

What do U.S. agricultural policies have to do with trade, especially in terms of the developing world? As discussed in Chapter 11 on agriculture, the U.S. government subsidizes U.S. farmers and agribusinesses, enabling and encouraging them to produce large amounts of farm products, such as wheat, rice, corn, cotton, and tobacco. When these large supplies of agricultural products enter world markets, they force down global market prices, to the detriment of low-income developing country farmers. (You know the routine: an increase in supply causes a reduction in price.) Cotton is a case in point; it is a crop that can be produced more cheaply in countries such as India and Uganda, where land and farm labor are cheaper than in the United States. Yet, despite their cost advantage, farmers in these poorer countries cannot compete with the U.S. farmers and agribusinesses that remain profitable due to the generous subsidies of the U.S. government. Poor-country farmers become poorer despite having the comparative advantage in production. ("Cotton suicides" by cotton farmers in India provide one widely publicized example of the desperation faced by the rural poor when they can no longer provide for their families. Indian farmers literally drink their pesticides when they are squeezed between low prices they receive from their sales and high prices they pay for their inputs.)[3]

U.S. agricultural subsidies have become part of a heated controversy in the current round of international trade talks of the WTO, as we shall see momentarily. Clearly, the policies legislated by the United States on topics as significant as agriculture have the means of promoting or negating the development needs of the developing world.

Global Trade Agreements

General Agreement on Tariffs and Trade
An international trade agreement, first negotiated in 1947, with the goal of reducing trade barriers among member countries of the world. It is now replaced by the WTO.

Except for the problems we've just considered, economists generally view free trade as a win-win situation for all trading countries. This was evident in the **General Agreement on Tariffs and Trade (GATT)**, an international agreement that took effect just after WWII. GATT was replaced by the WTO in 1995. Several rounds of discussions took place within the context of GATT, including the Kennedy Round completed in 1967, the Tokyo Round completed in 1979, and the Uruguay Round completed in 1993. These rounds were remarkably successful in reducing tariff barriers among member countries of GATT. The average tariff on manufactured goods decreased from 40 percent in 1947 to 5 percent in 1992. More recently, however, under the guise of the WTO, the Doha Round has met with difficulty. Named after the city in Qatar first hosted, the Doha Round failed to resolve the insistence by developing countries that the developed countries reduce their agricultural subsidies before they themselves offer any conciliation. The developing countries have felt powerless to effect any change in what they perceive as "trade restrictions"; that is, developed country agricultural subsidies. The WTO, as the introduction to the chapter indicates, is still a source of controversy in the new millennium of globalization.

Group of Twenty (G-20)
A group of twenty developed and emerging countries (Argentina, Australia, Brazil, Canada, China, France, Germany, India, Indonesia, Italy, Japan, Mexico, Russia, Saudi Arabia, South Africa, South Korea, Turkey, the United Kingdom, the United States, and the European Union). Its goals are to support international trade, investment, and development.

In 1999, a group of countries called the **Group of twenty (G-20)**, a take-off on the **Group of eight (G-8)**, joined together. The G-20 includes the following countries: Argentina, Australia, Brazil, Canada, China, France, Germany, India, Indonesia, Italy, Japan, Mexico, Russia, Saudi Arabia, South Africa, South Korea, Turkey, the United Kingdom, the United States, and the European Union. The G-20 includes the countries in the G-8 as well as many countries that were left out of that group but are important to the world economy. Argentina, Brazil, and China, for example, have become quite industrialized and have significant roles in the areas of international trade and finance.

Group of twenty meetings also include representatives from the IMF and the World Bank. The 2014 meetings also invited Mauritania as the 2014 chair of the African Union, Myanmar as the 2014 chair of the Association of South-East Asian Nations (ASEAN), Senegal as the representative of the New Partnership for Africa's Development, and others. The organization represents two-thirds of the world's population, 85 percent of global GDP, and over 75 percent of world trade. It certainly has the potential to have significant effects on the global economy. The mandate of this organization is to promote discussion of key issues related to global economic and financial stability. Among other goals are its commitments to global trade, investment, and development.

Group of eight (G-8)
A group of the largest industrialized countries of Canada, France, Germany, Italy, Japan, Russia, the United Kingdom, and the United States. Its purpose is to foster free trade and stabilize international finance, though many view it as favoring the developed countries.

Despite ostentatious goals, the G-20 has not succeeded in greatly reducing trade restrictions. The World Bank reported in February 2009 that since the first meeting of the

G-20 in November 2008, 17 member countries of the G-20 had adopted 47 measures designed to restrict trade. Russia had raised tariffs on used cars. China had tightened import standards for food and prohibited Irish pork. India prohibited Chinese toys. Argentina tightened licensing requirements on auto parts, textiles, and leather goods. Many other countries, including the United States, began subsidizing troubled automakers or car dealers. While some of the arguments were based on environmental or consumer safety issues, others definitely went beyond the norm of fostering free trade.[4]

Regional Trade Agreements

There are other, regional groups that seek to foster trade among themselves. We'll consider just a few.

One of the more prominent is the **North American Free Trade Agreement (NAFTA)**. This agreement between the United States, Canada, and Mexico went into effect on January 1, 1994. NAFTA allows each of the three trading countries more equal access to one another's markets, along with reductions in trade restrictions. Congress passed the NAFTA Transitional Adjustment Assistance program to provide worker retraining and assistance to American workers displaced from jobs as a result of NAFTA. It also provided "retooling" assistance to U.S. companies harmed by the agreement, helping them move into more competitive industries. As we've already discovered, the United States benefits when importing a product from a country with lower labor costs. Indeed, most economists see benefits to all three of the countries. Nevertheless, there have been some concerns.

A major issue is that some of the lower production costs in Mexico are caused by unfair circumstances. Mexico has had less restrictive controls on pollution, minimum wages, child labor, and working conditions in its factories. To deal with these circumstances, so-called side agreements were added to NAFTA, whereby businesses in Mexico were required to comply with child labor laws and laws requiring environmental protection, minimum wages, and safe working conditions. Many people believe that these requirements were inadequate and widely ignored,[5] thereby harming the Mexican worker and the Mexican environment. Others are concerned that unfair production cost differentials between the United States and Mexico may be forcing U.S. firms to go out of business or to relocate in Mexico. Your parents will recall when Ross Perot, a former U.S. presidential candidate, once referred to the potential U.S. job loss associated with NAFTA as a "giant sucking sound."

In fact, economists believe that very few U.S. workers have become permanently unemployed and that others have found jobs in our export industries as a result of NAFTA. The Mexican share of U.S. imports did increase, but the Mexican share of U.S. exports increased as well. Ross Perot's "giant sucking sound" seems more like a moderate breath. Nevertheless, problems of pollution and poor working conditions continue in Mexico. These issues of sweatshop labor and environmental destruction are raised in protests against globalization.

The **European Union (EU)** is another regional trade association, though it goes far beyond efforts to expand trade among member countries. It also coordinates international finance and economic stability and growth among its members. One of the major recent achievements of the European Union was the adoption of a new common currency, called the **euro**.

In addition to these regional trade agreements, there have also been movements under way to expand NAFTA into a larger Free Trade Agreement of the Americas. Also, a new agreement that includes the United States, Mexico, Canada, Japan, Vietnam, Australia, Peru, and 5 other countries and titled the Trans-Pacific Partnership may be promising.

North American Free Trade Agreement (NAFTA)
An agreement between the United States, Canada, and Mexico allowing more equal access to one another's markets. The agreement went into effect on January 1, 1994.

European Union (EU)
The European Union includes 28 European countries, including many in Western and Eastern Europe. It fosters free trade, finance, stability, and growth among its members.

Euro
The common currency of the European Union.

Ideally, this agreement would place environmental protections and worker rights directly into the agreement itself, increasing the likelihood that they would be respected. There are a number of other world trade agreements as well, including Mercosur (a trade agreement between Argentina, Brazil, Paraguay, Uruguay, Venezuela, and newcomer Bolivia), the Andean Community (a group including Bolivia, Colombia, Ecuador, and Peru), the ASEAN (a group including Brunei, Cambodia, Indonesia, Laos, Malaysia, Myanmar, the Philippines, Singapore, Thailand, and Vietnam), and the Southern African Development Community (Angola, Botswana, Lesotho, Republic of Congo, Madagascar, Malawi, Mauritius, Mozambique, Namibia, Seychelles, South Africa, Swaziland, Tanzania, Zambia, and Zimbabwe). In addition, we've mentioned the African Union and the New Partnership for Africa's Development. Many economists believe that since developing countries often suffer under the policies of developed countries, they benefit by establishing their own regional trade organizations.

Politics and Trade

Although international trade is an economic issue, it has often become politicized. The United States became the victim of politics during the Arab Oil Embargo in 1973–1974 and the Iranian Oil Embargo of 1979. In each case, oil was cut off from the United States, causing an energy crisis in our nation.

Trade embargo

Restrictions on trade with another country for political reasons.

Sometimes, the United States restricts trade to bring about political goals. It commonly restricts trade with communist countries. Cuba is a case in point. In 1959, the Cuban revolution created a communist country headed by Fidel Castro, who confiscated certain U.S. property in Cuba. The United States responded in 1960 with a **trade embargo**, as well as subsequent policies to "punish" some of the countries that trade with Cuba. The embargo severely harmed the well-being of the Cuban nation and its people, at least initially. Many people in the United States are opposed to Cuba's dictatorial political system, and they charge the Castro government with violating the human rights of Cuban people. Many others feel that far from violating human rights, Cuba has provided high-quality health care and education to all of its residents, despite the poverty of the country. In the year 2000, the House of Representatives struck a deal to allow the sale of food and medicine to Cuba (under highly restricted conditions) for the first time in four decades. President Bill Clinton signed this bill a few months later. President Obama has stated his desire to reduce some of the restrictions between the United States and Cuba, and early in his administration he established policy that would permit Cuban-Americans to visit relatives in Cuba as often as they wish. Many Americans believe that the United States suffers more from the trade embargo than does Cuba. In early 2015, President Obama surprised the world with an announcement of improved relations with Cuba in a number of respects, including trade, travel, remittances, and placement of a U.S. embassy in Cuba. And, as this text goes to print, the world is anxiously waiting to see what changes may take place in the Cuban economy when the frail and elderly Fidel Castro passes away and his brother, newly appointed President Raul Castro, assumes total control over the country.

Efforts have also been under way in the United States to reduce politically motivated restrictions on trade with other countries. The same 2000 bill that reduced U.S. sanctions against Cuba reduced sanctions against four countries under embargo by the U.S. government: Iran, Sudan, Libya, and North Korea. In the case of North Korea, the embargo had been in effect since the early days of the Korean War in 1950. The new plan allows U.S. firms to sell goods, especially farm products, to North Korea and allows that nation to sell raw materials and finished goods to the United States. However, under the George W. Bush administration, the efforts to improve trade relations with many of these countries tapered off or halted entirely. New issues, in the form of weapons tests and uranium enrichment, have troubled U.S. relations with North Korea and Iran, and genocide in the Darfur region of western Sudan strained relations between the Sudanese government and the United States, as well as with other Western governments. Sudan's further conflicts with South Sudan have continued to strain its relations with the United States.

China and Vietnam are two countries whose trade relations with the United States have been improving. Both countries have socialist economies in partial transition toward capitalism. Vietnam, like Cuba, provides its entire population with health care and education. Yet, both Vietnam and China have communist political systems that are opposed by the United States. China has a long history of human rights violations, which angers many U.S. citizens and makes them hostile toward the easing of trade restrictions. Many feel that maintaining trade restrictions is the only leverage that the United States has for improving human rights in China. Others argue that only through normalized relations will improvements be generated. They argue that free trade would benefit both the United States and China.

Our relations with China took a turn during the economic and financial crisis. While the United States has for some time taken offense at China for our large trade deficit with the country, China has recently expressed concern about its huge financial investment in the United States. (The trade deficit is financed by Chinese financial investment. This will make more sense in the Appendix that follows.) The Chinese concern is *voiced* as a fear that the United States will not be able to make good on U.S. government bonds and other securities. Of course, that will not be the case. We will discuss government borrowing through the issuance of government bonds and other securities in Chapter 15.

The United Nations also has a history of enacting sanctions on various countries. Examples include the 1965 sanctions on Rhodesia's white minority government (now independent of this minority government and named Zimbabwe), the 1963 sanctions on the white minority government in South Africa due to its system of apartheid (separation of whites and blacks), the 1990 sanctions on Iraq for its invasion of Kuwait, and the 2010 sanctions on Iran for its nuclear proliferation.

Finally, a more recent example of politically motivated trade restrictions is the 2014 placement of sanctions on Russia for its intervention in Ukraine. The United States and the European Union dealt a blow to Russian efforts to develop future oil sources in the Arctic and elsewhere by barring Western companies from providing high technology for Russian deep water exploration. They also placed limits on American and European capital markets, making it more difficult for Russian banks to obtain long-term loans. Russia, of course, vowed to retaliate.

Those who believe in free trade believe that it will improve not only trade relations but also other relations between the United States and foreign countries. Opportunities for foreign investment may open up. In addition, travel restrictions may fade. Fewer restrictions on immigration may encourage greater inter-country mobility of workers, raising some issues addressed in Chapter 14 on unemployment. All of these topics arise in the debates and regular protests over globalization.

A Final Comment

When using economic theory, economists often implicitly make the assumption of free markets, even though free markets are rarely the case. This is true of the theory underlying comparative advantage and the gains from specialization and trade. In the real world, there may be severe impediments to free markets. For example, consider the coffee industry. Farmers in remote villages in Ethiopia may grow the best coffee beans in the world, but if their only option is to sell them is to a single buyer who periodically visits the village, they will be forced to accept any very low price that is offered. They have no alternative but to do so. The coffee beans are then sorted, washed, dried, bagged, and shipped to corporations such as those in the United States, where they are packaged, marketed, and sold at exorbitant prices due to the market power within the concentrated coffee market (market power is discussed in more detail in Chapter 13). The consumer pays a high price for coffee, while the impoverished grower receives next to nothing. The common assumption of free trade is often inappropriate.

You, the Student

There is a rapidly growing movement in support of "fair trade," where products are certified as fair trade and consumers are assured that the farmers receive fair prices for their products. This often works through farmer-owned cooperatives; and by cutting out many of the "middle men" and the profits of the corporations, consumers can buy a superior product at a reasonable price, knowing that the benefits of the sale will accrue to the poor farmer and his or her village. If you are interested in exploring this important means of alleviating world poverty, check out the Web site listed in the Discussion and Action Questions at the end of this chapter. You can also look around the town you live in (yes students, you should get to know your college town) and see if any vendors sell fair trade coffee, tea, chocolate, and other products. You can support them. You can also talk to your campus food service, and perhaps organize other students to join a petition, to encourage the food service to provide fair trade products. Many campuses provide as many fair trade products as is feasible.

View*Point*   Conservative versus Liberal

Historically, the lines have been drawn fairly clearly between traditional conservative and liberal views when it comes to the international economy, particularly in discussions of international trade. Economic conservatives within the United States have generally favored free trade. They have felt that free trade results in the efficiencies that arise in general from free markets. Economic liberals, on the other hand, have been concerned about the effects of free trade on U.S. workers and businesses. They have argued that government intervention in the form of quotas and tariffs is necessary to protect U.S. citizens from "unfair" trade practices in foreign countries. If, for example, foreign businesses keep labor costs artificially low by subjecting their workers to unsafe conditions or by avoiding any environmental controls, they have an unfair cost advantage relative to U.S. businesses. Labor in both the United States and the foreign country suffers and environmental destruction occurs.

The line between conservatives and liberals is no longer drawn so clearly. There appears to be much greater consensus that free trade will generally benefit the United States. NAFTA is a case in point. The Clinton administration lobbied hard for the passage of NAFTA, and the legislation received conservative and liberal support. Liberals are probably a bit more concerned about the effect of the trade agreement on U.S. labor and the environment than conservatives.

Development economists and policymakers have traditionally held the same types of views when it comes to the trade relations affecting poor countries. Liberals have been concerned about the effects of globalization on developing countries, including many of the economic justice issues that have been raised. Conservatives have traditionally focused more on the inefficiencies associated with trade restrictions. They have promoted freer markets for international trade. Liberals and conservatives have generally come together in their attention to market forces and the promotion of exports, and they have both come to realize the harm created by U.S. agricultural subsidies and trade restrictions on the people of developing countries.

SUMMARY

International trade and finance are becoming increasingly important for the United States, as well as for the rest of the world. Our imports provide important products for U.S. consumers, and our exports provide jobs for our workers. Residents of other countries around the globe benefit from trade in this manner as well. Indeed, as long as countries specialize along the lines of comparative advantage and exchange through trade, the world as a whole produces more output, providing higher total consumption levels for all trading countries.

The benefits of free trade are not equally distributed within a trading country. Although consumers and exporters gain from free trade, companies and workers displaced by imports lose. The plight of the latter parties triggers arguments for trade restrictions. Two common restrictions are quotas and tariffs, which both reduce the economic benefits

of trade. As an alternative to trade restrictions, governments might provide direct assistance to and retraining/retooling programs for displaced workers and companies.

The theory of specialization and exchange sometimes breaks down in practice, especially in the case of many poor countries. Among the problems that these countries frequently encounter is a lack of diversity of exports, reliance on primary commodities with unstable prices, declining terms of trade, overreliance on essential imports, food insecurity, and economic injustice.

Some trade issues are political, as well as economic, such as politically motivated trade embargoes. Yet, throughout the world, countries have been moving toward far-reaching regional trade agreements, including the NAFTA. This agreement and the WTO are aimed at reducing trade restrictions among member countries.

DISCUSSION AND ACTION QUESTIONS

1. How does international economics affect you directly as a consumer and as a future worker? How do international events and circumstances touch you as a student in a U.S. university or college?

2. Find out about the WTO by checking out its home page (http://www.wto.org). Click "The WTO" (in the menu that runs along the top of the page); then click "What is the WTO?" Check out the "10 benefits of the WTO trading system" and "10 common misunderstandings about the WTO."

3. Have you ever considered trying to become self-sufficient, producing for yourself all the things that you need and want? What would be the benefits of this attempt? What would be the drawbacks?

4. Look up information about the trade situation of some of the countries listed in Table 12-1 in the CIA *World Factbook* Web site (http://www.odci.gov/cia/publications/factbook). Select a country, then click the link to the economy, read the economy overview, and scroll to the trade statistics. Discover the major exports and imports of the country, along with its trading partners. Is the country in deficit or surplus? What is the effect of warfare in some of the countries? Are there any reasons that statistics may be underreported? Remember this CIA Web site because it will provide you a wealth of information about any specific country that you may research in the future.

5. What are some goods in which you think the United States has an absolute advantage in production? What about low-wage countries such as Thailand and

Pakistan? What about tropical countries such as Costa Rica and Cuba?

6. Based on the information in Table 12-2, and assuming a trade ratio of four DVDs for three pairs of shoes, what would the production possibilities curve (without trade) and the consumption possibilities curve (with trade) look like for Greenland? Does Greenland benefit from specialization and trade?

7. Suppose that the U.S. Congress passes trade restrictions on imports of French wine into the United States. What will be the effect of these restrictions on (a) U.S. consumers of wine, (b) U.S. producers of wine, (c) French producers of wine, (d) U.S. farmers producing agricultural goods for export, and (e) the United States as a whole?

8. Why do U.S. companies and workers within particular industries that are harmed by trade tend to have more political influence than the consumers who benefit from this trade? Do U.S. consumers have a good understanding of how they benefit from trade? Are they a cohesive political lobby?

9. Suppose a concentrated U.S. industry, such as the aluminum industry, is successful in getting trade restrictions on aluminum imports passed through Congress. Because these restrictions will reduce the foreign competition faced by the American aluminum industry, they will also enhance the market power of American firms within this industry. What then is a possible impact of the trade restrictions on U.S. employment within this concentrated industry?

10. What are some of the problems of international trade that are faced by developing countries? What suggestions

would you have for the government of a developing country as it plans its trade strategy?

11. Draw a graph of the market for a product, such as cocoa beans, assuming that the demand is inelastic (draw the demand curve relatively steep). Now draw in a supply curve that fluctuates from year to year (try to shift the supply curve forward and backward about the same distance as in Figure 12-5). Now repeat the exercise for *processed* cocoa, but assume that demand for this product *does not* have inelastic demand (draw the demand curve relatively flat). Shift the supply curve around in the same fashion as you did for cocoa beans. Is the price fluctuation larger or smaller in the second case? What does the answer tell us about developing country commodity exports for which demand generally is inelastic? What does it tell you about the effect of processing a commodity such as cocoa beans into a product such as cocoa?

12. Use a browser to search for sweatshop labor. Do you believe you've found an impartial source of information on sweatshop labor? What are some things that you as a consumer can do about sweatshop labor? For example, can you begin a campaign at your school to find out where the sweatshirts and T-shirts that carry your school's logo are manufactured? Can you find a Web site that organizes student responses to sweatshop conditions in the garment manufacturing companies involved in producing school clothing?

13. Read the home page of the Anti-Slavery organization (http://www.antislavery.org) to find information on the issue of cocoa slavery. What can you as a consumer do about cocoa slavery?

14. Use a browser to search for child labor. How extensive is the problem of child labor? How do you think child labor affects the child's daily life? How does it affect the child's future? What about the child's family? How can the use of child labor harm labor markets in both developing countries and the United States? What do you think of a global project that might provide food and even small amounts of money to the families of children who go to school (instead of the job market)? There is further discussion of student activism on behalf of ending child labor at the end of Chapter 14.

15. Are "fair trade" coffee and other products available in your community? Are they available on your campus? Would you be interested in checking out the "action guide" of the TransFair Web site at http://www.transfairusa.org/content/support/campus.php (or some similar organization, found by typing "fair trade coffee campus" on your browser) and beginning a local campaign to adopt fair trade products on your campus?

16. What benefits do you think the United States receives from the NAFTA? What problems do you think the United States experiences as a result of NAFTA? How do you think the United States can benefit from the economic growth of Mexico, which is an expected result of the agreement?

17. U.S. agricultural policy was discussed in this chapter and Chapter 11. As a result of what you've learned, are you interested in talking with others (including your legislators) about any concerns you may have about the effects of U.S. agricultural policies on the poor of the developing world?

18. (Refer to the Appendix to answer this question.) Why would Japanese residents demand U.S. dollars? Why would U.S. residents demand Japanese yen? Draw a graph of the market for the U.S. dollar relative to the Japanese yen. In August 2014, the exchange rate between the U.S. dollar and the Japanese yen was 102.04 yen per 1 U.S. dollar. This is from the same source as in footnote #6.

NOTES

1. Mark Landler, "As Trade Barriers Rise as Slump tightens Grip," The St. Paul Pioneer Press, 3-23-09.

2. More information on sweatshop labor and slavery in the cocoa trade may be found on the Web site of CorpWatch (http://www.corpwatch.org), an educational and activist organization that seeks to "foster democratic control" over global corporations, especially in the areas of human rights, labor rights, and environmental justice. You can also search on-line for the Walk Free Foundation, an anti-slavery organization that published some of the information on slavery that is found in the text.

3. Indian farmers literally drink their pesticides when they are squeezed between low prices they receive from their sales and the high prices they pay for their inputs.

4. Mark Landler, "As Trade Barriers Rise as Slump tightens Grip," The St. Paul Pioneer Press, 3-23-09.

5. Jacqueline Brux, "Neo-Liberalism in Mexico," 2000. Available from author.

6. The exchange rate between the U.S. dollar and the Mexican peso was 1 U.S. dollar per 13.16 Mexican pesos in August 2014, www.x-rates.com/table/.

7. There is one additional reason why residents of many countries wish to acquire U.S. dollars. This is because the dollar is a relatively stable currency, whereas the currencies of many other countries fluctuate. People who fear the decline in the value of their own currency may acquire (demand) dollars in order to protect against this risk.

Appendix 12-1

International Finance

When residents of two countries engage in trade or when they transfer funds for other purposes, they must deal with the matter of foreign currency. If a product is worth $500 in U.S. currency, how much is it worth in terms of Mexican pesos? If I wish to invest my $1,000 in a Japanese company, how many yen does this amount represent? To answer these questions, we need to understand the concept of exchange rates and how these rates are determined. This is not as difficult as you might think, since you understand demand and supply!

Exchange Rate Determination

An **exchange rate** is simply the price of one country's currency in terms of another country's currency. We can say, for example, that 1 U.S. dollar is worth about 13.16 Mexican pesos. This is the exchange rate between dollars and pesos. Alternatively, we can say that 1 Mexican peso is worth about $0.08 (8 U.S. cents). (This exchange rate is calculated by taking the equation $1 = 13.16 pesos, and dividing each side by 13.16. We end up with $1/13.16 = 13.16 pesos/13.16; or $0.08 = 1 peso.) The two expressions are identical: we can talk in terms of 13.16 pesos per dollar or 7 cents per peso. Note, however, that an exchange rate always expresses the value of one currency in terms of another. There is no such thing as an absolute value for a currency; exchange rates are always relative.[6]

Most of the industrialized world uses a **flexible (floating) exchange rate system**, in effect since 1973. Under this system, exchange rates are determined on the basis of demand and supply. Using simple techniques with which you are already familiar, we can see how the exchange rate between the dollar and peso is determined.

To simplify matters, pretend that there are only two countries in the world, the United States and Mexico. This oversimplification enables us to use a graph and does not detract from the analysis. Let's consider the market for the dollar and determine the value of the dollar in terms of the Mexican peso. This market is portrayed in Figure 12-6 on page 310.

Note the demand curve D is the demand for dollars by Mexico's residents. (Remember that there are only two countries in the world.) Why would Mexico's residents demand dollars? There are a number of reasons. An obvious one is that Mexican people may wish to travel in the United States. They will need to pay their hotel bill and taxi fare in dollars; hence, they first need to exchange their pesos for dollars. This process of acquiring dollars represents a demand for dollars.

There are more important reasons for demanding dollars, however. Suppose a Mexican resident wishes to purchase a General Motors car. GM wants to be paid in dollars.

Exchange rate
The price of one country's currency in terms of another country's currency.

Flexible (floating) exchange rate system
A system whereby exchange rates are determined on the basis of international demand and supply for a currency.

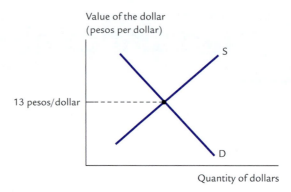

Figure 12-6 • The Market for the U.S. Dollar
The demand curve D represents the demand for U.S. dollars by Mexican residents. The supply curve S represents the supply of U.S. dollars by U.S. residents, which is synonymous with the demand for Mexican pesos by U.S. citizens. The intersection determines the equilibrium price, or exchange rate, between the U.S. dollar and the Mexican peso. This exchange rate is 13 pesos per dollar.

© Cengage Learning

Although the Mexican customer won't need to come up with dollars, the Mexican company that imports the GM vehicle into Mexico will. The process of exchanging pesos in order to acquire dollars with which to purchase the vehicle represents a demand for dollars. Suppose another Mexican resident wishes to invest her savings in a U.S. financial market, perhaps by purchasing a U.S. government or corporate bond. She will have to first acquire dollars with which to pay for the bond; this transaction also represents a demand for dollars. Suppose a Mexican company wishes to buy and operate a plant in the United States. The owner will have to purchase the plant and pay the workers with dollars, thereby first exchanging pesos for dollars. This transaction again represents a demand for dollars. **Although there are other reasons to acquire (demand) dollars, these are four important ones: to travel in the United States, to purchase U.S. goods and services, to invest in U.S. financial markets, and to buy and operate plants in the United States.**[7]

Now consider the supply curve S in Figure 12-6. This curve represents the supply of U.S. dollars by American residents. Why would U.S. citizens wish to supply dollars? The answer to this question is very easy if we recognize that the process of U.S. residents supplying dollars is the same as the process of U.S. residents demanding pesos. **In a two-country world, our process of acquiring one currency is the same as our process of supplying the other: we exchange our dollars for pesos.** Consequently, the supply of U.S. dollars by U.S. residents can be simultaneously viewed as the demand for Mexican pesos by U.S. residents.

Why do U.S. residents demand pesos? For the same reasons that Mexican residents demand dollars! Many of us wish to travel to Mexico City, or purchase Mexican clothing, or invest in the Mexican stock market. Many of our companies want to buy and operate plants in Mexico. All these desires create a U.S. demand for Mexican pesos. And this makes our picture complete. We have a demand for dollars and a supply of dollars (demand for pesos). The intersection of the demand and supply of U.S. dollars determines the equilibrium exchange rate between the dollar and peso. This intersection occurs at the exchange rate of about 13 pesos per U.S. dollar in Figure 12-6.

We can extend this analysis by recognizing that either the demand or supply curve of Figure 12-6 can shift in response to changing economic conditions. The demand for U.S. dollars by Mexico's residents will increase if Mexican incomes increase. This is because higher incomes permit Mexican people to buy more U.S. goods and invest in more U.S. financial markets. This outcome is demonstrated in Figure 12-7. Note that the equilibrium exchange rate will change to 14 pesos per dollar, representing an increase in the value of the dollar relative to the peso (just what we would expect when the demand for dollars increases). Another way of saying this is that the dollar has **appreciated** (increased in value) relative to the peso. Because the value of one currency is always expressed relative to the other, we can also say that the peso has **depreciated** (decreased in value) relative to the dollar.

Is a higher value of the dollar good or bad? You may be used to this answer by now: it depends! In particular, it depends on who you are. For a U.S. consumer of Mexican clothing imported into the United States, a high dollar is good. It means that the peso is low, so that fewer dollars are needed to pay for the clothing denominated in pesos. That is, Mexican products become cheaper for the U.S. consumer. On the other hand, a high dollar is not so good for a U.S. exporter. When the dollar is high, more pesos are needed to pay for U.S. products denominated in dollars. That is, U.S. products have become more expensive for Mexican residents, who may now reduce their purchases somewhat. U.S. exports may fall.

Appreciate
The value of one country's currency increases relative to another country's currency.

Depreciate
The value of one country's currency decreases relative to another country's currency.

Economic Policy

Economic policy in the United States (or any other country) can have an impact on exchange rates. Recall the earlier discussion of U.S. trade restrictions imposed on imports of cotton cloth. These restrictions reduce U.S. purchases of foreign cotton cloth. If our purchases of foreign cloth decline, so too does our demand for foreign currency with which to pay for the cloth. As our demand for a foreign currency falls, the value of that currency decreases (and the relative value of the dollar increases). A rising value of the dollar makes our exports more expensive to foreign consumers, who will likely purchase fewer of them. *Now we see the harm to U.S. producers of export goods when we impose trade restrictions designed to protect our cotton cloth industry. We may help one sector of the U.S. economy, but hurt another.*

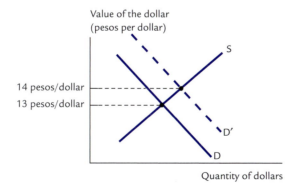

Figure 12-7 • A Shift in the Demand for U.S. Dollars
Increased advertising of U.S. products in Mexico will probably increase the demand for U.S. products by Mexican residents. This will cause Mexican residents to increase their demand for U.S. dollars with which to pay for the U.S. products, causing the demand for dollars to increase from D to D'. The new equilibrium exchange rate is 14 pesos per U.S. dollar.

© Cengage Learning

Consider another example of economic policy. Suppose U.S. policymakers decide to raise interest rates. A rise in U.S. interest rates relative to interest rates in other countries of the world means that U.S. financial markets now become more attractive to foreign investors. Why should a Norwegian citizen deposit her savings in a Norwegian financial institution when she can receive higher interest earnings by depositing her savings in a U.S. financial institution? Of course, she would first have to exchange her Norwegian Kroners for U.S. dollars (thereby creating a demand for dollars). This increase in the demand for dollars with which to make the deposit pushes up the value of the U.S. dollar. **Indeed, one of the most important factors affecting the value of a currency is the relative interest rate in different countries.**

By the way, the economic and financial crisis in the United States certainly had its impacts on international finance. We've already noted that foreigners who invested in U.S. mortgage-backed securities suffered when many U.S. mortgage repayments became unlikely and the value of both these mortgages and mortgage-backed securities fell. This brought the international community together in an effort to limit the rippling effects of what was now a global economic and financial crisis, as we will see in the following section.

International Management of Exchange Rates

Although much of the industrialized world uses flexible (floating) exchange rates, the real-world system is not based entirely on the market forces of demand and supply. Individual countries may intervene, buying and selling currencies, to influence exchange rates. This action is sometimes referred to as a "dirty float." Since 1986, an entire group of countries has coordinated their policies in an effort to influence exchange rates. These countries have already been referred to as the **Group of Eight (G-8).** A major goal of G-8 is to stabilize exchange rates of major world currencies within an acceptable range of one another. It is felt that all member countries benefit from greater stability among these rates. Other countries have joined associations that manage and stabilize their exchange rates.

Part IV

Efficiency and Stability Issues

© Konstantin L / Shutterstock.com

Chapter 13

ROAD MAP

Chapter 1
Introduction
The pure competition assumed in the tutoring example contrasts with the market power discussed in Chapter 13

Chapter 10
World Poverty
Higher prices due to market power contribute to declining terms of trade and international debt problems in developing countries

Chapter 11
Global Agriculture
Concentration is increasing in the agricultural sector

Chapter 13
Market Power

Chapter 12
International Trade
Imports decrease domestic market power. As European markets become more free, U.S. antitrust agencies will cooperate more with their European counterparts

Chapter 15
Government Macroeconomic Policy
Failures in the concentrated U.S. auto industry contributed to recent U.S. recession and the fiscal stimulus included efforts to aid this industry

The Economic Toolbox

- Market power
- Competition
- Barriers to entry
- Price taker
- Monopoly
- Price maker
- Oligopoly
- Concentration ratio
- Economies of scale
- Natural monopoly
- Product differentiation
- Collusion
- Cartel
- Price leadership
- Price discrimination
- Antitrust
- Declining terms of trade
- Elasticity of demand (appendix)

Market Power

The statements above suggest that businesses and their practices that subvert the free market harm U.S. consumers. Certainly we have gone through a period where one must have had one's head in the sand to be ignorant of the excesses, failures, and frauds perpetrated by our nation's largest financial and other corporations, as well as the failures of government regulation and control, that led to the financial crisis of 2007–2008 and subsequent global recession. President Obama's assistant attorney general for antitrust makes it clear that he intends to reverse the sideline behavior of the antitrust division that contributed to this crisis. What does this all mean to you?

What are the implications of the bailouts, takeovers, and bankruptcies of the last decade? Do you ever worry about the effects of powerful firms? Have you ever written to your senator about the high price of automobiles? Have you ever questioned how the electric company is regulated? Have you ever wondered whether Microsoft has monopolized portions of the computer industry? Have you ever demonstrated against additional fees you've had to pay when you buy tickets for a rock concert?

A good guess is that you have not. Perhaps you haven't realized that the way markets are structured has serious implications for prices, output levels, employment, efficiency, income distribution, and political influence. Much of the American public seems uninterested in, or at least unaware of, the effects of market power in the United States. Some people naively assume that because we have antitrust laws and economic regulation of some monopolies, we do not have a problem. Others argue that regulation decreases business efficiency and it should therefore be eliminated. Others are simply uninterested—long-term consumer Ralph Nader had once noted that the general public views antitrust matters as "too complex, too abstract, and supremely dull."

We have just gone through a period where the excesses of big business have come to the fore. Although "big" doesn't necessarily equate with "market power," several of the corporations that have required government intervention do indeed have considerable market power, including those in the automobile industry and the financial industry. We've reached a point where considerable government intervention has been undertaken to prevent the 2007–2008 financial crisis from exploding, including government takeover of the government-sponsored enterprises Fannie Mae and Freddy Mac, which invest in mortgages and mortgage-backed securities. (This is discussed in more detail in Chapter 7 on housing.) The government has also bailed out financial corporations Goldman Sachs,

There is no more important work we do. Those who conspire to subvert the free market system and injure U.S. consumers are prosecuted vigorously and penalized –appropriately... Our successful efforts to detect and prosecute cartels also reflect the broad consensus in the United States that schemes to deny consumers the benefits of competition have no place in the free market and merit significant punishment.

—BILL BAER, ASSISTANT ATTORNEY GENERAL, ANTITRUST DIVISION, U.S. DEPARTMENT OF JUSTICE, SEPTEMBER 10, 2014.

Morgan Stanley, American Investment Group (AIG), and Citigroup and automobile companies Chrysler and General Motors (GM). Major companies, such as Chrysler, GM, and Lehman Brothers, went bankrupt. Many of these large firms have had little or no regulation, and this raises the issue of what types of government regulations and intervention are now appropriate for the future well-being of our economy.

In this chapter, we will look at the effects of market power on the American economy. The implications for consumers are significant. We can consider these in a way that is neither complex and abstract, nor dull! To gain an understanding of the problem of market power, you must first learn something about three market structures: competition, monopoly, and oligopoly.

Competition

Recall that the markets in Chapter 1 were described as competitive. Because there were many small buyers and sellers, no one producer could influence the "going market price" of its product. Another way of saying this is that no individual supplier had any **market power**. The examples suggested that if one tutor out of many identical tutors decided to charge an exorbitant price, consumers would simply buy the services of other competing suppliers. Thus, competition protected consumers from potentially unreasonable prices.

A market structure in which the seller cannot influence price is what economists call **competition**. A competitive market has three characteristics:

1. Many small buyers and sellers
2. A standardized product
3. No barriers to entry or exit

Let's consider each of these characteristics separately. As we've just noted, the first characteristic has bearing on the going market price. Because many small buyers constitute the total demand in the market, no individual buyer is powerful enough to extract a lower price on the product. Because so many small firms are selling the product, no one supplier can charge a higher price for the product. If it has occurred to you that the terms *small buyers* and *small sellers* are not very specific, you are correct. Firms can be large in absolute terms and do many million dollars of business annually, but by perfect competition, we mean they are small relative to the entire market. Agricultural markets are often viewed as competitive. We have many small suppliers of corn, for example. Even the largest corn producer in the country produces only a very small share of the entire supply of corn in the country.

Second, in a competitive market, the products of all producers are standardized or roughly identical. Most agricultural products, if we carefully specify the grade, are standardized. So are the markets for standard-sized rubber bands, pencils, and floppy disks. See if you can think of other standardized products. The importance of this standardization is that the buyer will not care which seller she buys from, because the products are roughly the same. Therefore, she will not be willing to pay a higher price for one firm's product since that firm's product is no better than any other firm's product.

Third, a competitive market has no barriers to entry. A **barrier to entry** is some condition that makes it difficult or expensive for a new producer to enter the market. Perhaps start-up costs are so huge that a great deal of capital must be raised before a new firm begins operations. Or the government may require a firm to obtain a license before it can sell its goods or services. Or the products of existing firms may be protected by patents, so that production of a similar product carries the risk of a patent infringement

Market power
The ability of an individual firm to influence the market price of its product.

Competition
A market in which many small producers sell a standardized product to many small buyers.

Barrier to entry
A market characteristic that prevents new firms from entering the market.

lawsuit. These barriers to entry are not present in a competitive market. If they were present, there would not be "many small sellers."

An important implication of these characteristics is that the competitive firm will be a **price taker**. That is, it will take the market price as given and will not (by itself) have any influence over this market price. Any level of output that it could possibly produce is too small to affect the market price. Consider Figure 13-1, which shows the market for fresh fish offered for sale in one week by fishing boat operators in a northwestern U.S. port.

The market price of $120 per hundredweight (100 pounds) is established by the interaction of total market demand and supply. At this price, 7,000 hundredweight of fish will be sold in the port's commercial fish market. Let's assume that Mr. Diaz can offer for sale any quantity between 0 and 50 hundredweight this week, but any of these quantities is too small to influence the market price. Even if he doubled his output from 25 to 50 hundredweight, or if he reduced his output to 0, his behavior would have no real effect on the market supply of fish. Therefore, Mr. Diaz offers his desired quantity of fish to the market and charges the market price of $120 per hundredweight. He takes this market price as given.

Why doesn't Mr. Diaz charge a price higher than $120? The answer is simple. If he does, his customers will buy from other producers. His fish are no different from fish caught by other fishing boat captains. If he tries to get a higher price, he will lose all his business.

Perhaps Mr. Diaz believes that if he lowers his price, he can sell more fish and increase his revenue. However, he is pretty much guaranteed that he can sell all of his fish at the going market price, so that lowering the price would merely reduce his revenue. (The intersection of market demand and supply means that quantity demanded will equal quantity supplied at the market price.)

The competitive market price is a reasonable one; the market demand curve reflects the value of fish to all the buyers in the market, and the market supply curve reflects the costs of production incurred by producers in this market. (Recall from Chapter 1 that cost of production is one of the most important factors that influence supply.) Mr. Diaz (and all other fish suppliers in this market) will be prohibited from

Price taker
A firm that is unable to influence the market price of its product.

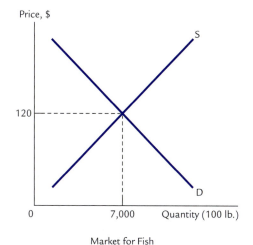

Figure 13-1 • A Competitive Market for Fresh Fish
The competitive market determines the price per unit of fish. Equilibrium price is $120 per unit (hundredweight), and equilibrium quantity is 7,000 units.

© Cengage Learning®

charging a price higher than the market price. This is not a legal or even a spoken prohibition; it is just the way that competition works to assure that consumers are not charged exorbitant prices. This outcome is one of the great advantages of competitive markets.

Monopoly and Oligopoly

Monopoly

A market in which only one firm produces a product with no close substitutes.

Monopolist

The single firm in a monopoly market.

Price maker

A firm that is able to influence the market price of its product.

The opposite of a competitive market is a monopoly. A **monopoly** is a market with only one seller of the product. We can also refer to this single seller as a **monopolist**. The product produced by the monopolist has no close substitutes, so if buyers want the product, they have no choice but to buy it from the monopolist. The monopolist is not a price taker but a **price maker**. Another way of saying this is that the monopolist has market power. Again, market power is defined as the ability of an individual firm to influence the market price of its product. This ability does not mean that the firm will simply set the highest possible price; it means that the firm can raise its price by decreasing the quantity that it supplies. Unlike the competitive firm (which accepts the market price as given), the monopolist knows that its output level will help determine its price. The monopolist faces the entire downward-sloping market demand curve (since it is the only supplier in the market). When it offers for sale a particular quantity, it is establishing where along the market demand curve the market equilibrium quantity is located. This simultaneously establishes the market price.

Consider Figure 13-2, which shows a market demand for cable TV service. The price is the monthly fee for basic cable services, and the quantities are the numbers of subscribers in the area in the month. Only one cable supplier provides service in the area. Note that if the cable TV company sells 25,000 units, it can get a price of $15, but if it decides to sell only 20,000 units, it can charge a price of $20. The way that the firm influences its price is by controlling its quantity. By selling fewer units, it can charge a significantly higher price for those units that it does sell. Also note that its revenue will be greater if it

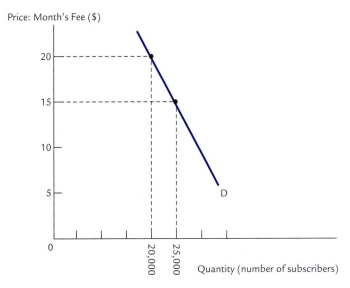

Figure 13-2 • Cable TV Demand
Because the cable TV company's demand curve is downward sloping, the company simultaneously establishes a price when it supplies a certain quantity. By reducing its output to 20,000 units, it can increase its revenue.

© Cengage Learning®

sells only 20,000 units. A firm's total revenue is always the product price times the quantity sold. If the cable TV company sells 20,000 units at $20 each, its revenue will be $400,000. But if it sells 25,000 units at $15, its revenue will be only $375,000. (For more information about the elasticity conditions that are necessary for the monopolist to reduce output and increase revenue, please see the Appendix to this chapter.)

When a monopoly dominates the market, the competitive supply curve based on the costs of production of many small producers simply no longer exists. Instead, the monopolist will choose to supply a lesser amount of the product to get a higher price and receive a larger profit. **So, compared with a competitive market, a monopoly with the same production costs will charge a higher price, produce a smaller quantity, and receive higher revenue and profits than would competitive producers. As a consequence of producing smaller quantities, they will also employ fewer workers**. Keep in mind that while the monopolist controls its supply, it does not control its demand. The demand curve faced by the monopoly firm is controlled by consumers of the product.

The United States has few true monopolies. As competition develops, such as satellite television, monopoly fades (though significant market power may still exist). Most of the monopolies that do exist are regulated by some government agency (we will look at the controversy over regulation later). Historic examples are long-distance phone service and the post office. AT&T once was a monopoly supplier of long-distance phone service until the government broke up this monopoly and more providers of long-distance phone service entered the scene. Similarly, the U.S. Postal System was once a monopoly supplier of letter delivery. (United Parcel Service, or UPS, delivered only packages.) Now, suppliers of letter delivery include UPS, Federal Express, and other companies. In addition to these, local areas often have monopoly suppliers of services to the locality. These might include the provision of electricity, water, sewage, garbage pickup, bus service, and others. At least at the local level, these would be considered monopolies. To exist as a monopoly requires that there be some force, such as government regulation, that effectively keeps other firms from entering the market. To summarize, let's note that a monopoly has the following characteristics:

1. It is a single firm.
2. It offers for sale a unique product with no close substitutes.
3. Its market has strong barriers to entry.

In addition to these limited numbers of monopolies, our nation faces market power in another type of market structure, referred to as **oligopoly**. An oligopoly is a market in which only a few large firms dominate the market. The individual firms in these markets are referred to as **oligopolists**. These firms produce a large enough share of the total market supply of their product so that each of these large firms can influence the market price. When we speak of the "big three" automobile companies, or the "big four" ready-to-eat cereal companies, or the "big five investment banks," we are referring to oligopolies. All of these companies have market power. In addition, if oligopoly firms agree to get together and cooperate on their output levels, they can set a price as high as if they were a monopoly.

Oligopoly
A market in which only a few large firms dominate.

Oligopolists
Individual firms in an oligopoly market.

Measuring Concentration

One of the best ways to assess market power is to measure the level of concentration within a particular market. When there are only a few relatively large firms in a market, we say that the market is concentrated. Concentration implies the existence of market power. We often measure concentration by means of the **concentration ratio**, which is

Concentration ratio
The percentage of output produced by the four largest firms in an industry.

usually defined as the percentage of output produced by the four largest firms in the industry. **The higher the concentration ratio, the greater is the concentration in the industry**. If there are four or fewer firms in the industry, the concentration ratio will be 100. That is, the four largest firms produce 100 percent of the output. If the industry contains many small firms, the concentration ratio will be very low. A concentration ratio of 10 would mean that the four largest firms produce only 10 percent of the output and that the industry probably contains many competing firms. The U.S. government calculates concentration ratios every five years, and releases them with a lag. The most recent statistics were calculated for 2007, and revised in 2013. Table 13-1 shows the concentration ratios for a number of U.S. industries.

Many economists consider a concentration ratio of 80 to 100 to represent very high concentration. Examples include cigarettes, breweries, and breakfast cereals. Industries with concentration ratios between 50 and 80 would represent oligopoly with significant market power and would include automobiles and ammunitions. A concentration ratio of 40 or less would indicate less market power. However, when using concentration ratios, we must be careful. Although they are useful indicators of possible market power, they are not perfect measures of market power. Some cautions are therefore in order.

First, concentration ratios are based only on domestic (U.S.) production and exclude foreign competition. Some industries face significant competition from imports. The American automobile industry is a case in point. Although there are only three major domestic car manufacturers, imports make up a large share of U.S. auto sales. American automobile markets are therefore more competitive than the concentration ratio of 71 implies. As U.S. industries face increasingly more global competition, U.S. concentration ratios tend to overstate their market power.

Second, the concentration ratios in Table 13-1 are calculated for the entire nation, yet many markets are in fact local or regional. Take quick printing for example. The national concentration ratio of 4 is very low, indicating very little market power. However, if we look at a local market, such as your college town, there may be only one or two quick

TABLE 13-1 • Concentration Ratios for Selected Manufacturing Industries, Four Largest Companies, 2013[a]

Industry	Concentration Ratio
Cigarettes	98
Breweries	90
Breakfast cereal manufacturing	85
Ammunitions (except small arms) manufacturing	79
Dog and cat food	78
Bottled water manufacturing	76
Auto manufacturing	71
Chocolate manufacturing from cocoa beans	66
Sugar manufacturing	52
Dairy	30
Frozen food	29
Food	13
Quick printing	4
Retail bakeries	3

[a]2007, as revised in 2013.

Source: www.census.gov/eped/www/concentration.

printing facilities. Market power is considerable. The problem is more significant with other products, such as newspapers. Even if market power at the national level is very low for newspapers, most cities have only one or two local newspapers. These smaller newspapers may have significantly more market power on the local market than the concentration ratio suggests, especially in shaping opinions about current issues.

These problems do not mean that concentration ratios are useless as approximations of market power. They do mean, however, that concentration ratios are not perfect measures of market power. They should be used carefully and adjusted when necessary to conform to the realities of the market. At the same time, keep in mind that a more broadly defined product (such as food, with a concentration ratio of 13) will have less concentration than a narrowly defined product (such as dairy or frozen foods, with concentration ratios of 30 and 29, respectively). This is because many businesses produce food, and there are no real substitutes, but fewer businesses produce dairy or frozen foods.

Barriers to Entry

The principal reason that some markets are dominated by only a few large firms is that there are barriers to entry into these markets, just as there are in the case of monopoly. New firms therefore find it difficult, if not impossible, to begin operations. Barriers to entry are the source of the existing firms' market power and the reason that concentrated markets remain concentrated year after year.

Let's consider seven of the most commonly encountered barriers to entry.

Economies of Scale

First, some markets are characterized by **economies of scale**. This means that a large amount of the product can be produced at a lower cost per unit than a small amount of the product. For example, a bakery may be able to produce 100 loaves of bread at a cost of $1 per loaf, or 1,000 loaves of bread at a cost of $0.50 per loaf. Economies of scale arise from the technology used in manufacturing the product, as well as the organization of labor and any discounts that a producer may receive on large purchases of inputs. In the case of the bakery, perhaps the company can purchase 100-pound bags of flour (when producing large quantities of bread) at a much lower price per pound than if it purchases only 10-pound bags of flour (sufficient for producing the small quantities of bread). Similarly, the bakery may organize its workers into an assembly-line production process which is more efficient than having each worker produce entire loaves of bread, but which is only feasible for large quantities of bread. For example, a bakery producing large quantities of bread may have one worker mix the dough, another worker bake the bread, and another worker slice and package the loaf. The smaller bakery may be unable to efficiently use more than one worker at a time.

Although the bakery demonstrates the idea of economies of scale, the issue really becomes quite significant when we consider industries such as automobiles, steel, aluminum, or aircraft. An automaker may be able to keep the cost of producing each car relatively low only if it produces on a very large scale. The cost of producing each car may be extremely high if the company produces relatively few cars. In this type of market, it is impossible to start small and grow. If a new firm enters the market and produces a small number of cars, it will not be able to compete with established large firms that are already producing large numbers of cars. Starting small eventually leads to failure, not growth. This lesson was learned by a number of firms that have tried to enter the automobile industry during the past 45 years. Consider the entry of the Bricklin and the DeLorean into the sports-car market. Although both were exciting vehicles, their

Economies of scale
A situation whereby a large amount of a product can be produced at a lower cost per unit than a small amount of the product.

producers eventually failed because they could not match the low per-unit costs of the comparable cars produced by established firms.

Exclusive Franchises

Natural monopoly
A market with significant economies of scale.

A second barrier to entry occurs when the government becomes involved and permits a single firm to monopolize the market. This is often the case when there is a **natural monopoly**, which occurs when economies of scale are extensive. In these circumstances, the government may step in and issue an exclusive franchise to one producer. An **exclusive franchise** gives the firm the sole right to conduct business in a particular geographic area. Because the exclusive franchise is granted to the firm, the firm is usually regulated by an agency of the government to ensure that consumers receive some of the benefits of large-scale production. Examples of regulated natural monopolies are your local natural gas company and electric company. If economies of scale are truly significant in these markets, the granting of an exclusive franchise simply recognizes the inevitable. The market will be concentrated with or without the government's action, but at least regulation will help protect the consumer. However, the exclusive franchise acts as a barrier to entry into the market, because new firms cannot legally enter the market. A problem arises when natural monopoly-type regulation is imposed on sectors that are potentially competitive. In this situation, regulation is the source of monopoly power within the industry, and the outcome is much inferior to that in a competitive market.

Exclusive franchise
Permission by the government (often a local government) for a monopoly firm to exist. (It is normally accompanied by government regulation.)

Control of Essential Raw Materials

Third, a firm's control of essential raw materials to manufacture a product will serve as a barrier to entry into the market because new firms will not be able to obtain the raw materials to begin operations. Consider, for example, the aluminum industry. The essential ingredient in the production of aluminum is bauxite. When aluminum was first produced, the Aluminum Company of America (Alcoa) cornered the market on bauxite and for many years had a monopoly on the production of aluminum.

Patents

Patents
A government grant of exclusive rights to use or sell a new technology or product for a period of time.

Fourth, some products are protected by patents, which serve as barriers to entry. **Patents** are limited-term monopoly grants from the government to the inventor of the product. Our government gives patents for new products and new processes to encourage innovation and invention. After all, firms incur costs in developing new products. If a firm is not guaranteed the benefit of its new invention because its competitors begin selling the new product shortly after it does, how can we expect the firm to put money into research and development? When a firm has a patent on a product, it can protect itself by bringing a patent infringement suit against any new firm that tries to produce a similar product. Although patents do encourage invention, they also encourage the development of market power in three respects: (1) The holder of the patent will be the sole producer of the product for many years. The patent will enable the firm to establish itself in the minds of consumers as the pre-eminent seller of the product, giving the firm a competitive advantage even after the patent has expired and other firms can legally begin production of the product. (2) Patents can be misused. Established firms sometimes "blanket" the patent by seeking and obtaining patents that they have no intention of using. In other words, they obtain patents on many more variants of the product than they will actually produce simply to prevent other firms from producing a similar product. Only about one-half of the patents granted are actually used. (3) The common practice of aggressively defending patents with patent infringement lawsuits discourages would-be competitors from producing close substitutes.

Product Differentiation

Fifth, products are frequently differentiated, and product differentiation acts as a barrier to the entry of new firms. **Product differentiation** is any characteristic that makes the product of one firm different from another firm in the eyes of the buyer. The difference may be real (style, quality, color, or taste) or it may be entirely artificial (created solely by labeling and advertising). A good example of a differentiated product is household laundry bleach, which is simply a solution of sodium hypochlorite. Despite the uniformity of the product, Clorox has dominated the bleach market for many years, commanding a higher price than other brands because many consumers are convinced that Clorox is a better product than the other brands on the market. Product differentiation acts as a barrier to entry because new firms must spend a great deal of money on advertising their product in an effort to compete against the established brand name of the firm already in the market. The expenditures are too high for a business firm just starting up production of the product. Some differentiated products are film, breakfast cereals, and automobiles.

Product differentiation
The creation of the image that one firm's product is different from or somehow superior to other similar products.

Licensing

Sixth, the government requires new entrants to obtain a **license** before beginning operation in many professions and trades. We license doctors, dentists, lawyers, beauticians, barbers, and undertakers, among others. The reason for licensing is fairly obvious. We accompany the granting of the license with the passing of an examination to ensure some minimum level of competency. But licensing also restricts entry into fields.

License
A permit to operate in a trade or profession.

Behavior of Established Firms

Seventh, the actions of established firms can also deter entry into the market. For example, these firms may occasionally lower the prices for their products so that new firms wanting to enter the market would have to match these low prices in order to compete with the existing firms. Although the established firms can afford temporarily low profits arising from the price cuts, newer entrants into the industry cannot. This type of price-cutting by established firms can drive new firms out of business or prevent firms from entering the industry in the first place.

A good example of this type of behavior comes from the cigarette industry, which was dominated by three large firms back in the 1930s. These firms sold established brands of cigarettes nationally and accounted for about 90 percent of cigarette sales. Many small local tobacco companies sold only in limited geographic regions. When one of the small firms would increase its sales, the big three would retaliate by introducing "fighting brands," which were off-label cigarettes sold at below cost. A market with a history of such predatory competition is not an attractive market for new firms to enter. Can you think of other examples in which firms temporarily lower their prices in order to drive out or prevent competition? (For example, have you ever noticed "gasoline price wars," where all gas stations within a locality temporarily lower their prices? Do you think they were successful at eliminating some of their competition?)

These seven examples of barriers to entry keep markets concentrated over time. Because the firms in the industry will be relatively few and rather large (relative to the total market), they will be able to control the supply in the market and to charge a price higher than the competitive market price. They will possess market power.

Implications of Market Power

We have already discussed some of the effects of market power. The firms will charge a higher price, produce a smaller quantity, employ fewer workers, and receive higher revenue than would competitive producers. Figure 13-3 compares the price, output, and revenue levels under conditions of competition versus monopoly in the market for a new hypothetical pharmaceutical drug called "anti-age." Let's assume that this drug reduces the aging process and that no other drug makes or advertises this claim. Assume first of all that there are many firms of relatively equal size so that the market is competitive. The supply curve labeled S_c is the total supply curve under competition and is made up of all of the supply curves of all the individual firms that provide anti-age totaled together. The intersection of demand and supply gives us equilibrium point A, and indicates that the price will be $2.00 per monthly supply and the quantity will be 20,000 monthly supplies under competition. Alternatively, assume that only one firm supplies the drug. We don't actually draw a supply curve in the case of monopoly, but we just indicate some point along the demand curve to show the quantity that the monopolist intends to supply. For example, this point might be point B, with a quantity of 10,000 monthly supplies, and a corresponding price equal to $20 per monthly supply.

Notice that the total revenue to all the firms combined in the competitive alternative will equal price multiplied by quantity, or $2.00 × 20,000, which equals $40,000. On the other hand, the revenue to the monopoly firm will be $20 × 10,000, or $200,000. *The monopolist raises its revenue by reducing its output level below the competitive level.* And since the monopoly produces a smaller quantity (and therefore employs fewer people), its costs are lower than they are for the competitive firms all together, indicating that the profits will be higher in the monopoly market than in the competitive. (Once again, see this chapter's Appendix for elasticity conditions.)

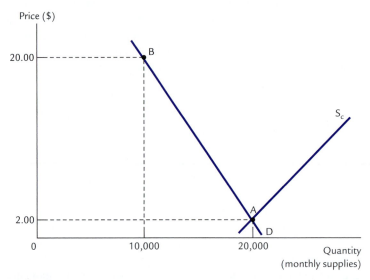

Figure 13-3 • Output, Price, and Profits under Competition and Monopoly
Note that output is lower and that price and profits are higher under a monopoly than they would be under competition.

In addition to affecting price, output, employment, and profits, market power and concentration often lead to collusion, inefficiency, and price discrimination. Let's discuss these phenomena one at a time.

Collusion

Collusion is better known as price-fixing. It occurs when firms cooperate to restrict the total market output and thereby obtain a higher price. For collusion to be successful, all the firms in the market must cooperate. If some firms collude to charge a higher price, while others do not, consumers will simply buy from the noncolluders at a lower price. Collusion is therefore more likely in markets with relatively few firms and substantial entry barriers.

The two types of collusion are cartel agreements and price leadership. A **cartel** is a group of producers that has an explicit agreement among themselves to limit output and charge a price higher than the competitive price. Cartels with which you might be familiar are the Organization of Petroleum Exporting Countries (OPEC), an organization of 13 of the world's largest oil-producing nations, and the DeBeers diamond cartel, which has controlled the world's supply of diamonds. A colorful and illegal cartel known as the "electrical equipment conspiracy" existed for many years in the United States. It included 29 electrical equipment companies headed by industry giants General Electric (GE) and Westinghouse. When the conspiracy was uncovered, GE, Westinghouse, and 44 of their executives were charged with conspiring to fix prices over a 25-year period by rigging bids in the sale of billions of dollars worth of heavy electrical equipment. The firms took turns offering the low bid. This low bid had previously been agreed on by the cartel and was actually at a high level. The colluders had devised ingenious schemes to coordinate their bidding. A firm would know whether to bid high or low, for example, by the phase of the moon.

Price leadership is a more subtle form of collusion. It occurs in markets in which firms never *explicitly* agree to collude, but instead somehow come to the realization that it is in their best interests to charge similar prices and to restrict output to maintain these higher prices. When this happens, one of the firms emerges as the price leader and the other firms adjust their price whenever the leader changes its price. American Tobacco was long the price leader in the cigarette industry, Kellogg in the cereal industry, Campbell's in the canned soup industry, and GM in the automobile industry. (Incidentally, the long-established practice of price leadership in the American automobile industry collapsed in the early 1980s when the industry began contending with substantial competition from imports.)

As you perhaps know, collusion is illegal under our antitrust laws. And indeed, firms that form cartels are subject to severe penalties should they be caught. Our antitrust system has been quite effective against cartels. The sad truth, however, is that the system is ineffective against price leadership. Without convincing evidence that firms have formally met and agreed to collude, proving that they are guilty of price-fixing is nearly impossible.

Inefficiency

A second problem with market power is that firms in concentrated markets have less incentive to be efficient than do firms in competitive markets. A competitive firm must minimize the cost of its product in order to survive. But the firm in a concentrated market, protected by entry barriers, has no such incentive. Security breeds laxness, and costs rise. *The Wall Street Journal* and other business publications abound with examples of dominant firms

Collusion
Price-fixing.

Cartel
A group of producers that explicitly engages in price-fixing.

Price leadership
A form of collusion in which firms follow the price increases of a leading firm.

that suddenly faced with competition cut costs substantially. Caterpillar Tractor Company, the long leading U.S. producer of construction equipment, found it possible to cut costs by more than 20 percent when suddenly besieged by Japanese competition in the early 1980s. When the American automobile industry was hit hard by foreign competition in the late 1970s, GM, Ford, and Chrysler were able to reduce their costs by 20 to 30 percent. When the Harley-Davidson motorcycle company lost its market dominance to Japanese competitors in the 1960s, it first sought protection in the form of import tariffs on motorcycles, which were in place during much of the 1980s but slated to end in 1988. By 1988, Harley-Davidson had cut its inventory by two-thirds, improved productivity by 50 percent, and reduced its rate of defects by 70 percent. As you may have realized when you read these examples, the business publications reported the successful cost-cutting measures, lauding the "lean and mean" American firms. But the firms had substantial excess costs to cut, and it was competition that forced them to do so.[1] Competition, whether domestic or international, promotes efficiency and benefits consumers.

Other sources of inefficiency in concentrated markets are related to the product differentiation in which these firms engage. In order to attract consumers, oligopolists, for example, spend huge amounts of money on marketing and advertising their products. Frequently, this includes prime time TV commercials and color glossy ads in national magazines. In addition, firms in the auto industry spend enormous amounts of money on the annual style changes of their automobiles. Firms in the breakfast cereal industry spend large amounts of money on the packaging of their products so that they appeal to children, often with games on the back of the packages and prizes within the boxes. When marketing activities serve to inform customers about the product, then the money spent on marketing may be useful to consumers. Unfortunately, much of the marketing efforts are designed more to manipulate consumers than to inform them. These expenses of product differentiation are wasteful and represent a significant drain on society's scarce resources.

Price Discrimination

Price discrimination

Charging different groups of buyers different prices (when price differentials are not justified by cost differences).

Another consequence of market power is **price discrimination**, or charging different prices to different groups of customers when the price differentials are not justified by differences in costs. Firms charge "what the market will bear," and different market segments will bear substantially different prices. Price discrimination is profitable for the discriminators, but it is only possible when firms have significant price-making power. Price discrimination is extremely common in the United States.

Let's consider some examples, beginning with the automobile industry, which has a rich history of price discrimination. As you undoubtedly know, American car manufacturers produce a variety of vehicles, ranging from small economy cars to luxury models. The markup over cost varies substantially with the model. Because purchasers of small economy cars tend to be more price conscious than purchasers of Cadillacs and Lincolns, firms take a smaller markup over cost on the economy models. The price differences reflect not only cost differences but also differences in what the market will bear.

Another way that automobile companies discriminate is illustrated in the area of replacement parts and optional equipment. The markup is much higher on parts and options than on the car itself. If your car is not running because it needs a new part, you are not particularly price conscious about the part. You may be horrified when you see the repair bill, but if you consider the car worth keeping, you have little choice other than to pay it. Also, the high markup on options explains why the salesperson pressures you so much to buy many options when you shop for a new car (one of the most frustrating events in American life). The auto industry is, by the way, not the only industry that discriminates in the sale of replacement parts. The practice is exceedingly common. If you don't believe this, price a replacement plate for your microwave oven.

The drug industry, the products of which are usually protected by patents, uses extensive and systematic price discrimination. Drugs that will ultimately be consumed by hospital patients are often priced higher than drugs that will be consumed by retail buyers. Large buyers such as the Veterans Administration can obtain drugs at far lower prices than can retail druggists. The drug industry claims that the huge price differences are the result of differences in the cost of packaging and selling drugs to different groups, but such differences are small, and Senate testimony in the 1970s revealed that druggists often paid prices more than three times that paid by the Veterans Administration for the same patented drug. Can you think of more recent examples in the drug industry? Can you think of other examples of price discrimination? The issue of price discrimination is discussed in relation to elasticity in the Appendix to this chapter.

Forces That Decrease Market Power

Market power obviously produces some undesirable consequences that harm the consumer, whereas competition benefits the consumer. Let's now consider the forces that decrease market power. These forces are (1) technological change, (2) antitrust activity, (3) deregulation of unwisely regulated sectors, and (4) import competition.

Technological Change

Technology is a major force on market structure in the economy. Economies of scale, which characterize natural monopolies, are often eroded by the forces of technological change. Take, for example, the telephone industry. When phone messages were carried on wire cables, the industry was characterized by extensive economies of scale. Fiberoptic and microwave transmission of phone messages, however, involve lesser economies of scale, and long-distance telephone service, which was once a natural monopoly, is now potentially competitive. Since the divestiture of AT&T, consumers in most localities have had a choice of long-distance carriers, and competition has decreased the price of long-distance calls. Now, additional competition is coming from cell phones, a still newer innovation.

Consider next the railroads, which had significant market power during the late 1800s and the early part of the twentieth century. Technological change since then has resulted in new competitors for the railroads. The invention of the internal combustion engine and the subsequent development of cars, trucks, and airplanes led to a significant level of inter-industry competition for the railroads. Once the dominant force in American transportation, railroads are now a slowly declining industry.

The U.S. Antitrust System

Our **antitrust** system is a set of weapons designed to combat market power. It consists of laws passed by Congress, agencies empowered to administer these laws, and a court system to try cases under the laws. The first federal antitrust law (*trust* is simply an old-fashioned word for monopoly) was the Sherman Act, which was enacted in 1890. The Sherman Act's provisions made monopolization and conspiracies in restraint of trade illegal. The law was quite generally written. Congress made known its intent and left it up to the Justice Department and the courts to apply the law to specific cases. As time passed, it became evident that the courts and agencies had difficulty interpreting the law, and

Antitrust
Our laws, agencies, and court system established to control market power in the United States.

Mergers
The combining of two firms into one.

another more specifically written law was passed. This was the Clayton Act of 1914. The Clayton Act contains many provisions that make it illegal to engage in actions that would "substantially lessen competition." The Clayton Act has been amended several times, most notably in 1950, when the passage of the Celler-Kefauver Act strengthened the law against **mergers** that would adversely affect competition.

The principal agencies charged with administering antitrust law are the Antitrust Division of the Justice Department and the Federal Trade Commission (FTC). The FTC is also the federal agency with jurisdiction over marketing practices such as deceptive advertising, so its resources—not great to begin with—are split between its two functions. The Antitrust Division is staffed at its lower levels with people who make a career of enforcing the antitrust laws, but its head is a political appointee, as is the attorney general to whom the chief antitrust officer reports. The vigor of antitrust prosecution therefore varies with the presidential administration, not only because the people at the head of the agency set its goals but also because the agency's budget is politically controlled. This is not to say that antitrust is ever abandoned. Every administration prosecutes price-fixers when they are apprehended. But prosecution of other antitrust cases, especially mergers, waxes and wanes.

The position of the Reagan administration (1981–1988) was that the economy is in fact more competitive than simple examination of concentration ratios would indicate. The administration argued that even markets with high concentration ratios seldom have barriers to entry so high that they are not subject to the "potential competition" of new entrants. It was assumed that the threat of this potential competition constrains the behavior of the established firms and leads them to behave in a relatively competitive manner. Finally, it was argued that firms must be large and unconstrained in order to compete effectively internationally. These arguments were used to curb antitrust budgets and decrease antitrust activity. Both the Antitrust Division and the FTC have always been small when compared to their job. Their resources had grown, however, until the Reagan administration cut their budgets by about 30 percent in inflation-adjusted dollars. The number of attorneys employed by the Antitrust Division and the relevant section of the FTC declined from 435 to 221 in the period from 1980 to 1989. Government actions against mergers were virtually eliminated under the Reagan administration, and as a result, one of the heaviest periods of merger activity in U.S. history began in the 1980s.[2] Reagan antitrust policy is relevant as a precursor to the views of President George W. Bush.

First, however, it is useful to mention that both of the presidencies of George H. W. Bush (1989–1992) and Bill Clinton (1993–2000) were somewhat more activist with regard to antitrust than was President Reagan. The budgets and staff of antitrust agencies were increased. A price-fixing case against Archer Daniels Midland Company and the corn-processing industry was brought and won by the government. Proposed mergers were examined more closely. For example, the only two acute-care hospitals in Dubuque, Iowa, were prevented from merging. A single hospital would have resulted in an unacceptable level of market power. Another example occurred when the U.S. Antitrust Division and its European counterparts blocked the proposed merger in 2000 of Sprint and WorldCom, two large telecommunications firms. The telecommunications market is global, and the merger would have significantly decreased competition in telecommunications throughout the world. On the other hand, the 1997 merger between McDonnell Douglas and Boeing, which left the United States with one civilian aircraft manufacturer, was permitted because it was argued that international competition in aircraft manufacturing is substantial.

The administration of President George W. Bush (2001–2008) was truly nonactive in antitrust matters. It did not file a single case against a dominant firm for engaging in monopoly behavior. This appears to be different with the Obama administration, as indicated in the quote that opens this chapter. Indeed, the Department of Justice has taken action against a number of firms, including Apple, NGK Spark Plug Company, Shingo Okuda, Amex, Bazaarvoice, Bridgestone Corporation, and U.S. and American Airways. For whatever reasons, Hewlett/Packard and EBay have broken up. On the other hand, pharmaceutical and media mergers have recently been the highest since the Great Recession.

An antitrust case that may well be relevant to your interests involved Ticketmaster, the world's largest seller of event tickets. Ticketmaster is based in West Hollywood, California, but it has operations in many other countries as well. Ticketmaster acts as an agent for its clients involving stadiums, arenas, and theaters, and sells the tickets that these clients provide. Ticketmaster charges markups, sometimes large, on the tickets it sells.

In 1993, Ticketmaster was sued by the rock band Pearl Jam (your author's favorite) for using monopolistic practices and refusing to charge lower service fees for the band's tickets. At the time, Pearl Jam wanted to keep ticket prices under $20 and believed that the Ticketmaster service fees were too high. Ticketmaster threatened to cancel contracts of any venues that would host Pearl Jam's concerts without using Ticketmaster as a distributor. This resulted in the cancellation of the Pearl Jam tour. Ticketmaster was nevertheless found not guilty of violating antitrust law. Ticketmaster, the lawsuit, and the pros and cons of the outcome continue to be discussed in blogs and other forums on the Internet.[3]

A more recent antitrust action, under President Clinton, was the 2000 decision of District Court Judge Thomas Penfield Jackson that Microsoft Corporation was a monopoly, that it had illegally abused that power, and that it should be broken up. This, of course, is another antitrust example that probably affects you. The case was filed in 1998, when the government accused Microsoft of monopolizing the market for computer operating platforms with its 90 percent Windows market share. Furthermore, the government charged that the company had used its monopoly power to stifle competition by bundling its Internet Explorer Web browser into the Windows operation system, polluting Sun Microsystems, Inc.'s Java programming language to diminish its competitive threat to Windows, and threatening IBM and Compaq. As a result, innovations that would benefit consumers were never developed.

The decision was, of course, appealed. Microsoft and its defenders argued that breaking up the firm would result in slower technological progress in the software industry. Furthermore, they argued that Microsoft's product is admired and used by millions of consumers. Microsoft argued that putting new features into old products is a natural part of technological progress. For example, cars include stereo systems and air conditioners, which were once sold separately, and cameras come with built-in flashes. The same is the case with operating systems. Over time, Microsoft has added many features to Windows that were previously stand-alone products. This has made computers more reliable and easier to use because consumers can be confident that the pieces work together. Microsoft argued that integration of Internet technology was the natural next step.

Microsoft subsequently settled with the George W. Bush administration and most of the 19 states that had signed on to the government case. Among other things, Microsoft agreed to reduce the price it charges its competitors that want to use Microsoft's operating system in their software. By 2003 Microsoft was complying with the terms of the settlement. The settlement did not end Microsoft's antitrust troubles, however. In recent years, the company has had to contend with several private antitrust suits, as well as suits brought by the European Union that allege a variety of anticompetitive behaviors. And this raises a final issue.

Microsoft is not the only media company to face lawsuits. An antitrust suit was brought against Apple, Google, Intel, Adobe, Pixar, Lucasfilm, and Intuit that accuses them of conspiring against their own employees by agreeing not to not to directly solicit each others' employees. The suit alleges that this limits the engineers' mobility and pay to the benefit of the companies. While the companies have offered a settlement to their employees, the case has not yet been accepted for the first four companies mentioned and the case may yet go to trial. Additionally, antitrust investigators have examined Google's practices of bundling advertising services together in a way that prohibited rivals from competing for the business of its advertisers. Another battle with Google took place over the company's plan to digitize books in opposition to the Authors' Guild and other authors' organizations. Finally, Apple was charged with scheming with major book publishers to drive up the price of electronic books. All of these examples are in various stages of completion.

A question now facing U.S. antitrust authorities is how and to what extent they should cooperate with similar agencies in the European Union. As European countries have realized that they must protect competition within their economies, they have established agencies similar to our antitrust agencies. Furthermore, technological advances in communications have resulted in more markets that are truly global. International cooperation is necessary to protect competition in such markets.

Although antitrust laws and actions do not eliminate all market power, they do constrain the activities of dominant firms. It can be argued that the antitrust system thus confers important benefits to consumers.

Regulation and Deregulation

Natural monopolies that exhibit substantial economies of scale are generally regulated by state or federal government agencies such as your state public service commission. Regulation involves limitation of market entry by the granting of exclusive franchises to firms. As we have already discussed, these franchises eliminate any real or potential competition. The natural monopoly is then regulated with respect to rates charged and level of service offered. Rates (prices) are set after hearings in which firms present data on their costs, and citizens' groups present testimony about the probable adverse effects of rate increases. The accounting data presented by the firm are scrutinized by the professional staff of the regulatory agency. The result is a compromise between the interests of the firm and those of its customers. Because markets with substantial economies of scale tend to be highly concentrated, regulation can greatly improve the outcome.

The major problem with regulation occurs when a public utility-type of regulation is imposed on industries that are not natural monopolies because they do not have substantial economies of scale. When this happens, regulation shelters the firms from competition and actually causes inefficiency. In markets in which competition is possible, it should be encouraged. Regulation tends to be less flexible than competitive market forces, which would lead to a better outcome in terms of prices, services, and level of output.

Consider, for example, the trucking industry, which is not subject to economies of scale. Small and large trucking firms can compete on a relatively equal basis. However, interstate trucking was regulated by the federal government in 1935 and continued to be strictly regulated until 1980. Firms could not begin operating on particular routes without obtaining licenses to do so from the Interstate Commerce Commission (ICC), the agency given jurisdiction over highway carriers. The ICC limited entry into the industry to protect existing carriers, eliminating potential competition. Many trucking firms' licenses were for specific commodities, so all firms could not carry all commodities. If these firms could not obtain a load of their regulated commodity at the end of a trip, they simply traveled back to their terminal empty. This practice obviously created inefficiency. All similar carriers charged the same regulated price. Since they could not compete on the basis of price, they competed on the basis of frequency of service and therefore often hauled loads that were less than their vehicles' capacity. This too was inefficient. Trucking regulation did not benefit consumers. Shippers paid significantly higher rates because of the industry's inefficiency, and these higher rates were passed along to consumers in the form of higher prices. In

1980, the industry was substantially deregulated. Because regulation was unwise in this case, efficiency improved and consumers benefited.

Deregulation simply means lessening regulatory restrictions, either in part or in total. Many formerly regulated industries were deregulated in the late 1970s and the 1980s. Because these industries were quite competitive without regulation, deregulation was appropriate. Among the industries deregulated in this period were natural gas production, airlines, railroads (the monopoly position of which had been eroded by inter-industry competition), and, of course, trucking. *The bottom line with regard to regulation is that it can improve the performance of natural monopolies but that it is inferior to competition when competition is possible.*

It is important to note that our discussion of regulation has thus far focused on the issues of competition and market power. Our government also imposes regulations in the areas of environmental protection, consumer and worker safety, and so on. Deregulation in these areas during both the Reagan and George W. Bush administrations has been accused of endangering the safety of our citizens and the protection of our environment. Thus, as with regulation to curb the excesses of market power, these other forms of regulation are controversial.

It is now well known that there were significant lapses in the regulation of the financial industry, particularly in terms of mortgages and mortgage-backed securities, as was discussed in Chapter 7 on housing. For example, although commercial banks are regulated by the Federal Reserve, many other financial institutions are not subject to the same regulations. These other institutions became increasingly important in supplying credit in the years leading up to the 2007–2008 financial crisis. Both these institutions and the regulated commercial banks took on significant debt burdens without adequate capital to back them, and they increasingly made high-risk loans. Subsequent losses affected the ability of financial institutions to lend, which slowed economic activity and contributed to the global recession of 2008–2009. We will discuss some of these issues in Chapter 15 on macroeconomic policy and in Chapter 17.

Import Competition

Finally, competition from imported products curbs the market power of domestic firms. The presence of Toyota, Nissan, and Volkswagen provides some degree of competition for the big three U.S. auto companies. The industry's abandonment of price leadership in the 1980s stemmed not from government action but from competition from abroad. Ultimately, American consumers have benefited from import competition, though as we will see shortly in the discussion of the automobile industry, the existence of competition by itself has not been sufficient to protect the American consumer.

Import quotas and tariffs that limit competition from foreign imports are often called upon to protect American firms. The powerful firms that lobby Congress to limit imports are often in concentrated markets. Restricting imports protects the market power that exists in these concentrated industries, but does not benefit the American worker or consumers. The protection of market power in these concentrated industries ultimately causes lower output levels, lower employment, and higher prices to consumers, described as consequences of market power earlier in this chapter. *Neither the U.S. worker nor the U.S. consumer benefits from trade restrictions.*

The Extent of Market Power

How serious is the problem of market power? The answer is not simple. Various researchers have tried to address the issue of whether concentration (and market power) has increased over time. A classic study was conducted by William Shepherd for the time period 1939 to 1980. Shepherd concluded that market power fell from 1939 to 1958, and fell again from 1958 to 1980. He believed that greater competition was achieved through increased international trade, reduced government regulations, and vigorous government antitrust activity.

The major issue is whether concentration and market power have changed *since* 1980. Some factors have contributed to lower concentration, including international trade and the information revolution (consumers now have better information about products and prices nationally and internationally, which thereby diminishes the market power of local monopolies). On the other hand, public resources devoted to antitrust are now well below their level in the years prior to President Reagan. According to the American Antitrust Institute (AAI), "Antitrust budgets remain too low, staff is stretched too thin, and the agenda is haunted by a 'laissez faire mentality.'"[4] As a result, the AAI believes that large segments of our economy are becoming more concentrated. What is clear is that merger activity has abounded since 1980 and that concentration ratios are quite high in many industries.

Local Aspects of Market Power

Walmart epitomizes a big-box organization that, in the minds of many, wields considerable global, national, and local market power. Walmart is the world's largest privately owned company, employing millions of workers and earning profits of tens of billions of dollars. It is the center of controversy as critics charge that its business practices are unethical and aimed exclusively at maximizing company profits. Among these charges are that it does not pay its employees a living wage, it does not allow its workers to form unions, it does not provide adequate health insurance for its employees, and it discriminates by failing to promote women to management positions. It is also accused of purchasing products from unsafe global sweatshops and employing foreign workers at wages below minimum and with hours above those permitted in its operations in their country. Some of these topics were addressed in Chapter 12. Of course, many other large companies face similar charges, including Apple, which has been accused of tolerating poor working conditions in some of its foreign factories, including low wages, long work hours, bad conditions, and the charging of exorbitant fees by third party recruiters to the factory jobs. Critics have charged that these fees amount to bonded servitude. Apple has since begun audits of its foreign factories to assure improvements.

Wal-Mart recently made changes in its operations. In early 2015, it announced that all of its workers would receive a minimum of $9 per hour. Target subsequently followed suit, and it's possible that other major retailers will do the same. The wage announcement may be the result of Wal-Mart's desire to improve worker morale, to respond to years of organizing by Wal-Mart employees, to address its concern about political efforts to raise state and federal minimum wages, or any number of these factors. Wal-Mart has also initiated a plan to hire more veterans, buy more U.S.-made merchandise, and help move its part-time workers into full-time jobs.

Wal-Mart has also initiated stricter measures to address concerns about global suppliers of its merchandise. This followed the deadly fire in a Bangladesh clothing factory that was mentioned in Chapter 12. The company said it will have a "zero-tolerance" policy on subcontracting with producers that do not have a Wal-Mart employee stationed in the country to ensure safety compliance. Wal-Mart stated it would drop companies immediately if they subcontract their work to factories that hadn't been authorized in this fashion. It also stated it would publish a list of factories not authorized to manufacture goods for the company on its corporate website. Critics argue that Wal-Mart's moves are inadequate and that the company (and other companies) need to pay their suppliers more so they can cover the costs of improvements in the factories. Do you think Wal-Mart is sincere in its new efforts, is it a response to consumer pressure, or is it a maneuver to gain goodwill in the local and global community?

Back to the local issue, the effect of Walmart (and other big-box stores) on local communities is controversial. Critics argue that the prices charged by Walmart will drive local establishments out of business, destroying the small town atmosphere and financial standing of the community. While beneficial to consumers, the low prices may come at the expense of others, as suggested in the preceding paragraph. Furthermore, critics allege that these lower prices may disappear when local businesses fail and Walmart utilizes its enhanced market power to raise prices. Others argue that Walmart, in fact, enhances competition, thereby assuring lower prices to consumers. They also maintain that the increased traffic resulting from large numbers of Walmart shoppers visiting local communities will actually increase the business of downtown merchants. What is your opinion?

International Aspects of Market Power

We've already considered one aspect of market power, which is the role of international trade in reducing industry concentration. For example, Table 13-1 indicates that the concentration ratio for the American automobile industry is 71, suggesting a very concentrated industry with considerable market power. And while the auto industry is indeed concentrated and has market power, it is considerably less than if there were no imported automobiles competing with domestic producers. The fact that American consumers can purchase a Toyota, Volvo, Volkswagen, Mazda, Kia, or Rolls Royce reduces the market power held by Ford, GM, and Chrysler. A broader discussion of international trade took place in Chapter 12.

There is another implication of market power on international trade that should be mentioned here, however. Many developing countries have experienced **declining terms of trade**, which is a decline in the value of their exports relative to the value of their imports. This makes it very difficult for these countries to acquire needed foreign currency. While there are many reasons for the relative decline in the value of developing country exports, market power has been an important factor in the relative increase in the value of their imports. As a result of the market power of OPEC along with Western oil companies, the price of energy imports in many developing countries has often been very high. In addition, market power in the developed countries, including the United States, has resulted in high prices of manufactured goods imported into the developing countries. This has reduced the ability of developing countries to repay their international debt and has forced them to undertake policies that are often undesirable as a result. This is discussed in greater detail in Chapter 17.

Declining terms of trade
A decline in the value of a country's exports relative to the value of its imports.

Too Big to Fail?

We've noted that market power does not necessarily equate with "bigness," though it can. What happens when a concentrated industry that is far bigger than "big" threatens to go belly-up? This is exactly what happened with the U.S. automobile industry in 2008–2009.

We've noted that the concentration ratio for the U.S. auto industry is 71, meaning considerable market power for GM, Ford, and Chrysler (although, as we've noted, foreign competition does decrease the extent of domestic market power). The "automobile crisis" was triggered by a number of events, some of them long in coming. First, rising energy prices since 2001 (see Chapter 3) encouraged consumers to reconsider their purchases of pickup trucks and large sport utility vehicles (SUVs), which were favored by U.S. automakers due to their high profit margins. U.S. car producers utilizing union workers and paying them higher salaries, benefits, health care, and pensions than their foreign competitors (including those operating in the United States) had undertaken production of the larger vehicles in order to compete more effectively with foreign producers. Many commentators also believe that the U.S. auto industry was less competitive than its foreign contenders due to a variety of poor business practices. By 2008, the subprime mortgage crisis and attendant financial crisis dried up credit and pushed up interest rates, making it more difficult for consumers to finance automobile purchases. Finally, by 2009, the global economic slowdown had reduced vehicle purchases of all kinds, creating large declines in car sales, buildup of inventories on new car lots, and discounts designed to attract wary consumers.

With fewer consumer purchases of automobiles, the U.S. auto industry began reducing production and laying off workers. Thus these major lay-offs in the automobile industry were caused by the economic recession, and in turn, exacerbated it. By 2009, Chrysler and GM had filed for bankruptcy. The nation was shocked. For the industry to fail completely would have caused unrivaled unemployment and misery for the American public. The auto industry, just like the financial industry before it, was considered too big to fail. The government stepped in, bailing out Chrysler and GM and extending a line of credit to Ford. In return for the bailouts, the government took control over restructuring. Among the required changes, GM was forced to sell off a number of its models and the CEO was forced to resign. Chrysler was forced to partner with the Italian automobile company, Fiat.

A Final Note

Markets consisting of large and powerful firms may lobby our government for protection of their interests. Outcomes may be reduced regulations, limited antitrust activity, and trade restrictions. All of these may be conducive to greater market power within already concentrated industries. Trade restrictions, for example, may effectively limit the competition faced by U.S. firms, thereby serving as a barrier to entry and enhancing the market power already existing in the industry. Unfortunately, consumers do not have the same level of influence over government policy as large and powerful business firms operating in unison. To the extent that we believe in democracy, we like to think that one person's vote counts just as much as any other person's vote. This may not be the case when oligopoly firms (or other firms, for that matter) have greater political clout through their lobbies and contributions to political campaigns. One area where this has recently become controversial is in what President Eisenhower referred to many years ago as the "military-industrial complex." In the context of war in Afghanistan and Iraq, contracts for reconstruction activities were given to firms such as Halliburton and Bechtel, companies that had strong ties to the Bush administration. This affected their profitability and left some people wondering whether potential profits were an inducement for the U.S. invasion of Iraq in the first place.

Regardless of your view on this latter issue, it *is* true that market power can have considerable implications in our economy and perhaps our politics, and many economists argue that we need policies that limit market power.

You, the Student

Are you concerned about market power? Are you concerned about the accusations toward companies such as WalMart, including unfair practices toward workers, women, and foreign labor? If so, you can boycott the company. Alternatively, you can talk to the manager about your concerns. Keep in mind that Wal-Mart is just an example. Other companies may be utilizing the same kinds of practices.

View*Point*   Conservative versus Liberal

Conservative and liberal economists differ greatly in their attitudes toward market power, antitrust activities, and economic regulation. Conservatives, who believe in a limited government role in the economy, feel that market power is seldom a serious problem. They believe that barriers to entry are seldom so high as to eliminate the threat of competition from new firms entering the industry. Furthermore, technological change erodes established monopoly positions. Thus, conservatives seldom see a need for antitrust or economic regulation, and they believe that such policies usually create inefficiency.

Liberals (and some conservatives), on the other hand, believe that competition creates efficiency, and that the government must act to reduce the market power that impedes competition. There is greater liberal support for active antitrust policy and government regulatory authority.

One of the ways in which conservative and liberal economists differ most is in their attitudes toward mergers. Conservatives argue that any increased market power that is created when firms merge is controlled by potential competition from new entrants into the industry and by technological change. Liberals, on the other hand, generally feel that the antitrust system is needed to control excessive market power and that proposed mergers should be scrutinized closely before they are allowed to take place.

With respect to public utilities, liberals believe that they should be regulated to protect the consumer from monopolistic excesses. Conservatives, however, argue that the government actually creates monopoly power by granting the utility companies exclusive franchises. They argue that the problem is the government monopoly grant, not the economies of scale that result in a natural monopoly. Thus, conservatives consistently view economic regulation largely as a source of inefficiency and too much expansion of the government role.

With the recognition that insufficient regulation was a major factor in the recent economic and financial crisis, there will undoubtedly be greater support across the economic spectrum for judicious and responsible regulation.

SUMMARY

Market power exists when there are only a few dominant firms in a market. These firms are sheltered from competition by barriers to entry. Barriers to entry can include economies of scale, exclusive franchises, control over essential raw materials, patents, product differentiation, licensing, and behavior of firms such as price-cutting. Firms in concentrated industries can significantly influence their own prices by restricting the quantity of their products. The adverse consequences of market power are often higher prices, higher profits, lower quantities of goods available, lower

employment, inefficiency, price discrimination, and collusion, as well as the potential for untoward political influence.

The major factors that can inhibit the development and abuse of market power are technological change, our antitrust system, economic regulation of natural monopolies, and import competition. Our antitrust system has a colorful history, including litigation against Microsoft and Ticketmaster. There are several reasons to conclude that market power exists in many U.S. industries, as is evident by large mergers, high concentration ratios, and limited government antitrust activity.

DISCUSSION AND ACTION QUESTIONS

1. What characteristics are necessary for a market to be competitive? Are there many competitive markets in the real world?

2. What are the disadvantages of market power for society? (*Hint:* Discuss price, output, employment, profits, price

discrimination, etc.) Be sure you understand why these result from market power.

3. What are barriers to entry? Why must barriers to entry be present if market power is to exist in a particular market?

4. Discuss the following barriers to entry: (a) economies of scale, (b) exclusive franchises, (c) control of essential raw materials, (d) patents, (e) product differentiation, (f) licenses, and (g) price-cutting. Describe how each functions as a barrier to entry by new firms.

5. Can you think of any examples of price-cutting that may exist in your community? Are you aware of any such activity involving some of the products that you purchase?

6. What are some examples of product differentiation in industries other than those discussed in the text? Especially think in terms of some of the products that you purchase.

7. Can you think of other examples of price discrimination besides those mentioned in the text? What about the way that airlines charge their business clients one price (noting that businesspeople often purchase fares just before they travel and that they have little flexibility in when and whether they travel) versus fares charged to vacationers (who often have alternative means of travel, choice over the time of travel, and the ability to purchase tickets in advance)? Can you explain the different fares charged by the airlines in terms of price discrimination?

8. Can you explain why adult and child moviegoers are often charged different amounts when going to the movie theater, keeping in mind that both an adult and a child each takes up an entire seat?

9. How do tariffs and import quotas harm the consumer? How do they harm the U.S. worker?

10. Are you a liberal or a conservative with respect to antitrust and economic regulation?

11. You are undoubtedly aware that most of the tickets that you purchase for rock concerts and other events go through Ticketmaster, and, of course, there is always a fee connected with this. Do you believe that Ticketmaster uses its market power to charge unnecessarily high fees for its service? Do consumers (and rock bands) have any alternative to using Ticketmaster? Are you aware of any bands that have chosen to supply their tickets without using Ticketmaster? If so, how successful have they been? One forum for views about Ticketmaster is on Wikipedia, the free encyclopedia, at http://en.wikipedia.org/wiki/Ticketmaster.

12. Open the Department of Justice's antitrust page (www.usdoj.gov/atr), and click What's New. List the new cases that have been initiated.

13. Go back to the Department of Justice Web site at www.usdoj.gov/atr. Find the page that explains how to report possible antitrust violations or potential anticompetitive activity. Read the confidentiality page with respect to reporting violations.

14. Check out the Census Bureau Web page that focuses on concentration ratios (http://www.census.gov/econ/concentration.html). Can you find concentration ratios for markets that are not reported in this book? Find one market you are interested in and determine whether it is competitive or concentrated. By the time you read this book, you may be able to find updated concentration ratios. (Note that concentration ratios are published every five years with a lag of five years for revision.)

15. Go to the Web site of the AAI at http://www.antitrustinstitute.org. This institute is an independent Washington-based nonprofit organization dedicated to education, research, and advocacy to assure competition and challenge unduly concentrated power in the United States and world economies. Read the organization's mission on its home page. Would you say that this is a liberal, conservative, or centrist organization?

16. Google purchased YouTube for $1.6 billion in 2006. Now, in addition to a search engine, Gmail, calendar, chat room, and other applications and tools, Google owns the popular video-sharing Web site. What implications might this purchase have for market power and concentration?

NOTES

1. Much of the discussion of inefficiency is based on the work of William G. Shepherd. See, for example, *The Economics of Industrial Organization*, 4th ed. (Englewood Cliffs, NJ: Prentice Hall, 1997).

2. Much of this is from William G. Shepherd, *Public Policy toward Business*, 8th ed. (Boston: Irwin, 1991), p. 191.

3. Some of this information is from Wikipedia, the free encyclopedia, at http://en.wikipedia.org/wiki/Ticketmaster. You too can contribute to this and various blogs!

4. American Antitrust Institute (AAI) (http://www.antitrustinstitute.org/about.cfm).

Appendix 13-1

Market Power and Elasticity

L et's think a bit about the role of the elasticity of demand in relation to market power. Two issues in particular relate to elasticity.

Elasticity and Monopoly Profits

First, since the monopolist supplies a unique product with no close substitutes, it is likely that the demand for this product is inelastic (since the only alternative that consumers have if the price rises too high are to pay the price or go without the product). As discussed in Chapter 2, we know that when demand is inelastic, consumers do not alter the quantities that they purchase very much when the price of the product changes. Monopolists take advantage of this situation by recognizing that even a small reduction in the quantity will be associated with a much higher price (because of the inelastic demand). This is reflected in the relatively steep demand curve in our earlier Figure 13-3, which is repeated below as Figure 13-4. Since we calculate revenue as price times quantity, and

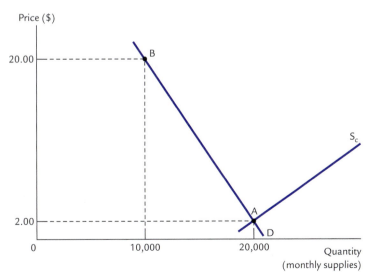

Figure 13-4 • Output, Price, and Profits under Competition and Monopoly
Note that output is lower and that price and profits are higher under a monopoly than they would be under competition.

since the price variable will be going up more in percentage terms than the quantity variable will be going down, the monopolist can increase its revenue by supplying a smaller quantity of output. In this case, as the monopolist moves away from the competitive equilibrium at point A, it is reducing quantity from 20,000 monthly supplies to 10,000 monthly supplies, a 50 percent decrease in quantity. (This is calculated as $(20,000 - 10,000)/20,000 = 10,000/20,000 = 0.5 = 50\%$.) The corresponding price increase is 900 percent (calculated as $(\$20 - \$2)/\$2 = 18/2 = 9.00 = 900\%$). Clearly the decrease in quantity is smaller than the increase in price in percentage terms.

Since the monopolist is producing a smaller amount of output, its costs of production will be lower as well. The fact that costs fall and revenue rises means that the monopolist can increase its profits by restricting its output. If the demand for the monopolist's product was not inelastic, the monopolist would be unable to increase revenue by reducing its quantity.

Elasticity and Price Discrimination

We can also consider the relation between the elasticity of demand and price discrimination. Recall that price discrimination occurs when a business firm charges different prices to different groups of consumers. Let's use the example of long-distance telephone service, prior to the existence of competition, and simplify by assuming that there are only two different groups of consumers of long-distance phone service. One group of businesspeople often must call their clients during business hours. They may have few alternatives to making the phone call. However, a different group of non-business consumers is more flexible. These consumers of phone service can perhaps write a letter or an e-mail instead, and they can often make their phone calls during evenings or weekends. The differences between these two groups of consumers can be explained in terms of elasticity of demand.

The first group of businesspeople has an inelastic demand for long-distance phone service. The businesspeople are inflexible and unable to cut down much on their phone calls when the price of making the calls goes up. The supplier of long-distance phone service can increase its revenue by raising its price (since it knows that this group of consumers will cut down on long-distance phone calls very little). Recalling that revenue equals price times quantity, we know that the price will increase proportionately more than the quantity will fall. As a result, the firm increases its revenue by raising its price. This graph would be similar to the one we just considered in Figure 13-4, with a relatively steep demand curve.

But what about the flexible group of consumers? Since they have more alternatives to making their long-distance phone calls during business hours, they can manage to be price conscious and will reduce their phone calls considerably if prices rise. For this group of consumers, the firm will increase its revenue by reducing its price. This is because when demand is elastic, people will increase their number of phone calls proportionately more than the price falls. Since revenue equals price times quantity, the price reduction will be more than offset by an increase in quantity, and the revenue to the supplier of long-distance phone service will increase. By charging the different prices to the different groups of consumers, the firm can increase its revenue and profits. A graph would show a relatively flat demand curve.

Of course, the conditions that must be met for this type of price discrimination to take place include the existence of market power (otherwise, the firm could not alter its price) and the ability of the firm to segment consumers into different groups with different elasticities. The phone company does this by offering high rates during business hours and low rates during evenings and weekends.

Many more examples of price discrimination exist. For example, can you explain the different fares charged by airlines for businesspeople versus vacationers? (*Hint:* Use the same type of reasoning as in the case of long-distance phone service.) What about different charges for adult and child moviegoers? In all of these and other cases, the firm with market power can increase its revenue by charging higher prices to the group with inelastic demand and by charging lower prices to the group with elastic demand. In such a fashion, the price-discriminating firm can increase its overall profits.

Chapter 14

ROAD MAP

Chapter 5
Discrimination
How extensive is job-related discrimination? How do unemployment rates vary for people of different race or ethnicity? How are migrant and immigrant workers treated within U.S. labor markets?

Chapter 6
U.S. Poverty
There is a close link between poverty and unemployment. Minimum wages, unemployment compensation, and the earned income tax credit help protect against poverty.

Chapter 12
International Trade
Many fear that trade leads to the loss of U.S. jobs.

Chapter 13
Market Power
Market power can contribute to restricted output, less employment, and higher prices in concentrated industries. Market power contributed to the recent U.S. economic crisis.

Chapter 14
Unemployment and Inflation

Chapter 17
Globally Free Markets for the Twenty-First Century?
Have global economic reforms worsened or improved the problems of unemployment and inflation?

Chapter 15
Government Macroeconomic Policy
Unemployment and inflation can be corrected by proper macro policy.

The Economic Toolbox

- The macroeconomy
- Gross domestic product (GDP)
- Recession
- Labor force participation rate
- Unemployment rate
- "Discouraged workers"
- Frictional, structural, and cyclical unemployment
- Full employment
- Minimum wage (price floor)
- Inflation
- Consumer price index
- Cost-of-living adjustment (COLA)
- Barter
- Hyperinflation
- Purchasing power
- Demand-pull, cost-push, and profit-push inflation

Unemployment and Inflation

President Barack Obama began his presidency in the midst of a recession. This recession began in late 2007 and continued into 2009. By 2014, though, when the president spoke, our economy had turned around and unemployment rates had fallen. The president was correct in stating that we need to create even more jobs, and in particular, we need to make sure our labor force has the skills and education to take these new jobs. Ours is no longer the manufacturing economy of the past, and now relies much more heavily on the service sector. Our labor force must be prepared to address our changing economy and to be able to compete globally.

If you are a traditional student in your late teens or early twenties, you have only been familiar with the relatively recent healthier economy. The stories of massive job layoffs and unemployment lines were just that—stories from years gone by. Perhaps your grandparents lived during the Great Depression of the 1930s. Ask them to tell you about the one out of every four people who couldn't find work, the bread lines, and the frugality of that era. Perhaps your grandparents still won't throw anything away, despite being comfortably well off. The lessons of hard times are difficult to erase.

Maybe your parents remember the inflation of the 1970s, with skyrocketing energy prices and long lines at gas stations. Since energy is used in the production of virtually everything, from manufactured goods to agricultural goods to services, rising energy prices resulted in rising prices of virtually everything else. Inflation rates were like we had seldom seen before and have never seen since.

We will consider both unemployment and inflation in this chapter. We must ask what a healthy economy means for us? What does it mean for you as you look to your job horizon and to your spending habits as an American consumer? What does it mean when you choose your major and strive to excel in your field? And equally important, how long will it be before the health of our economy fails again and you must be prepared to deal with that?

The Macroeconomy

As you recall from Chapter 1, when we study unemployment and inflation and the policies designed to control them, we are focusing on the **macroeconomy**. Indeed, **macroeconomics** is the study of the overall economy. In previous chapters, we've considered individual markets such as the markets for health care, housing, and agricultural products. The study of

[We have] the lowest unemployment rate in over five years. ....The ideas I've outlined so far can speed up growth and create more jobs. But in this rapidly-changing economy, we have to make sure that every American has the skills to fill those jobs. ....I've asked [for] across-the-board reform of America's training programs to make sure they have one mission: train Americans with the skills employers need, and match them to good jobs that need to be filled right now.... Of course, it's not enough to train today's workforce. We also have to prepare

Macroeconomy
The total economy.

Macroeconomics
The study of the total economy.

Microeconomics
The study of individual aspects within the total economy.

Gross domestic product (GDP)
Real value of total output in an economy.

Recession
A decline in a nation's gross domestic product (output) associated with a rise in unemployment. Technically, there must be a decline in real GDP for at least two consecutive quarters.

Labor force
All people age 16 and older who are working for pay or actively seeking employment.

individual markets within the economy is part of the study of **microeconomics**. Some economists refer to microeconomics as the study of the trees, whereas macroeconomics is the study of the forest. We're looking at the same economy, but contrasting the individual parts with the overall picture.

Recall our study of agricultural markets in Chapter 12. We were interested in the output of corn or wheat and how the prices of these agricultural goods were changing. **In macroeconomics, we are concerned instead with the quantity of *total output* in our economy (which we call gross domestic product, or GDP) and how the *average price level* for all of this output is changing**. An increase in the average price level is what we mean by inflation. And although employment within any individual market is closely related to output in that market, in macroeconomics we are more concerned with employment for the country as a whole, which is closely related to total production, or GDP.

Also notice that we used the term *recession* in the first paragraph of this chapter. This term will be used occasionally throughout this chapter and discussed in more detail in the next chapter. For now, let's just say that a **recession** is a decline in a nation's output, which results in a decline in the number of people hired to produce this output.

Unemployment

Let's begin our study of macroeconomics with topics related to unemployment. To do so, we need to understand what is meant by the concepts of the labor force and the labor force participation rate.

The Labor Force Participation Rate

The **labor force** refers to all people age 16 and older who are working for pay plus all people in this age range who are actively seeking employment. Think about this definition for a moment. Clearly, the concept of the labor force goes beyond just those people who are working. It also includes those who would like to be working and who are looking for a job. We sometimes refer to the labor force as the workforce. It refers to those actively interested in working.

Who is not included in the labor force? Obviously, not children. But neither are retired people, full-time homemakers who do not desire a job outside of the home, full-time students who do not wish to work for pay while pursuing their education, people in institutions such as prisons and mental hospitals, nor anyone else who is not actively seeking a job. The labor force is clearly a subset of the entire population.

Why is this concept of the labor force important? First, it demonstrates the quantity of our labor resource available for the production of national output. It also reflects societal trends and attitudes. In the 1950s and 1960s, for example, many women did not work outside of the home. Indeed, many in society believed that a woman's place was in the home, and not in the labor force. This attitude was not prevalent during earlier wartimes or in recent years. Attitudes have also changed about the work habits of teenagers, single mothers, and even fathers of newborns; and financial necessity has increased the likelihood that many college students support themselves with part-time work.

The phenomenon of working mothers is very interesting. In the early 1960s, only about one-fourth of married mothers worked outside the home, whereas more than one-half of single mothers did. Over the next few decades, the share of working married mothers increased dramatically, but the share of working single mothers remained stable. By the mid-1980s, the share of working married mothers exceeded that of single mothers, and by the late 1990s, almost two-thirds of married mothers worked.[1] What do you think are the reasons for these trends?

The **labor force participation rate** is the share of the population age 16 and older that is in the labor force. It is calculated as the number of people in the labor force divided by the total number of people age 16 and older. **We can think of the labor force participation rate as the percentage of all "adults" who are actively interested in working.** Table 14-1 shows the U.S. labor force participation rates for men and women, individually and combined, in 1964, 2008, and 2013. Overall, the labor force participation rate has increased since 1964, but in 2013, it is below what it was in 2008. Many people feel that they cannot find jobs, that they have the wrong skill set, or that wages are too low to justify child care and other expenses, causing them to drop out of the labor force entirely. Many older residents are retiring and many younger ones are going on to higher education rather than entering the labor market. None of these people are in the labor force. Also notice that the participation rate of men has decreased substantially since 1964, whereas the participation rate of women has increased dramatically (though falling from 2008 to 2013). The labor force participation rate remains much higher for men than women, however. What do you think are the reasons for some of these trends and changes?

Labor force participation rate
The ratio of the number of people in the labor force to the number of people age 16 or older in the population.

TABLE 14-1 • U.S. Labor Force Participation Rates for Men and Women, Individually and Combined, Selected Years

Year	Men (%)	Women (%)	Men and Women (%)
1964	82	39	59
2008	73	60	66
2013	70	57	63

Source: U.S. Department of Commerce, Bureau of Labor Statistics, www.bls.gov.

The Unemployment Rate

Ask your friends how they think the unemployment rate is calculated. Unless they've had an economics course, they will probably stammer a little and then make some vague statements about people without jobs. Unfortunately, this answer is not adequate for economic analysis.

The **unemployment rate** is defined as the percentage of the labor force that is unemployed. The unemployment rate is calculated as follows:

$$\text{Unemployment Rate} = \frac{\text{Number of Unemployed People}}{\text{Number of People in the Labor Force}}$$

Unemployment rate
The percentage of the labor force that is unemployed.

To qualify as an **unemployed person**, a person must be in the labor force. As you already know, the U.S. concept of the labor force refers to all people age 16 and older who are working for pay plus all people age 16 and older who are actively seeking employment but unable to find a job. The latter are considered unemployed.

Think about this definition for a moment. Some people are not counted in either the numerator or the denominator. *The only people who are classified as unemployed are those who are actively looking for jobs.* That is, they must be answering want ads, sending out vitae, engaging in job interviews, or doing whatever is necessary to find a job. Therefore, full-time homemakers and students who are not seeking employment for pay are not categorized as unemployed. (As we've noted, neither are children, retired people, volunteer workers, people in prison or mental hospitals, or those who would simply rather not work.)

Because the labor force consists of people who are either employed or unemployed, it may sound as though the labor force and the total population are the same. This is not the case! Remember that all of the homemakers, students, retired people, children, and so on that were excluded from the numerator of the unemployment rate are excluded from the denominator as well. Your great-grandmother and the next-door "stay at home" mother are not unemployed, nor are they part of the labor force. Nor are you and other students, if you are not working or seeking a job for pay.

Unemployed person
A person age 16 or older who is actively seeking employment but is unable to find a job.

The Unemployment Data

What is the national unemployment rate? Just what is considered low, and what is high? How do current rates compare with those of the recent past? Do all groups of people within our economy face the same probability of becoming unemployed? What are your chances of becoming unemployed?

The National Unemployment Rate

Let's begin to answer these questions by looking at the annual unemployment rates for our nation in recent years. Table 14-2 displays these data.

Notice that the year 2000 unemployment rate was extremely low by historical standards, even when compared to the prosperous years of the 1960s, not to mention the periods of high unemployment rates in 1975, 1982–1983, and 1992. The low unemployment rate in the year 2000 had a lot to do with the expansion of our economy since 1992. By 2010, however, we see the extremely high unemployment rate of 9.6, but dropping down to 6.2 percent in 2014. Not shown in the table are still lower rates of 5.7 percent and 5.5 percent in January and February of 2015, respectively. These lower unemployment rates correspond with the economic growth that followed the recession we've referred to in 2007–2009. We will consider the issue of recession again shortly. The unemployment rates from 2000 through 2014 are shown more visibly in Figure 14-1.

TABLE 14-2 • U.S. Unemployment Rates, Selected Years[a]

Year	Unemployment Rate (%)	Year	Unemployment Rate (%)	Year	Unemployment Rate (%)
1960	5.5	1983	9.6	2011	8.9
1970	4.9	1990	5.6	2012	8.1
1975	8.5	1992	7.5	2013	7.4
1980	7.1	2000	4.0	2014	6.2
1982	9.7	2010	9.6		

[a]Data from 2000 onward are not strictly comparable with earlier years.

Source: U.S. Department of Commerce, Bureau of Labor Statistics, **www.bls.gov**.

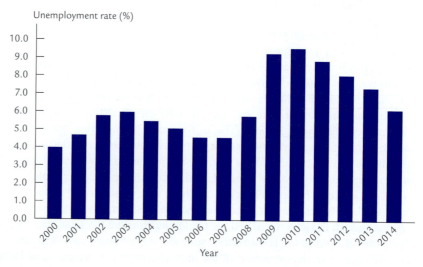

Figure 14-1 • Change in Unemployment Rates Since 2000 (Based on Data from the U.S. Department of Commerce, Bureau of Labor Statistics, **www.bls.gov**.)

Unemployment Rates for Selected Groups of People

Like the national unemployment rates indicated in Table 14-2, the relative unemployment rates of certain groups of people are important for national policy. Table 14-3 displays these data for 2013. The national average unemployment rate for this year was 7.4 percent. We can use this number as a benchmark for comparing the unemployment rates of individual groups of people.

Notice first of all that the unemployment rate for men is higher than the unemployment rate for women. This is not always the case. In fact, some economists believe that unemployment rates for women are lower than those of men during and immediately after recessions. They explain this in terms of "discouraged workers," which is described momentarily. In any event, in any one year the unemployment rate may be a little higher for men, whereas in the next year it may be a little higher for women. Keep in mind that to be classified as unemployed, a person must be actively seeking employment. Therefore, any full-time homemakers who are not seeking outside employment are not included in the unemployment statistics.

Second, notice the very high unemployment rate for teenagers, more than three times the national average. This group of young people has the highest unemployment rate of any age group, year after year. Part of the difficulty for teenagers is that they lack the education, skills, and experience that are often required by employers.

Finally, notice that the unemployment rate for white people is well below the national average and far below the unemployment rates for African-Americans and Hispanics. The unemployment rate for African-Americans is often about twice that for whites, and the unemployment rate for Hispanics is between the rates for African-Americans and whites. Again, we are referring only to people who are actively seeking employment. The unemployment rate for Asian-Americans is below the national average. Clearly, the burden of unemployment is not borne equally by all groups. *Although there are many reasons for the differing unemployment rates for people of differing race and ethnicity, the numbers suggest that the equal opportunity and affirmative action policies discussed in Chapter 5 continue to be very important.*

Problems in Measuring Unemployment

The official unemployment rate gives us a rough idea of how the economy is doing. We believe the economy is doing better if this rate falls. But measurement problems may cause the official statistics to understate the economic hardship of unemployment.

TABLE 14-3 • U.S. Unemployment Rates for Selected Groups, 2013

Group	Unemployment Rate (%)	Group	Unemployment Rate (%)
Nation	7.4	Whites	6.5
Men	7.6	African-Americans	13.1
Women	7.1	Asian-Americans	5.2
Youth ages 16–19	22.9	Hispanics	9.1

Source: U.S. Department of Commerce, Bureau of Labor Statistics, www.bls.gov.

Many economists believe that the unemployment rate understates the true extent of economic hardship from unemployment in our country for two reasons. First, anyone working at least part time for pay is considered to be employed. Although many people prefer part-time work, many others prefer full-time employment and need full-time work to support their families. When these people can find only part-time jobs, they experience economic hardship even though they are officially classified as being employed.

Second, some people who would like to work and who have actively sought employment have become so discouraged in their search that they have given up looking for jobs. In many ways, these **discouraged workers** are perhaps the ones most severely affected by unemployment, yet they cease to be tallied in the unemployment statistics as soon as they stop their active job search. When the economy is depressed, the number of discouraged workers increases, and the understating of unemployment becomes more severe. Despite recently falling unemployment rates, there are large numbers of discouraged workers (as well as part-time workers and workers receiving very low pay).

We've just noted that unemployment rates for women are often lower than unemployment rates for men during and immediately after recessions. This may be the case if more women become "discouraged" and drop out of the labor market in times of limited employment. They may decide that wages are too low to justify child-care costs, and they may decide to stay home to care for their young children. This means that even though women may face more difficulty in the labor market, their actual unemployment rates may be lower than those of men, masking the problems they experience.

Economists believe that mismeasurement of the unemployment rate can have serious ramifications. First, many of our macroeconomic policies are based on the unemployment rate, and if unemployment is understated, policymakers may not take the problem seriously enough. Second, changes in our economy can have a misleading impact on official unemployment rates. When the economy is in a downturn, for example, many people who are unable to find employment give up their job search. At that point, they fall out of the unemployment statistics entirely, because they are no longer classified as being unemployed. Thus, simply because these workers are now ignored in the statistics, the official unemployment rate may be decreasing as the economy is worsening!

Discouraged workers
People who would like to work, but have become so discouraged in the job search that they have stopped actively seeking employment.

The Effects of Unemployment
Personal Effects

The effects of unemployment on individual workers and their families are obvious. Clearly, the income of the family will fall when the breadwinner(s) lose a job. *Many people are unaware that most unemployed people do not receive unemployment compensation.* Unemployment compensation is an income transfer from the government to the eligible unemployed person. To be eligible, one must first have had a job. Even then, government data show that minority of those who are laid off from their jobs receive unemployment compensation, and benefits are less likely among the lower-income workers who need it most. For those who do receive unemployment compensation, their benefits are usually well below their former income and exist for only a limited period of time. Labor economists have frequently argued that the unemployment compensation program must be updated to reflect current employment conditions.

Beyond the income loss, the unemployed person suffers other tangible losses. One such loss might be employment-related health benefits, thereby harming the health of the family. Another loss is on-the-job experience, which might reduce the unemployed person's productivity and marketability.

Unemployment causes a variety of problems, not just strictly economic ones. Researchers at Johns Hopkins University and other organizations have noted a high correlation between unemployment rates and a variety of social ills. When unemployment rates go up, we typically see an increase in domestic violence, divorce, alcoholism, child abuse, and suicide.

Macroeconomic Effects

The problem posed by unemployment to the macroeconomy is quite different from the problems it poses to individuals. Recall the production possibilities curve of Chapter 1. This graph is repeated in Figure 14-2.

Recall that when we use society's resources and technology to their fullest, the economy is represented somewhere along the production possibilities curve. The economy may choose to produce at a point such as point C, with production of 90 tons of bread and 40 tons of roses. However, if some of our resources sit idle, we will not be able to produce to our full potential. With unemployed workers, we may instead be at a point such as point U, perhaps producing only 60 tons of bread and 40 tons of roses. **The macroeconomic problem of unemployment is the reduction in our nation's output that it causes**. As long as there is scarcity in our world, we must be concerned when we are not producing to our full potential.

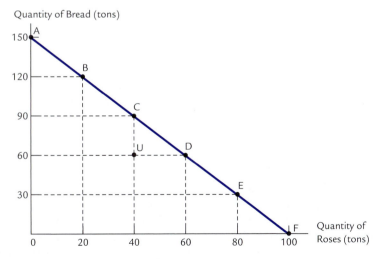

Figure 14-2 • Production Possibilities Curve

© Cengage Learning

Types of Unemployment

There are three basic types of unemployment: frictional, structural, and cyclical unemployment.

Frictional Unemployment

Do you remember looking for your first part-time job? Did you expect to apply, interview, be hired, and begin work the moment you began your job search? Of course not! Similarly, when you graduate from college with your degree in hand, you should not be surprised when it takes time to find that long-awaited "real" job. There is a normal time delay before finding a job—or, for that matter, when changing jobs or reentering the labor force after a period of absence. This is an expected situation and is referred to as **frictional unemployment**. The name reflects the "friction" present in the labor market—that is, our imperfect information about job vacancies and business firms' imperfect information about job seekers. It takes time for employer and employee to get together, to discover their compatibility, and to move through the red tape that is necessary before the job vacancy is filled.

Because frictional unemployment is very normal and is assumed, by definition, to be temporary, it is not generally considered to be a serious form of unemployment. In fact, many consider some frictional unemployment to be necessary for a healthy economy. We need to have people move to better jobs to maintain an efficient economy. Of course, the longer the job search, the more serious the situation becomes. Hence, we are interested in programs that can improve job information for employers and job seekers. Your college career services office, state job service office, and local employment agency provide this type of service. At the national level, computerized job searches can minimize the time spent seeking information and ultimately bring together employer and employee.

Frictional unemployment
Temporary unemployment caused by a normal time delay when a person seeks a first job, changes jobs, or reenters the labor force after an absence.

Structural Unemployment

Now consider a more serious problem than the time delay in finding your first postcollege job. Suppose you are majoring in elementary education, with the hope of teaching at the primary level. Perhaps the demand for elementary teachers was very high at the time you planned your career and you have been intently preparing yourself since then. Now, suppose a shift is taking place in our economy, or at least in the community in which you wish to teach. The number of schoolchildren may be decreasing, thereby reducing the overall demand for elementary teachers. At the same time, the demand for more specialized schoolteachers may be increasing, as more school districts seek to meet the needs of children with emotional or learning disabilities. There may be unfilled vacancies for specialized teachers at the same time that many nonspecialized teachers remain unemployed. This situation is an example of structural unemployment.

As the name suggests, **structural unemployment** is caused by structural shifts within our economy. Consider, for example, how the structure of demand has changed within our economy over the last several decades. Consumer demand is on the increase for a variety of services such as health care, technology services, personal care, social assistance, construction, professional services, and business, whereas in previous years, demand was higher for manufactured goods. As a result, job opportunities have opened up in specific occupations such as retail sales, registered nurses, home health aides,

Structural unemployment
Unemployment that results from structural changes in our economy, such as changes in demand or technology.

personal care aides, office clerks, and programmers; whereas jobs have been lost in the manufacturing sector.[2] On a personal note, these are good areas for you to consider for your future career, and you will also be well served by studying, in addition to economics, the fields of science, technology, engineering, and math.

Technological advance is another example of structural change within our economy. Robotics in the auto industry has enabled machines to replace welders, creating job loss in the auto industry, at least in the short run. At the same time, jobs have opened up as a result of other forms of technological advance—in the computer industry, for example. The welders who lost their jobs in the auto plant, however, probably do not have the skills to take the jobs in the computer industry. Changes in international trade relations also cause structural unemployment. As the demand for our imports and exports change, people (and businesses) must adapt to these changes.

The point is that with structural unemployment, a job vacancy may exist for each unemployed worker, but because of structural circumstances within the economy, the unemployed worker is not suited to the particular job. The laid-off welder is available, but lacks the skills for the computer industry. The laid-off steelworker lacks the education necessary for a job in the health care field. These are precisely the types of problems that the president referred to in his comments that open this chapter. We need training and education to prepare people for the new jobs of the present and of the future.

Other structural factors that prevent people from taking available jobs may be present. Some workers may lack necessary child-care facilities, face discrimination, or live in an inner city or a part of the country where jobs are scarce. The fact that jobs are available in Florida's service sector means little to the unemployed person on the Minnesota Iron Range, who is unable to participate in that job market.

Many people believe that these latter factors are serious enough for the government to take action. These include the provision of child-care facilities and the enforcement of antidiscrimination policies. Mass transit may be helpful to inner-city commuters, and relocation assistance may be needed for workers who must move to find jobs. Many of the European countries provide these services as a matter of course. These interventions (and those affecting frictional unemployment) represent microeconomic policies by nature.

Cyclical Unemployment

Cyclical unemployment is the type of unemployment most closely linked to the macroeconomy and to macroeconomic policy. Hence, it is the type of unemployment with which we are primarily concerned in the two chapters that follow.

Cyclical unemployment is defined as unemployment that results from a drop in economic activity in our economy as a whole. Whereas structural unemployment has to do with changes in sectors within the economy, cyclical unemployment has to do with the macroeconomy in total. When our economy is expanding and producing larger levels of output, the number of jobs expands as well, for we need workers to produce higher levels of output. On the other hand, when our economy contracts and produces lower levels of output, the number of jobs will contract as well. Many people lose their jobs in a downturn of the economy, and many are unable to find first-time jobs.

Notice that only with cyclical unemployment do we assume that the economy has an insufficient number of jobs. With frictional unemployment, a job is available for the job seeker. He or she simply hasn't found it yet! With structural unemployment, there are job losses in one sector or geographical area of the economy, but there are job vacancies in

Cyclical unemployment
Unemployment that results from a drop in economic activity in our economy as a whole.

others. There is simply a mismatch between available jobs and workers, who lack the skills, education, location, or other forms of access to these jobs. Only with cyclical unemployment is the number of jobs insufficient. Macroeconomic policy is necessary to expand the economy and create new employment opportunities.

We've noted that we currently have a problem with structural unemployment. This requires one set of policies to correct it. However, even with the elimination of structural unemployment (though we cannot ever eliminate all of it), we still do have a problem with cyclical unemployment. We need government policy of a different nature to correct this. We will discuss macroeconomic policy more carefully in Chapter 15.

Full Employment

Full employment

A situation in which there is no cyclical unemployment; all unemployment is frictional or structural.

Have you ever heard the term *full employment*? It's natural to assume that full employment means a job for everyone who wants one, but this is *not* the definition of full employment! **Full employment** is defined as a situation in which there is no cyclical unemployment; that is, enough jobs are available for all who want to work. It doesn't mean that everyone is suited to a job that exists, or that everyone has actually found a job. *It means is that any unemployment that exists will be structural or frictional, not cyclical.* An unemployment rate of 4 to 5 percent or slightly higher is often considered by economists to represent full employment.

Although it appears deliberately misleading, the full-employment concept is, in fact, useful. When the economy achieves full employment, there may be a need to provide better information, training, education, or other services; but there is no need for macroeconomic policy to correct the economy. On the other hand, when the economy does not experience full employment, macro policies must come into play.

Employment and Wage Effects of Immigration

In the United States and abroad, immigration is a controversial issue. Some of the animosity toward immigrants stems from bigotry, and much stems from fear—fear that large-scale immigration will increase unemployment and cause wage rates to fall. The fact that significant numbers of immigrants enter the United States illegally only increases this fear.

The polar attitudes in the United States toward immigrant workers can be expressed by the following statements: (1) immigrants work for next to nothing and take jobs away from native-born Americans, or (2) immigrants work hard and only take jobs that native-born workers wouldn't want anyway. The truth, as is often the case, is probably somewhere between these two extremes. While immigrants may displace some native-born labor, others are doing jobs that wouldn't have existed without immigration.

Emotions run stronger than usual when our economy is doing poorly and many Americans are unemployed. Evidence of animosity toward immigrants permeates our public policy. Some legislators have sought to restrict *legal* immigrants' eligibility for welfare benefits and impose new requirements that recipients of welfare and applicants for citizenship use English on their forms and exams. This requirement is especially onerous for elderly immigrants who have difficulty learning a new language. Others have sought to deny public assistance, health care, and public education to the children of *illegal* immigrants, despite the fact that these children, if born in the United States, are indeed legal citizens of the United States. At the other extreme, we are reminded that most immigrants, legal and illegal, are seeking the same kinds of work and better lives for their families as were sought by the immigrant ancestors of most Americans. Immigrants hope to be welcomed as friends and neighbors in our schools, workplaces, and communities, just as we all do. Nevertheless, immigrants can find themselves linguistically and culturally isolated and more vulnerable to exploitation and discrimination because of their legal status and language barriers.[3]

The debate over immigration became intense during President George W. Bush's second term of office. The president proposed a dual program of providing work visas for illegal immigrants already in the country, along with tighter border control to prevent further illegal immigration. Conservatives in his own party were split on the issue, with many opposed to any overtures to the illegal workers in the country and others supportive of business access to cheap immigrant labor. Liberals, church organizations, and others concerned with equity issues opposed an initial House bill that would place severe sanctions on illegal immigrants, including a requirement to display documentation before receiving health care. Ultimately, disagreement between the House and the Senate killed any immediate chance for passage of an immigration bill. Circumstances changed, however, with the election of a Democratic majority in the 2007 Congress, and President Bush once again addressed immigration reform in his January 2007 State of the Union Address. Calling for a temporary worker program and a path toward citizenship, the president argued that "We need to uphold the great tradition of the melting pot that welcomes and assimilates new arrivals."[4] Ironically, President Bush had more in common with many congressional Democrats than Republicans on immigration issues. More recently, the Obama administration's immigration policy had initially been accused as being in shambles. Unable to gather any consensus in Congress, no sweeping immigration bill has been passed. Obama's presidency was initially marked by widespread deportations, and the immigrant community, normally an ally of Democrats, was offended by this issue. This was perhaps a factor in the loss of Democratic congressional and governor seats in the Obama midterm elections. Obama claimed he carefully followed the law in the hope that this would create the opportunity for bipartisan support for a new immigration law. However, without adequate support for new legislation, President Obama instead announced in 2014 executive action that would allow up to 5 million illegal immigrants to remain at least temporarily in the United States, without fear of deportation, though Congressional Republicans vowed to reverse this action once the new Republican Congress took over in 2015. Many believe that only after acquiring legal status can immigrants move freely within the labor market, integrate themselves into communities, and end the horrible exploitation that often takes place in the illegal workplace.

Since economics is at the root of at least some of the immigration debate, let's consider the economic implications of immigration for U.S. labor markets. Let's focus our attention on low-skilled immigrants in the short run, noting that large-scale immigration increases the supply of low-skilled workers and lowers the wage rate for these workers. The graph of the low-skill labor market is shown in Figure 14-3. This graph is similar to all of the demand and supply graphs we have considered for various goods and services. But instead of the quantity of a product (such as bushels of corn), we have the quantity of labor (such as the number of workers) on the horizontal axis. The vertical axis represents the price of labor, which is the wage rate. The demand curve D is the demand for low-skilled workers by business firms (and anyone else who hires low-skilled workers). S is the supply of native-born U.S. workers who offer their labor services to the low-skill labor market. The equilibrium wage rate is $8 per hour, and the equilibrium number of U.S. workers is 100,000. All of the quantities in this example are unrealistic, but are used for simplicity.

Now let's show the effects of large-scale immigration of low-skill workers. With such immigration, the supply of low-skilled workers increases to S′, which includes both U.S.-born and immigrant workers. The increase in supply causes the equilibrium wage rate to fall to $7.25 per hour. Employment increases to 200,000 workers. But notice that the number of employees supplied by the U.S. native-born labor force is now only 50,000. The remaining jobs are worked by immigrant workers. **So, we could summarize**

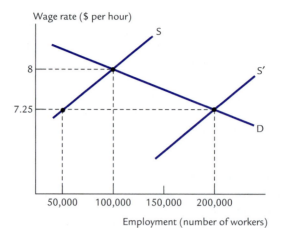

Wage rate ($ per hour)

Figure 14-3 • A U.S. Labor Market for Low-Skilled Workers With and Without Immigration
The quantity of labor (the number of workers) is shown along the horizontal axis, and the price of labor (the wage rate) is shown along the vertical axis. The demand curve D is the demand for low-skilled workers, and S is the supply of native-born U.S. workers who offer their labor services to the low-skill labor market. The equilibrium wage rate is $8 per hour, and the equilibrium number of U.S. workers is 100,000. The immigration of low-skilled workers increases the supply of labor to S′, thereby lowering the wage rate to $7.25 per hour. As a result, the number of native-born workers is just 50,000 workers, while the total number of workers is 200,000.

the *short-term* **labor-market effects of large-scale immigration of low-skill workers by saying that such immigration increases the supply of low-skilled labor, thereby decreasing the wage rate in low-skilled labor markets**. At the lower wage rate, fewer U.S. workers take the low-skill jobs, and immigrants fill more of these jobs. Some specific low-skill labor markets, such as the markets for domestic workers, hotel chambermaids, roofers, and seasonal agricultural labor, may be affected in this way by large-scale immigration. However, studies show that these effects are small, if they exist at all.[5] Others argue that immigrants take jobs that non-immigrants are unwilling to take. If this were true, the supply of labor curve would not really shift forward and the wage rate would not fall. Also note that the increase in supply and decrease in the wage rate are exaggerated in our example in order to show the theoretical result.

Over a longer time period, the effects of immigration are less clear. Lower wages decrease business firms' costs of production, thereby increasing their profits. This situation may encourage businesses to expand, resulting in more employment opportunities. And, American consumers can purchase a larger array of consumer goods and services at lower prices. **Thus, a larger labor force resulting from immigration encourages expanded productivity, economic growth, and jobs**. And, of course, immigrants are also consumers. As they purchase food, clothing, and housing, this increases the demand for labor to produce these goods. All of these factors contribute to economic growth and job creation. In addition, research shows that immigrants, as a group, are entrepreneurial and that they are more likely to start up businesses than are native-born citizens.

We must also remember that many immigrants to the United States are indeed highly skilled and educated. Because of our immigration laws, they are often permitted to immigrate to meet the needs of U.S. businesses that cannot find adequate numbers of U.S. workers with the same qualifications.

Two final factors on U.S. immigration bear mentioning. First, the real solution to illegal immigration is not bigger walls, more powerful guns, and increased numbers of border guards. The real solution is a reduction in poverty in other countries that makes people so desperate to come to the United States that they will risk death and dignity to enter the country illegally. And finally, from a noneconomic perspective, we benefit from greater cultural diversity. After all, we are a nation of immigrants.

Immigration is not just an issue in the United States. Many people from North Africa, Syria, and elsewhere have been driven by desperate conditions of poverty or violence to attempt dangerous migrations across the Mediterranean Sea in small dilapidated boats to get to Europe. Thousands have died in the process, including almost 3,500 in 2014 alone. Others have died in similar circumstances. Global efforts are necessary to try to assist these people and ideally, to remove the circumstances that lead to their desperation in the first place.

The Employment Effects of the Minimum Wage

Another issue concerning unemployment and labor markets is the **minimum wage**. The federal minimum wage was, with a few exceptions, $7.25 per hour in 2015. Individual states and cities have the option of having a higher minimum wage, but it may not go lower than the federal one. As of 2015, 29 states exceed the federal minimum wage. Seattle has a minimum wage of $15 per hour and San Fransisco is using a tiered approach to reach $15 within a few years. President Obama has proposed raising the federal minimum wage to $10.10 per hour, but this proposal has stalled in congress.

To analyze the effects of the minimum wage, we can return to the type of graph of the low-skill labor market that we examined in the discussion of immigration. In Figure 14-4, the horizontal axis shows the quantity of labor (number of workers), the vertical axis shows the wage rate, D represents the demand for low-skilled labor, and S represents the supply of low-skilled labor. In this example, we'll assume that the equilibrium wage rate is $5.00 per hour and that the equilibrium quantity of labor is 100,000 workers.

Suppose the government decides that a wage rate of $5.00 per hour is too low. People may argue that this wage is a poverty wage and doesn't compensate the worker for the value of a hard day's work. The wage is considered to be inequitable. As a result, the

Minimum wage
A legally imposed minimum price (wage) for labor.

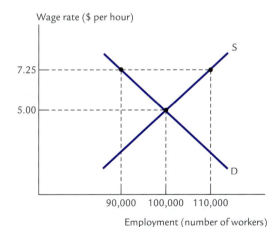

Figure 14-4 • The Minimum Wage in a Market for Low-Skilled Workers
The quantity of labor (the number of workers) is shown along the horizontal axis. The demand curve D is the demand for low-skilled labor, and the supply curve S is the supply of low-skilled labor. The equilibrium wage rate is $5 per hour, and the number of workers is 100,000. A minimum wage of $7.25 results in a quantity of labor supplied of 110,000 workers and a quantity of labor demanded of 90,000 workers. The result is a surplus of 20,000 (unemployed) workers.

© Cengage Learning

Price floor

A legally imposed minimum price for a good or service.

government decides to establish a minimum wage at $7.25 per hour. A minimum wage is similar to the **price floors** discussed in Chapter 11 on agriculture. Price floors are intended to help the supplier, whether it is a supplier of corn or a supplier of labor. The price floor makes it illegal to pay a price (wage) below the established price floor. Therefore, it represents a *minimum* price (or wage).

The minimum wage of $7.25 is indicated in Figure 14-4. Notice that the minimum wage is above the equilibrium wage in this market for low-skilled labor. If the minimum wage is not set above the equilibrium wage, it will have absolutely no effect on the market. Recall that the minimum wage merely prohibits payment of a wage rate below the minimum. It doesn't prevent payment of wages above the minimum. If the minimum wage is below the market equilibrium, the normal equilibrium wage rate will take over.

We can see the effects of the minimum wage in the graph by extending this wage rate to the demand and supply curves for low-skilled labor. We hit the demand for labor curve at a relatively low point on the demand curve, a point corresponding to a quantity of labor demanded of 90,000 workers. This quantity demanded is reasonable, because business firms will try to cut back on the quantity of labor they hire when labor becomes more expensive. Indeed, some of them may go out of business entirely. We hit the supply of labor curve at a relatively high point on the curve, a point corresponding to a quantity of labor supplied of 110,000 workers. This quantity supplied is also reasonable, because more people may be willing to work when wages are higher. The result is a disequilibrium situation in which the quantity of labor supplied (110,000 workers) is greater than the quantity of labor demanded (90,000 workers). A surplus of labor exists, which is another way of saying that the minimum wage has created some unemployment. Although the minimum wage has benefited some workers (those who are able to find jobs and receive the higher wage), it has harmed other workers (those who become unemployed). Business firms also lose as they are forced to pay higher wages. Thus, the results are mixed.

Although our graphical representation of the minimum wage may be appropriate for some low-skilled professions, it is not appropriate for most occupations in our country. Certainly, the minimum wage is below the equilibrium wage rates in these higher-wage-paying professions, and therefore the minimum wage becomes ineffective in these professions. It does not raise wages, and it does not create unemployment. The analysis is valid therefore for only the low-skill occupations we've discussed. Even then, some economists believe the effect of minimum wages on employment is small, if at all.

Is there a better way to ensure adequate incomes for hard-working individuals other than the minimum wage, since the minimum wage creates problems (unemployment) as well as benefits (higher wages)? *Most economists dislike artificial prices, whether they are price ceilings or price floors.* They oppose these measures because they create disequilibrium situations (shortages and surpluses) and distort incentives in markets. *Therefore, direct assistance to targeted groups of people is often preferable.* If our concern is for workers who receive poverty wages, a direct solution would be for the government to simply pay the worker the difference between his or her market wage and the wage necessary for an adequate income. Many people are averse to this type of solution because it appears to amount to a handout, but it avoids the market distortions caused by the minimum wage. Indeed, we do have an example of the alternative solution in the form of the Earned Income Tax Credit, which was discussed in detail in Chapter 6 on U.S. poverty. This **Earned Income Tax Credit (EITC)** reduces the taxes owed by (or provides a payment to) workers with incomes below a certain level. It has certainly helped low-income working people, though many of these workers are still poor, and expansions of the tax credit have been proposed.

Earned Income Tax Credit (EITC)

A federal income tax credit for low-income workers and families.

Inflation

Inflation has not been a serious problem in the United States since 1980, when the Iranian Revolution resulted in the cutoff of petroleum to the United States, thereby pushing up its price (and other prices along with it). But certainly by the year 2000, the problem in the economy was not inflation, but unemployment.

We have noted earlier in this chapter that **inflation** is a rise in the average price level. As you might expect, therefore, **deflation** is a decrease in the average price level. Most of our recent experience is with inflation, so this is the topic that will concern us. But first, to learn how economists calculate the inflation rate, we need to review the **consumer price index (CPI)**.

The consumer price index is what we usually mean when referring to the cost of living. It is defined as a weighted average of the prices of a fixed basket of goods and services purchased by a typical urban household. In the early 1980s, studies were done to determine which goods and services, and which quantities of these items, were purchased by American households. The average, or typical, urban household is then determined. The basket of goods and services purchased by this typical household is assumed to remain fixed over time, until a new survey is done. The prices of items within this fixed basket are based on prices in a variety of urban stores, and a weighted average of these prices is calculated by weighting the prices of large-quantity items more heavily than low-quantity items in the basket. That is, if the typical household purchases 10 pairs of jeans and 1 movie video, the price of jeans receives a weight 10 times the weight of the video when calculating the average price of this basket.

Because the CPI is an index, the weighted-average price of this basket of consumer goods and services is manipulated further. We leave the actual construction of the consumer price index for the appendix to this chapter. Keep in mind, though, that the resulting CPI does not actually tell us the prices that exist in a particular year. It tells us only how prices in one year compare with those in another year.

Using the consumer price index to calculate the inflation rate is easy. We subtract the CPI for one year from the CPI for the prior year, and then divide the answer by the CPI for the earlier year. For example, if the CPI is 200 in 2020 and 180 in 2019, we can calculate the 2020 inflation rate as follows:

$$\frac{(2020 \text{ Inflation Rate} - 2019 \text{ Inflation Rate})}{2019 \text{ Inflation Rate}}$$

or:

$$\frac{(200 - 180)}{180} = \frac{20}{180} = 0.11 \text{ or } 11 \text{ percent.}$$

In this example, the 2020 rate of inflation is 11 percent. (Notice that a decimal, such as 0.11 here, can be translated into a percent by moving the decimal point to the right by two places. That is, 0.11 becomes 11 percent.)

Inaccuracy of the Inflation Rate

We noted earlier that the unemployment rate tends to understate the true problem of unemployment. *We will see that the consumer price index tends to systematically overstate the true problem of inflation for two reasons, both of which have to do with the notion of the fixed basket of consumer goods and services.*

Inflation
A rise in the average price level.

Deflation
A decrease in the average price level.

Consumer price index (CPI)
A weighted average of the prices of a fixed basket of goods and services purchased by a typical urban household.

The basket of goods and services purchased by a typical household is deliberately assumed to remain fixed for several years so that changes in the prices of the basket reflect changes in prices only, not changes in the quantities of the goods and services themselves. Thus, if a typical household purchased 100 hamburgers, 1 computer, and 1,000 gallons of gasoline in the survey year, we assume that the typical consumer purchases the same quantities of these items in later years. Then if the consumer is spending more money in later years, it is because the prices of these items have increased and not the quantities (which we have assumed remain constant).

However, when we ignore quantity changes, we are ignoring the fact that consumers tend to conserve on items for which price is increasing. During a period of rising energy prices, for example, such as we've been experiencing in various years, consumers may reduce the amount of energy they consume. They may insulate their homes, drive more fuel-efficient cars, turn down their thermostats and air conditioners, and so on. When we assume a fixed basket of consumer goods, we ignore the fact that consumers are reducing the amount of energy they purchase (including gasoline), thereby reducing the price of their actual basket of consumer items below the price of the fixed basket. Hence, the inflation rate, based on the assumption of a fixed basket, is overstated.

Similarly, some quality changes within the basket of consumer items are taken into account, but many other quality changes go unrecorded. A price increase may be recorded for a particular item, such as a personal computer, without taking into account some of the quality improvements of this computer. We think of an increase in price as an indicator of inflation, whereas at least some of the price increase may be caused by a change in the nature of the product (its quality). In this fashion, the consumer price index again overstates the problem of inflation.

The issue of the accuracy of the inflation rate is not entirely academic. Certainly, if policymakers are to design appropriate policy, they must know with accuracy how serious the problem is. If the problem of inflation is overstated, macroeconomic policies designed to reduce inflation may at times be inappropriate. Other practical issues involve the **cost-of-living adjustment (COLA)** that is made in some wage contracts, Social Security benefits, and other payments that are adjusted for inflation. As was mentioned in Chapter 9 on Social Security, politicians have sought to reduce Social Security benefits by offering a lower revised estimate of inflation than that provided by the consumer price index, thereby making a more modest inflation adjustment to Social Security benefits. This unpopular measure was never enacted.

Cost-of-living adjustment (COLA)
An adjustment that automatically increases incomes or benefits when the average price level rises.

The Data

Despite problems with the consumer price index, economists and policymakers continue to use it. Table 14-4 shows inflation rates based on the consumer price index for selected years between 1970 and 2013. We can see the very high inflation rate of 13.5 percent in 1980, and relatively low inflation rates since 2010. In fact, inflation rates have been low since the early 1990s.

TABLE 14-4 • U.S. Inflation Rates, Selected Years[a]

Year	Inflation Rate (%)	Year	Inflation Rate (%)
1970	5.8	2010	1.6
1980	13.5	2011	3.2
1990	5.4	2012	2.1
2000	3.4	2013	1.5

[a]Based on the CPI being the average of the time period 1982–1984.

Source: U.S. Department of Commerce, Bureau of Labor Statistics, 2014 www.bls.gov.

The Effects of Inflation

Inflation is generally not as serious a problem as you might think, at least not in the ways you might expect. Most people assume that a rise in the average price level means that we as a people cannot afford to buy as many goods and services as we did before— that is, inflation harms our **purchasing power**. In fact, a period of inflation in and of itself does not have that effect because our purchasing power depends on both the price level and our incomes. If the average price level rises by 10 percent at the same time that our incomes rise by 10 percent, our purchasing power is not altered. *Unless some other factors are present, the income for the country as a whole does rise along with the price level during a period of inflation.* Therefore, the purchasing power of our nation is not harmed.

There are, however, other problems associated with inflation. They can be categorized as problems of redistribution, uncertainty, menu costs, and international effects.

Redistribution

Even though the purchasing power of our people as a whole is not harmed by inflation, certainly some people in the country will gain and some people will lose. The economic situation of others will remain unchanged.

Consider Social Security recipients as an example. Because the Social Security program has an automatic cost-of-living adjuster built into it, Social Security benefits will rise at the rate of inflation. If the rate of inflation in any given year is 4 percent, for example, Social Security benefits will also rise by 4 percent. In this way, the purchasing power of Social Security recipients is unchanged during a period of inflation.

On the other hand, the purchasing power of other people will suffer if their incomes do not increase as rapidly as the price level. Retirees receiving private pensions (not Social Security), workers who have signed a long-term labor contract, welfare recipients, and minimum wage workers may all experience a decrease in their purchasing power. Civil servants, including professors at public colleges and universities, may also experience such a decrease. The negative effects of inflation on these people will be offset by the positive effects on others who see their incomes rise more rapidly than the average price level (such as workers protected by powerful unions). Although these various groups of people will offset one another so that the purchasing power of the nation is unchanged, it is clear that some people within the country benefit while others lose during a period of inflation.

Borrowers are said to gain during a period of inflation, whereas lenders are said to lose. Imagine that you lend $100 to your best friend and agree to charge an interest rate of 3 percent. One year from now, you expect to receive your $100 back, plus $3 to compensate yourself for the year you went without your $100. Imagine, however, that the rate of inflation over the year is 7 percent. Your $103 at the end of the year will not buy as much as the $100 when you lent it to your friend. You lose, but your best friend (still your best friend?) gains.

Realize, however, that most lenders will recognize the significance of inflation when entering into a lending contract. If a bank wishes to charge an interest rate of 10 percent and anticipates an inflation rate of 5 percent, it will charge an interest rate of 15 percent (10 percent plus 5 percent) when it makes a loan. In this way, the bank protects itself from the harmful effects of inflation. Borrowers gain and lenders lose during inflation only if inflation is unanticipated. When inflation is highly variable, borrowers and lenders

Purchasing power
The ability to buy goods and services.

may be less willing to engage in loan contracts because of uncertainty, resulting in slowdowns in economic activity.

Uncertainty: Inefficiency and Risk Aversion

This suggests another problem with inflation: the inefficiency that results from uncertainty about prices. Suppose that the rate of inflation has been 3 percent per year for the past 20 years. In this case, we have good, reliable information on which to base our economic decisions. But suppose, instead, that the inflation rate has varied considerably from year to year, and no one can reliably predict what the rate of inflation will be over the next few years. You will not know now whether you can afford your tuition four years from now. Others will not know whether it's to their advantage to buy a car or a house in a few years when their finances are in better shape, or whether to buy it now before the prices go up too much. Businesspeople will not be able to predict their costs of production, revenues, or rates of return over the next few years and will not know whether they should pursue a particular investment project. Our collective decisions may be incorrect in the face of uncertainty about inflation. Furthermore, if we are all risk-averse, meaning that we prefer not to undertake risks, we may all choose to do nothing rather than risk doing the wrong thing. You may decide not to go to college, others may decide not to buy the house or the car, and the business may decide to forgo productive investment. As we slow down our economic activities, we slow the growth of our economy. People and businesses are unwilling to engage in long-term contracts and activities. The uncertainty effects of inflation are most severe when inflation rates are extremely high or volatile.

Menu Costs

Menu costs

The costs associated with reprinting menus, revising cost schedules, adjusting telephones and vending machines, and so on, when inflation occurs.

When inflation is 2 percent per year, the owner of a restaurant will likely reprint the menu with higher prices at the end of the year. If inflation is 15 percent per year, however, the restaurant owner will likely redo the menu every month or even every week! The costs associated with making adjustments due to inflation are what is meant by the **menu costs** of inflation. However, these menu costs are not restricted to the restaurant example. They apply whenever airlines and bus lines must revise their price schedules and whenever vending machines and pay phones must have their prices and coin slots altered. These costs are not usually considered too serious, but they (like the uncertainty effects of inflation) tend to be more problematic when inflation rates are high or fluctuating rapidly. In the 1990s, pay telephones in Russia were the greatest bargain around simply because officials were not able to change the sizes of the coin slots as rapidly as inflation made this procedure necessary! Obviously, as computers are used to re-write and publicize these price changes, menu costs become minimal.

International Effects

Finally, another problem of inflation in any one country is that it can result in prices in that country being higher than those in other countries. If the United States has an inflation rate of 4 and Japan has an inflation rate of 1 percent, the prices of Ford vehicles are probably rising more rapidly than the prices of Toyotas. American and Japanese consumers alike will be encouraged to buy Toyotas rather than Fords, thus increasing our imports while reducing our exports. However, as the world becomes increasingly interdependent, inflation in one industrialized country can sometimes spread to other industrialized countries as well. It may therefore become less likely that only the United States will experience inflation and not our trade and financial partners.

Types of Inflation

Different types of inflation are identified according to the conditions that lead to them. We consider these types now so that they are familiar to you in the next chapter, in which we see how inflation is caused in the context of the macroeconomy. First, **demand-pull inflation** is caused when any sectors of the economy (consumers, businesses, or government) increase their demand for goods and services. **Cost-push inflation** occurs when there are increases in costs of production, such as rising energy prices or wages. (Cost-push inflation is the type of inflation that occurred when energy prices were increasing in the 1970s.) Finally, **profit-push inflation** occurs when, as a result of market power, businesses deliberately restrict output to drive up prices and profits, as we described in Chapter 13.

> **Demand-pull inflation**
> Inflation that occurs when any sectors of the economy increase their demand for goods and services.
>
> **Cost-push inflation**
> Inflation that occurs as a result of increases in the costs of production.
>
> **Profit-push inflation**
> Inflation that occurs when businesses use market power to restrict output in order to push up prices and profits.

Which Problem Is More Serious: Unemployment or Inflation?

Policymakers are often faced with the question: which is more serious, unemployment or inflation? It's an important question. The answer depends largely on who has been asked the question. An unemployed person will naturally feel that unemployment is the more serious problem. Yet, the effects of unemployment on the individual can be alleviated somewhat with government transfers. Thus, unemployment in a country such as the United States will be less problematic for the individual than will unemployment in a country such as Mexico, for example, which lacks an adequate safety net for its unemployed. Unemployment will nevertheless be very serious for many people in the United States. Furthermore, the effects of unemployment on our nation's output cannot be reversed. Output that is forgone today as a result of resources sitting idle will never be available for consumption tomorrow.

A person living on a fixed income will consider inflation the more serious problem. It is indeed a serious problem for individuals whose incomes do not rise as rapidly as the price level. Many have suggested that incorporating a cost-of-living adjuster into all economic contracts can minimize this problem. Thus, all wage contracts, pension plans, lending and rental agreements, welfare programs, and the minimum wage would provide incomes or benefits that rise along with the average price level, just as Social Security benefits do. Although this measure would eliminate some inequity, uncertainty, and inefficiency, it would not rectify the problems of menu costs and international effects.

Policymakers must face the world as it is and make difficult decisions about the outcomes of policy on unemployment and inflation. **As we see in the next chapter, there is often a trade-off in the sense that one policy will reduce unemployment while increasing inflation, and vice versa.** If we are combating unemployment, we want to stimulate the economy, which may cause inflation. If we are concerned about inflation, we try to contract the economy, which increases unemployment.

As we've looked at the data, we've noted that although our economy can be prosperous one year, it can be problematic the next. Our history is dotted with serious problems of unemployment and inflation. Although our policymakers today have the wherewithal to prevent the types of situations that existed during the Great Depression, certainly less serious levels of unemployment can occur at any time. Such is the nature of business cycles, or the ups and downs of economic activity. In the next chapter, we will examine the types of policies that the government can use to prevent severe instability and to deal with problems of inflation and unemployment.

Global Unemployment and Inflation

It is interesting to compare the United States with other countries in terms of their unemployment and inflation rates. The World Bank publishes these indicators on a yearly basis, using their most updated data. These numbers are shown for selected countries in Tables 14-5 and 14-6. Note the extremely high unemployment rates in some of the Eastern European countries of Macedonia, Bosnia and Herzegovina, Armenia, and Albania, as well as the African countries of Lesotho, Gabon, and Botswana. Greece stands out as a Western European country with an extremely high unemployment rate, akin to the rate in the United States during the Great Depression of the 1930s. Much lower unemployment rates occur, perhaps surprisingly to you, in countries such as Vietnam, Thailand, and Rwanda.

TABLE 14-5 • Unemployment Rates in Selected Countries, 2012[a]

Country	Unemployment Rate (%)	Country	Unemployment Rate (%)
Macedonia	31.0	United States	8.1
Bosnia and Herzegovina	28.2	United Kingdom	7.9
Lesotho	26.5	Canada	7.2
Greece	24.2	Germany	5.4
Gabon	20.3	Uganda	4.2
Armenia	18.5	Vietnam	2.0
Botswana	17.7	Thailand	0.7
Albania	14.7	Rwanda	0.6

[a]Or most recently available year 2009–2012.

Source: World Bank, World Development Indicators 2014. www.worldbank.org.

We also see a wide variety of inflation rates in Table 4-6. As with unemployment rates, we see very high inflation rates in some of the Eastern European and African countries, though not all of them. We also see an extremely high inflation rate in Venezuela, which is typical of (though higher than) Latin American countries in general. Note the very low and even negative inflation rates at the end of the table. Economists do not necessarily regard such low inflation rates as a positive thing, as prices are not always keeping up with GDP growth.

TABLE 14-6 • Inflation Rates in Selected Countries, 2013[a]

Country	Inflation Rate (%)	Country	Inflation Rate (%)
Venezuela	40.6	Brazil	6.2
Iran	39.3	United Kingdom	2.6
Malawi	27.3	United States	1.5
Belarus	18.3	Latvia	0.0
Guinea	11.9	Sweden	0.0
Ghana	11.6	Switzerland	−0.2
Angola	8.8	Ukraine	−0.3
Afghanistan	7.6	Georgia	−0.5

[a]Or most recently available year 2008–2011.

Source: World Bank, World Development Indicators 2014, www.worldbank.org.

Hyperinflation Around the World

We in the United States consider any inflation rate above 10 percent to be exceedingly high. But many countries of the world experience inflation rates far above this, as we've seen in the table. In the past, many Latin American countries have commonly experienced annual inflation rates in the range of several hundred, or even several thousand, percent. Examples from the 1980s and 1990s include Brazil (2,739%), Argentina (3,080%), Peru (7,650%), and Nicaragua (14,316%). Many Eastern European countries have experienced extremely high inflation rates during their transition to market-based economies with market-based prices. The inflation rate in Russia, for example, was 1,353 percent at one point during the year 1992.[6] In 2008, the *monthly* inflation rate in Zimbabwe was in the hundreds of thousands percent! In the context of the extremely high inflation rates, money becomes almost worthless. No one is willing to save, because the value of savings decreases rapidly as the average price level rises. The smart course of action appears to be to spend your money as soon as you get it, because things hold value, whereas money does not! On a recent trip to an African country, your author changed a $10 bill to buy souvenirs. Because of inflation, she ended up carrying a bag full of 20,000 small units of the African currency. In other countries, people have literally gone shopping with wheelbarrows or baby buggies filled with money.

Even with wheelbarrows and armloads of money, the prices of groceries in an economy hit by severe inflation may be rising before the customer can leave the store. Theater prices may increase while you're watching the movie! Lodging prices may double while you are sleeping! (Indeed, your same author had this experience while peacefully sleeping in a small apartment in Russia!) In any of these cases, even a cart full of money may not be enough to pay the bill. In such situations, people may resort to **barter**, because their money is worth nothing. Inflation this severe is what we mean by **hyperinflation**.

Many people fear inflation because they believe it will lead to hyperinflation, but hyperinflation almost always occurs in countries experiencing war, revolution, or other severe disruptions of their economies. Hyperinflation should not be a concern for the United States—even if severe economic disruptions were to occur, the policies of the Federal Reserve System and the government could mitigate their impact on inflation rates. We examine these policies in the next chapter.

Barter
The direct exchange of goods and services for other goods and services rather than for money.

Hyperinflation
Extremely high inflation, whereby money becomes almost worthless.

You, the Student

Child labor was mentioned in Chapter 12 on international trade. It is also relevant to our discussion of employment issues in this chapter. According to the International Labour Organization (ILO) of the United Nations, more than 200 million children in the world today are involved in child labor, doing work that is damaging to their mental, physical, and emotional development. Child labor is usually the result of poverty, and by preventing children from receiving an education, it only perpetuates their poverty. Children work because their survival and that of their families depend on it, and it exists even where it has been made illegal. Sometimes, the fact that it is illegal drives it underground, making conditions even worse for those children who are working. Almost three-quarters of working children are engaged in the worse forms of child labor, including armed conflict, slavery, sexual exploitation, and hazardous work.[7]

You can learn more about child labor by visiting the ILO Web site at http://www.ilo.org. Perhaps your class or student organization may wish to do a project that creates greater public awareness of the problem of child labor. The ILO Web site provides materials, including posters, brochures, and bookmarks, as well as suggested classroom activities to raise awareness of child labor.

View*Point*   Conservative versus Liberal

It is difficult to place the issues of unemployment and inflation into the traditional framework of conservative versus liberal. Certainly, both conservatives and liberals alike prefer to see lower rates of unemployment and inflation. Some specific policy actions may correspond more with one philosophical viewpoint than the other, however. For example, the federal government could become more involved in offering computerized national job search programs in an effort to minimize frictional unemployment. More important, liberals may wish to see the government heavily involved in reducing certain types of structural unemployment. For example, they may want to see government provision or subsidies for child-care services and greater government enforcement of affirmative action and equal opportunity legislation. Both efforts would remove some constraints that prevent groups of people from obtaining available jobs. Another government role could be in expanding training and education opportunities, thereby qualifying more people for available jobs. The government might offer retraining, relocation, and retooling assistance to people laid off and businesses shut down as a result of technological change or international trade. All of these government efforts may be viewed cautiously by those conservatives who are reluctant to see an expanded role of government in the economy and who have more confidence in the private sector to solve our economic problems. More often than not, however, both liberals and conservatives see the value of programs such as these.

As we look at macro policies designed to reduce cyclical unemployment and inflation in the next chapter, we see that conservatives as well as liberals are concerned with these problems. But they support very different types of macro policies, depending on their general view toward government involvement in our economy.

SUMMARY

Unemployment and inflation are two important topics in the context of the macroeconomy. A person is considered to be unemployed when he or she is actively seeking employment but is unable to find a job. Inflation is defined as a rise in the average price level. With the recent recession, the national unemployment rate was very high, and certain age groups and racial and ethnic groups are always more likely than others to experience unemployment. The recent unemployment rate has fallen and the annual inflation rate has recently been relatively low.

Unemployment is categorized as frictional, structural, or cyclical. Inflation is classified as demand-pull,

cost-push, or profit-push. Both unemployment and inflation can cause serious problems in our economy. Unemployment creates both monetary and nonmonetary problems for the unemployed person and reduces output for our nation as a whole. Inflation, especially when severe, creates problems of redistribution, uncertainty and inefficiency, menu costs, and international effects. Policies to correct these problems are an important consideration in the next chapter on government macro policy. Both unemployment rates and inflation rates vary considerably around the world.

DISCUSSION AND ACTION QUESTIONS

1. What does it mean when we say that macroeconomics is the forest, whereas microeconomics is the trees? Which topics are important in macroeconomics? Which topics are important in microeconomics?

2. Why do you think the labor force participation rate of men is higher than that of women in the United States? Why has the labor force participation rate of women been increasing so dramatically?

3. Some economists believe that unemployment rates of women may be lower than those of men during and immediately after recessions. Can you explain this phenomenon?

4. Have you ever been unemployed? (Remember the technical definition of unemployment.) If so, which type of unemployment did you experience?

5. Ask your friends or family how the unemployment rate is calculated. Are they able to give the proper technical procedure?

6. Check the Bureau of Labor Statistics Web site (www.bls.gov) to find out the current unemployment rate. Would you say that our economy is currently experiencing full employment? (Remember, full employment doesn't mean *full* employment.)

7. Can you explain why it is sometimes the case that unemployment rates increase while additional jobs are being created in our economy? And why is it sometimes the case that unemployment rates decrease while jobs are being lost in our economy? (*Hint*: Think in terms of discouraged workers.)

8. What are the effects of unemployment on the individual unemployed person? What are the effects on the economy? Which effects are more serious?

9. What are some policies that can be used to reduce structural unemployment? Try to come up with some of your own ideas.

10. In June 2000, 58 illegal Chinese immigrants were found dead in a sealed area of a truck, smothered by heat and lack of air during a five-hour journey to Britain. It was said that the victims had died "a most terrible death." Similar situations occur frequently as illegal Mexicans cross the U.S. border, often locked in small, airless vehicles, and as Cubans traverse stormy waters in poorly equipped boats. Who do you think is to blame for these situations? Is it the desperate immigrants, the crime syndicates that provide the transportation, a rigid immigration system, a public attitude of hostility toward immigration, or a global economic system that permits poverty in one country alongside prosperity in another? Defend your answer.

11. Many U.S. companies have been charged with buying their products from "sweatshops" operated in poor developing countries. This is discussed in more detail in Chapters 12 and 13. While any job is conceivably better than no job for poor unemployed workers, there is still the equity issue involving dangerous and low paying jobs. Find out what you can do about sweatshop labor by simply googling "sweatshop labor."

12. Why is the understatement of unemployment statistics a problem? Why is overstatement of inflation statistics a problem?

13. Look up the Census Bureau Web site for the Bureau of Labor Statistics (http://www.bls.gov) and see if you can find the current and last year's consumer price index. Use these numbers to calculate the current inflation rate.

14. How are you affected by inflation? Think carefully about the effects discussed in this chapter. Are you a gainer or a loser?

15. Which problem do you believe is more serious: unemployment or inflation? Defend your answer.

NOTES

1. David T. Ellwood, "Anti-Poverty Policy for Families in the Next Century: From Welfare to Work and Worries," *Journal of Economic Perspectives* 14, No. 1 (Winter 2000), pp. 187–198.

2. Forbes, www.forbes.com, for the Universityy of Iowa, www.uiowa.edu; and the Bureau of Labor Statistics, www.bls.gov. You will note that some of the occupations listed do not command a high salary. Some high demand jobs with high salaries include software developers (applications and systems software), market research analysts, personnel training and development specialists, financial analysts, physical therapists, web developers, logisticians, database administrators, meeting/convention planners, translators, and information security analysts.

3. These latter sentiments were expressed by Bishop Nicholas DiMarzio of Brooklyn in a statement released August 23, 2006, and cited in Patricia Zapor, "Labor Day: Challenges, Rights of Immigrants," Catholic News Service, *The Superior Catholic Herald*, August 31, 2006.

4. President George W. Bush, State of the Union Address, January 23, 2007.

5. Roger Lowenstein, "The Immigration Equation," *The New York Times Magazine* (July 9, 2006), pp. 36–43, 69–71.

6. The World Bank, *World Development Indicators 2014* (Washington, DC: The World Bank, 2014).

7. The International Labour Organization, *Child Labour*, http://www.ilo.org/global/Themes/Child_Labour.

Appendix 14-1
Construction of the Consumer Price Index

An index is constructed first by choosing a base year, such as 2002. We then calculate the 2002 consumer price index by dividing the actual weighted-average price of the fixed basket of consumer goods and services by the same value and multiplying the result by 100.

Let's calculate the consumer price index for a small hypothetical country. If the 2002 weighted average of prices of the basket of consumer items is $4,000, we calculate the 2002 index as follows:

$$
\begin{aligned}
(2002 \text{ average price level}/2002 \text{ average price level}) \times 100 &= (\$4{,}000/\$4{,}000) \times 100 \\
&= 1 \times 100 \\
&= 100
\end{aligned}
$$

The consumer price index for the base year will always be 100. Now suppose that we want to calculate the consumer price index for the year 2020. Suppose the weighted-average price of the fixed basket of consumer items is $8,000 in 2020. We calculate the 2020 consumer price index by dividing the $8,000 by the average price level for base year 2002, then multiplying by 100. That is, we calculate the 2020 price index as follows:

$$
\begin{aligned}
(2020 \text{ average price level}/2002 \text{ average price level}) \times 100 &= (\$8{,}000/\$4{,}000) \times 100 \\
&= 2 \times 100 \\
&= 200
\end{aligned}
$$

A consumer price index of 200 means nothing to us by itself. An index is not an average price of anything. However, we can use the CPI to compare prices in one year with those in another year. In our example, we can say that prices have doubled between 2002 (with a CPI of 100) and 2020 (with a CPI of 200).

Chapter 15

ROAD MAP

Chapter 6
U.S. Poverty
Government macro policies can serve to increase or decrease the extent of poverty.

Chapter 7
Housing
A fiscal stimulus was used to assist the U.S. housing market.

Chapter 12
International Trade
What is the effect of macro policy on international trade and finance?

Chapter 13
Market Power
Greater government and Federal Reserve regulation is being urged to protect our economy against further financial market crisis and abuse of market power.

Chapter 15
Government Macroeconomic Policy

Chapter 14
Unemployment and Inflation
Government macro policies can improve or worsen unemployment and inflation.

Chapter 17
Globally Free Markets for the Twenty-First Century?
Will U.S. macro policy and the policies of other countries continue a conservative or liberal trend?

Chapter 16
Taxes, Borrowing, and the National Debt
Government taxes and borrowing contribute to the state of the macroeconomy.

Chapter 15

The Economic Toolbox

- Aggregate Demand
- Aggregate Supply
- Gross domestic product (GDP)
- Real versus nominal GDP
- Composition of GDP
- Distribution of income
- Demand-pull, cost-push, and profit-push inflation

- Recession
- Stagflation
- Full-employment GDP
- Fiscal, monetary, and supply-side policy
- Federal Reserve
- Trickle-down

Government Macroeconomic Policy

N ow it is time to jump into a complete discussion of the macroeconomy. In doing so, you will find that you can more easily understand the issues of unemployment and inflation, as well as other important economic issues facing our nation today. You will also discover the meaning of government macro policies such as fiscal policy and monetary policy, terms that everyone has heard before, especially in light of the recent severe recession, but that few people really understand. Because you already understand demand and supply, you will have no difficulty understanding these macroeconomic topics.

In the long run, we are all dead.

—JOHN MAYNARD KEYNES

Graphing the Macroeconomy

You undoubtedly remember that I promised to present only two basic types of graphs for most of the book. But also remember that I told you we could get a lot of mileage out of these graphs. In particular, we can revise our thinking about the demand and supply graphs of Chapter 1 and use the graphs to represent our economy as a whole.

Recall that each demand and supply graph in Chapter 1 was used to represent the market for a particular good or service, such as tutoring services. The graph representing the market for tutoring services is repeated in Figure 15-1.

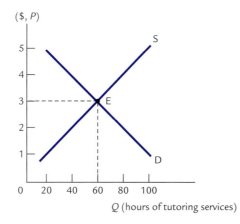

Figure 15-1 • The Market for Tutoring Services, One week
The market will clear at point E. At the price of $3 per hour, quantity demanded equals the quantity supplied (60 hours) of tutoring services.

Now let's transform this graph into one representing our economy as a whole. Let the *P* on the vertical axis no longer represent the price of tutoring services, but the average price level for the economy as a whole. That is, *P* in Figure 15-2 now represents the average price of all output produced in our economy. (For example, *P* could be measured by the consumer price index discussed in Chapter 14.)

Instead of the *Q* on the horizontal axis representing the quantity of tutoring services, let's use the symbol GDP to represent total output of all goods and services in our economy. Note that GDP stands for gross domestic product, which was introduced in Chapter 1 and is defined as our nation's total output. We will consider GDP in greater detail and define it more precisely shortly.

Aggregate demand

The quantity of total output (GDP) demanded (purchased) at alternative average price levels.

Now let's redefine the downward-sloping demand curve as AD rather than D, where AD stands for **aggregate demand** and is defined as the quantity of total output (GDP) demanded (*purchased*) at alternative price levels. This definition sounds very similar to the definition of demand, except that now we are looking at the total demand for GDP by all sectors of the economy. Keep in mind that aggregate demand refers to the "purchasing" side of our economy—that is, the quantity of GDP that will be purchased at various average price levels. **AD represents all people in the world who purchase U.S. GDP.**

Aggregate supply

The quantity of total output (GDP) supplied (produced) at alternative average price levels.

Similarly, we will use the symbol AS for the supply curve, where AS stands for aggregate supply. **Aggregate supply** is defined as the quantity of total output (GDP) supplied (*produced*) at alternative price levels. Here, we are looking at the total supply of GDP by all producers in our economy. Keep in mind that aggregate supply refers to the "production" side of our economy—that is, the quantity of GDP that is produced. **Aggregate supply represents all the people who produce U.S. GDP.**

Notice in Figure 15-2 that aggregate demand is downward sloping (just like a normal demand curve), whereas aggregate supply is upward sloping (just like a normal supply curve). The reasons for the upward slope of aggregate supply are very

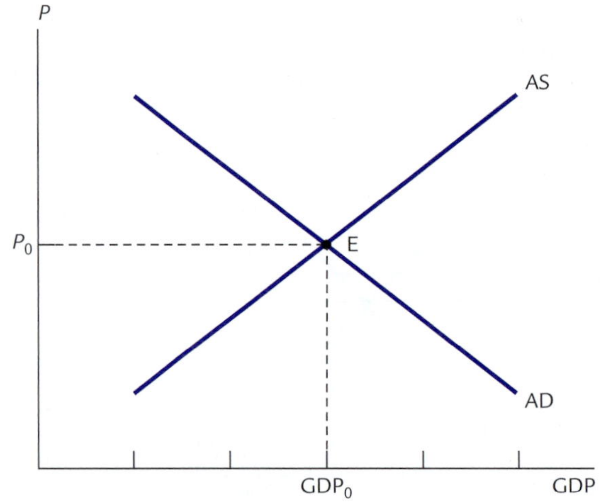

Figure 15-2 • The Macroeconomy

In the graph of the macroeconomy, *P* represents the average price level, GDP is total output, AD is aggregate demand, and AS is aggregate supply. At equilibrium E, the average price level is equal to P_0, and GDP is equal to GDP_0.

© Cengage Learning

similar to the reasons for the upward slope of a supply curve in an individual market. Higher prices for products give producers greater incentive to produce their products; hence, the quantity of output supplied increases when the prices of output increase.

The reasons for the downward-sloping aggregate demand curve are very different from the reasons for the downward-sloping demand curve in an individual market, however. In considering the market for oranges, for example, people are willing to buy more oranges when the price falls because they can more easily afford them. They also might substitute oranges for other types of fruit such as apples and bananas. This kind of substitution is not possible when we are considering aggregate demand, because we are looking at the total demand for *all* output, and substituting *all* output with something else is impossible. Similarly, realize that a decline in the average price level does not make GDP more affordable, since our purchasing power depends on both incomes and prices. We generally assume that overall income in the economy declines as the average price level declines, unless other factors are at work. This concept was discussed in more detail in Chapter 14 on inflation. These considerations suggest that there must be other reasons why the quantity of GDP demanded increases when the average price level falls. These reasons have to do with trade, assets, and interest rates and are discussed in detail in Appendix 15-1 to this chapter.

Finally, notice that aggregate demand and aggregate supply intersect at point E in Figure 15-2. At this equilibrium point, we can see that the average price level is designated as P_0 and actual gross domestic product is equal to GDP_0.

Gross Domestic Product

A Definition of GDP

Gross domestic product (GDP) is defined as the market value of all final goods and services produced in the economy in a given time period, usually one year. We need to think about this definition in detail. First, realize that final goods and services include all products (for example, cars and dishwashers) as well as all services (for example, haircuts and health care) that are purchased as final products. Suppose you buy a bag of flour from the supermarket. This bag of flour is a final product, because it will not be processed and resold later. (You may bake a cake and eat it, but you will not sell the cake.) However, suppose the bakery downtown purchases large bags of flour and uses the flour to produce doughnuts and cookies for sale. In this case, the flour is an intermediate product, and the doughnuts and cookies are the final products. Only the final stage of the product is included in gross domestic product to avoid double counting. The value of the flour is incorporated into the price of the bakery's products; we do not want to count the value of the flour twice.

Second, note that all of the goods comprising GDP must be produced during the particular year. If, for example, you sell your 10-year-old home this year, the value of your home does not constitute part of this year's GDP. However, if you employ the current services of a realtor, the value of the realtor's services is included in this year's GDP because they are current services. Similarly, if a car is produced in one year but is held over as inventory to be sold in the following year, it is counted as part of GDP in the year that it is produced. We consider the car to have been "purchased," for the time being, by the producer, who holds it in the form of inventory.

Gross domestic product (GDP)
The market value of all final goods and services produced in the economy in a given time period (usually one year).

Third, recognize that it is necessary to define gross domestic product in value terms, specifically dollars in the United States. We could not add up all the apples, oranges, refrigerators, and television sets produced in our economy, nor could we determine whether GDP was higher in one year in which we produced lots of refrigerators than in another year in which we produced lots of television sets, because we can't compare refrigerators with televisions. And we could not compare the GDP of the United States—let's say it produces plenty of baseball cards, beer, and hot dogs— with that of Russia—let's say it produces large amounts of potatoes, vodka, and caviar—because we can't compare the quantities of these countries' respective products. You are probably getting the picture: we cannot add apples and oranges, nor can we compare them.

For these reasons, we must first attach value to the physical quantities of output produced; then we can add them up to tabulate total domestic product. We use market prices to value the physical quantities of output. **Market price** includes the retail price of the product plus any sales and excise taxes paid by the consumer. Once output is valued in dollars, we can simply add up the dollar values of output to tabulate total GDP. Money serves as a common denominator.

Finally, notice that the definition of gross domestic product refers to goods and services produced in the economy. This little word *in* is significant, because it distinguishes gross domestic product from gross national product.

Because some statistics rely on data for gross national product, abbreviated GNP, it is useful to define GNP as well. **Gross national product (GNP)** is defined as the market value of all final goods and services produced by the economy over a particular time period. The only difference between the two definitions are the words *in* and *by*!

When we refer to goods and services produced *in* the economy, we mean they are produced within the physical boundaries of the United States. If, for example, a Mexican citizen comes to the United States during the summer to pick tomatoes, the value of these tomatoes would be included in U.S. gross domestic product, because the tomatoes are produced within the physical boundaries of the United States. If, however, a U.S. citizen spends the summer making and selling earrings in Mexico, the value of the earrings would not be part of U.S. GDP, because the earrings are not produced within the physical boundaries of the United States.

On the other hand, when we refer to goods and services produced *by* the economy, we mean by U.S.-owned factors of production (that is, by U.S. workers, business owners, and so on). Now, for example, if a U.S. citizen paints pictures in Mexico, the value of the pictures is counted as part of U.S. gross national product. It doesn't matter where the earrings are produced, as long as a U.S. citizen produces them. Handbags produced by a Canadian citizen in the United States would not be tabulated as part of U.S. GNP (because the producer is a foreign citizen) but would count as part of U.S. GDP (because they are produced in the United States).

Gross domestic product is the concept generally used by the U.S. government and generally used in this textbook. However, GDP data are occasionally not readily available, and GNP is used instead. In either case, the concepts can be viewed as roughly identical for our purposes, both depicting our national production.

The United States has the highest GDP in the world, valued at almost $17 billion in 2013. While we consider other measures such as gross national income in other chapters, total GDP might be considered as a measure of the total economy. In that regard, no other country even comes close. China has the second highest GDP, at about $9 billion. The 10 countries with the highest levels of GDP are shown in Table 15-1.

Market price
The retail price of a product plus any sales and excise taxes paid by the consumer.

Gross national product (GNP)
The market value of all final goods and services produced by the economy in a given time period (usually one year).

TABLE 15-1 • Gross Domestic Product (GDP) of the Top Ten Countries in the World, 2013[a]

Country	GDP (billions of dollars)
United States	16,800,000
China	9,240,270
Japan	4,901,530
Germany	3,634,823
France	2,734,949
United Kingdom	2,521,381
Brazil	2,245,673
Russia	2,096,777
Italy	2,071,307
India	1,876,787

[a]2013 or most recently available data from 2009–2012.

Source: World Bank, World Development Indicators 2014, www.worldbank.org.

Real versus Nominal GDP

Whenever we use any variable expressed in value terms, including gross domestic product, we must be careful about comparing different time periods. Suppose GDP doubles over the time period 1990 to the year 2000. Does this increase mean that actual output doubles, that just the prices of this output double, or that both output and prices have risen? If we are interested only in whether actual output increases, we need to think in terms of real GDP, rather than nominal GDP.

Real GDP is defined as GDP calculated at **constant prices**. Constant prices refer to the prices that exist in a particular base year. If 1982 is the base year, for example, real GDP in 1990 is calculated by valuing the 1990 production of apples and oranges (and everything else) at the prices that existed in 1982. Similarly, real GDP in the year 2000 is calculated by valuing the year 2000's production of apples and oranges (and everything else) in the prices that existed in 1982. Then, when we compare real GDP in the year 2000 with that in the year 1990, any increase in real GDP will be caused by increased output, and not rising prices (because the prices are kept constant). This example is shown below.

Real GDP
GDP calculated at constant prices.

Constant prices
Prices that exist in a base year.

$$1990 \text{ Real GDP} = 1990 \text{ production} \times 1982 \text{ prices}$$

$$2000 \text{ Real GDP} = 2000 \text{ production} \times 1982 \text{ prices}$$

Nominal GDP is defined as GDP calculated at **current prices**, which are actual prices during a particular year. Nominal GDP for the year 2000 would include the production of all those apples, oranges, and everything else, valued at prices that exist in the year 2000; 1990 nominal GDP is valued at 1990 prices. This example is shown below.

Nominal GDP
GDP calculated at current prices.

Current prices
Actual prices of a particular year.

$$1990 \text{ Nominal GDP} = 1990 \text{ production} \times 1990 \text{ prices}$$

$$2000 \text{ Nominal GDP} = 2000 \text{ production} \times 2000 \text{ prices}$$

Nominal GDP is the number we want to consider when we are trying to make sense of information for one year only, such as in Table 15-1. Real GDP is the number we want to use when we are comparing information over different time periods. **Real GDP is adjusted for inflation; nominal GDP is not.**

Flaws of GDP

Gross domestic product is typically used as an indicator of economic activity, as well as a measure of standards of living. When GDP is high, the assumption is that the economy is doing well and that standards of living are high. When GDP is growing over time, the assumption is that economic activity and standards of living are increasing. These assumptions have some flaws, however. Nonmarket activities, the underground economy, and the distribution and composition of national output make GDP an imperfect measure of economic activity and our standards of living.

Nonmarket Activities

Remember that GDP is defined as the market value of all final goods and services produced in the economy. What if a good or service is produced but not marketed? What if you paint your own apartment, eat food from your own garden, or volunteer your services at the local hospital? Or perhaps more important, what if you provide homemaking services in your own home, preparing meals, caring for children, and cleaning the house? All of these activities are productive, but because they are not bought and sold in the marketplace, no market value is attached to them, and they are excluded from GDP statistics.

The exclusion of nonmarketed goods and services serves to understate the full value of productive activity in our economy. Many would argue it also undermines the value of homemaking services, traditionally the domain of women. Failure to fully value these important services may translate into failure to fully appreciate the contributions of women (and an increasing number of men) in our economy.

Exclusion of nonmarketed goods and services also distorts comparisons. During the 1950s, most women stayed home as full-time homemakers. By the 1990s, many women had entered the formal labor market, paying out money for services that they had previously provided themselves. As soon as a babysitter is hired, a housekeeper is paid, and fast food is purchased on the way home from work, these goods and services enter into GDP statistics. *GDP is artificially higher in the 1990s and 2000s than it was in the 1950s in part because people are now being paid to provide the homemaking services that went unrecorded in the 1950s.*

Comparisons of countries' GDPs are distorted as well. In developing countries, families often grow their own food, build their own homes, and gather their own water and fuel, and GDP statistics are very low in part because many of these nonmarketed activities go unreported. Once again, the services of many women (who perform most of these activities) go unrecorded and are undervalued.

Underground Activities

The underground economy involves economic activity that is never reported to the government, either because the activity is illegal or the participants wish to evade taxes. Such underground activity causes GDP to understate actual economic activity.

Suppose you are engaged in illegal activity such as gambling, prostitution, or drug trade (I hope not!). You will naturally report your income from this activity to the government—not! For obvious reasons, illegal economic activity goes unrecorded in gross domestic product statistics. Although we do not know how much underground activity exists, we do know that for many countries it is sizable. In some countries, such as Afghanistan and Colombia, a large share of economic activity consists of illegal drug sales.

Similarly, any time a person engages in under-the-table exchange, usually to avoid payment of personal income taxes, the activity is not recorded and therefore doesn't enter GDP statistics. This type of exchange might include legal activity, such as informal house painting or babysitting, but if payment for the service is unreported, it never enters the GDP statistics. People who underreport their tips distort the GDP statistics in a similar fashion. Again, the magnitude of such underground activity is unknown, but it is thought to be significant in the United States.

Composition and Distribution

There are two more important reasons why gross domestic product is not an adequate indicator of people's standards of living. These reasons are discussed at length in Chapter 7 on world poverty. *For now, let it suffice for us to mention that the* **composition of GDP** *is as important as the total value of GDP.* If a small country primarily produces armaments and other military hardware, for example, its people may not be achieving the same quality of life as those of another country that has a similar level of GDP but primarily produces health care, educational services, and other goods and services directly meeting the needs of people.

Composition of GDP
The goods and services of which GDP consists.

The distribution of GDP or, more technically, the **distribution of income** generated from the production of GDP is also highly significant. It makes a great deal of difference whether a nation's income flows primarily to a small, select, elite group of people or is distributed more equally within the country. The masses of people will live much better in the latter situation. *For this reason, standards of living may depend just as much on the distribution of income as the total value of gross domestic product.*

Distribution of income
How national income is distributed within an economy.

One final note: suppose that the GDP of a country is growing quite rapidly over time, but at the same time, the country experiences more and more pollution, congestion, and depletion of natural resources. Or what if the people of the country must work more and more hours each week in order to produce the high levels of output? Or what if the *Exxon Valdez* disaster, Midwest floods, and Hurricane Katrina all were associated with increased GDP in the cleanup phase? Can we really say that standards of living are improving? *Even though we focus a great deal of attention on total gross domestic product, be sure to tuck away somewhere in your mind that for all of these reasons, high GDP is not necessarily synonymous with high standards of living.*

Aggregate Demand and Supply

Because aggregate demand refers to the quantities of U.S. gross domestic product demanded at alternative price levels, it is useful for us to think of the various sectors that purchase this GDP and that are represented along the aggregate demand curve. In doing so, we can also think through the factors that will shift aggregate demand. For simplicity, let's just think in terms of the factors that might increase aggregate demand. **Aggregate demand will increase whenever any sectors of the economy increase their purchases.** Let's consider each of these sectors in turn.

What Sectors Are Represented by Aggregate Demand?

Consumers

Individual consumers such as you and I purchase U.S. durable and nondurable goods and services. **Durable goods** are products with a life of longer than one year, whereas **nondurable goods** are those that usually last less than one year. Durable goods include items

Durable goods
Products with a life of longer than one year.

Nondurable goods
Products with a life of less than one year.

such as appliances, furniture, and automobiles; food is an example of a nondurable good (assuming you clean out your refrigerator at least once a year—let's hope so!). Household purchases of services such as haircuts and doctor visits are included in the consumer category as well. Indeed, consumer purchases represent the largest component of aggregate demand. It is a relatively stable component as well, particularly the portion consisting of nondurable goods. Regardless of whether the economy is doing well or poorly, people tend to purchase products such as food on a steady basis. Durable goods are less stable; when the economy is doing poorly, many people are forced to reduce their purchases of large-ticket items such as automobiles and home entertainment centers. When the economy picks up, purchases of these items pick up as well.

Consumers will increase their purchases of goods and services as a result of a variety of factors. When consumer incomes rise, consumer purchases go up (since we are richer). When consumer wealth (the value of our stocks, bonds, houses, and rock band equipment) increases, our consumer purchases go up (since we feel richer). When consumer expectations of the future improve, consumer purchases also go up. (If you expect a promotion in the near future, you may well go out and start celebrating now!)

Consumer incomes can be directly affected by government policies. Policies to reduce personal income taxes, for example, will serve to increase our after-tax income. Our consumer purchase will increase as well. Similarly, government policies that increase government income transfers will also increase consumer incomes. An **income transfer**, as you may recall from Chapter 6 on U.S. poverty, is a cash transfer from the government to an individual for which no good or service is provided in return. Examples of income transfers include Social Security payments, unemployment compensation, and veterans' cash benefits. When these income transfers rise, our incomes increase. Once again, when income transfers increase, our consumer purchases increase as well.

Consumers are also responsive to changes in interest rates. When interest rates fall, the cost of borrowing money declines. As a result, consumers are more willing to purchase expensive items that they must buy with borrowed money (houses, cars, and appliances). **Since consumers represent part of aggregate demand, all of the factors that increase consumer purchases will increase aggregate demand.**

Finally, note that although U.S. consumers buy some foreign-produced goods (such as Toyotas and Acer computers), these purchases are not part of U.S. GDP. Therefore, these purchases of imports are not represented along the aggregate demand curve for U.S. GDP.

Income transfer

A cash transfer from the government to an individual for which no good or service is provided to the government in return.

Businesses

Private business firms in our economy also purchase U.S. GDP. They buy a variety of equipment such as machinery, tools, and computers. They also purchase structures such as factories, office buildings, retail outlets, restaurant buildings, and warehouses. Finally, businesses "purchase" their **inventories**, which are unsold goods and materials. These inventories include any unsold final product, the product in intermediate stages of production, and raw materials and component parts.[1]

Business inventories may be held for a variety of reasons. An automobile company, for example, may hold huge inventories of finished cars because the managers anticipate a large demand for the cars in the near future or because demand for the cars has currently fallen off and the product remains unsold. Whatever the reason, increases in inventories are included in aggregate demand as business "purchases." We can envision these

Inventories

Unsold goods and materials.

inventories as though they are purchased by business firms, even though manufacturers do not actually purchase their unsold inventories.

Business purchases are a relatively small component of aggregate demand, but they tend to fluctuate a lot. When the economy is in a downturn, owners of businesses are reluctant to expand by purchasing new factories and equipment. When the economy improves (and business owners are convinced it will last), they are willing to increase factory and equipment purchases.

Business purchases are influenced by a variety of factors. Expectations of the future are an important factor. If the economy is improving and businesses expect their sales to boom, they may begin purchasing new factories and equipment now to meet the future consumer demand. Furthermore, businesses, like consumers, are influenced by interest rates. A decline in interest rates means that new factories and equipment are cheaper and easier for businesses to buy. **Any of the factors that serve to increase business purchases will serve to increase aggregate demand.** However, as with the consumer sector, we are including only business purchases of U.S. GDP and not foreign products.

Government

Government purchases of goods and services represent the third component of aggregate demand. The government purchases a variety of items, including food for government nutrition programs, office supplies for government administrators, and the university computer with which I am writing this book. The government also purchases services, including the services of police officers, firefighters, military personnel, and public teachers (including your author!). Last, the government purchases structures, such as prisons and school buildings. Again, only government purchases of U.S. GDP are represented along the aggregate demand curve.

Note that income transfers are not included in the category of government purchases of goods and services, since the government is not really purchasing anything. Instead, when the income transfers are eventually spent by the recipients, their purchases of U.S. GDP are included in the consumption component of aggregate demand, as we've just noted.

The decisions of government can have important impacts on aggregate demand. *Because government purchases of goods and services are included as part of aggregate demand, an increase in government spending on national health care, the space program, public education, or any other program will directly increase aggregate demand.* In terms of the effect on aggregate demand, it doesn't matter what it is that the government purchases. Thus, if the country goes to war, and the government purchases military hardware and the services of the armed forces, aggregate demand will increase just as if the government had chosen to increase its purchases of public parks and libraries. Of course, in other respects, it certainly does matter what the government purchases.

Don't be confused between government *purchases* of goods and services and the *production* of these goods and services. For now, we are only talking about the purchase of these. The production of these goods and services takes place on the aggregate supply side of the market.

Also keep in mind that government policies can also *indirectly* affect aggregate demand. The decrease in taxes or increase in income transfers mentioned previously will increase the (after-tax) incomes of consumers, which will cause their purchases to increase. These government policies influence the consumption component of aggregate demand. We examine these more carefully shortly.

Foreign Purchasers

As the final component of aggregate demand, we recognize that foreigners purchase some of our production, around 10 percent of U.S. GDP in recent years. These foreigners include individual people, businesses, and governments of other countries, and we refer to their purchases as U.S. exports.

Anything that causes foreign purchases of U.S. GDP to increase will result in an increase in aggregate demand. The size of these exports is largely determined by factors out of U.S. control. Because foreigners are purchasing our exports, their purchases depend on variables such as foreign incomes.

Shifts in Aggregate Demand

An increase in aggregate demand caused by an increase in purchases by consumers, businesses, government, or foreigners is represented as a forward shift in aggregate demand. This shift is shown in Figure 15-3. Similarly, a decrease in purchases by any of the four sectors causes a backward shift in aggregate demand.

Shifts in Aggregate Supply

Aggregate supply can shift for the same kinds of reasons that the supply of tutors in Chapter 1 could shift. An increase in aggregate supply would occur if the costs of production (such as energy prices or wage costs) decrease. Aggregate supply would also increase if technological advance makes production of our nation's output cheaper and easier. In the case of agricultural production, construction, and the services of the tourism industry, aggregate supply would increase if the weather is good. Some economists and politicians believe that the government can use policies to influence a shift in the aggregate supply curve; this issue is discussed shortly. **An increase in aggregate supply for any of these reasons causes the aggregate supply curve to shift forward to the right, as shown in Figure 15-4**.

We are now ready to translate this analysis into a discussion of inflation, employment, and government macro policy.

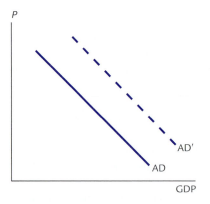

Figure 15-3 • An Increase in Aggregate Demand
When aggregate demand increases, it shifts forward from AD to AD′.

© Cengage Learning

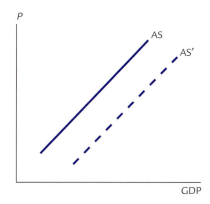

Figure 15-4 • An Increase in Aggregate Supply
When aggregate supply increases, it shifts forward from AS to AS′.

© Cengage Learning

Inflation Revisited

In Chapter 14, we defined the three types of inflation and noted that these could be more easily understood in the context of the macroeconomy. Let's consider each type in terms of the graph of aggregate demand and aggregate supply, focusing on different periods of time in the U.S. economy.

Demand-Pull Inflation

Recall that demand-pull inflation is caused by an increase in aggregate demand. Consider the graph in Figure 15-5. Initial gross domestic product is GDP_0, corresponding to an average price level of P_0. Now consider circumstances that might cause an increase in aggregate demand. The aggregate demand curve would shift forward to AD′, resulting in an increase in gross domestic product to GDP′, as well as an increase in the average price level from P_0 to P'. The rise in the average price level is what we mean by inflation; and in this case, it represents demand-pull inflation.

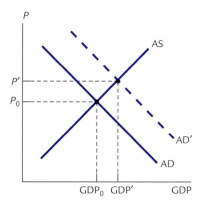

Figure 15-5 • Demand-Pull Inflation
An increase in aggregate demand from AD to AD′ results in a higher average price level (P') and a higher level of gross domestic product (GDP′).

© Cengage Learning

An example of demand-pull inflation would be the conditions that existed during the early 1960s. President John Kennedy had initiated a variety of social programs, which were expanded during the Great Society years of President Lyndon Johnson. All of these programs represented increases in government purchases of goods and services (such as food for needy citizens), as well as increases in government income transfers to low-income people. Personal income taxes were also cut in 1963, resulting in higher after-tax income, and consumers increased their purchases of goods and services as a result. Finally, the war in Vietnam consisted of a demand by the U.S. government for armaments and other military supplies, as well as purchases of the services of armed service personnel.

Cost-Push Inflation

Recession

A decline in a nation's gross domestic product (output) associated with a rise in unemployment. Technically, there must be a decline in real GDP for at least two consecutive quarters.

Cost-push inflation was defined in Chapter 14 as inflation caused by an increase in the costs of production. Inflation rates were very high in the mid- and late 1970s. These rising prices can be explained as cost-push inflation. Cost-push inflation is shown in Figure 15-6. In this figure, the backward shift in aggregate supply results in a decrease in gross domestic product to GDP', as well as a decrease in employment, and an increase in the average price level to P'. The rise in the average price level is the problem of inflation, whereas the decline in GDP is what we mean by **recession**, as defined in Chapter 14.

An example of cost-push inflation occurred in 1973–1974, when oil supplies were cut off to the United States by Arab countries in response to U.S. support for Israel during the Arab-Israeli wars. Oil prices rose as a result. And in 1979, the Shah of Iran was over-thrown during the Iranian Revolution and Iranian oil was once again cut off to the United States. This time, oil prices soared. All these events occurred in the context of increasing market power by OPEC, the Organization of Petroleum Exporting Countries. OPEC used its market power to initiate overall increases in the price of oil. Because oil and related energy products are important components of our nation's overall purchases, the rise in oil prices *directly* caused an increase in the average price level. But beyond this, we also know that energy is an important input in the production of virtually all goods and services. Thus, rising energy prices represented an increased cost of producing virtually everything. The increased costs of production contributed to the decrease in the aggregate supply curve that is shown in Figure 15-6 and was an *indirect* cause of inflation.

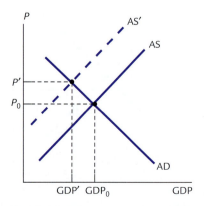

Figure 15-6 • Cost-Push Inflation

A decrease in aggregate supply from AS to AS' results in a higher average price level (P') and a lower level of gross domestic product (GDP').

© Cengage Learning

During a recession, total production declines, and employment falls off as well. (Fewer workers are needed to produce lower levels of output.) There is a correlation between employment and GDP; a rise in one is associated with a rise in the other, and a fall in one is associated with a fall in the other. Thus, the United States experienced the double whammy of simultaneous inflation and recession. This situation is referred to as **stagflation**. Despite the fact that these problems in the macroeconomy were caused by oil price increases, President Jimmy Carter was largely held accountable for them. Many believe that these problems are the reason that President Carter was voted out of office and President Ronald Reagan was voted in during the 1980 presidential election.

Stagflation
Simultaneous inflation and recession.

Profit-Push Inflation

This form of inflation results from the market power of various industries within the U.S. economy. When business firms use their market power, discussed in Chapter 13 as the ability to influence market prices, output is deliberately restricted to drive up prices and profits. If market power is extensive, these conditions show up as a backward shift in the aggregate supply curve. The graph would look identical to Figure 15-6. Although many fail to recognize it, U.S. market power restricts output and employment in the United States and raises the prices of our products, especially manufactured items, thereby harming workers and consumers alike. The rising prices of manufactured products have also had negative implications for developing countries that import these products, as discussed in Chapter 12.

Government Macro Policy

We are now in a position to analyze the policies available to the government to deal with the problems of unemployment and inflation. You have probably heard the terms *fiscal policy* and *monetary policy*. And beginning with President Reagan's first term of office, the nation became familiar with the term *supply-side policy*. Despite our familiarity with these terms, most Americans do not understand exactly what they mean. We consider each of them in turn.

Fiscal policy
The use of government spending and tax policy to shift the aggregate demand curve.

Fiscal Policy

Fiscal policy is defined as the use of government spending and taxes to shift the aggregate demand curve. Fiscal policy can be either **expansionary** (shifting the aggregate demand curve to the right) or **contractionary** (shifting the aggregate demand curve to the left). John Maynard Keynes, who is quoted at the beginning of the chapter, was the economist who developed the idea that the government could use active fiscal policy to correct the economy. He felt that government should act while the problem was occurring, rather than wait for the long-run time period when "we are all dead."

The effects of expansionary policy are shown in Figure 15-7 on page 380. Suppose that the economy is operating with gross domestic product at GDP_0, and the average price level at P_0. Let's assume that full-employment GDP occurs at GDP_F. We define **full-employment GDP** as the level of gross domestic product associated with full employment of the labor force. At full-employment GDP, cyclical unemployment is zero. **Full-employment GDP is a hypothetical concept, and it is the level of GDP that we aspire to reach whenever actual GDP is at some lower level.**

Expansionary fiscal policy
Fiscal policy that increases aggregate demand, thereby expanding the economy.

Contractionary fiscal policy
Fiscal policy that decreases aggregate demand, thereby contracting the economy.

Full-employment GDP
The level of gross domestic product associated with full employment of the labor force. (It is a hypothetical concept.)

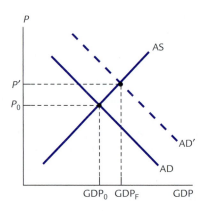

Figure 15-7 • Expansionary Fiscal Policy
Expansionary fiscal policy shifts the aggregate demand curve forward, resulting in a higher level of gross domestic product (GDP_F) and a higher average price level (P').

If expansionary fiscal policy is successful, the aggregate demand curve will shift forward (increase). Gross domestic product will rise to GDP_F, increasing employment in the process. (We need more workers when we produce higher levels of GDP.) The average price level will increase as well.

You already understand the tools that can be used by the government to cause the shifts in aggregate demand. They are government purchases of goods and services, government taxes, and government income transfers. Recall that government purchases of goods and services represent a component of aggregate demand. Thus, whenever the government increases its purchases, aggregate demand will shift forward.[2] Alternatively, the government can reduce personal income taxes. The higher after-tax income of consumers encourages them to increase their purchases, thereby increasing the consumer component of aggregate demand and causing the aggregate demand curve to shift forward. Finally, an increase in government income transfers will serve to raise consumer incomes, again causing the aggregate demand curve to increase. Keep in mind that in all of these cases, the forward shift of aggregate demand represents an increase in aggregate demand.

Any or all of these fiscal policy tools can be used independently. The government may increase its purchases of goods and services while lowering taxes, for example, because there are other ways it can finance its purchases besides raising tax dollars. Therefore, when any one of these policy tools is used, do not necessarily assume that another tool is used simultaneously.

Examples of Fiscal Policy

The 1990s and Early 2000s. When President Bill Clinton took office in 1993, the nation had been experiencing some difficulty with recession. Unemployment rates were higher than normal, and Clinton was seeking ways to increase GDP. That is, he was seeking some form of expansionary fiscal policy. One of his first policy proposals was an increase in national highway construction. The government purchase of construction materials and the services of construction workers served to effectively increase aggregate demand.

President George W. Bush was elected to the nation's highest office in 2000. President Clinton had left him with an unemployment rate that was extremely low at 4.0 percent, and an inflation rate that was relatively low at 3.4 percent. The government budget was in surplus, a conservative welfare system was in effect, and an eight-year stretch of economic growth had continued unmitigated. George W. Bush left no doubt about his intentions to reign in government spending, reduce taxes, and privatize portions of Social Security, health care, and education. Of course, these policies would represent contractionary fiscal policy.

As you now know, our economy changed dramatically in the few years after President Bush entered office. Our nation first experienced a recession that was relatively minor, but with the highest unemployment rates in a decade. Our country experienced 9/11, a war with Afghanistan, and an invasion of Iraq. Apart from military expenditures (which economic conservatives often have favored), taxes and spending on domestic programs were cut. In these ways, President Bush maintained a conservative agenda, similar to the conservative supply-side policies of the 1980s. And except for national defense, his conservative objective was to reduce the role of government in the economy.

As President Bush left office at the beginning of 2009, we faced a very different economy. The nation was in serious recession and was reeling from a housing and financial crisis. A new economy called for new policies and a new president who was willing to use fiscal policy and call for monetary policy that would create economic recovery, as well as correct for the failures and excesses of a deregulated financial sector. President Obama's more liberal economic philosophy ties in well with the government spending needs for a recovering economy and the regulation of a faulty financial sector.

The 2007–2009 Recession. We've previously noted that President Obama faced the economic challenge of a lifetime when he entered office in 2009 in the midst of the greatest recession we've faced since the Great Depression of the 1930s. Unemployment rates were 9.6 percent, 8.9 percent, and 8.1 percent, respectively, by 2010, 2011, and 2012. Expansionary fiscal policy was in order and the president ordered the American Recovery and Reinvestment Act, more commonly referred to as the stimulus bill. This bill was passed by Congress and amounted to $787 billion in new spending and tax cuts that were designed to slow the economy's downward spiral and then help it recover over time.

The increase in government spending, which included an increase in transfer payments as well as the reduction in taxes, is exactly the type of tool of expansionary fiscal policy that we have been considering in this chapter. But this was a major recession. No one expected that the stimulus bill would create an immediate recovery and, indeed, it was designed as a combination of short-term and longer-term stimulus. Nor was it expected to immediately reduce unemployment rates. Most economists believe that improvement in unemployment rates lags by up to 6 to 12 months after a recovery begins and GDP starts to grow, because there are always new entrants into the labor market and because labor productivity continues to rise (so that the number of newly created jobs is always less than would otherwise be indicated and the newly created jobs do not all go to previously unemployed workers).

Short-term stimulus items included an almost immediate reduction in tax withholding from payrolls, putting more income in the hands of consumers immediately. Unemployment insurance benefits were also increased and extended, and there was a one-time increase in social security benefits, both of these transferring more money to consumers. Economic theory tells us that these increases in after-tax consumer income will cause them to increase their purchases almost immediately. This means more income to more computer producers (for example), who then purchase more furniture (for example), and the entire process continues to spiral. It takes a while at each stage of consumer spending to result in the hiring of more employees to produce more of the product and to take home more income and then to increase their own spending. These multiplier effects take place over the longer term.

Other short-term stimulus items included funding for states to avoid cuts and to cover increased caseloads in Medicaid, thereby bolstering the health care industry and providing care to people who could not otherwise afford it, and greater funding for the Food Stamp Program (now called SNAP). Over the longer term, states will be able to continue health care and education programs that might have otherwise been cut and to avoid taxes that might have otherwise been raised. These items also inject more spending into the economy. Some infrastructure projects were undertaken immediately with the stimulus bill, thereby creating immediate employment of construction workers, engineers, and so on. Other projects are scheduled to take place over the longer term. These include spending for mass transportation, highway construction, and energy projects. One popular program was the "cash for clunkers" program, which provided rebates of up to $4,500 to consumers who brought in their old cars and purchased new ones. A number of the stimulus items were designed to improve the environment as well as the economy. And, of course, the President and Congress enacted the Affordable Care Act, commonly referred to as Obamacare, expanding spending on health care (though the act provided for savings in health care as well).

More recently, in his second term of office, President Obama continued his expansionary fiscal policy by enacting or proposing expanded education and training, construction of roads and ports, new hubs for high-tech manufacturing, and loans to small businesses to expand their operations. Spending was limited, and indeed cuts were enacted, as a result of the sequester, which will be discussed in Chapter 16.

Summary of Fiscal Policy

To summarize, expansionary fiscal policy consists of one or more of the following tools:

1. An increase in government purchases of goods and services
2. A reduction in government taxes
3. An increase in government income transfers

Similarly, contractionary fiscal policy consists of one or more of the following tools:

1. A decrease in government purchases of goods and services
2. An increase in government taxes
3. A decrease in government income transfers

Monetary Policy

Monetary policy

Changes made in the nation's money supply to shift the aggregate demand curve.

Federal Reserve

The U.S. central banking system.

Monetary policy is defined as changes that are made in the nation's money supply in order to shift aggregate demand. Whereas fiscal policy is under the control of the government (the president and Congress), monetary policy is under the control of the **Federal Reserve**. The Federal Reserve (often abbreviated as the Fed) is our nation's central bank. The seven members of the board of governors of the Federal Reserve are appointed by the president and approved by Congress. They serve staggered 14-year terms, such that a member is generally appointed every two years. Thus, although the membership of the board of governors is determined by the government, the role of any one presidential administration is limited. Therefore, the Federal Reserve is somewhat immune to politics. The current chair of the Board of Governors of the Federal Reserve is Janet Yellen.

Among other things under the control of the Federal Reserve is our nation's money supply. Changes in the nation's money supply will affect the interest rate. (Although economists refer to *the* interest rate, in fact there are many interest rates, each depending on the type of loan or financial investment. These rates do tend to move up and down together, however.) Think of the interest rate as the price of money. An increase in the supply of money will cause a reduction in the interest rate (just as an increase in the supply of corn will cause a reduction in the price of corn). A decrease in the nation's money supply will cause an increase in the interest rate.

Monetary policy affects the economy through its effects on interest rates. A fall in the interest rate will cause a rise in business purchases of factories and equipment, as well as an increase in consumer purchases of cars, houses, appliances, and other expensive items. Businesses and consumers must borrow money to finance these major purchases, and falling interest rates lower the cost of borrowing. Many business firms and consumers decide that they can now afford to purchase the items because of the low cost of borrowing money. **Thus, an increase in the nation's money supply will cause a fall in interest rates, causing an increase in consumer and business purchases, and therefore an increase in aggregate demand.** An increase in the nation's money supply reflects **expansionary monetary policy** (monetary policy that increases aggregate demand, thereby expanding GDP). A decrease in the nation's money supply will decrease aggregate demand, and is therefore called **contractionary monetary policy**. It will contract GDP.

Thus, monetary policy, just like fiscal policy, is an aggregate demand-side policy. Students sometimes get confused when they think of the term *money supply* and they assume it affects the supply side of the economy. Rather, monetary policy, just like fiscal policy, is designed to influence aggregate demand.

Examples of Monetary Policy

1981–1983. The Federal Reserve may choose either expansionary or contractionary monetary policy, depending on the state of the economy. A good case in point is the situation encountered by newly elected president Reagan in 1981. As a result of the rise in oil prices already described, the president faced a serious problem of inflation. Although the president has no direct control over monetary policy, President Reagan did make a national plea to the Federal Reserve to engage in contractionary monetary policy to reduce aggregate demand. The Federal Reserve complied; the results are indicated in Figure 15-8, with the decrease in aggregate demand and consequent decline in GDP.

As the Federal Reserve reduced the nation's money supply, interest rates soared. The construction industry and the automobile industry were particularly hard hit, as businesses and consumers were unable or unwilling to borrow at such high interest rates

Expansionary monetary policy
Monetary policy that increases aggregate demand, thereby expanding GDP.

Contractionary monetary policy
Monetary policy that decreases aggregate demand, thereby contracting GDP.

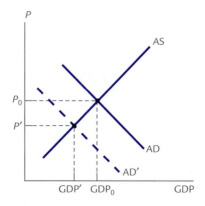

Figure 15-8 • Contractionary Monetary Policy
Contractionary monetary policy shifts the aggregate demand curve backward, resulting in a lower level of gross domestic product (GDP′) and a lower average price level (P′).

© Cengage Learning

and were therefore unable to finance purchases of factories, houses, and automobiles. The consequent recession resulted in the high unemployment rates of the early 1980s. Inflation was controlled, but at the cost of severe recession and unemployment.

2009–2014. Another example of monetary policy took place with the Great Recession beginning at the end of 2007 and continues as of 2014. The situation called for classic and drastic expansionary monetary policy, as well as expanded regulations over the nation's financial and monetary system. The Federal Reserve, first under Ben Bernanke and then Janet Yellen, engaged in expansionary monetary policy, which resulted in lower interest rates and increased borrowing and spending by consumers and businesses and a consequent increase in aggregate demand. Consumers bought more cars and computers and businesses bought more factories and equipment. In this case, expansionary monetary policy was used to its fullest, bringing some interest rates down to zero and enabling banks to lend at lowest possible interest rates.

2015 and beyond. By 2015, with recovery from the Great Recession well underway, there was considerable talk of the Federal Reserve reversing its years of monetary expansion and allowing interest rates to rise once again. This would prevent any possible inflation from developing, but others are fearful that employment would suffer at the same time. Janet Yellen has made it clear that her primary concern is unemployment, and made this visible in an early 2015 photo op with unemployed workers standing behind her. Still, with the economy recovering, many expect a rise in interest rates in the near future.

Summary of Monetary Policy

To summarize, expansionary monetary policy consists of Federal Reserve action to increase the nation's money supply, which causes interest rates to fall, which encourages consumers and businesses to increase their purchases of goods and services. Contractionary monetary policy consists of Federal Reserve action to decrease the nation's money supply, which causes interest rates to rise, which encourages consumers and businesses to decrease their purchases of goods and services. In the first case, aggregate demand increases, along with GDP, employment, and the average price level.

The Trade-Off Between Unemployment and Inflation

These examples of fiscal and monetary policy demonstrate one shortcoming of policy that operates on the aggregate demand side of the economy. An increase in aggregate demand, as in the case of the expansionary fiscal policy in the early 1960s, results in an increase in GDP and employment, but at the cost of creating inflation (the rise in the average price level). A decrease in aggregate demand, as in the case of the contractionary monetary policy in the early 1980s, reduces the problem of inflation, but at the cost of creating recession (the decrease in GDP). Recession creates unemployment. **Thus, aggregate demand-side policy creates a trade-off between the problems of unemployment and inflation, at least in the short run.** (This trade-off is modified somewhat in Appendix 15-1 with a bit more realistic view of the aggregate supply curve.)

Supply-Side Policy

Wouldn't it be nice to come up with a policy that would simultaneously reduce inflation and unemployment? This objective underlies supply-side policy and was the reason for the widespread jump onto the supply-side bandwagon of the Reagan administration of 1981–1984. **Supply-side economics** was a revolution in thought. Adopting a general philosophy that promoted less involvement of government in the economy, President Reagan undertook supply-side policies with the stated objective of increasing aggregate supply. President George W. Bush also shared some of Reagan's perspectives. **The idea behind supply-side policy is that by increasing aggregate supply rather than aggregate demand, GDP and employment will rise, and the average price level will simultaneously fall.** This phenomenon is questionable and quite controversial among economists. It also had very negative side effects. For these reasons, we will relegate this topic to Appendix 15-2.

Supply-side economics
The view that conservative economic policies can be used to increase aggregate supply.

The Post-Great Recession Economy

The Great Recession officially began in late 2007 and ended in 2009. Since then, GDP began rising slowly and then steadily gathering speed. By late 2014 and 2015, the economy was doing quite well, with growth spurred in part by falling oil prices. As you know, with consumers spending less at the pump, they have more money to spend on consumer purchases, which in turn spur on the economy. Unemployment rates have fallen, though serious problems of discouraged workers, part-time workers, and low wages for many have remained. Thus, the picture isn't quite as rosy as we would like.

The Great Recession in the United States had serious negative ramifications for the rest of the world. Slowdowns were severe in China, Japan, Russia, much of Europe, and of course, the developing world. More recently, oil producing countries, including Russia and others, have suffered even more severely as their income from oil exports plummeted. Many countries are beginning to recover, though slowly. While conditions in the United States have major implications for the rest of the world, slow growth in the rest of the world has less impact on the United States, largely because the United States is far less dependent on trade (as was discussed in Chapter 12).

You, the Student

In Norway, and in other European countries, it is taken for granted that the government will assist people in managing their home lives with their employment. For example, pregnant women receive paid sick leave for morning sickness. They receive one full year of paid maternity leave. Fathers are required to take three months of paid paternity leave. Women or men who choose to stay at home with their small children are paid by the government to care for them, rather than placing them in day care. We can say that these policies are extremely family friendly. Do they encourage excessive births? Probably not, as the birth rate in Norway is extremely low. If you would like to see these types of policies in the United States, you could try writing to your legislators at www. senate.gov and www.house.gov. Ask them how they feel about these measures.[3]

ViewPoint | Conservative versus Liberal

Any one of the tools of fiscal policy or the use of monetary policy can successfully expand the economy. Theoretically, the use of supply-side policy can do the same. Even if all these expansionary policies are equally effective, people will disagree about the type of policy to be used. Liberals, you should note, would be in favor of fiscal policy that increases government purchases and transfers, especially if the government purchases are for domestic social programs. Conservatives would also prefer to see fiscal policy that reduces taxes and places more purchasing power in the private sector of the economy, though conservatives are often supportive of high levels of defense-related spending. Conservatives would also prefer the use of monetary policy, which, by lowering interest rates, enables private consumers and businesses to increase their purchases.

Thus, although the various policies may be similar in terms of their desired impact on the macroeconomy, the philosophies underlying them vary greatly. And even though these policies may cause identical change in the size of our gross domestic product, the composition of GDP and the distribution of income will certainly be affected. We may have more national defense, but less national health care. We may have more money in the hands of the rich, but no change in the incomes of the poor. And we may have more purchases of homes and factories, but fewer purchases of public school buildings. Certainly, the composition of GDP and the distribution of income are as important as the size of GDP itself.

SUMMARY

We can analyze the macroeconomy with a graph of aggregate demand and supply. Aggregate demand is the quantity of total output demanded at alternative average price levels, whereas aggregate supply is the quantity of output produced at alternative average price levels. The intersection of aggregate demand and supply determines the country's average price level and actual level of gross domestic product. Actual GDP is correlated with the nation's level of employment. GDP refers to the market value of all final goods and services produced in the economy, usually within a one-year time period. Aggregate demand consists of the purchases of consumers, businesses, government, and foreigners. The government and the Federal Reserve can use policies to shift aggregate demand and supply in an effort to reduce inflation or unemployment. The two types of policies used to shift aggregate demand are fiscal policy and monetary policy. Fiscal policy includes changes in government spending and taxes, whereas monetary policy works by changing the nation's money supply to alter interest rates.

DISCUSSION AND ACTION QUESTIONS

1. Many have argued that the government should attach a value to homemaking services and include this value in gross domestic product statistics. Do you agree? Why?

2. Is gross domestic product an accurate measure of the standard of living? Why or why not?

3. Describe the effect on gross domestic product, employment, and inflation of each of the following: (a) war, (b) elimination of environmental regulations, and (c) cuts in welfare benefits.

4. Look up the current level of GDP at the Census Bureau's Web site (http://www.census.gov). What is the value of nominal GDP? What is the value of real GDP? What is the base year(s) used in calculating real GDP?

5. Look up the current unemployment rate at the Bureau of Labor Statistics Web site (http://www.bls.gov). Would you say we currently have full employment?

6. Conservatives favor a lesser role for government in the economy, whereas liberals favor a greater role. How would each of these groups feel about a fiscal policy that increases government purchases and income transfers? Fiscal policy that reduces taxes? Monetary policy that reduces interest rates?

7. What is your opinion about the role that government should play in the economy?

8. Go to the Web site of the president (http://www .whitehouse.gov) and search for a recent speech by the president that focuses on government spending or tax policies. What type of macroeconomic policy is being promoted? Do you agree?

9. Do you believe in trickle-down philosophy? (See Appendix 15-2.)

Notes

1. Don't be confused by the fact that business purchases of GDP include intermediate goods. Even though the definition of GDP includes final goods and services only, business purchase of intermediate goods is included because of an accounting technique. This technique relies on "value added"; in other words, only the *additional* value of a good or service at each stage of the production process is measured as GDP, thereby avoiding the double-counting problem of including intermediate as well as final goods in tabulating GDP. Either technique—adding up value added at each stage or only adding final goods and services—will give us the same value for GDP.

2. There is a multiplier effect associated with increased government spending. Not only is there the initial spending on highway construction, for example, but when construction workers get hired and paid, they go out and increase their demand for consumer purchases, let's say of automobiles. More autoworkers are hired and paid, and they go out and increase their demand for consumer purchases, let's say computers. As more computer producers are hired, they increase their demand for consumer purchases. All of this spending was triggered by the initial government spending on highway construction and all of it results in an increase in aggregate demand. This multiplier effect also works in reverse. If government purchases of highway construction fall, construction workers lose their jobs and reduce their purchases of cars. Car producers lose their jobs and reduce their purchases of computers, and so on. Finally, the multiplier effects occur with fiscal policy that operates through changes in transfers and taxes as well. Our simplification of ignoring these multiplier effects in the text do not alter the final conclusions.

3. Your author's daughter is a resident of Norway with two small children. The comments are based on her experiences.

The Slope of the Aggregate Demand Curve

I t was noted earlier that the aggregate demand curve slopes downward, as shown in Figure 15-9. The downward slope indicates that the quantity of gross domestic product demanded increases when the average price level falls and that it decreases when the average price level rises. The relationship between the quantity of GDP demanded and the average price level is negative for three reasons. They are not the reasons you would normally expect, as indicated earlier in the text.

First, let's consider the international trade effect of a rise in the average price level. If the average price level in the United States rises relative to the price levels in other countries, then American consumers will tend to buy more foreign goods and fewer American goods. Thus when we noted earlier that there are no substitutes for the purchase of U.S. GDP, there are in fact substitutes in the form of foreign-produced GDP. The price of a Ford vehicle may rise, for example, in comparison with the price of a Toyota. U.S. consumers (as well as the consumers of other countries) will probably buy more Toyotas and fewer Fords. This reduction in U.S. GDP demanded occurs as a result of the rise in the U.S. average price level.

Second, a rise in the average price level reduces the value, or purchasing power, of our wealth (assets). Our wealth is what we own, such as houses, stocks, bonds, and even money. The money you have tucked away in a savings account (or under your mattress, for that matter) is no longer worth as much when the average price level rises. That is, a

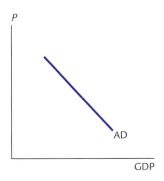

Figure 15-9 • A Downward-Sloping Aggregate Demand Curve
A downward-sloping aggregate demand curve means that the quantity of gross domestic product demanded (*purchased*) increases when the average price level falls and decreases when the average price level rises.

© Cengage Learning

fixed amount of money loses its purchasing power when the prices of purchased items increase. Less wealth means that people cut back their purchases (because they feel less wealthy). Thus, the quantity of GDP demanded falls when the average price level rises.

Third, a rise in the average price level has implications for interest rates. When people experience a loss in the value of their assets as we have just considered, they need to borrow more money from their banks in order to make their purchases. Borrowing this money represents an increase in the demand for credit and pushes up the price of credit—in other words, the interest rate. As interest rates rise, people and businesses reduce their purchases of big-ticket items, such as cars, homes, and factories. Thus, the quantity of GDP demanded decreases as the average price level rises.

In all of these examples, we have considered why a rise in the average price level causes a reduction in the quantity of GDP demanded. Realize that a decrease in the average price level will cause the opposite effect, that is, an increase in the quantity of GDP demanded.

Keep in mind the difference between factors that cause a movement along the aggregate demand curve and factors that cause a shift in the aggregate demand curve. Because the average price level is on the vertical axis of the graph of aggregate demand, any change in the average price level that causes changes in the quantity of GDP demanded is reflected as a movement along the demand curve. On the other hand, changes not precipitated by a change in the average price level—such as changes in population size, consumer incomes (not wealth), or government fiscal or monetary policy—will cause a shift in the entire aggregate demand curve.

The Slope of the Aggregate Supply Curve

The actual slope of the aggregate supply curve is important when it comes to policy prescription. Throughout the chapter, we've used a simplified version of the aggregate supply curve, one with a straight-line upward-sloping shape, as is shown in Figure 15-10. This shape is responsible for one of our conclusions in this chapter: that aggregate demand-side policy creates a trade-off between unemployment and inflation. This trade-off is not quite so clear-cut if we look at the aggregate supply curve more carefully.

Economists have come to various conclusions about the shape of the aggregate supply curve, depending on whether they consider the long run or the short run, as well as other

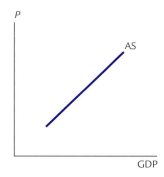

Figure 15-10 • A Straight-Line Upward-Sloping Aggregate Supply Curve
A straight-line upward-sloping aggregate supply curve means that the quantity of gross domestic product supplied (*produced*) rises when the average price level rises and falls when the average price level falls.

© Cengage Learning

assumptions. We can simplify, however, and draw an aggregate supply curve that incorporates many of these views. This supply curve is depicted in Figure 15-11.

Notice that the aggregate supply curve in Figure 15-11 has a flat range (Range A), an upward-sloping range (Range B), and a vertical range (Range C). The upward-sloping range corresponds to the aggregate supply curve in Figure 15-10 and can be viewed as reflecting a normal state of the economy—that is, one with moderate changes in GDP, employment, and the average price level. *Any shift of aggregate demand within this range will create the trade-off between unemployment and inflation.* (See the shift from AD_2 to AD_3 in Figure 15-12. GDP increases from GDP_2 to GDP_3, and the average price level increases from P_2 to P_3.) Employment rises along with the rise in GDP.

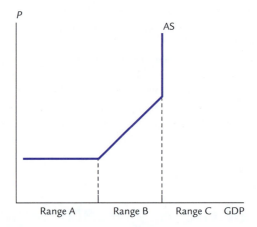

Figure 15-11 • An Aggregate Supply Curve with Three Distinct Ranges
The flat region (Range A) represents low output and employment, the upward-sloping region (Range B) represents a moderate level of output and employment, and the vertical region (Range C) represents high output and full employment.

© Cengage Learning

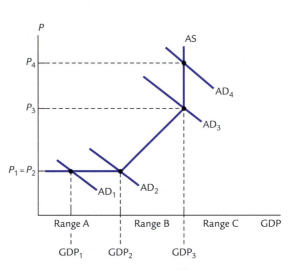

Figure 15-12 • Shifting Aggregate Demand in the Three Ranges of the Aggregate Supply Curve
An increase in aggregate demand causes an increase in just GDP in Range A of the aggregate supply curve, an increase in GDP and the average price level in Range B, and an increase in just the average price level in Range C.

© Cengage Learning

The flat range of the aggregate supply curve is sometimes called the Keynesian range, because it is typical of the depression era when John Maynard Keynes developed his theory of the economy. Specifically, GDP was low, unemployment rates were extremely high, and workers were willing to work for whatever low wages were being offered at the time. Capital equipment (factories and machinery) was underutilized, operating perhaps only one shift per day instead of two or three. In this context, firms can easily expand production to meet expanded demand. Production costs per unit of output (per car, for example) will not rise, since wages and capital prices will not be pushed upward. Without rising costs of production, firms have no reason to raise their prices to consumers. *This means that within the flat Keynesian range of aggregate supply, any increase in aggregate demand will increase output and employment, without causing any attendant inflation.* This situation is shown in Figure 15-12, where the shift in aggregate demand from AD_1 to AD_2 increases GDP from GDP_1 to GDP_2, but P_2 remains equal to P_1.

Finally, the vertical range of aggregate supply corresponds to a situation of high GDP and a fully employed economy. Keeping in mind the definition of full employment from Chapter 14, expanding production beyond this level is very difficult. If aggregate demand increases, for example, and the manager of an automobile company wishes to expand production to match the additional demand, the only way to hire additional workers will be to offer higher wages. Similarly, if capital is fully utilized, any expansion of car production will require additional capital. Both of these situations will create rising costs of production, which firms will try to pass on to consumers in the form of higher prices. Despite the inflation, however, overall GDP will not expand, because the only way to hire additional resources in a fully employed economy is to bid them away from other firms. The automobile company may be able to expand car production, but a refrigerator company, for example, may lose employees and end up reducing output. *An increase in aggregate demand in this context of full employment will only create inflation, without creating any additional output or employment.* This outcome is shown in Figure 15-12, where aggregate demand increases from AD_3 to AD_4. The average price level rises from P_3 to P_4, but GDP does not increase.

Although the economy is generally not in a state as extreme as Range A or Range C, we can understand that an increase in aggregate demand when employment is low will fairly easily result in expanded output and employment, without triggering much inflation. On the other hand, an increase in aggregate demand when employment is high will largely create inflation, without triggering much of an increase in production or employment.

Appendix 15-2

Supply Side Economics

Recall that aggregate supply refers to the "production" side of our economy—that is, the quantity of GDP that is produced. Aggregate supply represents all the people and businesses that produce U.S. GDP. It is the quantity of total output (GDP) supplied (produced) at alternative average price levels.

Tools of Supply-Side Policy

The supply-side tools of President Reagan included cuts in personal income tax rates, cuts in government transfer programs, and cuts in government regulations. These policies are relevant today, because they are the same types of policies that economic conservatives, including President George W. Bush, have enacted and other conservative politicians are proposing and enacting. Each of these policies is considered in turn in the following sections. They can all be depicted in Figure 15-13.

Cuts in Personal Income Tax Rates

Supply-side policy
The use of various tools to improve the incentives for workers and businesses to produce more output, thereby increasing aggregate supply and GDP.

This policy tool is a little confusing, because fiscal policy as well as **supply-side policy** can utilize cuts in taxes. Recall that in terms of fiscal policy, a tax cut will place more income in the hands of consumers, who will increase their consumption purchases. This phenomenon is reflected in an increase in aggregate demand. The effects of the tax cut are very different from the perspective of a supply-side theorist, however. From this perspective, the tax cut must take the form of a reduction in tax *rates*, because it is assumed that tax rates influence our decisions (incentives) about work effort. A reduction in tax rates is considered tantamount to an increase in hourly wages, and it is assumed that people will respond to the incentive of higher after-tax wages by increasing their work effort. That is, some people will take second jobs, others will accept overtime hours, and still others will take a job that they previously were unwilling to take. *Supply-side policies typically center on incentives, and here the incentive is to increase work effort. If the nation's workers respond as desired, the increased work effort will result in expanded production, which will increase the supply side of the economy.* Aggregate supply will shift forward, as in Figure 15-13, resulting in expanded GDP and a decreased price level.

In 1981, President Reagan proposed a series of large, three-year tax rate cuts. Although Congress scaled back the magnitude of the cuts somewhat, they were the largest tax cuts in our nation's history up to that time. The tax cuts were subsequently criticized, because high-income households received by far the largest tax reductions, whereas low-income households received very little benefit.

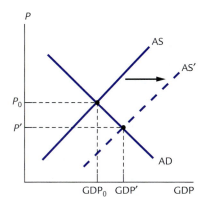

Figure 15-13 • Supply-Side Policy
If supply-side policy is effective, it will shift the aggregate supply curve forward, enabling an increase in GDP without an attendant increase in the average price level.

© Cengage Learning

More recently, President George W. Bush pushed similarly large federal income tax rate cuts through Congress, as well as cuts in other taxes. Although he stated that everyone who pays income taxes deserves a tax cut, in fact his tax proposals were designed once again to primarily benefit higher-income earners. While President Bush claimed that the tax cuts were intended to create economic growth, we can't ignore the fact that they were motivated by a conservative agenda, as was the case of the tax cuts under President Reagan. The Bush tax cuts are discussed further in Chapter 16.

Cuts in Income Transfers

Like cuts in taxes, cuts in income transfers can be construed as both fiscal policy and supply-side policy tools. In terms of fiscal policy, the cuts in income transfers would lower recipients' incomes, causing their consumption purchases to fall. This outcome would be reflected in a decrease in aggregate demand. In terms of supply-side policy, incentives again become important. Many conservatives argue that transfer programs provide incentives for people to be lazy, seeking handouts from the government instead of going to work. By reducing transfers, people are forced to seek employment. With more people working, production expands and aggregate supply increases.

President Reagan enacted large cuts in government income transfers, primarily social welfare programs. All of these had a major impact on the nation's poor. As discussed in Chapter 6, our recent welfare reform has gone beyond work incentives, now *requiring* that participants work. Whether the issue is incentives or requirements, the intention is to increase people's work effort, thereby increasing production and aggregate supply. Of course, a welfare system that relies on work runs into trouble in a recession, where work opportunities are scarce. This was the situation faced by low-income people during the 1981–1983 and 2007–2009 recessions.

Deregulation

A third supply-side tool used by President Reagan was that of **deregulation**, which refers to reductions in government regulations affecting American businesses. The largest cuts were made in the areas of environmental protection and worker safety. The Reagan

Deregulation
The reduction of government regulations.

administration argued that these regulations tie the hands of business and increase the costs of production. Deregulation also works through incentives; lower costs of production raise profit margins, giving businesses greater incentives to produce. By reducing these regulations, President Reagan argued that businesses would expand production, thereby increasing aggregate supply. The conservative agenda of President George W. Bush was really no different in this respect. Economic conservatives believe that reducing government regulations not only creates greater incentives for businesses to expand production, but they like the idea of restricting the role of government in the economy as well.

In addition to deregulation in the areas of environmental protection and worker safety, the financial sector also experienced deregulation through the early 2000s. This, as you know, was a key factor triggering the financial and housing crisis, followed by the recession in late 2007. Regulation of the financial sector will be discussed in more detail in Chapter 17. In the meanwhile, realize that there is considerable disagreement over the future role of the Federal Reserve in preventing such further crises. Whether the Fed's regulatory powers will be extended, or whether the Fed will stick primarily to monetary policy, remains to be seen.

Effects of Supply-Side Policy

Were the supply-side tools of the early 1980s successful in increasing GDP? Have the more recent conservative policies of the first decade of the 2000s been effective in expanding our economy? Answering these questions is difficult because supply-side policies do not operate in a vacuum. Implemented simultaneously with the supply-side policies of the early 1980s was the contractionary monetary policy already described. The effects of the monetary contraction by far dwarfed any expansionary supply-side effects that may have occurred. Similarly, the effects of supply-side policy in the first decade of the 2000s were much smaller than other forces that have served to alter aggregate demand. As is discussed in the next chapter, these latter forces include increased spending by the Bush administration on warfare, national defense, and homeland defense.

We have reasons to question supply-side effectiveness. Cuts in tax rates have a limited effect, if any, on work effort. Most people are unable to alter the number of hours they work each week, so increased incentives for work effort will not change the number of hours worked. Others may increase their work hours when their after-tax wages go up because the incentive to do so is now greater. Still others may decide to cut their work hours because tax rate cuts allow them to maintain their desired level of income while working fewer hours. Many labor economists believe that the overall impact of changes in after-tax wages is probably close to zero, meaning that overall work effort remains largely unchanged.

Many have argued that just like tax rate cuts, cuts in government transfers do not result in expanded work effort. After all, transfer programs have often been meant for women with small children and others who were unable to work. Furthermore, many participants in our current welfare system (TANF, as discussed in Chapter 6) will not be able to work unless their needs for child care, transportation, job training, and education are met. Finally, given the possibility of recession at any time, jobs may simply be unavailable (as was the case in the early 1980s and in 2007–2009). Just because a person has an incentive (and with TANF, a requirement) to work does not mean that he or she will find a job. Clearly, jobs must exist if the incentives are to be effective in increasing work effort and aggregate supply.

Finally, in terms of deregulation, there can be serious implications for workers and the environment. And, of course, the deregulation of the housing and financial sectors just mentioned had disastrous effects on our economy, including the sharp decline in GDP and employment.

Keep in mind that the supply-side policies of the early 1980s, as well as the conservative policies of the early 2000s, all have as their objective a reduced role for government in the economy. Supply-siders would reduce government domestic spending and involvement in social programs, reduce taxes so as to increase the spending ability of the private sector, and reduce government regulatory control over business. *The conservative objective of reducing the government role in the economy is at the root of supply-side policies.*

If we question the effectiveness of supply-side policy to create economic growth, then we must wonder what other factors might be more successful? The forces that *do* serve to increase long-term aggregate supply are discussed in Chapter 17, where we look at economic conditions in the twenty-first century. In fact, we merely need to think in terms of the production possibilities curve, whereby economic growth is signified by an long-term outward shift in the production possibilities curve. The factors that create this growth include an increase and improvement in factors of production and technology. These are the factors that the president correctly referred to at the beginning of this chapter.

Trickle-Down

Did President Reagan's willingness to reduce taxes for the rich and to reduce government spending for the poor mean that he and other supply-siders were interested in helping the rich and hurting the poor? Did President George W. Bush's support for further reductions in taxes for the rich and support for welfare reform that emphasizes work mean that he once again created a choice of the rich over the poor? Supply-side economists and politicians would answer with a resounding no! Instead, they argue that these policies are necessary to generate economic growth. They argue that economic growth will improve the prosperity of the nation, and eventually the benefits of this prosperity will trickle down to everyone, rich and poor alike. No wonder this approach to economics has been dubbed **trickle-down philosophy**! We'll leave it to you, the reader, to decide if this conservative approach to economics indeed provides benefits to all, or whether the poor will continue to be left behind from the prosperity of the nation. This issue is important because the conservative agenda of many politicians incorporates trickle-down philosophy to this day.

Trickle-down philosophy
The view that supply-side policy will generate economic growth and prosperity, the benefits of which will eventually "trickle down" to all.

Chapter 16

ROAD MAP

Chapter 2
Crime and Drugs
Taxes could be used to discourage drug use if drugs became legal

Chapter 3
The Environment
Taxes can create incentives to protect the environment

Chapter 5
Discrimination
Property-tax financing of public education leads to unequal educational opportunities for segregated minorities

Chapter 6
U.S. Poverty
Many of our taxes heavily burden the poor. The Earned Income Tax Credit helps the working poor

Chapter 9
Social Security
Social Security taxes are among our most regressive taxes

Chapter 12
International Trade
Taxes (tariffs) are a form of trade restrictions

Chapter 16
Taxes, Borrowing, and the National Debt

Chapter 14
Unemployment and Inflation
These two macro problems are affected by government taxes and borrowing

Chapter 15
Government Macroeconomic Policy
Taxes and borrowing enable government spending and affect the macroeconomy

Chapter 17
Globally Free Markets for the Twenty-First Century?
Raising taxes as part of global economic reform stabilizes budgets but creates hardships for the poor

The Economic Toolbox

- Government securities
- Tax rate
- Tax base
- Tax credit
- Earned Income Tax Credit
- Refundable
- Dividends
- Capital gains
- Payroll tax
- Excise tax
- Progressive, proportional, and regressive taxes

- Tax burden
- Loanable funds
- Crowding out
- Budget deficit
- National debt
- Perfectly inelastic demand (appendix)
- Perfectly inelastic supply (appendix)
- Interest rate (appendix)
- Loanable funds (appendix)
- Crowding out (appendix)

Taxes, Borrowing, and the National Debt

So far, we have considered a variety of government expenditures, including spending on social and poverty programs, control over pollution and big business, ensuring equal opportunity, expenditures on agriculture and the control of crime, and government spending to increase aggregate demand and stabilize the economy. Most recently, we have seen large increases in military spending. In particular, government spending has increased dramatically in relation to the U.S. wars in Afghanistan and Iraq and U.S. air strikes against Al-Qaeda and the Islamic State (ISIL). We have also seen large increases in government spending in terms of stimulus money to expand our economy and to cover the retirement and health needs of an increasingly aging population. But we have not yet carefully addressed a critical question: how does the government come up with the money to finance these programs and policies?

One of the most obvious ways that the government acquires revenue is through taxes. By taxing the public (including individual income earners, property owners, businesses, and consumers), the government acquires a large portion of the expenditure dollars that it needs. The other means of financing government spending is by government borrowing. The government borrows when it issues **government securities**, which include government bonds, treasury notes, and treasury bills. A government security is really just an IOU: it is a piece of paper saying that the government has borrowed money from you, for example, and promises to repay it, plus interest, at some future point in time. The government sells these pieces of paper to banks, corporations, some foreigners, and a large number of ordinary American citizens. If you own some government savings bonds, it means you are lending your money to the government. We will consider these two basic means of financing government spending in the sections that follow.

Government securities
Government bonds and treasury bills.

Government Taxes

As Benjamin Franklin states, all we can be sure of is death and taxes. While this is a humorous simplification of the world, civic-minded people certainly do recognize that government spending requires government revenue, so that taxes *are* a certainty. Still, people want these taxes to be fair and reasonable.

Government taxes come in various forms and are imposed by the federal government as well as state and local governments. We will consider these various taxes and then analyze their impact on the macroeconomy, the distribution of income, and individual markets within the United States. We'll begin with federal taxes.

In this world nothing can be said to be certain, except death and taxes.

—*BENJAMIN FRANKLIN (1706–1790), COMPLETE WORKS, 1887–1888*

Federal Taxes

Figure 16-1 displays the principal federal taxes and the proportion of 2013 federal tax revenue accounted for by each type of tax.

The Federal Personal Income Tax

We can see from Figure 16-1 that the federal personal income tax is the most important of the taxes levied by the federal government. The personal income tax brings in roughly 47 percent of total federal tax revenue. This tax is placed on most forms of individual income and has been dropping as a federal tax source for many years now.

Tax base

The value of income, earnings, property, sales, or other valued items to which a tax rate is applied. In the case of the personal income tax, the tax base is incremental income.

Tax rate

The percentage of the tax base that must be paid to the government as tax.

In this case, taxable income is called the **tax base**. The first portion of your income is covered by one tax bracket and a corresponding **tax rate**; the next portion of your income is in the next bracket and covered by a higher rate, and so on. Until 1986, there were 14 different tax brackets. The portion of the income of highest-income individuals that was in the very highest bracket was taxed at the highest rate. This maximum tax rate was 90 percent until 1964, when it underwent the first of several reductions over the next five decades. The number of tax brackets has also been sharply reduced over time. In 2014, the maximum tax rate was 39.6 percent, and there were six additional tax brackets with tax rates of 10 percent, 15 percent, 25 percent, 28 percent, 33 percent, and 35 percent.[1]

The drop in the maximum tax rate from 90 percent in 1964 to 39.6 percent in 2014, and the reduction in the number of tax brackets, is significant. It has largely benefited the rich, and as we shall see shortly, has also reduced the amount of taxes taken in by the

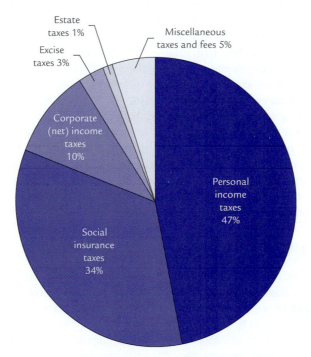

Figure 16-1 • Revenue From Federal Taxes as a Share of Total Federal Tax Revenue, 2013

Source: The Department of Commerce, Census Bureau, www.census.gov, 2015.

federal government. The impetus for these changes came primarily from the conservative administrations of President Ronald Reagan (1981–1988) and President George W. Bush (2001–2008).

Americans can take advantage of several tax breaks in the federal personal income tax. Households can claim **exemptions** for each family member. In 2014, this personal exemption was $3,950, though it phases out at higher levels. Households can also deduct various expenditures (deductions) from their taxable income. One example of such a deduction is a household's mortgage interest payments, discussed as a benefit especially to middle- and upper-income homeowners in Chapter 7 on housing. There are also deductions for parents of children and for college students. Alternatively, households may take the **standard deduction**, which is a fixed amount of income that taxpayers can deduct from their taxable income if no other deductions are claimed. In 2014, the standard deduction was $6,200. Taxpayers might also be eligible for various **tax credits** that directly reduce their tax amount payable to the government.

Aside from reducing the number of tax brackets and reducing tax rates, the 1986 tax code eliminated many deductions, increased the standard deduction, and increased the Earned Income Tax Credit. The **Earned Income Tax Credit (EITC)** has continued to increase in size over time and is available to eligible low-income workers. It is **refundable**, meaning that it provides a refund to eligible workers even if their earnings are too low to be taxed. Many economists see the EITC as an effective policy tool for reducing poverty among the working poor, maintaining incentives for people to work. (This is effective as long as there are jobs to be had.) While there is popular support for higher minimum wages for low-income workers, many economists believe that a larger EITC that is available to more workers would be a more direct and effective means of improving the standards of low- and middle-income workers. (Be sure to check the discussion and action questions in Chapter 6 to see if you are eligible for the earned income tax credit!)

Other economic issues related to the federal personal income tax rates on dividends and capital gains, and whether to tax these as ordinary income. **Dividends** are the profits earned from stock ownership and generally flow to the very wealthiest people in our nation. **Capital gains** refer to the net income received when an asset is bought at a particular price and subsequently sold at a higher price. For example, if you purchase a share of corporate stock for $100, but later sell it for $150, you will receive $50 worth of capital gains. It would be nice for you if there was a very low tax, or even no tax, on these capital gains.

The Bush Administration enacted large, though temporary, cuts in the dividends and capital gains taxes. These, along with the changes in the federal personal income tax brackets and tax rates, primarily benefited the very rich. Since very few low and middle income citizens receive much of their income in the form of dividends and capital gains, it has been estimated that a large portion of the benefits of the cuts in these taxes went to the richest 1 or 2 percent of all taxpayers. (According to the Center on Budget and Policy Priorities, almost half of all long-term capital gains in 2012 went to the top 0.1 percent of households!) In addition to equity issues, economists are concerned that large cuts in taxes that are paid by very high-income people cause a substantial decline in government tax revenue, unlike tax cuts for the poor who pay relatively lower taxes to begin with.

Payroll Taxes

The second largest federal category of taxes is for social insurance. Taxes in this category are also called **payroll taxes**, because they are deducted directly from your paycheck or

---

Exemptions
Amounts of money for each household member that can be deducted from household income before personal income tax rates are applied.

Standard deduction
A fixed amount of money that taxpayers can deduct from their taxable income when calculating their personal income taxes, if other deductions are not claimed.

Tax credits
Amounts of money by which the income taxes payable to the government can be directly reduced. A person or business must meet certain criteria to be eligible for a credit.

Earned Income Tax Credit (EITC)
A federal tax credit for low-income working individuals and families. State governments may also utilize an EITC for their personal income taxes.

Refundable
A refund is available even if an income earner does not pay taxes, as long as he or she files a tax form.

Dividends
Profits from the ownership of stock.

Capital gains
The net income received when an asset is bought at a particular price and sold at a higher price.

Payroll taxes
Taxes based on earnings from work and usually deducted directly from the paycheck.

paid by your employer to fund various social insurance programs. The worker and the employer are taxed an equal amount for the two major social insurance programs, Social Security and Medicare. These two programs provide income to retired workers and their dependents, disabled workers, and survivors of deceased workers, as well as hospitalization and basic medical care for retired and disabled persons. All social insurance taxes together represent 34 percent of federal government tax revenue. They are discussed in greater detail in Chapter 9 on Social Security.

Miscellaneous Taxes: Corporate, Excise, and Estate Taxes

Corporate profits are taxed according to the corporate income tax. This is actually a *net* income tax, because it taxes business income minus expenses, or in other words, profits. The corporate (net) income tax generates about 10 percent of federal tax revenue.

Excise taxes

Taxes applied to the purchase of specific goods or services.

Excise taxes, operating like sales taxes but levied only on particular goods and services, bring in approximately 3 percent of federal tax revenue. Finally, estate and gift taxes bring in about 1 percent of the total. Miscellaneous taxes and fees make up an additional category representing 5 percent of the total.

Furthermore, under President Bush, heirs to very large estates (valued over $5 million for an individual) became exempt from paying estate taxes (which are distinct from the personal income tax). Clearly, one must be exceedingly wealthy in order for this tax to kick in. There is continued pressure by conservatives to eliminate all estate taxes and to make this effective permanently. Because only very wealthy people own the highly valued estates that are subject to the estate tax, elimination of this tax would benefit the nation's wealthiest individuals. Bush, as well as other conservatives, have often referred to the estate tax as a "death tax." Some commentators suggest that this is done to make voters think that people are taxed just for dying. Regardless of politics, the opening quotation of this section on taxes links together the certainty of death and taxes. By calling the estate tax a death tax, we link the concepts of death and taxes even further!

State and Local Taxes

State and local governments also impose various taxes, and they each place different emphasis on one tax or another. Figure 16-2 displays the various state and local taxes, as well as the relative importance of each type of tax in 2013. Keep in mind that these numbers represent averages over all states and localities and are not necessarily typical of any one particular state.

As revealed by Figure 16-2, the property tax brings in the largest share of state and local tax revenue (35%). The property tax is primarily levied by local governments. These taxes are levied directly on owners of buildings and land, and they depend on the value of this property. Economists usually assume that much of the property tax is passed from owner to renter (in the form of higher rents) in the case of rental housing. Property taxes are used to fund local public schools, as was discussed in greater detail in Chapter 4 on education and Chapter 7 on housing. Because property values are low in low-income school districts, this low tax base results in educational opportunities that are often poor in these areas.

The sales and excise tax comes in close as the second highest tax source, bringing in 34 percent of the total. Sales and excise taxes are levied on goods and services sold within the state, locality, or both. Some states exempt certain items, such as medicine

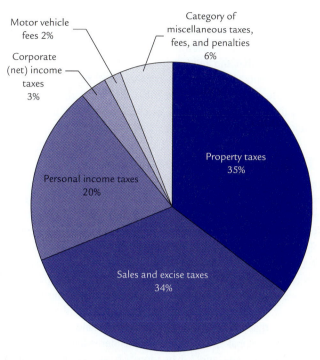

Figure 16-2 • Revenue From State Taxes as a Share of Total State Tax Revenue, 2013

Source: U.S. Internal Revenue Service, *IRS Data Book,* 2014, http://www.irs.gov.

and food. Other states do not. Excise taxes are placed on the sale of goods such as cigarettes, gasoline, tobacco, and alcohol. (State and local excise taxes are often placed on the same products as are federal excise taxes.) In the case of sales and most excise taxes, the tax base is the market value of the purchased item. In some cases, the tax base for the excise tax is some unit of the purchased good (such as a pack of cigarettes).

Most states (and a few localities) also have a personal income tax, bringing in 20 percent of the total. Personal income taxes vary by state. In some states, there are different tax brackets and rates, as at the federal level. In other states, one tax rate applies to all people's taxable income. (The latter tax would be an example of what is often referred to as a *flat-rate tax.*) Note that various exemptions, deductions, and credits may apply to state personal income tax systems as well as those at the federal level. For example, some states have an EITC built into their state personal income taxes.

Finally, the corporate income tax brings in 3 percent, and motor vehicle license fees represent 2 percent of the total. Miscellaneous taxes, fees, and penalties, as well as statistical discrepancies, bring the total share up to 100 percent.

Comment

State and local governments have encountered a great deal of financial difficulty in recent years. The poor economy has reduced their tax revenue (because people with lower incomes and lower property values pay lower taxes, and these same people also purchase fewer taxable goods and services that create sales tax revenue). At the same time, transfers from the federal government to state and local governments have been limited. Many also claim that the federal government places more mandates (rules) on state and local governments, but does not provide funding to meet these mandates. In recent years, many state and local governments have faced the problem of scarcity and opportunity cost as they have been forced to choose between the schools, prisons, and other programs that they wished to support.

Effects of Taxes on the Macroeconomy

Recall the aggregate demand curve of Chapter 15. Remember that aggregate demand is the total output (U.S. GDP) demanded (*purchased*) by all sectors of the economy at alternative average price levels. The sectors comprising aggregate demand include individual consumers, business firms, the U.S. government, and foreigners. Government taxes play a role in the buying decisions of people within some of these groups. Let's consider the effect of taxes on consumers.

Let's begin by assuming that the federal government increases spending on public parks by $1 million. As we know from Chapter 15, this greater spending will increase aggregate demand, as indicated by the arrow in Figure 16-3, panel A. Real GDP increases from GDP to GDP'. Now suppose that the government wishes to finance this $1 million expenditure through an increase in personal income taxes. Consider what happens when the government raises these taxes. As you and I pay more of our income to the government, we have less after-tax income to spend as we wish. As a result, our consumption spending

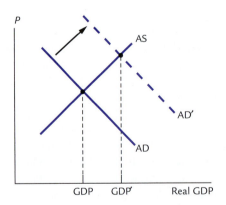

Panel A. Increased Government Spending on Parks.

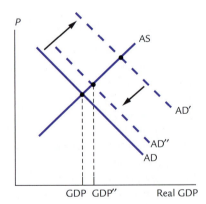

Panel B. Increased Government Spending on Parks, Financed by Increased Taxes.

Figure 16-3 • Increased Government Spending on Public Parks, Financed by Increased Taxes versus Government Borrowing

Panel A shows the increase in aggregate demand that occurs as a result of the increased government spending on parks. A relatively large increase in GDP results from GDP to GDP'. Panel B shows the impact of the increased government spending on parks, assuming that this spending is financed by increased government taxes. Aggregate demand increases as a result of the increased government spending, but it shifts back as a result of the increased taxes, which result in lower after-tax income for consumers, thereby reducing some of their consumption spending. The net increase in aggregate demand is very small, resulting in just a very small increase in GDP from GDP to GDP''.

goes down. As the consumption component of aggregate demand decreases, aggregate demand decreases as well, as shown by the second arrow in panel B of Figure 16-3.

Even though aggregate demand falls, it will not fall as much as the increased government spending on public parks caused it to increase in the first place. The reason is that the $1 million spent on parks represents a direct component of aggregate demand, whereas the increase in taxes of $1 million causes a decrease in spending by consumers, but not by the full $1 million. The reason is that we rarely change our consumption spending by the full amount of an income change. If our income goes up by $100, we may go out and spend an additional $80. We will save the rest. When the income of consumers as a whole goes down by $1 million, they will reduce their spending by less than $1 million. Thus, spending may fall by $800,000 rather than the full $1 million.

The point of this discussion is that the rise in aggregate demand caused by increased government purchases (expenditures) will be substantially offset by the decline in aggregate demand through decreased consumer spending when taxes go up. This will not be a total offset. That is, the combined effect of the increase in government spending and taxes will be a small net increase in aggregate demand. A small expansion in the economy is represented by some small increase in GDP (from GDP to GDP$''$ in panel B).

The important point is as follows: **If the government finances its increased expenditures through increased taxes, only a moderate expansion of the economy will occur.** A moderate expansion may be appropriate if the economy is operating at a high level of capacity; too much expansion would put undesired upward pressure on the price level. **On the other hand, if the goal of government is to substantially expand the economy, raising taxes to finance increased expenditures is not the most effective way to proceed.** As we shall see shortly, it would be preferable to finance the increased expenditures by government borrowing.[2]

The Effects of Taxes on Income Distribution

In addition to their effect on the macroeconomy, taxes have an important impact on the distribution of income. Indeed, taxes can be designed specifically for this purpose. When economists consider the redistributive effect of taxes, they usually classify taxes according to three basic types: progressive taxes, proportional taxes, and regressive taxes. Each of these has a different impact on income distribution.

A **progressive tax** is one that takes a larger percent of income from high-income people than from low-income people. Note that the key phrase is *percent of income*. We are not concerned here with absolute dollar amounts of taxes; we are concerned with the taxes that people pay *relative to their incomes*.

The prime example of a progressive tax is the rate structure of the federal personal income tax. Many state income taxes have a progressive rate structure as well. A progressive tax rate structure relies on different income brackets. As we have previously discussed, the first portion of a person's income goes into the first tax bracket and is taxed at a corresponding tax rate. The next portion of income goes into a higher tax bracket and is taxed at a higher tax rate. This procedure continues until the last increment of a person's income is placed into the highest appropriate tax bracket. Thus, the higher the person's income, the higher are the tax rates applied to increments of income. As a result, a higher-income individual pays a larger percent of his or her income to the government; a lower-income individual pays a smaller percent of his or her income. This type of tax places a greater burden on the higher-income individual, thereby redistributing income away from high-income households. Recall that changes in the last three-plus decades have greatly reduced the progressivity of the federal income tax rate

Progressive tax
A tax that takes a greater percentage of income from high-income people than from low-income people.

structure by reducing the number of brackets and by lowering the maximum tax rate. *Also note that once various exemptions, deductions, and tax credits are taken into account, the actual income tax may be less progressive, or perhaps no longer progressive at all, because many of these tax breaks are targeted to the middle- and upper-income classes, not to the poor. (The deduction of mortgage interest is a case in point.)*

Proportional tax

A tax that takes the same percentage of income from people of all income levels.

A **proportional tax** is one that takes the same percentage of income from people of all income levels. An example of this type of tax is the flat rate personal income tax levied by various state governments. Some have proposed that a flat rate income tax be used at the federal level as well. Because a flat rate tax takes the same percentage of income from people of all income levels, it does not redistribute income. Again, bear in mind that the proportionality of actual flat rate taxes will depend on the existence of various exemptions, deductions, and credits combined with the taxes. The overall result may well be a regressive tax.

Some people wish to simplify the federal personal income tax by using a flat rate tax. They fail to realize that it isn't the tax rate structure that is complicated. Rather, it is the list of deductions and credits that makes filing the tax so difficult. A flat rate tax also prevents the tax from serving a redistributive role.

Regressive tax

A tax that takes a greater percentage of income from low-income people than from high-income people.

Finally, a **regressive tax** is one that takes a larger percent of income from low-income households than from high-income ones. Most of the taxes in our country are regressive. Does this surprise you? Our regressive taxes include sales taxes, most excise taxes, property taxes, and the Social Security tax. Because some of these taxes are not levied directly on income, seeing why they are regressive is sometimes difficult. Let us consider a state sales tax as an example.

Suppose that a state levies a sales tax of 5 percent of the value of taxable goods purchased within the state. *The 5 percent is the tax rate, whereas the value of taxable goods is the tax base.* Actual percentage rates vary by state, as do the taxable goods covered by the tax. Let's consider two typical families, a higher-income family with an annual income of $500,000, and a lower-income family with an income of $21,000. The situations of these two families are outlined in Table 16-1.

Although the numbers chosen are made up, they provide realistic results. Note that the higher-income family spends $300,000 per year on taxable goods, whereas the lower-income family spends only $20,000. A lower-income family can be expected to have smaller consumption expenditures than a higher-income family. But note that the lower-income family spends a larger *percent* of its income on taxable consumer goods ($20,000 divided by $26,000 equals 77 percent), than the high-income family ($300,000 divided by $500,000 equals 60 percent). The reason is that lower-income families must spend their income on necessities and they have little income left over for saving. Higher-income families, on the other hand, can afford to save a larger share of their income (by placing it in various forms of investments), thereby "consuming" a smaller share.

TABLE 16-1 • Effects of the Sales Tax on Two Hypothetical High- and Low-Income Families in One Year

	High-Income Family	Low-Income Family
Income	$500,000	$21,000
Purchases of taxable goods	$300,000	$20,000
State sales tax rate	5%	5%
Amount of sales tax paid	$15,000 (= 0.05 × $300,000)	$1,000 (= 0.05 × $20,000)
Amount of sales tax paid as a percent of income	3% (= $15,000 / $500,000)	5% (= $1,000 / $21,000)

Because the higher-income family does spend more money on taxable goods, in absolute terms, it will also spend more money on the state sales tax, again in absolute terms. When these tax amounts are expressed as a percent of family income, however, we see that the lower-income family pays a higher percent of its income (5%) on the tax, whereas the higher-income family pays a smaller percent (3%). **The 5 percent sales tax results in the lower-income family paying a higher *percent of its income* on the tax. Thus, the tax is regressive.**

Property taxes and excise taxes are regressive for very similar reasons. Low-income families tend to spend a larger percentage of their income on goods covered by excise taxes and on housing (either owned housing or rental housing) than do higher-income families. The latter is due to the fact that we generally assume any property taxes are passed on to renters in the form of higher rent.

The Social Security tax is also highly regressive, but for different reasons. First, the Social Security tax is levied only on income earned by working: that is, on wages and salaries. Because lower-income families receive most of their income in the form of wages and salaries, all of this income is taxed. On the other hand, most of the income of high-income people may be in the form of interest, capital gains, dividends, and so on. Therefore, most of their income may not be taxed for Social Security purposes. As of 2014, the Social Security tax rate on eligible income is 6.2 percent. (Medicare is taxed separately at 1.45 percent, which is why the total is often expressed as 7.65 percent.)

Social Security taxes also are regressive in that they are assessed on earnings only up to a certain limit. Beyond this limit, earnings are not taxed. This earnings limit as of 2014 is $117,000. Any income earned beyond this level is not taxed for Social Security purposes. Therefore, all of the income of low-income earners may be taxed, whereas some (or even most) of the income of high-income earners may not be. Table 16-2 shows how the Social Security tax applies to two hypothetical high- and low-income people. In this example, the high-income person pays 1.1 percent of income on the Social Security tax, whereas the low-income person pays a much larger 6.2 percent of income.

As a result of the earnings limit and the taxation of only work-earned income, low-income families pay a much larger share of their income on the Social Security tax than do high-income families. Remember that once Social Security benefits are taken into account, the overall Social Security system loses some (or all) of its regressivity. This situation is discussed more completely in Chapter 9 (on Social Security).

Regressive taxes redistribute income in favor of the rich and to the detriment of the poor. Progressive taxes do the opposite. *Over the course of the 1980s, through the early 2000s, a number of factors helped to make our overall tax system increasingly regressive.* Large cuts made during the Reagan administration in personal and corporate income tax rates, our two most important progressive taxes, have reduced the significance of these two taxes as tax revenue sources. In addition, large increases in Social Security, excise,

TABLE 16-2 • Effects of the Social Security Tax on Two Hypothetical High- and Low-Income People in One Year

	High-Income Person	Low-Income Person
Income from working	$150,000	$10,000
Income from other sources	$450,000	$0
Income taxed for Social Security	$117,000	$10,000
Amount of Social Security tax paid	$0.062 \times 117,000 = \$7,254$	$0.062 \times \$10,000 = \$620$
Amount of tax paid as a percent of total income	$\$7,254/(\$150,000 + \$450,000) = \$7,254/\$600,000 = 1.2\%$	$\$620/\$10,000 = 6.2\%$

sales, and property taxes have occurred over the same time period. Thus, we are seeing less emphasis on progressive taxes and increasing emphasis on regressive ones. Changes by President George W. Bush that we've already considered have also resulted in a far more regressive overall tax system. These have provided the greatest benefits to high-income individuals and further reduced the potential of the federal personal income tax to be a progressive tax in the overall tax system.

President Bush justified the tax cuts on personal income, dividends, capital gains, and multimillion-dollar estates, all of which benefit the rich, by claiming that since high-income people pay the most taxes, they should therefore benefit from the largest cuts. While this rationale may be valid in terms of the income and estate tax, it is less applicable in the case of our *overall* tax system (where low-income people pay a heavy burden in terms of Social Security, excise, sales, and property taxes). In other words, there has been a move to reduce the taxes that burden the rich, but not a commensurate move to reduce the taxes that burden the poor. Finally, other proposals have been made by conservative politicians from time to time that include replacing the current federal personal income tax structure with a flat rate tax or with a national sales tax. These would also make our overall tax structure far more regressive.

As already discussed, President Obama has focused on expansionary fiscal and monetary policy and not the conservative policies to cut taxes that have just been described. Part of his concern conforms with that of many economists who fear that since our tax system overall is becoming more regressive, with high-income people taking advantage of tax breaks and low-income tax payers bearing a greater burden, the broader implication is that overall tax revenue received by federal and state governments is likely to fall.

Effects of Taxes on the Microeconomy of Individual Markets

Excise and property taxes affect markets for specific goods. Consider an excise tax in a hypothetical local market for gasoline.

Demand and supply for gasoline are indicated by the curves D and S in Figure 16-4. Without any excise tax, equilibrium occurs at point E; equilibrium quantity equals 100 gallons,

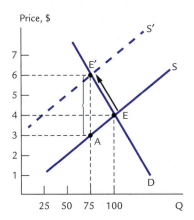

Figure 16-4 • Effects of an Excise Tax on a Hypothetical Market for Gasoline
A $3 per gallon excise tax will shift back the supply curve for gasoline. At the new equilibrium E′, the price is $6 per gallon and the quantity of gasoline is 75 gallons. The excise tax of $3 per gallon is paid by the suppliers of gasoline to the government. Because consumers pay more and suppliers keep less, both groups bear part of the burden of the excise tax.

and equilibrium price equals $4 per gallon. Now consider the imposition of an excise tax of $3 per gallon. We can view this excise tax as an additional cost of production because the supplier of gasoline must actually hand the tax dollars to the government. Just as the supplier must pay wage costs, energy costs, rental costs, and so on, it now must pay an additional cost of $3 per gallon on each gallon of gasoline sold. Recall that any increase in the costs of production will cause supply to decrease. This is shown by the backward shift of the supply curve, as indicated by the new supply curve S′.

With the imposition of the excise tax, a new equilibrium is established at point E′. Equilibrium quantity has fallen to 75 gallons, and the equilibrium price has risen to $6 per gallon. What has happened is that supply has decreased, causing gasoline prices to rise. In response to higher prices, consumers have moved back up along their demand curve (shown by the arrow from E to E′), reducing the quantity they wish to buy. Both quantity demanded and quantity supplied are now at the lower level of 75 gallons.

Why has the price risen from $4 to $6, and not by the full $3 excise tax per gallon? The actual price increase is the result of demand and supply. Note that the vertical distance between the two supply curves (measured by the bracket from A to E′) represents the $3 per gallon excise tax. The cost of supplying each gallon of gasoline has gone up by exactly this amount. But the market price of gasoline has risen by only a portion of this amount, in this case by $2 per gallon. The implication is that the **burden of the tax** has been borne by suppliers and consumers alike. Consumers bear a portion of the full burden of the tax in the form of the extra $2 they must pay for each gallon of gasoline they purchase. Suppliers bear a portion of the full burden in the form of lower profits; they now must pay an additional $3 for each gallon that they sell (the tax), but they receive only an additional $2 from consumers. The difference ($1) comes out of their pockets.

The results of this exercise are fairly typical. As a consequence of the imposition of the excise tax, a smaller quantity of the product is produced and sold, the price is higher, and both consumers and suppliers share the burden of the tax. Realize, however, that the burden need not be shared equally by these two groups. The price of a product upon which an excise tax is imposed could rise substantially, perhaps even the full amount of the tax. In this case, consumers bear the entire brunt of the tax. Likewise, the price could rise only negligibly. In this event, suppliers bear the greater burden. Appendix 16-1 to this chapter considers some of the circumstances that determine which group actually bears the greatest burden of any particular excise tax. *Generally, consumers bear a large share of the burden of the gasoline excise tax.*

The effect of an excise tax imposed on gasoline is interesting because it can influence consumer behavior. As discussed in Chapter 3 on the environment, an excise tax that causes a significant rise in the price of gasoline can encourage consumers to reduce their gasoline use, thereby reducing pressure on a finite resource and slowing the emission of greenhouse gases. It is also a good source of government tax revenue because consumers do not cut down on their purchase by large amounts, enabling the government to continue to receive excise taxes on the amount of gasoline sold.

Property taxes can operate in a similar way. Recall our earlier assumption that at least a portion of the property tax is passed along from the owners of the rental housing to the renters. This analysis shows how and why some of this tax is redirected, and why renters will indeed bear part of the burden of the tax. Consider a local market for rental housing, depicted in Figure 16-5 on page 408. Demand and supply determine an equilibrium quantity of housing.

Burden of the tax
The impact of the tax that is felt by producers and consumers. Consumers bear the burden in the form of higher prices paid for the product; producers bear the burden in the form of lower profits.

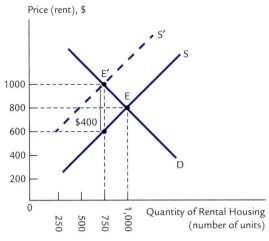

Figure 16-5 • Effects of the Property Tax on a Hypothetical Market for Rental Housing
The $400 per month property tax on rental housing will shift back the supply curve, resulting in a new equilibrium at E′. At the new equilibrium, the rental price of housing has increased from $800 to $1,000, but the landlord must pay $400 to the government in property tax. Because the tenant pays more and the landlord keeps less, both groups will bear part of the burden of the property tax. Note that the equilibrium quantity has decreased.

In this case, the equilibrium quantity of housing is 1,000 units and the market rental price is $800 per unit per month. Adding a property tax of $400 per month can be viewed as an additional cost of supplying the housing, as property ownders must hand the tax dollars to the government. The higher cost will be reflected in a backward shift of the supply curve to S′. A new equilibrium will be established at point E′. Quantity has decreased to 750 units, and the market rent has gone up to $1,000 per unit. In reality, the rental price to the renter will often go up much higher and the burden for the landlord will be much lower.

Global Comparisons in Taxes

It is interesting to compare tax revenues in the United States with other Western industrialized countries in the world. An appropriate way to do this is to look at total tax revenue as a share of GDP. These data are shown for most Western industrialized countries in Table 16-3 for the year 2012. There is quite a range, from a low of 10 percent in the United States to 34 percent in Denmark. Of course, those countries that collect the most taxes as a share of GDP will have the

TABLE 16-3 • Total Tax Revenue as a Share of GDP in Western Industrialized Countries, 2012[a]

Country	Taxes as a Share of GDP (%)	Country	Taxes as a Share of GDP
United States	10	France	22
Switzerland	10	Greece	23
Canada	12	Italy	23
Germany	12	Belgium	26
Austria	19	Luxembourg	26
Finland	21	Norway	27
Netherlands	21	United Kingdom	27
Sweden	22	Denmark	34

[a]Or most recent year.

Source: World Bank, *World Development Indicators,* www.worldbank.org.

greatest ability to provide services to its citizens. Those countries with low taxes will leave more money in the hands of private individuals and businesses.

Government Borrowing

Listen to this! As of October 15, 2014, the Obama administration announced that the federal government budget deficit, which is the amount of money the government has borrowed this fiscal year, is $483 billion! Sound like a lot to you? Well, this is $197 billion less than it was for fiscal year 2013, $165 billion less than was forecast previously by the president, the lowest it has been since 2007, and less than the average of the last 40 years![3] Yet Americans remain perennially worried about government budget deficits, far more so than economists tend to be. The source of this concern may well be the proverb quoted above, but it is more likely that individual households recognize that they themselves cannot borrow indefinitely year after year and they feel that this should be the case for government as well.

Nevertheless, individual people and families do borrow money. In doing so, they go into debt. The debt may be good or bad for the family, depending on a number of factors. They may use it to improve their education and job skills so that they ultimately earn higher income than they otherwise would. They may need to purchase a car in order to get to work. And they almost certainly need to borrow money in order to finance the purchase of a home. But what about government borrowing? Is the country well or poorly served when the government borrows money and in doing so goes into debt? The next several pages will help us answer this question. The main thing to realize is that the government is not a household. This distinction is what separates the valid concerns of individual families about their own borrowing with the less valid concerns about government borrowing.

Recall that the government can finance its expenditures not only through taxes but also by borrowing. The latter process occurs as the government issues securities. Anyone can purchase a government security: another level or agency of government, a bank or other financial institution, a corporation or other form of business, and individual people like you and me. When I purchase a government bond, I am lending my money to the government. At some specified point in the future, I will receive my money back, plus interest. Because no coercion is involved, presumably this deal is a good one for both the government and me. Is it a good deal for the economy?

To answer this question, we must consider the impact of government borrowing in a couple of respects. Just as with taxes, we will analyze the effect of government borrowing on the macroeconomy and income distribution. We will also consider its relation to the national debt. Finally, in Appendix 16-2, we will consider the effect of government borrowing on interest rates.

Effects of Government Borrowing on the Macroeconomy

Recall our earlier scenario in which the government wishes to increase spending on (purchases of) public parks by $1 million. As indicated before, these higher purchases are part of aggregate demand and will cause the aggregate demand curve to shift forward. This is shown in both panels A and B of Figure 16-3. In panel B, the government financed its purchases of public parks by raising taxes, which caused a subsequent backward shift in aggregate demand as consumers reduced their own purchases in response to lower after-tax income. Very little expansion of the economy ultimately occurred.

In panel A, however, the government is not financing its purchases by raising taxes. It is borrowing the money it needs to purchase the additional public parks. There is no reason for the aggregate demand curve to shift backward as in panel B. Panel A shows a significant expansion in the economy. Whether this result is desirable depends on the

Neither a lender nor a borrower be.

—*PROVERB*

state of the economy. If the economy is operating at high capacity, the expansion is most likely to bring unwanted price rises in its wake. On the other hand, if the economy is operating well below capacity and perhaps is in recession, the expansion is exactly what our economy needs. **Government spending financed by borrowing expands the economy more than government spending financed through increased taxes.**

Effects of Government Borrowing on Income Distribution

If I buy government bonds, I will benefit from this decision. The government will repay me at some future time, with interest to boot. Who will finance the interest payment? One possibility is that the government will merely borrow again to finance its interest expenditures. There is nothing intrinsically wrong with this practice. Unlike you and me, the government can borrow indefinitely. Alternatively, the government may increase taxes to finance my interest payment. If you pay the additional tax and I receive the interest benefit, income is redistributed from you to me. I will be happy, but you will not.

The redistribution of income that occurs in this process may in fact cause greater income inequality in our country. Bond owners tend to be middle- to upper-income people; rarely do low-income people have the means to participate significantly in this type of investment activity. On the other hand, we have seen that our tax system has become increasingly regressive. **To the extent that low-income people bear a greater burden of tax payments, and high-income people receive a greater benefit in the form of interest income on bonds (and other forms of income from government securities), income redistribution occurs from the poor to the rich.**

This redistribution does not mean that government borrowing is bad, per se. We can alter the impact of government borrowing on income distribution without reducing the government's borrowing ability. We can devise means to restructure government securities in ways that make them more accessible to low-income people. And, of course, we can alter our national system of taxation to achieve greater progressivity, if we have the desire to do so. The negative impacts of government borrowing on income distribution could be dealt with directly in this fashion. Finally, we know that both tax revenue and borrowed funds can be used by the government to finance policies and programs that foster greater or less equality, depending on the nature of the policies and programs they choose to finance.

Effects of Government Borrowing on the Government Budget and the National Debt

The federal government is too big and it spends too much money. [We need] a constitutional amendment that mandates a balanced budget.

—President Ronald Reagan, 1988

We must bring the federal budget into balance.

—President George H. W. Bush, 1989

We have an obligation to leave our children a legacy of opportunity, not debt.

—President Bill Clinton, 1996

Together, we can restrain the spending appetite of the federal government, and we can balance the federal budget.

—President George W. Bush, 2007

There is, of course, another responsibility we have to our children. And that is the responsibility to ensure that we do not pass on to them a debt they cannot pay.

—President Barack Obama, 2009

Every U.S. president in recent memory up through President Obama has spoken out strongly against budget deficits. Until the late 1990s, our national concern was how to manage government budget deficits. With the turn of the century, the issue became how to manage government budget surpluses. By 2002, our concern once again reverted to dealing with budget deficits, in this case, massive ones! It is ironic that President George W. Bush (and President Reagan) always spoke so passionately of balancing the federal budget, when the military spending and tax cuts during the administrations of these two presidents greatly increased budget deficits. However, the budget deficit as President Obama entered his first term of office was also massive, in part due to existing military spending and in part due to the recession and efforts to create an economic recovery. We will consider President Obama's economic policies momentarily.

Effect of Government Borrowing on the Government Budget

The **budget deficit** is simply the difference between federal government spending and federal government tax revenue in a particular year. If the government spends $1,500 billion and brings in tax revenue of $1,300 billion, we have a budget deficit of $200 billion. The deficit is the amount by which the government is currently in the red: that is, the amount that the government must borrow to make up the difference. **The budget deficit is an *annual concept*; it represents the difference between government spending and government tax over the course of any one year.**

The opposite of a budget deficit is a **budget surplus**. If the government brings in tax revenue that is greater than government spending, we have a budget surplus. Thus, if the government spends $1,500 billion and brings in tax revenue of $1,700 billion, we have a budget surplus of $200 billion. Just like the budget deficit, the budget surplus is an annual concept.

Effect of Government Borrowing on the Macro Economy

The effect of government purchases of goods and services that are financed by government borrowing is quite different than when these purchases are financed by increased taxes, as discussed in the previous section on taxes. In that case, the increased taxes caused a large offset in the effect of increased government purchases on GDP. **If the government finances its increased purchases by borrowing, there is no offset and the macro economy receives the full increase in GDP**. Which situation is preferable depends on the state of the economy. If GDP is low or the economy is in recession, certainly we need a large increase in GDP and it is preferable to finance the increased government spending by borrowing. On the other hand, if GDP is already high or perhaps at full employment GDP, then the increase in government purchases without the tempering effect of increased taxes will result in an over-heated economy and a serious risk of inflation. This topic is addressed in Appendix 15-1 of Chapter 15.

Recent History

While budget surpluses tend to be rare in recent times, our nation did have a string of surpluses from 1999 to 2001. The surplus that existed during these early years of the new century ushered in vast disagreement over the best use of this money. There were those who urged the government to use the surplus to finance increased spending on social programs and transfers. Others argued that the surplus should be used to shore up the Social Security program. President George W. Bush argued that the bulk of the surplus should be used to finance tax relief. In the absence of deliberate decisions such as these, the surplus would automatically go toward reducing the national debt.

Unfortunately, the disagreement over the use of budget surpluses ended rather abruptly by 2002 and 2003, when spending for homeland security, national defense, the

Budget deficit
The difference between federal government spending and federal government tax revenue in any one year.

Budget surplus
The difference between federal government tax revenue and federal government spending in any one year.

fight against terrorism, and the wars in Afghanistan and Iraq caused government expenditures to spiral upward. At the same time, President Bush pushed forward the tax cuts that were discussed in the previous section.

Deficits were booming by the time President Obama took office. Furthermore, large companies were going bankrupt, the financial and housing sectors were failing, and the nation was in recession. People were out of jobs and receiving lower incomes. With lower incomes to citizens, this means lower tax revenue to government and higher government spending on transfers to the needy (such as unemployment compensation and welfare assistance). The recession, by automatically lowering tax revenue and increasing government spending, automatically contributed to worsening budget deficits.

Unfortunately, the way to improve matters required additional government spending, at least for a period. President Obama put into effect expansionary fiscal policy, which he referred to as his stimulus plan. Government spending on a number of projects, such as construction, increased. This meant that as construction workers were hired, they began paying taxes and receiving fewer government transfers. Other sectors of the economy responded to the stimulus in a similar fashion. As a result, the nation pulled out of the recession and budget deficits began to fall.

Despite these improvements in the economy and in the size of budget deficits, certain members of Congress were nevertheless concerned. In 2011, Congress passed a law stating that if they couldn't agree on a plan to reduce the deficit by $4 trillion, including the $2.5 trillion in deficit reduction that lawmakers in both parties had already accomplished over the previous few years, approximately $1 trillion in automatic and across the board budget cuts would begin to take effect in 2013 and continue through 2021. *These cuts were referred to as the sequester.* The entire idea behind these arbitrary cuts was to make them so unattractive and unappealing that Democrats and Republicans would certainly get together and find a good compromise of sensible spending and tax cuts, including the closing of tax loopholes. Congress did not come together, however, and the sequester went into effect. Rather than a careful cutting of inefficient or ineffective programs, all programs across the board (with few exceptions) were cut. These include programs that we've already considered to be funded at inadequate levels, including Section 8 housing, other programs for the poor, education programs, and many others. Aside from the effect of the sequester on important programs, it has certainly had the effect of slowing the recovery of our economy and the improvement in the labor market. It merely shows the impact that non-economists who do not understand and are overly concerned about budget deficits can have on our country.

The National Debt

National debt

The total amount of money owed by the federal government. It represents the accumulation of all funds borrowed by the federal government that have not yet been repaid.

The national debt is different but closely related to the budget deficit. **The national debt is the total amount of money owed by the federal government.** *It represents the accumulation of all funds borrowed by the federal government, up to the present, which have not yet been repaid.* A budget deficit in any one year will increase the size of the national debt (whereas a budget surplus will decrease the national debt). Is there anything wrong with the government running a budget deficit and incurring an increasing national debt? Most politicians say yes. Most citizens also say yes. As we've noted, people often make an analogy between the government and individual households. They say that we ought to be responsible. We ought to spend within our means. We ought to repay prior debts before borrowing more. We cannot borrow forever. Eventually, a day of reckoning will arrive. If individual households must exhibit financial responsibility, certainly our government should do the same.

This analogy is not entirely appropriate, however. As we've noted, the government *can* continue to borrow indefinitely. Unlike individual households, the country does not have to answer to the frowning face of the bank loan officer. With no limit on borrowing, the government can continually "roll over" its debt; that is, it can continue to borrow money to repay previously borrowed money. No day of reckoning will arrive. There will be no day of bankruptcy. There will be no shortage of people and businesses willing to lend to the government.

Does this mean that the national debt causes no problems? Again, many of our politicians and citizens believe that it does cause problems, though they often misunderstand the types of problems it creates. To complicate matters, economic conservatives have traditionally opposed a large national debt and the deficits that contribute to it, whereas economic liberals have typically been less unconcerned. More recently, these positions have become somewhat reversed, for reasons such as military spending that are discussed in the ViewPoint section of this chapter. To analyze the concerns about the national debt, we should begin by considering the actual size of the debt and the owners of the debt, and then we can examine the impact of the debt on our economy.

The Size of the National Debt

Recall our discussion of gross domestic product (GDP) in Chapter 15 on government macroeconomic policy. We recognized that any variable that is expressed in dollar terms and compared over different time periods must first be adjusted for inflation. Otherwise, increases in the value of the variable may simply express a rising average price level, not a rise in the real variable itself. The same care is necessary when considering the size of the budget deficit, as well as the size of the national debt. If we are comparing their size over time, we must adjust for inflation to eliminate the impact of rising prices. Often, when the sizes of the budget deficit and the national debt are reported in newspapers and compared over different years, the writer neglects to adjust for inflation. *This failure to adjust for inflation results in the reporting of a grossly exaggerated increase in the size of the deficit and the debt.* It is also important to use an appropriate benchmark when considering the size of the deficit and the debt. Gross domestic product represents one such reference. A simple illustration should demonstrate why we should be interested in the size of the deficit relative to GDP (which is really our capacity to produce and repay), and not just in the deficit's size alone. Consider a simple economy with the following budget deficit in a particular year.[4]

GDP	= $100,000
Government spending	= $20,000
Government tax revenue	= $18,000
Budget deficit	= $2,000
Budget deficit relative to GDP	= $2,000/$100,000 = 2%

In this example, the budget deficit is $2,000. This deficit represents 2 percent of gross domestic product. This $2,000 is contributing to the size of the national debt. Now suppose the economy has doubled over time:

GDP	= $200,000
Government spending	= $40,000
Government tax revenue	= $36,000
Budget deficit	= $4,000
Budget deficit relative to GDP	= $4,000/$200,000 = 2%

The size of the budget deficit has doubled, from $2,000 to $4,000. Yet, nothing in this example should alarm us. As GDP doubles, it appears quite natural for government spending to double (as well as consumer and business spending), for government tax revenue to double, and for the size of the deficit to double as well. Relative to GDP, however, the deficit has not grown; it remains at 2 percent of GDP. Although an enormous doubling of the budget deficit would appear to contribute to an enormously rising national debt, this example suggests no cause for concern. The national debt will grow, but we should be more interested in the size of the debt relative to GDP, just as we are interested in the size of the budget deficit relative to GDP.

What it all means is this: if we wish to accurately consider the growing size of the budget deficit or the national debt, we must consider the size of the variable relative to GDP. The data in Table 16-4 show the size of the national debt relative to GDP for the selected years over the time period 1940 to 2013.

We see from Table 16-4 that the size of the national debt relative to GDP was 53 percent in 1940, increasing to 122 percent in 1946. This dramatic increase in the national debt was caused by huge government spending during World War II. The debt relative to GDP was quite low by 1980, but it increased steadily up to the present. This is due to the cuts in taxes that we have discussed, as well as increases in government spending on the military and homeland defense, Social Security, and efforts to pull the nation from recession. The relatively low recent budget deficits will undoubtedly lower the ratio of the national debt to GDP in the near future This money, along with less tax revenue, had to be borrowed, thereby increasing the debt.

Who Owns the National Debt?

Recall that anyone can purchase government securities. Buyers of these securities are the owners of the national debt. Recent data are hard to come by, but we do know that in 2013, about two-thirds of the national debt was owed to U.S. citizens, banks, corporations, and the Federal Reserve. Much of this money (perhaps half) is owed to Social Security trust funds and private pensions, thereby protecting the retirement years of our older citizens. Much of it is also intergovernmental (between federal agencies and state and local governments). About one-third of the total debt is owed to foreigners. When we think of the national debt in these terms, recognizing that no one is being forced to lend to the government and that it is presumably a good investment for people, the national debt sounds less ominous.[5]

The Impact of the National Debt

The implications of the national debt are really the implications of government borrowing that we have already considered. The negative effects of government borrowing involve

TABLE 16-4 • The Size of the National Debt Relative to Gross Domestic Product, Selected Years From 1940 to 2013

Year	National Debt/GDP (%)	Year	National Debt/GDP (%)
1940	53	1980	33
1946	122	1990	56
1960	56	2000	63
1970	38	2013[a]	72

[a]Estimate.

Source: www.cia.gov/library/publications/the-world-factbook/rankorder.

an inequitable income redistribution and rising interest rates (appendix). And certainly interest payments made to foreign people generate particular concern for some, because they represent a real transfer of income out of the United States. Some people are also concerned about a potential burden passed on to our children. This burden would take the form of taxes imposed on future generations to make interest payments to current owners of government securities.

On the other hand, government borrowing can have positive consequences. It enables the government to expand the economy as needed and to make expenditures that can specifically benefit our society. Whether these are programs benefiting us directly in the present, such as Social Security and poverty reduction, or programs that invest in future generations, such as programs of health and education, the benefits accrue to our nation. These benefits must be considered whenever we concern ourselves with potential problems with the national debt.

Proposals to Require a Balanced Budget

No discussion of budget deficits and the national debt is complete without a discussion of the many proposals that would require a balanced budget by the federal government. An annually balanced budget would disallow any government borrowing, hence, no addition to the national debt. It would mean that all government expenditures must be financed by tax revenue and that any increased government spending increase must be matched by an increase in tax revenue.

Unlike politicians, economists see many problems with a requirement that the federal government balance its budget. First, balancing the budget in any given year is extremely difficult. Too many variables are unknown. Suppose, for example, that the nation must deal with extensive flooding or hurricane destruction (such as Hurricane Katrina). By declaring a national emergency, the federal government is committed to spending additional amounts to assist in the cleanup. Or even more to the point, suppose that the nation goes to war and increases its military spending. These unplanned events would create a budget deficit. It's true that the government could change the tax code or establish additional taxes, but such measures would not be feasible on a regular basis. It's also true that the government could reduce its spending on other programs, but these funds may have already been committed. (Halting highway construction already under way, denying Social Security benefits already promised, or closing federal prisons just because the budget is headed into deficit would be inappropriate!)

Second, suppose that our nation is entering a recession. As you will recall from the discussion of fiscal policy in the previous chapter, the government would like to pull the nation out of the recession by increasing government spending or by reducing government taxes. In the context of a balanced budget requirement, the government can do neither because each would create a budget deficit. The government's hands are tied, as it can no longer use fiscal policy to correct the economy.

Now let's take this discussion one step further. During a recession, people lose their jobs. When people lose jobs, their incomes decline. We've noted that when people's incomes decrease, they pay fewer taxes. And, they also are more likely to receive unemployment compensation and welfare assistance. **For these reasons, an economy in recession creates an** *automatic decrease* **in government tax revenue and an** *automatic increase* **in government spending.** Together, this revenue decrease and spending increase create an automatic increase in the budget deficit. (The opposite would be the case in an expansion of the economy.) Now, according to a balanced budget requirement, the government must eliminate the deficit by initiating either an increase in taxes, a decrease in government spending, or some combination of the two. Although difficult, carrying out these measures is possible. But they are exactly the *wrong* policy prescription for a nation in recession! What the government must do to correct the recession is to increase its spending or decrease taxes. *In other words, complying with the balanced budget amendment would exacerbate the recession and create even greater instability for the economy.*

The proposals for a balanced budget requirement have come in the form of proposals for new legislation and proposals for a constitutional amendment. The proposals have varied somewhat; those that allow exceptions for periods of recession, and those that require the budget to be balanced over several years rather than in one year, mitigate some of the problems we've considered. We should keep in mind that philosophies about government spending and taxes have motivated proposals that require a balanced budget. These proposals reflect the conservative viewpoint that less government involvement in our economy is best.

You, the Student

The Earned Income Tax Credit (EITC) was discussed earlier in this chapter and in Chapter 6 on U.S. Poverty. The EITC is an important means of assisting the working poor—except that many of these workers are not aware of it. If workers' earnings are low enough that they are not required to file the federal personal income tax form, they often fail to realize

View**Point**   Conservative versus Liberal

As you might suspect, conservatives and liberals hold disparate views on the issues of government taxes and borrowing. Conservatives generally favor reductions in government taxes for several reasons. First, they prefer to see income remain in the hands of the private economy, rather than turned over to the government. And, they prefer to see private sector spending rather than public sector spending. Second, they worry about the effect of various taxes on incentives. They believe that if personal income taxes are too high, people will work less. If business taxes are too high, businesses will produce less. If income from savings is taxed too much, people will save less. And the list goes on. On the other hand, liberals are more comfortable with government taxes and spending, as long as the taxes do not heavily burden the poor and the middle class. They also like to use tax credits to support what they consider worthwhile activity, such as spending on higher education or the care of elderly people. Liberals and conservatives might both support excise taxes, such as those on gasoline, if they encourage conservation, though liberals might be concerned about the regressive nature of these taxes.

High levels of government spending that are financed by government borrowing have historically been a real problem for conservatives. They have been concerned that attendant increases in interest rates will crowd out private spending (appendix), and they worry about the increased government spending that government borrowing permits. They have strongly and publicly argued in favor of legislation or a constitutional amendment that requires a balanced budget. Ironically, conservatives generally feel differently about government spending and budget deficits when it comes to expenditures for national defense (as with the war in Iraq). The huge budget deficits resulting from a combination of reduced taxes and increased defense and wartime expenditures in the last several years have not overly concerned many conservatives of the Bush administration. There is historical precedent for such a view. In the 1980s, another conservative president (Ronald Reagan) was unconcerned with the budget deficits that resulted from tax cuts and massive increases in national defense.

that they may still be eligible for the EITC—that is, if they file their income taxes! One of the most important things that can be done to assist the working poor is to make them aware of this tax credit, which provides a refund even if the person paid little or no federal personal income taxes. Some individual states provide an EITC as well. If you belong to a service-oriented student organization or perhaps an accounting or tax class, your group may wish to perform a public service by making information about the EITC available to low-income people. You can do this by obtaining copies of the EITC tax form and information booklet from Internal Revenue Service (http://www.irs.gov) or from locations in your community where tax brochures are provided (the post office, the public library, city hall, and so on). Then request permission to disperse them, along with a notice, in locations where low-income people are likely to congregate: local soup kitchens, food shelves, thrift stores, the Salvation Army, low-income health clinics, and so on. This simple project is an easy way to put your knowledge into action to help people.

SUMMARY

The U.S. government has two means of acquiring financing for its expenditure programs: taxing and borrowing. The largest source of federal government tax revenue is the personal income tax. Other federal taxes include social insurance (payroll) taxes, the corporate income tax, excise taxes, and estate taxes. Individual state and local governments commonly levy property, sales and excise taxes, personal income taxes, and corporate income taxes. Government expenditure programs that are financed by taxes have a moderate impact on the macroeconomy in terms of expanding gross domestic product. In addition, taxes have important implications for income distribution, depending on whether they are progressive, proportional, or regressive. The federal personal income tax—and some state personal income taxes—have progressive rate structures. Sales and excise taxes, property taxes, and social insurance taxes are all regressive. Finally, excise and property taxes have an impact on the markets for specific goods such as gasoline, alcohol, cigarettes, and rental housing. They generally cause prices (and rents) to rise and quantity consumed to decrease. Changes in our tax code over the last three-plus decades have served to create greater inequality in income distribution, which ultimately threatens overall government tax revenue.

Government borrowing occurs whenever the government issues government bonds and treasury bills. When you and I purchase a government bond, we are in effect lending our money to the government. Government expenditures, financed by borrowing, cause the greatest expansion of the macroeconomy in terms of increasing gross domestic product.

Government borrowing also has an effect on income distribution in that it benefits higher-income owners of government financial securities and harms lower-income taxpayers. Finally, government borrowing has the effect of raising interest rates, which may serve to reduce private investment expenditures within the economy. This process is referred to as crowding out (see Appendix 16-2).

The budget deficit is the difference between government spending and government tax revenue. The deficit is an annual concept; it represents the amount that the government borrows in a particular year. Similarly, the budget surplus is the difference between government tax revenue and government spending. When the budget is in deficit, politicians argue about how to reduce the deficit. When the budget is in surplus, politicians argue over how to spend the surplus. The national debt is the total amount of money owed by the government. A budget deficit in any one year will increase the size of the national debt.

The size of the national debt is exaggerated when we do not make adjustments for inflation and properly compare the debt with the nation's gross domestic product. Much of the national debt is owed to various levels and agencies of government; other shares are owed to businesses and financial institutions, individuals, and foreigners. Any negative effects of government borrowing and the national debt must be considered relative to the positive results of government borrowing. These results include expansion of our economy and spending on government programs that may benefit our nation.

DISCUSSION AND ACTION QUESTIONS

1. Consider recent changes in the federal personal income tax. What is the effect on income distribution? Do you believe this is fair? Why or why not?

2. Consider other proposals to replace the federal income tax structure with a flat rate tax structure or to replace the income tax with a national sales tax. How would these

actions affect income distribution? Do you agree with these proposals? Why or why not?

3. How do you feel about the elimination of the estate tax on extremely high values of inheritance? Why did the Bush administration refer to this tax as a "death tax"?

4. How do you feel about a reduction in the capital gains tax? An increase in the Earned Income Tax Credit? What is the effect of these on income distribution?

5. Should the Social Security tax be overhauled to reduce its regressivity? Why or why not? How might this be done? (Hint: See Chapter 9.)

6. Why does the government place excise taxes on goods such as cigarettes and alcohol? Is it because these products are "sinful"? (These taxes are often called "sin taxes.") Do you believe that excise taxes reduce consumption of these goods by very much? What does your response to this question imply regarding the amount of government excise tax revenue?

7. What sort of tax system do you feel is the fairest? What are the advantages and disadvantages of regressive, progressive, and proportional taxes?

8. What do you think of the European approach to encouraging conservation in gasoline use by imposing very large excise taxes on gasoline? Do you think this would work in the United States? Do you think it makes a difference if we are considering a short time period (such as two months) versus a longer time period (such as two years)? Why?

9. Visit the Census Bureau Web site (http://www.census.gov) to find current information on federal government spending and tax revenue. What is the major spending category? What is the major tax revenue source?

10. Visit the Treasury Bulletin Web site (http://www.fms.treas.gov/bulletin) to determine the current size of the budget deficit and of the national debt. How have these figures changed, if at all, from the data in this textbook?

11. Do you believe that the current budget deficit should be reduced? If so, how should it be done? Should taxes be increased? Should government spending be reduced? If so, which specific programs should be reduced? What would be the effect on the economy?

12. Are you concerned about the national debt? Why or why not? Has your opinion changed as a result of what you have learned in this chapter? Has your opinion changed as a result of the large buildup of military expenditures related to the wars in Iraq and Afghanistan and the U.S. air strikes in Iraq and Syria? Has your opinion changed as a result of the 2008–2009 recession and stimulus spending by government?

NOTES

1. Unless otherwise stated, all tax rates in this chapter refer to individuals and not married couples. The source is U.S. Internal Revenue Service, http://www.irs.gov, 2014.

2. In the macroeconomic examples in this chapter (as in Chapter 15), we deliberately simplify the effects of changes in purchases (spending) by ignoring the multiplier effect. The *multiplier effect* is a "spiraling effect" of initial spending changes on larger ultimate spending changes in the economy. For example, if the government "purchases" more public parks, it will pay the construction workers for their work. These construction works will increase their purchases with their new higher incomes, buying, for example, new cars. U.S. automakers will hire more autoworkers, and they will spend their additional income on furniture, for example. This process continues. This multiplier effect results in far more consumer spending that further increases aggregate demand, employment, income, and spending. There is a similar downward spiral of a multiplier effect when the government raises taxes. With less after-tax income, people reduce their purchases of things such as computers. The computer industry responds by producing fewer computers and laying off some workers. These workers have less income and therefore reduce their purchases of appliances, for example. The multiplier process continues to spiral its way downward. The simplification of ignoring the multiplier effects does not detract from the conclusions of this chapter.

3. *The New York Times*, October 15, 2014.

4. It is not necessary to adjust the size of the national debt for inflation when we are considering the debt as a share of GDP. This is because we would adjust both the numerator and denominator of the fraction and the inflation adjustment would cancel itself out.

5. America's Foreign Co-Editors, *The New York Times*, July 19, 2011.

Appendix 16-1

The Impact of Excise Taxes with Perfectly Inelastic Demand and Supply

We have already considered the impact of an excise tax on gasoline and the closely related case of a property tax on rental housing. Let's consider a few additional cases of excise taxes to further "observe" the workings of our economy. For additional discussion of elasticity, refer to other chapters and in particular, to the appendices of Chapter 2 on crime, Chapter 13 on market power, and Chapter 15 on government macroeconomic policies.

Consider a hypothetical market for cigarettes. In Figure 16-6 on page 420, an extreme assumption is made. The supply curve is drawn with its usual shape, but the demand curve is perfectly vertical. Consider what this vertical demand curve means. Although price is free to move up and down, the quantity demanded will always remain fixed. That is, people wish to buy a particular quantity of cigarettes and refuse to adjust this quantity *merely* because of a price change. Economists refer to this lack of adjustment to price changes as a **perfectly inelastic demand**. Of course, perfectly inelastic demand isn't entirely realistic. Although many people are so addicted to cigarettes that they appear willing to pay almost any price for the product, at least some smokers (particularly teenagers) will adjust quantity demanded in response to price changes. But we'll ignore this possibility and assume for simplicity that cigarette smokers will pay any price, as long as they can get their desired quantity of cigarettes. Equilibrium occurs at point E, with a market price of $6 per pack, and an equilibrium quantity of 5,000 packs of cigarettes.

Now consider the imposition of a $2 per pack excise tax. As you know, this tax represents an increased cost of production and will result in a decrease (backward shift) in the supply curve to S′. A new equilibrium results at E′, at which point a higher price is charged for the cigarettes. Recall that the vertical distance between the two supply curves represents the amount of the tax. Note that the price has gone up by the full amount of the tax, from $6 to $8 per pack. Equally important, the quantity of cigarettes bought and sold has not changed at all.

What has happened is that supply has decreased, pushing up the market price of cigarettes. But consumers have *not* responded in the usual fashion; they have refused to cut down on their purchases of cigarettes. As a result of this inflexibility (inelasticity), they incur the full burden of the tax. They pay the full additional $2 in the form of a higher price; suppliers bear no burden whatsoever.

Although this case is an extreme and somewhat unrealistic one, it does demonstrate an important principle. **As consumers are more unresponsive to price changes (that is, as they have a more inelastic demand)**, *they will bear a larger burden of any excise tax.* This is true in the case of excise taxes on gasoline and alcohol and the similar case of property taxes on rental housing as well. It is also true of the highly addictive drugs mentioned in the appendix to Chapter 2 (on crime and drugs) and the agricultural goods

Perfectly inelastic demand
Demand in which buyers are completely unresponsive to changes in price.

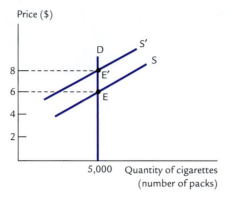

Figure 16-6 • Effects of an Excise Tax in a Hypothetical Market for Cigarettes With Perfectly Inelastic Demand

The original equilibrium at Point E corresponds with a price of $6 per pack and 5,000 packs of cigarettes. An excise tax of $2 per pack of cigarettes will cause a backward shift in the supply curve from S to S'. At the new equilibrium E', the price of cigarettes has increased from $6 per pack to $8 per pack, the full amount of the tax. Consumers will bear the full burden of an excise tax when the demand curve is perfectly inelastic.

mentioned in Chapter 12 (on international trade). All of these products have an inelastic demand (though not perfectly vertical).

Now let's consider an opposite case, shown in Figure 16-7. Let's analyze the local farmers' market in your town, where local growers try to sell their tomatoes. On any given day, let's assume that growers have a fixed supply of tomatoes. This quantity is available for sale, regardless of the price it can command, because the tomatoes have

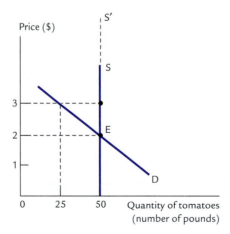

Figure 16-7 • Effects of an Excise Tax in a Hypothetical Market for Tomatoes With Perfectly Inelastic Supply

An excise tax of $1 per pound of tomatoes would ordinarily be reflected in a backward shift of the supply curve. When supply is perfectly inelastic, we can express this shift as a vertical extension of the original supply curve. Equilibrium remains at point E, and the price remains at $2 per pound. Because the supplier must pay $1 per pound to the government, but receives no increase in the price paid by the consumer, the supplier bears the full burden of the excise tax when supply is perfectly inelastic.

already been picked. No others are available on this day, and those already picked cannot be saved for another day (let's assume they turn into mush on day two). This kind of situation results in a market for tomatoes in which the demand curve has its normal slope, but the *supply curve* is now perfectly vertical. Equilibrium occurs at point E, with a market price of tomatoes of $2 per pound and an equilibrium quantity of 50 pounds of tomatoes.

Now consider an excise tax imposed by local authorities on the sale of tomatoes. Let's suppose this tax is $1 per pound. We would like to shift the supply curve by the vertical distance of the tax. There is no way to go but up, however. We cannot shift the curve in the usual fashion; we can indicate the shift merely as a vertical extension S′. The equilibrium remains at point E, with no change in quantity or price.

Why doesn't the price change? Why don't the growers say to heck with the market (or something similar) and raise their price by $1 anyway? Well, they're certainly free to do that. But look at the problem that would result. At a price of $3 per pound, quantity demanded falls to 25 pounds, but quantity supplied remains unchanged (as we know it must). A surplus of tomatoes is the result. The natural process we considered in Chapter 1 will result in a bidding down of the price as the only means of eliminating the surplus. *Farmers are stuck with the realities of the market; their inability to alter their quantity supplied means they are stuck with the entire burden of the tax.* They pay an extra $1 to the government, but they receive not one extra penny from consumers. This time, producers have the **perfectly inelastic supply**. **This extreme example gives way to the more general result that the more unresponsive suppliers are to price changes (that is, the more inelastic their supply), the greater the burden of the excise tax they will bear.**

The results of the cigarette and tomato cases can be generalized in a number of respects. **First, the group—be it consumers or producers—that is more unresponsive (inelastic) to price changes bears the greater burden of any excise tax. Second, this principle applies to any situation in which production costs increase**, whether because of excise taxes, government regulations for safety or pollution standards, increased energy prices, higher wages, or whatever. *When rising costs of production cause a decrease in supply, the price will rise by some amount that depends on the relative elasticity of demand and supply*. The more inelastic the demand, the more the increased cost will be passed on to consumers in the form of increased prices. The more inelastic the supply, the more the cost will be borne by producers in the form of lower profits, and the less probable it is that prices will rise very much.

Perfectly inelastic supply
Supply in which producers are completely unresponsive to changes in price.

Appendix 16-2
Effect of Government Borrowing on Interest Rates

Interest rate

The percentage of borrowed funds that must be paid to the lender (or investor) for the privilege of using the funds.

Loanable funds

Money that is borrowed or lent.

We can analyze the impact of government borrowing on interest rates if we view market interest rates as simply the price of loanable funds. An **interest rate** is the percentage of borrowed funds that must be paid to the lender (or investor); **loanable funds** refers to money that is borrowed or lent. To see how interest rates are determined, we must consider the market for loanable funds. This task is not difficult because our demand and supply analysis works in the market for loanable funds just as easily as it does in the market for rental housing, computers, or watches.

Figure 16-8 shows the market for loanable funds. The quantity axis represents the quantity of loanable funds. The demand curve for loanable funds represents all who wish to borrow money: business firms, individuals like you and me, and, of course, our government. The curve is downward sloping, indicating that we are more willing and able to borrow money at low interest rates than at high interest rates. The supply curve for loanable funds represents all who wish to lend money, including commercial banks and credit unions. The supply of loanable funds also incorporates all individuals who place money in savings accounts (lending their money to banks) or who purchase government or corporate securities (lending their money to the government or corporations). The supply curve is upward sloping, indicating that we are more willing to lend as the interest rate that we

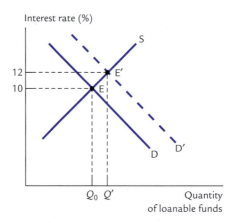

Figure 16-8 • Effects of Government Borrowing on a Hypothetical Market for Loanable Funds
The demand for loanable funds curve D represents the demand for borrowed funds by consumers, businesses, and government. If the government wishes to increase its spending on goods and services and chooses to finance these expenditures by borrowing, the demand for loanable funds will increase to D′. This increase in demand will cause an increase in the interest rate from 10 percent to 12 percent and an increase in the amount of money borrowed and lent to Q′.

rate." In fact, there are many rates, depending on types of loans, their lengths of maturity, and whether you are borrowing or lending. We are ignoring these differences and perhaps looking at what might be an average market interest rate. Equilibrium will occur at point E, with quantity Q_0 being borrowed and lent and a market interest rate of 10 percent.

Now suppose the government wishes to finance its expenditures by issuing government securities—that is, by borrowing money. This is reflected in the increased demand for loanable funds, as shown by the new demand curve D′, which results in the new equilibrium E′. In this new equilibrium, the quantity of funds both borrowed and lent has increased to $Q′$, and the market interest rate has risen to 12 percent. What has happened is simply that the demand for loanable funds has gone up, causing an increase in the "price" of loanable funds. Lenders have moved up along their supply curve, increasing the quantity they are willing to lend to match the increase in quantity demanded.

As a result of government borrowing, interest rates go up. The amount depends on the state of the economy and the market for loanable funds. The most serious concern about rising interest rates is their impact on business and consumer spending. As we've noted before, when interest rates are high, business firms are less likely to purchase factories and other capital equipment, and individuals are less likely to purchase big-ticket items such as cars, houses, and appliances. We simply are less willing and able to pay the higher costs of borrowing. Economists refer to this situation as **crowding out**. **Government spending, financed by borrowing, has caused interest rates to rise. As a result, individuals and businesses in the private economy choose to borrow less and therefore spend less.** *Government spending has partially crowded out private spending.* To the extent that business purchases of factories and capital equipment fall, we have a smaller investment in our future economy and productive capacity. Plus, those who wish to see a reduced role for government in our economy, and consequently an increased role for the private sector, are particularly concerned about crowding out.

Crowding out is certainly an issue, but we must keep it in perspective. First, crowding out is never complete, at least in the short run. Suppose that the government borrows and increases its spending by $1 million. This government borrowing of $1 million does not mean that there is $1 million less for the private sector to borrow and spend. Remember that the rising interest rates increase the willingness of people to lend; thus, more funds are available for everyone. Individual people and businesses now borrow and spend less, but not by the full $1 million that government borrowing and spending increases. Second, rising interest rates need not occur. Recall that monetary policy can be used to control these rates. An increase in the money supply will cause interest rates to fall, offsetting the impact of the increased government borrowing on interest rates. Whether this policy is desirable again depends on the state of the economy. *In an overheated economy, a simultaneous expansionary fiscal policy (increase in government purchases) and expansionary monetary policy will probably cause an overexpansion of the economy and a threat of inflation.* In a less-active economy, economic expansion may again be just what the doctor ordered. Economists, like politicians, are divided on the desirability of the various options. But understanding the impacts of the policy choices is important to forming an intelligent opinion.

Third, even if business investment falls as a result of rising interest rates, the government borrowing that initiated the process may result in government funds to be used for public forms of investment, such as road and highway construction and human capital (public education, training, and so on). These benefit society just as private investment does.

Finally, note that a rise in interest rates, for any reason, will have some implications for international trade and finance. These implications were considered in Chapter 12 (on international trade and finance).

Crowding out
A situation in which government spending, financed by borrowing, causes interest rates to rise, which results in less spending by the private economy.

Part V

You and the World Around You

Chapter 17

Globally Free Markets for the Twenty-First Century?

Chapter 17

ROAD MAP

Chapter 1
Introduction
Is our global economy shifting to the economic right or left?

Chapter 3
The Environment
How does environmental protection affect economic growth?

Chapter 6
U.S. Poverty
Do the factors contributing to U.S. economic growth increase or reduce U.S. poverty?

Chapter 10
World Poverty
Do the factors contributing to worldwide economic growth increase or reduce world poverty, or does it do both?

Chapter 12
International Trade
How does international trade affect worldwide economic growth—for better or worse?

Chapter 13
Market Power
How does worldwide market power affect the developing country economies?

Chapter 17
Globally Free Markets for the Twenty-First Century?

Chapter 16
Taxes, Borrowing, and the National Debt
How does tax policy and government borrowing affect economic growth?

Chapter 15
Government Macroeconomic Policy
What is the link between fiscal, monetary, and supply-side macro policy and economic growth?

The Economic Toolbox

- Capitalism
- Socialism
- Liberalism
- Economic growth
- Savings rate
- Capital gains
- Consumption tax
- Labor productivity

- Economic transition
- Price decontrol
- Safety net
- Economic reform
- International debt
- Capital flight
- Conditionality

Globally Free Markets for the Twenty-First Century?

I s the market a force for good or ill? Does it require modest government intervention, or does it demand greater government watchfulness? Free markets or regulated markets? More government or less government? These have been the debates throughout the last several decades, as well as throughout this textbook. As we shall see, the world had embraced a direction decidedly in favor of globally free markets—markets characterized by minimal government involvement, at least until very recently. But what about the future?

The title of this chapter ends with a question mark. Although the direction of change has been clear until recently, there is no reason to expect that free markets will work for all countries and all times. There is also no reason to assume that the recent transition to free markets will go smoothly for all nations or that a return to policies of the past will not occur. Indeed, several countries, especially Latin American ones, have begun to shift to the left. Let's examine the trends.

Markets

Throughout this book, there have been repeated references to demand and supply and the workings of markets in general. There have also been repeated references to government intervention in the economy. The proper role for government versus the proper role for the marketplace has prompted heated discussion among economists and politicians for decades. The respective roles for government and market have been the focal point for the ViewPoint sections throughout this text. In terms of economic philosophy and in U.S. terminology, those who favor a limited role for government are generally referred to as economic conservatives, whereas those who favor a greater role for government are regarded as economic liberals. **The conservative view maintains that free markets are efficient and they provide the proper incentives for economic prosperity and growth to occur.** Market failures are believed to be minimal, and government interference in properly functioning markets can only create inefficiencies and restrict growth. Limiting the government's role as much as possible is best.

This conservative view was evident in the discussion of supply-side policy in Chapter 15 (on government macroeconomic policy). Supply-side economists favor reductions in government regulations, taxes, domestic programs, and transfers. Their view is that the marketplace

Nor is the question before us whether the market is a force for good or ill. Its power to generate wealth and expand freedom is unmatched, but this [recent economic] crisis has reminded us that without a watchful eye, the market can spin out of control—and that a nation cannot prosper long when it favors only the prosperous. The success of our economy has always depended not just on the size of our gross domestic product, but on the reach of our prosperity; on our ability to extend opportunity to every willing heart—not out of charity, but because it is the surest route to our common good.

—*PRESIDENT BARACK OBAMA, INAUGURAL ADDRESS, JANUARY 20, 2009*

Capitalism
An economic system wherein the economic decisions are made by the private sector via the marketplace and the means of production are owned by the private sector.

Socialism
An economic system wherein the economic decisions are made by the public (government) sector and the means of production are owned by the public sector.

Western industrialized world
The industrialized capitalist countries of the world.

Eastern industrialized world
The industrialized ex-socialist countries of Eastern and Central Europe.

Developing world
The developing countries of the world.

Liberalism (or neo-liberalism)
A movement toward freer (more capitalist) markets. This is another term for *economic reform* or *economic transition.*

works efficiently; we must untie the hands of businesses and consumers to enable them to make their own private decisions, and the economy will be better as a result.

Liberals, on the other hand, see the marketplace as imperfect and market failures as serious. In their view, markets are not necessarily equitable, and sometimes not even efficient. Furthermore, society has goals, such as environmental protection, care for the poor and elderly, and economic stabilization that cannot be met by the marketplace operating freely on its own. Liberals believe that the government must intervene in markets to achieve these goals. Our recent crises in the housing market and financial markets, the automobile industry, and indeed our national economy as a whole would suggest that entirely free markets do not work, that some degree of government intervention is necessary. But what is the proper extent of government involvement?

Most economies favor some combination of markets and government involvement. Some countries are more heavily capitalist, whereas some are predominantly socialist. Under **capitalism**, the private sector (individuals and private business) makes economic decisions via the marketplace and it owns the means of production (factories, equipment, and land). Under **socialism**, by contrast, the public sector (the government) makes economic decisions and owns and controls the means of production. Under capitalism, consumers and producers interact through the marketplace, responding to market-determined prices. Under socialism, the government has a more prominent role in determining which goods will be produced, how they will be produced, and what their prices will be.

Keep in mind that capitalism and socialism refer to economic systems. They imply nothing about political systems, such as democracy and communism. Certainly, a socialist economy may exist under either communism (Vietnam) or democracy (Chile); and a capitalist economy may exist under communism (Hong Kong) or democracy (the United States). In this text, we are focusing our attention on economic systems.

The movement toward free markets has been a recent global phenomenon, the direction entailing different circumstances in different parts of the globe. We will consider each of the three major regions of the world in turn. We will define the **Western industrialized world** as the industrialized capitalist countries of the world, including the United States, Canada, most of Western Europe, and other countries (including Japan) that have achieved high economic performance through predominantly stable market conditions. We will define the **Eastern industrialized world** as the industrialized ex-socialist countries of Eastern Europe. These countries include the former Soviet Union and much of the rest of Eastern and Central Europe. Finally, the **developing world** encompasses all of the developing countries, including most countries of Africa, Asia, and Latin America.

One more term should be clarified. Economists often refer to the changes taking place in the formerly socialist and developing countries as **liberalism** (or sometimes neoliberalism). This term is confusing, because it refers to a movement toward markets with *less* government intervention, rather than the traditional liberal philosophy we have described. Do not confuse the words *liberal* and *liberalism*. The first implies government involvement in the economy; the latter implies change toward free markets.

The Western Industrialized World: Economic Growth

Conservative Republicans controlled the U.S. presidency for the 12 years from 1981 to 1992. And although a Democrat (President Clinton) became president in 1993, conservative Republicans took control of both houses of Congress in 1994. A conservative Republican

(President George W. Bush) once again took the presidential office in 2001. The conservative views toward tax policy, education, health care, the environment, Social Security, and government regulation of this era generally reflected the familiar undercurrent of supply-side economics and a philosophy of free markets with a minimal economic role for government.

This conservative framework was not unique to the United States. Many of the larger democracies of the Western industrialized world, including Britain, France, and Germany, took on a conservative philosophy that resulted in restricted government involvement in their economies and more focus on free markets. Domestic social programs declined, and economic growth was the driving interest in Western Europe in the beginning of the new century.

With the election of President Barack Obama and the beginning of his administration in 2009, the United States took a decidedly leftward turn. To the extent that this translated and will continue to translate until the end of his terms into more liberal policies depends greatly on Congress. (It will continue to depend on Congress and the next president.) Furthermore, the global recession of 2007 to 2009 necessitated greater government involvement in the economies of the United States and the other Western industrialized countries, as discussed in Chapter 15 on macroeconomic policy. Since economic growth is generally the principal objective of conservatives, let's begin by considering **economic growth**, defined here as an increase in average annual growth in GDP.

Economic growth
A sustained increase in production, represented by an outward shift of the production possibilities curve. An increase in gross domestic product (GDP) (or GDP per capita) over an extended time period.

Economic Growth Rates

Table 17-1 reveals the average annual growth rates in GDP for the Western industrialized world.

TABLE 17-1 • Average Annual Growth of GDP, Western Industrialized Countries, 1990 to 2000, 2000 to 2007, 2009, 2013[a]

Country	1990 to 2000	2000 to 2007	2009	2013
Austria	2.4	2.0	−3.8	0.3
Belgium	2.1	2.0	−2.8	0.2
Canada	3.1	2.7	−2.7	2.0
Denmark	2.5	1.8	−5.7	0.4
Finland	2.6	3.0	−8.5	−1.4
France	2.0	1.8	−3.1	0.2
Germany	1.8	1.0	−5.1	0.4
Greece	2.2	4.3	−3.1	−3.9
Ireland	7.5	5.5	−6.4	−0.3
Italy	1.6	1.0	−5.5	−1.9
Japan	1.3	1.7	−5.5	1.5
Netherlands	2.9	1.6	−3.7	−0.8
Norway	4.0	2.4	−1.6	0.6
Portugal	2.7	0.9	−2.9	−1.4
Spain	2.6	3.4	−3.8	−1.2
Sweden	2.2	3.0	−5.0	1.6
Switzerland	1.0	1.8	−1.9	1.9
United Kingdom	2.7	2.6	−5.2	1.7
United States	3.5	2.6	−2.8	1.9

[a]Most recently available data from 2010 to 2014.

Source: World Bank, *World Development Indicators 2014*, World Bank (Washington DC: World Bank, 2014).

Table 17-1 shows some very interesting results. First compare results for the time periods 1990 to 2000 and 2000 to 2007. In most cases, growth rates were higher in the earlier time period. This is the case for the United States, which grew at an average annual rate of 3.5 percent over the 1990s and only 2.6 percent from 2000 to 2007. Results took a big turn for the worse by 2009. The U.S. recession that began in late 2007 left a big toll on GDP by 2009, and the U.S. recession spread throughout most of the Western industrialized world. *Note that all GDP growth rates were negative in 2009!* This means that GDP was falling, at often very high rates. The worst was Finland at −8.5; the U.S. rate was −2.8. Almost all other countries did worse than the United States, especially Finland, Ireland, Denmark, and notably the big global players of Japan, Germany, and the United Kingdom.

By 2013, most GDP growth rates were low, but positive. The rate for the United States was 1.9 percent, tied for highest in the Western industrialized world. The recovery was later and lower for France, Germany, and Japan. The U.S. growth rate has been rising steadily since 2013, averaging 3.9 percent in the third quarter of 2014. Since 2013, the European economies have continued to struggle, and Japan announced it was in recession by late 2014.

The increase in GDP that is revealed in Table 17-1 can be discussed in the framework of aggregate supply (in the short-run) and production possibilities (in the long-run).

Economic Growth in Terms of Aggregate Supply and Production Possibilities

Supply-side philosophies are based on the idea that reductions in government regulations, programs, taxes, and transfers create incentives for greater productivity, thereby increasing aggregate supply. This forward shift in the aggregate supply curve would be associated with an increase in GDP. Supply-side policies and their effects were discussed in Appendix 15-2 of Chapter 15 (on government macroeconomic policy). Figure 17-1 summarizes the desired effects of supply-side policy.

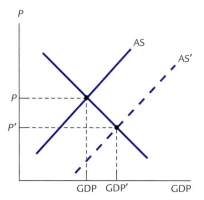

Figure 17-1 • Effects of Supply-Side Policy on the Macroeconomy
Supply-side policy is designed to cause an increase in aggregate supply, as shown by the shift of the aggregate supply curve AS to AS′. The result is an increase in GDP to GDP′ and a reduction in the average price level from P to P′.

Supply-side policies are intended to increase GDP, but a sustained expansion of GDP requires further policies that create long-term changes. These fundamental changes can be analyzed in the context of the production possibilities curve discussed in Chapter 1. The production possibilities curve from Chapter 1 is repeated here in Figure 17-2.

Recall that the production possibilities curve shows the alternative combinations of the maximum amounts of output that an economy can produce if all of its resources and technology are fully and efficiently utilized. The economy can achieve higher levels of production if the production possibilities curve shifts outward over time. We have defined economic growth as a sustained expansion of output. The factors that cause this outward shift in production possibilities include an increase in the quantity or quality of society's resources or an improvement in technology. These factors can generate a sustained expansion of output—that is, economic growth.

Let's consider four specific examples of the factors contributing to economic growth. These are an increase in capital, an improvement in labor productivity, an improvement in technology, and a decrease in unnecessary regulation. As we examine these dynamics, we can consider government policy with respect to each of them.

An Increase in Capital

Economic growth can occur if there is a sustained increase in the quantity of physical capital: that is, an increase in our nation's stock of factories, equipment, machinery, and the like. Even infrastructure such as roads and bridges can be considered to be physical capital. This increase in capital is made possible by an increase in investment, and investment is made possible by saving—either private saving by households and businesses or public saving through government taxes.

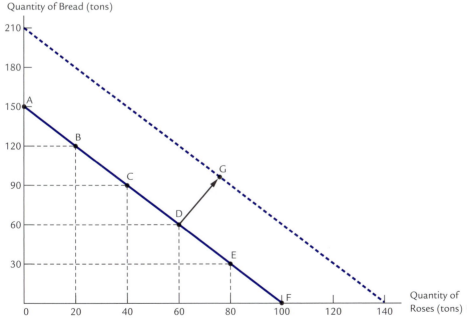

Figure 17-2 • Production Possibilities Curve with Economic Growth
Points A through F show alternative combinations of bread and roses that the economy can produce. More of both bread and roses can be produced when the production possibilities curve shifts outward as a result of economic growth.

Savings rate

Total savings (private and public) divided by GDP.

Capital gains

The net income received when an asset is bought at a particular price and sold at a higher price.

Consumption tax

A hypothetical tax on the portion of income that is spent on consumer goods and services, as opposed to income that goes into savings.

High investment activity necessitates a high **savings rate**, which is defined here as total savings divided by total GDP. Savings rates in the Western industrialized world are shown in Table 17-2 and range from a low of 11 percent in Greece to a high of 39 percent in Norway. The U.S. savings rate is 17 percent, somewhere around the middle. Although not shown here, China has a very high savings rates of 51 percent and East Timor has an astounding rate of 248 percent.

Some expect the U.S. savings rate to increase in the twenty-first century as the baby-boomer generation grows older, enjoying higher incomes and finishing their payments for houses and education for their children. However, government savings and dissavings will play a role as well. When the government spends less than it brings in through tax revenue, it engages in saving. When it spends more than its tax revenue, it engages in dissaving. The temporary spate of budget surpluses at the turn of the century encouraged those who sought a higher U.S. savings rate. However, the more recent major tax cuts of the Bush administration, coupled with greatly increased expenditures on the military, rapidly increased U.S. government dissaving. Budget policies under Obama, however, created the lowest budget deficits in many years.

Numerous efforts and proposals have been made to increase the national savings rate through supply-side policy. These efforts and proposals have been aimed at increasing incentives for households and businesses to save and invest. The 1981 tax law accelerated tax write-offs for new investment by businesses, greatly reducing corporate income taxes. The 1981 and subsequent tax laws provided tax breaks to households placing income into individual retirement accounts (IRAs) and 401(k) accounts. The capital gains tax has been reduced. As discussed in Chapter 16 on taxes, a **capital gain** is the net income earned when one sells an asset at a higher price than was paid for the asset. Taxes on dividends, received by shareholders, have also been reduced. The latter two tax cuts have been very controversial because while the Bush administration argued that the cuts contribute to economic growth, the vast majority of the tax benefits accrued to the wealthiest Americans, the ones who are more likely to have these forms of investment income. Some of these tax cuts were intended to be temporary. The Republican Congress of 2015 or later may well vote to continue them.

Furthermore, there have been repeated proposals for a **consumption tax** to replace our current federal personal income tax. Like a hypothetical national sales tax, a consumption tax would tax only the share of household income that is spent on consumer goods and services; it would not tax the portion of income that is saved. Although the

TABLE 17-2 • Savings Rates,[a] Western Industrialized Countries, 2012[b]

Country	Savings Rates (%)	Country	Savings Rates (%)
Austria	25	Japan	22
Belgium	25	Netherlands	28
Canada	21	Norway	39
Denmark	24	Portugal	15
Finland	21	Spain	21
France	18	Sweden	29
Germany	26	Switzerland	35
Greece	11	United Kingdom	13
Ireland	18	United States	17
Italy	18		

[a]Savings rate calculated as total savings divided by GDP.
[b]2012 or most recent available year 2005 to 2011.

Source: World Bank, *World Development Indicators 2014*, World Bank (Washington DC: World Bank, 2014).

goal is to provide greater incentives for saving, this tax would place the greatest burden on low-income individuals, who by necessity must spend virtually all of their incomes on consumption. This would represent a very regressive tax (recall that the definition of a regressive tax is one that takes a larger percent of income from lower-income people).

Finally, many conservatives believe that business taxes deter business firms from starting up and from expanding, all presumably preventing an expansion of the nation's capital stock. In this regard, it is interesting to compare the various business tax rates that exist throughout the Western industrialized world. Defined as total business taxes divided by profits, these tax rates are displayed in Table 17-3. We see that the highest rates of 67 and 65 percent are found in France and Italy, whereas the lowest rates of 21 and 22 percent are found in Canada and Luxembourg. The United States, with a rate of 44 percent, is somewhere in the middle.

If the types of policies discussed in this section prove successful in increasing savings rates and business investment, we would expect to see an expansion of our nation's factories, equipment, and machinery that would result in an expansion of GDP—that is, in economic growth.

Although most of the conservative emphasis has been on providing incentives for increased private saving and investment, liberal interest in increasing government investment should not be overlooked. The government can play an important role by investing in highways and mass transit, as well as schools and health care facilities. Since all of these forms of investment can improve the business environment, as well as the productivity of workers, they can enhance both the physical and human capital of our nation. Indeed, these are the types of stimulus policies President Obama set in motion in response to the recession of 2007 to 2009. Unfortunately, these policies were hampered by the sequester, which began in 2013 and is discussed in more detail in Chapter 15.

A Decrease in Regulation

The government regulates business in a variety of ways, including protections for consumers of pharmaceuticals, food, and manufactured goods; safeguards for workers in industry; and protection of the environment. In light of recent deaths caused by unsafe tires, airbags, and certain pharmaceutical drugs, the necessity for wisely developed government regulations is clear. On the other hand, unwise and unnecessary regulation merely increases business costs and decreases output. Therefore, cutting unwise regulation is a desirable policy and is conducive to economic growth. The problem, of course, is recognizing which regulations are harmful and which are beneficial.

TABLE 17-3 • Total Tax Rate (as percentage of profits), 2014[a]

Country	Total Tax Rate	Country	Total Tax Rate
Austria	52	Japan	51
Belgium	58	Luxembourg	22
Canada	21	Netherlands	39
Denmark	26	Norway	41
Finland	40	Portugal	42
France	67	Sweden	49
Germany	49	Switzerland	29
Greece	50	United Kingdom	34
Italy	65	United States	44

[a]2014 or most recently available year from 2010 to 2013.

Source: World Bank, *World Development Indicators 2014*, World Bank (Washington DC: World Bank, 2014).

Generally speaking, economic conservatives prefer less government regulation, whereas economic liberals prefer more. The supply-side policies since the early 1980s include widespread cuts in government regulations. Environmental protection is a good case in point. President Ronald Reagan and President George H. W. Bush greatly reduced government regulations in this area. Many of President Bill Clinton's proposed regulations met a hostile Congress and were not passed. President George W. Bush continued the trend toward less environmental regulation and a more industry-friendly environmental policy. Although this policy may have provided some short-run benefit to the economy through a reduction in the compliance costs of business and a resulting increase in aggregate supply, the long-run costs might outweigh this benefit. Just as an increase in productive resources will shift the production possibilities curve outward over time, a decrease in our natural resources caused by environmental damage and resource depletion will shift the curve inward. The capacity of our nation to produce and grow will be compromised, and the quality of life of our citizens will decline.

As suggested in Chapter 3 on the environment, environmental protection is a global necessity. Deforestation and the burning of fossil fuels contribute to global warming and loss of precious biodiversity. Acid rain destroys crops, waterways, and capital structures across countries. Use of certain chemicals destroys the ozone layer. Air and water pollution know no boundaries.

In 2014, President Obama signed an agreement with China that would mutually and dramatically reduce greenhouse gas emissions. Republicans in Congress were furious and vowed to reverse this once the new Congress took over in 2015. Other Obama policy decisions to reduce greenhouse gas emissions were done by executive authority without the consent of Congress. These also stand to be reversed.

We can see the overall regulatory picture in the data in Table 17-4. It shows an "ease of doing business index" that measures the overall regulatory environment. This includes not just the number of regulations, but presumably also includes the ease of dealing with government bureaucracy regarding these regulations. The index ranges from 1 to 189, with the lowest numbers indicating the greatest ease. The countries in Table 17-4 have indices ranging from a low of 4 in Denmark to a high of 61 in Greece. The number for the United States is 7, which shows a high degree of ease of doing business. This confirms what we have just been considering—that regulations have been eroded over the last several decades. If one were to examine numbers from other parts of the world, including much of Africa,

TABLE 17-4 • Ease of Doing Business Index (lowest number has greatest ease),[a] Western Industrialized World, 2014[b]

Country	Ease of Doing Business Index	Country	Ease of Doing Business Index
Austria	21	Japan	29
Belgium	42	Luxembourg	59
Canada	16	Netherlands	27
Denmark	4	Norway	6
Finland	9	Portugal	25
France	31	Sweden	11
Germany	14	Switzerland	20
Greece	61	United Kingdom	8
Italy	56	United States	7

[a]Index is from 1 to 189. Ease of doing business means a regulative environment conducive to business.
[b]2014 or most recent available year from 2010 to 2013.

Source: World Bank, *World Development Indicators 2014*, World Bank (Washington DC: World Bank, 2014).

some in Latin America (such as Venezuela at 182) and some in Eastern Europe (such as Tajikistan, Ukraine, and Uzbekistan at 166, 96, and 141, respectively), we would see why these countries are generally not favorable environments for businesses to start up.

In addition to deregulation in the areas of environmental protection and worker and consumer safety, the financial sector also experienced deregulation during the 1980s.

We've recently seen the effects of this latter failure, to ensure the health of the finance industry. Deregulation, as you know, was a key factor triggering the recession in late 2007. Part of the problem was a dual system of finance. On the one hand, commercial banks had typically been responsible for traditional mortgage lending, a process that is discussed in detail in Chapter 7 on housing. Commercial banks are regulated by the Federal Reserve and have traditionally been quite cautious in terms of risks undertaken by the bank (or the homebuyer) regarding potential default. On the other hand, the development of changes in the traditional form of mortgage lending (such as lending to less creditworthy borrowers and lending with an adjustable rather than fixed interest rate) along with the rapid development of investment in securities that are backed by mortgage loans—"mortgage-backed securities"—changed the nature of the finance industry. Financial institutions engaged in the latter forms of lending were not regulated in the same way as the commercial banks, and inordinate risk-taking resulted in the collapse of the financial system and housing market and contributed to the recession in late 2007–2009.

As a result of the regulatory shortfalls, President Obama implemented greater regulations over the financial industry, favoring an approach whereby the Federal Reserve would supervise the various investment banks and a separate agency regulate consumer protection services in areas including mortgage lending and credit cards. Congress, of course, is mixed in its opinion.

An Improvement in Labor Productivity

Labor productivity is defined as GDP per person employed. U.S. labor productivity growth, which lagged in the 1970s and 1980s, has now increased to much higher levels. For example, U.S. labor productivity was 2.7 percent in 1992, but had increased to 3.0 percent by 2008.[1] **Labor productivity hinges on the type and amount of capital and technology used in conjunction with labor, and these, of course, have improved in recent years.** Keep in mind, however, that labor productivity also depends on human capital. Human capital includes the skills and abilities of people. Once again, government support for training programs, education, health, and nutrition all remain important for ensuring high levels of human capital and have been featured as part of President Obama's stimulus policies.

Labor productivity
GDP per person employed.

An Improvement in Technology

Technology can be thought of as ways of using available resources to produce output. Improvements in technology enable us to produce more output, given our limited resources. These improvements are embodied in new and more efficient machines, new products, and new methods of production.

One way government policies can encourage technological advance is by providing patent protection to developers of new products. A **patent** is a government grant of exclusive rights to use or sell a new technology for a period of time. Without patents, other businesses might copy the new technology or product, thereby creating profits for themselves at the expense of the developer. Without patents, businesses have little incentive to develop new products. Patents have been extremely important in areas such as pharmaceuticals, communications technology, and consumer goods. The numbers of patent applications in the Western industrialized countries are

Technology
Ways of using available resources to produce output.

Patent
A government grant of exclusive rights to use or sell a new technology or product for a period of time.

shown in Table 17-5. Japan has the highest number in the world, with 287,010 patent applications. The United States has 268,780 patent applications. Keep in mind that these numbers are not adjusted for population size or size of GDP, placing a limit on their usefulness.

Technology can also advance through spending on research and development. One way the government can influence the development of technology is by funding research and development by businesses and universities. For example, the government can provide funds to universities for their faculty to conduct research and can provide tax breaks to businesses to encourage their research and development. Table 17-5 also shows the total amount of spending on research and development as a share of GDP. These amounts range from a low of 0.7 percent in Greece to a high of 3.6 percent in Finland. The United States spends 2.8 percent of GDP on research and development.

Finally, nowhere has technological advance been more prominent than in the area of computers. Indeed, investment in information technology, including computers, software, communications networks, and Internet infrastructure, have contributed to a large share of economic growth in recent years. Users of computer technology include students, other individuals, businesses, and governments. They (we) all become more efficient with the use of computer technology. Imagine that your author researched and typed her doctoral dissertation without use of a computer! (She did manage to use a computer to construct a sophisticated model and conduct advanced econometric analysis through access to the university's mainframe computer—no personal computers at that time!) Certainly computer technology helps businesses and others in the United States and other countries to produce more and better products at the same or lower costs of production (including our time). It has also been a major factor in improving labor productivity. The number of Internet users per 100 people is one way we can examine how widespread is the use of the Internet in individual countries. These numbers are revealed in Table 17-6.

TABLE 17-5 • Patent Applicants (number of residents) and Research and Development Spending (as a percent of GDP), 2014[a]

Country	Patent Applications	Research and Development Spending
Austria	2,260	2.8
Belgium	760	2.2
Canada	4,710	1.7
Denmark	1,410	3.0
Finland	1,700	3.6
France	14,540	2.3
Germany	46,620	2.9
Greece	630	0.7
Italy	8,440	1.3
Japan	287,010	-
Luxembourg	110	1.4
Netherlands	2,380	2.2
Norway	1,010	1.7
Portugal	620	1.5
Spain	3,270	1.3
Sweden	2,290	3.4
Switzerland	1,480	-
United Kingdom	15,370	1.7
United States	268,780	2.8

[a]2014 or most recent available year from 2010 to 2013.

Source: World Bank, *World Development Indicators 2014*, World Bank (Washington DC: World Bank, 2014).

TABLE 17-6 • Number of Internet Users per 100 People, Western Industrialized World, 2013[a]

Country	Number of Internet Users per 100 Population	Country	Number of Internet Users per 100 Population
Austria	81	Japan	86
Belgium	82	Luxembourg	94
Canada	86	Netherlands	94
Denmark	95	Norway	95
Finland	92	Portugal	62
France	82	Sweden	95
Germany	84	Switzerland	87
Greece	60	United Kingdom	90
Italy	59	United States	84

[a]Or most recent available year 2010 to 2014.

Source: World Bank, *World Development Indicators 2014*, World Bank (Washington DC: World Bank, 2014).

Note that Denmark, Norway, and Sweden have the largest numbers of Internet users per 100 people in the Western industrialized world (95), whereas the United States has quite a bit fewer (84). Perhaps this is due to the large size of the United States and the fact that much of it is rural. Nevertheless, schoolchildren and others without access to the Internet are at quite a disadvantage in today's modern world. Once again, it is pertinent to mention that research and development, computer technology, and other aspects of technological advance have been tempered by the restrictions put in place by the sequester. Nevertheless, President Obama has proposed expansions in research and development, as well as expanding the reach and lowering the cost of high-speed Internet service, stating that "Today, high-speed broadband is not a luxury; it's a necessity."

Implications of Growth for the Twenty-First Century

The market-oriented growth policies of the Western industrialized world are now in question. A Republican Congress took over in 2015, but with two remaining two years of Obama's presidency. It is not clear if any major action will be taken in the near future, or whether that action will be reversed in years to come. We can hope that because of the excesses and failures of the financial and other industries, tougher regulations put in place in this area will remain. Nevertheless, some of these were relaxed in a compromise bill passed in late 2014 that would maintain budgetary spending for government for fiscal year 2015. Beyond this, there definitely seems to be a cyclical movement of philosophy from a restricted government role to an expanded government role, and perhaps it will shift back again if dissatisfaction with any current direction takes place. Certainly, cyclical shifts seem to occur whenever drawbacks of either extreme become evident. In the United States, post–World War II economic growth did little to mitigate extremely high poverty rates. The war on poverty and the civil rights movement of the 1960s addressed the needs of the population to which the prosperity of the 1950s did not trickle down. Yet, the liberal policies of the 1960s and 1970s brought forth a conservative backlash as many politicians (and Supreme Court justices) in the 1980s, 1990s, and early 2000s sought to reverse years of affirmative action and antipoverty policies. Conservatives argued that government social policies caused inefficiency and reduced work incentives. In the twenty-first century, concern for the people left behind from the prosperity of worldwide economic growth may well again precipitate a greater call for government response.

The Eastern Industrialized World: Economic Transition

The recent changes in Eastern Europe are nothing short of revolutionary, something that most students who came of age within the last few years cannot fully comprehend. The Cold War ended. Germany is reunified, and the Berlin Wall is down. The Soviet Union no longer exists; it has been divided into some 16 independent nations (the largest of which is Russia). And, the former socialist economies of Eastern and Central Europe are now undergoing an **economic transition** toward capitalism.

Economic transition
A shift in policies and institutions that move economies from socialism toward capitalism.

We are using the term *Eastern industrialized world* to include the formerly socialist Eastern and Central European countries, even though some would define a few of these countries as part of Asia. The economic transition toward capitalism has achieved varied levels of success, as evidenced by diverse economic growth rates. Table 17-7 displays the variation in growth rates for countries of the Eastern industrialized world over various time periods.

TABLE 17-7 • Average Annual Growth of GDP, Eastern Industrialized Countries, 1990 to 2000, 2000 to 2007, 2009, 2013[a]

Country	1990 to 2000	2000 to 2007	2009	2013
Albania	3.5	5.3	3.3	1.3
Armenia	−1.9	12.7	−14.1	3.5
Azerbaijan	−6.3	17.6	9.4	5.8
Belarus	−1.7	8.3	0.2	0.9
Bosnia & Herzegovina	NA[b]	5.3	−0.9	0.4
Bulgaria	−1.8	5.7	−5.5	0.9
Croatia	0.6	4.8	−6.9	−1.0
Czech Republic	1.1	4.6	−4.5	−0.9
Estonia	0.2	8.2	−14.1	0.8
Georgia	−7.2	8.3	−3.8	3.2
Hungary	1.6	4.0	−6.8	1.1
Kazakhstan	−4.1	10.0	1.2	6.0
Kyrgyzstan	−4.1	4.1	2.9	10.5
Latvia	−1.6	9.0	−18.0	4.1
Lithuania	−2.7	8.0	−14.7	3.3
Macedonia	−0.8	2.7	−0.9	3.1
Moldova	−9.6	6.5	−6.0	8.9
Poland	4.6	4.1	1.8	1.6
Romania	−0.6	6.1	−6.8	3.5
Russia	−4.7	6.6	−7.8	1.3
Serbia	−4.7	5.6	−3.5	2.5
Slovak Republic	1.9	6.0	−4.9	0.9
Slovenia	2.7	4.3	−7.9	−1.1
Tajikistan	−10.4	8.8	3.8	7.4
Turkmenistan	−4.8	N/A[a]	6.1	10.2
Ukraine	−9.3	7.6	−14.8	1.9
Uzbekistan	−0.2	6.2	8.1	8.0

[a]2013 or most recently available year from 2010 to 2014.
[b]N/A = not available.

Source: World Bank, *World Development Indicators 2014*, World Bank (Washington DC: World Bank, 2014).

Growth Rates

Look at the growth rates for the periods 1990 to 2000 and 2000 to 2007. These growth rates are fascinating! First, about two-thirds of the average annual growth rates for the time period 1990 to 2000 are negative. This means that GDP declined on average each year during the time period. Nevertheless, all of these growth rates turned positive over the time period 2000 to 2007. Sometimes, the reversal is incredible. For example, Tajikistan had the largest negative growth rate (−10.4 percent) from 1990 to 2000, but close to the highest average annual growth rate (8.8 percent) over 2000 to 2007! Other countries with very high growth rates from 2000 to 2007 include Armenia, Azerbaijan, Kazakhstan, and Latvia. Russia's negative average annual growth rate from 1990 to 2000 (−4.7 percent) reversed to a positive rate in 2000–2007 (6.6 percent). *Note that the reversal from negative to positive growth rates for the Eastern industrialized countries is in stark contrast to the Western industrialized countries, which generally had lower growth rates in the more recent time period.*

We can see in the table that growth rates in 2009 were very low or even extremely negative. Note the negative growth by 7.8 percent in Russia, for example. These low and negative GDP growth rates were, of course, the result of the global Great Recession. What began as a U.S. recession had rapidly spread to the Eastern industrialized world, just as it did to the Western industrialized world. Finally, we can see improvement in growth rates by 2013, with only a few negative rates. In Russia, the growth rate of GDP was 1.3 percent. Keep in mind, however, that the dramatic cuts in petroleum prices had not yet occurred until 2014 and beyond. These caused dramatic slowdowns in oil exporting countries such as Russia. We will return to this shortly.

The most prominent elements of the transition to capitalism have been the movement toward market-determined prices and the process of privatization, as well as the development of entrepreneurship. Russia experienced some of the difficulties inherent in the transition process. Nevertheless, in terms of entrepreneurship, there is no question that everyday Russian citizens immediately embraced entrepreneurial activities; whether in the form of kiosks lining the streets of Moscow's famous Arbat and metro stops, babushkas selling homemade fast foods and household articles at every metro stop, teenagers selling gasoline along highways near the long lines at gas stations, professionals moonlighting as translators and drivers, and residents seeking Western partners in Russian joint ventures.[2] Problems in Russia were more evident in the areas of prices and privatization.

Market-Determined Prices

Recall the efficiencies associated with market-determined prices. Demand and supply equate so that shortages and surpluses are eliminated. (It is when the government intervenes by setting rental ceilings in housing or price supports in agriculture, for example, that we end up with shortages or surpluses.) In a free market, the high prices of scarce goods encourage consumers to be frugal in their use of the goods and encourage suppliers to expand production of the goods. Shortages do not result. On the other hand, the low prices of plentiful goods encourage consumers to use the goods more extensively and encourage suppliers to produce fewer of these goods and shift production away from these goods and toward a greater number of goods more desirable to consumers. Surpluses are thus prevented.

Under pure socialism, the government sets the prices of goods and services. Prices had traditionally been set artificially low in the socialist economies of Eastern Europe.

For example, consumers had been able to afford basic items of food, clothing, and gasoline. **Artificially low prices operate like price ceilings, however, and shortages are the result.** So, although people could afford to purchase needed items, these goods were often unavailable in stores. People would expend considerable time and energy standing in long lines and leaving their jobs to rush to stores whenever rumors of new supplies arrived.

Decontrol of prices

Removal of government controls on prices.

These shortages are largely relics of the past. Prices of most items have been allowed to rise to market-determined levels in most Eastern European countries. In other words, **decontrol of prices** has occurred. Governments no longer set all of the prices. However, in cases where wages have not risen as rapidly as prices, the purchasing power of consumers has declined. Supplies are now plentiful, but many people cannot afford the goods. **Inflation is always a short-run effect of extensive price decontrol.**

Price decontrol in Russia was abrupt. Within days, prices on 80 to 90 percent of wholesale and retail goods were decontrolled.[3] The rise in prices of so many goods and services naturally caused a sudden rise in the average price level. The inflation rate soared, peaking at approximately 2,520 percent per year at the height of price decontrol in 1992. Inflation has since subsided but is still considered to be a serious problem. (The average annual inflation rate over 1990 to 2000 was 99 percent and only about 7 percent in 2013. This is still high, but nowhere near the problem it was previously.)

Privatization

Privatization

The transfer of government-owned enterprises or responsibilities to the private sector.

Privatization refers to the sale of government enterprises to the private sector. Throughout Eastern Europe, governments have owned everything from industry and businesses to agricultural land, energy facilities, agricultural marketing boards, and transportation networks. The process of privatization presumes that private ownership of the means of production enhances efficiency and growth.

Once again, Russia presents an interesting example of this process of privatization. The Russian privatization program started in April 1992 with the sale of municipally owned shops. At the same time, the government began the process whereby state and collective farms converted to private ownership. In June, the government began to convert large- and medium-sized firms into shareholding companies[4] (meaning that individuals may own shares in the company). Finally, in October the government began to issue to all Russian citizens a voucher that can be used to purchase shares in such companies. (Your author even managed to purchase a voucher, a "piece of Russia," in a secondary market to a secondary market—that is, in an illegal transaction in a hallway outside of an auction site.)

The Russian privatization program has not been without difficulty. First, different elements of the Russian government have disagreed greatly over the pace of privatization. Second, small businesses, mostly shops and services, have been sold off more rapidly than larger enterprises. The largest enterprises are far more difficult to privatize. Third, machinery and equipment in many Russian enterprises were outmoded and in poor repair. Productivity in these enterprises was very low. As privatized businesses became more profit oriented, and as government subsidies to these businesses declined, many firms went bankrupt, resulting in worker layoffs. **Unemployment is always a short-run result of extensive privatization.** Fourth, Russian enterprises tended to be monopolies. Before the transition, Soviet planners had categorized industry into 7,664 "product groups." Of these product groups, 77 percent were produced by single firms.[5] Even as these government-owned monopolies became privatized, there remained the problems associated with monopoly that were discussed in Chapter 13 on market power. Finally, a large, though unknown, share of Russia's industries had been defense related. Since the end of the Cold War, Russian military expenditures are much lower. (Nevertheless, Russian military expenditures are still quite high in comparison to the rest of the world. Russia spent 3.6 percent of GDP on the military in 2007, in contrast to the United States, which spent 4.2 percent of GDP. Only a few other countries spend more.) All of this suggests that Russia will continue to face hurdles in the forms of privatization and demonopolization. Despite all this, Russia has now successfully established many small- and medium-sized private firms. The country reported over 442,000 new businesses established just in 2012, more than any other country except the United Kingdom with 457,000. (Data for the United States are not available.)

Effects of the Transition

The objectives of the transition from socialism to capitalism throughout the Eastern industrialized world are greater efficiency and growth. But this transition has posed many problems for people. Inflation made it difficult for consumers to afford basic necessities. Farmers were hard hit by increases in the prices of inputs such as fertilizer, while the prices they received for their food products remained artificially low. Workers were laid off in defense industries, government jobs, and privatized businesses, and other workers frequently were unpaid. Corruption is still often widespread, and organized crime is sometimes rampant. Whereas many people have struggled to make do in light of these difficulties, others have profited from liberalization, creating blatant inequality. Alcoholism and suicide rates in some countries rose, and life expectancies even declined in the early years of the transition. A quotation from a young Russian woman studying in the United States summarizes some of these difficulties early in the transition.

> *The situation in Russia is very difficult for the ordinary citizen. My father recently lost his government job, though he was soon hired into a different job. My mother, who works at a bank, did not lose her job but she was not paid for seven months. Imagine, a bank with all that money, and my mother not being paid! Lost jobs and nonpayment of wages are common. People get by moonlighting. Old women beg or sell homemade food, used clothing, or anything that anyone will buy. Pensions are often very small, as low as $30 per month or less. This will buy maybe a loaf of bread and a bottle of milk each day, plus a little bit of meat each week. With wages falling behind prices, it now takes about seven days of work at a typical wage to purchase a tube of mascara, and two months of work to purchase a good pair of shoes. Twenty rubles will buy a bottle of bad vodka. Many people drink. In the meanwhile, middle-aged men flaunt their wealth and drive their Mercedes, Audis, and BMWs. It is easy to recognize the Mafia.*[6]

The Twenty-First Century?

The twenty-first century is a question mark. Although policies of liberalization will undoubtedly continue, the struggles and dissatisfactions of ordinary people may slow down or change the nature of the transition. In some countries, the transition may even be reversed. In Russia, the rise in power of politicians who wish to return to the policies of the past exemplifies the dissatisfaction of people with the current political and economic situation. Opinion polls at different times have shown that large shares of the population wish to return to the "old days," when they were provided with housing, jobs, child care, and health care. In other Eastern industrialized countries, some policies of liberalization have been reversed and some socialist-leaning politicians have been elected. In still other Eastern industrialized countries, significant minorities favor the return to socialist economies.

By 2014, Russia was in the midst of a serious economic crisis, precipitated by the global fall in oil prices, Russia's important export. Falling oil prices led to a decline in the value of the ruble, which meant that imported goods became expensive and beyond the reach of ordinary Russians. (You can refresh your memory of how this works by referring to Appendix 12-1.) In late 2014, Russia tried to shore up the value of the ruble by raising interest rates, a certain way to slow down the economy beyond what it was already experiencing (as discussed in general terms in Chapter 15). As this text is written, a severe recession is threatened.

Another problem for Russia has been its support for pro-Russian rebels in the eastern part of Ukraine. Sanctions were placed on Russia as a result, which add just another problem for Russian economic growth.

*One of the critical issues in the transition to freer-market economies in the Eastern industrialized countries is a **safety net** for people.* Under socialism, governments had guaranteed jobs, housing, child care, and medical coverage for all citizens. As ordinary citizens now experience a loss of jobs and purchasing power, governments must ensure that people's basic needs are met. Otherwise, the transition will proceed neither smoothly nor successfully.

Safety net

Government programs, such as housing, nutrition, and health care, to maintain the well-being of people.

The Developing World: Economic Reform

Economic reform

Change in policies and institutions that moves economies to freer (more capitalist) markets.

Much of the developing world is undergoing a process referred to as **economic reform**. This means that developing countries are adopting policies that move their economies toward freer markets; or to use another word, they are engaged in liberalism. The economic growth rates reported in Chapter 10 indicate much variation in the success of the developing countries in increasing GDP per capita. (The Great Recession in the United States had certainly affected them as well, with major slowdowns in countries that include the "emerging nations" of China, India, and Brazil.) The economic reforms predominant in the 1990s and 2000s have their roots in the international debt crisis of the 1980s. And that crisis has its roots in the world economic conditions of the 1970s.

The 1970s: Oil Crisis

The most significant economic events of the 1970s revolved around oil: the restriction of oil supplies by the Organization of Petroleum Exporting Countries (OPEC), the Arab oil embargo in 1973 to 1974, and the Iranian Revolution in 1979. These events restricted oil supplies to the West and sent world oil prices skyrocketing. The OPEC countries, including several countries in the Middle East, as well as Nigeria, Libya, Algeria, and Gabon in Africa; Venezuela and Ecuador in South America; and Indonesia in Southeast Asia; received massive increases in their *earnings* from oil exports. However, the non-oil-exporting countries, including most developing countries, suffered huge increases in their *spending* for oil imports. The effects of the oil shocks were threefold.

First, the OPEC nations began a process of "recycling" their oil revenue; that is, they deposited much of their oil revenue in U.S. and European financial institutions. These **petrodollars** (so named because petroleum prices are denominated in dollars) greatly enhanced the lending capacity of these Western commercial banks and other financial institutions. Second, many developing countries began to borrow heavily. The non-oil-exporting developing countries borrowed to finance their oil imports, while several

Petrodollars

Money earned from the sale of petroleum. (Petroleum prices are denominated in dollars.)

of the oil-exporting developing countries, such as Mexico, borrowed to develop their oil sectors and diversify their economies. Some developing countries borrowed in order to finance economic development, while others had other purposes in mind (as we shall see). At the time, the cost of borrowing was low because interest rates were low and the lending capacity of the Western financial institutions was high. Commercial banks were quite willing and able to lend. Third and finally, the rising oil prices of the decade triggered worldwide inflation. (This was described as an example of cost-push inflation in Chapter 15.) This inflation set the stage for the events of the 1980s.

The 1980s: Debt Crisis

The 1980s began with great concern in the United States over the inflation that was largely generated by the escalating oil prices. In 1981, the Federal Reserve engaged in **contractionary monetary policy** (recall the discussion in Chapter 15 on macro policy in the early 1980s). The consequences of this were several. (1) Inflation was brought under control, but at the expense of skyrocketing interest rates and consequent U.S. recession that later spread worldwide. (2) Rising interest rates meant that interest payments by developing country borrowers increased as well. (3) Rising interest rates in the United States had a secondary effect of pushing up the value of the dollar. The rising dollar made developing country payments for oil imports even more difficult because oil is valued in dollars. It also made repaying predominantly dollar-denominated debt more difficult for the developing countries. Developing country **international debt** was now a full-blown crisis.

By 1988, the developing countries had borrowed more than a trillion dollars, and the amount was increasing. They borrowed for a variety of reasons, including those related to the oil market, which we've noted. Many developing countries also borrowed for other laudable purposes, including investment in infrastructure and industry and development of agricultural and export sectors. In many developing countries, however, borrowed funds were grossly misused. Banks had so much lending capacity that they neglected to take adequate care in who they lent to and for what purpose. Countless stories tell of funds that were squandered on grandiose but inefficient government projects, on luxury goods for the rich, and on the coffers of wealthy businesspeople and government officials. For example, Tyler Bridges, then a writer for the *Washington Post*, examined Venezuela's use of borrowed funds in the mid-1980s. He wrote:

> *I discovered that the government hadn't kept track of where the money had gone, though various sources indicated that only a portion of the money was invested in projects fostering long-term growth.... [In one example,] thanks in part to a presidential decree requiring that every public bathroom and elevator have an attendant, public-sector employment tripled from 1974 to 1984.*[7]

Another problem was that of capital flight. **Capital flight** is a process whereby borrowed funds are reinvested in financial markets or real estate abroad. Corrupt government officials or businesspeople with access to borrowed funds often invested these funds overseas, rather than using them for local projects. Capital flowed outward, profits and interest earnings accrued to wealthy investors, and developing countries failed to benefit from the borrowed money. When governments fail to invest borrowed funds productively, this naturally hampers the ability of borrowing countries to repay their debt. As an analogy, when you borrow money to finance your education, you are making yourself more productive (recall the discussion of an investment in human capital), and this means that you will eventually earn more money with which to repay your loan. When borrowed funds are used unproductively, the ability to repay becomes tenuous. In the case of developing

Contractionary monetary policy
Reductions in the nation's money supply that serve to raise interest rates and reduce aggregate demand.

International debt
The amount of money owed by one country to a foreign country or institution.

Capital flight
A process whereby developing (or other) countries invest funds in foreign countries.

country borrowing, the fault may lie with an inefficient or corrupt government, but it is the residents of the borrowing countries who then bear the burden of the debt.

The enormous burden of the debt becomes clear when we carefully consider the process by which a country must still try to pay off its debt. First, the amount of money that must be paid on the debt each year (interest payment plus repayment of principal) may represent a very large expenditure. Since the income of developing countries is generally low, the demands on this limited income represent a bewildering array of choices in a typical low-income country trying desperately to develop. Large expenditures must go to satisfying the basic consumption needs of people: food, shelter, and medical care. Government expenditures are also necessary for a variety of social services, public education, and infrastructure. With a population at the margin of subsistence and with a driving need for development, any expenditures diverted toward repaying the debt will directly harm the well-being of people. This state of affairs explains a commonly made observation: "In poor countries, the debt crisis has a child's face." *The reallocation of spending toward repaying the debt harms the well-being of people, the most vulnerable of whom are typically the very young.*

In addition to finding money to repay the debt, there is the problem of the form that this money must take. **Debt repayment must be made in the form of the currency initially borrowed; thus, repayment must typically be in U.S. dollars or in the currency of other major countries.** We'll refer to this currency as "hard currency," meaning that it is widely accepted throughout the world. Developing countries have very limited means of obtaining hard currency with which to make their payments. They may earn foreign currency through their exports to other countries. Typically, these export earnings have been limited, in part due to global recessions in the early 1980s, early 1990s, and late 2007 to 2009. (Do you recall the problem of developing country declining terms of trade discussed in Chapter 12 on international trade?) A country may also acquire foreign currency through foreign investment by other countries and through international assistance. A final option, and one that has been frequently chosen by developing country governments, is to continually borrow to repay past debts. Obviously, the latter results in a vicious cycle of continuous borrowing in which developing countries have little hope of becoming debt free.

In a country with limited opportunity to earn hard currency, such currency must be carefully spent. When that currency must be used for debt repayment, it cannot be used for other important activities such as the purchase of foreign capital or technology or the import of important food and energy products. Yet, perhaps the direst implications of debt repayment take place in the long term. Countries that are desperate for hard currency earnings to repay their debt will undertake overall development policies that are quite different from the ones they might otherwise undertake. *Countries under pressure to acquire export earnings may feel forced to expand patterns of export cropping that can worsen the income distribution, use up limited resources, harm food security, and cause environmental problems.* They may succumb to pressures to encourage indiscriminate foreign investment that may not be the most conducive to their overall development objectives. They may emphasize industrial over agricultural sector development. Under more ideal conditions, a country might well pursue very different, and more beneficial, paths to development. (These were discussed in more detail in Chapter 10 on world poverty.)

The 1990s: Economic Reform

The final phase of the debt crisis occurred as many countries were forced by their inability to meet payment schedules to seek financial assistance from the

International Monetary Fund (IMF). IMF assistance is helpful, but it has typically involved **conditionality**, forcing countries to undertake the economic reforms (often called "austerity measures") referred to earlier as a condition for assistance. In other words, there were "strings attached" to the assistance. These reforms include requirements that governments reduce their spending and privatize government enterprises. Governments are also required to allow food and other prices to rise to market levels and to reduce their controls on foreign trade and investment. In other words, they must move toward freer markets, reducing the government's role in the economy and allowing the market to determine prices. Some countries have voluntarily adopted economic reforms, but most others have had these reforms imposed on them. Some of these reforms have created tremendous hardship for governments and residents alike. One African leader expressed his frustration this way:

> *You do not talk of "austerity" to a [person] who has not tasted food for days, who can conceive of no more ecstatic pleasure than to have a few drops of water to wet his [or her] lips and tongue.... Enforced increases in food prices are meaningless mutterings to the mother brushing the flies off her baby's eyes, watching [the child] starve to death by the minute because there is no food or milk or water.*[8]

The Twenty-First Century?

Developing countries have had mixed reactions to economic reforms. In many countries, such as Nigeria and other African countries, privatization resulted in massive layoffs of public-sector employees. The private sector has not yet been able to restore employment adequately in these countries. In other countries as diverse as Kenya, Indonesia, and Mexico, rising food prices were met with riots or demonstrations by urban consumers. In still other countries such as Chile, economic reforms created rapid economic growth and national prosperity despite the fact that large segments of the population remained abysmally poor. *One thing that is clear is that developing countries undergoing economic reform, just as Eastern industrialized countries undergoing economic transition, need a safety net to protect those citizens harmed by the changing economy.*

Many developing country residents are rejecting the notion that economic reform, along with capitalism and a market-based economy, will ultimately benefit the poor. While maintaining democratic elections, they are turning toward modified versions of socialism in reaction to the failures of conservative economic policy. This is especially true in Latin America, where many socialist presidents have recently been elected (often with overwhelming victories). Some examples are Venezuela, Bolivia, Chile, Ecuador, Nicaragua, and Venezuela. Former president Hugo Chavez of Venezuela nationalized (took government ownership of) companies in the oil industry. Bolivia nationalized its natural gas sector and its largest airport operations; and the former leftist government of Chile pledged itself to be an alternative economic model for the developing world. While current Chilean president Michelle Bachelet, elected in 2014, is still considered a socialist, her policies have been strongly market-oriented, with trade liberalization and strong financial institutions and other stabilizing policy. President Rafael Correa of Ecuador vowed to put Ecuador's poor ahead of foreign debt payments as he was sworn into power in January 2007 (and reelected in 2013), yet he also put in place economic reforms that helped create stronger economic growth. President Daniel Ortega of Nicaragua, a socialist elected in 2007 and reelected in 2013, has the United States as its largest

International Monetary Fund (IMF)
An international organization, largely funded by Western industrialized countries, which provides conditional loans and financial assistance to needy countries.

Conditionality
The obligation to meet certain requirements in exchange for financial assistance.

export partner and Canada as its second. In all of these cases, it is important to keep in mind that the shift has not been to *pure* socialism, with complete government control over the economy. Most property has remained in the hands of the private sector and most prices remain market determined. Furthermore, these changes may not be permanent.

Once again, in all of these examples, it is important to keep in mind that we are seeing neither a total shift to socialism nor a total shift to capitalism. Just as countries such as Vietnam and Cuba are adopting aspects of capitalism in the context of socialist economies (as we noted in Chapter 10), other countries such as Bolivia and Venezuela are adopting aspects of socialism in the context of capitalist economies. As some of the countries we've mentioned emerged from the great recession, they were doing quite well with a 2013 economic growth rate of 5.4 percent in Vietnam, 6.8 percent for Bolivia, and 5.6 percent for Venezuela (2012), 4.1 percent for Chile, 4.0 percent for Ecuador, and 4.6 percent for Nicaragua. (Recent rates for Cuba are unavailable.) Unfortunately, as oil and natural gas prices began falling in 2014, growth rates will fall for those countries dependent on these exports.

President Obama startled the nation with the announcement of an easing of relations with Cuba in late 2014, including the restoration of diplomatic relations and the establishment of an embassy in Havana. Travel, trade, communications, and remittances (money sent by Cuban-Americans to relatives in Cuba) were eased. In a trip to study the effects of economic reforms in Cuba in the late 1990s, your author was pleased to find the high standards of living that were discussed in Chapter 10. While housing standards were poor in Havana, all children, no matter how remotely they lived, received health care and education. The same was discovered in her mid-1990s trip to Vietnam. Both governments were also making concerted efforts to reduce migration to large cities, which we know often results in poor living conditions, by assisting families with land acquisition, home construction, and some market-determined prices of agricultural products. While these two countries still maintain nondemocratic governments, their shifts toward capitalism have improved conditions for their citizens. Hopefully restored relations between Cuba and the United States will improve conditions to an even greater extent.

The main point of this chapter, however, is that the world is neither moving toward pure capitalism nor pure socialism, but rather somewhere in-between. While this may be reassuring to some, it still remains to be seen how the developing countries and the Eastern industrialized countries (as well as the Western industrialized countries, for that matter) will react to the failures of extreme capitalism and socialism. Will they push forward with even more conservative policies, hoping that benefits will trickle down to the poor? Or will they react like some of the Latin American examples and seek policies to soften, or even nullify, the market-oriented policies of economic transition and reform? Just as the title to this chapter ends with a question mark, so too does this paragraph.

You, the Student

Has your teacher asked you to read the Epilogue to this book (directly following this chapter)? If not, please go ahead and read this two-page finale that I've written to you anyway, as it challenges you to take a stand in making this a better world. As an educated citizen, you have the opportunity and responsibility to make a difference in our world!

View**Point**   Conservative versus Liberal

This chapter has examined a conservative movement throughout the world toward capitalism and globally freer markets, though this movement is not uniform across the world. Economists vary in their views of the movement toward capitalism. Market economies often lead to efficiency and growth, but issues of equity may be neglected. If this is the case, and if governments fail to provide adequate programs for the poor and the unemployed, the benefits of a market economy will fail to trickle down to the needy. In the new millennium, the disparity between the rich and the poor may become greater. Liberals tend to be more concerned than conservatives about this equity issue.

On the other hand, if socialist interventions go so far as to reduce the usefulness of the price system and the incentives of the marketplace, economies may stagnate and fail to grow. Conservatives tend to be more concerned than liberals about these issues of incentives and efficiency.

The ideal economy will seek a balance between conservative and liberal policies. After all, the efficiencies of the marketplace mean little if shares of the population fail to benefit from them. Similarly, the equity achieved by more socialist economies cannot provide maximum benefits if inefficiencies prevent economic growth and productivity.

Just where is the balance between conservative and liberal? You have studied this contrast throughout the course, whether the issue is poverty, the environment, health care, housing, or agriculture. You now have the information and insight you need to analyze this issue by yourself and to come to the policy conclusions that make sense to you.

SUMMARY

The Western industrialized world, the Eastern industrialized world, and the developing world have all embarked on a movement toward freer markets for their economies. Much of the Western industrialized world has embraced conservative economic policies in the hope of generating economic growth. Many of these countries, including the United States, have at times shifted leftward. Most formerly socialist industrialized countries are experiencing a revolutionary transition from socialism to capitalism. And finally, large numbers of developing countries have adopted economic reform policies, voluntarily or involuntarily, that are designed to make their economies more market oriented. Both socialism and capitalism have their successes and failures, and the long-term outcomes of these economic systems remain to be seen.

DISCUSSION AND ACTION QUESTIONS

1. Are you an economic liberal or conservative? What is your view of government social programs, taxes, and regulation of business?

2. Consider the U.S. supply-side policies under President Ronald Reagan and President George W. Bush (as discussed in Appendix 15-2), such as cuts in taxes, transfers, and regulations. Do you expect these types of policies to achieve efficiency and economic growth? Do you expect the benefits of these policies to trickle down to all?

3. What do you think about some of the specific conservative tax policies and proposals, such as replacing the personal income tax with a consumption tax and reducing the capital gains and dividends tax? Do you think these would be effective in creating economic growth? How do you feel about the effect they would have on U.S. income distribution?

4. How might the U.S. government encourage greater research and development? How would R&D benefit the economy?

5. Suppose that the government of a formerly socialist country decontrols prices and permits them to rise to market levels. How can the government assist low-income consumers who might be unable to afford higher food and other prices?

6. Assume that the process of privatization continues successfully in Russia. Would all the problems of Russian industry by solved? What other policies may be necessary?

7. Use the Central Intelligence Agency (CIA) *World Factbook* at http://www.cia.gov/cia/publications/factbook to look up the current economic situation in any one of the Eastern industrialized countries. Has GDP been increasing or decreasing? How high is the inflation rate? What are some of the standards of living (life expectancy, infant mortality rate, and so on)? How do these compare with other countries in the Eastern industrialized world?

8. How have international conditions outside the control of developing countries exacerbated the problem of international debt? Do you believe it is right for the International Monetary Fund (IMF) to stipulate conditions when providing financial assistance to debt-ridden developing countries?

9. Go to the International Monetary Fund (IMF) Web site at http://www.imfsite.org. It provides links to countless statistics, reports, and other global information, including the transformation of countries to capitalism.

10. Go again to the International Monetary Fund (IMF) Web site (http://www.imfsite.org) and click "Conditionality" to learn more about the history, role, operation, and effectiveness of IMF conditionality (in the IMF view).

11. Use the World Bank Web site (http://www.worldbank.org) to look up debt information on a developing country of your choice. Look for the debt service ratio, which expresses the ratio between debt service (annual repayment of debt plus interest) and export earnings and which is written as Total Debt Service/Exports. This ratio is the best indicator of the debt burden of an individual country.

12. Go to the home page of the World Bank at http://www.worldbank.org to discover the wealth of information on worldwide economic and social indicators, including information on savings rates, standards of living, international debt, and many others Many of these statistics are arranged in easy to read tables showing all major countries of the world (see "indicators"). You can also obtain data quickly on any country of your choice by clicking on the name of that country.

13. What type of safety net is necessary for residents of formerly socialist and developing countries as they move toward market economies?

14. What do you think of the normalizing of relations between the United States, as announced by President Obama in late 2014? Do you think they will be effective in improving living conditions for people in Cuba? Do you think they will assist in improving the political climate in Cuba?

15. Do you believe that the global movement toward freer markets will continue well into the twenty-first century, or will it reverse itself? Why?

NOTES

1. World Bank, *World Development Indicators 2014*, (Washington DC: World Bank, 2014). Unless otherwise indicated, this or earlier versions are the source for other data in this chapter.

2. Jacqueline Brux and Jacques Foust, "Doing Business in the Russian Economy in Transition" (paper presented at the Midwest Economic Association meetings, Chicago, Illinois, March 1994).

3. U.S. Department of Commerce, Business Information Service for the Newly Independent States (BISNIS), International Trade Administration, *Commercial Overview of Russia*, Moscow, January 28, 1993.

4. "Russia Reborn," *The Economist*, December 5, 1992.

5. Ibid.

6. Yana S. Yurgelyanis, in a conversation with the author.

7. Tyler Bridges, "Before Bailing Them Out, Plug the Leaks," *Washington Post National Weekly Edition*, March 22–April 7, 1989.

8. Bread for the World Institute, *Africa: Crisis to Opportunity*, 1995, http://www.bread.org.

Epilogue
You and the World Around You

Twenty-six years ago, after two children and one miscarriage, I had another miscarriage. It was especially sad, since this time my odds were not good and I knew that I didn't have the courage to put my family and myself through this again. Nevertheless, I wanted to do something meaningful and long-lasting and since I felt there existed no good textbook that covered the economics of social issues, I decided to write this book. You are now reading the sixth edition, and it has indeed become long lasting! You can decide if you think it is meaningful!

You have finished this particular study of economic issues in the world today. You have used economic tools to analyze a broad spectrum of social issues. In the process you have learned techniques that you can use to analyze other issues. You have developed critical and analytical thinking skills that you can use all your life. You will be better able to understand how government policy affects you and your family. You have learned the vocabulary to understand what you read in the newspaper, see on the TV news, or read on Internet news sites. You can understand the meaning of statistics, their flaws, and their biases. Indeed, you are now a better-educated citizen.

What does this mean? Are you a "better" person? Will you have a better quality of life? Will you contribute to a more just society? Will you make an impact on the world in which we live?

I hope your answer is yes to all of the aforementioned questions. Or at least I hope that you now have an interest in improving the world around you. You will be among the 38 percent of the population over age 25 in this country who has a college degree. You will be among the most educated people in the world. What all of this means is that you have both the ability to affect the world and the responsibility to do so.

Beginning in high school, I have always been an activist. I have exercised my right to free speech by organizing demonstrations and planning events. These were always peaceful, lawful, and respectful, as they must be if they are to be effective. I have exercised my right to vote and I have written letters to the editor and contacted my legislators.[1] I have campaigned for candidates: working the phones, distributing leaflets, and offering rides to the polls. I have organized social justice groups and list-serves, worked in soup kitchens, and collected food and clothing for the poor. My work overseas has always had the poor in mind. I have agreed with U.S. government policy and I have disagreed. I like to think that I have made a difference. *You* can make a difference! *You are an educated citizen!*

I am calling on you to be an ethical, socially concerned global citizen. The text, and in particular, the sections "You, the Student" and "Discussion and Action Questions" at the end of each chapter have challenged you to become involved, whether you wish to lobby for fair trade coffee on your campus, boycott "big-box" superstores in your community, struggle against homelessness in your country, or improve the environment on your planet. You are a privileged person with a high education in a high-income country. Along with privilege comes responsibility. I call on you to use your education to make this a better world.

The issues we have analyzed in this book will not go away. You will finish your formal education (no one ever finishes learning), and you will go on to your career. I hope some of you will take more economics courses and perhaps even become economists. But you will be workers of all sorts and in all types of circumstances. Your investment in your education will make you a more productive worker wherever you go to work. I hope you will remain concerned about issues of poverty and discrimination, pollution, homelessness, abuse of market power, and others. The real world forces you to take ethical positions on these issues as they are related to your workplace, your life, and the lives of those around you.

Finally, you are part of a global economy. The events of 9/11 brought this home to us. In polls subsequent to September 11, 2001, Americans showed an alarming inability to locate Middle Eastern countries on a map, and a total misconception of which countries the perpetrators of 9/11 were from. Results of a National Geographic-Roper Global Geographic Literacy Survey that polled young adults age 18 to 24 revealed the following: Only 13 percent of those surveyed could locate Iraq or Iran, only 14 percent could pinpoint Israel, and only 17 percent could locate Afghanistan on a map. Fifty-eight percent of those polled could not locate Japan, 65 percent couldn't locate France, and 69 percent couldn't locate the United Kingdom on a map. And, unbelievably, about 11 percent of the young Americans polled couldn't even locate the United States on a map! In comparison, the survey found that young people in other countries, notably Sweden, Germany, Italy, France, Japan, Canada, and Great Britain scored above young people in the United States. Among the countries polled, only youth in Mexico scored below the U.S. youth.

As a citizen of the world, you will increasingly be called upon to understand international issues, to work in businesses with international linkages, and very likely to travel in foreign countries yourself. The world has indeed become a global village. And you are a resident of that village!

What this means is that you must continue your education. In order to stay in tune with worldwide events and issues, you must become a lifelong learner. For now, take international courses, and if your courses do not have international content, explain to your teachers that you *need* an international education. And make sure you don't only learn about the Western industrialized countries. Some four-fifths of the world's population will soon reside in the developing countries of Asia, Africa, and Latin America. Talk with international students and faculty. Browse the Internet and use care to assess the statistics you read: what is the source, what exactly is the unit of measurement, and what is the year? It is easy to use statistics to misrepresent a point someone wants to make, but you are now better equipped to recognize this. Watch informative news shows and read high quality newspapers. When you come to articles about foreign countries, be sure to read them! Always have a map or a globe handy. When you read your first article about Burundi, you will wonder where this nation is located and why you should know about it. But the next time you read about Burundi, you will recognize it. Pretty soon you will know more, not just about Burundi, but about the entire global economy than any of your friends and family. You will truly be an educated citizen (and impress everyone around you!).

I am proud of you, for the academic success you have achieved thus far and for your continued studies. I will be proud whether you become a parent who places their child above all others, a nurse's aide who washes the bodies of those who cannot do it themselves, a professor of economics, or a Nobel Peace Prize winner. And, I will be proud of you for being an ethical, involved citizen. Finally, as they say in Africa, if you think you are too small to make a difference, try sleeping in a closed room with a mosquito!

Sincerely,
Dr. Jacqueline Brux
(Jackie)
jacqueline.m.brux@uwrf.edu

P.S. Even though I don't know you personally, my readers, I do feel great affection for you. Please feel free to write to me with any suggestions you may have for this book, or just to write! I would love to hear from you and I promise to personally write back!

NOTE

1. You may contact your U.S. senators at the U.S. Senate Office Building, Washington, DC 20510, and your U.S. representatives at the U.S. House of Representatives, Washington, DC 20515. You may leave a telephone message for either at (202) 224-3121. You may write the president at The White House, Washington, DC 20500, or leave a message at (202) 456-1111. You may also send an e-mail to the president at President@Whitehouse.gov. Web sites and e-mail addresses of members of the U.S. Senate and House of Representatives are available at http://www.senate.gov and http://www.house.gov, respectively, as is information about schedules, bills, committees, and so on.

Glossary

A

Absolute advantage A situation whereby a country can produce a good at a lower resource cost than another country.

Absolute poverty A situation in which people experience the hardship of poverty according to some objective criterion.

Adjustable-rate mortgages (ARMs) Mortgage loans on which interest rates are adjusted to market levels.

Adverse selection A process by which insured people's choices lead to higher-than average loss levels for the program's sponsor.

Affirmative action Efforts to provide equal opportunities in terms of employment and education to underrepresented groups of people.

Aggregate demand The quantity of total output (GDP) demanded (purchased) at alternative average price levels.

Aggregate supply The quantity of total output (GDP) supplied (produced) at alternative average price levels.

Agricultural subsidies Government programs to assist agriculture.

Aid to Families with Dependent Children (AFDC) Our nation's former welfare program that provided cash assistance to eligible low-income families with children.

Antitrust Our laws, agencies, and court system established to control market power in the United States.

Appreciate The value of one country's currency increases relative to another country's currency.

Assets Property that is owned, such as land.

Average life expectancy The age to which a baby born in a particular year can be expected to live.

B

Barrier to entry A market characteristic that prevents new firms from entering the market.

Barter The direct exchange of goods and services for other goods and services rather than for money.

Block grant A lump sum of money given by the federal government to state governments to use as they wish within broad federal guidelines to develop programs to meet a broad category of need.

Budget deficit The difference between federal government spending and federal government tax revenue in any one year. (If spending exceeds tax revenue, the budget is in deficit.)

Budget surplus The difference between federal government tax revenue and federal government spending in any one year. (If tax revenue exceeds spending, the budget is in surplus.)

Buffer stock A mechanism for stabilizing agricultural prices, whereby an agricultural product is purchased and placed in storage during years of high production and released from storage and sold during years of low production.

Bumper crop An unexpectedly large crop resulting from good growing conditions.

Burden of the tax The impact of the tax that is felt by producers and consumers. Consumers bear the burden in the form of higher prices paid for the product; producers bear the burden in the form of lower profits.

C

Capital flight A process whereby developing (or other) countries invest funds in foreign countries.

Capital gains The net income received when an asset is bought at a particular price and sold at a higher price.

Capital goods Goods such as machinery and factories that are used to produce other goods.

Capital-intensive technology Technology utilizing large amounts of capital relative to labor.

Capitalism An economic system wherein the economic decisions are made by the private sector via the marketplace and the means of production are owned by the private sector.

Cartel A group of producers that explicitly engages in price-fixing.

Closing costs The total amount of money paid at the time a person purchases a house.

Coefficient for the Price Elasticity of Demand The percentage change in quantity demanded divided by a percentage change in price

Coinsurance payment A percentage of medical expenses that the insured person must pay over and above the deductible (or maximum out-of-pocket expense).

Collusion Price-fixing.

Comparative advantage A situation whereby a country can produce a good at a lower opportunity cost than another country.

Competition A market in which many small producers sell a standardized product to many small buyers.

Composition of GDP The goods and services of which GDP consists.

Composition of poverty The number of poor people in each group of the population as a share of the number of poor in the nation.

Concentration The domination of a market by a few large firms.

Concentration ratio The percentage of output produced by the four largest firms in an industry.

Conditionality The obligation to meet certain requirements in exchange for financial assistance.

Constant prices Prices that exist in a base year.

Consumer goods Goods that are consumed (used) by consumers.

Consumer price index (CPI) A weighted average of the prices of a fixed basket of goods and services purchased by a typical urban household.

Consumption possibilities curve A curve that shows alternative combinations of the maximum amounts of two products that can be consumed within a country during a particular time period.

Consumption tax A hypothetical tax on the portion of income that is spent on consumer goods and services, as opposed to income that goes into savings.

Contractionary fiscal policy Fiscal policy that decreases aggregate demand, thereby contracting the economy.

Contractionary monetary policy Monetary policy that decreases aggregate demand, thereby contracting the economy. Reductions in the nation's money supply that serve to raise interest rates and reduce aggregate demand.

Contractual right A right that is specified in contract between parties.

Cost shifting The practice of recovering the unpaid costs of some patients by charging higher prices to other patients.

Cost-benefit analysis A study that compares the costs and benefits of a policy, program, or activity.

Cost-of-living adjustment (COLA) An adjustment that automatically increases incomes or benefits when the average price level rises.

Cost-push inflation Inflation that occurs as a result of increases in the costs of production.

Crowding out A situation in which increased government spending that is financed by borrowing causes interest rates to rise, which results in less spending by the private economy.

Current prices Actual prices of a particular year.

Cyclical unemployment Unemployment that results from a drop in economic activity in our economy as a whole.

D

Declining terms of trade A decline in the value of a country's exports relative to the value of its imports.

Decontrol of prices Removal of government controls on prices.

Deductible A payment on an annual or per-service basis that must be made by the insured person before the insurance company's payments begin.

Defensive medicine The ordering of unnecessary tests and services by health care professionals solely to protect themselves from charges of malpractice.

Deficiency payments The target price minus the market price, multiplied by the number of units sold.

Deflation A decrease in the average price level.

Deforestation The clearing of forested areas in an unmanaged fashion.

Demand curve A graph showing quantities that consumers are willing to buy at alternative prices during a specified time period.

Demand schedule A table showing quantities that consumers are willing to buy at alternative prices during a specified time period.

Demand-pull inflation Inflation that occurs when any sectors of the economy increase their demand for goods and services.

Depreciate The value of one country's currency decreases relative to another country's currency.

Deregulation The reduction of government regulations.

Desertification The encroachment of desert on previously fertile land.

Design standard A regulation that specifies both the required level of performance and the means of compliance.

Developing world Developing countries of the world.

Direct cost Actual paid expenses.

Discouraged workers People who would like to work, but have become so discouraged in the job search that they have stopped actively seeking employment.

Discrimination Action that treats individuals differently on the basis of some arbitrary characteristic.

Distribution of income The distribution of income between different income groups.

Dividends Profits from the ownership of stock.

Down payment The amount of a homebuyer's own money required by the lender for the purchase of a home.

Dumping Exporting goods at low prices, even below the cost of production.

Durable goods Products with a life of longer than one year.

E

Early retirement effect Social Security's effect of increasing private savings by encouraging earlier retirements.

Earned Income Tax Credit (EITC) A federal tax credit for low-income working individuals and families. State governments may also utilize an EITC for their personal income taxes. The credit is available whether or not the worker pays federal personal income taxes.

Earnings Money received from labor market activities.

Eastern industrialized world The industrialized ex-socialist countries of Eastern and Central Europe.

Economic conservative A person who believes in very low levels of government involvement in the economy.

Economic development A multifaceted process that involves improvements in standards of living, reductions in poverty, and growth in GDP per capita.

Economic growth A sustained increase in production, represented by an outward shift of the production possibilities curve. An increase in gross domestic product (GDP) or GDP per capita over an extended time period, sometimes averaged over several years.

Economic liberal A person who believes in high levels of government involvement in the economy.

Economic reform Change in policies and institutions that moves economies to freer (more capitalist) markets.

Economic transition A shift in policies and institutions that move economies from socialism toward capitalism.

Economies of scale A situation whereby a large amount of a product can be produced at a lower cost per unit than a small amount of the product.

Efficient Using resources in such a way as to maximize the desired output.

Effluent fees Taxes on production causing water pollution.

Elastic demand Demand in which buyers are relatively responsive to changes in price.

Emissions fees Taxes on production causing air pollution.

Employment discrimination Not hiring certain workers on the basis of some arbitrary characteristic.

Endowments Income-earning investments of a school or other institution.

Enrollment cap A maximum limit on the number of students allowed to enroll in a school.

Entitlement A payment that eligible citizens have a right to receive by law.

Equilibrium A state of balance; a point at which quantity demanded equals quantity supplied.

Equity Fairness.

Euro The common currency of the European Union.

European Union (EU) The European Union includes 28 European countries, including many in Western and Eastern Europe. It fosters free trade, finance, stability, and growth among its members.

Exchange rate The price of one country's currency in terms of another country's currency.

Excise tax A tax applied to the sale of a specific good or service.

Exclusive franchise Permission by the government (often a local government) for a monopoly firm to exist. (It is normally accompanied by government regulation.)

Exemptions Amounts of money for each household member that can be deducted from household income before personal income tax rates are applied.

Expansionary fiscal policy Fiscal policy that increases aggregate demand, thereby expanding the economy.

Expansionary monetary policy Monetary policy that increases aggregate demand, thereby expanding the economy.

Export cropping Agricultural production for export, rather than production of food for local consumption.

Exports The value of goods and services sold to foreigners.

Externality The cost or benefit of an economic activity that spills over onto the rest of society.

F

Fair market rent An amount determined by HUD to be reasonable rent for low-income housing in that area.

Federal Reserve The U.S. central banking system.

Fee-for-service The charging of a specific fee for provision of a specific health care service.

Fiscal policy The use of government spending and tax policy to shift the aggregate demand curve.

Flexible (floating) exchange rate system A system whereby exchange rates are determined on the basis of international demand and supply for a currency.

Free-rider problem A situation in which individuals that do not pay their share for a good or service nevertheless enjoy its benefits.

Frictional unemployment Temporary unemployment caused by a normal time delay when a person seeks a first job, changes jobs, or re-enters the labor force after an absence.

Full employment A situation in which there is no cyclical unemployment; all unemployment is frictional or structural.

Full-employment GDP The level of gross domestic product associated with full employment of the labor force. (It is a hypothetical concept.)

Fully funded Having sufficient reserves to pay all expected liabilities; it is a legal requirement of private insurance.

G

General Agreement on Tariffs and Trade An international trade agreement, first negotiated in 1947, with the goal of reducing trade barriers among member countries of the world. It is now replaced by the WTO.

Gentrification The conversion of low cost apartments into middle- and upper middle-class housing.

GNI per capita Gross national income per person on average. Calculated by dividing total gross national income by total population.

Government securities Government bonds and treasury bills.

Gross domestic product (GDP) The market value of all final goods and services produced *in* the economy in a given time period (usually one year).

Gross national income (GNI) The income generated from the production of a nation's output. Gross national income is the broadest of all income concepts.

Gross national product (GNP) The market value of all final goods and services produced *by* the economy in a given time period (usually one year).

Group of eight (G-8) A group of the largest industrialized countries of Canada, France, Germany, Italy, Japan, Russia, the United Kingdom, and the United States. Its purpose is to foster free trade and stabilize international finance, though many view it as favoring the developed countries.

Group of Twenty (G-20) A group of twenty developed and emerging countries (Argentina, Australia, Brazil, Canada, China, France, Germany, India, Indonesia, Italy, Japan, Mexico, Russia, Saudi Arabia, South Africa, South Korea, Turkey, the United Kingdom, the United States, and the European Union). Its goals are to support international trade, investment, and development.

H

Health maintenance organizations (HMOs) Health insurance plans under which the covered care is limited to designated providers and the use of services is coordinated by a patient's primary care physician or physician group. HMOs often encourage preventative care.

Homeowner's insurance Insurance that covers the replacement cost of a house and its contents.

Housing voucher Housing subsidies in the amount of the difference between the fair market rent and 30 percent of a poor family's income.

Human capital discrimination Anything that prevents certain groups from acquiring the level or quality of education or training to which other groups have access.

Hyperinflation Extremely high inflation, whereby money becomes almost worthless.

I

Imports The value of goods and services purchased from foreigners.

Incidence of poverty The distribution of poverty within the country.

Income distribution The division of total income in an economy among people of different income groups.

Income transfer A cash transfer from the government to an individual for which no good or service is provided to the government in return.

Income Money received from all sources.

Increasing opportunity costs As more of one good is produced, society must give up increasingly larger amounts of the alternative good.

Index of dissimilarity A measure of segregation.

Indigenous People who are of native born ancestry.

Indirect cost The opportunity cost of forgone alternatives.

Individual equity The principle that benefits received are proportional to amounts paid in.

Indivisible A characteristic of public goods in that they are impossible to divide into units sufficiently small to be sold in private markets.

Inefficiency Using resources in such a way as not to maximize the desired output from them.

Inelastic demand Demand in which buyers are relatively unresponsive to changes in price.

Inequity Unfairness.

Infant mortality rate The number of babies who die within their first year of life per every 1,000 live births.

Inflation A rise in the average price level.

Informal employment sector An employment sector consisting primarily of service occupations in an unofficial setting.

Infrastructure Social overhead capital, including facilities for transportation, communication, marketing, and extension services.

In-kind transfers Transfer of goods or services (or access to goods or services) from the government to an individual for which no good or service is provided to the government in return.

Interest rate The percentage of borrowed funds that must be paid to the lender (or investor) for the privilege of using the funds.

International debt The amount of money owed by one country to a foreign country or institution.

International Monetary Fund (IMF) An international organization, largely funded by Western industrialized countries, which provides conditional loans and financial assistance to needy countries. The global organization established in 1944 with the goal of providing loans and reducing world financial instability.

Inventories Unsold goods and materials.

Investment in human capital Spending that is designed to improve the productivity of people.

L

Labor force participation rate The ratio of the number of people in the labor force to the number of people age 16 or older in the population.

Labor force All people age 16 and older who are working for pay or actively seeking employment.

Labor productivity GDP per person employed.

Labor-intensive technology Technology utilizing large amounts of labor relative to capital.

Law of demand There is a negative relationship between price and quantity demanded, all other things equal.

Law of supply There is a positive relationship between price and quantity supplied, all other things equal.

Liberalism (or neo-liberalism) A movement toward freer (more capitalist) markets. This is another term for economic reform or economic transition.

License A permit to operate in a trade or profession.

Life expectancy The age to which a baby born in a particular year can be expected to live on average.

Literacy rates The percentages of populations that can read and write.

Loanable funds Money that is borrowed or lent.

Lorenz Curve A graph that displays the income distribution.

Luxury good A commodity for which demand is highly sensitive to changes in income.

M

Macroeconomics The study of the total economy.

Malpractice insurance Insurance carried by health care professionals to protect themselves from large malpractice damage awards.

Market power The ability of an individual firm to influence the market price of its product.

Market price The retail price of a product plus any sales and excise taxes paid by the consumer.

Marketable pollution permits Tradable permits that allow the owners of the permits to produce a given amount of pollution.

Maternal mortality rate The number of deaths of women for pregnancy related reasons per 100,000 live births.

Means-tested A way of determining who is eligible for a program, based on the person's low-income status and possibly low asset ownership.

Median (middle) If there is a series of numbers from low to high, the median would be the one exactly in the middle.

Medicaid A government program providing medical coverage for eligible low income people.

Medical savings account A type of insurance in which the purchaser makes payments into an account that can be drawn against in times of illness.

Medicare A government program providing medical coverage largely to elderly people.

Menu costs The costs associated with reprinting menus, revising cost schedules, adjusting telephones and vending machines, and so on, when inflation occurs.

Mergers The combining of two firms into one.

Microeconomics The study of individual areas of activity within the total economy.

Microenterprise credit Small loans that are used for small entrepreneurial purposes.

Minimum wage A legally imposed minimum price (wage) for labor.

Minority A group with less access to higher positions in society.

Monetary policy Changes made in the nation's money supply to shift the aggregate demand curve.

Money income All household income from any source, including income transfers, calculated before taxes.

Monopolist The single firm in a monopoly market.

Monopoly A market in which only one firm produces a product with no close substitutes.

Mortgage insurance Insurance that pays off a mortgage if the borrower defaults.

Mortgage-backed security (MBS) A financial security that is backed by mortgage debt.

N

National debt The total amount of money owed by the federal government. It represents the accumulation of all funds borrowed by the federal government that have not yet been repaid.

National health insurance Health care systems that involve government assurance of universal coverage of the population.

Natural monopoly A market with significant economies of scale.

Negative income tax A taxation system that taxes people with incomes above a certain level and pays people with incomes below that level.

Net benefits The excess of benefits over costs.

Newly industrializing countries (NICs) Singapore, South Korea, Taiwan, and other countries achieving rapid growth through industrialization.

Nominal GDP GDP calculated at current prices.

Nondurable goods Products with a life of less than one year.

Nonexcludable A characteristic of public goods in that their benefits cannot be kept from persons who do not pay for the goods' provision in a private market.

Nonrivalrous A characteristic of public goods in that use by one person does not prevent use by others.

Normal retirement age The minimum age at which workers can retire with full Social Security benefits.

North American Free Trade Agreement (NAFTA) An agreement between the United States, Canada, and Mexico allowing more equal access to one another's markets. The agreement went into effect on January 1, 1994.

O

Occupational crowding Crowding of some groups of workers into a limited number of jobs.

Occupational discrimination Not hiring some groups of workers for particular jobs, resulting, for example, in men's jobs and women's jobs or minority jobs and white jobs.

Oligopolists Individual firms in an oligopoly market.

Oligopoly A market in which only a few large firms dominate.

Opportunity cost The best alternative forgone in order to produce or consume something else; what you give up to get something else.

Overallocation of resources The production of more than the socially optimum amount of a good or service.

P

Patent A government grant of exclusive rights to use or sell a new technology or product for a period of time.

Pay-as-you-go system A program in which current taxes pay current benefits.

Payroll taxes Taxes based on earnings from work, usually deducted directly from workers' paychecks.

Perfectly inelastic demand Demand in which buyers are completely unresponsive to changes in price.

Perfectly inelastic supply Supply in which producers are completely unresponsive to changes in price.

Performance standard A regulation that specifies the required level of performance but not the means of compliance.

Petrodollars Money earned from the sale of petroleum. (Petroleum prices are denominated in dollars.)

Physician sovereignty A medical doctor's control over the demand for medical procedures.

Points Fees charged by a lender at the time it grants a mortgage.

Pollution Waste that is not recycled.

Poverty line A level of income below which a household is considered poor.

Poverty rate The percentage of the population that is poor.

Preferred provider organization (PPO) A health insurance plan under which a group of medical providers contract to provide the insured patient's medical care at discounted rates.

Prejudice A prejudgment on the basis of stereotypes and hearsay, plus the refusal to consider evidence that conflicts with the prejudgment.

Premium A payment to purchase and keep in force an insurance policy.

Price ceilings Legalized maximum prices for goods or services.

Price discrimination Charging different groups of buyers different prices (when price differentials are not justified by cost differences).

Price floors Legally imposed minimum prices of a good or service.

Price leadership A form of collusion in which firms follow the price increases of a leading firm.

Price maker A firm that is able to influence the market price of its product.

Price supports Legally imposed minimum prices of goods or services. Price supports are specific examples of price floors.

Price taker A firm that is unable to influence the market price of its product and takes the market price as given.

Primary commodities Unprocessed raw materials and agricultural products.

Private goods Goods produced or purchased by business firms and individuals.

Private insurance A private program provided by for-profit insurance companies and funded by premiums. Its purpose is the pooling of risk of losses.

Private schools Schools that are not operated by the government and that are mainly financed by student tuition and endowments.

Private Individual people and businesses.

Privatization The transfer of government-owned enterprises or responsibilities to the private sector.

Product differentiation The creation of the image that one firm's product is different from or somehow superior to other similar products.

Production possibilities An economic concept explaining scarcity and the need for choices; alternate combinations of the maximum amounts of two different goods that can be produced during a particular time period if the economy's resources are efficiently and fully employed.

Profit-push inflation Inflation that occurs when businesses use market power to restrict output in order to push up prices and profits.

Programs to reduce supply Policies to decrease the amount produced and offered for sale.

Progressive tax A tax that takes a greater percentage of income from high-income people than from low-income people.

Property taxes Taxes levied by local governments on land, buildings, and other property to fund services such as education and police protection.

Proportional tax A tax that takes the same percentage of income from people of all income levels.

Public Government.

Public assistance Any government program that is targeted to aid low income people.

Public goods and services Goods and services often provided by the government because their unique characteristics make it unlikely that the private market will provide them in sufficient quantity.

Public goods Goods produced or purchased by government.

Public housing Housing units owned and operated by a local public housing authority but federally subsidized and often federally regulated.

Public schools Schools that are operated by the government and are financed by tax revenue.

Purchasing power The ability to buy goods and services.

Pure competition A market in which many producers sell a standardized (identical) product to many buyers.

Q

Quota A restriction on the quantity of an imported good; rigid numerical requirements in hiring.

R

Rate of return The "benefit rate," computed by dividing the net benefit by the amount invested.

Rationing function of price The ability of a flexible market price to clear the market of shortages and surpluses.

Real GDP GDP calculated at constant prices.

Real price Price as adjusted for the effects of inflation. We do this when we consider price changes over time.

Recession A decline in a nation's gross domestic product (output) associated with a rise in unemployment. Technically, there must be a decline in real gross domestic product (GDP) for at least two consecutive quarters.

Redlining The practice of denying mortgages in certain minority neighborhoods.

Refundable A refund is available even if an income earner does not pay taxes, as long as he or she files a tax form.

Regressive tax A tax that takes a greater percentage of income from low-income people than from high-income people.

Regressivity A situation in which a larger percentage of income is taken from low-income people than high-income people.

Relative poverty A situation in which people are poor in comparison to other people.

Rental ceilings (rent controls) Legally imposed maximum rents on rental housing.

Replacement rate The percentage of the worker's last working year's earnings that is replaced by Social Security retirement benefits.

Resources Land, labor, machinery, and other inputs used to produce goods and services.

Retaliation A situation in which one country responds to the trade restrictions of another country by imposing trade restrictions of its own.

Reverse discrimination Discrimination against white males.

Rural–urban migration The movement of people from the rural sector to the urban sector, often in search of better living conditions.

S

Safety net Government programs, such as housing, nutrition, and health care, to maintain the well-being of people.

Savings rate Total savings (private and public) divided by GDP.

Services Activities such as haircuts, health care, and education that are consumed (used).

Shortage A situation in which quantity demanded is greater than quantity supplied. This occurs only when the price is lower than the market level.

Social adequacy The principle that benefits are sufficient to provide a minimum level of economic security to the population as a whole.

Social costs of production The total costs of production, including both private costs and spillover costs.

Social insurance Any government program funded by payroll taxes on employers, employees, or both. It is targeted to aid certain eligible groups of people, and a person need not have low income in order to be eligible.

Social Security wealth effect The tendency of the population to substitute Social Security for private saving, thus decreasing private saving.

Social Security A federal program that provides income transfers to retired workers, the survivors of deceased workers, and disabled workers.

Socialism An economic system wherein the economic decisions are made by the public (government) sector and the means of production are owned by the public sector.

Spillover A costs or benefit of a private market activity that is shifted onto society at large; alternatively called an externality.

Spillover benefit A positive externality; the benefit of an economic activity that is shifted onto society.

Spillover cost A negative externality; the cost of an economic activity that is shifted onto society.

Stagflation Simultaneous inflation and recession.

Standard deduction A fixed amount of money that taxpayers can deduct from their taxable income when calculating their personal income taxes, if other deductions are not claimed.

Standards Maximum levels of pollutants that are acceptable by law.

State Children's Health Insurance Program (SCHIP) A federal program providing health care coverage for children in low-income working families.

Statistical discrimination Judging an individual on the average characteristics of his or her group.

Statutory right A right that is specified by law.

Structural unemployment Unemployment that results from structural changes in our economy, such as changes in demand or technology.

Subprime mortgage A mortgage loan made to a borrower with less than "prime" borrowing characteristics.

Subsidies Payments from the government for some given action, such as recycling.

Subsidize The payment of some of the costs of an economic activity by the government.

Subsistence food crops Crops grown primarily as food for the family. A small amount may be marketed.

Supply curve A graph showing quantities that suppliers are willing to sell at alternative prices during a specified time period.

Supply schedule A table showing quantities that suppliers are willing to sell at alternative prices during a specified time period.

Supply-side economics The view that conservative economic policies can be used to increase aggregate supply.

Supply-side policy The use of various tools to improve the incentives for workers and businesses to produce more output, thereby increasing aggregate supply and GDP.

Surplus A situation in which quantity supplied is greater than quantity demanded. This occurs only when the price is higher than the market level.

T

Target prices A program in which farmers are paid the difference between the target price and the market price.

Tariff A tax on an imported good.

Tax base The value of income, earnings, property, sales, or other valued items to which a tax rate is applied. In the case of the Social Security tax, the tax base is earnings through working.

Tax credits Amounts of money by which the income taxes payable to the government can be directly reduced. A person or business must meet certain criteria to be eligible for a credit.

Tax rate Percentage of the tax base that must be paid to the government as tax.

Technology Ways of using available resources to produce output.

Technology forcing Standards that force firms to use specific pollution control technologies.

Temporary Assistance for Needy Families (TANF) A block grant from the federal government to state governments to be used in state welfare programs in compliance with federal guidelines. (Pronounced TAN-EF.)

Third-party payment A health care payment made by someone other than the patient or the patient's family.

Tokenism Hiring minorities to comply with the law, not for their abilities.

Trade balance The value of a nation's exports minus its imports.

Trade deficit The amount by which a nation's trade balance is in deficit (imports exceed exports).

Trade embargo Restrictions on trade with another country for political reasons.

Trade surplus The amount by which a nation's trade balance is in surplus (exports exceed imports).

Trickle-down philosophy The view that supply-side policy will generate economic growth and prosperity, the benefits of which will eventually "trickle down" to all.

Trust fund Taxes collected and invested specifically to pay future Social Security benefits.

U

Underallocation of resources The production of less than the socially optimum amount of a good or service.

Underemployment A situation in which people work limited hours or with low productivity.

Unemployed person A person age 16 or older who is actively seeking employment but is unable to find a job.

Unemployment rate The percentage of the labor force that is unemployed.

Unemployment A situation in which resources are not fully used in production.

Universal entitlements Payments (or programs) to which eligible citizens have a right by law.

Usury laws Laws establishing a maximum legal interest rate.

W

Wage discrimination Paying equally productive workers different wages on the basis of some arbitrary characteristic.

Western industrialized world The industrialized capitalist countries of the world.

World Bank An international organization whose mission is to end extreme poverty and boost global prosperity by promoting leadership, scholarship, and loans to countries in need.

World Trade Organization (WTO) The global organization, established in 1995, with the goal of reducing barriers to trade among member countries.

Index

J